Schumann

A Chorus of Voices

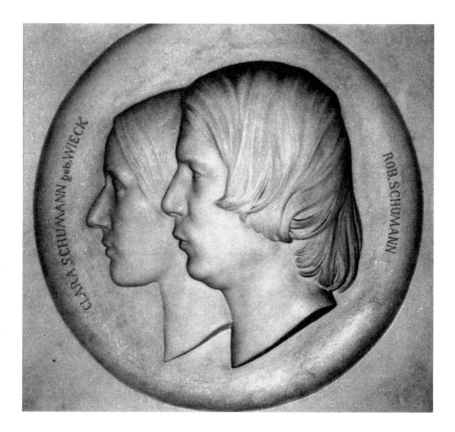

Schumann

A Chorus of Voices

Interviews and Conversations
with John C. Tibbetts

AMADEUS
PRESS

Amadeus Press
An Imprint of Hal Leonard Corporation
New York

Frontispiece: This relief medallion can be found on the central stairway of the Schumann-Haus, Zwickau.

Published in 2010 by Amadeus Press
An Imprint of Hal Leonard Corporation
7777 West Bluemound Road
Milwaukee, WI 53213

Trade Book Division Editorial Offices
19 West 21st Street, New York, NY 10010

All photographs are from the author's personal collection unless otherwise specified.

Printed in the United States of America

Book design by Snow Creative Services

Library of Congress Cataloging-in-Publication Data

Tibbetts, John C.
  Schumann : a chorus of voices / interviews and conversations with John C. Tibbetts.
      p. cm.
  Includes bibliographical references and index.
  ISBN 978-1-57467-185-8
  1. Schumann, Robert, 1810-1856—Criticism and interpretation. 2. Music—19th century—History and criticism. 3. Musicians—Interviews. I. Title.
  ML410.S4T43 2010
  780.92—dc22
  [B]
                                            2010016923

www.amadeuspress.com

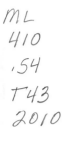

With love and admiration to Nancy B. Reich,
an unfailing inspiration during the many years
of this book's preparation

There exists a secret bond between kindred spirits in every period. You who belong together, close your ranks ever more tightly, that the Truth of Art may shine more clearly, diffusing joy and blessings over all things.

—Robert Schumann, "New Paths," 1853

Contents

Foreword

Emanuel Ax

I hope that when people come to *Schumann: A Chorus of Voices*, they won't mind listening to us musicians and biographers and commentators talk about the many things—"the politics, the literature, the people," as Schumann himself said—that inform the life and music of this wonderful composer. And maybe they can learn something about us in the process! Informal, spoken conversations like the ones you find here can go off in freer, more unexpected directions than what you would find in a more "academic" book. This bicentenary year in 2010 of Schumann's birth gives us a chance for a veritable free-for-all of talk! A few years ago, I had a wonderful experience sitting down with my colleagues and friends at the Library of Congress to talk about piano performance and traditions. The late Eugene Istomin presided over our group, which included Charles Rosen, Leon Fleisher, and Yefim Bronfman. These conversations, which are now available on video through the Library of Congress website, were a rare opportunity for all of us to get together and just go with the topics wherever we wished. And at this writing I'm planning a series for

John C. Tibbetts with Emanuel Ax.

the CBC about ten selected piano concertos, talking about them as well as playing them. It's the world we live in; these days, performers like us are seen and heard in so many different ways via so many different media. We find ourselves talking from the stage, too, which in the past wasn't very acceptable. I find myself speaking more and more during recitals. It makes me relax and makes me feel that I'm communicating more with individuals. I'm even happy if they respond to me. Why not? All this sort of thing should be part of the awareness and training of young musicians today as they enter the profession.

But ultimately, there's always the music. The music. On some level, of course, you enjoy Schumann without referring to words at all, although a book like this reminds us that many extramusical contexts inform his music. But in the end, the best education is to just listen. And maybe then there will be a time when you will want to know more about what lies behind his life and music. And then this book will be there, waiting for you. That's the way I am with sports. I knew nothing about football when I arrived in the United States. And after a time I became fascinated by it. And now I'm to the point where I understand the referees' signs. It's very exciting. It makes me a kind of participant in a sense. If I had the chance, I'd love to be a coach for the New York Giants!

April 11, 2009

Preface

"THE STEREOSCOPIC VIEW"

[Man] has always cared more for truth than for consistency.
If he saw two truths that seemed to contradict each other, he
would take the two truths and the contradiction along with
them. His spiritual sight is stereoscopic, like his physical sight:
he sees two different pictures at once and yet sees all the
better for that. . . . The whole secret of mysticism is this: that
man can understand everything by the help of what he does
not understand.
                                    —G. K. Chesterton, *Orthodoxy*

Robert Schumann once advised that the public should be "spared the intimacies of the genius's workshop." Moreover, he advised the artist to "keep his labor pains to himself" lest "monstrous things might be disclosed." Undaunted by Schumann's caveat, this book takes a stereoscopic view of his life and work, seeking the interior realities of his mind and his art while mapping the exterior world of his age of romantic culture, society, and politics. Schumann himself, after all, ignored his own advice. As the finest music critic of his time, he dissected and disclosed the works of his contemporaries to public view. As a composer, he bared his soul in some of the most unabashedly confessional music ever written. And ever attentive to his legacy, he left us a more detailed record of his daily life and compositional activities than any composer in history.

Moreover, for a composer notorious for his enigmatic silences, baffling behavior, and private mysteries, Robert Schumann enjoyed a lifelong pleasure in convivial society. "One wants so much to associate with people," he told Clara in the first weeks of their marriage in 1840.* He belonged to social groups, clubs, and associations of all kinds. Early and late in his life, in and out of universities, cafés, musical groups, and at home, he surrounded himself with congenial friends and colleagues. While still in his teens in his hometown of Zwickau, he formed a *literarischen Schulerverein*, a literary group, whose aim was to introduce its members

---

* Schumann's Marriage Diary entry, September 13–20, 1840.

to the works of major European authors—many of whom inserted artistic collectives of their own into their books and music. In the late 1820s he formed his own private piano quartet. In the 1830s he gathered around him his celebrated Davidsbund, or League of David, whose members, both real and fictitious, promoted the cause of new music. Late in life, in his status as "the Master," he surrounded himself with a younger generation of amiable spirits, including Albert Dietrich, Joseph Joachim, and Johannes Brahms.

Schumann: A Chorus of Voices is dedicated to that amiable collective spirit. Over the course of thirty years, spanning the late 1970s to the present, I have sought out and interviewed a new Davidsbund of Schumann enthusiasts—a "league of our own," as it were.* This is no mere conceit. The many biographers, musicians, critics, archivists, and commentators in these pages do indeed constitute a privileged circle. I'm reminded of the words of Edvard Grieg: "The mere mention of Schumann's name is enough to send shipboard strangers into each other's arms."

This book is that warm embrace. The speakers here represent all age groups, span several generations, and come from far-flung locations. They speak out in their own voices. These are not written documents, but transcriptions of conversations in which people share their own backgrounds, research activities, and insights. They inquire, argue, dispute, and celebrate, by turns, aspects of the life and music of a composer they all agree is seminal to nineteenth-century romanticism in the arts. Thus, in significant ways, this book is as much about them as it is about Schumann. Because some of these conversations go back three decades, it has been necessary to update many of them. Others, because the contributors have since passed on, have been allowed to remain in their original contexts. From the latter group are the late biographers John Daverio (interviewed just a few months before his untimely death), Peter F. Ostwald, and Joan Chissell; conductors Erich Leinsdorf and Lukas Foss; pianists Eugene Istomin, Malcolm Frager, and Samuel Sanders; and scholars Eric Sams and Tim Mitchell. At the other extreme are those younger scholars and musicians who today represent fresh fields of inquiry and performance, notably conductor Marin Alsop; pianists Ronald Brautigam, José Feghali, and Steven Spooner; violinists Peter Zazofsky and Thomas Zehetmair; cellist Steven Isserlis; and scholars Lawrence Kramer, Jonathan Kregor, Katherine Kolb, Laura Tunbridge, Roe-Min Kok, and Erika Reiman.

---

* Brief excerpts of some of these interviews originally appeared in my radio series *The World of Robert Schumann* (2004). This fifteen-part series has been broadcast worldwide on the WFMT Radio Network. For information on this series, go to www.johnctibbetts.com.

In between are figures long established in their fields, including singers Dietrich Fischer-Dieskau and Elly Ameling; pianists Vladimir Ashkenazy, Jörg Demus, Paul Badura-Skoda, and Charles Rosen; cellist Lynn Harrell; cultural scholars Jacques Barzun, John Fetzer, and Albert Boime; Robert and Clara Schumann biographers Nancy B. Reich, Ronald Taylor, Leon Plantinga, and John Worthen; archivists Thomas Synofzik, Ute Bär, Gerd Nauhaus, Margit McCorkle, and Joachim Draheim; and specialists of those composers intimately and/or professionally associated with Schumann, including Leslie Howard and Michael Saffle (Franz Liszt), D. Kern Holoman and Katherine Kolb (Hector Berlioz), R. Larry Todd (Felix Mendelssohn), and Charles Rosen and Garrick Ohlsson (Frédéric Chopin).

All of them, and more, past and present, have given freely of their time and supported and encouraged this book. Astonishingly, all have allowed me to preserve—with minimal editorial intervention—their idiosyncratic, conversational voices, as opposed to the more rigorously academic rhetoric of their professional writing and performances. (My own questions are indicated parenthetically in the conversations, and my additional remarks are enclosed within brackets.) Moreover, while the colloquy is hardly comprehensive, the purview is wide, ranging from Schumann's earliest years, his relationship with his wife, Clara, and his last days; from his most popular keyboard, symphonic, and vocal works, to the more unjustly neglected dramatic choral works, chamber works, and ballets (yes, Schumann was a ballet composer, in the broadest sense!). There are speculations about his emotional and physiological illnesses, reports from scholarly archives, and accounts of Schumann's influence on today's composers. There are even comments about some of the extant motion picture dramatic biographies.

To all of them, I dedicate this book. As neither a musicologist nor music historian, I make no pretensions that this is an "academic" volume. I simply hope this collection of amiable conversations and informal testimonies expands the circle of enthusiasts you meet in these pages to a wider readership likewise intrigued and curious about Schumann. And just as Schumann himself enjoyed striding into the fray of controversies, these contributors are by no means entirely in accord in their views. For example, sparks fly when psychiatrist Peter F. Ostwald and musical cryptologist Eric Sams lock horns in their opinions about the nature of Schumann's final illness. Pianists Garrick Ohlsson and András Schiff differ sharply on the organization and meanings of the piano cycles. Cellist Steven Isserlis and violinist Peter Zazofsky disagree about Schumann's idiomatic writings for strings. Conductors Lukas Foss, Christoph von Dohnányi, and Marin Alsop review the ongoing debate concerning Schumann's abilities as an orchestral composer; Jacques Barzun and D. Kern Holoman grapple with the issue of "program music." And everybody, it seems, has a say, pro and con, about those ongoing issues, such as the role that Clara played in his life and the relative merits of Schumann's last works. I suggest that you take time to get to know these contributors and their connections with Schumann's life and music as profiled in the Introduction: "The Company Assembled"; and, if you are so disposed, attend further to their more extended autobiographical remarks in the closing Appendix, "In the Workshop."

As we approach Schumann's 200th birthday in 2010, we wonder, as the commotion of the voices in these pages echoes in our ears, if any of the riddles and mysteries of his life and work have been resolved. As John Daverio has astutely noted in one of the conversations recorded in this book, Schumann was an elusive, sometimes seemingly unstable compound of many things, "a forward-looking artist and visionary, a conservator of classical traditions, a poet and an enigma, a tragic figure, and someone to whom no single genre was central to his development." Any attempt to shoehorn this elusive figure and his music into a conveniently symmetrical model or set of hidebound systems and conclusions is bound to fail. Dietrich Fischer-Dieskau seems to be saying the same thing in this book's Epilogue: "In the end we will not know what kind of man Schumann was. And it is good that we will not know. We have no idea how he managed to do what he did. And that's for a genius the best way."

Schumann: A Chorus of Voices can do no more (and no less) than follow the form Daverio himself proposed in his estimable biography, *Robert Schumann: Herald of a "New Poetic Age,"* still the indispensable single volume in English on Schumann. "The model for Schumann's creative work," Daverio writes, "is less a perfectly rounded whole, a circle with a midpoint, than a constellation of fragments." A single energy, he concludes, lends coherence to those fragments—"the notion that music should be imbued with the same intellectual substance as literature. Schumann developed this conviction while he was still a teenager; he held to it until the end of his career."* Appropriately, the contributors to these pages share that conviction and purpose. Like Schumann's wonderful piano cycles of the 1830s, whose fragments and fractures revolved in erratic orbits around their interior meanings, the individual voices in this book collide, bounce, and rebound against each other, creating that collective "Innere Stimme," or interior voice, that in itself is not heard so much as inferred.

What that voice says, dear reader (and listener), is up to you.

---

* John Daverio, *Robert Schumann: Herald of a "New Poetic Age"* (New York: Oxford, 1997), 19.

Further Acknowledgments

In addition to the those contributors already cited, I wish to thank John Cerullo, Jessica Burr, and Angela Buckley of Amadeus Press and longtime friend and adviser Harry Haskell for their editorial advice. And "Hats off!" to Simon Callow for his robust support and encouragement. My appreciations also go to my colleagues at the University of Kansas for their assistance—James Smith and Charles Gibbs of the Music and Dance Library; and Bärbel Goebel for her assistance in the translations of the German texts. To all those Good Companions appearing in this book—thanks on behalf of Schumannians everywhere. And, as always, my love and thanks go to Clara Schumann's biographer Nancy B. Reich. Without her indispensable advice and unfailing, selfless generosity over a span of many years, this book would have not been possible.

John C. Tibbetts
University of Kansas
August 18, 2009

Introduction

The Company Assembled

Why should we be mere idle spectators? Let us go to work to improve matters, and restore the true poetic quality of music.
—Robert Schumann

Gerd Albrecht

German-born Gerd Albrecht (1935–) was a first-prize winner at the International Conductors Competition in Besançon at age twenty-two. From 1994 to 1996 he was principal conductor of the Czech Philharmonic. Subsequent appointments have included chief conductor of the Danish National Radio Symphony Orchestra and the Yomiuri Nippon Symphony Orchestra. His enthusiasm for Schumann has led to recordings of *Genoveva* and the complete *Manfred*. Interview: Washington, D.C., 1995.

Theodore Albrecht

Theodore ("Ted") Albrecht is a professor of music at Kent State University. A specialist in German choral music and performance, he has also published extensively on Beethoven, including the multivolume *Letters to Beethoven and Other Correspondence* (1996) and *Ludwig Van Beethoven: A Guide to Research* (2001). Interview: Kansas City, March 2006.

Marin Alsop

With her appointment as music director of the Baltimore Symphony Orchestra, Marin Alsop becomes the first woman to head a major American orchestra. Among her many awards and honors, she is especially proud of the MacArthur Foundation award, with which she is developing educational programs for the schoolchildren of Baltimore. Her busy schedule includes making numerous guest conducting appearances, broadcasting for National Public Radio, and continuing a highly praised recording project for Naxos of the Dvořák symphonies. Currently, she is planning a Schumann bicentenary festival. Interview: Denver, Colorado, March 24, 2009.

Elly Ameling

The outstanding Dutch soprano (1933–) studied in Rotterdam and The Hague. She completed her training with Pierre Bernac. In 1958 she won first prize at the Concours International de Musique in Geneva. Her extensive repertoire ranges from Monteverdi and Bach through Benjamin Britten and Gershwin. It is Schumann and Schubert, however, in which she particularly excels, and her recordings with Jörg Demus and Dalton Baldwin are highly prized. She retired from public performance in 1995. Interview: Kansas City, Missouri, 1983.

Styra Avins

Published in 1997, Styra Avins's *Johannes Brahms: Life and Letters* was the first comprehensive collection of Brahms's letters in English. Heavily annotated, it debunked many prevailing myths about the composer and his relationship with Robert Schumann. Interview: New York City, 1998.

Emanuel Ax

One of the most beloved pianists of his generation, Emanuel Ax was born in 1949 in eastern Poland and began studying piano with his father in Warsaw. Relocated to New York, he enrolled in the Juilliard School and at sixteen won the Young Concert Artists' Michael Award. He has gone on to many honors, including the first Arthur Rubinstein International Piano Competition in 1974 and the Avery Fisher Prize five years later. He recorded the Schumann Piano Quartet and Quintet with the Cleveland String Quartet in 1986. Three interviews: Lawrence, Kansas, 1983; Kansas City, 2005; and New York City, April 2009.

Paul Badura-Skoda

Now in his early eighties, pianist Paul Badura-Skoda continues to perform at major international music festivals with such renowned conductors as John Eliot Gardiner and Zubin Mehta. Born in 1928, he is regarded as an authority on early music performance, and his many recordings include the complete piano sonatas of Schubert, Mozart, and Beethoven, many of them performed on original instruments from his own collections. Interviews: Kansas City, 1987; and College Park, Maryland, 1992.

Ute Bär

Professor Bär is one of the primary researchers involved with the *New Edition of the Complete Works of Robert Schumann,* an ongoing project through research centers in Zwickau and Düsseldorf, Germany. Interview: Zwickau, Germany, April 2009.

Jacques Barzun

One of the foremost humanists of our time, Emeritus Professor Jacques Barzun was born in France in 1907 and came to the United States in 1920. After graduating from Columbia College, he joined the faculty as Seth Low Professor of History and, for a decade, dean of faculties and provost. He is a specialist on romanticism, and his pertinent books include the groundbreaking *Berlioz and the Romantic Century* (1950), an edited edition of Hector Berlioz's *Evenings with the Orchestra* (1956), and *Classic, Romantic, and Modern* (1961). He received the Gold Medal for Criticism from the American Academy of Arts and Letters. His most recent book is the monumental *From Dawn to Decadence* (2000). Interview: New York City, December 1986.

Erik Battaglia

Erik Battaglia is a professor of lied and oratorio at the G. Verdi Conservatory in Turin, Italy. His compositions include *Variazioni su un tema di Webern,* and his literary works include volumes on Goethe lieder and a translation of Gerald Moore's *The Unashamed Accompanist.* His friendship with the late music historian/critic Eric Sams led to his founding in 2006 of a website, "Centro studi Eric Sams" (www.ericsams.org), which consists of the online publication of Sams's complete works. Interviews: Turin, Italy, November 2008.

Edmund Battersby

A graduate of the Juilliard School, where he studied with Sascha Gorodnitzki, Edmund Battersby is currently a member of the faculty of Indiana University–Bloomington. He frequently performs romantic repertoire on early keyboard instruments. Interview: Lawrence, Kansas, April 2009.

Herrmann Baumann

One of the world's leading horn players, Hermann Baumann was born in Hamburg in 1934. He was principal horn in several German orchestras before turning exclusively to solo performing in 1967. He excels in both the valve horn and the "natural," or valveless, horn. Interview: Düsseldorf, June 1991.

Gordon Boelzner

Gordon Boelzner (1937–2005) worked with the New York City Ballet for many years before becoming its music director in 1990. Interview: New York City, April 1988.

Albert Boime

Albert Boime is a professor of art at UCLA. His more than 140 publications include *Thomas Couture and the Eclectic Vision* (1980), *The Academy and French Painting in the Nineteenth Century* (1986), *Art in an Age of Revolution, 1750–1800* (1987), and *The Art of Exclusion: Representing Blacks in the Nineteenth Century* (1990). Interview: Los Angeles, June 1990.

Victoria Bond

The multifaceted Victoria Bond is an acclaimed conductor, composer of operas and orchestral pieces, and pianist. She was born in Los Angeles into a family of professional musicians. She studied at the Mannes School and the Juilliard School. In 1977 she became the first woman to earn a doctoral degree in orchestral conducting. A devotee of Robert Schumann, she conducted the North American premiere of *Genoveva* in 1987. Interviews: New York City, 1989 and April 2009.

Ronald Brautigam

Dividing his time between the fortepiano and the modern concert grand, Amsterdam-born Ronald Brautigam (1954–) studied with Rudolf Serkin and has garnered an international reputation for his widely ranging repertoire. Recently, his Mozart and Beethoven performances on fortepiano for the BIS label have received ecstatic acclaim. He lives in Amsterdam. Interview: Amsterdam, March 20, 2009.

Simon Callow

British stage, screen, and television actor Simon Callow was born in Streatham, London, where he attended the London Oratory School and studied at the Drama Centre. His acclaimed theatrical performances include the role of Mozart in the original production in London of *Amadeus* in 1979 and several one-man shows, including *The Mystery of Charles Dickens*. His films include *A Room with a View* (1985) and *Four Weddings and a Funeral* (1994). He has also written biographies of

Orson Welles and Charles Laughton. With conductor Roger Norrington, he made a film about Robert Schumann. Interviews: Kansas City, 1985; London, 2003.

Joan Chissell

Joan Chissell (1919–2007) worked as a writer, journalist, and music critic for more than thirty years for the *Times* in London. After receiving a scholarship to the Royal College of Music in 1937, she studied theory with Herbert Howells. Shortly thereafter she began her long tenure with the *Times*. Her books include *Chopin* (1965), *Schumann* (1962), *Schumann's Piano Music* (1973), and *Clara Schumann: A Dedicated Spirit* (1983). Interview: London, September 1988.

Katherine Ciesinski

Katherine Ciesinski (1950–) is a leading American opera singer and voice teacher. She was a first-prize winner of both the Geneva International Competition and the Concours International de Chant de Paris. In addition to the standard operatic and song repertoire, she is a champion of nineteenth-century women composers. Her recording of songs by Clara Schumann was released by Leonarda Records in 1981. Interview: Kansas City, 1989.

Roger Cook

Before becoming the chair of the Department of German and Russian Studies at the University of Missouri, Professor Roger Cook received his PhD in German at the University of California, Berkeley. He is the president of the Heine Society of North America and the author of *By the Rivers of Babylon: Heinrich Heine's Late Songs and Reflections* (1998) and the editor of *A Companion to the Works of Heinrich Heine* (2002). Interview: Columbia, Missouri, 2004.

John Daverio

The untimely death in April 2003 of John Daverio, one of the world's most renowned Schumann scholars, was a staggering loss to the musical community and to Schumann scholarship in particular. He was just forty-eight years old. A professor of music at Boston University, he wrote *Robert Schumann: Herald of a "New Poetic Age"* (1997), which is among the very select indispensable volumes on the composer. Other books include *Romantic Music and the German Romantic Ideology* (1993) and *Crossing Paths: Schubert, Schumann, and Brahms* (2002). Interview: Columbus, Ohio, February 2003.

Jörg Demus

Jörg Demus's career spans the entire history of long-play recording technology. Born in 1928 (?) in Austria, Maestro Demus studied at age eleven at the Viennese State Academy for Music and Dramatic Art and made his New York debut in the mid-1950s, after launching in 1948 a highly successful recording career on the Remington and Westminster labels, and establishing a legendary four-hand and duo-piano partnership with Paul Badura-Skoda. He won the Busoni Prize in 1956. He has been the highly sought-after accompanist for Dietrich Fischer-Dieskau, Elly Ameling, and Elisabeth Schwarzkopf. He recorded the first complete issue of Schumann's piano music in 1968-70. Three interviews: Kansas City, Missouri, 1983; and Düsseldorf, 1991 and 1994.

Christoph von Dohnányi

Born in Berlin in 1929, Christoph von Dohnányi claims a distinguished heritage, including the theologian Dietrich Bonhoeffer, an uncle on his mother's side, and pianist/composer Ernst von Dohnányi, his grandfather. After receiving the Richard Strauss Prize from the city of Munich, Maestro Dohnányi studied at Florida State University with his grandfather and subsequently was appointed general music director of the Lübeck Opera (1957–63). After several other appointments, he achieved lasting fame during his tenure with the Cleveland Orchestra (1984–2002) and upon his retirement was named first-ever Music Director Laureate of the Cleveland Orchestra. His recording of the complete Schumann symphonies was released by London Records in 1988–89. Interview: Cleveland, Ohio, July 1988.

Joachim Draheim

Joachim Draheim is a professor of Latin in the Gymnasium of Karlsruhe. He appears on camera in Steven Isserlis's *Schumann's Lost Romance* (1996). Interviews: Düsseldorf, 1991 and 2009.

Christoph Eschenbach

A pianist and orchestra conductor of international standing, Christoph Eschenbach was born in Breslau, Germany, in 1940. He won first prize in the Clara Haskil Piano Competition in 1965 and studied conducting with George Szell and Herbert von Karajan. His conducting posts included the Tonhalle Orchester-Zürich (1982–86), the Houston Symphony Orchestra (1988–99), and the Philadelphia Orchestra (2003–7). Maestro Eschenbach is currently slated to be the music director of the National Symphony Orchestra, beginning in 2010. Interview: Düsseldorf, June 1994.

José Feghali

Winner of the gold medal at the seventh Van Cliburn International Piano Competition in 1985, José Feghali was a child prodigy in his native Brazil, where he made his recital debut at the age of five. He studied with Christopher Elton at the Royal Academy of Music in London and subsequently has enjoyed a full concert career as well as the appointment of artist-in-residence at Texas Christian University. He played Schumann's *Carnaval* in his Van Cliburn appearances. Interview: Chicago, February 2006.

Vladimir Feltsman

The Russian-born Vladimir Feltsman (1952–) debuted with the Moscow Philharmonic at age eleven and a few years later studied with Yakov Flier. In 1971 he won the grand prize at the Marguerite Long international piano competition in Paris. After eight years of political repression, he was finally able to leave the Soviet Union in 1987. Currently he holds the Distinguished Chair of Professor of Piano at the State University of New York. He became an American citizen in 1995. Interview: Kansas City, October 1989.

David Ferris

David Ferris is an associate professor of musicology in the Shepherd School at Rice University. He received his PhD in music from Brandeis University and before going to Rice taught at Amherst College and the Massachusetts Institute of Technology. His book *Schumann's Eichendorff "Liederkreis" and the Genre of the Romantic Cycle* (2000) is a major contribution to Schumannian research. Interview: Rice University, May 2003.

John Fetzer

Professor John Fetzer is a specialist in German romantic literature. His books include *Romantic Orpheus: Profiles of Clemens Brentano* (1974). Interviews: Urbana, Illinois, spring 1989, and Davis, California, March 2009.

Dietrich Fischer-Dieskau

One of the consummate musicians of our time, Maestro Dietrich Fischer-Dieskau has excelled in the worlds of art song, opera, and oratorio since his first public appearance in 1947. He was born in 1925 in a suburb of Berlin. He studied with Hermann Weissenborn. Following two years' imprisonment by the American Allies near the end of World War II, when he performed for prisoners of war, he launched a meteoric career. Numerous appearances, recordings, and writings have followed, establishing him as one of the most erudite, as well as accomplished, performers in history. Perhaps more than any other singer, he has championed the vocal music of Robert Schumann. He is an honorary member of the Robert Schumann Society. Interview: Düsseldorf, June 1994.

Erik Fokke

After his graduation from medical school, Erik Fokke worked from 1984 to 1988 as a resident in urology and microbiology in Amsterdam and at National Institutes of Health (NIH) in Bethesda, Maryland. Since 1990 he has worked as a general practitioner in Amsterdam. Next to his medical training, he was a student in musicology at the Schumann Akademie in the Netherlands from 1999 to 2005.

Lukas Foss

The late Lukas Foss (1922–2009) enjoyed acclaim as a conductor, composer, pianist, and educator. He left his native Berlin in 1937 and studied conducting at the Curtis Institute in Philadelphia with Fritz Reiner. As the organizer of the Improvisation Chamber Ensemble, and as the music director of the Brooklyn Philharmonic, the Buffalo Philharmonic, and the Milwaukee Symphony, he composed many works and brought new repertoire to his listeners. Interview: Kansas City, June 1988.

Malcolm Frager

Before his untimely death at age fifty-six, Malcolm Frager (1935–1991) was a "pianists' pianist." Fiercely honest in his playing and an avid researcher into original manuscripts, he was instrumental in recovering and performing a huge body of manuscripts by Mozart, Beethoven, and Schumann. He studied with Carl Friedberg, a pupil of Clara Schumann, and won two prestigious awards in 1959–60, the Leventritt in New York and the Queen Elisabeth in Brussels. Interview: Kansas City, Missouri, October 1987.

Claude Frank

A distinguished educator as well as pianist, Claude Frank was born in Nuremberg, Germany, in 1925. He abandoned Nazi Germany in 1937 and continued his studies with Artur Schnabel throughout the war years. Following his Town Hall recital debut in 1947, he appeared with most of the major orchestras, including a debut with Leonard Bernstein in 1959. He is a renowned specialist in the repertoire of Schubert, Beethoven, and Schumann. Interviews: Lawrence, Kansas, 1987 and 1988, and New York City, 2002.

Peter Frankl

One of the first pianists to record Schumann's complete piano works (a project begun in 1973), including the works for piano four hands (with András Schiff), Peter Frankl (1938–) has also enjoyed considerable success on the international concert circuit. Born in Hungary, he studied at the Franz Liszt Academy in Budapest. He is currently a visiting professor at Yale University. Interview: New York City, summer 1987.

John Eliot Gardiner

Sir John Eliot Gardiner is acclaimed as one of the foremost conductors of our time. Born in 1943 in Dorset, England, he took up the baton at age fifteen and before graduating Cambridge founded the Monteverdi Choir. In the next decade, between 1964 and 1968, he also formed the Monteverdi Orchestra and the English Baroque Soloists. In 1990 Maestro Gardiner formed a new period instrument orchestra, the Orchestre Révolutionnaire et Romantique. Long considered a specialist in baroque performance, in recent years he has expanded his repertoire into nineteenth-century works by Schumann and others. He was knighted at the June Birthday Honours in 1998. Interview: Kansas City, February 1989.

Richard Goode

Born in East Bronx, New York, Richard Goode (1943–) studied piano with Elvira Szigeti, Claude Frank, and Rudolf Serkin. His many prizes include the first prize in the Clara Haskil Competition in 1973 and the Avery Fisher Prize in 1980. He was the first American-born pianist to record the complete Beethoven piano sonatas, a project he began with a performance cycle in Kansas City. With the Chamber Music Society of Lincoln Center, he has performed many of the late chamber pieces by Schumann. Interviews: Kansas City, 1987 and 1988.

The Guarneri String Quartet

In 2009 the Guarneri Quartet celebrated its forty-fifth anniversary. Founded in 1964, it comprised Arnold Steinhardt and John Dalley, violins; Michael Tree, viola; and David Soyer, cello. Peter Wiley has been the cellist since 2001. The members are in residence at the University of Maryland and are faculty members of the Curtis Institute of Music in Philadelphia. It has been announced that the quartet will retire in 2009. Interviews: Kansas City, March 1989.

Rufus Hallmark

Rufus Hallmark, professor of music at Rutgers University, has taught at Brown, MIT, Holy Cross, and Queens College (CUNY). He served as director of the Aaron Copland School of Music at Queens and as chair of the Music Department at Rutgers. His musicological research has focused on text–music relations and source-critical work in solo song, chiefly the German lieder of Schumann and Schubert. He received an MA from Boston University and a PhD from Princeton. His publications include *The Genesis of Schumann's "Dichterliebe"* (1979) and *German Lieder in the Nineteenth Century* (1996). Interview: Düsseldorf, June 1994.

Thomas Hampson

Now in the forefront of the world's great singers, Thomas Hampson (1955–) has performed in most of the major opera houses round the world, from Düsseldorf, Germany, where he made his operatic debut in 1981, to the Metropolitan Opera, where he made his American debut in 1986. He has studied with Martial Singher and Elisabeth Schwarzkopf. His devotion to the song literature—from the songs of Stephen Foster, Cole Porter, Gustav Mahler, and Robert Schumann—has won him several Grands Prix du Disque. A recent project is his recording with Wolfgang Sawallisch of a "restoration" of the complete Schumann *Dichterliebe*, which reveals his scholarly, as well as his musical, accomplishments. Interview: Omaha, Nebraska, November 1993.

Lynn Harrell

Born in New York in 1944 to musician parents (his father was the celebrated baritone Mack Harrell), Lynn Harrell studied with Leonard Rose at Juilliard and made his Carnegie Hall debut with the New York Philharmonic in 1961. In addition to a stellar concert and recording career that has firmly established him in the front rank of cellists of his generation, he excels as an educator and became the first holder of the prestigious Piatigorsky Chair of Cello at the University of Southern California, Los Angeles. Interview: New York City, 1988.

Margaret Hillis

The late Margaret Hillis (1921–1998) was the first woman to conduct the Chicago Symphony. She appeared as guest conductor with many American orchestras but preferred to work as one of the great choral conductors of our time. She studied at Indiana University in Bloomington and later studied choral conducting with Robert Shaw at the Juilliard School. In 1957, at the behest of Fritz Reiner, she founded the Chicago Symphony Chorus. She received nine Grammy awards for her choral work for Georg Solti. Interview: Kansas City, February 1988.

Heinz Holliger

Regarded as the world's finest oboist, the Swiss-born Heinz Holliger (1939–) grew up in Bern, Switzerland, where he studied at the Conservatory of Music. An indefatigable conductor, traveler, and composer (he studied composition with Pierre Boulez), he tirelessly champions what he fears is most lacking in our lives—the appreciation and understanding of contemporary music. To date, more than eighty works have been written for him by Elliott Carter, Frank Martin, I Sang Yun, Krzysztof Penderecki, and others. As a composer himself, he has written three stage works based on the writings of Samuel Beckett (*Come and Go, Not I,* and *Where When*), choral works like the *Scardanelli Cycle* (inspired by the poems of Hölderlin), and several musical homages to his favorite composer, Robert Schumann, including *Gesänge der Frühe.* Interview: Kansas City, 1991.

D. Kern Holoman

A professor of music at the University of California–Davis, D. Kern Holoman (1947–) is an authority on Hector Berlioz. His books include *Berlioz* (1989) and *Masterworks: A Musical Discovery* (1998). Interviews: Davis, California, June 1999 and April 2009.

Leslie Howard

Renowned as one of the foremost Liszt scholars and performers of our time, Leslie Howard (1948–) was born in Melbourne, Australia, and relocated to London in 1972. Possessing one of the most eclectic repertoires of any living pianist—from Handel to Glazunov to Grainger—Howard began his epoch-marking series of recordings of the complete solo piano music of Liszt for Hyperion Records in 1986. The series now numbers more than a hundred discs, complete with Howard's own scholarly liner notes that are themselves worth the price of admission. He is president of the London Liszt Society. He was awarded the Franz Liszt Prize from the Hungarian government in 1986. Four interviews: Kansas City and London, 1987–2007.

Steven Isserlis

Steven Isserlis has rapidly established himself as one of the foremost cellists in the world. He has a particular affinity and passion for the music of Robert Schumann. Born in 1959 in England, he was the youngest in a family of musicians. After seven years of study with Jane Cowan, at age eighteen he went to Oberlin and studied with Richard Kapuczinsky. Many recordings, concerts, and festivals have followed. He has two abiding ambitions: one is to perform the complete cello music of Schumann, and the other is to bring classical music to young readers with his splendid series of books, including the happily titled collection of stories *Why Beethoven Threw the Stew*. Interview: London, May 2009.

Eugene Istomin

Born in New York City of Russian-Jewish parents, Eugene Istomin (1925–2003) was as famous for his chamber work with the legendary Istomin–Stern–Rose Trio as for his exemplary solo career. He inherited a priceless legacy of musicianship from his first teachers, Alexander Siloti, Sergei Rachmaninoff, Rudolf Serkin, and Pablo Casals. He won the Leventritt Award in 1943 and began appearing publicly that year. In 1975 he married Marta Montañez Martínez, the widow of Casals. Shortly before his death he received a commission from the Library of Congress to create a video series, "Great Conversations in Music." He won a Grammy Award in 1970 for his trio's recordings of Beethoven, and a year later received the French *Légion d'honneur*. Four interviews: New York, Washington, D.C., and Kansas City, 1987–98.

Paul Katz

Born and raised in Los Angeles, renowned cellist Paul Katz performed with the Cleveland Quartet from 1969 to 1995, which made more than 2,500 appearances on four continents. The recipient of many awards, including the Richard J. Bogomolny National Service Award (America's highest honor in the field of chamber music), he has taught at Rice University and the Eastman School of Music, and currently is on the faculty of the New England Conservatory. With pianist Emanuel Ax, he recorded the Schumann Piano Quartet and Quintet in 1986. Interview: Lawrence, Kansas, October 1987.

Walter Klien

Internationally acclaimed for his authoritative performances of the Viennese School, Walter Klien (1928–1991) recorded the complete works of Mozart, Schubert, and Brahms. He was born in Graz, Austria, and studied with Arturo Benedetti Michelangeli. Shortly before his death he was honored with the Joseph Marx Music Prize in 1987 and the honorary gold medal of the city of Vienna in 1989. He has recorded many of Schumann's piano works.

Hans Joachim Köhler

Professor Köhler edited the Peters edition of Schumann's complete songs and piano music. Interview: Düsseldorf, June 1991.

Roe-Min Kok

Born into a minority Chinese community in Muslim Malaysia, Professor Roe-Min Kok wrote her PhD dissertation at Harvard on Robert Schumann. She represents Canada at CHOMBEC (Centre for the History of Music in Britain, the Empire and the Commonwealth). Currently she is an assistant professor at McGill University. She is continuing her studies in the culture of childhood and, in particular, Schumann's contributions to that culture. Her book *Rethinking Schumann* (coedited with Laura Tunbridge) is forthcoming. Interview: Montreal, Canada, May 5, 2009.

Katherine Kolb

Professor Katherine Kolb teaches in the Foreign Languages and Literatures Department of Southeastern Louisiana University. Her studies in literature and music have naturally led her to Schumann and Berlioz. Her work has appeared in *Berlioz Studies* (1992). Interview: Minneapolis, June 1990.

Lawrence Kramer

Lawrence Kramer is professor of English and music at Fordham University and the coeditor of *Nineteenth-Century Music*. He has published six books, including *Music as Cultural Practice, 1800–1900* (1990), *Classical Music and Postmodern Knowledge* (1995), and *Musical Meaning: Toward a Critical History* (2002). He is a pivotal figure in the development of the controversial New Musicology, which integrates the study of music with social and cultural issues. Interview: Bard College, June 1991.

Jonathan Kregor

Born in 1978 in Peoria, Illinois, Jonathan Kregor is an assistant professor of musicology at the College Conservatory of Music, University of Cincinnati. Currently, he is working on a book on Franz Liszt's transcriptions of songs and instrumental works. Interview: Lawrence, Kansas, April 5, 2009.

Anton Kuerti

Austrian-born Anton Kuerti studied with Mieczyslaw Horszowski and was the recipient of the prestigious Leventritt Award. One of today's most-recorded pianists, Kuerti performs an extensive repertory that includes many recordings of Schubert, Beethoven, and Schumann. He is an officer of the Order of Canada, where he currently makes his home. Interviews: Kansas City and Toronto, 1987–88.

Erich Leinsdorf

The late Erich Leinsdorf (1912–1993) was one of the most acclaimed conductors of our time. Born in Vienna, Maestro Leinsdorf studied conducting at the Mozarteum in Salzburg and later at the Vienna Academy of Music. His many posts included music director of the Cleveland Orchestra (1943–46), the Boston Symphony (1962–69), and the (West) Berlin Radio Orchestra (1978–80). His books include *Cadenza: A Musical Career* (1976) and the posthumously published *Erich Leinsdorf on Music* (1997). He is especially noted for his performances of Schumann's *Scenes from Faust*. Interview: Chicago, April 1989.

Svyatoslav Levin

Pianist Svyatoslav Levin was born in 1955 in the far east of the Soviet Union, almost on the border to China. Nine years later he relocated to Tbilisi, the capital of Georgia. From 1975 to 1983 he studied at the Moscow State Tchaikovsky Conservatory, where he took a doctoral degree in music performance. With his wife, Svetlana (also a graduate of the Moscow Conservatory), and daughter, he immigrated to the United States in 1989. They now live in Kansas City as naturalized citizens. Interview: April 2009.

John M. MacGregor

Art historian and former psychotherapist John M. MacGregor (1941–) has been a pioneer in the study of the relationship between insanity and creativity, psychiatry and art. Born in Montreal, he studied painting on his own before embarking on psychoanalytic research at the Menninger Foundation and the Hampstead Clinic in London. He studied art history at McGill University and took his PhD from Princeton. His *The Discovery of the Art of the Insane* (1989) has been hailed as a landmark as the first scholarly study of the "mad" artist and public attitudes toward insanity and creativity. A second volume, *Henry Darger: In the Realms of the Unreal*, aroused controversy with its publication in 2002. Interview: San Francisco, November 1990 and April 2009.

Akio Mayeda

Akio Mayeda (1935–) is a founding member of the Robert-Schumann-Gesellschaft in Düsseldorf and one of the organizers with Klaus Wolfgang Niemöller of the *Neuen Robert-Schumann-Ausgabe*, whose volumes began appearing in 1991. His books include *Robert Schumanns Weg zur Symphonie* (1992). Interview: Düsseldorf, June 1991.

Susan McClary

Specializing in the cultural criticism of music, Susan McClary is a professor of musicology at the University of California, Los Angeles. She is best known for her books *Feminine Endings: Music, Gender, and Sexuality*

(1991) and *Conventional Wisdom* (2000). She has revealed a special interest in gender considerations in the music of Robert Schumann. Interview: Minneapolis, June 1990.

Margit McCorkle

After completing a thematic catalogue on Johannes Brahms in 1984, Margit McCorkle published her *Robert Schumann: thematisch-bibliographisches Werkverzeichnis* in 2003. As part of the ongoing *Robert-Schumann-Ausgabe* (New Robert Schumann Complete Edition), it is an indispensable volume for the Schumann specialist. Ms. McCorkle lives in Vancouver. Her current projects include project work on a Carl Maria von Weber *Ausgabe* and plans to launch a website under the auspices of Henle Verlag to update recent scholarly findings on the Schumann catalogue. She received the Zwickau Schumann Prize in 2007. Interviews: Düsseldorf, June 1991 and Vancouver, May 2009.

Timothy F. Mitchell

The late Tim Mitchell (?–1993) was a professor of art history at the University of Kansas from 1979 to 1993 and a specialist in the life and work of the nineteenth-century German painter Caspar David Friedrich. He is the author of *Art and Science in German Landscape Painting, 1770–1840* (1993). His special interest concerned the connections between Friedrich's landscape paintings and the songs of Robert Schumann. Interview: Lawrence, Kansas, April 1986.

Gerd Nauhaus

The former director of Robert-Schumann-Haus in Zwickau was born in 1944. His publications include *Dichtergarten für Musik: eine Anthologie für Freunde der Literatur und Musik* (2007), *Schumanniana Nova: Festschrift Gerd Nauhaus zum 60 Geburtstag* (2002), *The Marriage Diaries of Robert and Clara Schumann* (with Peter Ostwald, 1994), and *Robert Schumann: eine Lebenschronik in Bildern und Dokumenten* (with Ernst Burger, 1999), and *Robert Schumann Tagebücher, 1836–1856* (1987). In 1986 he was the recipient of the Schumann Prize from the city of Zwickau. Interviews: Düsseldorf, June 1988, and Zwickau, June 1994.

Wolfgang Nehring

Wolfgang Nehring is a professor of German at UCLA. His special interests include German romanticism and the turn-of-the-century German literature of Hugo von Hofmannsthal and Arthur Schnitzler. He has published an edition of Wilhelm Wackenroder and articles on Eichendorff and E. T. A. Hoffmann. Interviews: Los Angeles, 1989 and 2009.

John Nelson

One of today's most versatile and accomplished conductors, John Nelson was born in Costa Rica of American parents. He studied at Wheaton College and at the Juilliard School. Currently the Directeur Musicale Honoraire of the Ensemble Orchestral de Paris, Maestro Nelson has also held posts with the Indianapolis Symphony Orchestra (1976–87) and the Caramoor Festival (1983–1990). His particular love is for the big choral works of Berlioz and Schumann. Interview: New York City, October 1991.

Garrick Ohlsson

Since his triumph at the 1970 Chopin International Piano Competition and the reception of the Avery Fisher Prize in 1994, Garrick Ohlsson (1948–) has established himself as a pianist of the first rank with an enormous repertoire, including recordings of the complete Chopin piano music. He was a student of Claudio Arrau and has recently performed all-Busoni concerts at Lincoln Center. Interviews: Kansas City, October 1987 and 1989.

Peter F. Ostwald

Before his untimely death in 1996, Dr. Peter F. Ostwald was internationally recognized for his work on the interaction between music and psychiatry. His books on Schumann include *Schumann: The Inner Voices of a Musical Genius* (1985, winner of an ASCAP Deems Taylor Award) and his translations of *The Marriage Diaries of Robert and Clara Schumann* (1993). Both belong on the shelf of essential works on Schumann. The Berlin-born Ostwald received his medical degree from the University of California–San Francisco in 1950. Six years later he joined the staff of the Langley Porter Psychiatric Institute. His other books include *Vaslav Nijinsky: A Leap into Madness* (1991) and *Glenn Gould: Ecstasy and Tragedy of Genius* (1997). Four interviews: San Francisco, 1985–89.

Elizabeth Paley

Elizabeth Paley (1967–) earned a doctorate in music theory from the University of Wisconsin–Madison and is currently an organist, pianist, and freelance writer living in Durham, North Carolina. She has served on the faculty of the University of Kansas and Duke University. Her publications have appeared in *The Astrophysical Journal, 19th-Century Music, The Cambridge Companion to Schumann, South Atlantic Quarterly,* and (under a pseudonym) *The Chronicle of Higher Education.* Her research interests include narratology, feminist theory, the intersections of music and the supernatural in nineteenth-century melodrama, and, in the case of Schumann, *Paradise and the Peri* and *Manfred*. Interview: Durham, North Carolina, April 2009.

Leon Plantinga

Leon Plantinga is an emeritus professor of music history at Yale University. Since his retirement in 2005, he has served as director of the Yale Collection of Musical Instruments. He is the author of *Schumann as Critic* (1967), *Clementi: His Life and Music* (1977), *Romantic Music: A History of Musical Style in Nineteenth-Century Europe* (1984), and *Beethoven's Concertos: History, Styles, Performance* (1999). Interview: New Haven, Connecticut, July 1990.

Simon Preston

During his illustrious career, Simon Preston (1938–) has distinguished himself as one of the great organists of modern times, as well as one of the most illustrious musicians in the history of English cathedral music. He was born in Bournemouth, England, and studied the organ with C. H. Trevor and Sir David Willcocks. Interview: Kansas City, 2004.

Nancy B. Reich

Independent scholar Nancy B. Reich is the author of the definitive *Clara Schumann: The Artist and the Woman,* winner of a Deems Taylor Award in 1985. The revised version, which was published in 2001, contains a valuable catalogue of works. She has taught at Queens CUNY, Manhattanville College, and Bard College. In 1996 she was awarded the Robert Schumann Prize of the city of Zwickau, Germany. She lives in Hastings-on-Hudson, New York. Six interviews: Hastings-on-Hudson, New York City, Kansas City, and Düsseldorf, Germany, 1985–2008.

Erika Reiman

Erika Reiman (1968–) attended Mount Allison University, McGill University, and the University of Toronto, where she earned her PhD in historical musicology. Since the publication of her book *Schumann's Piano Cycles and the Novels of Jean Paul* (2004)—the best volume in English on the subject—she has concentrated on piano performance. In 2007 she premiered a piano concerto by David Fawcett, a composer living in Hamilton, Ontario. Interview: Montreal, Canada, April 2009.

Aribert Reimann

A distinguished opera composer and pianist, Aribert Reimann was born in Berlin in 1936. After studying composition at Berlin's Hochschule für Musik, he made his reputation as a composer with several literary operas, including *King Lear* (written for Dietrich Fischer-Dieskau) and *The Castle*. Among his works relating to his lifelong interests in Robert Schumann are the *Seven Fragments for Orchestra, in Memoriam Robert Schumann* and an instrumentation for mezzo-soprano and orchestra of the *Maria Stuart* song cycle. He won the Arnold Schoenberg prize in 2006. Of special note is the fact that in 1993 Reimann obtained the diary of Dr. Richarz (Schumann's doctor in Endenich) from the nephew of Richarz's aunt's godson. He handed it over to the Archives of the Academy of the Arts, Berlin. Interview: Düsseldorf, 1991.

Joshua Rifkin

Musicologist, pianist, and conductor, Joshua Rifkin (1944–) studied with Vincent Persichetti at Juilliard. Although widely known for his work with the Bach Ensemble, beginning in 1978, he is also noted for his research in the fields of Renaissance, Baroque, and ragtime music. Interview: Lawrence, Kansas, 1989.

Charles Rosen

Charles Rosen is a professor of music and social thought at the University of Chicago and has been the Charles Eliot Norton Lecturer at Harvard. His books include *The Classical Style: Haydn, Mozart, Beethoven* (1971), which won the National Book Award; *The Romantic Generation* (1995); and *Romantic Poets, Critics, and Other Madmen* (1998). He is a concert pianist, musicologist, and theoretician whose authority extends from Bach to Boulez and whose erudition encompasses painting, languages, and literature. A specialist in Schumann, he recorded for Globe Records in the Netherlands—later released by Nonesuch Records—the "Revolutionary Masterpieces," which restored our attention to the original manuscripts of Schumann's piano cycles of the 1830s. Two interviews: New York City, 1988, and Kansas City, 2008.

Michael Saffle

A professor of music and humanities at Virginia Tech, Michael Saffle earned his PhD at Stanford University. He has published articles and reviews in the *Journal of the American Musicological Society*, *Acta Musicologica, Notes,* the *Programmhefte* of Bayreuth's Wagner Festival, *Music & Letters,* and the *Leonardo Music Journal*. His books include *Franz Liszt: A Guide to Research,* revised and republished by Routledge in 2004 and again in 2009. In 2006, on his sixtieth birthday, he was honored with a *Festschrift* published as an issue of the cultural-studies eJournal *Spaces of Identity*. Interview: Blacksburg, Virginia, May 17, 2009.

Eric Sams

The interests and accomplishments of the late Eric Sams (1926–2004) were many. Cryptologist, musicologist, Shakespearean scholar, and specialist in the music of Robert Schumann, he grew up in a working-class household in Essex, England. After distinguishing himself as a code breaker in the Intelligence Corps during World War II, he won a scholarship to Corpus Christi College, Cambridge; joined the Civil Service in the Department of Employment; married; and began his extensive series of reviews and articles in publications like the *Musical Times*. Several books followed, in which he applied his cryptoanalytic methods in pursuit of what he called "tonal analogues" in music; all of these have become standard texts: *The Songs of Hugo Wolf* (1961), *The Songs of Robert Schumann* (1969), and *The Songs of Johannes Brahms* (2000). For further information, consult the website www.ericsams.org, which has been organized by Professor Erik Battaglia of the Verdi Conservatory in Torino, Italy. Interview: Sanderstead, Surrey, October 1988.

Samuel Sanders

The late Samuel Sanders (1937–1999) was an esteemed and beloved recital partner for many of the great singers and instrumentalists of our time, including Robert White, Itzhak Perlman, and Mstislav Rostropovich. He was born in the Bronx and, despite a congenital heart ailment that would later take his life, made his New York piano recital debut when he was thirteen and subsequently made his reputation as an accompanist (he preferred the term "collaborator"). As a faculty member of the Juilliard School, he established a master's degree program for accompanists. Interview: New York City, 1992.

Helma Sanders-Brahms

Helma Sanders-Brahms was born in Emden, East Frisia, in 1940. After studying literature and drama at the University of Cologne, she became a trainee in film production under Pier Paolo Pasolini. Her films have aroused controversy, dealing with mental illness, feminism, and Germany's Nazi past. Several of her films have dramatized the lives of artists, including *Mein Herz*, about Gottfried Benn, and *Geliebte Clara*, about Clara Schumann. No other female filmmaker from Germany has had more movies at the Cannes Film Festival.

Wolfgang Sawallisch

Acknowledged one of the world's greatest conductors, Maestro Sawallisch (1923–) was born in Munich, Germany. He made his conducting debut in Augsburg in 1950. Among his many subsequent posts were general music director at Hamburg, principal conductor of the Vienna Symphony Orchestra, and music director of the Philadelphia Orchestra, from which he retired in 2003. A gifted pianist, he has performed in recitals with Dietrich Fischer-Dieskau, Elisabeth Schwarzkopf, and Thomas Hampson. He has recorded all the Schumann symphonies. Interview: Düsseldorf, June 1988.

András Schiff

Born in 1953 in Budapest, Hungary, András Schiff has become one of the most respected pianists of his generation. He began his formal studies at the Ferenc Liszt Academy and in 1974 was the gold medalist in the Tchaikovsky Competition in Moscow. Active in all phases of music making, he has excelled in conducting and in organizing music festivals all over the world. His Schumann performances include the complete music for piano four hands (with Peter Frankl), and his honors include the Claudio Arrau Memorial Medal from the Robert Schumann Society in Düsseldorf in 1994. Interview: Kansas City, April 1998.

Maurice Sendak

Acclaimed artist and illustrator Maurice Sendak was born in Brooklyn, New York, in 1928. Best known as an award-winning author and illustrator of numerous books, including the celebrated *Where the Wild Things Are* (1963), he has also illustrated the tales of the Brothers Grimm and designed sets for operas. His many awards include the Caldecott Prize and the National Medal of Arts. In 2003 he was the first recipient of the Astrid Lindgren Memorial Award for Literature. Interview: Kansas City, Missouri, October 1989.

Steven Spooner

Recipient of many awards, including the top prize of the Hilton Head International Piano Competition and prize winner of the New Orleans International Piano Competition, Professor Steven Spooner has studied at Loyola University, Paris Conservatory, the Moscow and Tbilisi conservatories, and Indiana University, Bloomington (where he completed his doctorate). He has released two solo recordings of works by Schubert and Liszt on the EMR Classics label. He is currently assistant professor of piano at the University of Kansas. Interview: Lawrence, Kansas, April 2009.

Richard Stoltzman

The first wind player to win the Avery Fisher Prize (1986), Richard Stoltzman (1942–) stands in the front rank of clarinet performers. Born in Omaha, Nebraska, he first learned the instrument from his father, and later he studied with Professor Keith Wilson at the Yale School of Music. He has performed in every possible music style and in every conceivable media environment. His recordings of the clarinet music of Brahms have won him two Grammys. Interview: Kansas City, October 1990.

Thomas Synofzik

Thomas Synofzik (1966–) is the director of Robert-Schumann-Haus in Zwickau, Germany, Schumann's birthplace. Dr. Synofzik studied musicology, church music, and historical keyboard instruments in Cologne and Brussels. He taught at music colleges in Trossingen, Essen, Cologne, Dortmund, and Detmold. His first publication devoted to Schumann was a 1993 edition of Schumann's letters housed in the Bonn municipal archives. His dissertation in 2000 was devoted to Heinrich Schütz and his contemporaries. He published a monograph on Schumann and Heine, and a book with photographs from Clara Schumann's photo albums and several articles and musical first editions. Interview: Zwickau, March 2009.

John Taras

John Taras (1919–2004) danced with Michel Fokine's American Ballet Theater. Interview: New York City, April 1988.

Ronald Taylor

Author of many books, including *E. T. A. Hoffman* (1973), *The Romantic Tradition in Germany* (1970), *Richard Wagner: His Life, Art and Thought* (1979), *Robert Schumann: His Life and Work* (1982), and *Kurt Weill: Composer in a Divided World* (1991). Taylor is an emeritus professor of German at the University of Sussex. He is a well-known translator of German literature and of critical and scientific works on a broad variety of subjects. Interviews: Champaign-Urbana, Illinois, April 1992, and London, January 2008.

R. Larry Todd

Professor R. Larry Todd has been hailed by the *New York Times* as "the dean of Mendelssohn scholars in the United States." A professor of music at Duke University, he has published several books on Mendelssohn, including *Mendelssohn: A Life in Music* (2003); *Mendelssohn and His World* (1991); and *Mendelssohn and Schumann: Essays on Their Music and Its Context* (1984), coedited with Jon W. Finson. He is also the general editor of the Schirmer series *Studies in Musical Genres and Repertories,* for which he contributed *Nineteenth-Century Piano Music* (1990). Interviews: Bard College, August 1991, and Durham, North Carolina, March 2009.

Uriel Tsachor

Uriel Tsachor is professor and head of the piano area of the University of Iowa School of Music. He was born January 1, 1958, and took his degrees from the Juilliard School and the Tel Aviv Rubin Academy. Winner of the Busoni and Queen Elisabeth competitions, he has concertized worldwide and has an extensive discography on EMI and Musical Heritage Society, including many works by Schumann. He is a Steinway Artist. Interview: May 12, 2009, Iowa City, Iowa.

Laura Tunbridge

Professor Laura Tunbridge is a lecturer in music analysis and critical theory at the University of Manchester. Her dissertation from Princeton examined Schumann's music for Byron's *Manfred* and Goethe's *Faust*. Her *Schumann's Late Style* (2007) is a valuable reassessment of Schumann's later works. Interview: London, May 2008.

Charles Wadsworth

Charles Wadsworth (1929–) was for twenty years the presiding genius behind the Chamber Music Society of Lincoln Center, which he formed in 1969. A native of Newnan, Georgia, he is also the artistic director of several other chamber music series, including, since 1977, the Spoleto Festival USA. He has received the Handel Medallion for his contributions to the cultural life of the City of New York. Interview: New York City, June 2000.

Sarah Walker

Sarah Walker is one of the greatest mezzo-sopranos of our time. Born in Gloucestershire in 1943, she studied voice with Vera Rózsa at the Royal College of Music from 1961 to 1965. In addition to having a wide operatic repertoire, she is a patron of the London Song Festival and a staunch advocate of lieder singing and the song repertoire. Her recording of the Schumann *Maria Stuart* lieder with pianist Roger Vignoles was released by CRD in 1982. Interviews: Kansas City, Missouri, October 1988, and London, February 2009.

Gillian Weir

An internationally renowned organist, Gillian Weir was born in 1941 and studied piano with Cyril Smith and organ with Ralph Downes. She made her debut in 1965 at the Royal Albert Hall playing the Poulenc Organ Concerto. Since then she has won renown for her performances of the complete works of Olivier Messiaen. In 1996 she was made a Dame Commander of the British Empire, the first organist to receive this accolade. She has recently been appointed Distinguished Visiting Artist at the Peabody Conservatory. Interview: Kansas City, November 1989.

Robert Winter

A formidable scholar/pianist/multimedia artist, Professor Robert Winter earned his PhD at the University of Chicago and is currently professor of music and interactive arts at UCLA. He has written important books about Beethoven history and performance (*The Beethoven Sketchbooks: History, Reconstruction, Inventory,* 1985), broadcast on American Public Radio, and pioneered interactive software about a wide range of subjects in music history. He has become an articulate international spokesperson for the role of content and the arts in a digital world. In 2008 he was honored with UCLA's Distinguished Teaching Award. Three interviews: Kansas City, Los Angeles, and Columbus, Ohio, 1987–2002.

John Worthen

Before becoming Professor of D. H. Lawrence Studies at the University of Nottingham, where he remains emeritus professor, John Worthen taught at universities in North America and Wales. In addition to his biographical work on Lawrence, he has published *The Gang: Coleridge, the Hutchinsons & the Wordsworths in 1802* (2001) and *Robert Schumann: Life and Death of a Musician* (2007). Interview: London, July 2007.

Peter Zazofsky

Boston-born Peter Zazofsky (1955–) studied violin with Joseph Silverstein and Dorothy DeLay. Among his many prizes are the 1980 Queen Elisabeth competition and the grand prize of the 1979 Montreal International competition. He is associate professor of violin and chamber music at Boston University. He has recorded violin works by Robert and Clara Schumann. Interview: Kansas City, September 1988.

Thomas Zehetmair

One of today's most outstanding violinists, chamber performers, and conductors, Thomas Zehetmair (1961–) was born in Salzburg, Austria, and studied at the Salzburg Mozarteum. He formed his own string quartet in 1994. He frequently performs Schumann's violin works with his fellow enthusiasts Heinz Holliger and Christoph Eschenbach. Interview: Düsseldorf, June 1994.

David Zinman

One of the world's finest conductors, David Zinman was born in New York in 1936 and began studying the violin at age six. After graduating from the

Oberlin College Conservatory of Music, he became one of the youngest conductors of the Netherlands Chamber Orchestra in Amsterdam. From 1985 to 1998 Maestro Zinman was the music director of the Baltimore Symphony Orchestra. Since 1998 he has been music director of the Aspen Music Festival and chief conductor of the Tonhalle Orchestra in Zürich. Interview: Kansas City, March 1990.

Eugenia Zukerman

Acclaimed flutist, accomplished broadcaster, and best-selling author, Eugenia Zukerman was born in Boston. After graduating from Barnard College as an English major, she turned to music and at the Juilliard School from 1964 to 1966 was the pupil of Julius Baker. In 1980 she added to her concert career the position of arts correspondent for the *CBS Sunday Morning* program, for which she has produced more than three hundred artist interviews/stories. Interview: Kansas City, June 1988.

1

"The Extravagant Gaze"

Romanticism

Commentators: *Theodore Albrecht, Jacques Barzun, Albert Boime, Roger Cook, John Daverio, David Ferris, John F. Fetzer, D. Kern Holoman, Katherine Kolb, Lawrence Kramer, John M. MacGregor, Susan McClary, Tim Mitchell, Wolfgang Nehring, Leon Plantinga, Nancy B. Reich, Erika Reiman, Joshua Rifkin, Charles Rosen, Maurice Sendak, and Ronald Taylor*

HISTORICAL BACKGROUND

> *I am affected by everything that goes on in the world, politics, literature, and people. I think them over in my own way, and then I express them in music. That's why so many of my compositions are difficult to understand, because they relate to distant interests.*
>
> —Robert Schumann, letter to Clara Wieck, April 1838

> *We have a duty, if we want to understand a composer like Robert Schumann, to enter as fully as we can into his world. We must go outside the individual personality in order to see him in the round. There is no question that Schumann was aware of and responded to the whole spectrum of history, arts, and ideas around him.*
>
> —Jacques Barzun

EDITOR'S NOTE

On what basis does historian Professor Robert Winter declare in these pages that Robert Schumann is the "quintessential romantic, the point-man in the left-wing platoon"? Such questions and answers are best approached by placing Schumann in the contexts of the revolutionary ferment, turmoil, and creative exuberance of the late eighteenth and early nineteenth centuries. Like his immediate contemporaries—Hector Berlioz, Richard Wagner, Frédéric Chopin, Felix Mendelssohn, Franz Liszt, and Giuseppe Verdi, among others—his life and work are compounded of the energies and contradictions of those times.

Eighteenth and Nineteenth-Century Contexts and Nationalist Movements

Jacques Barzun

Romanticism was the great surge of genius, of enthusiasm, of a sense of exploration, and of a constructive impulse coming after the end of the Napoleonic Wars that affected all of the arts and produced that collection of masterpieces that we still haven't totally absorbed. That generation of Schumann, Berlioz, Liszt, Heine, and the others had been made highly self-conscious by the turmoil of twenty-five years of revolution and war all over Europe. And they no longer had the rather simplistic view of the eighteenth-century French neoclassicism that intellect, reason, was all-sufficient. They knew there were other elements to the human organism, and they observed them. Introspection was their great art. They wanted to be all-inclusive. They wanted to know about

Jacques Barzun's books on romanticism are central to the study of the subject. (Photograph courtesy of Jacques Barzun)

the whole world, not just western Europe. And they wanted to know about the whole man, not just the top part of his head.

I fail to see why so many intelligent people cannot grasp what romanticism was about—why it came to be and how it flowed into a vast delta of separate tendencies, realism, naturalism, symbolism, surrealism, and all that. And still such people continue to use the word *romantic* or *romanticist* as a term of general abuse; or, if not merely that, as a term for wildness or incoherence. The analogue, of course, is the way Shakespeare was first taken, as someone who didn't know what he was about and who bursts out in wild inspirations and formal irregularities. It's taken over three hundred years to absorb Shakespeare, and maybe it'll take three hundred years (and we're not there yet) to absorb romanticism. That baffles me. I have people who read my books and write to me and talk to me and say, "I see, I understand"; and in the very next sentence they show they haven't understood.

Leon Plantinga

Romanticism is a very, very puzzling phenomenon. None of us are very sure we really know what we are talking about when we talk about romanticism. People are called romantics who have widely differing notions about intellectual and cultural stances. As you probably know, some scholars have thrown up their hands in horror at trying to pin it down. I'm not quite so despairing about it. There are some things that we can associate with the term. It was about the beginning of the nineteenth century that a conscious, self-designating romantic period, or romantic movement, came to life, primarily in Germany. Friedrich Schiller, a younger friend of Goethe, was a central character in this transaction. He wrote a book in which he was trying to make distinctions among several kinds of literature. Some he thought as belonging to a classical tradition; others he regarded as *not* of that tradition at all. So, we have to go back and ask, what does *classical* mean?

That is part of a European civilization that we've had with us since the fifteenth century or so, this glorification of ancient culture, and most particularly of Greek culture. There were attempts to re-create it, emulate it, derive principles from it. And in the seventeenth century the academic system in French letters was founded on the notion of establishing and codifying principles based on what they thought was ancient Greek culture. However, in the eighteenth century in England came signs of rebellion. There was a new enthusiasm for original genius, something that was *natural,* something you were *born* with, not something you got from education or from civilizing agencies. It was a notion of "genius" that was a sort of attendant, personal spirit hovering around like a genie above your head, which connects you to a higher reality. So, the man behind the plow can be just as much a genius as the man born in a palace. This ran directly counter to the old notions of cultivation of art, which is subject to precept, subject to norm, or art which is supposed to represent universal values, things that are apprehendable by everyone. Anybody can be a genius, but it's not democratic in that anybody can, through his own efforts, *become* one. Either you are or you aren't.

Then, in Germany at the beginning of the nineteenth century, you have Schiller and the brothers Schlegel, Friedrich and August, proceeding to define a second tradition, not the old classical tradition, but one that is defined as a *departure* from it. There's a new interest in medieval literature, which had been scorned by the classicists. They had regarded the Middle Ages as a "middle" period, a dark abyss, which they dismissed as a time when absolutely nothing was going on, a time between the glories of Greece and Rome and the present day. Thus things like romance, the stuff about knights and kings and courtly love, were regarded as nonsense. But now there's a new interest in all that. The term *romanticism* comes from *Roman,* or *romance*—the "roman de la rose," a very much admired medieval treatise. Art comes to represent a way to get at the truth that is not available through other routes. It becomes almost a replacement for religions, for philosophy. Part of this is simply a collapse in the faith of reason, the ability of human reason to figure out what the world is about, what action ought to be, what society ought to be. It's a response to the old bromide that the rationalists say, that if you just give us enough time, allow us to formulate our questions in a clear and unequivocal way, the answers will be in some way self-evident. As it says in our Declaration of Independence: "We hold these truths to be self-evident, that all men are created equal . . ." (Well, why in the world should this be *self-evident?*) That's a characteristically rationalist stance. But in the early nineteenth century, people don't believe that anymore. Rationalism had gotten us into all kinds of trouble. Particularly in Germany they tended to look into their own psyches and into feelings and nonverbal apprehensions of things. Art—particularly this romantic view of art, which includes a transcendental, cognitive value in art—holds sway.

The situation in the nineteenth century in England was very different. England never had been the center of a musical current before this. The last important English composer had been Henry Purcell! The reason for that, it seems to me, is that it was not thought that to be a composer was socially respectable. Charles Burney had done his best in the 1780s and 1790s to establish a national conservatory. It was always an uphill battle in England because of the social stigma attached to entertainers.

Entertainment was the sort of thing one *buys* but not what one *does*. After all, marketing and trade and mercantilism had begun in England before anywhere else. Despite the notable exceptions of the Lake Poets, the Gothic novelists in English culture, and someone like Jeremy Bentham, a positivist view of English society was much more characteristic.

Albert Boime

People were becoming self-conscious during this period. They suddenly became *aware* of possibilities, because classicism was being undermined; there was a self-consciousness about art that previous masters, previous critics didn't have. Suddenly you were aware there was more than one possibility. Romanticism is there. By the time of the July Monarchy in France, it's in place and has to be dealt with. It's no longer being treated as the bastard stepchild of some other—of the Revolution, for example. As a result, this self-consciousness gives people a greater awareness of themselves, greater self-understanding and at the same time greater awareness of themselves in history. And I think it's that self-consciousness that we see in eclecticism. Eclecticism is a highly self-conscious style in which young artists find themselves confronted with two or more possibilities;, and each one pulling for his or her attention . . .

Since his seizure of power in France in 1799 and his claim to be emperor five years later, Napoleon became an icon that dominated the first quarter of the nineteenth century. His model is always there in place. Balzac wanted to do with the pen what Napoleon did with the sword. And of course everyone talks about "Napoleonic" complexes. People had enough at this period of that Caesarian kind of domination. I think they wanted something else to loosen the strain of Napoleon. Curiously enough, Napoleon was a highly eclectic person, who ordered and regimented all the fine arts and culture and everything else in society. It's a kind of hybridized style that emerges in the Napoleon epoch of realism. It fuses links with the past with a sense of the modern age.

For example, he rejects as inappropriate the idea of allegory in David's painting "The Oath of the Eagles." He's also very disturbed that his image atop the Vendôme Column was going to be in classical garb, although his advisers finally convinced him it was appropriate because the column itself was based on Trajan's Column in Rome, so that classical garb seemed to be appropriate. But he was very disturbed by it. He had a modern sensibility; he was very much involved with science, technology, and industry in the period. But he also had a responsibility, an urgent need to persuade everyone that he had a legitimate place within French history. In order to shore up this position, which after all was the result of usurpation— Napoleon had no right to be there, in terms of history—he had to link himself with former rulers. So he was constantly trotting out images of Charlemagne and Henry III, always making these connections to the historical past, as if he himself represents historical links with the past. He was in a double bind. He had to persuade the French public that he was part of the mainstream of French history. And at the same time he had a personal need to live in the present. He was mastering and conquering space and time in a way that demanded realism. So there is that kind of collision between the past and the present in Napoleon.

Napoleon was welcomed abroad as a unifying figure. Although he tightened the reins at home, abroad he overcame centuries of authoritarian and feudalistic rule. So in some ways when he went abroad, he was welcomed by the local people. There was usually a Bonapartist party in place to see him and were glad to see the old feudal system go. All those remnants of aristocracy and clericalism disappear. For example, when he went to Spain, he got rid of the Inquisition. When he went to Germany, he administrated it in a bureaucratic way that made sense. And he collapsed all those principalities and fiefdoms into a very efficient working bureaucratic apparatus. So I think that people did appreciate him wherever he went. Not everyone understands that. On the other hand, his opponents were there, as well. So there was always conflict. Out of that conflict comes the great nationalist tendency of the nineteenth century. Nationalism of course is the great basis for romantic painting and romantic music. I would say that Napoleon's occupation in all those generated this kind of nationalism. This rethinking of one's roots.

Certainly wherever the Napoleonic armies went, there was a force in place. Either people were "Napoleonophiles," and were inclined to be sympathetic to Napoleon and the French, or there were Frenchmen positioned to guide things in the interim. So, one could say that all activities in Germany during the Napoleonic period were monitored, especially after the defeat of the Germans at Jena in 1806. People who opposed Napoleon had to speak, write, or paint covertly in order to do that. This is not new in the history of art. For example, William Blake passed many of his own ideas into very cryptic, unexplainable forms just because things were so rough, especially during the time of the Revolution there in England.

In Germany you have the philosopher-patriot Johann Fichte, for example, talking about the great German future in terms of education, culture, although he comes pretty close to condemning Napoleonic incursions. Fichte's addresses to the German people were done through the medium of culture. So he's addressing the situation in an *indirect* form. The painter Caspar David Friedrich and others are also doing allegorical paintings. Medievalism becomes an important cultural manifestation of this connection between past and present. It was a moment in German history when there was unification, and the German state was free from European—I should say, from foreign—domination.

Jacques Barzun

Although Napoleon had been tramping all over the towns of Germany, he was also liberating them from ancestral constraints of a social, political, and moral kind. He was the bringer of liberty by force in a manner we don't readily imagine nowadays. But he certainly made the Rhineland and north Italy modern regions, taking a step of 150 years in 15 years. I don't know how long it would have taken the rest of Europe to make the same giant step. Thus he encouraged nationalism in two ways. First of all, he embodied the French Revolution, the nation in arms, the great new nation dedicated to the rights of man. Second, when his ambitions really got to be much too much, these disparate duchies and principalities united in a nationalist feeling *against* him. So he brought in the idea of liberty, and then the idea was turned around against him—quite properly. People were disillusioned because they discovered—the way Wordsworth did—that the latter phases of the Revolution systemized by Napoleon in his domestic rule were tyrannical (although by modern standards he was a gentle tyrant, quite large-minded about many things). They were disappointed because the ideal couldn't be worked out practically. He couldn't keep the nation and half of Europe together without decrees of an oppressive sort. And that brought about the disillusionment, particularly among literary and artistic people, who tend to think that no rules of any kind should obtain in the social realm.

Albert Boime

Nationalism is a very stimulating force for artists. It gives artists a reason to be, in a sense. And you find a number of artists being swept along with the grand nationalist fervor in all these countries of this period. Before this, artists were supposed to be apolitical in their work, from the "invasion" of ideas political, social, and other. I think this is a distortion of the artist's role in history. The artist, like any other individual, responds to what's happening in the world. And I think that artists are much more political than usually thought as being.

Theodore Albrecht

You have to remember that nationalism was on the rise as a part of romanticism. Goethe, both as poet, playwright, novelist, and Friedrich Schiller were Germans writing in German for Germans and creating a new national language. Much as Manzoni would do in Italy in the nineteenth century. And we can't forget people like the Brothers Grimm who were collecting old folktales. They were not just tales to tell the kiddies before they went to bed. They were part of a systematic oral history of going out and collecting folktales before the Industrial Revolution killed them off.

Germany was a geographical, philosophical, and social construct that was now united by language. This is why we have in the nineteenth century an August Hoffmann von Fallersleben, who can write "Deutschland, Deutschland, über Alles," which was not a proto-Nazi poem or proto-Nazi anthem, but a poem that simply expresses nationalistic tendencies, nationalistic boundaries of the German language, which extended from west of Cologne to east of Berlin and down into the Austrian lands as well. This was a concept of a "gross-Deutschland" that went across nationalistic boundaries, went across religious boundaries, and was determined by the language. And again, we go back to the Brothers Grimm. We forget about the Grimm brothers as far as their work on the German language. They were the first to put together a huge dictionary of the German language, what the Oxford Dictionary is for us today. Its meanings, literary associations, and histories of words are all part of the Grimm dictionary of the German language that took decades to compile.

Remember, what we now call Germany had consisted of hundreds of principalities and free cities, especially in central Germany, extending from Hamburg down through the Rhinelands; down through Cologne, Düsseldorf, Mainz; down the Rhine to Freiburg; going down through Zelle, Hanover, Fulde, Frankfurt. Each owed its allegiance to larger principalities, larger kingdoms. What we tend to forget is that some of these were much closer aligned to France than they were to Germany, especially some of the outlying Habsburg tributaries. Think, for instance, of Bonn. Who was the ruler of Bonn? In Mannheim? Those rulers were generally younger brothers of the current emperor, whoever he happened to be. Remember that in the imperial household, any household of nobility in those days, the eldest son inherited all. The second son would be designated for the military. If the eldest son died, then the military son could take over the running of the principality, of the family fortunes, et cetera. If there were third and fourth sons, they often became prince-archbishops, electors, cardinals. Think, for instance, of Beethoven's patron, the archduke, Cardinal Rudolf, the younger brother of the emperor, a nephew of Emperor Joseph II (who we all know from *Amadeus*). He was far enough down the family line that he was going nowhere, unless the rest of the family was wiped out. Rudolf, who would never ascend to the throne, was designated for the priesthood.

Within the two years that Beethoven left Bonn, Bonn was French. The French took over the west bank of the Rhine by 1794. The Habsburg prince, archbishop, elector that ran Bonn, had to flee back to Vienna. The west bank of the Rhine became French, and the official language became French. This is quite typical. We have these cultural divisions. People in this area especially had this divided cultural loyalty. Napoleon was able to bring them together as a unified, large France—a "gross-France," a "gross-Frankreich." This much was good. What he also did was encourage economic development that could not have been there otherwise.

Once Napoleon was gone, you had the Congress of Vienna in 1815, which reestablished a lot of those principalities. The Germans hated that. A foreign government had imposed these good things on them, but it was still a foreign government. What you've got now is Prince Metternich sitting over in Vienna. He's looking at this situation and he starts to see Catholic and Protestant Germany uniting against the Holy Roman Empire. There's more autonomy for Bavaria than there was in the past, because at one time Bavaria extended to the Rhine River. Metternich looks on and sees a Germany that is not part of the Holy Roman Empire. He sees Catholic Germany in the south, but he sees unification coming together from the Protestant lands in the north. And any good Catholic German looks suspiciously on any good Protestant German and vice versa. Little by little, these religious barriers were starting to break down as these economic barriers broke down as well. By the same token, Metternich saw a weakening Habsburg Empire, and he did not want to see the traditions that were growing in a strengthened Germany undermine the Holy Roman Empire. So he tried his best to keep intrigues afoot so everyone would be suspicious of the other. He was very much a man who tried to get back to the old state of things. He was almost a monarch.

At this time the typical radical German nationalist patriot was looking toward a more intellectual Germany. He was a student. He was highly idealistic. Religion meant less to him than to his forebears a generation or two before. He was more inclined to put together a Catholic German with a Protestant and say—again, "Deutschland, über Alles." Whatever we are, We're Germans and we have to have this 'Germany' in the fore-front of our mind."

Tim Mitchell

A sense of German nationalist identity can be seen in the landscape paintings of Caspar David Friedrich [1774–1840]. His work was highly politicized. Friedrich paints landscapes in which he predicts the imminent defeat of Napoleon. There would be a deep forest with a single soldier looking into it. And you know if he ever goes in, he will not come out again. This was Friedrich's prediction that the French would never prevail against the Germans. There might be an eagle swooping over the valley, showing the continuing Germanic spirit. When I say "Germany" today,

I'm talking about a country that didn't really exist then. There were many principalities and dukedoms, et cetera. He was born a Swedish national. All his life he thought of himself as a German-speaking Swede. He was a nationalist and wanted a unified Germany. In fact, he even refused to correspond with his brother as long as he was on French soil. But after the defeat of Napoleon, the old forces came back to power. And there was an outlawing in Germany of wearing the old costumes. This was offensive to the new German powers. Friedrich's paintings often portrayed people wearing these costumes with their wide-brimmed hats. When you see these in the paintings, he's referring to a nationalist spirit.

PHILOSOPHICAL/ARTISTIC CONTEXTS

> *It is precisely from music that philosophers could learn that it is possible to say the profoundest things in the world. . . . Wonderful sound-meanings knock at every human heart with the quiet question, "Do you understand me?," but are by no means understood by everyone.*
> —Robert Schumann, 1834

EDITOR'S NOTE
No composer in the romantic period was more thoroughly steeped in the German, French, and English philosophers, novelists, poets, painters of his time than Robert Schumann. The discussions here examine pertinent philosophers Kant, Schopenhauer, and Rousseau; the aesthetic theories of August and Friedrich Schlegel; writers Goethe, Wilhelm Wackenroder, Novalis (Friedrich von Hardenberg), Joseph von Eichendorff, Heinrich Heine, Ludwig Tieck, Clemens Brentano, E. T. A. Hoffmann, and Jean Paul Friedrich Richter; and painters Delacroix and Caspar David Friedrich. Also examined are the Shakespeare and Bach revivals and the significance of the Orpheus myth in romantic thought and sensibility.

Aesthetes, Philosophers, and Critics

He saw himself on the threshold of the distance which he had often before gazed at in vain . . . and which he had mentally

painted in exotic colors. He was on the verge of immersing himself in the blue waters of the distance.
—Novalis, *Heinrich von Ofterdingen*

John F. Fetzer

I think we best understand the aesthetic contexts surrounding Schumann and his generation if we examine that enduring metaphor for the romantic spirit, the myth of Orpheus. This involves what I call the "threshold effect." From the broadest possible view, the romantic epoch in Germany literature falls roughly between 1796 and 1826. Europe in the 1790s felt itself on the threshold of something new in governmental rule, after centuries of monarchial domination. Romantic artists straddle the threshold between tradition and revolution, conservative tendencies and radical trends. In much of my research in romantic music, painting, and literature, I refer to this "threshold" effect. One example of this is that the artist yearns for some higher realm but, at the same time, is caught in the reality of everyday, practical living. The concept of the threshold assumes a position poised or wedged between viable alternatives. I personally don't think that the romanticist ever attains—or even deep down wants to attain—that higher realm that he's yearning for. Or, maybe he does want to, but knows it's impossible.

The fate of Orpheus, that quintessential poet-musician, embodies this "threshold effect." According to the myth, Orpheus descends into Hades, wins back Eurydice through the power of his words (poetry) and his music (the lyre), and attempts to bring her back with him to the upper world. But out of a basic human failing—or is it some divine intervention?—he doesn't have faith in his artistry, and he does the very thing he is forbidden to do—he looks back. At the moment he turns around to see her, he loses her. He is left on the threshold between fulfillment and frustration.

You look back and you see the impossibility of the dream. We call this the "romantic irony" or "romantic agony." You can agonize over it; or you can ironize the situation; but if you cross the threshold, once a decisive step is taken in either direction, we can no longer speak of romanticism. And that's your lot in life. It often happens that the romanticist sometimes deliberately destroys or leaves incomplete some of his creations. He'll set you up for a mood, and then by some trick dispels the mood, because he's aware that what he's looking for can never be attained. He can't really take that step across the threshold, but he has to stay there, unable to proceed. And that's why I think so many romantic works end as fragments, because there can be no solution that you can move toward. There's no closed circle where we can say, "Ah, gee, I see what he was getting at."

We're left in a kind of a limbo. We can only stand there at the threshold and seek a way of life and understanding that adjusts to this basically tragic situation we're in. The painter expresses the same thing. Think of the paintings of Caspar David Friedrich, where you see lonely individuals standing at an open window, on the seashore, on high mountain peaks, at doors or in doorways or some other transitional point. These are thresholds that open out to a beckoning outer life; but, at the same time, they are barriers across which they cannot cross.

Consider by contrast the eighteenth century, where the artist knew what was what. Jonathan Swift could write in his "A Modest Proposal," "Let's slay all the children and eat them!" But you knew as a rational individual that he was not really proposing this. Swift and his readers were secure in the meaning. But the romanticist lives in ambivalence and ambiguity. He has sympathy for both sides of the equation. Heine is a case in point. On the one hand, he loves the romantic dream and he sets it up in six strophes of a poem. But in the last line of the poem he equivocates with some biting little quip at the end. He wants us to believe in the dream, but he also knows it's impossible.

So the romanticist, like Orpheus, is an outsider, trapped on the threshold between the dream and the reality. Think about this in terms of musical enharmonics. You think you are in a tonal center, but all of a sudden, with a subtle shift, you're in another, but related, one. So the listener is not quite sure what tonal realm he's in. Schubert does this all the time. And so does Schumann. They are standing on the threshold between tonality and the disorienting atonality of the twentieth century. I see this as a kind of counterpart to the ambivalence of language, where the romantic poet realizes that words are not definite denotators of things but more connotators of things. Denotation would be the counterpart to taking that full step across the threshold into another realm. But the ambivalence of language, its connotative function, means straddling possible meanings. That's one reason why the romantics like Novalis and Eichendorff loved the construction "as if" (in German, "als ob"). The most famous poem by Eichendorff, to which Schumann put music, has the line, "It was as if Heaven kissed the Earth, so that [the Earth] had to think of [Heaven] as a kind of cosmic embracer." And the last stanza then reads, "My soul spread out its wings, flew through the quiet landscape, as if it were flying home." The "as if" construction is an ambivalence, a threshold between possibility and impossibility. So we are left in this "hovering" situation between a realization and a nonrealization. That is so characteristic of the romantics.

Orpheus also symbolizes a "lost Eden" of the union of words and music. What has happened over the course of the centuries is that a division has set in, a separation, where we confine music to one area and the word to another. To bring them back together again is one of the romantic ideals—to go back to a golden age when they were one and lived together in harmony. But we've lost that Eden because of our divided consciousness. The possibility to make music one with poetry is a kind of symbolic attempt to go back to that golden age that has been lost. Again, the romantic can only hover helplessly, trapped in the threshold between them.

The romantics in their time envisioned a crisis in communication and the discreditation of art and the artist. Language alone is not felt adequate to really express what we're trying to say. The most famous essay is the one everybody knows in German literature. It's written by Hugo von Hofmannsthal around 1900, and it's called "Letter to the Lord Chandos." In the poem a young poet laments to his benefactor, Chandos, "I can no longer write poetry, because the words crumble in my mouth like rotten mushrooms." You see, language no longer conveys the essence of things. It's just rotting mushrooms, decaying and incapable of conveying anything. You have the ability to write in a beautifully written idiom but an inability to really articulate anything. Ironically, by the way, Hofmannsthal after his Chandos Letter produced some of his best and purest poetry.

At the same time, words and music cannot be joined. One can hover only on the threshold between them. The alternatives for the composer and the painter invite a kind of nihilism. Poets like Clemens Brentano had the growing suspicion that silence might be preferable to song. This problem begins right with the romantic period but becomes a really crucial issue in the twentieth century. The path leads from lush romanticism to the austere atonality and the mathematical calculation of the Schoenbergian serial row down to the minimalism of Philip Glass and, finally, the "silent" compositions of John Cage. But we never get to the essence of what we want to "say."

With regard to the pictorial arts, we have the trend away from representation to abstraction of color, form, and painterly application in the twentieth century; and finally to the blank canvas.

But let's go back to this "threshold" business. Romantic agony, or romantic irony? How about yet another view? I'm fond of quoting the words of Mabel Dodge, a real-life counterpart to a character in a novel by Friedrich Schlegel, *Lucinde* [1799]. Listen to what Dodge tells her lover, John Reed, as they experience the beginnings in 1917 of the Russian Revolution: "Oh, Reed, darling, we are just at the Threshold and nothing is ever so wonderful as the Threshold of things."

Ronald Taylor

Let's first go back to the philosophical and literary roots of romanticism, which began in the eighteenth century. I start with people like Herder and go through Goethe and Schiller and the big philosophers, Kant, Hegel, Schelling, Fichte; and down through the nineteenth century with Jaspers and Heidegger. It is impossible to go very far in German literature in the nineteenth century without coming across the need to concern yourself with some philosophical issues of the time. This is not true, not the same with English literature. You do not need to read English philosophers in order to appreciate Shakespeare, Milton, Wordsworth, Keats, Shelley, Tennyson, the rest. But Germany has a heavily biased philosophical tradition. And this raises the need very soon to be concerned with matters of this kind.

Goethe is, of course, a huge figure. There is nobody else like Goethe in German culture; and Goethe has so many facets that he is intimidating. I think it very important not to turn Goethe into a philosopher. Goethe is, I think, primarily a poet. Great poetry contains a philosophy. Great poetry is about life. You cannot write about life, whether you write an essay or a sermon or a poem, without expressing some kind of—what I would call in the broadest sense—a philosophy. What one calls the "message" of poetry. If the man had wanted to write a philosophical treatise, if the man had wanted to give a sermon, he would have done so. He did not, he wrote poetry. And I think it's a very important distinction to make.

Another big name is Immanuel Kant. Kant dominates thought in Germany at the turn of the century, from the eighteenth to the nineteenth century. Kant determines the limits of what is knowable. If you look back into the eighteenth century, this is of course an exercise in rationalism. There is no point in talking about what we can never know about; let us talk about what we can know about, so that once the limits are drawn, we may know what our proper area of activity is. This is the backward-looking side, back into the eighteenth century, into the Enlightenment, into the Age of Reason. The forward-looking side, through the nineteenth century, is the side which influenced E. T. A. Hoffmann, Schopenhauer, and the German romantics in general. They said, "Right, if these are the limits of what we can know, we nonetheless realize that there is a huge area which is left untouched by investigations of that kind." And they assumed, because it is not amenable to the disciplines of rational argument, in Kantian terms, that what had been left over was all the more important; that the most important things in life are the things we *cannot* talk about, that we cannot reduce to rational criteria. Who does not know the emotion of love, who would dare to define what love is, perhaps the most important single reality in any man's life? Yet it remains a mystery, it remains peculiar to that man. And here you have, I think, the beginnings of romanticism, to which E. T. A. Hoffmann belongs, to which Schopenhauer belongs, and so on. The accent is on the subjective experience, that love for one man is not love for the next man; the mystery that goes with the spiritual reality of love, the spiritual reality of beauty, the aesthetic perception—all these things which cannot be reduced to rational criteria; and which by romantic definition are all the more important for that reason.

Of course, Robert Schumann, the most literate of the romantic composers, would have read Kant and Hoffmann. Hoffmann had studied with Kant in Königsberg and is certainly one of the many who came with the Kantian message, like Fichte, Schelling, and Schopenhauer. All these figures in the early nineteenth century were unthinkable until Kant, as it were, released the floodgates of this subjective experience.

Albert Boime

People are choosing the careers of composers, painters, novelists in the nineteenth century who might not have had the opportunity or inclination or even the possibility to make those choices prior to the French Revolution. A person can say, "When I grow up, I'm going to be an artist." This is unusual, unexpected in the nineteenth century. And I think it has to do with the historical change. More people, for example, can make this choice without necessarily undergoing that intensive preparation which we associate with the academy, which we associate with the central educational institution in the art world in, say, the eighteenth century and to an extent in the nineteenth century as well. And people can make the choice of being an artist or painter or writer without benefit of academic training. Because now their work no longer depended upon an academic system of rules and regulations. It had more to do with some vision, something that is beyond rules. There you get the concept of the genius. The genius is not available to larger and larger populations.

David Ferris

At the turn of the nineteenth century, writer-aestheticians Friedrich Schlegel and August Wilhelm Schlegel are certainly the most important spokespeople of German romanticism; and you find this concept in the writing of other romantics, too, such as Novalis, certainly, and E. T. A. Hoffmann and Jean Paul. They all influenced Schumann a great deal. Friedrich Schlegel himself contrasts the classical and the romantic aesthetic and form. To begin with, he was a scholar of ancient Greek art; and he considered the art and poetry of his own day to be not all that interesting. He was very conservative at first in his viewpoints. But, gradually, he came to see what he regarded as the "imperfections" of an artwork of his own day was in fact the strength of it. It was trying to get beyond itself and move on to something else. And so he contrasts the classical as something that is complete and whole and finished with the romantic, which is always becoming and never completed and never perfect.

Poets, Novelists, Painters

Goethe, Schiller, Novalis, Wackenroder, Eichendorff, Gautier, Hugo

Wolfgang Nehring

German romanticism is difficult to summarize, but it's a very, very rich period. What so many of the novelists and poets have in common is their background in German idealism. For Germans, Goethe and Schiller are not romantics but classicists. Tieck and Hoffmann are the models preferred by many of the romantics. Germans have called this contrast *Vollendung* and *Unendlichkeit*: the first is something complete and fulfilled; the latter is unfulfilled and has no end. So, the romantics have one ideal and the classicists have the other. However, when you look closer, this distinction is not so clear-cut. You find that classicism and romanticism reveal certain affinities. I mean, if you look at the personal relationships among the German authors, you see that the romantics esteemed Goethe highly (but it was not vice versa), and the classicists in their younger years were attracted to the *Sturm und Drang,* or "storm and stress," phase of revolution in the theater. They praised Shakespeare because he broke all the rules in the drama, like the rigid adherence to the "unities" and the artificial separations between tragedy and comedy. The romantics, too, had much in common with the early *Sturm und Drang.* They, too, rejected the idea of classicism as a closed, or contained, world, a world where you always tried to stay within reality. The romantics were more of a *centrifugal* than a *centripetal* force, you might say; they always strove to transcend reality. For the romantics, the irrational plays an important role, since it transcends the borders of the present world; whereas in *Vollendung* you need some kind of borders in order to have a complete work. This may also explain why so many romantic novels by Novalis, Clemens Brentano, Ludwig Tieck, Jean Paul, and Joseph von Eichendorff are mostly fragments. They can't resolve, or achieve completion.

The generation born before Schumann felt the strongest attraction to Goethe's novel *Wilhelm Meisters Lehrjahre*. When the novel appeared in 1794, Novalis, Schlegel, Eichendorff, and Wackenroder were all in their late teens or early twenties. Schlegel said the novel was of a level of the French Revolution in its impact on them. I take exception to calling *Wilhelm Meister* a *Bildungsroman*. That term refers to the development of the mind and the personality. I prefer the term *Entwicklungsroman*, which considers the development of the whole person, how one develops through experiences in the mind and in reality and sensuality. In such novels, the young man travels and encountered experiences of the senses, the mind, of spirituality. He changes into a more complete human being. He returns to the bourgeois middle class with a better understanding of reality and society.

The romantics had a reaction against this. Novalis had first considered *Wilhelm Meister* as an excellent and fascinating book. But later he called it an "unpoetic" work, and he rejected the idea that Wilhelm should become part of a trivial and bourgeois world. Novalis wanted to defend the artist and show how the romantic sensibility would change the world. So his unfinished novel, *Heinrich von Ofterdingen* [published posthumously in 1802] became a kind of "anti–*Wilhelm Meister*." In the first part (the book was unfinished), there are many chapters about dreams and fairy tales that poeticize the whole world. Love and poetry, Novalis says, can rule the world, or provide the best way to understand and change it.

Another influential book is the *Outpourings of an Art-Loving Friar* by Wilhelm Wackenroder, which appeared in 1797. The character of the composer-conductor Joseph Berglinger is the hero of a short piece in the collection. It is an early example of what we call the *Künstlerroman*, or "novel of the artist." It is a tradition that goes all the way through the nineteenth century in later works by E. T. A. Hoffmann, Jean Paul Richter, Hugo von Hofmannsthal, and Thomas Mann. In all these works, you must answer the question, how do you reconcile art with life? Wackenroder was a student of law, but he died very young from tuberculosis. Although he was not as well known in his brief life as his friend Ludwig Tieck, he had a great impact on romantic authors such as Ludwig Tieck, Friedrich Schlegel, E. T. A. Hoffmann, and Clemens Brentano. You could say in some ways Berglinger is a predecessor of the Hoffmann character that influenced Schumann so much, Johannes Kreisler. Like Kreisler, Berglinger is a composer/conductor, but, unlike Kreisler, he is not a madman. He is very troubled, and he is obsessive about music; but he is not mad. Moreover, he is not an alter ego of Wackenroder, like Kreisler is of Hoffmann.

Even though Joseph von Eichendorff is a romantic, in my opinion he is still very close to Goethe in many respects. He, too, feels a bias against Hoffmann. He prefers looking for harmony and solutions to tensions and problems. He recognizes problems but issues his "Beware!"—"Watch out!"—warning, "Don't get into it too far!" He wants us pull back from the demonic aspects of romanticism. He was born in Silesia in 1788, which is a Catholic region, and he was a Catholic poet (one of the few genuine authors in romanticism). He had a very happy childhood, but when the family lost its fortune, he had to study law and work for his livelihood. This was difficult in the Protestant region of Prussia. He never felt at home. In a way, you can say that he led a kind of double life. He was a conscientious government official who did his job; but in his poetry and stories you find a longing for an escape and freedom from this philistine existence.

Eichendorff's work, particularly his novels *Ahnung und Gegenwart* [1811–12] and *From the Life of Taugenichts* [1826], can be compared to works of the painter Caspar David Friedrich and to Ludwig Tieck's novel *Franz Sternbald's Wanderings* [1797]. This classic romantic novel is a true *Entwicklungsroman,* about the travel, landscape, and experience of a young painter, [and] was in many ways a model for Eichendorff's work. And you also have to think about the great German landscape painter of this time, Caspar David Friedrich. Eichendorff and Friedrich portray a very suggestive kind of landscape, which doesn't have many specific details, just a few that come back again and again in story after story. They know how to activate the fantasy of the viewer and the reader in this way: they can *complete* the scenes that are just sketched in. Although they both use landscapes as allegory, I think we too often exaggerate that *all* their landscapes have allegorical meaning. But it is true that often these landscapes are *more* than landscapes, more than just a picture or a description.

Eichendorff often describes the time of twilight. One of his most famous poems, "Zwielicht," or twilight—which Schumann sets to music in one of his great song cycles [*Liederkreis*, Op. 39]—comes from one of the many poems in his novel *Ahnung und Gegenwart*. It describes getting on to night and people are losing one another and the landscape transforms into something scary. There's always a close parallel with landscape and mind and soul. It's not that the landscape is just a reflection of the soul, but often the soul adjusts to the landscape and the time of the day. People really do feel differently at such times. There is a demonic quality to this time of twilight, and also sometimes at noon, when everything is still and hot and not moving. When all is quiet, the inner life dies out; everything can become scary, and strange things can appear.

Ahnung und Gegenwart means "premonition" and "present." The title is hard to understand in the context of the novel. Scattered through the text are many of Eichendorff's most famous poems. He considered this book to be about his own contemporary time, approximately 1809, when Germany fell into the hands of Napoleon. At the end of the story, there is a war going on, corresponding to the Tyrolean Uprisings of 1809 and the resistance of Austrian government against France. We have here an *Entwicklungsroman,* rather like Goethe's *Wilhelm Meister,* about young Count Friedrich, who goes into the world for experience and education. The plot is very complicated. To be brief, in the first book of the novel, he falls in love, makes friends, and finds his life mostly satisfying. In the second book he goes into the city to the court of a prince and now wants to study and be useful to society. But he finds out he's the only person who takes court life seriously! They are all just playing around. In the last book, after his big disappointment, he goes to war. His cause is defeated, and he loses his fortune. He rediscovers his roots, his family and religious connections. He ends up in a monastery. He's not completely resigned to this life, but he does feel he now wants to reform mankind from the new perspective of this life.

David Ferris

Joseph von Eichendorff was, as you may know, a devout Catholic. He was very spiritual and held out a profound attraction to Schumann. Unfortunately, for a time after his death he was not taken very seriously by scholars, and in a sense he fell out of favor. Much of his work had a "folklike" tone that some regarded as superficial. But he was very popular in his lifetime. Only in our time, in the late 1950s and early 1960s, did scholarly people start to appreciate him anew. He transforms the Christian schema in a way that is typical of the romantics, in that he centers it much more on the human consciousness than on God. So the idea is you have this golden age of the past, this Edenic time, which contrasts starkly with the sense of alienation we feel in the present. We strive to return to the golden age, but with a heightened level of consciousness. You might think of this trajectory as a kind of cycle, or spiral, where you're always trying to better yourself. And so that is a way, I think, that the romantics take the Christian idea and secularize it, or focus it more on human consciousness.

Katherine Kolb

Even though we talk about French romanticism exploding in the 1830s, all during the early decades of the century you had writers who were already open to these new currents. The most famous of whom, of course, was Chateaubriand. His novel *René* is a kind of a French *Werther,* published thirty years later, in 1802. All of these writers had a new sensibility toward music as something evocative, simple, that speaks to the soul but not to the mind. One of these writers, Senancour, says that the ideal music is that of female voices singing in unison in a language one can't understand.

Théophile Gautier says that Delacroix, Hugo, and Berlioz constitute a kind of romantic trinity. He sees in each one a seminal figure of the romantic revolution in France. And he sees each one of them as a giant in his respective art. Ironically, each one of them had rather little to do with each other and had little understanding of what the other was doing in terms of revolution in their own arts. Yet each one of them did indeed revolutionize the arts in various ways. In another essay Gautier talks more specifically about the parallels between Hugo and Hector Berlioz. For instance, you have Hugo's liberation of rhythm in words and music in *Hernani*. The classical alexandrine line in French from the time of Louis XIV had very strict parameters. It was supposed to stop after twelve syllables, and the meaning was not supposed to go over the line. Not only that, but each line was supposed to be evenly divided into two parts—six syllables each; there were very strict rules about rhyme schemes. There were incredibly strict rules about all of it. Now, Hugo dared to subvert that by liberating that kind of line by his enjambments. In diction, also, he took liberties. The classical French language, which had been restricted in the vocabulary it could use—i.e., only "noble" words. You couldn't talk about serious subjects with humble words, or say ordinary things, like "What time is it?" (which Hugo had one of his characters say in the play). You couldn't say a word like "handkerchief" on the stage. But Hugo confuses, or merges, these vocabularies. What Berlioz does with the melody is the same sort of thing. He liberates the melody, he goes beyond these four-square bars. You're supposed to have in a classical piece balanced phrases, four bars answered by another four bars; and then you have eight; and then that's answered by another eight. It must be even and always regular. Schumann noticed this right away when he wrote about the piano score of the *Symphonie fantastique*. He wrote a whole page in his review about how Berlioz seemed to be going back to the origins of poetry in writing music *before the bar line*, before the meter had been regularized. But how do rules get established? They can only get established by trial and error. This is what Hugo and Berlioz kept saying in their manifestoes.

Jean Paul Friedrich Richter

Erika Reiman

A lot of Schumann studies talk about the influence on him of the novelist Jean Paul Friedrich Richter [1763–1825]. But they categorize Jean Paul as a romantic. I think that he is more deeply rooted in the Enlightenment, as was the case with his contemporary, Goethe. And he's not really a part of the so-called Jena School, where you see many leading young literary figures at the university, like Novalis, the Schlegel brothers, and Wackenroder. No, Jean Paul doesn't really have that *Sturm und Drang,* melodramatic quality, for the most part. You rarely find the angst you associate with Byron's *Manfred,* for example. When you look at the history of German literature, Goethe is classified as *"klassik"*—to which I would add some of Jean Paul— and it's Wackenroder, the Schlegel brothers, Novalis who are the true early romantics.

He had an unusual background among the writers of this time. He was born to very modest circumstances in Franconia, which is in northern Bavaria, geographically not that far from Schumann's birthplace. He found literature to be his salvation, I think. He had many friends and relatives that died young, and he was forced to confront his own mortality. In 1790 he wrote a letter to himself in which he confronted his own mortality. After that he started writing his novels and connecting his thoughts to the wider world. Before that, he had been writing mostly satire.

All of the major novels come in at something like 750 to 1,000 pages and appear in a cluster around 1793 to 1820. The first novel, *Die unsichtbare Loge* (The Invisible Lodge), about a secret society, was unfinished. It became the basis for his first completed novel, *Hesperus.* This was the novel which gave him fame across the German-speaking lands, particularly with female readers. Already we're seeing his penchant for paired characters. And in the next novel, *Siebenkäs,* which is the name of the main character, you see in the forefront two characters who look like twins but who have opposing personalities. The character of Siebenkäs is the mild-mannered lawyer, and Leibgeber is the crazy philosopher. Jean Paul is not idealizing one over the other. The next is *Flegeljahre* (Fledgling Years). Following that is *Titan,* a funny title, because there's not really a "titanic" figure in the novel, but it's about somebody who *might* be destined to become the heir to a throne. It's very much a *Bildungsroman,* or maybe more of an *Entwicklungsroman,* about all kinds of development, not just philosophical or educational. After that are no more novels on that scale. There was a late novel, *Der Komet,* but it never achieved the popularity of the earlier works. He lived twenty-five more years after that.

John Daverio

I have to say I haven't read the whole of Jean Paul, not even the half. He presents special problems to English translation, which can make it difficult for us to understand fully his impact on Schumann. But we must try. There are writers whose works are very much tied to the language and the linguistic peculiarities of the language for which they are written. You know, German lends itself to the inventing of words and making up words and combining little words into larger ones in ways that other languages don't. And this is one aspect of Jean Paul's own writing that makes it difficult to translate and makes it difficult for the modern reader. Jean Paul also obviously had a very facile and quick mind, and he sees all kinds of unusual connections and makes all kinds of strange comparisons and stops to ruminate upon them. It makes him a challenge. He likes to tell stories, stories within stories, so we lose track of the main narrative. So I think that Jean Paul's writings, his novels, are intended for a kind of reader who is not as stressed and constrained by time as the modern reader is. To generalize, the modern reader wants the author to get to the point and get on with it. These writings are products of an age where there are no movies and no TV and where reading aloud was an important aspect of a lot of nineteenth-century literature. Not just to be read silently, but to be read aloud. We know that Schumann tried to interest Clara in doing this in the early years of their marriage. She didn't share his passion for Jean Paul.

Wolfgang Nehring

I must admit I am not a big fan of Jean Paul. He definitely is an anti-classical author, someone who doesn't present a harmonious world. He enjoys very much a playful way of contrasts and ambivalence, wit, and allusions. His books like *Hesperus, Titan,* and *Siebenkäs* are very hard to read. They are not straightforward. There is no clear plot, but the story digresses into many episodes. They read like dreams, or daydreams. They are sometimes very sweet dreams. He has a sense for the idyllic life. Many of his characters live in reality but build within it a separate enclave. The reader can see the harsh reality around them, but the characters themselves live an idyllic life without knowing very much about the harsh reality around them.

It puzzles me how Jean Paul was so popular in his time. It must be because of his appeal to feelings, which is very strong. He is a good example of someone who can combine feelings with wit in a very intricate style. I think he was particularly popular among women readers. Even now today there are Jean Paul circles. I know a professor in Switzerland who teaches nothing else but Jean Paul, one seminar after another. Jean Paul is famous for his characters that appear in pairs. The two that most deeply affect Schumann, Walt and Vult, from *Flegeljahre,* are typical. They are two separate characters who supplement one another to become one complete character. One is more practical, the other is more sentimental; one more active, the other more a dreamer. They can grow together into a single character. But you should not confuse this with the device of the *Doppelgänger.* This is a person that appears like another person and stands for separate parts of the same personality. There is something that is *uncanny* about the *Doppelgänger,* and in Jean Paul there is never this uncanny quality.

Heinrich Heine

Roger Cook

I think Schumann found in Heinrich Heine [1797–1856] something that touched him profoundly. Two of his best song cycles [*Liederkreis,* Op. 24; *Dichterliebe,* Op. 48] are based on his poetry. Heine was a very complicated figure. The word *ambivalence* says it all. I'm talking about every aspect of his thinking: the political, his ideas on the poetic soul, love and religion. Any one view that focuses on one aspect of Heine is barely touching the surface. He had a stormy career as a student. He was expelled, or suspended, at one point for dueling. By 1826 he was looking for some kind of job that would be permanent. That's the main reason he was living in Munich at the time. He was hoping that King Ludwig of Bavaria would sponsor a position as professor. When he finally did secure employment, it was as editor of the *New Political Annals,* a literary journal. He left it after only six months, because he felt it was beneath him. His real fame came from the *Reisebilder,* or "Travel Pictures," which he started writing in 1825 and published in 1826–27. About that same time he also published the *Buch der Lieder.* It was not until the 1830s, and in part because of the musical settings that romantic composers gave to his songs, that the *Buch der Lieder* [1827] eventually became a famous book. In the preface to the second edition years later, he seemed almost apologetic about having bared his romantic soul in verse. By that time, in the late 1830s, he was back writing very politically oriented prose. Still later in his life, he began to appreciate more the kind of moments of fullness that he thought romantic poetry caught, as opposed to the larger, more politically historical view of seeing yourself always working toward a future. At the same time, there's this aloofness about it all. It's like he's laughing at his own vulnerability, even while he writes about it. And yet he can still relish the passion of being caught up in those romantic moments.

Throughout his life Heine was slim, with a sleek face and wit that women found attractive. He certainly had lots of charisma, and it is mentioned often in letters that he would be the one at a dinner party singled out for his charm and eloquence. But although he certainly had a lot of affairs when he was young, he had no successful love relationships. In particular, there were the painfully unrequited loves for his cousins Amalie and Therese. For me, the essence of Heine's poems is the idea behind unrequited love. It's not simply unrequited love and the pain that it causes, but that love itself, or a kind of passionate romantic love, contains as much sorrow as bliss. Many of the poems in Schumann's *Dichterliebe* cycle bring out that point. Even when love seems successful and happy, the pain and sorrow always wins out in the end.

The 1830s and 1840s for Heine were mainly times of prose writing, journalism, and social and political criticism. In Paris he corresponded with and knew some of the earliest communist thinkers, particularly Karl Marx. He was very much attracted to communism as a form of social justice. However, it made him sad to think that the triumph of social justice and material equality would spell the end of his poetry. His poems, he said, would be worth little more than wrappings for fish in the marketplace. In his book *The Romantic School* [1836], he was quite critical of the conservative bent of romanticism, and he made fun of the Schlegel brothers. He was more serious, even prophetic in his critique of nationalism. Not only did he personally reject what he feared was its inherent anti-Semitism, but he knew it would lead to the upheaval and overhaul of European ideology, which, in our hindsight, we know led to the fascist and national socialist movements of the last century.

E. T. A. Hoffmann

Wolfgang Nehring

The two great opposites of German literature at this time are Goethe [1749–1832] and E. T. A. Hoffmann [1776–1822]. Goethe is not always favorable to the romantics. He says the classical mode is the healthy mode, and the romantic mode is the sickly mode. I have no doubt he is referring to Hoffmann. I definitely think Hoffmann was influenced by hypnotism, called "mesmerism" at the time. He talked about dreams, about the dark things happening in the inner self. Freud liked to read him. In his "Essay on the Uncanny," he talks about Hoffmann's "Der Sandmann." Goethe did not really care to read Hoffmann, but he knew about him because there was a passionate Hoffmann circle in Weimar. Goethe's knowledge and judgment of him was mostly secondhand, because they came mostly through reading Walter Scott's famous article on Hoffmann. Scott had referred to him as somebody who should be seen by a doctor, a physician! Of course, Goethe was right in seeing Hoffmann as an anti-classical writer. Hoffmann didn't strive for reason and the harmony of art and reality. Rather, he thought the artist's mind was so complicated that it was on the brink of madness. He cultivated that a little bit. Goethe, by contrast, always refrained from harmful things. But Hoffmann was always looking for them.

Ronald Taylor

Among the many writers who influenced Schumann, E. T. A. Hoffmann is one of the most interesting. He was, as you know, a very versatile man. Regardless of his reputation as a writer of grotesque fantasies, we must never forget he was also a painter, a musician, and a judge. He was a highly respected, very progressive appeals judge who defended many what we would call liberal, progressive causes in a regime that was politically repressive at that time. He spent his days sitting on the bench, then came home in the evening, met with a number of similarly romantically inclined friends, went out and drank late into the night, came back home at three o'clock in the morning, and wrote his fantastic stories between three and six. The next morning at nine o'clock he was sitting in court again. Now, this is not a madman.

Interestingly enough, the music that he wrote is very different from what you would expect him to have written. If you know only his stories, which are of course fantastic and romantic, the sort of music he writes is very eighteenth-century, very reminiscent of Mozart. He saw himself as a musician and wanted to be remembered as a musician almost to the end of his life. It was only, I think, in the last five years of his life that he accepted the rather cruel fact that it was not as a musician that he was going to be remembered. True, there has lately been a certain revival of interest in his compositions, but I suspect that is less for their intrinsic value than out of simple curiosity.

We were talking a moment before about the blending of these various arts under the supremacy of music, the point I was making that not only musicians, but the writers and painters of this time were governed by the prediction that music was somehow the dominant art and held in this mysterious way, which the other arts did not have. And Hoffmann has this fascinating alter ego, an eccentric musician named "Johannes Kreisler," who appears in several stories and in that fantastic novel *Kater Murr* [1822]; and whom Schumann depicted in his *Kreisleriana* piano music. In one story, Kreisler sits down at the keyboard and starts to rhapsodize, to extemporize. In the mysterious, dim light, he gives a rhapsodic commentary to his friends as he modulates and improvises at the keyboard. And here I quote: "What are these strange, rustling sounds I hear all about me? Invisible wings sweep to and fro, I am floating on the fragrant air; but the fragrance gleams in circles of flame, mysteriously intertwined. These I now see to be delectable spirits, who beat their golden wings in notes and chords of rapturous beauty . . . They are bearing me into the land of eternal desire. But as they grasp me, pain shoots through my body, seeking to tear my breast asunder, and to escape."

And so he goes on and on. His passion mounts, it becomes *fortissimo*, with repeated chords of C minor. Kreisler is, of course, by many people's reckoning, simply mad. But he works himself into a state of ecstasy; he doesn't know where he is, he collapses into exhaustion after a performance of this kind. And of course this again raises this very interesting question that people so often want to discuss. Are people like Hoffmann as mad as Kreisler himself is—on this very hazy borderline between sanity and madness? What is madness; are we not all at certain ecstatic moments no longer fully in control of ourselves, as Kreisler here is obviously no longer in control of himself?

Katherine Kolb

E. T. A. Hoffmann not only took Germany by storm, but he was revered in France. It happened in the late 1820s, when two translators successfully rendered him into French. Like Edgar Allan Poe later, Hoffmann just clicked with the French—maybe even more with them than with the Germans. I mean, everyone had to read him. In 1835 Janin, one of the most famous journalists of the day, wrote an article in a dictionary of conversations labeling him with the word "fantastic." You couldn't go anywhere without hearing that word. They took his tales and they called them *Contes fantastiques*. Hoffmann didn't always use that word, you know. His stories were just "tales." But he does use "fantastic" in the title of a set of tales, which Schumann takes over in his *Fantasiestücke* [Op. 12] piano pieces. But it's the French who use that label, and it really takes off. So Berlioz's *Symphonie fantastique* goes right along with that vogue. It's not only in Germany that you find this tradition. Back in the rationalist seventeenth century, you have Cyrano, who wrote a kind of science fiction. He was rediscovered by the romantics, in fact.

The Shakespeare Revival

> *Shakespeare's world incites me, more than any thing beside, to quicken my footsteps forward into the actual world, to mingle in the flood of destinies that is suspended over it, and at length, if I shall prosper, to draw a few cups from the great ocean of true nature, and to distribute them from off the stage among the thirsting people of my native land.*
> —Goethe, *Wilhelm Meister's Apprenticeship*

Charles Rosen

Schumann, of course, knew his Shakespeare and turned to him often throughout his life. There's this myth that the romantics revived Shakespeare. Shakespeare had never been absent. But what happened with the romantics was interesting. Before this time, Shakespeare had been criticized as a genius who was completely wild, who broke all the rules, a child of nature who just wrote from the flood of his genius. In fact, that's basically how Shakespeare was considered during his lifetime by Ben Jonson. When they told Ben Jonson that Shakespeare had never blotted a line, he said, "I wish he'd blotted a thousand!" He thought there were a lot of mistakes in Shakespeare. But now Shakespeare began to be considered as a role model. The founder of German romanticism, Friedrich Schlegel, said that Shakespeare was the most "correct" poet that ever lived. Similarly, when E. T. A. Hoffmann wrote about Beethoven, he said that Beethoven was not at all the wild, untamed genius that people think he is, but the most sober and correct musician who ever lived. What Hoffmann was doing would have been understood at the time but might not be understood today: He's comparing Beethoven to Shakespeare and saying Beethoven is our Shakespeare in music.

Katherine Kolb

It is essentially true that thanks to the translations and criticism of Gotthold Lessing and the Schlegel brothers in the latter part of the eighteenth century, the Germans were the first to really catch on to Shakespeare. You have to remember Shakespeare is sixteenth-century, and the French in fact in those days had just as much power in language as the English. But there was no real equivalent to Shakespeare in the French tradition. In the Shakespearean historical plays, for instance, you have no limits of place, or time. You can freely range about in time or place. With the reign of Louis XIV in the seventeenth century, this sort of thing was disallowed. Much later in the eighteenth century, Voltaire went to England and got very excited about Shakespeare. Later on, of course, he in fact did incorporate certain aspects of Shakespeare into his plays, even though he is still thoroughly imbued with classical notions and the grandeur and glory of Louis XIV. Therefore, he ends up calling Shakespeare a "barbarian," which, according to neoclassical rules, he is. It's not until the 1820s that the French are overwhelmed by Shakespeare, even though many did not understand English. They responded to a "liberation," of sorts, of rapid scene changes and varieties in diction and styles of acting. Berlioz and Schumann will take this formal freedom that they learned from Shakespeare to extremes in their music.

Albert Boime

The painter Eugène Delacroix compulsively draws upon Shakespearean texts for his works, like his *Hamlet and the Grave-Digger* and *Macbeth*. This would be true for the writers, Victor Hugo and others. If not adapting directly, they are certainly influenced by Shakespearean plays in incorporating them into their work, such as *Burgraves* and *Hernani*. So there is a definite influence coming from Shakespeare's work. Which for these people suggests the breaking of traditional boundaries as well. The Aristotelian unities are overthrown, in a sense, by Shakespearean work. Also elements of mystery and wordplay and color and darkness and moods that Shakespeare represents are far removed from classical tradition. And I think that Shakespeare came on the scene as a very stimulating force in French letters and arts at this moment. Ophelia is another character we see painted over and over again. John Everett Millais does this incredible image of Ophelia, and the Pre-Raphaelites incorporate a great number of Shakespearean images into their paintings.

Leon Plantinga

For Germans at the beginning of the nineteenth century, the person who embodied the rebellion against, or departure from, classical civilization was William Shakespeare. He seemed to oppose everything that the French academic system upheld. He didn't observe the "unities" of time, place, and action in drama. His characters were wildly eccentric types, and they didn't fit into the sort of pigeonholes that characters were supposed to represent in classical drama. His language was enormously varied and rich, whereas in Racine's classical drama the vocabulary is very small, particularly according to the higher positions of the characters. A king, for example, was someone who spoke hardly at all. Shakespeare, by contrast, puts wild figures of speech into the mouths of characters in all stations of life and class. All of this was regarded as the absolute antithesis of classical form and regard for the integrity of genre.

MUSIC IN THE ROMANTIC AGE

> *Musical tones are the life and the form of night, the sign of everything invisible, and the children of longing.*
> —Clemens Brentano, *Godwi*

> *The most divine, most glorious miracles occur in the innermost recesses of the human soul; and it is the duty of man to*

proclaim these miracles to the world in whatever form he can, be it in word, in sound, or in color.

—Robert Schumann

EDITOR'S NOTE

Music's relationship to and expression of the first flush of the romantic period—herein roughly defined as 1770–1830—is examined, including discussions of its peculiar aptness to the age, its role in folksong and nationalism, and its programmatic considerations. We conclude with observations on the impact of Franz Schubert on Schumann.

Music as the Ultimate Romantic Expression

Ronald Taylor

I have a theory that in every age there is a particular art which seems to express the spirit of that age better than the other arts. One has to phrase this rather carefully. I don't mean to imply, for example, painting is predominant to the extent that the literature is insignificant. This does not happen; rather that when one looks at certain periods, certain arts seem to express, as I said, most completely the spirit of that particular age. And we are talking basically about the romantic period. And I think that in the romantic period it is music which expresses most completely everything that was going on in the world at this particular time.

Music is very much a part of this subjective experience. Music is a mystery. And Kant himself did not go into music; but of course Schopenhauer did and Hoffmann did. You cannot describe music. If you ask, for example, what is Shakespeare's *Hamlet* about, you can give some sort of answer. You can say this is the story of a man in a particular predicament, what his family problems are, what sort of psychological situation he is in. You can ask what a painting is about. If it's a portrait, you can describe who the man is, you can give something about his historical importance, you can talk about the age in which he lived, his relationship with the sitter. If it's landscape, you can say where it is; you can talk about the relationship of that aspect of nature as it stands to the painting.

But when it comes to music, when you ask the question, what is Beethoven's Fifth Symphony about and tell me what it *says,* you realize the impossibility of answering that question in the same way. You cannot describe a piece of music unless, of course, it is overtly "program music."

This is also a subject in itself and quite close to Schumann and to the romantic tradition. But the basic question from which you started, the subjective experience, this is, I think, the essence of the romantic experience of music.

Ultimately, the key figure—I keep coming back to Schopenhauer—will do nothing less than propose music as the mysterious center of the universe. Let us not question things to which there are no answers. Let us accept this inexpressible reality at the core of existence; we can all absorb it, we can all feel it, and that is enough. Let us not try to explain it. And I think this is a matter of common experience. This is very difficult to avoid, overphilosophizing over this particular subject. Perhaps we all feel this; we all know the extent music has a power over people, which, for example, literature does not. To read a poem takes effort. We have to sit down; we have to appreciate aesthetic values against the content and the message. We have to *work,* in a sense. And it requires a certain amount of education before we would pick up a volume of poetry and study it. But you can fill concert halls with people who will listen to Beethoven's Fifth Symphony, without knowing what key it's in, what the instruments are, without knowing anything about Beethoven. Yet they will be overwhelmed by the experience; they will be knocked off their feet by what goes on, because of this power of music, as it were, to infiltrate into the human experience.

Wolfgang Nehring

In Schumann's day, novels and stories are appearing that feature composers and musicians as their main characters. One of the earliest and best known is a story by Wilhelm Wackenroder [1773–1798] about the composer-conductor Joseph Berglinger. It is one of the most important early romantic novels about music. Berglinger grows up in the home of a strict, dull medical doctor. He is dissatisfied with his life. He keeps his real love, which is for music, a secret from his family. Despite his lack of formal instruction, he fantasizes at the piano. He feels it elevates him beyond reality, beyond his surroundings. It makes him a better man. He wants to live in this pure, heavenly world. He feels music speaks to the higher sensibilities in everybody. It's not a craft that you can learn, but an expression of the soul. If he is in a concert or in church, it takes him away from the ordinary and the dull, and he feels that it cleanses him and exalts him.

But at home his father hates the arts and he is angry that Joseph is neglecting his medical studies. Finally, troubled by what to do for a career, Joseph leaves the house and achieves some success as a conductor in the city. But this comes at a cost. He suffers the torments of having to learn the craft of composing, the science of making music. He also scorns the life at court and the dullness of his audiences. He feels he is sinking down and down. He begins to feel only he understands his music. It isolates him.

Then—and this is unusual in German romanticism—Berglinger has a bad conscience that he has neglected his family. He finds out that while he has been living the good life, his father lies dying and sisters have fallen into disrepute. Wackenroder is saying that while art is a high calling, it has a negative side, too, when it detracts from important issues in daily life. This tension finally destroys him.

Katherine Kolb

Music and musicians are also important themes in French novels, too. It has been so drummed into us that romanticism begins with the English and the Germans, and that the French were belated in all this, that we forget that it was the French writings of Rousseau and Diderot that were so influential on Goethe. Rousseau, of course, not only wrote about music but was a musician. His *Dictionary of Music* was something that was known to every music lover ever since he wrote it around 1760. His whole outlook, his whole philosophy of the self, of the individual, the emotions, was a validation of instrumental music. That's one of the great ironies of history, of course—that Rousseau thought music was only "melody," simple, beautiful, melody. The simpler, the better for Rousseau, who scorned harmony. Music, he says, was essentially something to dream to. Think of Rousseau and his *Reveries*. He says in an incredible passage, "Music can even make *silence* speak." As if where words fail, music can enter in. And there's Diderot, who was tremendously seminal in all of this with *Rameau's Nephew,* whose main character is a musician, and which consists of one of those crazy dialogues that go off every which way. He has some tremendously interesting things to say about music. Everything that he had learned told him that instrumental music was an inferior form of the art, but in some of his private letters he's always swooning over pieces of instrumental music.

Jacques Barzun

Writings by Rousseau, Wackenroder, and others took music away from rigidly bound rules and prescriptions. Don't forget, you have the so-called Paris School in France, the composers of the French Revolution and all the foreigners who were in Paris, including Reicha, Cherubini, Spontini, and so on. They had premonitions of romanticism in their works and contributed to the great outburst that comes with Weber, Berlioz, Liszt,

Schumann, Chopin, and so on. In fact, romanticism did not replace its parental heritage, rationalism and classicism. The eighteenth century lingered on. It's a paradox that what survived into the nineteenth century is what is most frequently attacked as unique to romanticism. By the time romanticism had been purged of sentimentality and grandiloquence, it had found its own unique character. I've always been struck by Beethoven's admiration for the Paris School, which he expressed many times. And there came the great shift from seeing opera as the main carrier of dramatic music to the idea that Beethoven and theorists from the Jena School, like the Schlegel brothers, established that instrumental music alone, orchestral music, could contain drama within itself. In that category we might say also that Mozart was a proto-romantic composer, certainly at the end of his life.

Music and Revolution

Katherine Kolb

Music had a decidedly revolutionary function in France. The "Marseillaise" was originally a political tool in the hands of Rouget de Lisle. In the 1790s he was a captain in the French Army of the Rhine. He took the verses from the revolutionary rhetoric of the posters around at the time. The melody was a simple line, no harmony at all. By 1792 it spread throughout France. Later, in 1830, you see Berlioz going out into the streets and leading a chorus of "Marseillaise." That's a great moment, a privileged moment. This was the kind of populist fervor against the Restoration Monarchy that carried over from the Great Revolution. Berlioz thought of it as essentially a *battle* piece. It's the first known instance of Berlioz using music to inflame patriotism. He believed firmly in music's function as a means of binding the people together, and he composed his own choral version of it. It's instructive to realize that he gave the verses to a man's voice, then a woman's voice, and then a child's voice. So, this emphasizes the notion of the citizenry participating in this call to arms. Ironically, in 1852, it is banned by law. You're not allowed to sing it during the time of the Second Empire.

Already this notion of music as something beyond the political, beyond the real, is taking root. Ever since Plato, people have said that music did have a kind of power. The French Revolution simply grasped that again in a particularly powerful way in a particularly volatile environment with something like the "Marseillaise." Nothing that powerful had ever been seen or heard before. Music comes to be regarded as powerful in its own right, and you have someone like Beethoven who produces symphonies that seem extraordinarily expressive of revolution. Yet they have no words. So no one can tell you outright what they have to say. But it's clear that they are powerful. The poets had been used to having the upper hand. Words had always been superior, and of course the romantic poets for the first time in France in two centuries were taking off and writing great stuff. They wanted to maintain their supremacy. It's because of music's power of the *ineffable,* the feeling, that is beyond the words, that gives a new freedom to the poets themselves. And in his music Berlioz *invents* languages for eerie effects in the "Ride to the Abyss" in his *Damnation of Faust.* Nonsense words had been used before in opera—but always for comic effect. When asked about a specific program to music, say, to Berlioz's *Symphonie fantastique,* Schumann says, "Leave that to the French. The French are the ones who say music has to do with words."

The Bach Revival

Joshua Rifkin

Germany was a country that prior to the nineteenth century had been fragmented. But now it was beginning to feel those schisms very keenly. People began to reach out to the arts as unifying elements. After all, in the arts Germany had always played second place to France and Italy. So now it was terribly important to claim a great German composer. The discovery—or, I should say, the reclamation—of Bach in the romantic period was one of the great agendas of the ongoing rediscovery of the musical past. The early nineteenth century was the first really history-conscious era that had had its beginnings in the previous century. It was a time when you were not only interested in what is current, but what is carried over from the past.

Moreover, it was the more *recent* past that was becoming very, very meaningful. This is just at the time when the classical music repertory begins to get set up. The romantics are discovering things that are speaking to them and addressing their own condition. Thus Bach was still enough in the recent past that they would not have had the time to gain a certain kind of historical distance; and this meant that he was still in a way *living* repertory, which can be adapted to their present circumstances. There is a religious dimension here, because the striving for a unified Germany was very much bound up with the church. Although Germany had two religions, unification was spearheaded though the Protestant territories. And so there was a great expression of Lutheran faith and, subsequently, in Bach. He is not a church musician, exactly, but a musician who all his life was in the service of political entities. And since religious devotion was an integral part of state life, it became a great part of his duties. I'm not saying he was not a religious man. Clearly, he was. But with him music could serve in both sacred and secular contexts. He adapted secular works for sacred use quite frequently. That's rather different from what we know today. But with Bach, there was no real distinction. It was all considered part of a single, unified universe. And so, music is neither more explicitly religious nor less explicitly religious but implicitly bound up with the notion of God's creation. His dramatic and vocal style, the narrative, the instrumental colors, the differences between choruses and arias all spoke very much to the romantic sensibility. It was not so much the simple keyboard music or the learned fugues; it was the very dramatic, vital, and operatic music. So all of these elements come together in Bach.

Charles Rosen

You have this myth that Bach was rediscovered by the romantics. Better to say he was revived. There had already been generations of musicians who were influenced by Bach. Mozart discovers Bach and arranges *The Well-Tempered Clavier* for string quartet and for string trio. He even arranged one of the fugues from *Art of the Fugue*. Beethoven was brought up playing *The Well-Tempered Clavier* and played a few of them from memory when he was thirteen years old. It got in the newspapers! All these people were raised on Bach; that's how they learned music. Czerny had an edition of it. He taught it to Liszt. Chopin was raised on it. Schumann was raised on it. The so-called Bach Revival was actually a revival of the *choral* works. The young Mendelssohn revived the *Saint Matthew Passion* in a performance that was very heavily cut and abridged. From then on, Bach was regarded as the great composer of choral music.

The People's Music: Choral Music and Folk Song

John F. Fetzer

Everywhere in the nineteenth century, from Von Weber and Schumann to Brahms and Mahler, you see the German romantic preoccupation with folk song. This is often misunderstood. The collection of hundreds of German folk songs called *Des Knaben Wunderhorn* (The Youth's Magic Horn) [1804–7] was actually a deception. The people who edited it, Achim von Arnim and Clemens Brentano, claimed these were old German songs which they had found and collected. But it's been shown that a lot of them were not old German songs at all, but songs they wrote themselves and palmed off as old German songs! I mean, how do you know the melodies of a folk song from more than a century back? It might be conveyed from mouth to mouth, but what happens in the transition, just like a story that is passed on and on, is that it gets embellished, it gets changed, added to, subtracted from. So what you get a hundred years later is really not the original melody; it certainly is not the original text. So even if they had genuine folk songs, they were not necessarily original. This has come to light lately. What is interesting, though, is that even though there was falsification, it inspired people. It's like the phenomenon of Ossian in the eighteenth century. It was a fad that swept Europe, that had people ecstatic for what they thought was this ancient bard from the Scottish moors. But all of a sudden, it turned out to be a fraud. A man named Macpherson wrote the poetry and palmed it off as the work of this fictional "Ossian." But so what? It still had an effect on people's interest in ancient poetry. It was a fruitful forgery. And in a sense that's what happened with *Des Knaben Wunderhorn*.

Consider the case of the Brothers Grimm, who claimed philological accuracy. And Clemens Brentano and Achim von Arnim attacked them mercilessly, saying, "You can't really do that; this is not accurate." But, of course, the Grimms palmed themselves off as philologists and that they got their stories from the people. Now, today, several books have appeared—one by John Ellis, called *One Fairy Story Too Many*—which point out that they were forgeries that actually changed the fairy tales to make them fit the mold they thought fairy tales should have. Yet the tales did inspire an entire generation to think about the "Märchen" tradition, even though you can't claim them to be wholly authentic.

Theodore Albrecht

Music for the *Volk,* the people, played an important role in German nationalist sentiments. I refer to the *Liedertafel* and *Liederkranz* movements. During the Napoleonic occupation in Berlin, Carl Friedrich Zelter, whom most people remember as being Goethe's unofficial musical adviser, had developed something that he called the *Singakademie,* the "Singing Academy." It was a large music school that taught choral singing for mixed choruses and young people. By 1809 Zelter decided it might be nice to have a patriotic organization, and he founded what he called the *Liedertafel,* which literally means "song table." He called together twenty-four poets and musicians, mostly amateurs. They would sit around a table, eat dinner, and share with one another the poems and songs they had composed during the preceding weeks. Because we're dealing with a very romantic Germany, the songs would be about the love of forests, of the rivers and the trees, and the wide-open skies of beautiful Germany. It wasn't yet the blatantly patriotic stuff. As a matter of fact, they had initially in their bylaws that politics would not be discussed. Of course, we know that organizations go against their bylaws constantly, even today, and that time was no exception. There was also kind of an unwritten agenda looking toward the reinstatement of a Prussian king and queen upon the throne.

Hamburg and Cologne had *Liedertafeln* by 1812. The movement extended down the Rhine River; and Düsseldorf had one by 1820. Indeed, by 1820 most every large town and many, many small towns in north Germany, the Protestant lands, had *Liedertafeln*. In Zürich we find a publisher/composer by the name of Hans Georg Nägeli. He is probably best known to people today as a composer of German folk songs and the publisher of Beethoven's Op. 31 piano sonatas. Nägeli put together a male chorus that he called the *Liederkranz,* or "Song Crown." And this was organized on a more folklike and more pedagogical foundation than the *Liedertafeln* up north. The *Liederkranz* movement grew from German Switzerland, Zürich, to southern Germany, to Munich and Stuttgart. Stuttgart had its *Liedertafel* by 1821–24. Its most famous conductor and composer was Friedrich Silcher, whom classical music lovers know best as the man who arranged Beethoven symphonies and sonatas as songs and chorus.

And so, the *Liederkranz* movement moved north, and the *Liedertafel* moved south. In 1828–29 there was a very small *Sängerfest,* a "singers' festival," held in Würzburg, along the Main River. The participants loved it so much that two years later they had a huge *Sängerfest* in Frankfurt-am-Main. Frankfurt was symbolic for any number of reasons. Frankfurt was a free city, a neutral ground where Protestant and Catholics together could sing of the glories of Germany, of the German people, of the German homeland, the fatherland.

This was music that was available and *singable* for Germans with a beer or two under their belts. It was for Germans who could hardly read music, who had to have each line pounded out for them on the piano. It had an essentially homophonic texture. However, you do find that within the homophonic texture, which is essentially chordal, or hymnlike, a certain amount of imitation and a certain amount of antiphonal work. First and second tenors would sing one line, and the baritones and basses would sing another line. We're dealing essentially with a four-part male chorus: Tenor one, tenor two, bass one (which is baritone), and bass two. You find the same kind of division in the female choirs. It's highly accessible stuff intended for a wide audience, which is going to immediately understand the music and the words.

Program Music

Tones all by themselves actually cannot paint anything which emotion has not painted before; if I think about my childhood or the year 1826, A minor and similar keys come to mind; if I think about last September, it dissolves itself as if of its own accord into hard, dissonant pianissimo notes. Whatever occurs to [the composer], he seeks to express through tones.
—Robert Schumann, 1829

It is no empty figure of speech when a musician says that colors, fragrances, rays appear to him as sounds and that he beholds a wonderful concert in their intermingling. A sensitive physicist says that hearing is internal seeing; likewise, to the musician seeing becomes internal listening, listening to the innermost sense of music, which, as it resonates in harmony with his soul, sounds forth from everything his eye comprehends.
—E. T. A. Hoffmann

Jacques Barzun

It was inevitable that there would be a need to explain to the public what was happening in dramatic music, as E. T. A. Hoffmann did, as Berlioz tried to do, as Weber and his writings did, as Schumann did. The public was accustomed to following a narrative line only in opera, not in orchestral music. Reviewers would make up a program just to help the audience along. And then a negative reaction comes and you see Schumann himself crossing out the titles he had given to his pieces, which had probably referred only to associations between what he was composing and what he remembered. But such a connotation, as I prefer to think of it, is not, as it were, ironbound. It is *a* connotation, *an* association. There could be twenty interpretations about the same piece of music, all of them legitimate and none of them compulsory. I've tried to elucidate that, but it seems to be extremely difficult for people to understand that something written about a piece of music may lead us into it; but it is not the music. It is just something at the bottom of the verbal experience and the musical experience that is the core from which both spring—some sort of visceral, intuitive feeling for which there are no words.

D. Kern Holoman

What's terribly important is that most music, in my assessment, is *about* something. I see a piece of music like a painting or a book, as being about multiple things, all at once. I can well imagine a piece of music with no title and no overt reference to anything still being about things like conflicts, about sensuality, about passion, about literature—all at one time. I can imagine what was going through the composer's mind. And to deny that those things take place, that this work is as much about schizophrenia, as much about bedroom life, or even "D-flatness" is to miss what we call the inevitable "web of associations."

We confront this today. It's a hard thing to grasp, what sounds are about. Think of people who find Haydn harsh and difficult. Think of Beethoven not succeeding. So, it was quite common, particularly once the "Pastoral" Symphony had came along, to attach to music explications of one kind or another that can make "difficult" music a little easier to understand. And the more difficult the music, the more prone the explainers were to explain it in terms that were accessible to people.

To attach descriptions and then later to remove them is a common thing throughout the nineteenth century. Berlioz did it with his *Symphonie fantastique,* and Schumann did it with those names "Florestan" and "Eusebius." Jacques Barzun says that you're really not supposed to be thinking about guillotines and witches and things like that while listening to the *Symphonie fantastique.* He argues that Berlioz himself later quit distributing the program at the concerts. Well, much as I admire the level of Barzun's accomplishment, that's poppycock. Berlioz quit distributing the program because it was too expensive to print, and everybody knew it. And that's the only reason. When he gave the piece out of town in Germany, he had those notes translated into German and distributed so people could understand what it was about. I don't believe for a minute that Berlioz ever retroactively thought that a story or description wasn't important to the *Symphonie fantastique.* No, there are witches growling at you and there are funeral knells. My goodness, there's a head falling into the basket after the guillotine! If you don't believe that's happening in the *Symphonie,* you've missed a third of what's intriguing about it. Look at his masterpiece, *The Trojans.* The score is peppered with descriptives and long paragraphs about what color costumes characters are supposed to be wearing. In the "royal hunt and storm" sequence, we know in which direction the nymphs are going and from which directions the dogs come onstage, and all of that stuff. It's all written in the score. All you have to do is open the score and you see "here come the nymphs darting out of the reeds" and "here come the hunters' dogs." Think about the "tomb scene" in his *Romeo and Juliet.* Certainly that kind of measure-for-measure description of events that the man is seeing in his brain, waking up and gasping for air and palpitations and their last ecstasy together and all that stuff. Their heartbeats stopping at different rates. That's a kind of descriptive music for which there's very little precedent.

Leon Plantinga

Apart from illustrating stories in vocal works, music had not been thought to be particularly articulate in itself. Instrumental music was, at best, a mere imitation of vocal music. If you don't have any words, how can you know what it is *about*? However, in the early nineteenth century, this gets changed all around. It's thought that words are an impediment to music, that music has connotations that lead you to experience, to feel, to apprehend things that are utterly incapable of being expressed in words. Suppose you sit down and listen to the Variations movement from Beethoven's Op. 131 String Quartet, or the slow movement of the Mozart Clarinet Concerto; and afterward somebody asks, What did you think of it? What can you say? What is it that makes it seem so profound? Well, that's what the romantics were trying to get at. They knew that music operates on a realm not accessible to verbal discourse, not subject to the ordinary workings of human rationality. They don't take up the category of the sublime like the eighteenth-century writers like Edmund Burke and Immanuel Kant did (as in Kant's *Third Critique*)—at least not as a strict category. But scattered through the writings of E. T. A. Hoffmann and Wackenroder, and even in a philosopher like Schopenhauer, the sublime does play at least a part in describing the ultimate effect and signification of music. The sublime was too overwhelming to be described very well. Kant says it's too huge for us to assimilate. Whereas for him, as for any good eighteenth-century person, "beauty" can somehow be defined.

Franz Schubert

> *Although he has died only recently, hardly over thirty years of age, Schubert will always remain the favorite of youth. He gives what youth desires—an overflowing heart, daring thoughts, and speedy deeds. He tells of what youth loves best—of knights and maidens, romantic stories and adventures . . . He gives wings to the performer's own fancy—as no other composer has done save Beethoven.*
>
> —Robert Schumann

John Daverio

I can't say exactly why it is that Schumann developed this incredible passion for Franz Schubert, but it's clear that Schubert was the first of the great composers that Schumann became passionately involved with. And I think it's kind of interesting that it was mainly the instrumental music that touched him in this way. Yes, he had a fascination with Schubert as a composer of songs, like "Erlkönig," but as a critic he had some reservations about them. It was really the instrumental music that touched him. I suppose this grew out of the kind of musical culture that Schumann emerged from, where playing four-hand pieces for piano was very common. Schubert's four-hand music spoke to him, especially dances and dance music. If we think of various musical types or genres as forming a hierarchy, this is convivial music for the most part, music intended to be played at home for fun by amateurs. Schumann also wrote a fair amount of this music. He took these lowly forms, or musical types, and idealized them in certain ways. To give a simple example, *Papillons* is for solo piano, but it begins with an opening texture that sounds like four-hand music. You have the tune in octaves in the right hand and this kind of waltz accompaniment in the left hand. You listen and do a double take. If you close your eyes, you might imagine there are two pianos playing when in fact there's just one.

Eventually, of course, Schumann developed an attachment to the more serious works. He writes extensively about the E-flat Piano Trio, which seems to move him and touch him in many ways. While halfheartedly studying law in Leipzig, he had this amateur group of players, and they played Schubert. There's a letter he writes to Friedrich Wieck in which he speaks of being "psychologically" connected with Schubert. Most probably it's because in Schumann's mind there was a connection between Schubert and the novelist Jean Paul. It's all about storytelling. I think that Schumann tended to hear music, especially in his younger days, as if it were unfolding a story. And what gripped him about Schubert was that he doesn't tell a story in a straightforward kind of way. There are lots of digressions and cul-de-sacs and unusual twists and turns. And this very much spoke to him.

I think we can hear some of this in Schumann's own music. I think that in some ways he tries to do the impossible, which is to synthesize the Beethovenian approach, which is more driven, more goal-directed, with the more reflective and ruminative approach in Schubert.

Erika Reiman

Schumann's pairing in his mind and in his writings of the novelist Jean Paul and Schubert is very important. Schumann is showing great insight in linking their works, their attitudes, their organizational methods together. Schubert was esteemed at the time, but Schumann's idolatry of him was unusual. He revered Beethoven, but he didn't quite connect with him like he did with Jean Paul. Schubert's dance music has not been examined very much in this light. It's very much worth a look. Schumann took a lot from it and transformed it in his own works. He takes the formal outline of a Schubert dance, which is very simple and not intended for public performance, and transforms it into his piano cycles. He takes the markers of the rhythms and the oom-pah-pah accompaniments and *defamiliarizes* them, i.e., changes the rhythms, lengthens them, adds crazy modulations, sticks in material in the chain of waltzes that are not 3/4, et cetera. Suddenly, you're not sure just what you're listening to anymore. When Schumann links Schubert and Jean Paul, I think he's aware that whole universes are being created, very much like when Mahler later said that in his symphonies he wanted to create a whole world.

TRAVEL AND THE ROMANTIC LANDSCAPE

God favors those who
Go forth into the wide world
And see His many wonders
In mountains and forest, river and field.
 —Joseph von Eichendorff

"You miners are almost astrologers in reverse," said the
hermit. "Whereas they gaze incessantly at the heavens and
stay through those immeasurable spaces, you turn your gaze
into the earth and explore its structure. They study the
powers and influence of the constellations, and you investi-
gate the powers or rocks and mountains and the manifold
effects of the strata of earth and rock. To them the sky is the
book of the future, while to you the earth reveals monuments
of the primeval world."
 —Novalis, *Heinrich von Ofterdingen*

EDITOR'S NOTE

Like so many painters, novelists, poets, and musicians of the day, Schumann was eager to travel and experience at first hand the world around him. "Das muß ein schlechter Müller sein, dem niemals viel das Wandern ein" (It must be a terrible person who does not want to travel), said the poet in Schubert's song cycle *Die schöne Müllerin,* 1828. It should be noted that this thirst for travel and knowledge was not limited to the world *above*ground, but to those more mysterious regions *below*ground, as well.

Albert Boime

The idea of traveling for the romantic artist, the middle-class youth, and the aristocrat is absolutely indispensable in Schumann's day. Not so long prior to this, travel was formalized in the form of what the English called "the Grand Tour." So that the English upper-class youth as part of a finishing process, sort of a finishing school, had to take the tour of Europe and eventually Rome. Rome became the center of this journey, where one got classical education, was exposed to culture, and cultivated art of every type.

Gradually the Grand Tour opened up to include other segments of the population. Still middle-class, you don't find the poor, the proletariat, making these trips—although I should say that you have the journeyman in France and Germany, for example, the *journey* man, the man who goes on a journey and enlists in the workshops or building programs of master masons throughout the country. So, in a sense, there is that journey in a way that complements the upper-class grand tour. I think you find this journeyman concept greatly appealed to the romantics. I think of *Franz Sternbald's Wanderings* [1795–97] by Ludwig Tieck. This person hits the road, and many important things happen to him on the journey. So it's a quest, a quixotic question to find oneself through encounters with others. Particularly in Goethe's novel *Wilhelm Meister's Apprenticeship* [1795–96], you see this journeyman stage in the life of Wilhelm Meister as he leaves home, works as an errand boy for a theatrical troupe, becomes an actor, portrays Hamlet, and, enlightened in the ways of the world, ultimately returns to a bourgeois life.

You see the need to move beyond one's regulated sphere, the domain of everyday life, of tradition, of rules, of patriarchal authority. You see this again in *Wilhelm Meister,* to move beyond the domestic sphere, even though it takes place in the framework of the patriarchal desire for Wilhelm Meister to have this education or to learn the business trade. Nevertheless, so many other experiences happen along the way that are beyond the parental control, especially the father's control—the *Sehnsucht,* the yearning.

You'll find that almost every painter dreamed of traveling. Often in the paintings of Caspar David Friedrich you have images of people looking out of windows, gazing at nearby views and landscapes. By showing a person from behind, the spectator invariably identifies with this figure and participates in the view. It's one of the devices that Friedrich uses over and over again to tremendous advantage. A phrase has emerged. I don't know who first used it, but in Friedrich's case it's called the *Rückenfigur,* which means "figure seen from the rear." But it's so distinctive in his work that they had to coin a phrase in order to distinguish it or discuss it.

Other painters actually hit the road, as it were. Delacroix, for example, goes along with a mission during the July Monarchy to Morocco and Tangiers and paints images there. Many of these painters also wrote about their voyages and recorded them and sometimes proved themselves as gifted as writers as they were painters. It was very important, traveling, with its new insights and new visions, to stimulate the imagination. This is very important and mentioned over and over again. So traveling becomes part of a way of freeing oneself from the dictates of society—once again, to break the rules.

The railroad train was perhaps the most exciting innovation of the nineteenth century. It supplants the horse. Of course, we remember the joke, the race between the horse and the locomotive, in some cases the horse being the quickest. There is this need to shift from one technology to the other. And the locomotive seems to herald the most advanced type of technology that's available to the human imagination at that time. The railroad of course forces people to see things differently, whereas there were tremendous separations between town and village and countryside. Suddenly the locomotive arrives and telescopes these distances, and one sees the landscape change perceptibly in a short time. The desire to record that becomes very paramount in the work of the artists. Daumier and Turner and Couture talk about the locomotive, and others are fascinated with it. Of course, in the period of transition, the image they create for the locomotive strikes us as somewhat anomalous. They saw it as a great beast. They discuss it as if it were a fiery dragon, some unleashed animal out of control. That was one way they could deal with something so new that they didn't have the terminology to describe it. They came up with mythological terms to describe it. Again, as in the case with the horse, those that resist technological change, or want to make a statement about it, take the same imagery and subvert it by showing the opposite. In the case of Courbet, for example, in *Bonjour, M. Courbet,* we have an example of the artist on the road, walking with his knapsack, and in the background we see an elegant vehicle loaded down with baggage. And clearly Courbet is making a statement about his rejection of such elegant means of transportation in favor of walking around the countryside and meeting with people and demonstrating a more humble kind of existence, rather than the luxurious one of being in a horse-drawn vehicle of luxury.

The locomotive brings with it also the harnessing of people. The mechanization of labor that's scary to a lot of people. The locomotive is the first case where you see a real split between those who favor technology as a panacea for all ills, who see in it the emancipation of human beings from drudgery; and the others who see in it the possibility of the regimentation of human society, the mechanization of human beings like locomotives. So you have that tension played out throughout the nineteenth century to our own time, of course.

Ronald Taylor

Now, this of course is an age where in the natural sciences all kinds of investigations of worlds seen and unseen are going on. We come back to the Kantian dualism, in a way, of what can be seen and what can't be seen. Now, what cannot be seen, of course, are the events of the mind; we cannot peer into our heads and see what is actually going on. Equally, we cannot just look underneath the ground where our feet are standing to see what if anything is going on. There is mining for practical purposes, but there is also investigation into the treasures of the earth for scientific research purposes—the investigation of precious stones and all the rest of this. This did hold a fascination for the romantics, and if we are looking for stories in which this is exploited, then certainly one very readily occurs to me, "Der Runenberg," by Ludwig Tieck [1773–1854]. It's about a magnetic attraction exerted by nature, mysterious nature beneath the surface, behind the mountains, in the forest, in the caves, in some inaccessible area, somewhere where we cannot penetrate. A man who has opened his mind to the mysteries that lie beneath the surface can never escape them. And in this story of the Runenberg we see a perfectly respectable man who marries his childhood sweetheart, has a child, and comes in the course of his wanderings to a mysterious land. He meets a sort of folk-tale figure who talks to him about mysterious characters and mysterious forces under the ground. Suddenly, he is greatly attracted by these forces. He goes home, but after a few days he realizes he can no longer cope with his family or with practical, day-to-day domestic life anymore. He disappears again. Years later he is discovered as a sort of hermit wandering around with no material possessions and no interest in the acquisition of wealth or position in the world. All this he has thrown away. We learn from this the power that the romantics felt from the mysterious forces of nature— a power from which no man will escape who has once exposed himself to their influence. Once you're caught by this you are never, as it were, a sane man again. You have completely abandoned the realistic side, the rational side of life, in return for a higher reality, but a destructive one.

Tim Mitchell

It's interesting that in the very year of Schumann's birth, 1810, you find Friedrich having his first success in Berlin when he displayed his "Monk on the Seashore." It's an amazing landscape painting that is reduced to three bands of color—the bottom is a sandy tone, which is the shore; there's a strip of ocean with a sharp horizon; and above we have the dark and cloudy sky. And in the middle on the beach is a small figure. There is no structuring of space in depth, no framing trees on either side, no softening of visual effect. Heinrich von Kleist wrote that when he looked at it, it was as if his eyelids had been cut away. That tells us how truly shocking it was. Here was a direct, emotionally perceived experience. From that eventually grew the concept of abstraction, that you didn't need a subject matter. Think of the twentieth-century movements in painting, Die Brücke and Blaue Reiter, artists who called themselves "new romantics," modernizing what the earlier romantics had established.

Indeed, 1810 is an important year for lots of reasons. It is also the year when a group of young artists leave for Rome and become the Nazarenes and set off another movement in art history. Old things are ending and new things are beginning. Landscape paintings and artists had been generally restricted to peripheral areas, like making prints for pocket books. Not until Friedrich do you find the landscape becoming a dominant element, with figures reduced in scale. There's no way to avoid the fact that this is a *landscape,* and the figure is there to reflect the landscape and not the other way around. Obviously, it becomes extremely important here and elsewhere. It is fair to say that the principal center for the elevation of landscape comes in Germany in the early nineteenth century.

The painters' sensitivity to geography played an important part in the romantic sensibility. Actually, these ideas go back to ancient times. There was discovered in the sixteenth century a text by Tacitus about the German tribes who lived in the forests. There grew up the sense that in some way there were two major cultural forces in Europe that were in some ways in opposition to each other—the southern and the northern. The southern in the Mediterranean was characterized by certain lifestyles, certain mental attitudes, but also governed by certain climatic conditions—soft light, soft skies, generalized landscape forms, and the ocean. Whereas northern Europe's rugged hills, gnarled oaks, and dramatic cloud forms gave rise to different attitudes and lifestyles. Much of this comes out in art history, philosophy, and literature in the writings of Winckelmann, the great art historian. He wrote the two basic texts on the history of ancient art, published in the middle of the eighteenth century. He said that images were products of climate. Art was inextricably bound to climate, culture, and system. This led to Germans in their own cultural products stressing the ruggedness and the sublime emotions of peaks and valleys and rushing torrents.

Wolfgang Nehring

Joseph von Eichendorff's *From the Life of a Taugenichts* [1826] is one of the great travel novels. Indeed, almost all the novels of the romantics are about traveling. It is literally about a *Taugenichts,* a character who is a "good-for-nothing." He is the most romantic character in Eichendorff and is now almost a part of German folklore. We never know his name, beyond simply "Taugenichts." His father calls him that because he doesn't want to work like the others, but to enjoy the spring and lie in the sun. His father throws him out of the house. This is fine with this young man. He thinks the world revolves around him. He has a strong feeling for nature, so he feels he can now fly free like the birds (they don't want to sit around the house in the spring, either!). Several times, he finds himself in the danger of settling down too early in life. He has no money, so he has to work as a gardener. But that is too bourgeois for him; he prefers to be a hunter. But he's always "saved" by his naive confidence in God. All his mistakes turn out to be good for him. He loves a young girl, but because he mistakenly thinks she's a married countess and above him in station, he decides he should leave her. He goes to Italy and Rome, but all his disappointments bring him back to this girl, whom he now recognizes as a just a maid. He sees her for who she really is. He has finished a great circle of life. And everything ends nicely for him.

Everywhere in these books the geography is mixed up. Just as Friedrich the painter will combine aspects of different landscapes to create a sort of combined or composite world, so Eichendorff confuses his readers with locations and terrain that make no geographical sense. Taugenichts can go in just one day from Italy to Vienna on a boat on the Danube River. But there is no Danube on this route; and certainly you couldn't make this journey in one day! The landscape *adjusts* to the psychological longings of the characters. This is how it works when longing determines reality. And you see that often Friedrich's paintings and Eichendorff's books have people looking down at the land and the sea from a high mountain or from the treetops. He writes about a spring night, when a "Jacob's Ladder" reaches down from the heavens. You can climb to the top and walk out onto the branches into the open. From above, you can see the landscape below. In fact, his characters are always climbing trees! Whenever they feel restricted and the world seems too narrow around them, they just climb a tree and find themselves in a new world, feeling free and easy to breathe, glimpsing the transcendent in life. If they go into houses, they have to open the windows. By the same token, think about Friedrich's paintings, and you see people with their back to you, either on a mountaintop gazing into the wide spaces, or, if they're inside, looking out of doors and windows.

ALTERED STATES: ROMANTICISM AND THE DARK SIDE

All of life, everything had become only a dream and a presentiment. He was always saying that any man, although imagining himself to be free, was in fact only the horrible plaything of dark powers, which it was vain to resist.
— E. T. A. Hoffmann, "The Sandman"

EDITOR'S NOTE
Robert Schumann was not alone in his fascination with, fear of, and ultimate decline into madness. In the post-Enlightenment age of political, philosophical, and social revolution, all the romantics, in their own ways, busily charted the outré capacities and emotions of mankind, investing them in the artist hero, on the one hand, and the mad genius, on the other. Their art recorded and expressed these unconscious, dreamlike, even demonic forces.

Jacques Barzun
The dark side of nature was an important discovery of romanticism. And it came out in a great burst, because it had been officially suppressed for so long. I don't mean suppressed by the civic authorities, but by the writers and thinkers in pursuit of single-minded reason. It was bound to explode like a volcano at some point, and it did then. It was in part the motive power of the romanticists' genius and their art; and it was in another way something they had to cope with in their own lives and in society. And we've had that struggle ever since, haven't we? It begins in the latter part of the eighteenth century. Voltaire wrote a poem about the Lisbon earthquake in 1755, a disaster which killed more than thirty thousand people. It was a break in the Newtonian machine, contradicting the idea that a Creator had perfected a smoothly running system ["Oh wretched man, earth-fated to be cursed. . . ."].

Bishop Percy collects the border ballads [the *Reliques* of 1765], which are full of demons and superstitions and the like. And poets write about the pleasures of the imagination. William Collins in England and Goethe in Germany write about the importance of superstition in the artistic sensibility. Linked with that is the discovery of the common people. The "folk" have a spirit, knowledge, and wisdom of their own. And it expresses itself in their traditions and their superstitions, such as their legends about the Brocken, witches, goblins, and so on. So it all hangs together rather beautifully, because it was perfectly natural. No one sat down one day and said, "Now we're going to rediscover the demonic." What they did was to acknowledge it and to study it rather than ignore it. I personally relish ghost stories and have contributed to a recent encyclopedia on the ghostly and the horrible [*The Penguin Encyclopedia of Horror and the Supernatural,* 1986].

Albert Boime

The insane person is an emblem for the romantic spirit. During this period there's a tremendous preoccupation with the insane, with monomania and other delusions. The upheavals of the Revolution in the Napoleonic period obviously dislocated and disoriented numbers of people who had to be institutionalized. You'll find in this period that psychoanalysis as a separate discipline—although an offspring of the medical profession—begins to define itself. The painter Théodore Géricault, for example, is commissioned by Dr. Georget to depict images of institutionalized monomaniacs, kleptomaniacs, people who have a gambling mania, and others. Goya, also, depicts people in the institutions of Saragossa. So there is tremendous interest in this period in the insane. Another factor in this is the political repressiveness in the aftermath of the Napoleonic incursions. In fact, many people who were dissidents were accused of being insane and institutionalized. The insane asylum became a weapon to be used against dissenters. Prince Metternich [1773–1859], the Austrian politician, suppressed nationalistic and democratic trends in central Europe and found insanity very convenient. Anything and anyone that deviated from the system, who dared speak about change or revolution, was automatically calumnied and labeled a threat to the body politic—and therefore a social deviant, a heretic who needed to be incarcerated. So in a sense, this became a self-fulfilling prophecy: The greater the repressiveness, the greater the tendency to break out. And in a sense, the insane individual then is no longer considered a social deviant but somebody who embodies a sense of freedom from this repression, a possibility for moving beyond. The artist, I think, inclines toward a sympathetic understanding of the monomaniac, of the person considered a deviant; because in some way the artist now is operating within a society which sees the painter in a similar way—a social deviant. There's a bond of sympathy which is established between the insane person (who is another marginalized figure, like the criminal, or the poor person, the rural farmer).

I think that Géricault's interest in the insane is certainly tied to the idea of creativity, that there is also a state of mind that one can achieve under a neurosis, that seems to be exalted, to speak to a creative state, that seems very closely connected to the creative state. So there is a fascination with the unstable, with the demented, with the neurotic, which in some way may be seen as a complement to the creative state of mind. And certainly Delacroix talks about madness in a way that suggests that he feels himself sometimes close to it. I think in the case of important romantics like the poet Hölderlin and composers Schumann and Lenau, you have several instances of actual insanity. Others think of themselves as coming close to it. Perhaps it is because the *idea* of madness is now being enlarged in their thinking to include the person who is in a sense "breaking the rules," breaking new ground. . . .

Because of people like Schumann and his suicide attempt, we are burdened with the stereotype of the self-destructive "mad artist." The only way we can understand an artist is if he can be classified as "mad." In other words, we don't have a place for the normative artist who does the same as everyone else and lives and tries to make a living out of art. We feel impelled to understand art and artistry generally as some sort of bizarre activity. So I believe we tend to overestimate the importance of madness. And in a way this sort of thing can be exploited for monetary gain as well. Think of how Hollywood has run with the stereotype in thousands of movies, ranging from horror films like *The Phantom of the Opera* [1926] to science fiction thrillers like *Forbidden Planet* [1955].

Meanwhile, artists themselves could use this as a way of protecting themselves, as a way of isolating themselves from a society that was hostile, and at the same time giving to them a stimulus for creativity. Classed by themselves as mad by these conventional terms was also to stimulate, provoke them to creation.

There is an underlying fear and anxiety about creativity. People feel they don't know how to deal with it. It's there, palpable; it has to be dealt with. The stereotype comes in here to help explain something that is unknown and mysterious to a lot of people. It's a way of *negotiating* it. Possibly it is a fear of *change,* more than anything else. Hence the creative act threatens a kind of sociopolitical structure, frees itself in a sense from the ties that bind individuals to their conventional life. It becomes fearful. And if one can isolate it, stigmatize it as something apart, something insane, something mad, it helps people get through.

Visionaries in particular often are deemed mad. Thomas Couture did the painting called *Le fou,* the mad person, showing the mad individual in a cell, explaining a point with his fingers. And this clearly is a portrait of an individual of a philosophical nature, trying to explain a system to others which deviates from the norm. In the nineteenth century, there were a number of utopian philosophers deemed mad. They had extravagant visions of the future, like Charles Fourier, Saint-Simon. They were far-seeing individuals who imagined a world of such extravagant proportion it seemed beyond the capacity of the present, and so therefore they were deemed crazy—Swedenborg, certainly, and William Blake in his own time. And what this referred to in a sense was a misapprehension, a mistaken notion of "mad" as the scientist who does not have feet rooted in reality. A visionary.

For the romantic, this is a positive image. For people who wanted *change,* they could look to these models, these possibilities as something to work for. But it wasn't long before these individuals were deemed mad by the very forces that wanted to keep society in a fixed position. They were threatened by change. This is also true of people who were threatened by female presences in the arts. A female who could write was always classified as "unsexed," for example. These people saw a threat to their status, to their situation, by these visions that seemed to herald a world in which there was great social injustice.

Tim Mitchell

We must remember that, in a way, romanticism was a continuation of the Enlightenment. The late eighteenth-century "Nightmare" paintings of Fuseli [1741–1825] can be seen as if they were proto-romantic works, exposing the dark side of the so-called Enlightenment. I prefer to see them as the Enlightenment's *recognition* that there is an irrational, dark side of man that should be studied. These paintings bring into the light those hidden aspects of the subconscious that people knew were there but didn't know what to do with. We see in this early romantic period a change from seeing the world as a mechanistic system to the world as an organic whole, spiritually elevated, internally alive with some kind of vital energy. Now, whether that vital energy is some kind of odd force, or whether it's the divine spirit of God, is debated by various people. Can you accept that the universe and the world and man are all parts of the same cosmic, organic whole?

John M. MacGregor

The romantics utilized the best possible metaphor to express the irrationality of their age, which is the horse. The horse is a major symbol appearing everywhere, in poetry, music, the novel, painting. It's endless; it just recurs and recurs and recurs all over the place. I think one of the most profound images of a horse is found not in the visual arts or in the rhythms of music; no, it's in the literature. Consider an example in Émile Zola's novel *Germinal*. You have the horse underground, in the mines, running wild, running uncontrolled in the darkness, during a mine disaster. And that image of the horse in the lower depths, running out of control, is an incredibly profound image of the id, the most primal, the most basic force—the irrational, unconscious force within man. There are many layers of meaning for the horse. I don't want to oversimplify it. But it is a male symbol, and one associated with the sexual drive and all the irrational forces within man. Plato understood that very well with the image of the dark horse. But the romantics didn't have to think about it, just create. You've got the painter Fuseli with that wild nightmare image of the horse suddenly intruding into this young girl's room. Unquestionably, there's sexual meaning to the horse. You don't have to be a Freudian to see that. And you have horse imagery in Stubbs, those wonderful, strange horses in Stubbs; and the horses of Géricault in the storms . . . Again and again the horse rears its head. And it's almost one of the most profound symbols within romanticism, of what romanticism's about, of the unleashing of the "beast" in man.

Several painters in the romantic period cultivated a fascination with madness. The British painter Hogarth went to Bedlam for some of his subjects. He was a social critic who used humor as his weapon. And Bedlam at the time was seen as a source of humor. So he went, as many Londoners did, to laugh at the insane and to poke fun. Géricault, on the other hand, was in a completely different situation. He was commissioned by a psychiatrist to do his work. He went to asylums with a major commission and a very different attitude toward the insane. In that sense, it was an amazing collaboration between him and the scientist, Georget. One of the miracles was that Géricault, who was rather a poor portraitist, quite an inferior portrait painter, rallied around the insane and produced some of the greatest portraits of the nineteenth century. Nobody could have anticipated that happening. So, a very great change had occurred between the time of Hogarth and the time of Géricault.

There was also an element of identification Géricault had with his subjects. That may have to do with an awareness of his own psychological problems. I don't think he was psychotic, but I think he was experiencing profound neurotic disturbances. But that's sufficient to establish an identification with insanity. But the point is he approached it as a realist. Somehow, his curiosity led him to a confrontation which eliminated romantic sentiments and let him record the truth—not a fantasy, not a romantic fallacy at all, but the truth. And his portraits are in that sense painful confrontations with the reality of madness. Those portraits are more important as *realist* paintings than they are as romantic images.

Other romantic artists were gifted at staying *away* from the reality of madness. And when they encountered it—and this is still true of artists—sometimes the reality is very frightening, and they turn away. The British essayist Charles Lamb, for example, was adamant that there was nothing "romantic" about madness. He wanted to make it very clear it was a rather horrible situation. His sister was profoundly ill and stayed that way. He lived with a tragedy associated with madness. Coleridge, on the other hand, had less experience with the reality of madness, and so he could look upon at it as a more romantic and creative state.

The French novelist Balzac had his own way of debunking the romantic image of madness. But he did it in a way that, for us now, leads to a new appreciation and respect for the art of the insane. Let me explain: His story *Le chef-d'oeuvre inconnu* ["The Unknown Masterpiece"] was intended to exploit to the fullest extent the romantic notion that great art might result from full-blown insanity. He leads you down the garden path in his tale of the painter, Frenhofer, who spends a lifetime on what he thinks is his "masterpiece." Finally at the end, you find out that it's nothing. Just nothing. As a result of the painter's obsessive and relentless efforts, the painting had deteriorated into something utterly incomprehensible to anybody. The suggestion is that his mental state has deteriorated to the extent that he's not capable of creating anymore, that it's absolutely been destroyed, that the work is ruined. At least, that's the way we were supposed to see it at the time. That story has taken an entirely new meaning for us now, because since that time the discovery of the art of the insane has occurred—at least for some people, particularly in Europe—and now we are enormously curious to see the painting that Frenhofer did! Suddenly we regard that "nothing" painting in a different light—as the first *abstract* painting! Picasso saw it that way when he illustrated the story: as something amazing—that somehow Balzac had anticipated the birth of abstract art.

ROMANTICISM AND GENDER

> *Ought I to neglect my talent to travel with you on your concert tours as escort? Or, should you allow your talent go to waste because I am tied to the newspaper and my piano? What will the world say? Yes, it is absolutely necessary for us to find a way to use and develop our two talents side by side.*
>
> —Robert Schumann, letter to Clara, 1842

EDITOR'S NOTE

The private and professional relationship between Robert and Clara Schumann is representative of perceptible changes in traditional gender roles in the nineteenth century. Many contemporary scholars are now arguing that the reconsiderations and shifts in conceptions of "feminine" and "masculine" at this time are not only emblematic of social, political, and artistic energies in the romantic period, but point the way toward today's fluid status of gender inquiry and identification.

Lawrence Kramer

During the nineteenth century we see a very slow but steady transformation in the idea of what an artist is. That can be briefly defined by the word *feminization*. As the century goes on, more and more of the capacities culturally ascribed to and expected of the artist become those that are traditionally assigned, or relegated to the feminine—emotional sensitivity, the capacity for relationships, irrationality, being in touch with deep, dark human forces, and so forth. Even sexuality, which in the nineteenth century was denied woman but in previous centuries had been made their particular (and dangerous) province. So this presented a serious problem to nineteenth-century male artists, for whom cultural prestige and cultural authority still rested on the public recognition of them as "masculine" men, but whose activity constantly exposed them to the threat of being regarded as "feminine." When Nietzsche in 1888 calls Wagner "an old woman" and an "old witch," there's nothing worse he could say. So that problem, and the definition of what artists are—what we expect of them and what we want them to do—is at stake here.

Schumann's relationship to this is less anxiety-ridden, though not certainly without anxiety, than many subsequent writers, poets, painters would be able to muster. I think the reason for that is that Schumann, for lots of reasons—social, psychological—felt very drawn to femininity. His sense of his marriage to Clara early on, before various kinds of problems set in, was they were going to be partners working together; they were going to complement each other. Schumann really took very seriously that music itself was in a certain sense "feminine." So he had a very strong fantasy identification with the feminine. After he finished the "Spring" Symphony, he said he felt like a woman who's just given birth—"I'm sick and sore, but I feel good." That kind of remark, particularly from a "manly man" in the early years of the nineteenth century, shows a genuine appreciation, love, envy, desire for the possibilities of feminine identity. And it's inevitable that it would express itself at very deep and real levels in the music.

Susan McClary

People who have been working in literature in the nineteenth century, or with representations in the visual arts, have been seeing a number of patterns in the way that women were understood and presented. First, there were these angelic creatures mostly operating within a domestic sphere, frequently posed as if they were madonnas and sometimes as tragic heroines—but usually desexualized. And then you find later in the nineteenth century the move toward the siren, toward the independently sexual woman—but as monster. This does not mean that when romanticism decided that a feminine sensibility was an important dimension of human experience, women suddenly were catapulted into the middle of artistic production. Quite the opposite. It had been much easier for women to participate in cultural production, actually, in the seventeenth and some of the eighteenth and nineteenth centuries.

There are a number of ways in which gender stereotypes can show up in the early romantic opera. One of the most obvious would be music in which you have a text or song in which it is clear that you are dealing with gendered characters. However, even when we enter into music at that angle, we're not dealing with a monolithic kind of position of whatever it is that constitutes masculinity versus femininity. You have a whole range always available. Music, as with literature and film, is always a site where a lot of different possibilities get negotiated. So that, for instance, when I say to people that I'm dealing with gender, a lot of people want to throw *Fidelio* in my face, because here is an opera where you have a very strong female lead. It seems to me there are ways in talking about *why* this is such an important thing for Beethoven to be doing at that particular moment in history. It doesn't mean gender isn't at stake. It seems to me *Fidelio* has gender very much at stake, which is being negotiated against other tensions, including class and the French Revolution. I doubt that anyone would want to argue that Beethoven is a feminist. There are reasons why a character like Leonore is empowered within a very patriarchal context to do the kinds of things she does. So we're not dealing with something that is automatically feminist in intent; rather, gender is being inscribed as very important in works like that.

There are other ways that gender becomes an issue in nineteenth-century music. The music that was understood largely to be "masculine" would have been the symphony, the large-scale sonata, and large-scale chamber genres. These are genres that are more concerned with structure and form; they are not heavily ornamented and are not intended for the domestic sphere.

By contrast, I've been looking at some of the genres that are usually understood *not* to have anything to do with gender, namely, instrumental music. But even in instrumental music you've got categorizations that follow the lines of gender. Professor Jeffrey Kallberg, at the University of Pennsylvania, demonstrates the very large extent to which genres such as the piano nocturne was typed as "feminine" [*Chopin at the Boundaries*, 1996]. First of all, because the nocturne was in line with the "serenade," it was presumed to be played for women at night. Indeed, small piano pieces in general were understood to be largely for feminine audiences or for women who were playing that kind of music in the home. The very high degree of ornamentation, of its decorative quality, was opposed to music that was more intellectually and structurally grounded—which was typed as "masculine." Now, keep in mind, I myself am not talking about something that is either strictly masculine or feminine. I'm talking about social codes and the way these things were understood. As a result of those kinds of associations, composers such as Chopin were understood by critics of his time and by generations afterward as being a "feminine" composer of nocturnes, those pieces that indulged, as it were, in the ornamental. You find that criticism that follows Chopin is very much involved with trying to defend it against what seemed effeminate traits; or it tries to demonstrate that underneath those ruffles actually is a very manly structure.

There is a real dilemma that someone like Clara Wieck or Fanny Mendelssohn would encounter when they come to write piano pieces of their own. Women had to write small pieces. It was hard to write larger pieces and get them performed; so the piano/vocal terrain had been something that they had been permitted to participate in. But now with the coding of the nocturne as a feminine genre, how does a woman go and write nocturnes without perpetuating certain kinds of stereotypes of the "feminine"? What does a woman do when she tries to go into those areas and compose? Does she simply reproduce the types, or do they reorganize and rechannel some of ways in which those genres operate? I think that's an area I would like to get into eventually.

In Robert Schumann we find an interesting tension between his ambitions to write symphonies, as represented by Beethoven, and his success in writing smaller pieces, which he would himself have understood as rather more "feminine." He is clearly drawn to both spheres. If nothing else, he was a man of tremendous contradictions. And I think that these contradictions get worked out in the music. Even if you looked at Schumann's critical writings, you find a lot of this coding going on, both in his language and in his responses to composers such as Schubert on the one hand, and Beethoven on the other. He attempts to come terms with both.

You find this gender coding in the very famous essay Schumann wrote regarding his discovery of Schubert's C-Major Symphony. It begins with Schumann reporting on his visit to a cemetery in Vienna to visit Schubert's grave. But then he quickly adds that he visits Beethoven's grave. Thus, throughout the essay, he organizes his points by leaping back and forth between Schubert, who is graceful, tender, lyrical (coded very much as "feminine"), as opposed to Beethoven, who is coded as manly, virile, potent, strong, powerful, and so on. It's as though Schumann can only bring himself to talk openly about how Schubert's piece moves him, if he can also hold on to Beethoven, and thereby locate himself halfway in between them. Near the end of the essay, he finally lets himself go and there is one of these very effusive passages (of which only Schumann is really capable) in which he talks very poetically about how moved he is when he listens to Schubert. But then he then suddenly pulls back and says, in effect: "I once discovered on Beethoven's grave a steel pen. I keep it and use it only on special occasions. I have written this essay with that pen. May its flow have been inspired." How interesting that is!—pulling back and positioning himself again with the more phallic dimension of musical production in order to write more "responsibly" about Schubert.

We are very sensitive about the sexualities of artists like Schumann and to the extent that their sexual orientations have been called into question over the years. We don't have discussions of what it means for him to have been the principal caretaker for his children during Clara's concertizing tours. Similarly, we don't find a lot of emphasis on Brahms as someone who took care of the children when Clara was concertizing and Schumann was institutionalized. No, you find people very determined only to uphold what seems to be the "proper" side of those figures. I think this is to the detriment of these men as well-rounded people who were very bravely trying to question some of the premises of gender organization. Moreover, it seems that some number of these composers were bisexual, if not homosexual (in the case of Schubert). And what has always interested me, in looking at biographies of these composers, is that you see no references to such possibilities, but instead rather funny, apparently unmotivated chapters that try to argue that Schubert had girlfriends. You say, where is this coming from? Why are we suddenly trying so hard to establish girlfriends for Schubert?

We have been in the West a society that is profoundly homophobic. It is terrified at the idea that art is being produced by men who are homosexual. I think part of that has to do with the fact that music can arouse very strong feelings in us. It also seems to me quite plausible that Schumann was in the earlier parts of his life engaged in homosexual behavior. That seems to me no problem. I don't see that's a cause for getting all upset about it.

It's interesting to see the lengths to which some musicologists will go to try to make good on their favorite composers. And it's also of course very sad to think that people still want to respond that way to homosexuality, when so many of our artists in music, literature, painting have been homosexual. Since Maynard Solomon has published his research on Schubert and suggested certain things about Beethoven, a lot of people have responded by saying, "Well, that was the composer's private business and has nothing to do with the work." We shouldn't be getting in to this thinking; it only frees prurient interests. I think it's important to accept that music is bound up with gender constructions and formulations of sensuality. And it would be very surprising if the way composers understood themselves with respect to gender and sexuality would not have a very strong influence on the music they wrote. Recognizing the tensions between the "masculine" and "feminine" zones within himself seems to be one of the most powerful things about Schumann's music. If Schumann is conflicted over whether he is heterosexual or homosexual—and maybe if he is determined not even to decide—then I think that we're dealing with something that is very rich and gives a lot of access into the music and its contradictions.

You could see Schumann as perhaps providing a model for music that is concerned with fusions, with negotiations between realms that in the rest of the world are held to be separate.

Nancy B. Reich

I didn't plan or think about being a feminist myself in my own studies, but I guess I am because I'm very interested in women and what women are doing and the fact they *should* have the opportunities to do it. I mean, the young men I know are really encouraging their wives, just as my husband did me, to work and to go ahead and travel if it's necessary and to lead interesting lives generally. These young women become so much more interesting as people, and their husbands appreciated it!

After the French Revolution, there were many new legal codes that granted rights and freedoms to men but not to women. In the Napoleonic Code, in the new Prussian Code, women were not allowed to participate in the French legislature. Even in England in the Reform Act of 1832, women were excluded from voting. It was a male privilege. (It was also an upper-class male privilege only.) So women were disenfranchised to a great extent. They became the property of their husbands. Even the wealthy women who had more control over their money in the eighteenth century lost some of that control in the nineteenth century. Before this, middle-class women worked with men in their home industries, but as industry began to move into the big urban centers, the men who ran the industries kept the women at home. In general, women did not have property rights. When a daughter married, she took the father's property as her dowry with her, and it became the property of her husband. And we know in divorce cases the father almost always got custody of the children. This is what happened when Clara's parents got divorced. Her father got custody, not only because the mother was blamed for an alleged affair with another man, but because the children were Wieck's property. Women from the bourgeois classes were forbidden to write, compose, paint, to do any of these things for money. They were expected to be ornaments, to keep a home as a haven and refuge for men. There were even laws legislating such functions as breast feeding. Motherhood was elevated to the position of sainthood. This was a whole new attitude that came in the romantic period.

I agree with Susan McClary that the smaller forms in music, like nocturnes and serenades, were considered more "feminine," perhaps because they were more suited to the home than the concert hall. However, I don't see that that means they were solely "women's pieces." We know that Maria Szymanowska, who was a Polish pianist and composer who lived from 1780 and died in 1828, wrote mazurkas and nocturnes that had had an influence on Chopin. But she didn't originate these forms, and even if she had, why would that brand them as merely "feminine" forms? Something that does make sense to me is when Dr. McClary speaks of music with great emotion being "feminine" and music that is more formally structured as "masculine." Yet here you have Schumann himself really throwing himself into the smaller forms, which are very emotional and unconventional formally. Does that mean we must think of *them* as feminine pieces?

For generations throughout the eighteenth century, women were employed usually in the court orchestras, often as singers and sometimes as instrumentalists—mainly as keyboard artists. There were a few women harpists in the Vienna Court Orchestra in the eighteenth century. So there had always been what I called a "class," a professional class of artist-musicians who worked at music for a living. The prejudices were against them mainly as composers. This was partly because of the whole romantic theory that the creative genius was always a male figure and that women's roles were more submissive and supportive. To be as a helpmate and so on. It was much harder for a woman who attempted composition. You remember how Fanny Mendelssohn was always squelched by both her father and her brother. They said, "A woman's first duty is to provide a beautiful home"; and Goethe said, "A woman has to provide the solace a man needs." Some men—and Robert Schumann was one—may have deliberately encouraged their own "feminine" side, but the women were not encouraged to develop their own "masculine' side."

Wolfgang Nehring

Several authors, like Friedrich Schlegel in his *Lucinde,* questioned traditional gender roles. His book proposed a different picture of femininity. A man can become sometimes like a woman, and a woman like a man. There are very many characters like this running through books at this time of indeterminate gender and are taken to be men. German romanticism is the one period when there was more emancipation of women than in any other period in German history. Women had a very similar position as men, particularly in the Jena circle of the early romantics, where Caroline and Dorothea Schlegel played a very important part in the survival of the circle. But this got lost later in the nineteenth century. (Later, there was Bettina von Arnim. She was never satisfied with traditional feminine roles. She never wanted to behave as she was told to do. All the writings that she did came against the advice of her brothers and friends.)

ROMANTICISM AND CHILDREN

> *"Does that mean," I said in some bewilderment, "that we must eat again of the tree of knowledge in order to return to the state of innocence?"*
>
> *"Of course, he said, 'but that's the final chapter in the history of the world."*
>
>   —Heinrich von Kleist, "The Marionette Theater"

> *I sang an old song, one of those ancient, original songs that resound in the paradise garden of our childhood, like memories and echoes of another world in which we were once at home. . . . By these songs poetic souls recognize each other in later, more mature years.*
>
>   —Joseph von Eichendorff, "The Marble Statue"

> *My* Song Album for the Young *will best show that I have chosen poems suitable for the young, by the best poets, and how I have striven to move from easy and simple pieces to*

more difficult ones. The child "Mignon" finishes the set, as she looks anxiously into a more troubled inner life.

—Robert Schumann, 1848

EDITOR'S NOTE

Even before Robert Schumann married Clara Wieck and long before he had children with her, he displayed great sensitivity and insight into what Novalis called the "extravagant gaze" of childhood. Admittedly possessing a "childlike" quality himself, as he admitted to Clara, he wrote music not only for and about children, but as tools in their musical education. Indeed, he is part of a generation of collectors and writers who collected fairy tales and peasant tales that held considerable appeal to young readers. They all exemplified what was little short of a revolution in changes in contemporary perspectives and attitudes toward childhood.

Albert Boime

Your mentioning that Schumann was described as having a "childlike" personality reminds me of the urgency that the romantic artist felt in assuming the position of childlike innocence at the point of creativity. Which is to say it was necessary to become spontaneous, to act free from rules, from authority. In this case, it's the bad child who operates outside the system, who flouts the rules, who becomes the model for artistic creativity. Similarly, in painting you have the sketch, which is spontaneous and does not conform to academic tradition. It's an embryonic state—perhaps even pre-childhood. So all those are qualities that are sought for, and the sketch becomes the material expression of that . . . Everything is new for the child. Every experience that comes out happens for the first time. Later on, these experiences become codified, rigidified. But the child has to improvise, because every confrontation in life is a new situation that requires creativity and improvisation.

Childhood is a subject that is endlessly appealing to the painters of this period, just as it was a very critical issue in the history of world society from the period of the Revolution onward. The child at one point has been seen as a miniature adult. And you see this in painting the way the child is garbed. Usually these clothes are just miniaturized versions of what the parents are wearing. Later on, however, we see changes. The children are given special kinds of outfits of their own to wear. Children's clothing and children's toys now are given a signification that is relatively new. This parallels the development of middle-class consciousness. The sense of development, of trying to create a new society that is non-aristocratic, that opens up the potentials that were heretofore denied or isolated. Again, you see this in Locke's idea of the babe born with the "tabula rasa," which is then impacted upon by experience. This means that any child, regardless of background (having nothing to do with birth or specific origin), is open and available to experience.

In Rousseau's novel *Émile* [1762], you have a discussion of childhood that is treated in depth. The child holds a vision of the world which is no longer available to the adult. The child is *open* to possibilities, to the visionary experience. This constitutes an interesting perceived link with how the romantics regarded the insane. The insane person and the child, like the savage, were all treated as a unit, all had accessibility to exalted states of mind which the artist relished for creative activity. So I think the child becomes the symbol of the innocent and the naive—and you see this also expressed in the concept of the artist's sketch. Both are that same need to get to that innocence, the sincerity, that speaks of openness to experience rather than the congealed impact of adulthood and regulated existence. The model of the child for creative expression is very important. On the other hand, as in the Brothers Grimm and other cases, the child also has a malevolent, a dark side, and that vision is frightening. Childhood is also the site of horror, of terror, the unknown, the mysterious.

Again, in a politically changing world it's also important to think of education, of training the child in appropriate behavior. This would be social systems of education, of trying to raise a new society as a manifestation of a new idea. And you have a tremendous amount of emphasis on education. You have the kindergarten concept of education, trying to raise the child to fit in certain kinds of bureaucratic and administrative structures. To what extent compulsory education is applied is an issue that is still debated in this country.

Wolfgang Nehring

The romantic authors were fascinated by the world of the child. They felt it was a spontaneous and innocent time, and they longed to return to this semiconscious world. A composer like Schumann even writes a lot of music that penetrates, or evokes, this world. Children play a big part in the stories of the Brothers Grimm. These tales had been told by the village elders while the women were working on their handcrafts. What is important is that children were either the heroes or the victims. Germans always felt that their confrontation with cruelty in these stories does not do harm to children. My personal experience is that children go along with the stories because the things presented in the tales are very clear-cut. There's never a bad ending, always a happy ending that says good will always be rewarded and the bad will be punished. Those that are treated cruelly are always the bad ones. I'm always surprised that in America the endings are altered. The cruel treatment of the evil characters is taken out. In the original "Cinderella," the bad sisters have their eyes picked out by the pigeons. And the bad queen in "Snow White" has to dance to death wearing hot shoes.

Maurice Sendak

Collecting the German *Märchen* and folk tales was started by the German poets Novalis, Achim von Arnim, and Clemens Brentano in the late eighteenth and early nineteenth centuries. We forget that the Brothers Grimm didn't collect their tales for children. They're not children's stories. They are *stories*. Period. They are great German folk tales, collected by the brothers not to amuse children, but to be saved for posterity. This was the beginning of the Industrial Revolution. The kind of horrors we're going through now were begun then. And the brothers were philologists and philosophers and collectors, and what they were afraid of was that these peasant tales were going to get lost in the shuffle. Napoleon was rampaging through German towns. The brothers wondered, what would be left after the Napoleonic Wars?

The tales did find a readership among children, that's true. Children have naturally good taste. And when these original stories came out, the brothers were appalled at first at the response by children. They had no idea that children were going to like them and read them so much. The question is, why did they like them so much? Because they had been given a lot of homilies and pap to read previous to that; and suddenly, here were marvelous stories that were linguistically available to them and were simply told. And, too, they were about life and death and murderous impulses and sex and passion and all the things children are interested in and hadn't been allowed access to. So of course they fell in love with the tales!

It was a form that everybody loved. Goethe and Tieck transformed them into what they called "literary fairy tales," a form of high art. E. T. A. Hoffmann simply adapted the form for his own purposes. His "The Sandman" is one of the most horrific stories ever written. And it was only natural that composers at the time, like Robert Schumann, would fasten upon them for their music and songs. And they all knew that going back to childhood was not some sort of "Peter Pan"-ey kind of thing. That is our own lopsided view of what childhood is and what adulthood is. The early romantics were more insightful than that. They saw in these tales the natural to-and-fro between the business of being a child and being a grownup. There was naiveté, yes, but there were premonitions of terrors, too. There was nothing eccentric or cute about it. It was just a natural state of things.

Later in the nineteenth century you still see the fairy and folk tales in writing and song. You go to Gustav Mahler, and you have his *Des Knaben Wunderhorn* (The Youth's Magic Horn) and his *Kindertotenlieder* (Songs on the Death of Children). I mean, *Des Knaben Wunderhorn* is a collection of poetry that is exactly the same thing as the Grimm fairy tales. Mahler wrote some of his best music in them. And his taste was impeccable. He got right back to it.

Now we have corrupted the folk and fairy tales into what are called "children's books." This was not the Brothers' idea at all. They didn't see them as something specifically for children; they were for *people*. It's hard to put ourselves back into that frame of mind, because we have so corrupted the form into idiocy, which is known as the "kiddie book."

2

"Establish the Light!"
Early Days and Career Conflicts

Commentators: Peter F. Ostwald, Nancy B. Reich, Eric Sams, Robert Winter, and John Worthen

YOUTH IN ZWICKAU

> *He stepped to the window. The choir of the stars stood out in the dark heavens, and in the east a white streak along the horizon heralded the coming day. Full of ecstasy, he cried out: "For me there is a dawning of the morn of an eternal day. The night is past. For the rising sun I shall kindle myself as an offering that shall burn forever."*
> —Novalis, *Heinrich von Ofterdingen*

> *When Florestan had ended, the master said: "No more words! . . . There shines a fresher blush in heaven. I know not whence it comes; but in any case, young men, strive on toward the light!"*
> —Robert Schumann, 1834

EDITOR'S NOTE

Robert Schumann was born in Zwickau, Saxony, on June 8, 1810. His father, August, was a bookseller who was noted for pocket-book editions of foreign literary classics, many of which he translated into German. His mother was the former Christiane Schnabel, of Zeitz. From his earliest years he showed a great interest in books and music. The death of his father in 1826 precluded an early direction in music studies. Instead, he received the usual grammar-school and gymnasium education, while dabbling in

Anonymous miniature of Schumann, Heidelberg, dated 1830.

music and composition on his own. In 1828 he entered Leipzig University, chiefly for the purpose of attending philosophical lectures, and a year later he went to Heidelberg to study law with Professor Thibaut, a sympathetic mentor and friend. Interests in music intensified, and in 1830 he relocated to Leipzig and the home of Friedrich Wieck to begin musical studies. But very soon he incurred a mysterious hand injury that dashed his ambitions to become a concert pianist. Attempts to alleviate the problem only worsened the condition.

Eric Sams

It is quite profoundly said, "Like father, like son." There can be no clearer case than Schumann, whose father, August, was certainly among the most literary persons of his generation. He was not especially creatively gifted, but a more bookish person it is impossible to imagine, someone who actually had his own lending library, his own bookshop, who edited, who wrote a bit, who contributed to gazetteers, who produced in Zwickau near Leipzig a personal one-man revolution in the history of German publishing. To this day this has not been sufficiently documented or studied. He was exceedingly influential, not only through his son, but at the production at an early informative stage of German literary studies in cheap pocket editions for ordinary persons. The social significance of this was far-reaching.

But let's not forget also that Schubert, his immediate predecessor, was in much the same position. His father was a schoolmaster and, though not as active as Schumann's father in the literary field, was an exceedingly well-read man; and it's hard for me to believe that any person, any German-speaking person of the nineteenth century, was better read and better equipped than Schubert, who actually had read the poetic sources that his songs derive from. And he had read all the works, apart from the songs that he actually selected to use. Not only that but he read all the journals of the time in which poems were printed in all manner of languages, Hebrew, English. All these he studied. He was an amazingly comprehensively literary figure.

Robert Winter

Schumann inaugurates a tremendous break with the musicians of the past, the Bachs, the Haydns, the Mozarts, Beethovens, Schuberts. They tended to be of humble origins and often from working-class parents. And their intellectual horizons were much more circumscribed than Schumann's. Schumann, of course, was the son of a bookseller, a dreamer, a visionary. At the outset of his career, he was the point man in the left-wing platoon. He was crusading against all the Philistines out there. He couldn't have been more overt and aggressive about it. His music was for him an extremely personal adventure. Beethoven, by contrast, was writing for a public, and Schubert was very, very much writing for a public. But with Schumann, one has the feeling so often—especially if you're a performer— that the audience isn't even there. You're playing it for yourself. By the end of his life, however, in the incipient wake of Wagner, he begins to represent a more conservative Mendelssohnian, Brahmsian wing. It's not that he went out of fashion. He just didn't have the longevity of a Haydn to get to his own voice and maintain it. That isn't to say, of course, that there aren't magnificent works from the last couple of decades of his life; but there is that sense of Schumann as a composer whose greatest promise perhaps came in the decade of the 1830s. In general, his whole life was in a sense an intellectual odyssey that set him apart and set a pattern for the Berliozes and the Liszts, the people that followed him. It's very much what we associate with romanticism. I think *that* in itself gives Schumann the right to be called the quintessential romantic.

Peter F. Ostwald

As a youth he was a very kaleidoscopic character. He was spoiled. He had a very unusual relationship with his mother, for whom he became really a kind of favored child. She was a powerful, unhappy, possessive person who soon became a widow. He himself became something of a playboy, a bit of a dandy, a social butterfly. On the other hand, he was also exceedingly shy, and much of the exuberance that one observed was a kind of forceful attempt to overcome his basic shyness and his social inhibition. He had great difficulty talking, for instance. That was a trait that was noticed by his friends already very early. He himself noticed it when he was in school. He had difficulty speaking. He would try to recite. He would get stuck. He would stumble, and later on he would often become quite inarticulate so that he would sit in a group of people and he would say almost nothing for hours. Occasionally, he would open up with someone with whom he felt very comfortable, and he could talk. But by and large, he was also a person who was quite inhibited, quite shy.

The River Mulde, just outside Schumann's hometown, Zwickau, Germany.

How serious was he as a student? From the beginning, we see him conflicted between the law and music. Today we think of college students as going to classes. Of course that wasn't really the way it was done in those days. Professors gave their lectures and sometimes students went, and sometimes they didn't; and a lot of studying was done at home. I think Schumann, by and large, did not really feel strongly compelled to be a lawyer. He registered at the university as a law student, but that was done mostly to comply with the wishes of his mother and his brothers. He really wanted to be an artist. I don't believe there's much of a controversy there anymore. Some people, of course, would say he never set foot in a lecture room, and others say he attended very dutifully. I think the truth lies somewhere in between. He probably went occasionally to a lecture, but we know that much of the time he was in his apartment playing the piano. For one thing, in Heidelberg he first developed symptoms of pain in his right hand. That was surely associated with overpracticing.

Eric Sams

In the midst of career conflicts and anxieties, Robert Schumann, no less than so many other young Germans of the early nineteenth century, traveled extensively. That was the way of the young German cultivated artist ever since Goethe—as in the earlier years, when the young Englishmen did the Grand Tour. Since Goethe, everyone had to go to Italy and everyone had to travel and see the world. And secondly, this was in any case a young man's natural impulse—to see the world a bit, to create, to receive impressions; and then, if one's an artist, to re-create those impressions in one's own way. And the more boundaries one could extend and the more horizons one can perceive, why, the more finished and complete an artist one is. Thirdly, Schumann as a composer in the romantic tradition naturally takes an interest in the whole known physical world, including world geography, because nothing less than the universal is his declared aim. When Schumann starts to write songs, he chose not only the German language but translations from English, Greek, French, et cetera. He wanted to master the literature of every known country and visit it if at all possible with his own person. It's just a general aspect of exploration, mental and aesthetic exploration, where you have to cover as much ground as possible, literally as well as metaphorically, and then come back and tell people what you've seen and experienced.

Peter F. Ostwald

He took the equivalent of the Grand Tour, of course. It was what so many students at that time did. And speaking personally for a moment, I would love to have gone with him on that trip to Italy in 1829. He was so happy when he was in Switzerland, for instance, walking in the Alps. But he was yearning for companionship. I would have loved to go along with him on that trip to get to know him better and also to keep him company, because I think he wanted so much to let people know what he was feeling, but there was no one very close to him. His mother was far away, and he wrote a lot of letters to her. She was almost like an imaginary companion. And I would have liked to have been with him then when he became ill in Venice. Something happened there which upset him very greatly, and I think I might have been able to help him with that a little bit and protect him from some of the stress he was experiencing.

All the while, he was extremely garrulous, so to speak, on paper. This is fascinating. He would write endlessly. He wrote something about himself every day; and of course, for ten years in the 1830s he was a newspaper journalist and editor of a newspaper. He wrote copious amounts of criticism, commentaries on music and musicians. He also wrote poetry, and when he was younger he attempted to write novels and short stories. Most of those have been lying in the archives. They were never finished and never published. His older brothers were publishers, but they never published any of his works. They realized, I think, that they were not first-rate work, and they wanted the name Schumann associated with the best. Now, when it comes to music, that's something else.

He had what we might think in retrospect were peculiar mannerisms. It was noticed when he was in college, for instance, he would make funny faces when he composed. He would sit at the piano, and he would have a cigar in his mouth and try to hum or sing his themes while he was playing, and cigar smoke would be getting into his eyes. I gather he also was something of a clown for a while. In the Wieck home, he would entertain the children by clowning for them and telling them stories. He had a tendency to have a very pensive expression with his lips somewhat puckered. I gather that when he was severely depressed, this would be more pronounced, as though he were whistling to himself. If you watch pianists playing or violinists, if you watch Perlman playing, you notice certain facial expressions that are associated with the performance. I don't see that as so distinctly pathological.

But there is a very interesting incident during his teenaged years. In Colditz he got to know a doctor, Ernst August Carus, who was the medical director of a hospital there. Carus's wife, Agnes, was a singer, eight years older than Robert. She and Robert used to play Schubert songs together. In fact, it was probably at Dr. Carus's house that Schumann met Friedrich Wieck and his daughter Clara. Here were two women who in various ways were important to Robert at the time. But it is likely that Robert felt tensions in that household, not only because Agnes was married, but because of the proximity to the hospital, which was also a lunatic asylum. You know, this gets us back to the Schumann family history of mental illness. Schumann was not the only member of the family who was disturbed. His sister Emilie was also mentally ill, and as far as I can tell, she had committed suicide. They don't know exactly how, but people in Zwickau think that she drowned herself.

Meanwhile, there was this need, this drive to differentiate himself from everyone, especially from his mother. He struggled in many different directions. And since he had this dual talent for writing and music, he was pushing constantly in these two directions. The only way to keep these two sides of himself in harmony was through art.

Schumann seems to have been sexually preoccupied, at least *interested,* in his student days. That would bother Friedrich Wieck later in the court trial concerning his daughter's marriage to Robert. But you have to be careful about drawing too many conclusions from Robert's diary entries. The fact that he writes about "prostitutes with fiery eyes" doesn't mean that he actually went to bed with prostitutes. We don't know what Schumann actually did, although one can assume from his later diaries when he was married that he was quite sexually active. I'm just not convinced that he was such a flagrantly promiscuous person as some of the biographers in the past seem to want to indicate. In fact, there are some entries in the diaries that he was very afraid of prostitutes, and that he would use excuses to stay away from them. There are entries where he talks about going to a house of prostitution, and he would flirt with the girls; but he was very relieved when his virtue was saved at the last moment. Or he would go to parties with his friend Rosen in Heidelberg to play games with the girls, but then he'd write "escaped with Rosen," or something like that, which makes me wonder how active he was, really. Interested, yes, but we don't know for sure.

I anticipate controversies here regarding my book [*Schumann: The Inner Voices of a Musical Genius,* 1985]. I don't know if Schumann had any homosexual experiences at this time. His diaries mention homosexuality several times. It's very difficult to know what to make of that. We know that he describes his feeling of love for a number of men, especially men that he lived with, including his roommate in college and another roommate in his twenties, Ludwig Schunke, who was a very, very close friend. Now, one has to understand in the context of this time that men were much more open in expressing love for each other. These could have been platonic relationships. We just don't know for sure. Also, they could have been overtly sexual relationships, because we know that's a very human thing; and nowadays we recognize that homosexuality is something that happens, might have happened in Schumann's day, too. It's something one couldn't talk about or write about in those days.

I think there was a tendency in the Victorian era generally to be very, very cautious about writing explicitly about sex. Now, I'm no expert about that. Peter Gay, the historian at Yale, has recently begun a whole series of volumes about sexuality in the Victorian era. I do know that in present-day biographies of musicians, one can speak more frankly about their sexuality. For example, Maynard Solomon's research on Beethoven goes to a great deal of trouble to try to identify who his "immortal beloved" was. It's expected nowadays to look into these things.

The fact remains that in many Schumann biographies there were no references to homosexuality. Then suddenly I read the Schumann diaries and hear references to homosexuality and I wonder, how do you handle that? Well, I thought the best way was to be honest about it.

John Worthen

I differ from Dr. Ostwald's contentions that Schumann displayed strongly homosexual tendencies. I think there's absolutely no evidence for that at all. Of course he slept with men. All men slept with men. Ostwald apparently doesn't realize that the single bed is an invention of the twentieth century, that you only had narrow beds if you had a very small room. Therefore men shared beds. Of course they did, what else were they supposed to do? Moreover, no sooner does Ostwald mention that the word "pederasty" appears in a notebook entry, in the next paragraph he claims that Schumann is engaging in pederasty!

Sure, Schumann is interested in sex. It's a compulsion in him, as well. You know, I have written extensively on D. H. Lawrence [*D. H. Lawrence: The Life of an Outsider,* 2007], but you mustn't think I'm transferring Lawrence's attitudes toward sex to my Schumann research! If anything, Lawrence was just the opposite from someone like Schumann. I think Lawrence was someone who found sex rather difficult and was brought into it, really, by his wife, Frieda, and was made to realize that sex was wonderful and fantastic. He had about three or four years where this was true; thereafter he felt rather differently about it. Simply stated, Schumann was, as I said, compulsively sexual, and he does make those interesting records in his later diary of the times he sleeps with Clara. Well, you could say he's noting that so she won't get pregnant. I don't think so. I think it's just because he loves recording things. The money, the sex, the events, the chess games, the places they've been—are very interesting for that.

We know now that at the time in 1831 when Schumann suffered his hand injury and noted his "illness," he had also been having a sexual relationship with a woman named "Cristel" (he also called her "Charitas"). We know practically nothing about her, not even her full name. We can speculate she might have been a servant or maid. There may have been a child. Daverio relegates this to a footnote, but the evidence is there, as I mentioned, that a child is born to someone who seems to be "Cristel," which occurs nine months after he starts sexual relations with her. There's really nothing more to know.

The only important thing here for Schumann was not to get found out, as you know. That's the rule. And I'm afraid servant girls were simply fair game. But at the same time you must distinguish between the "common woman," who is simply there for your own sexual gratification, and a middle-class girl, like Ernestine von Fricken or Clara Wieck, whom you do not lay a finger on unless you are seriously intending marriage.

Nancy B. Reich

When Robert Schumann came to the Wieck household to study music in 1830, he lived there for almost a year. He had never met anyone like this little girl, Clara. She had been brought up by her father, Friedrich Wieck, in a very practical, disciplined household. He sold, rented, and repaired pianos. He wasn't a piano *builder*, exactly, but he certainly could take care of any problems that arose. She was a very thin little girl until she was about sixteen. She had these two younger brothers and a very stern father who practically tied her to the piano (even though Wieck claimed she didn't practice every day, it was her duty, and she was always very conscientious about her duty). And she had an astonishing piano technique. She played her own pieces, which were very brilliant and virtuoso-like. There must have been great acclaim—and a great many bows and lots of money that the old man collected. Robert writes in his diary, "She just tosses off things and I have to slave away."

Clara and her father traveled and concertized extensively while she was still just a little girl. He would run the whole show. He was a combination stage father, teacher, and manager. He collected the money, sold engravings of her pictures, collected the tickets at the door. He put up the ads, got permission to play in each city, and often had to have the concerts approved, because in many cities in Europe in that time there were censors who had to pass on the program. He allowed her to perform her own works. Most of them were very flashy, virtuoso works which showed off her technique. It would have been interesting to see those early concerts. Sometimes they played together on the platform. They played duets on a small instrument called a "physharmonium"—something like a reed organ. There's a very famous incident in which something happened to the keyboard action when she pressed the pedal. He had to stand up and reach in and adjust the key every time it wouldn't spring back up. I mean, it was truly a partnership. Other times, she would play two or three pieces on her own. And there would usually be a singer to assist her, or a small orchestra. There might even be a small dramatic performance to fill out the bill.

It certainly would have been interesting to go those early concerts of hers. She would play perhaps two or three pieces. She had an astonishing technique, and she would play some of her own pieces, very brilliant. There must have been great acclaim and lots of bows and lots of money that the old man collected. She shared these concerts with others. There would always be a singer, and often there would be an orchestra to play an operatic overture. There might even be a small dramatic performance. At one of the concerts, in Hamburg, an improviser, a speaker, would pass out among the audiences slips of paper on which people could give him topics on which to declaim.

On a more personal level, at this point, the presence of Schumann must have been a great joy to her. She was still just a child, and she had never met anyone like this. He was so imaginative. He told the children ghost stories. They played scary games. Robert brought her a kind of joyousness and gaiety she had never had. She just fell in love with him immediately. This side of life she had never really experienced. In their letters back and forth, they would write things like, "The sunbeams are dancing on my piano, you must be thinking of me"; or, "When the clock strikes nine, you must put your music down," and so on.

Peter F. Ostwald

The damage to Schumann's hand dashed his hopes to be a concert pianist. It's been a controversial issue as to just what happened to him. I think Clara herself confused the issue by forgetting which finger was afflicted. In a nutshell, it's not that unusual a problem. One finds this not too uncommonly among musicians, especially pianists, who practice a great deal and who practice octaves and difficult passagework over and over again to the effect that they develop various muscular strains and sometimes mild neuropathies, as we call them, inflammations of nerves. Those are not unusual problems. The question is how are these things best treated? Well, Schumann consulted a number of doctors, and some of the treatments are not exactly what we would nowadays recommend. For example, there was one doctor who used what was called in that day an animal treatment, where you went to the butcher shop and you got yourself a freshly slaughtered pig or calf. Then you inserted your ailing hand into that animal, and you were supposed to absorb the healing powers from the animal warmth. It obviously disgusted him and dismayed him and made him very angry; and of course, it didn't help him. If anything, it probably stimulated some of his disturbing fantasies about death.

There are those that ascribe the injury to a first stage of syphilis. First of all, how people conceived of syphilis was different in those days. It was very, very problematical to make a correct diagnosis of syphilis. In terms of the hand problem, I've never seen that connection in any patient. I've never seen it described in any patients. I base my thinking essentially on a paper that came from two neurologists in England who reviewed the problem, and they seemed very skeptical that syphilis could produce that kind of a problem in the hand, and also they were very skeptical about the idea that treatment for syphilis would have anything to do with producing Schumann's symptoms.

And there is the issue of Schumann's hair. I was interested, of course, in the question of syphilis and mercury treatment, and one way I thought we could get closer to an answer was by testing the hair for mercury. If someone is exposed to mercury, that would be deposited in the hair. You can get hair in several places, you know. It was not too unusual in those days for people to save locks of hair, and Clara Schumann had quite a large, well-organized hair collection. In fact, I have hair samples of Johannes Brahms, Joseph Joachim, Clara Schumann herself, Schumann's father, and various other people. I think it was something that was done at the end of a party, let's say. Everybody would contribute a lock of hair, and then it would be tied with a little ribbon and pasted in a book. I found this collection in Dresden at the state library, and I was very fortunate to obtain permission from the director of the library to take a few strands of hair along and to have them tested. Well, I found that both Schumann's father and Schumann had traces of mercury in their hair. Mercury was commonly regarded as a "treatment" for syphilis. So that raises the question how did it get there? Not for syphilis, I think. Remember, in those days, hats were blocked with mercury. Mercury was an agent used by the hat blockers, hence the term the *mad hatter,* because hatters who worked with mercury would often develop toxic disorder due to the mercury. So the most likely explanation was the mercury got on the hair from the wearing of the hats. The other possibility, of course, is that he may have gotten mercury into his system from some kind of medication, and so I reviewed what the practices were of the physicians who actually treated Schumann. There was one doctor, a Dr. Muehler, in Leipzig, who used mercury very liberally. In fact, his textbooks were reprinted for many years. He used mercury very often to treat a number of symptoms that Schumann had, such as headaches, depression, weakness, very nonspecific symptoms, so it's not impossible Schumann was given mercury at some time. It would be administered in the form of a salve, or as drops in a solution.

Of course there have been other physical studies on Schumann. Someone went and exhumed his skull. That's not uncommon. There were many theories in the nineteenth century about intelligence and other mental functions being directly related to the configuration of the brain. You know, the whole idea of phrenology. You would have diagnostic experts who would palpate your head and, on the basis of the shape of your skull, would diagnose what your mental state was. After a person would die, the head often was removed and studied, and someone did that with Schumann's skull in 1885. Something happened. I don't know if it was lost, or if it was put away somewhere. At any rate, it's never been returned. The same thing happened, I understand, to Haydn.

Gerd Nauhaus of the Schumann-Haus told me about it. In fact, I have a very funny story to tell you about that. When I was in Zwickau, which at the time was in East Germany, I worked with Gerd. All the Schumann letters and diaries are kept in a safe deposit box, where they should be. Once, when Gerd took these things out, I saw another safe deposit box, and there was one section of it, a drawer, which had a heavy red seal on it. Gerd kept it closed. I was terribly curious, of course, to find out what was in that drawer. I decided one day to ask him, "Well, Gerd, I know what's in that drawer." And he became terribly pale and very flustered and said, "Oh you do? You know what's in that drawer?" And I said, "Yes, of course I know what you're keeping there. It's Schumann's skull." And the moment I said that, he relaxed and his color came back, and he said, "Oh I'm so glad that you don't know it. You see, in that drawer we keep the escape plans in case there's a bombardment, a nuclear holocaust. These are the escape plans for the city of Zwickau."

Eric Sams

Of course, the big problem about Schumann during this time of career conflicts—the one problem everyone comes up against straightaway—is what happened to his hand? What was the precise nature of the injury? His ambition to become a concert pianist was in jeopardy. There have been various theories about that, but it was always clear to me that there was something very mysterious about it. For example, Clara Schumann, in later life, when asked which finger he had injured, could not remember. It strikes me that there's something very strange indeed about that. If one actually has damaged a finger because of, as has often been suggested, injudicious overexercise at the keyboard, Clara Schumann (who knew him well at this time) would surely know what the cause of it was, what damage had been done, and how and what finger was affected. But these things she did not know, and the conclusion from that is, it seems to me, that no such thing had actually occurred; that he had *not* damaged his finger in the course of ordinary overexertion at the keyboard. Another reason for thinking that is almost nobody else has done that. There have been many pianists, but records of people who have practiced so assiduously as to cripple or disable themselves at the keyboard are very rare. It would be a very peculiar and odd thing to do so.

One has to look for some other explanation. One can't help noticing that the German biographies say pretty clearly, or hint rather extensively, that Schumann suffered from syphilis, as a great many poets and composers did in the nineteenth century. And this was the reason for his later insanity. So many other cases come to mind—Baudelaire, for example, and Hölderlin, a German poet of the period. Is it possible to suggest that there is some one cause which explains the whole of Schumann's medical history, including the damage to his finger? There is the possibility that he did damage his arm or his finger by a fall or something—not by practicing, but simply by falling over, perhaps in one of his tipsy fits. He did drink very heavily in his youth and in his university days at the very time when this injury occurred.

What is your reaction to Dr. Peter Ostwald's supposition that perhaps the index finger—the trigger finger—was the one affected. Which is significant, since this was the time in his life when he was eligible for military service?

Well, I happen to think that no doubt it was the trigger finger that was affected. There *was* damage to the hand, and it did last. I think the archive evidence that I turned up does really rather suggest that there was genuine, actual damage to the hand, and the actual incidence was not in any way what is called psychosomatic. I find it very hard to believe that there was actually nothing wrong with his hand. Clearly something was wrong. But what caused it? I think not piano playing or piano practice or a fall. That would really be too absurd, for Schumann, who was not only a great composer but also a pianist of potentially world class, according to Friedrich Wieck, who was well placed to judge. He was going to make Schumann into a pianist of the capabilities of Franz Liszt, and turn him into a touring virtuoso. And indeed so much of the Schumann piano music does suggest that his technical abilities were of the off-the-list category. And we know that he was able to play, even when his hand was damaged. I happened to see in a German medical encyclopedia what kind of treatments were recommended for the kind of condition that Schumann had. I discovered that the treatments that he was prescribed by his doctors were treatments for, according to this encyclopedia, damage to the nerves, peripheral neuritis or palsy caused by metal poisonings. You know, mercury was used by other professions, like hatters in the nineteenth century, hence the expression "mad as a hatter," because it gives you the shakes and the palsy. And I reflected, might not Schumann's hand injury been caused by mercury medication poisoning, which he would have incurred in the ordinary course of his syphilis? That seems another plausible explanation to me. Now, the syphilis hypothesis explains all the manifestations of illness that Schumann displayed late in life, from the initial contraction, the expansion of the pupils, to the final general paralysis of the insane. The whole case history is a classic case of nineteenth-century syphilis, of which there is a great deal of medical record and expert testimony. All the illnesses and symptoms, including a genital lesion, which he describes in his diaries, are explained very simply. From that first genital lesion to the final death by general paralysis, the history of nineteenth-century syphilis could not be more classical or characteristic.

This was first published in December 1971 and later taken up by a great authority on both psychiatry and general medicine, Dr. Elliot Slater. He is notable in this country for his work, and, in an article published in a Schumann Symposium by Professor Alan Walker, argued that this was a plausible explanation of the hand injury, of the aggravation of the hand injury.

John Worthen

What finger was it? It all comes down to what exactly Clara meant when she said it was his "second finger." It was the right hand, certainly. Did she mean that the thumb was not the first finger? If so, I would think she meant the middle finger. That seems to be confirmed by almost every account. And how he damaged it—well, he practiced too much, and I think he tried to repair the damage from his own weakened finger by using a machine to strengthen the finger. He gets damage first, in Heidelberg as early as 1830, and when he tried various mechanisms to make himself better, he only made it worse.

Yes, I know Dr. Ostwald has suggested that Schumann might have fallen on his hand while drunk. That's awful. I mean, Ostwald says he merely exacerbated it by being drunk. No, I think that Schumann would have known by 1831 that he was not going to make it as a professional virtuoso pianist. I mean, there was Clara, nine years younger, and already the "real thing." Surely when Wieck took him on in 1830, he knew that Schumann should have started much earlier to become a great virtuoso pianist. But he probably reasoned that if Schumann somehow does turn out to be a virtuoso, then he, Wieck, would get the credit. And if Schumann doesn't turn out, well, that's only because he wasn't able to practice enough. So it's a win-win for Wieck.

3

"Intimate Voices"

Florestan/Eusebius
and the Tonal Analogue

Commentators: Albert Boime, John Daverio, Susan McClary, Peter F. Ostwald, Nancy B. Reich, Eric Sams, Ronald Taylor, and John Worthen

FLORESTAN AND EUSEBIUS

> *External forms are but the trappings of the man. My heaven or my hell is within.*
>
> —Schiller, *The Robbers*

> *The other day Eusebius came quietly into the room. His pale features wore the enigmatic smile with which, as you know, he seeks to arouse curiosity. I was sitting with Florestan at the piano: Florestan is one of those rare musicians who seem to sense strange new forces that lie in store.*
>
> —Robert Schumann, 1831

EDITOR'S NOTE

Schumann's readings of Jean Paul, particularly the novel *Flegeljahre* (1804), which featured the Faustian "two souls," the twin brothers Vult and Walt, seems to have inspired Schumann's invention of the pseudonyms of Florestan and Eusebius. With their mediator, Master Raro, they first appear in the early 1830s as the "authors" of several of Schumann's piano works and are present as "collaborators" in some of Schumann's early music criticism.

Albert Boime

This business of multiples, or divisions of personalities, goes along with this "eclectic" movement in the nineteenth century. People are very self-conscious now about the possible "roles" that one could play as the artist. For example, you have possible stylistic manifestations, which could be gendered as male or female, perhaps. By compartmentalizing them into certain types, certain well-defined categories, it made it easy for Schumann to integrate them into a whole. It's analytic and it's synthetic at the same time. Schumann certainly wasn't conflicted. Nowadays we might be tempted to speak of him as being "conflicted," tormented, or loosely apply the term "schizophrenic." But in point of fact what he was doing was taking various manifestations of his personality, assigning them certain kinds of definitions, and then reconciling them into some synthetic whole. To me, this is perfectly reasonable, almost Wagnerian in its implications.

Ronald Taylor

The split personality, the alter ego, the ability to portray yourself as you are in reality, and as you might be in a purely spiritual world, is of course a very romantic phenomenon. Which brings us back to a Kantian dualism. You have, on the one hand, the area of reality in which we are all forced to live, and on the other, the area of spiritual reality in which we suspect that the real, deepest values of life lie.

This does lead very naturally into the world of Schumann, who created in his music criticism these two characters Florestan and Eusebius. They are expressive of the conflicting side of life as Schumann saw them—Eusebius, the reflective, the quiet, the withdrawn, the otherworldly person; and Florestan, the enthusiast, the passionate, outgoing figure to express the other side.

Jean Paul's characters of Vult and Walt in *Flegeljahre* are precedents for Schumann. Yes, indeed, these are very important figures, as far as Schumann is concerned. One is always wanting to be what one is not, or what God does not give us to be, whichever way we want to put it. For a long while, Schumann was in doubt about whether his particular artistic bent lay in the direction of literature or music. He inherited a very powerful literary background from his father, who was a writer. He grew up surrounded by works of literature. And it was very natural that he should be very well informed, and exceptionally well informed about the romantic literature of his day—Ludwig Tieck, Wackenroder, Novalis, the people we've been talking about, and Jean Paul, of course, above all. And the dualism one finds, this familiar romantic dualism between the mind and spirit on the one hand and physical reality on the other, is extremely powerful in Schumann, as well.

How to reconcile, or least balance, them? E. T. A. Hoffmann's term *Besonnenheit* is not a word that I would apply generally to romanticism, but it does reflect the sort of life, or answer to the problems of life, a balancing act between the claims of reality and the claims of the spirit. We've already mentioned Florestan and Eusebius as the two conflicting sides, perhaps, of his personality as he chose to project them. There is a sense in which *Besonnenheit* could be matched by the figure of Master Raro in Schumann's writings, where he draws together these two figures of Florestan and Eusebius and he says, I quote here—"Florestan and Eusebius represent my double nature, the two sides of which I seek to fuse together, like Raro." The extent to which one can talk about *fusion* is highly debatable. From the cold, outside perspective it seems as if they were living two hectically double lives, which are really irreconcilable. And I suspect that is probably truer of reality than to talk about fusing these two. Because in the last analysis, it's like trying to mix oil and water. The most romantic of artists has to eat. He knows that there is a real side to the family life. Here is Robert Schumann living with Clara; there are practical aspects of bringing up their very many children, which of course occupy a totally different area of his mind than his writings or his compositions.

Eric Sams

I think what the romantic artist does is to relate himself directly to the world. Not merely in a trivial, romantic way by his telling us all about his life and loves and so on, but in a serious romantic way, because it's a music of the brain as well as the heart. He ought to tell us about his intellectual experience and the way he conceives the world philosophically; to see the world through his own eyes and his own personality. And in Schumann's case, that personality, perhaps not by chance, happened to be dual. It is a feature of the German nineteenth century that its songwriters certainly had cyclic tendencies, to put the thing mildly. In extreme cases they were manic-depressive psychotics. One could put it that way. Those ideas, I'm sure, were borrowed from the German romantic movement and from, in particular, novelist Jean Paul Richter, especially in a book called *Flegeljahre,* which is about two brothers, Walt and Vult, who indeed show these characteristics. Everything stems from, as it were, two different poles of our perception. It's like stellar parallax—if you have your two observatories a long way away from each other, you can see stars that are much farther away. It's like that, and if you understand the heights of exultation and the depths of despair through personal experience, you're that much better equipped as an artist, I reckon, to interpret and describe.

I've never heard any of this in Schumann's music, or his personality, or his psychology, as one reads it in his notebooks and diaries, to be anything other than something basically sound, sane, and human. If it's in way unusual, it's because of his genius; but it's not in any way neurotic or, least of all, psychotic.

As you know, he had a difficult youth. He was fatherless in his forma-tive years and spent many years undisciplined in a kind of mental chaos. But this is regular routine for romantic artists. Nothing is special or unusual in that. It's the way the world of art had evolved. It was then an emphasis not on society as an ordered structure, but society and human aspiration as perceived through the prism of the individual. That was his real function as an artist, to join in that movement and express it thus; and his psychological difficulties were, I'm sure, expressed in terms of two personalities. He started a novel, after all, on the same lines as Jean Paul, in which there are these two contrasting characters which were his own. In general, I think he was telling us no more than something rather deep and significant about the human artistic creative personality in general. That it is indeed bipolar. That it does consist of two different aspects and two different ways of looking at the world, and those two together make a great truth.

It is significantly a Schumannian thing to do, but within the context of the romantic movement of the nineteenth century. Schumann is not alone in this regard. There are many, many parallels in music and in other arts; and in England the great composer Edward Elgar had almost exactly the same kind of personality. It is the artistic way of expressing, I think, some deep and significant truth about human personality, namely, that you see things better if you see them from different points of view.

As for Master Raro, I can make something of that straight away. "R-A-R-O" is simply the last two letters of "Clara" and the first two of "Robert" conjoined. It's symbolic of their marriage and their union. I think we can be fairly sure that his Raro is his incantatory, Prospero-like persona. But I think it would be also true to say that all these appear-ances and apparitions are, first of all, aspects of Schumann but most of all, above all, aspects of the human situation, the human personality, the human problem. He wished to be a *universal* artist, not merely an auto-biographical one—to record the whole of human experience, and I think he did so with great success.

Peter F. Ostwald

If you read carefully in the diaries, you can see that Florestan and Eusebius were invented around 1831, at a time of terrible despair for Schumann. He was drinking heavily. He was very much afraid of going under. He was trying desperately to be a writer. And he felt he was a failure as a musician. He had, of course, been planning on writing a kind of novel called *Child Prodigies,* and he hadn't been able to finish it. Suddenly, it occurred to him to use these figures and to give them names. Now, Florestan appeared first, and then Eusebius came along. They existed only in his imagination.

They spoke to him. He heard them speak to him. They gave him guidance, support and encouragement and ideas. We know all too little about the creative process, but composers do seem to have compositions presented or music presented to their consciousness in very distinctive ways. They will hear entire works in their inner ear. That's why I use the term "the inner voices" of Robert Schumann. Yes, I believe that he heard themes and that he heard the voices of Florestan and Eusebius. I think these were very real manifestations for him.

I think the best piece to illustrate this is the *Davidsbündler Dances,* because in it he labels movements belonging to "F," for Florestan, or "E," for Eusebius; other movements Schumann designates with both names. At one point he makes references to Eusebius and his "quivering lips." And the identities of these two brothers, so to speak, weren't limited just to the music. He used them a great deal in his writing, in his literary work. He would sign articles as being written by Florestan or Eusebius.

It's been conjectured Schumann may have had a dual personality, but I don't know that these concepts in the clinical world have been clarified all that much. I don't see this as what we might call a "split personality." No, I don't think so. The term *splitting* is used very generally. And it became a very important concept in medicine when Eugen Bleuler, at the beginning of the twentieth century, introduced the idea of schizophrenia, which is literally a splitting of the mind. You know, everyone really engages from time to time in splitting. When this process achieves a kind of flamboyant, pathological significance, then we might call it split personality. I don't think Schumann was a true split personality in that sense. If anything, Schumann was more of a narcissistic or histrionic personality. Narcissistic qualities are often found in greatly gifted people who become, through an awareness of their superiority, quite self-centered and who, because of the feedback they get through audiences and admirers, begin to see themselves in a somewhat inflated or self-engrossed way. *Histrionic* refers to the quality of playacting, of putting on a show. Again, I don't think that's all that pathological. What this does mean is here is a personality who could easily project himself into another role, who could see himself enacting types of persons that he really is not in his everyday life.

And then you have Raro. Master Raro. He was the integrative element in Schumann. Schumann very cleverly anticipated something that Sigmund Freud described many years later. Freud called the libidinal, biological aspects of the self the id, and he called the assertive adaptive capacities of the personality the ego. And he also talked about a kind of superego, which contained moral and ethical principles. One sees a forerunner of that in Schumann's writings about himself. Whereas Eusebius represents the more dangerous, eroticized, feminine qualities of the self, the id and

Florestan is the masculine, assertive, aggressive, driving, adaptive side; you find presiding over them Raro, the superego figure, who lends a kind of moral, ethical, and integrative component. One can picture it that way. Again, I think it's part of Schumann's enormous genius to be able to anticipate the tripartite organization of the human mind—what later Freud, who was not a musician and who did not have much of a sense of music, conceptualized so brilliantly.

Significantly, as he grew older, Schumann wanted to disown his wild youth, so he did another edition of the *Davidsbündler Dances,* in which he removed the names and the commentaries from the score. I think he associated them with his premarital years. But now he became much more conservative and conventional. This was an about-face from the radical and revolutionary composer he had been.

John Worthen

I think your discussion with Dr. Ostwald that the Florestan–Eusebius–Raro triumvirate is a Freudian id, ego, and superego thing is dubious. We are all Freudians, and therefore we make it Freudian. I don't think it is. I think at times Raro is Friedrich Wieck, at other times Raro is clearly Schumann at his very best, when he is both Florestan and Eusebius put together. But when Schumann is either Eusebius or Florestan, he's actually doing something very interesting: he's dealing with a real discrepancy in himself. At times he is this extraordinary exhilarated outgoing person; at other times he is this very quiet and reflective one. And rather than saying, "When I am one, I want to beat myself up for not being the other," he says instead, "No, I am these two people and this is how I proceed." It's a very good kind of self-therapy that he's engaged in.

Eric Sams makes the analogy of observatories at opposite ends of the earth being able to sight farther into the heavens because of the parallax view.

Sams would, wouldn't he? I think Schumann is just a man realizing that he is two different kinds of people and knowing, how I say, not to beat himself up for being the wrong one at the wrong time. And to use those personae in his journalism and music. Well, that's extraordinarily intelligent, isn't it? It really is. To say, "I'm coming from here, I'm coming from there, I'm coming from both." It's a sign to the reader, as well.

Susan McClary

It's important, I think, to remember that Schumann locates both masculine and feminine features inside himself, in the personae that he calls, respectively, Florestan and Eusebius. And it's the productive tension between those two that gives rise to his writing, his critical writing, and also his musical composition. Now, I don't mean that *masculine* and *feminine*, as I'm talking about them here, mean "man" and "woman." No, I think you have this very strong tension inside him that he also nurtured and celebrated in others, like Beethoven, on the one hand, and Chopin and Schubert, on the other. He wants to cultivate both.

Nancy B. Reich

Florestan and Eusebius meant special things to Clara. They represented two sides of Schumann she had gotten to know when she was a very young girl and first falling in love with him. As she grew older, I think they became a reminder of those childhood days that had brought her such happiness. They wrote to each other about Florestan and Eusebius. He would sign letters to her sometimes by one, sometimes the other. I think they both took these two personae quite seriously. But it's interesting to notice that she preferred Eusebius, who was the quiet, dreamy, introverted side of Schumann. The picture of Schumann which she loved most, and which she kept after he died, was a portrait that showed the dreamy, Eusebius side. However—and this is interesting—she couldn't bring herself to play the pieces identified as "Florestan" and "Eusebius" when she played the *Carnaval*. She simply omitted them. She also omitted the "Chiarina" section, which is the movement describing herself. I suppose she did that out of modesty, because everyone knew it referred to Clara (the Italian word for *Clara*).

As for Raro, he represented a man with very high musical ideals. That was probably based on Friedrich Wieck. When Robert first came to Leipzig, Wieck was not only his teacher, but for a while became a kind of father figure. Remember, Robert's father had died. And the mother and the guardian he left behind in Zwickau were very much opposed to his studying music. But she did respect Wieck's judgment. And Wieck took the opportunity to say in that famous letter to Robert's mother, "I can make a great musician out of him, just leave him to me. See what I've done with my daughter, you know. Give me a few years and I will make him into a great pianist." Then he added, "But Robert must be disciplined; he must do what I say." I think he was already beginning to suspect some of the difficulties Schumann might present as a student.

After he decided to give up performance, after the accident with his finger, he still turned to Wieck. And when he decided to found his musical journal, Wieck was among the original editors. His name was right up there on the title page of the first issue, along with other of Robert's friends. And Wieck was one of the *Davidsbündler,* one of these close associates, this group of people that believed in the same musical ideals; and to whom Schumann gave fanciful names.

THE TONAL ANALOGUE

When I play Schubert, I seem to be reading a Jean Paul novel turned into music.

—Robert Schumann

EDITOR'S NOTE

There has been considerable debate on the alleged use of musical ciphers, or tonal analogues, in nearly all of Schumann's music. It is a tempting notion, inasmuch as the two great influences on Schumann's earliest creative years were composer Franz Schubert and novelist Jean Paul Friedrich Richter—music and letters seemingly united in Schumann's imagination. Commentators Eric Sams and John Daverio discuss their differing views of these allegations.

Eric Sams

When did you begin to be interested in Schumann and tonal analogues?

Well, I heard that in the music. I began as a linguist in the intelligence corps when I had to learn a bit of German. If you're interested in music and in German, well, you're bound to be interested in lieder. So I was interested in that, but I didn't hear cipher in Schumann until I heard the D-Minor Symphony. And what you hear in that is what everyone has heard in different generations. You hear monothematicism, to use one word for it. You hear the same thing and the same theme and almost in the same meaningful sense over and over again repeated almost obsessively. It's not obtrusive when you first hear the symphony, but when you get to hear this motif in your mind, this main theme that goes all through the work, you can't get it out of your head that it is saying something and you wish to know what it is saying. I think that in all these symphonies there is some basic motif, a kind of seed, a musical seed from which the entire work grows. And this was in many ways a novel method of composition. And it's absolutely characteristic of Schumann, it seems to me. He begins with the word in his songs; certainly, the seed is the *word*. Everything grows from that. You can hear it. What you hear in Schumann is a word or name, a basic central idea from which the whole marvelous music evolves.

You hear it in the first version of the symphony, at the beginning, in the Romance movement, and everywhere else, hundreds of times. And what it says is: C–B–A–G#–A. And it's perfectly clear that what it's actually saying is "CLARA." I don't mean that it's actually depicting her in her various moods, but I mean that Schumann throughout the length of the symphony had his wife and his relationship to her and his own feelings of guilt and unworthiness in that connection and his hope for later triumph and future happiness. I think they all come to the ears of the listener through an awareness of that theme. You later come to read Schumann's diaries and letters, and you see that in 1841 he says, "I will call my next symphony 'Clara.'" And really, nothing could be clearer, and that is what happened. It was his birthday present to her on the 13th of September, 1841. It was in connection with her birthday that he returned to it in 1853 and rescored it and added other interesting counterpoints, but generally thickened the textures. But what he also did was add additional "Clara" themes to reaffirm his devotion and loyalty and to reemphasize the meaning of the symphony. And when he comes to the end we see the theme again in the major. The last movement is kind of a triumphant finale. It's in the musical language of the manic-depressive—that he has been (and I'm sure he had good reason for thinking this) guilty and unworthy of Clara. But in the future, the music seems to say, all is going to be happiness, radiance, and light; and "I will prove worthy of her." In thinking of the Clara symphony, he isn't just saying things about her, he's saying things about himself and their relationship and making a programmatic type of music pattern.

It's the only symphony that he revised.

That's true. This symphony bridges the years from 1841 to 1853. The First Symphony, the "Spring" Symphony, is very similar in many ways, an autobiographical work, I'm sure, but it deliberately quotes a poem, a spring poem, and describes a kind of tonal analogue. It doesn't overtly describe anything, but it makes a musical tonal symbol of the inner life of the composer. It also tells you why those thoughts are worth having. And the Second and Third symphonies also are programmatic, I'm sure; and they deal with life's experiences and autobiographical material; and I dare say they're organized in much the same way.

John Daverio

This is a big and complicated topic and one that I've given a fair amount of thought to. Let me first say that Eric Sams has done a lot of important and very original and imaginative work about Schumann; he has some very sensitive ideas about the songs, in particular. What I find problematic is his contention that Schumann had invented a special code to represent Clara in music. We do know that he used musical ciphers for things like the letters in A–B–E–G–G in the *"Abegg" Variations*, or A–S–C–H in *Carnaval*, or G–A–D–E in one of the pieces for the *Album for the Young*. But these aren't ciphers. This isn't really musical cryptography. The point of musical cryptography, or any kind of cryptography, is to encode or to encipher a message in such a way that only the recipient will be able to understand it. Only the person in possession of the key to the code will be able to understand it. Now, what Schumann is doing with notes and letters in pieces like *Carnaval,* this is pretty poor cryptography. In the case of the *"Abegg" Variations,* the solution to the puzzle is right there in the title: "Variations on the name 'Abegg.'" As I've tried to explain in my book *Crossing Paths* [*Crossing Paths: Schubert, Schumann, and Brahms*, 2002], they are really more analogous to the kinds of puzzles and rebuses that one would find in books for children—especially in books that teach children how to read. And I think they represent one of the ways in which the worlds of the child and the adult interpenetrate in Schumann's creativity.

Now, getting back to Sam's "Clara" theme. This has been a bugaboo of mine for a long time. When I was working on my biography [1997], I had problems with this in basic musical terms. I didn't really have a chance to do all of the spade work that would allow me to demolish the theory. I hope to have done that in *Crossing Paths* (though some might deny that). But in a nutshell, Sams argued that Schumann made use of an early nineteenth-century manual on cryptography to develop a cipher system that would allow him not just to encipher "Clara" but just about any other message in music. This manual was written by a guy named Johann Kluber and contains a comprehensive discussion of cryptography. As far as I know, nobody else had taken a close look at this volume. I was struck by the fact that in Sams's own work, he never cites chapter and verse, the things one would expect, with page references and quotations and such. I managed to get my hands on this book, and instead of a pamphlet, it was a 400- to 500-page volume, a very thorough consideration of the science of cryptography.

Well, this book in no way does what Sams says it does. And therefore there's no reason to think Schumann would have done these things, either. We have no record that Schumann had this book. The evidence that he knew the book is nil. In one of Sams's articles, he quotes a number of passages from Schumann's letters and other documents, and he puts them next to passages from Kluber. And what I have tried to do is trace more likely sources for all these supposed correspondences. Just to give you an example, Schumann refers in a letter or a review to a kind of "language of the flowers." Sams sets that next to a reference to a "flower language" in Kluber. On the face of it, this is a sign that Schumann might have known this book. Well, Kluber was not the only person to talk about a language of the flowers. In a volume of well-known poems by Goethe, *Westöstliche Divan,* evocations of Persian poetry of the fourteenth century, there's a big appendix of notes in which he talks about the fourteenth- and fifteenth-century practice of sending message by flowers, *Blumensprache.* I think that if Schumann got this from any place it was from Goethe. He set poems from that book, and we know that he knew Goethe. This seems to me a more likely source.

In all of the cases where we know for sure that Schumann used musical ciphers, all the letters can be translated into musical pitches. This does not preclude the possibility that he had this other system. However, there's not a shred of evidence that he developed a whole other cipher system for Clara. Sams describes the Fourth Symphony as the "Clara" symphony. He quotes Schumann as saying, "My next symphony will be called 'Clara.'" Now, if you go to the diaries, he wrote this after finishing the First Symphony. And the very next thing that he wrote was not the Fourth Symphony but what was published under the title of the *Overture, Scherzo, and Finale.* He had referred to that work originally as a "symphony." So if there's a "Clara" symphony, it's opus 52! Looking at the issues in another way, I think there was a span of twelve years or so where *every* piece he writes is a "Clara" piece, a "Clara" quartet, song, oratorio, et cetera.

4

"We Kindred Spirits"

Schumann and His Circle

Commentators: Jacques Barzun, Leslie Howard, Jonathan Kregor, Garrick Ohlsson, Leon Plantinga, Joshua Rifkin, Michael Saffle, Eric Sams, and R. Larry Todd

> *What important personages we conceive ourselves to be! We think that it is we alone who animate the circle we move in."*
> —Goethe, *Wilhelm Meister's Apprenticeship*

> *Every age has a secret society of congenial spirits. Draw the circle tighter, you who belong to one another, that the truth of art may shine ever more clearly.*
> —Robert Schumann, "New Paths," 1853

MUSIC JOURNALISM AND CRITICISM

EDITOR'S NOTE

Schumann and his generation not only expressed in music a public and private record of the world around and within them, but they all found in words another important way of expressing themselves. None of these composers had more to write—and wrote it with more exuberance and imagination—than Robert Schumann and Hector Berlioz. From 1834 to 1844, Schumann was the editor of *Leipzig's Neue Zeitschrift für Musik* (*The New Magazine of Music; NZfM*). In competition with the more conservative *Allgemeine musikalische Zeitung*, it became one of the most influential music journals of the day, not only in Leipzig, but across Europe and England and in the United States and South America. Although at most it had only 500 direct subscribers, many, many more times that number saw and read it. Meanwhile, in Paris, Schumann's colleague in letters, Hector Berlioz, was

The newly restored Coffe Baum, site of the Davidsbündler meetings of the 1830s, Leipzig, Germany.

also establishing himself as an important critic and editor with the Revue et gazette musicale in Paris.

The launching of the NZfM was by no means coincident with the establishment of Schumann's Davidsbund, or League of David, a circle of music enthusiasts, critics, and musicians promoting the cause of progressive music. Schumann populated the league with contemporaries and colleagues, like Paganini, Mendelssohn, and Friedrich Wieck, and wholly imaginary personae, such as Florestan and Eusebius. He referred to the league by name in several of his piano works in the 1830s, including the Carnaval and the Davidsbündler Dances.

Jacques Barzun

I think musical commentaries like Schumann's both educated the reader and attempted to reveal in prose the poetry of the music. Here was music altogether new, really, in intention and in form. Even Beethoven's simplest symphonies were considered incomprehensible and monstrous and all that. So people who did get the point had to say—this is what it's all about; this is what you might experience if you opened your ears and shut your mouth. Above all, just *listen*. Today's critics would not have been possible if the preparatory work had not been done by these pioneers. Of course, I don't want to take up the whole question of theoretical criticism that we now have, which is abstract—so far removed from the work itself that nobody could accuse it of being educational and helpful. Rather, it's calculated disturbance to prevent enjoyment! But up to now the various kinds of criticism have been justified by their purpose and their results.

Leon Plantinga

The romantic period saw a collision between intellectual and social necessity. The old patronage system was dead. After the French Revolution there was very little left of it. Some musicians could occasionally function at court for a while, like Louis Spohr and Franz Liszt in Weimar. But this was simply no longer the pattern. It was not how a musician could make his daily bread. So what a musician has to do now is appeal to an anonymous public, to people out there he's never met and of whose tastes he cannot be sure.

When Carl Maria von Weber became director of the German Opera at Prague, and then at Dresden around 1818, he was in competition with the local Italian opera. He felt at a disadvantage, because he didn't have the better singers, and his company didn't have the kind of social clout that the Italian opera had. So he began to issue periodical statements in which he talked about the productions and general topics, like "German Opera vs. Italian Opera," and attacked the Italian conventions of the recitative-area format. He was trying to get the readers to understand what he's doing, precisely at a time when it's crucial to appeal to a general public. He advocated a longer dramatic line in the libretto, supported by the music.

To further his aims he formed an imaginary group called the *Harmonischer Verein,* or "Harmonic Union." These characters also appeared in a novel that he wrote, *The Life of the Composer.* They all expressed in Weber's writings their ideas about art and music. They sometimes agreed with each other, and sometimes did not. And around 1832 here is young Schumann, out of law school, writing this very imaginative stuff of his own, and he doesn't know if anybody will like or understand him. For precedents he draws upon the *Harmonischer Verein,* E. T. A. Hoffmann's *Serapionsbrüder* ("The Serapion Brotherhood"), and, of course, Jean Paul.

His outlet is the *Neue Zeitschrift für Musik,* or *New Magazine of Music.* Its circulation averaged about five hundred subscribers. It was published in eight leaves, that is, eight pages in a double bifolium, quarto-sized. It was not exactly the first magazine of its kind. There had been other musical journals in German-speaking countries. Johann Mattheson had a journal called the *Critica Musica,* or *Critical Music,* in the mid-1720s. A similarly named journal, the *Critische Musicus* by Adolph Scheibe, appeared in the 1730s and 1740s. There were a few others. They were like newsletters, had a very limited circulation, and were the products of single persons. In general, they were addressed to the community of scholars and musicians who could understand fairly technical matters. More to the point was the *Allgemeine musikalische Zeitung,* or *AmZ,* which was founded in 1798. Edited by a man named J. F. Rochlitz, it was addressed to a very different audience, a new middle class with interests in art, reading, and music. It wasn't just for a select readership but for a much larger circulation. It was published in Leipzig and distributed rather widely in German-speaking areas. There would be reviews of concerts and announcements of upcoming musical events—from questions about building instruments and whether it was proper to present opera during Lent. One new feature was particularly interesting, new reviews of published music. If you got your symphony published, you could get your copy off to the *AmZ* and expect to get it reviewed. This presented demands on music critics far different than today. Schumann, for example, when he started writing his criticism, had to review quartets by examining the score of *four individual parts.* He would line up four chairs and place the parts right next to each other, and his eye would scan from one part to the other in order to understand how the music was going. It really required a considerable amount of expertise, time, and concentration.

This sort of thing got to be a standard feature of musical journals in Paris, too. The one most like the *AmZ* was the *Revue et gazette musicale*, the *Musical Review and Gazette*. That, too, had regular reviews of published music. While Schumann wrote for German journals, Hector Berlioz did the same in Paris. Berlioz started writing music criticism because he needed the money. Nonetheless, he wrote elegantly, and he wrote sincerely on the subjects that were important to him. Schumann got into it from the beginning because he was outraged that the common denominator of musical culture in Germany was being debased. He thought that the kind of musical culture that was supported by and represented by the *Allgemeine musikalische Zeitung* was a scandal. He thought its appeal was to an uncomprehending middle-class audience interested only in money, that it was toadying to readers' need for conventional music. And this infuriated him. He wanted to apply to his music writings the high standards that were maintained in literature and literary criticism. There were genuine aesthetic and intellectual issues that had to be debated in an honest fashion. But he is confronting the dilemma of the romantic artist, namely, that although he is writing about music that is avant-garde, if you will, he also needs to reach a large and supportive audience.

Eric Sams

It is significant that Schumann would utilize alter egos and pseudonyms in his music criticism. What you're hearing in the best kind of romantic music is not just the composer but the whole man. He's speaking as an artist, as a musician, certainly, but also in his capacity as writer. Schumann was a great prose writer, and reader, in the kind of words he uses, the kind of music he prefers, all his utterances in any art form whatever. It's part of his expressive genius.

SCHUMANN AND FRÉDÉRIC CHOPIN

Chopin was here yesterday, and played for half an hour on my grand pianoforte—fantasies and new études of his own. . . . He affected me to a most uncommon degree. The sensitiveness of his imaginative style and character communicates itself immediately to the sensitive hearer: I held my breath while I listened.

—Robert Schumann, 1836

EDITOR'S NOTE

Schumann was an early champion of Chopin. On December 31, 1831, in the *Allgemeine musikalische Zeitung,* he greeted Chopin's "Là ci darem la mano" variations with the famous apostrophe, "Hats off, gentlemen, a genius!" His musical portrait of Chopin appears in *Carnaval,* and he dedicated his *Kreisleriana* to him; and Chopin, in turn, dedicated his F-Major Ballade to him. Although their relationship was never more than cordial (in later essays Schumann criticized him for lack of artistic development), they became the foremost exemplars of romantic piano music.

Garrick Ohlsson

Schumann and Chopin are the two greatest geniuses of the piano of their generation, with all due respects to Mendelssohn (who was more of a genius than many people think). But in terms of sheer depth, I think they both outclass Mendelssohn and Liszt at that time. But they didn't get along all that well. Chopin's most Schumannesque piece is the F-Major Ballade, which he dedicated to Schumann. It's has that Florestan-Eusebius series of contrasts you might expect. For such an elegant guy, Chopin's contrasts have no transitions at all; they are of such a brutality that they are almost unspeakable. But it hangs together, even though there's no reason that it should. He might have said, "Here, my dear Robert, this is *you*!" I do think that Schumann had a more generous temperament than Chopin. Schumann was more of a Californian, shall we say, in the sense of "Hey, man, wow, isn't it cosmic?!" And that was his reaction when he heard Chopin. He reacted with incredible generosity, and Chopin, being more of the Old World arrogant snob and polished aristocrat, was perhaps a bit disdainful of this overly mammalian enthusiasm. You can see all sorts of reasons why the two men did not click. Now, Chopin didn't think very much of Liszt, either, possibly for reasons of jealousy. And when Liszt began adding ornamentations to the études, Chopin said, "Keep that pig out of my garden!"

We have a very interesting comparison/contrast here. Chopin has many things in common with Schumann. They all did. Many things are in the air. At a given time you'll find that scientists in six different countries have the same ideas at the same time. Musicians did, too. They were all the children of Carl Maria von Weber. Although Weber was never as progressive as Beethoven or Schubert in their last years harmonically—Schubert and Beethoven went way beyond anything Weber ever did and pointed directly to the end of the nineteenth century—he invented the *sound* of the music of that generation around 1810–13, Schumann, Chopin, Liszt,

Mendelssohn, and Berlioz, although they are quite a diverse group in themselves. He almost invented the sound of these composers. Chopin and Schumann could not have been possible before then. They have things in common that other famous pairs of composers have had in common. How many music lovers have said, "I can't tell the difference between Haydn and Mozart"? But the more you know about them, the more their differences are crystal clear. Now, Chopin was kind of an exotic in this middle European world. He was like a flower from Tahiti dropped into the Paris musical scene, with his wild, Slavic temperament—but with aristocratic style and polish. He was the consummate technician and composer. He was refined and polished. And he had a sense of balance of texture and form that is really unparalleled. Now, Chopin was not great in large forms. In small forms he was a craftsman of a jeweler's precision. My feeling about Chopin was that he was in touch with his deepest demons and could control them like you would wild stallions. My feeling about Schumann was that his feelings got the best of him a lot of the time, compositionally and temperamentally. With Schumann, he gets inward, he gets self-involved and cliquish; and sometimes he gets so carried away with himself that he loses me. I also think it has something to do with the sheer flow of his inspiration and emotional flow, that perhaps he didn't edit very carefully. I get the feeling with Chopin that he chewed on his ideas to the point where you don't recognize any mastication. It's all done for you. With Schumann, maybe he should have chewed a little bit more. But I can't say there was another genius of his time to edit Schumann, unless it was Brahms; and he had his own music to write.

SCHUMANN AND HECTOR BERLIOZ

There is a divine spark in this musician. I hoped that maturity would improve and purify it to produce a clear flame. Whether this has happened I cannot tell.

—Robert Schumann, 1843

EDITOR'S NOTE

While Schumann was publishing his *Neue Zeitschrift für Musik* in Leipzig, Hector Berlioz was writing and editing the *Revue et gazette musicale* in Paris. Schumann's lengthy and perceptive critique of Berlioz's *Symphonie fantastique* was published in six installments in the *New Magazine of Music* in 1835. However, the two leading composer/critics of the day did not actually meet until January 1843, when their mutual friend Mendelssohn arranged a meeting in Leipzig. Although they never became close friends, Berlioz and Schumann nonetheless enjoyed mutual respect and shared many goals. Between their two journals, they covered most of the music activity between Leipzig and Paris.

Leon Plantinga

Schumann and Berlioz were very different in their origins. Very early on, when he began medical school, Berlioz was a part of the Parisian scene, a very urban, sophisticated milieu. From the beginning, he was in the "big time." Schumann had rather more earthy beginnings. He came from a little town in Germany, Zwickau, spent some time in Leipzig, then off to the University of Heidelberg, then back to Leipzig. Their musical backgrounds, however, were more similar. They were both somewhat self-educated—as nineteenth-century musicians tended to be. They weren't picked out to be musicians, as musicians from the eighteenth and seventeenth centuries usually were. So, Berlioz played his guitar and his flute and had a few lessons before coming to Paris; and he displayed nothing like professional competence as a musician. Likewise, Schumann, until 1830, was pretty much self-taught. He learned most of his music, it seems, at parties. You can tell by the textures here and there of his plain, two-hand piano music—it sounds like *four*-hand piano music. Thereafter, their interests diverged sharply. Schumann was profoundly interested in the piano, and piano music, and the expressive possibilities of both. Berlioz is not in the least interested in the piano. He is interested in dramatic music, in knowing how the world of Shakespeare might intersect with the world of music.

Leslie Howard

Hector Berlioz owed a great deal to Schumann and Liszt. Of course, there's the famous story about how the *Symphonie fantastique* came to the public consciousness. Berlioz couldn't get the score published. So Liszt made his piano transcription in 1834 with the sole purpose of bringing the piece to critical attention. Nobody had written a review of this piece, even though it had been played a few times (and Liszt had been at the first performance). It would be fourteen more years, by the way, before the score was published. In the meantime, Liszt had circulated it in a form which was more accessible.

Enter Robert Schumann, who wrote a review of the piece based on Liszt's transcription. There was no way he could have seen the original score, which Berlioz kept, as he did all of his music, in a suitcase which he took with him wherever he went. But Liszt had done the transcription so carefully—and had indicated the instrumentation to the best he could on two staves—that Schumann was able to get more than a rough idea of how the piece went. He wrote, I think, quite a perceptive and intelligent account of it. It's in two parts, one concerning musicological matters, and the other the more programmatic and emotional interpretation of it. That's how Schumann wrote criticism. If it's a piece that he really doesn't like, then he confines himself to musicological matters. But for others he waxes rhapsodic. It's really quite amusing to see him praising composers, any number of totally minor names that we'll never, ever encounter.

And Schumann even says here that while the Berlioz work is not exactly his cup of tea, he hastens to tell us that he respects it a lot. That's what a good critic ought to do. It's what some of those better composers in the nineteenth century ought to have done with Liszt. It's quite clear that Liszt wasn't Brahms's cup of tea, although when he started out, he was; and there are various things in the early works, the "Transformation" themes and the others in one of the piano sonatas, for example, where Brahms owes something to Liszt.

We use the nineteenth-century terms *fantasy transcription* and *paraphrase* very loosely. Liszt's work divides itself up into things which are more or less bar-for-bar arrangements of the original work, and the things which just take themes from the original and make a new piece out of them. There are one or two things which fall somewhere in between, where he more or less takes a section but is very free with it.

The *Symphonie fantastique* is bar for bar. Not only is it bar for bar, but it's quite interesting, because there are one or two passages which Berlioz altered later; and so we hear a version which we would otherwise not know. The second movement of the *Symphonie,* for example, I think is actually better in the version that Liszt worked from. I think it's a great pity when pianists play this version, and they think, "Oh, Liszt must have made a mistake," and so they "correct" it.

You can't actually transfer, or transcribe, to the piano *all* of the notes of the *Symphonie!* But what you can do is, you can do things on a piano which make you think of those notes. I think this is where he had it all over any other transcribers. When he transcribes the Beethoven symphonies, it's marvelous, because there are so many hack arrangements with which to compare them. You see at a stroke what he did and how sometimes he doesn't write down Beethoven's notes at all! He writes down some different notes, but they come out making the proper "sound" of Beethoven's symphony. That's because his ear was so marvelous. When you get right down to it, you cannot make a succession of notes on the piano sound more like an oboe than a clarinet, but you've got to do something in the way you play it just to illustrate that it is a different color. As far as achieving big "orchestral" effects, that's easily enough done. And Liszt does it very well. And the rest is just that he has such a variety of colors on the piano that it reminds you of the variety of colors of the orchestra.

Jonathan Kregor

A few years ago, when I was researching my dissertation, I found at the Harvard music library a copy of the *Neue Zeitschrift für Musik* [*NZfM*] containing Schumann's article about Liszt's transcription for solo piano of Berlioz's *Symphonie fantastique*. The library had opened a subscription to the *NZfM* in 1834. I must admit it was exciting to hold the article in my hands. You would think the pages would be falling apart by now, but they seemed to have used a good quality of paper, so it is preserved fairly well. Berlioz's *Symphonie fantastique* was premiered in Paris on December 5, 1830. He then revised it in 1832 with a rewrite of the third movement. Berlioz didn't publish the full score until 1845, after making still more revisions, particularly in the second movement. The 1832 version may be the one that Liszt used in his transcription for solo piano. We know that Liszt was at the premiere in Paris; and we know from Liszt's letters to Marie d'Agoult that he began working on his arrangement in 1833–34. What is interesting here is that Liszt included Berlioz in the work on the transcription. There is evidence that Liszt would transcribe portions, show them to Berlioz, and then receive advice on the details before he finally published it in 1834. Before this, audiences would have had at most only three or four opportunities to hear the whole work in its orchestral version.

I think Liszt turned to the Berlioz music not only because he was blown away by the music, but because he saw Berlioz as a kind of mentor figure, and he felt he had a lot of growing to do. At the same time, other composers were transcribing for solo piano works by lots of composers, including Beethoven; and Liszt on several occasions declared his intentions to do a better job on this sort of thing. He documented his Berlioz transcription in one of his "Bachelor of Music" letters to Adolphe Pictet, where he talked about his "new approach" to transcription that he had undertaken for the *Symphonie fantastique*. His letter was published in the *Revue gazette et musicale,* so it would have had a pretty wide distribution in France. This is where Schumann, who had not yet met Berlioz, first heard about the transcription. He habitually translated and printed such articles in his own journal. Even before this, there had been interest in Germany in Berlioz, and Schumann was ever watchful for composers on the rise.

Liszt's transcription for solo piano is top-notch, although it is very difficult to play. It contained some commentary written in French and some notes about the instrumentation that give you many insights into Berlioz's orchestra. Liszt was adamant that these be included. It also included the full program of the music. The program as we know it was in place by 1834. It's about an artist who is hopelessly in love and, after a series of encounters with the "Beloved" at a ball scene and in the country, is led to the guillotine. He descends to Hell, where he meets the Beloved, now grotesquely transformed. The last movement is the battle between a witches' dance and the religious Dies Irae; and that's how it ends. It's not just Harriet Smithson who is Berlioz' *idée fixe* here, but other women in Berlioz's life, notably Camille Moke, who had first attracted, then disappointed him. Berlioz relates in the *Memoirs* about traveling to Paris dressed as a maid, bent on shooting her and killing himself. But, fortunately, he got sidetracked. And of course we know that Berlioz's later marriage to Harriet Smithson was a disaster.

One of the reasons Schumann devotes so much space to the *Symphonie fantastique* in his journal is to rebut a critical review by François-Joseph Fétis. He had attacked the work and Berlioz in general. Not only did he take Berlioz to task for presuming to represent the story in music, but he charged that the work was "formless." As for the first attack, Berlioz defended himself at first by saying that the last two movements were in the nature of "a dream." But then later, he retreated a bit and said that the *entire* narrative was a dream. Liszt himself emphasized that this "program" is not a command for how we should hear the music, but merely an insight into how the story was an inspiration for the composer. This is an argument Liszt makes for other works, like Berlioz's "Harold" Symphony. Schumann himself ultimately makes a clear distinction between the program of the work and the work's identity without a program. He's trying to justify it as a work of "absolute" music. He is very forthright in saying, "As for the 'program,' let France keep it!" He also says it's insulting to Germans that they need to be instructed how to hear a piece of music. At this point in his life, he feels a "program" is not a prescribed thing, but an interpretive experience for the listener.

Schumann's agenda first and foremost was to show how the music worked as a valid composition. This necessitated a very thorough theoretical analysis, with all kinds of musical analysis, printed examples, and formal diagrams. He really touches all the bases. Secondly, his imagination allowed him to "hear" how a banal line on the piano transcription can be translated into the sounds of flutes and oboes and lower strings. Remember, he is not working from an orchestral score, but from Liszt's piano version. Some of Berlioz's musical effects were very new, after all,

Robert Schumann's writing desk, Robert-Schumann-Haus, Zwickau, Germany.

and Schumann responds to them with great insight. Even Fétis had had to admit that Berlioz is an incredible orchestrator. It's interesting to note that there was an error in Liszt's transcription. It gave the *Symphonie*'s premiere as being in 1820, instead of 1830. This accounts for Schumann's astonishment that such a work could have appeared before Beethoven's

Ninth Symphony and, moreover, that it had preceded Beethoven in the programmatic reach of the symphonic form.

Schumann's readers would not have known about this piece any other way. I know Berlioz was extremely pleased by this "news out of Germany," as he calls Schumann's notice. I think this marks the point where Berlioz seriously begins planning taking his music on tour in Germany. It opens the floodgates for Berlioz's reception in Germany. And Schumann singles out Liszt for his unbelievable transcribing abilities.

This is a foundational transcription for Liszt and, indeed, for the history of transcription in general. It is an extremely under-researched field. And Liszt has not been as careful as we now would have liked him to be in explaining to us what his process was as a composer–pianist–arranger. All those three elements freely intermingle in most of Liszt's works. This output is vast, and it is important to see how it fits into the larger culture. It's also important to Liszt's developing conception of himself as an artist. It's not too much to say that these endeavors contributed to Liszt's ideas about program music and thematic development.

Even though Schumann will not meet Liszt and Berlioz until years later, we can see at this time in 1834 a real kinship among them. For example, if we're to trust what Schumann says at the time, he tells Liszt in a letter, "I feel like I've known you my whole life." Coming from someone like Schumann, this is a very important thing to say.

SCHUMANN AND FELIX MENDELSSOHN

His judgment on musical matters, particularly on compositions, [is] the most profound and cogent that one can imagine. His life [is] a work of art—perfect.
—Robert Schumann, 1835

EDITOR'S NOTE
Schumann first met Mendelssohn in the autumn of 1835 when he settled in Leipzig to assume duties as conductor of the Gewandhaus Orchestra. Schumann immediately bestowed upon him the sobriquet "F. Meritis" in his League of David. They spent many productive and collaborative years together as the two leading lights of the Leipzig musical scene. Until Mendelssohn's death in 1847, Schumann continued to hail him as the greatest living contemporary composer.

R. Larry Todd

Schumann greeted Mendelssohn's arrival in Leipzig in the mid-1830s
enthusiastically and quickly dubbed him "Meritis" in the pages of his
journal. Schumann was essentially very much in awe of Mendelssohn.
Mendelssohn was the polished child prodigy who had composed in
nearly every genre. Schumann at that time was still very much a young
composer still trying to make his mark. And here was Mendelssohn, who
had composed the famous Octet when he was just sixteen years of age,
surely an incredible feat. The two men got together and formed a key part
of German musical life. They enjoyed a long, productive friendship for
many years. They overlapped in Leipzig, of course, where Schumann was a
journalist and had his paper, the *Neue Zeitschrift für Musik*. Mendelssohn
arrived there in 1835 as the conductor of the Gewandhaus Orchestra. In
the 1830s and 1840s, he was probably the most celebrated and distinguished composer in European music. In England he was revered by the
English. He made as many as ten trips to England, the first in 1829, the
last in the last year of his life, in 1847, when *Elijah* was performed before
the queen and Prince Albert. He definitely had private sessions with the
queen, playing for them piano duets of some of his *Songs without Words*.

One of Mendelssohn's great accomplishments in Leipzig was the
sense of history and programming that he brought to his concerts. He
expended a great deal of effort in bringing to the public the lost works of
Bach and Handel. He had several series of concerts in which he surveyed
various historical periods. This has proven to be important to us today,
because our notion of the canons of music, the mainline tradition—the
idea that Mozart is a classical composer, that Beethoven is a figure standing between the classical and romantic periods, and the idea of Bach as
culminating the baroque—a lot of this is systematized by the efforts of
Mendelssohn and his contemporaries.

And so what resulted was this general image of him as a kind of cheerful genius, somebody who effortlessly wrote music that was saccharine,
pleasant to listen to, but not very profound. He was quickly canonized in
the nineteenth century. There were a handful of compositions that became
entrenched in the public mind. One thinks of the Violin Concerto, the
"Italian" Symphony (although he never released it for publication), the
Octet, and the Overture to *A Midsummer Night's Dream*. For quite some
time it was thought that was about all there was to Mendelssohn. But we're
now discovering that composition was not easy for him. If you look at his
autographs, they are crammed with corrections. Measures are crossed out,
things reworked. He was a perfectionist very much as Beethoven was a
perfectionist. You see the same process in their manuscripts. They were
constantly refining, reworking, and they were never satisfied. He was not a

frail genius by any means. He was athletic and rather robust and certainly a workaholic. He had a sense of history about him that's quite striking. He tended to collect not only his manuscripts, which he ordered very carefully and had bound in volumes, but also his correspondence to himself he collected. We have about six or seven thousand letters addressed to him that survive in a collection in England. A person of enormous discipline, painstaking in every detail, in everything he did.

They complemented each other in so many ways—Mendelssohn making tremendous advances in the concert overture and in his later symphonies, Schumann focusing more on the piano music and the lied, the art song. Put the two together and you have a wonderful cross-section of the best in German music in the 1830s and 1840s. We know from Schumann's diaries that they were constantly meeting together, drinking together, and discussing music. Around them was a constant flux of musicians, singers, performers, pianists, virtuosos of all kinds coming to Leipzig to perform at the Gewandhaus concerts. Schumann the critic was constantly there, writing up reviews in his journal. And there's no doubt that there was a continual interchange of ideas between them.

As a result of much new research, we now are gaining a much clearer view of Schumann's relationship with Mendelssohn. It's strange how these things go in cycles. When I was a student, Schumann was regarded as much more serious composer of piano music than Mendelssohn. That's now all changed. Through Schumann's own writings we know he revered and emulated him in many ways. He dedicated his string quartets to him. It's clear that Mendelssohn could have advised Schumann on those works. And we know that Mendelssohn did advise him on the First Symphony. Schumann revised the opening horn call of his "Spring" Symphony on Mendelssohn's advice. Mendelssohn was heavily involved in promoting Schumann's *Paradise and the Peri*. Schumann, for his part, wrote many reviews about his work. (It is amusing to note that Schumann got it wrong when writing about Mendelssohn's Third Symphony. He got it mixed up with the Fourth Symphony, subtitled "The Italian," which was not published until after Mendelssohn's death. But Schumann had heard about the manuscript, so somehow in his review he wrote about "Mediterranean sunlight," when what Mendelssohn had intended was an evocation of heather and Hebridean fog!) Schumann's study with Clara of the music of J. S. Bach in 1845 was, I'm sure, under Mendelssohn's influence. And there is a Mendelssohnian strain that goes through not only much of his music but that of Clara, as well.

Another really interesting result of new scholarship is the renewed interest in Clara and Fanny Hensel. My major project of last year was finishing my biography *Fanny Hensel: The Other Mendelssohn* [2010]. These two women composers provide fascinating insights into musical life of the nineteenth century in general. They force us to reconsider everything we thought we knew. We know Clara performed many of Mendelssohn's piano pieces. Mendelssohn composed his *Allegro Brilliante* as a piano duet for her, which was premiered in the Gewandhaus. When she was fourteen, she composed her Piano Concerto in A Minor (to which Schumann added some orchestration), and it was premiered in the Gewandhaus under Mendelssohn's direction. Unfortunately, there was an incident where Schumann directed in private, in some of the household diaries, some anti-Semitic remarks about him. It is typical of the culture of the time. We have to remember that Mendelssohn's own teacher Carl Friedrich Zelter, in his correspondence with Goethe, also voiced such remarks. When those letters were published in the 1830s they were read out loud, and Felix's father, Abraham, was very hurt. Felix had to deal with this sort of thing through much of his life, despite the fact that he had already converted to Christianity. It goes a long way to explain why Mendelssohn was so close to the music of J. S. Bach, the musical Lutheran par excellence. In the end, Mendelssohn's death affected Robert profoundly. We know that sometime after his death, there was a dinner party where Franz Liszt spoke disparagingly of Mendelssohn, and Schumann was so offended he got up and left and refused to speak to Liszt for a time.

Joshua Rifkin

I think that Mendelssohn and Schumann and all that side of the romantic musical movement felt a very strong affinity for Bach. His harmonic richness, the sweep and spoken drama of his music, the rich (yet strict) counterpoint were all a great attraction. It's as if the expressive content was so wild that it had to possess a dialectic formal stringency. And remember that the romantics, like the earlier Gothic movement, were also fascinated by antique things. They loved Gothic cathedrals. They loved ruins to the point of building their own ruins. This was to them a "lost world" they could be nostalgic about. And Bach fits very much in with this preoccupation, as well, even though the romantics had a passionate involvement with their present-day world, too. In other words, the romantics wanted to live in two places at once—the present and the past.

When Mendelssohn came to Leipzig, he was prepared to lead a revival of Bach. His teacher, Carl Friedrich Zelter, led the *Singakademie,* a very prominent amateur chorus. In fact, it was the first great amateur choir and the model for the modern amateur choir. Zelter was a great Bach fan and owned a great many original Bach manuscripts, which he had used with the Singakademie. So, here comes Mendelssohn to Leipzig, and he conducted the revival of the *Saint Matthew Passion.* He was fired with enthusiasm for the work, even though Zelter was a little bit skeptical about its chances of winning broad acceptance. The performance was a tremendous success, partly because it had been well promoted in a press campaign.

You can compare the revival of Bach, let's say, to the ongoing life of a Broadway show. Take *Show Boat,* which over the sixty-odd years of its premiere has stayed in the repertory, but which has always been changed, rearranged, reorchestrated, shuffled about, and modified to suit present-day tastes. This is normal showbiz. But with Bach, nobody thought of this distance. It was just making his music a part of present-day life. And that is how it happened and has kept happening until more or less the present day.

SCHUMANN AND FRANZ LISZT

I have never found any artist, except Paganini, to possess in so high a degree as Liszt, this power of subjecting, elevating, and leading the public.
—Robert Schumann, 1840

Michael Saffle

Franz Liszt befriended an enormous number of performers and composers. Certainly the most famous of his many musically creative friends—although the friend in question did not always behave in an entirely cordial manner—was Richard Wagner. Less intense and ultimately less musically productive, but also less emotionally tumultuous, was Liszt's relationship with Robert Schumann. Schumann dedicated his Op. 17 *Fantasie* to Liszt, and Liszt replied with the gift of a lifetime: the dedication of his B-Minor Sonata to Schumann. Schumann, however, published his *Fantasie* in 1839, when he was still a Young Turk of a romantic. All this before the two musicians met face-to-face, and long before depression and finally insanity overcame Schumann. Liszt, on the other hand, waited until 1854 to publish the sonata, and by the time he completed it, Schumann had been committed to an asylum. It is unfortunate not only that Schumann never heard Liszt's masterpiece, but that he couldn't have heard it when he was still a young man. Both Liszt and Schumann grew less flamboyant with the passing years, but Schumann's music rapidly became more conservative than Liszt's. In 1848, when Liszt settled in Weimar, he was already working on his first symphonic poems. By 1848 Schumann had mostly given up musical experiments. And, of course, Schumann died in 1856. Liszt lived until 1886, long enough for the young Claude Debussy to listen to—and learn from—Liszt's own *Les jeux d'eau à la Villa d'Este.*

One of Schumann's gestures of friendship toward Liszt was to reprint, in German and in Schumann's own *Neue Zeitschrift für Musik,* a biographical article about Liszt that appeared originally in 1835 in several numbers of the *Revue et gazette musicale de Paris.* The author, Joseph d'Ortigue, did not always take careful aim at his subject (and at this point I shall indulge in an extended American metaphor). So, instead of playing sharpshooter, d'Ortigue fired once or twice from the hip. Of course he praised Liszt as a pianist, and it testifies to Schumann's sense of fair play that he reprinted the Frenchman's praise; he (Schumann) probably wouldn't have done that if he had envied Liszt's abilities as a performer or feared them. (Clara certainly envied Liszt's abilities and acclaim, and in later life she proclaimed him a "terrible" composer.)

Unfortunately, a few of the things d'Ortigue wrote were not only untrue, but extremely influential. One of these untruths appeared near the end of his article: Liszt, he gently suggested, wasn't an original composer because two of his earliest works were based on, or borrowed from, the works of others. Another untruth asserted Beethoven's presence at a concert "little Frantz" gave in Vienna in 1823. There is no solid evidence that Beethoven attended this concert and quite a bit of hearsay evidence that he didn't. Interestingly enough, however, d'Ortigue says nothing about the so-called *Weihekuss* (or "kiss of consecration") that Beethoven was long believed to have bestowed upon the young prodigy at the concert's conclusion. My own work as a musicologist might be cited here, because I recently published a reassessment of Lisztian biography, subtitled "Liszt after Walker"—a reference to the influential scholar and prose stylist Alan Walker—in which I examine again the impact of the *Weihekuss* story on music history. Anyway . . . apparently having forgiven d'Ortigue his factual errors and his notions about what makes music "original," Liszt wrote his lover the Countess Marie d'Agoult in 1839 that he planned to have the biography translated into English! Its success was due in part to Schumann, and Liszt's plan may be taken, if only implicitly and indirectly, as a form of thanks to his illustrious contemporary.

Leslie Howard

As he did for others, Liszt transcribed and paraphrased several of Schumann's songs. It's likely that more people heard them in his day through the piano versions than as works for voice. Liszt's work in that department has been often so misunderstood, but he was quite concerned to propagate unknown music as well as to exercise his imagination— which he couldn't fail to do anyway in writing variations of some of these song transcriptions. He writes different variations which correspond to the different verses, and which actually reflect the poetry. When you think he did fifteen Schumann songs, more than sixty of Schubert's, a dozen Mendelssohns, and twenty Beethovens—I don't know where he found time to do all that he did!

It's not so well known that Liszt did some transcriptions of some of Clara's songs, too. But I don't think he got as much as a thank-you out of her. Yet he gave all the royalties to her, just as he gave away practically everything he ever owned in his life. And you read that at first she did like Liszt when she first met him. Personally, I think she half fell in love with him. But maybe he wasn't interested in her, or maybe there was no sexual buzz there, or maybe he was too busy at the time dallying with the Countess d'Agoult. Who knows? But whatever, she never had a kind word to say about him for the rest of her life. Even when he was helping her.

5

"Hail, Wedded Love"

Clara, Courtship, and Marriage

Commentators: Joan Chissell, Katherine Kolb, Jonathan Kregor, Peter F. Ostwald, Nancy B. Reich, and John Worthen

---

EDITOR'S NOTE

Robert Schumann's courtship and marriage to Clara Wieck is one of the great romances in music history. Contrary to Hollywood myth, their relationship was fraught with strain and contentiousness, before and during the marriage. Although they had met before, they really got to know each other when Robert first came to study piano with Father Wieck around 1830. Despite the nine years' difference in their ages, within six years their friendship quickly blossomed into a romance. Her father's repeated attempts to block the relationship led to trial proceedings in Dresden and Leipzig, which eventually were decided in the couple's favor. They married in September 1840. During their marriage they had eight children and lived in three cities: Leipzig, Dresden, and Düsseldorf. Their union was rather unconventional at the time: Some of the time, Robert labored in relative obscurity at home with the children while Clara was the primary breadwinner on her concert tours. They collaborated on occasion as co-composers and co-arrangers. Clara premiered many of Robert's significant works, particularly chamber and concerted works; was the dedicatee of numerous compositions; and assisted with the production of his major stage and choral/orchestral works. She was also the executrix of his estate and, finally, editor-in-chief of the first collected edition of Robert's works.

EARLY YEARS, 1830–35

Yesterday I saw a scene I shall never forget. Professor Wieck scolded his son, Alwyn, who had not played well. "You wretch, you wretch!," he said, "—is this the pleasure you give your father?" The old man threw the boy onto the floor, pulled him by the hair, trembled and staggered, sat still to rest and gain strength for new feats. And, through all this, there was the little girl, Clara. She just smiled and calmly sat herself down at the piano with a Weber sonata. Am I among humans?

—Robert Schumann, 1830

Dear Mr. Schumann: I didn't write sooner because I got a mild case of scarlet fever. But I am recovered now and hope that soon you can come hear my next concert. I'm looking forward to Christmas. The piece of fruitcake that I'm saving for you is waiting to be eaten. Of course, I'll have to bake it first! Write to me soon, but please write legibly, for a change! Hoping to see you soon at our house, I remain, your friend, Clara.

—Clara Wieck, 1832

Young Clara

Nancy B. Reich

By the mid-1830s Clara Wieck was very well schooled and had studied with the best people in Leipzig and Berlin and Dresden. There are several instances at this time of her musical collaboration with Robert. One example can be seen in her Piano Concerto. When I was in the East Berlin Music Library, I asked for Clara Schumann's works, whatever they had, and they brought out a number of things. Among them was a most remarkable document. It was the manuscript of Clara's Piano Concerto, written when she was only fourteen. At the time she called it a *Concertsatz,* and what I had found later became the third movement. But the manuscript was definitely in *Robert's* hand. Apparently, he himself had orchestrated the third movement. Sure enough, entries in her diary confirm that out of friendship for her, he was going to orchestrate the work. It has been alleged that a theme by her became the basis for Robert's *"Clara Wieck" Impromptus.* But a few years ago, two scholars, working independently, found in Robert's diary (which was published in the 1860s) a melody which resembles that theme. In other words, it's possible it was originally *his* melody. He may have been fooling around with it at the piano, and maybe she heard it and improvised on it. Or maybe he forgot it was his melody. The thing is, they were both living and working in such close proximity that it's very difficult to say who thought of what first, although I must say she did stop composing when Robert died in 1856. I think she devoted herself to concertizing instead because of the public gratification and because she had to support the family.

Peter F. Ostwald

I think there was a nurturing, kindly, protective quality in Clara already when she was an adolescent. She loved to go on long walks with Robert, which was part of a health regimen which Wieck fostered. Schumann was nearsighted and somewhat clumsy, and Clara described how she would protect him from stumbling if they came close to a rock or some ridge in the road. She would hold his coat and pull him back. One gets this feeling of her protective interest in Robert from the beginning. This is an interesting phenomenon of the nineteenth century, because we know of a number of women who had this sort of nurturing influence over men, and who really spurred them on to create. Now, in Liszt's case this was the Countess d'Agoult; in Chopin's case it was George Sand; and in Schumann's case, it was Clara Wieck. Without Clara, Schumann would not have been the great composer that he is. When it comes to those early piano compositions, she certainly stimulated him a great deal. Because she was a performer, it gave him an opportunity to actually have his works heard in public, and for him to hear how they could be played. This was a great artistic relationship. No doubt about that.

COURTSHIP, 1836–40

> *You are the dearest thing in the world to me. A thousand*
> *times I have thought about everything, and everything tells*
> *me it has to be, if we want to and can manage it.*
> —Robert Schumann, letter to Clara, August 13, 1837

Peter F. Ostwald

Of course, Robert and Clara knew each other for many years before they actually got married. Already in those early years, there were problems. First of all, when they met, Clara was a mere child, whereas Robert was a college student. He was eighteen, and she was nine years old, so there was that kind of a discrepancy in the relationship. He hardly paid attention to her at first. It wasn't until she became an adolescent that he paid more attention to her. He, by that time, had become interested in other women, and he in fact, had become engaged to one of Clara's friends. That led to problems—disappointment and bitterness on her part, and a certain amount of anxiety and guilt on his part. Then, of course, there was the big problem which never ceased, namely her father's objection to the relationship; and he relentlessly attempted to keep them apart and did everything in his power to prevent the marriage. After they were married, he was not the ideal father-in-law, let's put it that way. Now, Clara was very loyal to her father, so there was a problem right there in the relationship.

Nancy B. Reich

After about 1835, there were times when they were kept separated, particularly when she was touring. They were able to correspond, but because she knew that her father would look at the letters, they worked out a secret underground correspondence, too. When she was in Paris, her father had no control over things, so they were able to correspond relatively freely.

The relief medallion of Robert and Clara Schumann, situated on the site of their last Bilkerstrasse residence, Düsseldorf, Germany.

Their letters indicate two things: first, that she was very much in love with him, and that was never any question of other men in her life; second, she was troubled when she was away from him—particularly about the break with her father. Should she remain with Robert? Should she break with her father? Who was right? What would this do to her career? She didn't admit any of this to Schumann; rather, she asked him things like, "How will we live; will we have enough money to live?" Clara's diary entries show that up to a few weeks before the marriage she was still saying things like, "I'm overwhelmed by my love for my father"; and things like, "Oh, what have I done to my father?" It must have been very difficult for Robert, who had been slandered in every way by him. I think Robert was exceptionally sensitive to her position in all this. Any other man would not have permitted, it seems to me, even the word "Wieck" to be spoken in his presence.

In her diaries and letters, Clara reveals her conflicts about how she felt about seeing her father so unhappy. She writes about having feelings of guilt. It was a very difficult period. I don't think she was really aware of the extent of Robert's depressions until the winter before they were married. But at that point she began to be troubled, as she realized that after the marriage the burden of many decisions might fall on her shoulders. Of course, she was remarkably mature. Although she was nine and a half years younger than he, she was very mature.

Jonathan Kregor

During those rather furtive courtship years, Clara really came into her own as a traveling concert artist. In the beginning of 1838, when she was eighteen—Clara and her father had been in Vienna for about a month— she played Beethoven's "Appassionata" Sonata at one of her concerts. By all accounts, it was a great success. [Note: On March 15 of that year, Clara received Austria's greatest honor, the *Königliche und Kaiserliche Kammervirtuosin* (Royal and Imperial Chamber Virtuosa).] The poet Franz Grillparzer took it upon himself to write a poem, "Clara Wieck and Beethoven," which was published in a Viennese newspaper. In a published letter Liszt, who had met Clara by this time and played four-hand music with her, quoted the Grillparzer poem. He quotes it again twenty years later in his book about Schumann. In translation, the poem goes:

> A Wizard, weary of the world and life,
> Locked his magic spells in a diamond casket
> Whose key he threw into the sea;
> And then he died.
> Common, little men exhausted themselves in vain attempts;
> No instrument could open the lock;
> And the incantations slept with their master.
> A shepherd's child, playing on the shore
> Sees these hectic and useless efforts.
> Dreamy and unthinking as all girls are,
> She plunges her snowy fingers into the waves,
> Touches a strange object, seizes it, and pulls it from the sea.
> Oh! What a surprise! She holds the magic key!

She hurries joyfully, her heart beating, full of eager
    anticipation.
The casket gleams for her with marvelous brilliance;
The lock gives way;
The genies rise into the air,
Then bow respectfully before their gracious and virginal
    mistress,
Who leads them with her white hand
And has them do her bidding as she plays.

Grillparzer presented this poem to Clara at a private gathering, and that presentation copy can now be seen at the Schumann-Haus in Zwickau. Robert's diary from 1838 documents the event, and he republishes the letter in the *Neue Zeitschrift für Musik* later in the summer. And he also recalls it in his diaries in 1844.

The poem is very audacious, in that it essentially claims that Clara is the legitimate interpretive heir of Beethoven. Remember, this is at a time when Thalberg and Liszt and many other competing pianists are coming through Vienna. Vienna is "ground zero" for great pianists. So, for Grillparzer—who wrote the funeral orations for Schubert and Beethoven—to anoint her in this way was a very big deal. Moreover, her gender plays a big role in this poem, bordering on erotic implications, with the focus on her "white fingers" and "virginal" state. Clara was very pleased by all this, and in her diary she waxes lyrical over the presentation. That whole Viennese trip was a huge success. But when "Fräulein Wieck" returns to Vienna years later as "Frau Schumann," she is now seen as beholden to her husband and not Beethoven, as if she has traded masters, and, in a lot of people's minds, she has traded down.

John Worthen

What are your conclusions about the possibility of sexual relations between Robert and Clara prior to the marriage?

I look into it, because it's been suggested that there were sexual relations. Dr. Ostwald says so. And in the novelization by J. D. Landis, *Longing* [2000], it is so depicted. It's all rubbish, of course. There's absolutely no evidence for it. One piece of evidence is that Schumann goes and stays in a hotel with Clara in Weimar. But actually, according to the evidence, he didn't. Clara was staying at the house of the mother-in-law of a musician at the time, not a hotel; so Schumann didn't go stay with her there. And that takes a large plank out of the possibility of it happening at that time. I'm perfectly sure they did not sleep together before they got married. People of that generation and that class did not.

You also say we should be guarded in our thinking that this romance between Robert and Clara was inevitable, their troth to each other was inevitable, their marriage inevitable. You really poked all that full of holes.

I'm afraid I do. I tend to work rather flat-footedly and say, what would have happened if—? And Carl Banck clearly was very close to Clara at one time, and if Becker and Clara hadn't responded the way they did in August 1837, then it seems a fair chance Schumann would have gone off with the other woman he was pursuing at the time. Her name was Robena Laidlaw. She's an important person here, and I think he would've pursued her. She was an eighteen-year-old pianist, and Schumann later said she had him "half in her net," as I think he put it. She said afterwards *he* was pursuing her. He certainly sent letters to her; and she in turn sent him some music and a lock of her hair. Her father sent him some cigars, which Schumann was very grateful to have. So, he was on good terms with the father in this case, as well. Clara was probably jealous of her. Personally, I don't think anything sexual transpired between them.

Clara was, of course, worried about Schumann's reputation as a sexual athlete, and I think she worried that when he was away from her for long periods, he would be interested in other women. Indeed, one time—around 1837—when she was away from Leipzig, she heard from her father that Schumann had been seen entering the house of a man called Nohr. She wrote to Schumann outraged about this. She said, in effect, "If I hear that you have been going to that house, that is the end of our relationship." The question that came to me was, what on earth is wrong with Schumann going to the house of this person? Well, I did some work, and there were two Nohrs I found in Leipzig at that time. One was an eminent, distinguished Leipzig violinist called Christian Nohr, whom Clara and her father had visited 1837. He can hardly be the culprit. Or, there was a man called Nohr who ran a pension and a restaurant. Again, it can't have been itself a distressful place, because Schumann and Clara actually dined there about ten years later while in Leipzig. Either Clara feared at the time that the place was notorious for its prostitutes, which is possible, where men went to pick up girls. Perhaps someone like Cristel, to whom she had reason to believe Schumann had been linked, worked there. Or, maybe the notorious "La Faneuse" perhaps was now acting as scullery lady in the house or something. Anyway, so Clara said, "If you go to that house, that is it." Schumann writes back, saying, "I can't talk about this; I wouldn't answer such a silly little question."

"La Faneuse" was someone in Leipzig he referred to in his diary around 1836. The name means "the winnower" in English. Schumann clearly had a relationship with her. I don't think it was Cristel, because he would not have fallen in love with her. The French name shows that she must have been rather well known, even notorious, with a "byline," shall we say. On one occasion he ends up disgracefully in a cellar with her in the summer of 1837 in what he called "a wicked relationship," before he gets back together with Clara. One of the very few things John Daverio gets wrong is when he says she was a lady with whom one could, quite literally, "make hay." Actually, making hay and winnowing are quite different activities! The only reason I can imagine for the nickname is that a winnower separates the light and unnecessary things from hard and useful things, and that's I guess what La Faneuse did.

THE TRIAL

> *I have endured everything. I have lost my father, I have stood up to him in a court of law, I have fought battles with myself; but Robert's love made up for all this.*
> —Clara Wieck, diary entry, January 17, 1840

Nancy B. Reich

A couple could not marry without the consent of parents of both the bride-groom and the bride. So when Robert and Clara wanted to marry, they needed permission from Clara Wieck's father and her mother. Robert's parents were both dead, so he could marry without permission. You remember that Robert went to Berlin—wrote to Berlin to get permission from Clara's mother, who was an ally. But the father refused to give permission, and that's why they sued the court for permission to marry. They appealed to the court. Each had two representatives. Wieck, the father, had to get a lawyer to represent him. At that time they lived in Saxony. The capitol was in Dresden, and they went to the court there. A judge listened to the evidence on both sides as presented by the lawyers. There were times when they all had to be there together. And Clara found this very difficult, because she had to face her father in the courtroom. There were times when the father didn't show up and they had to postpone it. That's why this whole thing took a long time.

Peter F. Ostwald

During the court procedure, Wieck did a sort of hide-and-seek game. Wieck was very clever. He would stall the proceedings repeatedly when a hearing was to take place, which required all the participants to be present. Wieck often at the last moment would send a letter to the court saying he's not going to be able to make an appearance; and then he would send another long letter with various demands and stipulations to the court. So there were not many times when they were all together in the courtroom. But there is a very poignant moment, in fact, when Wieck lost control over himself and became very emotional. Clara was caught in the middle. She was fighting against Wieck. She wanted to be married to Schumann. But also she felt such great pity for her father that it must have been very, very stressful for her. And this ambivalence must have disturbed Robert. Not only that, but the real possibility that the case would be decided against him.

By this time, you recall, Schumann had had some experience with the law through his studies. I mean, there is good evidence that he must have attended the law classes *sometime*. We know that he read law books, too. He was on friendly terms with some of the law students. He acquired some feeling for the law, and that helped him, not only in the law courts in Leipzig, but also in his finagling around contracts when he became the editor of *The New Magazine of Music,* which he ran almost single-handedly for many years. There is evidence of his precise, almost legalistic approach. I'm not suggesting he handled the Leipzig court procedure all on his own. Quite the contrary. I'm sure he had help, but he undoubtedly benefited somewhat from the legal experience that he had.

Clara actually was the first person to consult a lawyer. She was in Paris when she found out that Wieck was planning to deprive her of her earnings. She had been working as a concert pianist from childhood on, and Wieck had collected everything for her with the understanding that someday it would be returned to her. But she found out from a friend that Wieck was planning to take all of her property away from her. She and Robert at first attempted an out-of-court settlement. When Wieck wouldn't go for that, they had to go to court. There were substantial charges against Schumann. Wieck accused Schumann of being an alcoholic and being financially irresponsible. Those were the two main things he had to defend himself against. Incidentally, it's very interesting to me that Nancy Reich repeats the story that Schumann at this time was financially irresponsible. One sees that in all the biographies, but I simply don't believe it. If you look at the early diaries, you see that Schumann was very, very conscientious about money. He records every penny that he took in and every penny that went out. I do admit that he was very worried about money. During his student days, his mother and his guardian had kept him on a short leash. And it's true that he liked to spend money, but I don't see him as being financially irresponsible.

Wieck's objections also had a lot to do with Clara herself. She was his pride and joy, virtually his possession from childhood on. He didn't want to lose Clara, and he saw Schumann as a formidable rival. I also think that he knew that Schumann was mentally ill. As Clara did, certainly. Anybody who was close to Schumann would know this, and when you read the correspondence between Robert and Clara, you see Schumann makes no bones about it. He refers to his mental illness many times. In those days, and even today to a certain extent, people think that mental illness is something dreadful, something incurable, and is always going to lead to a terrible outcome. Madness is very frightening, and here was Schumann with some very definite episodes of mental disorganization and illness. I think that bothered Wieck.

John Worthen

Dr. Ostwald says two things which I object to. First, he implies that Clara's father knew that Schumann was mentally unstable. Ostwald states this much more clearly in his introduction to the marriage diaries that he published ten years after his *Schumann: The Inner Voices* biography. Now, in your interview with Ostwald, he actually says that Wieck knew about Schumann's mental disturbance. This is absolutely untrue. I have read all the records of what Weick said in the court in Leipzig, and his subsequent refutation of what the court had done, and if he'd had such information in his hands he would have used it. It was the best possible way. No court in the world would have stood up and said, "We allow this young woman to marry this madman." It wouldn't have done it. He used things like Schumann being so drunk he couldn't be given a key by his landlady. Wieck will play as dirty as he can get. If he'd had that, he'd have used it. He would have used the syphilis card, as well. And that would have been a way of "saving" Clara from Schumann. There's no question of that. The fact that he didn't play it shows he didn't have it, and didn't even suspect the existence of it. And Schumann himself would have said, "I don't have syphilis. I was cured. I've been healthy now for several years. I've had a bit of rheumatism, yes, but that's not syphilis, is it?"

MARRIAGE AND FAMILY

> *In a comedy we see marriage as an ultimate goal, reached only after surmounting obstacles which fill several acts. And at the moment when this goal is achieved, the curtain falls and a momentary satisfaction warms our hearts. But it is quite different in life.*
>
> —Goethe, *Elective Affinities*

*Times have changed with me. I used to be indifferent to the
amount of notice I received, but a wife and children put a different complexion upon everything. It becomes imperative to
think of the future now.*

—Robert Schumann, 1841

Nancy B. Reich

In many ways, for his time Robert was a remarkably sensitive husband and
father. He loved the children; he loved being the head of the household.
I've always been impressed with the care and support he showed Clara,
too. This is clear not only from his diaries, but from the household books.
He was really obsessive about keeping track of their lives. He kept diaries,
and he kept household books in which he recorded everyday expenses.
These are very important, because they tell us how much money he paid
the servants, how much bread cost, how much cigars cost, how much he
spent on postage and champagne. He also recorded the dates on which he
began and completed works, as the unfinished projects. He also kept track
of everything about the children, his daughter's first tooth, that sort of
thing. In the so-called *Ehetagebücher,* the Marriage Diaries, he continued
this obsessive kind of recording by organizing a diary which he and Clara
were to keep jointly. Now, some people have written that Robert wrote in
Clara's diary. It was a joint diary, and they were supposed to take turns.

She wrote one week, and he wrote another. He
did not keep a separate diary during that time.
Unfortunately, those diaries only covered the
years 1840–44. After that, there were no diaries, just household books until he went off to
the asylum in Endenich. We think that Clara
kept diaries from 1845 to the end of her life,
but those diaries have disappeared. They were
probably burnt after Litzmann used them for his
biography of Clara.

I think in a way Robert was a much more
loving and tender parent to the children than
maybe Clara was. He did feel, of course, that
his composing came first; and he made some
comments in the diary to the effect, "Clara has
done some very nice songs, but with children
and a husband who composes, it's difficult."
I think like all husbands who are proud of the

Nancy B. Reich is Clara Wieck-Schumann's biographer.

work their wives do, Robert had moments when he resented the fact that it interfered occasionally with his own work. For example, he was proud of the fact she was a concert artist, and he was very grateful that she introduced and played his own works. But accompanying her on a concert tour meant that he had to give up his own time, both as editor of his journal and as a composer. And of course he was in a difficult position, as any husband of an illustrious woman is. It's very difficult to be asked, "Are *you* musical, too, Mr. Schumann?" But despite his talking about wanting "a little wife at home," he needed the income from her performances. He also knew she was his best publicist and the person who introduced his work. On the other hand, there was no doubt that Clara had great pride in her playing. She relished her public appearances. I think she was the kind of pianist who needed an audience's support and approval and who did her best in front of an audience. She got enormous gratification from that. Besides, she had servants in the house. She always had nursemaids. She didn't nurse her own children. And when she went off on one trip to Copenhagen and left Robert behind with Marie, the first child, there was a maid and a cook in the house with them.

She did this without a concert manager. There were no professional concert managers until after 1850. It was particularly difficult for her, because she had to do all these "unwomanly" things like bargaining for fees, demand the right concerts, the right pianos, and oversee the right advertisements. She was usually chaperoned, usually with a female friend. She used public conveyances, which were probably a good deal safer than they are today. After 1839 there were railroads all over Europe. All the major cities had them, and she sometimes took her pianos, all boxed and crated, on the trains. She had to make all these arrangements herself. They were asked to come to America to earn money. They knew they could earn a lot, as their friend Jenny Lind had done. But they turned it down. It would have meant two years away, and she couldn't bear to leave the children for such a long period of time.

By the way, after she was married, she always wrote her compositions for Robert, for his birthdays or anniversaries, or as Christmas gifts. And they were always presented to him with a little note—those notes still exist on the manuscripts—in which she said, "Please have a little forbearance for this weak effort." Really sad inscriptions. She really didn't have much confidence in her own composing. At that point she was married to a great genius, and it must have been intimidating. But she was formed from a hard school. She was a tough lady and believed very much in discipline and hard work. I'm sure she was by far the more severe of the parents with children in terms of discipline and control. She always thought of their welfare, their physical welfare, but not so much of their emotional welfare. People were generally just not that aware of that sort of thing at the time. In those days, the German middle-class mother left much of the care of children to others. There were governesses, nannies, and servants. The whole family might have been together only for a few hours a day, at most. In the case of the Schumanns, both parents would go off do what they had to do—compose, concertize, plan tours, take walks together. I can only assume that there must have been times when the Schumann children must have felt abandoned, to some extent.

However, in many ways it's very clear, not only from his diaries, but from the household book, that Robert loved being a husband and father. He took careful note of the wages, the children's tuitions, the schools, the governesses. He played games and told stories to his children as he had done with Clara and her brother during their courtship. In fact, I have concluded that in the final analysis he may have been a more loving and tender father to the children than I think she probably was. I have been impressed to see how much care and consideration he took with Clara. He certainly supported Clara before they were married, because her father cut her off completely. And later, he was generous in things like remembering gifts to her brother and her mother.

On the other hand, he also had a social life. He would go out at night with his men friends and have his beer over at the local *Coffe Baum* in Leipzig, or other similar establishments in other cities where he lived. It was a kind of *two-sided* life: He was the genius who in an excess of work would fall into what he called a "Fugenpassion," or writing frenzy. He would write day and night, for four days and nights sometimes, to the point of exhaustion.

In the final analysis, the two personalities fit together very well. This was because of their differences, not their similarities. Clara was actually the more "masculine," so to speak, because she was the more dominating figure, more vocal and outgoing. Robert, on the other hand, was much more withdrawn and reticent. So they completed each other. They needed each other in every possible way—not only musically, but emotionally, as well. And in some sense, she may have been more of a mother figure to Robert than to the children.

Joan Chissell

Schumann was an extremely impressionable person and constantly fluctuated in his moods—one minute on top of the world, and the other minute in the blackest despair. I'm enormously impressed at all the new light that has been thrown on his personality now by the publication of so many diaries. I think Schumann scholars owe so much to Dr. Gerd Nauhaus of Zwickau, who has put all those diaries in print. First of all, there are the

Haushaltbücher, which I think are among the most remarkable things ever to have come from any composer. . . . The extraordinary thing about that is we always think of Schumann as a wild, undisciplined romantic, with no kind of practical sense whatsoever. And yet from the age of about twenty-eight until a fortnight before his breakdown, every single penny that he spent on anything is recorded in the *Haushaltbuch*—his rent, his insurance, his laundry book, what he spent on soap. And of course when he married, he always lists birthday presents and Christmas presents. We have very detail of his existence—where he ate lunch that day, what books he looked at, what people he spoke to. And every detail of his work, what was started, revised, finished. It's quite extraordinary he had time to record all these details. He even made a secret sign in the margin of the *Haushaltbuch* every time he and Clara made love. It's so astonishing that such a wild romantic could also be this meticulous accountant. I don't think any other composer in the world has ever done that. And it's such a contradiction, in a way, between the vision we have of a wild, youthful romantic and this scrupulous man of business.

I think possibly it was Wieck who was responsible in a way for Schumann starting the *Haushaltbuch*. Because Wieck had absolutely refused permission for him to become engaged to Clara when she was only about seventeen. One of the reasons he objected was Schumann's alleged irresponsibility over money. Maybe later Robert wanted to prove Wieck wrong—that he could in fact manage his financial affairs.

There are times when I found Clara slightly unsympathetic, in that I thought she didn't have enough humor and was too ambitious for her husband. But the more I thought about it all, the more I read Schumann's later diaries and really understood the problems that she had to face, I've now developed an enormous admiration for her, because I think he was an extremely difficult person in later years, partly because he was suffering so much. I think she had an awful lot to deal with in just coping with his moods and his difficulties and his problems. And also, of course, bringing up innumerable children. We now know there were several miscarriages, for which, ironically, she was extremely grateful. I think she tried to induce one or two. It wasn't entirely easy being Clara Schumann. I realize that now much more when I started writing about her.

John Worthen

I think some allegations that Schumann probably was not a very good father to the children are wrong. I owe this to Erik Jensen's recent book on Schumann [*Schumann*, 2001]. Jensen's very good on the children and points out that Schumann does a great deal more than just write music for them. One of the very few accounts we have of Schumann at home shows him playing with the children. That's in Düsseldorf. When he goes for walks, the children walk with him, particularly Marie, the eldest. And after a particularly long walk, he carries her in his arms. In this sense he is paying far more attention to children than most middle-class fathers at the period did. I mean, how can you generalize? He's not a perfect father in modern terms, but then, in the nineteenth century, no one was. I think, for a nineteenth-century person, though, he is being extraordinary loving, and caring, and playful. That little book of memories for the children he starts to keep for them is a very lovely little production, in fact. So he wants them not to forget their time together, so they will have this memory book. It's a very nice little family production.

Peter F. Ostwald

This is not your average married couple! Here were two geniuses, and that they were able to marry and do so much together and have these children—that in itself is a miracle. Many great composers did not marry. Beethoven is an example of that; Brahms is an example; Schubert; and Liszt never married, although he lived with various women.

When they began the marriage and decided to keep a marriage diary, it was very much understood that they were to be equal partners and that they would be interdependent. Actually, this was part of the romantic ideal that the man would develop certain of his feminine qualities, and the woman would develop certain of her masculine qualities, and Schumann was exceedingly generous with Clara. He gave her money and bought her a piano. She was in a very bad situation when Wieck took all of her funds away. Later on, Schumann supported her mother. He was always very generous, very giving. I don't see him as being a male chauvinist at all. He was very close to his own mother, and I think, yes, he did expect that Clara would occupy the role of housewife. I think she wanted herself to be that. She regrets, in some of her correspondence, that she was not prepared for that. I think they both sought in certain ways to achieve a kind of domestic bliss and a happy home. But then, both their professional aspirations interfered with that. She needed to concertize and travel, and he needed to be isolated to compose.

Yes, there were problems in that marriage from beginning to end. Clara describes them. He was never well from the beginning of the marriage. There were problems when they went on a concert tour to Russia. There were problems when they moved to Dresden and he was so sick. There was the Revolution beginning in 1848. At that time, Clara was giving very few concerts. She also had all those children to take care of, and there were not many opportunities for her to play. If she did give a concert, it was mostly for charity. Although she never stopped completely, her career went into decline while they were in Dresden. The opportunities were greater for her later in Düsseldorf, which was closer to Holland and to England, where she very much wanted to concertize. But it was precisely at that time that Schumann became very open in his criticism of her. In the past, when he was under better control, he had pretty much kept his criticism to himself or written it in his diaries. But as he moved closer to what we call this psychotic breakdown, then he became more overtly critical, and that must have been very difficult for Clara to deal with. That is a touchy subject. I think there were times when he was very unhappy with Clara. He complained about her playing, and at one point in Düsseldorf he even objected to her playing with the orchestra. She was trying to help him, actually. He was a very inadequate conductor, and she would come in and try to help lead from the piano. He said that was a man's job. I think he was at that point quite confused and quite disturbed.

Another problem in the marriage was they had so many children. You can't raise children very well under those circumstances, when the mother's out concertizing and the father's away composing. Who takes care of the kids? Fortunately, in those days, one could get governesses and nannies to do it. But I think, by and large, the children were probably neglected. The oldest child, Marie, became a sort of pseudo-parent for the younger children. As you know, the boys did not do well at all. One of them did not live very long—he died when he was just a year old; he was sick from birth. Another one became mentally ill and lived in a hospital for a great many years. A third one married and did pretty well for a while, but he became a morphine addict. The last child, whom Schumann never knew, developed tuberculosis and died in his early twenties. So that was very tragic. Of the four daughters, one of them, Julie, also died fairly young. She had married an Italian count in Turin and had some children. She succumbed to tuberculosis. The other three—two of them never married and became piano teachers and lived to a ripe old age. One of them did marry and lived in the United States for a while. That's why we have descendants of the Schumann family here in the States.

Katherine Kolb

Marriages like the Schumanns' that combined two careers were going on all the time in the nineteenth century. You had musician couples who were working together. There was little fuss or ado. It simply was a practical matter. The whole family would be musical, and they would contribute in their own ways. Louis Spohr, for instance, traveled with his wife, a harpist, who would be part of the performances. Now, with Berlioz, he may have envisioned such a thing. Before his marriage he was engaged to the pianist Camille Moke, who then later married the famous piano manufacturer Pleyel. It's nice to speculate on what might have happened had they in fact married. Whether it could have been that kind of marriage. As you may know from the *Memoirs*, Camille was faithless during the year that Berlioz went to Italy, and Berlioz never quite forgave her for that. He had it in for her all his life.

In the aristocratic tradition, you could have a certain equality of the sexes simply by virtue of the fact that no one had to work. The women, especially in France, were known in the aristocracies for being very independent, for holding their salons and having their own influence. But what happens in the nineteenth century is that women are expected to fulfill certain roles in a bourgeois, middle-class household, which has to support itself. Therefore, someone or other is going to have to take care of the children. It is true that you still have a proletariat that can provide household help. You still have that up to this century and partway into this century. And I think that part of the reason that Clara Schumann was still able to practice and concertize was that she had people to help her out in the household. Nonetheless, by Clara's time you are already seeing the problem in its modern form, which is how in the world are two people equally bent on their careers going to manage?

There are parallels between the courtship of Robert and Clara and Berlioz and Harriet Smithson. For each marriage to take place, the couples had to go through legal actions. The parents were violently opposed to both these marriages. We already know about the opposition of Clara's father, Friedrich Wieck. In Berlioz's case, there was strong prejudice from his parents against his marrying an actress. That was why his family was so opposed to Berlioz becoming a composer in the first place. In France, composing meant theater and the opera. And there was a tremendous prejudice against this. So Harriet, as an actress, was absolute anathema.

What this tells me in both instances is that at this time parents still had tremendous power over their children. Berlioz thought it was criminal that young couples should have their marriages arranged. The fact that he was so drawn to *Romeo and Juliet* is intimately bound up with his experience with Harriet. Unlike the Germany of Schumann, in France at this time marriages had to be, if not arranged, at least approved. You couldn't marry just anyone, because there was a whole family heritage that was to be transmitted. This was a carryover from the aristocracy. And the bourgeoisie carries this on, because the bourgeoisie have property. Even though it's not so much carrying on the name of the lord of the manor, they nevertheless stand on their dignity as a pseudo-aristocracy. And as transmission of property, they therefore control these marriages very carefully. It is during these years that Engels writes his essay on the family in which he talks about the fact that love and marriage cannot have anything to do with each other as long as you have these property questions that are involved with marriage. These things are totally extraneous to love. By contrast, the proletariat have no such concerns. Engels makes a distinction between a Catholic country like France and a Protestant country like Germany. He says in Germany there is at least a semblance, a pretense, of allowing the young people to choose their spouses. But that's essentially hypocritical. In fact there is still some control.

Franz Liszt seems to me an interesting example of someone who is not threatened by powerful, intelligent women. He had his two great loves, who were literary figures, writers of some note. Marie d'Agoult certainly kept up her writing when she was with Liszt. She also served as his mouthpiece. Liszt, in fact, had a certain inferiority complex, intellectually speaking. He still felt that he was part of that old generation of musicians who had not had what today we would call a proper liberal-arts education. But he was absolutely brilliant. He read everything. He could speak several languages fluently. He was at least as competent as Marie d'Agoult. Actually, there was no marriage in either of those cases. He wanted to marry Carolyne von Sayn-Wittgenstein, but she could not obtain a divorce.

6

"Multitudes of Winged Tones"

The Piano Music

Commentators: Paul Badura-Skoda, Edmund Battersby, Albert Boime, Ronald Brautigam, Jörg Demus, Christoph Eschenbach, José Feghali, Vladimir Feltsman, Malcolm Frager, Claude Frank, Peter Frankl, Richard Goode, Eugene Istomin, Walter Klien, Hans-Joachim Köhler, Roe-Min Kok, Lawrence Kramer, Anton Kuerti, Svyatoslav Levin, Tim Mitchell, Garrick Ohlsson, Peter F. Ostwald, Leon Plantinga, Simon Preston, Nancy B. Reich, Erika Reiman, Charles Rosen, Eric Sams, Wolfgang Sawallisch, András Schiff, Steven Spooner, Uriel Tsachor, Gillian Weir, and Robert Winter

> *Modern pianistic art wants to challenge the symphony orchestra and rule supreme through its own resources.*
> —Robert Schumann, 1839

EDITOR'S NOTE

Schumann's name will always be associated with the piano. Indeed, in the decade 1829–39—from the Op. 1 (*"Abegg" Variations*) to Op. 32 (*Vier Klavierstücke*)—he composed almost exclusively for piano. These years saw his studies with Friedrich Wieck, the injury to his hand and the abandonment of plans for a virtuoso career, his journalistic work, and the budding romance with Clara Wieck (who was a prime inspiration for most of these works). In 1848, after a few scattered works earlier in the decade, including the famous Piano Concerto in A Minor, Op. 54, Schumann returned to the solo keyboard with a profusion of works, in order of opus number: *Album for the Young*, Op. 68; *Four Marches*, Op. 76; *Waldszenen* (Forest Scenes), Op. 82; *Bunte Blätter* (Colored Leaves), Op. 99; three *Fantasiestücke* (Fantasy Pieces), Op. 111; *Three Sonatas for the Young*, Op. 118; *Albumblätter* (Album Leaves), Op. 124; and *Seven Pieces in Fughetta Form*, Op. 126. Among his last works in 1853–54 are the *Gesänge der Frühe* (Songs of the Dawn), Op. 133; and the *"Geister" Variations*. Other piano music for four hands includes the *Bilder von Osten* (Pictures from the East), Op. 66; *Twelve Pieces for Little and Big Children*, Op. 85; *Ball Scenes,* Op. 109; and *Children's Ball,* Op. 130.

Discussed in this chapter are the emergence of the romantic piano, Schumann's early experiences at the keyboard, the influence of novelist Jean Paul on his music, overviews of the entire corpus, recent musicological findings, a survey of the piano cycles, notes on his fugues and canons for pedal piano, and commentary on the piano music for and about children.

THE TECHNOLOGY OF THE ROMANTIC PIANO

Charles Rosen

During the romantic period of the 1830s, piano music was the most important music being written. It seems to me that one should play the music on the instruments that were inspired by the music. In other words, the imagination and vision of many composers exceed the instruments of their own time. You find in response to the new kind of music that was being written in the 1830s and 1840s further developments in the pianos of the 1850s and beyond. And there's no reason not to play Schumann and Chopin on the modern piano. It was due to the kind of music that Liszt was writing that Érard invented the metal frame for the piano. Today the concert piano is sort of like a dinosaur, dying out. People rarely buy a concert piano for your home. The home is not big enough anymore.

Leon Plantinga

Here in the instrument collection at Yale, we have a Bösendorfer piano from 1828 that is in almost mint condition because it was kept in a place that didn't have central heating all these years. It is a big piano, certainly large for the standards of 1828. Now, this is exactly the sort of instrument that Schumann played. We know he had a Viennese instrument. He gave Clara a wedding present that was a Viennese instrument they kept in their house. That instrument had the hammers facing back toward the player, a very different situation from a modern Steinway. I sat down at this piano and played the beginning of *Carnaval,* which we think is a *big* piece with big, full-fisted chords, which is always played for maximum resonance and the like. But what I heard was on a smaller scale with a more reedy sound, especially in the lower register. In other words, we're learning that at least up to the middle of the nineteenth century, we no longer think we have a clear idea of what the sounds in Schumann's ears were like.

Paul Badura-Skoda

Cristofori was the inventor of the fortepiano. He invented single-handed the most perfect mechanism, an action which actually could only be equaled by the modern actions, but not surpassed. His instruments reached great fame in the time of Bach and Scarlatti. Today we assume that Scarlatti knew and played the instruments, that Scarlatti brought them to Portugal, and later to Spain, and that a number of his sonatas most likely were written for the piano than for the harpsichord. It's rather recent knowledge. With regard to Mozart, the piano had reached a perfect stage by then, a well-balanced instrument with a perfect sensitive action, enabling you to play practically everything. Its only disadvantage, of course, was that it didn't have the powerful tone of the modern grand and was used in smaller hall or theaters. But it was still large enough to play with a chamber orchestra. These instruments, of course, have been revived in the last forty years, and the audience gets to recognize the beauty of these instruments. At first one is shocked because it is not the sound you expect from a piano; but then, later, you realize what wonderful tone colors it has, so much more transparent in the lower register. It has, in fact, more character and more variety of expression than the modern piano.

The question, of course, is if the piano used by Beethoven in his late years, by Schubert and by Schumann, would sound differently to our ears today. I can answer that in two ways. First of all, their instruments were the only instruments they knew, and therefore what was familiar to them to us is a little unfamiliar, even exotic to a certain degree. That is, I would say, a philosophical problem. The first reaction when you hear Beethoven on an original instrument is that it sounds a little strange. But given a chance, most people now like it. Secondly, it might be said that these instruments that are a hundred fifty or two hundred years old probably sounded differently, perhaps even better, when they were new. However, I think we can disclaim that for two reasons. Wooden instruments do not deteriorate as much as instruments with a metal frame, because there's not so much tension on the strings, and also since they have been in attics and in museums sometimes for a century, they were without tension at all. And also, of course, it is proven that even the best replicas do not really produce a larger or better sound than the original instruments. I am the happy owner of a rather well-chosen, priceless collection of instruments, dating from harpsichords of Bach's time until that of Brahms and Debussy, which includes quite a few modern grands.

We have had beautiful recordings on Schumann's original instrument, which is also in one of the Vienna museums. Vienna is very rich in this respect. And the collection at the Smithsonian includes over two hundred instruments. I think Clara Schumann's piano would not sound so unfamiliar to our ears. It might be more mellow, less percussive, which was quite a departure from the brilliant and the rather rich-in-harmonics sound of the early Mozart or Beethoven piano.

We have descriptions of Schumann playing with his foot all the way down on the pedal, letting the sounds mix and blur. Today I just practiced, for my own pleasure, "Des Abends" (In the Evening), the first of the *Fantasy Pieces,* Op. 12. I enjoyed this blurring of the harmonies, which re-creates, I would say, an optical illusion. At twilight you don't see objects very clearly, particularly if it's an autumn, a fall evening—then there might be a little mist, a fog. And I think this fogginess is something which was not invented by Debussy or by the impressionists, but can be heard in Schumann's and even Beethoven's music and their pianos, and also seen in contemporary paintings. I'm thinking in particular of the English painter Turner. If you see his paintings you would think he was a modernist, and yet he was a contemporary of Schumann and Chopin.

And of course it's interesting that there was a time when Schumann playing forbade the blurring of pedal. I'm thinking of a particular school of teaching in Russia and in France at the end of the nineteenth century. Whenever a person objected and said that Schumann, Beethoven, and Chopin wrote for these crazy pedals, then the inevitable answer was, "Yes, it worked well on their instruments, but it is not good for our modern instruments." May I say this is just nonsense! I've tested it. Bad pedaling can sound horrible on an old instrument as well as a new one. You have just to know how much and how little to use.

Edmund Battersby

Arthur Loesser, in his book *Men, Women and Pianos,* relates everything about the piano to social history. One of his points is that piano manufacture and piano sound change with shifts in the ruling class. People who were educated were no longer running things. Music perceived by the intellect was much less in fashion. I think that's true today. Thus one of the things that is most disturbing to people who hear early pianos for the first time, and who are used to the plush, homogenous sound of the modern instrument, is what they think is a "thinness" of sound. Fortepianists call this the "clarity" of the sounds. I'm referring to the separation of tones, the fact that you can hear everything, like all four parts of a string quartet. And people today are put off because there's so much more to follow in a performance. I've heard Alfred Brendel describe early piano performance as "x-ray music." To hear all the individual voices can be disturbing. It's harder to listen to that because you have to think more. It's much easier to hear the blended combination of sounds.

In the 1790s, every note sounded on the small instruments that Mozart, Haydn, and Beethoven played. As time went on, there was less individuality in the sound. The period we're talking about, 1792 to 1830, was the most extraordinary time in the development of the modern piano. In 1830 the cast-iron frame was introduced. Everything changed after that. There was a different aesthetic as people became more interested in the *fullness* rather than the *separation* of sounds. It's no accident that counterpoint is no longer in fashion in the romantic period. The less contrapuntal composers fell by the wayside, like John Field, Dussek, Hummel. We can't say Schumann and Chopin didn't understand counterpoint; they certainly did. But it got mixed up in a very rich tapestry in sound. It's more voicing than strict counterpoint. And in Chopin there's a tremendous amount of counterpoint, but it's not strict counterpoint, it's not fugal. We have to include Schumann with Chopin as a master contrapuntalist. He wrote canons and fugues and a lot of imitation. But strict counterpoint was not his thing—nor was it Mozart's, for that matter! In Schumann it comes out in the form of all kinds of references to hidden tones, motifs that are worked into complex passages behind tons of notes.

Schumann would have been alive to see the development of the seven-and-a-half-octave keyboard. I found that out recently when I tried to play Schumann's *Carnaval* on an 1830 Graf. The instrument didn't have enough notes! The *Fantasie* doesn't work on a Graf of that period, either. But I can play it on an 1854 Érard. Nonetheless, we know that Schumann had a Graf piano, which he gave to Clara when they were married. After he died, Brahms had that piano. The best musical chronicle of these changes can be seen in the Liszt piano works. He goes from very thin textures early in his music, to the 1840s, when he produces very thick textures. Late in life, he returns to the thin textures. As the pianos increase in sonority, Schumann thins out his textures. In a late work like *Waldszenen,* he uses a slender texture compared to, say, the earlier F-Minor Sonata. It's curious, because Chopin does the opposite. His Piano Sonata Op. 58 shows him taking advantage of the larger, stronger pianos and their increase in sound. I've found it difficult to find any comments from any of these people, including Clara Schumann, whether or not as time went by they missed the so-called limitations of the earlier pianos (of course, now we make a big thing about how marvelous these "limitations" were!). Clara's career spanned the whole development of the piano; and at the end of her career, she did talk about how fabulous the Steinway and other pianos were. I can't help but surmise that all these people probably found the newer pianos were improvements over the earlier ones. This is difficult for me to admit, since I do perform and record frequently on earlier pianos!

Peter F. Ostwald

Schumann took lessons on the organ when he was a small boy in Zwickau. And his father gave him then what is called in the diaries a Viennese grand piano. He played it and later requested that it be sent to his lodgings in Leipzig. He had access to pianos also in Wieck's piano shop in Leipzig. Most of the instruments he had access to were German or Viennese. There are several instruments you can look at in the Zwickau Museum. I believe they were Clara's instruments. She, of course, lived much longer and would have access to British and French instruments. They are smaller and not as sonorous, and the actions were lighter. It's often been remarked that Clara's playing especially was rather light and fast.

What Schumann's playing was like we can speculate through many descriptions published at the time. Even after he had his so-called hand injury, he continued to play. Some of the reports say that he played really very well, very fast; but he played in public, even as an accompanist. At that point he indulged much more in a kind of muted sound by keeping the pedal down and having the voices sort of flow into one another. These changes had much less to do with his so-called hand problem as it had to do with his very innovative approach to sound and his interest in structuring sounds in ways that nobody had ever heard before.

Ronald Brautigam

I am thinking of performing Schumann on the fortepiano. That's because, of late, I have been undertaking a project to record the complete solo piano music of Haydn, Mozart, and Beethoven on the fortepiano. But now that the end of the Beethoven is in sight, I hope to have more time for Schumann and Mendelssohn. If I can find the right instrument for it, I can imagine myself recording a great deal of Schumann's works on a period piano. I started playing the early instruments in the 1980s, when I was playing a lot of Mozart and Beethoven in the Netherlands with provincial orchestras. I found myself time after time with conductors with different ideas about the sounds I felt were needed. Whenever I played Mozart on a Bösendorfer, I couldn't get the sound I was looking for. I remember coming home one time from such a concert, quite depressed, wondering if this is what I have to do to make a living to the end of my days. So I picked up a magazine, which on the back page had an advertisement for pianos built by a gentleman named Paul McNulty. I found out he lived only three streets away from me! I think it was the only time in his life that he sent out such an advertisement! I walked over there and played some Mozart on one of his pianos, and I thought, "That's it! This is the sound I've been looking for!" It was a replica of a five-octave Viennese instrument by Anton Walter from 1792. Since then, I bought a second piano from Paul, which is a slightly bigger Walter. I use it more for my Beethoven, like the "Appassionata." It has just enough keys. After that, you need a bigger piano. Here at home I have my concert grand and the two fortepianos.

As far as the romantic repertoire is concerned, sometimes I think Schumann sounds better on the modern piano. But for the early Schumann, I've done the *Carnaval* on a Conrad Graf, like the one he and Clara owned. It works actually very well. One of the great advantages is the transparency of the sound. Schumann's music is often very busy, when he's in a sort of "Florestan" mood, and there's a lot of notes and melodies and voices at the same time. With the modern piano, the strings cross, so the bass strings run across some of the middle strings, which means it's very difficult to hear a clearly defined register. I mean, if you hit a note, it sounds all over the soundboard, whether it's a bass note or a treble note. With the earlier fortepiano, if you pay the bass it comes from that part of the piano; and if you play the treble, it comes from a completely different part of the piano. So, for the ear it's much clearer to hear all these differences between the registers of the piano. And when you play a scale going up, you can actually hear the sounds *traveling through the piano.* I definitely hope that with the upcoming Schumann Bicentenary, we will be hearing more of his music played on these instruments. And I'll probably do some of it on modern pianos, too. But once you know the touch and sound of the fortepiano, you can't play a big Steinway without changing something. I think my playing has become a little lighter and more transparent as a result. So you have to work a lot on the big piano with the heavier action.

JEAN PAUL AND SCHUMANN'S PIANO CYCLES

> *I have often asked myself where I would be if I'd never known Jean Paul: but he seems to be entwined with at least one side of me. . . . I would perhaps write in just the same way, but I wouldn't flee others' company as much, and I'd dream less.*
> —Robert Schumann, 1828

Erika Reiman

My book [*Schumann's Poetic Cycles and the Novels of Jean Paul*, 2004] explores in depth Jean Paul's novels and how they connect structurally with Schumann's piano music. Too much available literature has skipped around the topic. Sure, there's been a lot of focus on the *Papillons,* naturally, because of the Jean Paulian programmatic connotations, and there's been some attention to Schumann's own literary style in connection with Jean Paul. But there was little about what was happening in the music itself. I owe a lot to the late John Daverio, who was one of the peer reviewers of my book. He gave me great feedback. I met him briefly in 1998 at an American Musicological Society conference. His passing is a great loss. He was the premier figure in our field. And he was incredibly generous and positive.

Schumann was reading Jean Paul in the mid- to late 1820s, when he was an impressionable teenager. That wasn't uncommon at the time. Jean Paul was popular among young people. And because Schumann's father was a bookseller and writer, it was easy for Schumann to get his hands on the books. He writes several times, wondering where he would be as a composer were it not for Jean Paul. I think he's being very serious about this. And he's always a composer who tends to let us in on the workings of his own mind. Already, he is starting to imitate the literary style in his own attempts to write novels, like *Juniusabende und Julitage* (June Nights and July Days), which is very much modeled after the Jean Paul novels.

There are several concepts in Jean Paul's writings that have enormous influence in the way Schumann thought about music:

1. *Witz* is clearly explained in Jean Paul's own aesthetic treatise. In its simplest form, it's a collision of opposites, of things that you wouldn't think were related. Looking at it another way, it's finding commonalities between two seemingly opposite things. And that's what humor is, in the most general sense (but not necessarily to produce laughter). In Schumann's music, for example, at the beginning of the *Papillons,* you have a little waltz on the dominant, but it's only thirty-two bars long and it modulates several times. And then, suddenly, in the No. 2, in E-flat major, you have a *presto* in 2/4, which explodes all over the keyboard. The effect is of an incredible collision. Your idea of the waltz will get disrupted when Schumann tears it apart. He will write ten waltzes in a sequence in such a way that, apart from their time signature, seem not entirely waltzlike. You don't have to know the technicalities of this—about the key changes and rhythmic subtleties and all that—to feel the dramatic impact of the music. This is why these early works survive today. You don't have to know about the key changes and all that to feel the dramatic impact.

2. Jean Paul will often refer to a *Zweite Welt,* a "second world," where his characters go in their dreams and fantasies. It may be a momentary transformation, or, in the case of what he called a *Beiwerk,* it might be a more lengthy digression. But the characters never stay there; they

always return to earth, as it were. In fact, the highest happiness for
them ultimately comes from their real world of simple things and a
loving family. Mostly, these brief transformations occur between two
young lovers. And in *Hesperus* the main figure, Viktor, comes into
contact with the home life of an Indian guru. And as a result, Viktor
finds himself transported into a new realm, where everything is fantastic. But he does come back home. He doesn't stay there. So you get
sentence-level digressions, paragraph digressions, lengthy digressions
that might be published separately from the novel. I like the idea
that "Zweite Welt" anticipates what we know today in cyberspace as
"Second Life." I hear now that musicians are exploring the possibilities
of giving concerts in "Second Life" cyberspace. Both are idealizations
of reality, aren't they? A transcendence? You're still living in chrono-
logical time, but it doesn't feel that way. Schumann, too, frequently
unexpectedly departs from a main line with an extended idea, only to
return "home" again. You see this throughout those major cycles, the
Novelletten and the *Humoreske*.

3. The boundaries among the novels are very porous. Characters reappear from novel to novel. The character of Leibgeber in *Siebenkäs*, for
example, who is the alter ego of Siebenkäs, shows up in another novel,
Titan, where he's the alter ego of Schoppe, the crazy librarian. And
Jean Paul himself shows up in almost all the works. He comments on
the characters in his own voice. In one novel he shows up and becomes
the best friend of the main character and becomes the godfather to
the baby (who is named "Jean Paul"). He even footnotes his novels!
Can you imagine, footnoting works of *fiction*? All this is very much
a "meta-literary" approach, the sort of thing you associate with the
British novelist Laurence Sterne. And I know that Jean Paul read and
admired Sterne. I remember one of my thesis committee members
commented that the stuff I was writing about seemed more like post-
modernism than romanticism. You see examples of this porousness
in so much of Schumann's music, most obviously when Schumann
directly quotes passages from one work in other works. In all the cycles
you have fragmentary movements that don't really begin or end in a
recognizable way, so the boundaries *within* the works themselves are
porous. *Papillons* is quoted in *Carnaval* and in *Davidsbündlertänze*,
so that the boundaries *between* the works are porous. And the persona
of Schumann himself is present. Think of the endless "Clara" motives
that reappear everywhere in the piano and orchestral literature, and
those moments in the epilogues of *Kinderszenen* and the "Arabeske,"
where "the poet" steps forward to have his say.

4. And there's the issue of what I call "focalization." It's a question of viewpoint in the novels. Who are we supposed to be identifying with? From whose point of view are we seeing things? Thus you might be sharing a character's point of view and then, on the same page, switch to Jean Paul's point of view—the same situation described very differently from different angles. Musically, focalization in Schumann consists of him developing a musical structure with a simple motif, rather than a thematic or harmonic or melodic structure—or even an expected formal structure. If he starts off with a waltz melody, then all of a sudden, he changes the "angle," as it were, repeating it in a remote key or registrally transferring it to another region of the piano, or transforming it into a countersubject to something else.

5. So you see that whole notion of story and plot get confused in his novels. The Russian formalist critics will talk about *story,* the sequence of events chronologically, and *plot,* which is the sequence in which these events are presented to the reader. For a musical example, by Schumann's time listeners were trained for a piece to start in a tonic key, then move on to the dominant, or the relative minor or major (giving us another theme group or treatment of the main theme), then the development section, and a return to a restatement of the first theme in the tonic key. Schumann will have none of this. Many of his works start on a chord that cannot possibly be a tonic chord in any key, a dissonance, and then he'll take a lot of time establishing just what the tonic key is.

OVERVIEWS OF SCHUMANN'S PIANO MUSIC

> *The older I become, the more I see that the piano speaks essentially and characteristically in three ways: through multiplicity of voices and harmonic variety, through use of the pedal, and through volubility. In the first, one encounters the large-scale player; in the second, the fantasist; and in the third, the stringers of pearls.*
>
> —Robert Schumann

Jörg Demus

Playing and recording all of Schumann's solo piano works was a realization of a children's dream. Because when I was twelve, thirteen, I fell in love with the G-Minor Sonata. And then in the academy in the second and third year, I wanted just to study Schumann, and my teacher said,

"Well, unfortunately we have the regulations, we have the exams, we have to learn other things. It's not possible." And so I told myself, well, one day, I will do it all.

It finally happened in 1968–70, and it was a great project of the Austrian radio. I was considered already a Schumann specialist, but there was much I had to learn. There's simply too much literature. It was absolutely the first time for such a project. Another complete one on records, by Karl Engel, is not quite as complete as mine. It took me three years, but not continuously, because in between I always practiced, let's say, for the new series of sessions. I started with those works which I knew best. It was originally commissioned by a very small Japanese company, King Records, which doesn't even exist anymore. And they paid the memorable sum of five hundred dollars per record, and I thought, it's really not enough, but it gives me, at least, an incentive, a chance to learn this and to do that.

I had myself to arrange for the studio in Vienna. At the time I had my own Imperial Concert Bösendorfer grand. And it was also treated a little bit especially; I like a rather bright intonation. And I had invented in it a pedal, which I took from the upright piano, a pedal which brought the hammers halfway up and the keys sank halfway down, just as on some uprights. This very way you could get a splendid trill and pianissimo, and even the vibrato or tremolo of song. And I also had inserted a moderator. The old Hammerflügel had a felt, a very soft, lovely woven felt, between the hammers and the strings, which gave it a sort of harplike touch, and also such a moderator I had fit into my piano. So it had actually four pedals. I learned at the time editing sound; I did all the editing myself. And since then, four or five record companies have bought it and taken it over, including the Musical Heritage Society. My Schumann recordings are still alive, still on the market. I am the proprietor of the master tapes.

My major discovery, which I still maintain, is that there's not a bad note put out by Robert Schumann. You could say that in a hall of three thousand people, maybe the *Carnaval* is more effective than the *Kinderszenen* and the *Blumenstück,* but they are still considered among the masterworks of music. How like a little *Biedermeier* flower painting the *Blumenstück,* or "Flower Piece," is! He groups the individual blooms of our bouquet into little sections, I, II, III, IV, V, II, IV, II, and Coda (the numbers come from Schumann himself). The musical flower arrangement is apparently fortuitous, asymmetrical, just like a real bouquet! And now you ask where the aroma is coming from? Why, from the key of D major, of course!

And much of the late work, like the Fughetten, the Second Piano Concerto, Op. 134, and the *Gesänge der Frühe,* are very touching

Jörg Demus was the first pianist to record all of Schumann's piano music.

masterworks, just not as open and accessible to everyone. Schumann's polyphony is distinctly his own. He once compared it to a flower that hides its roots. He said Bach, not Mozart, was the origin of all that is poetic for his music.

There were many surprises. Schumann, before his Op. 1 and 2, had written a lot of compositions, some finished, some unfinished. There was a complete piano concerto in F major, but only the piano part exists. Then there was the early piano quartet, and a great many songs, and the *Beethoven Variations.* And more pieces from the *Album for the Young,* and so on. And several polonaises, which anticipate almost fifty percent of the *Papillons.* They were like studies for the *Papillons,* and they're only coming to light now. It helps explains a little bit the unexplainable miracles that Schumann, being considered a musical dilettante with no formal training at all, he can produce in his nineteen years such masterworks as *Papillons* and the *Intermezzi* and the *Toccata.* The *Papillons* are Schumann's apprentice work, his graduation piece, and his masterpiece all rolled into one. This *"neue Weis,"* or "new way," shows he had to prove himself by following in music his own character. It appears to simply have fallen from the skies into the lap of this happy Heidelberg law student. Originally, he had planned nothing else but to write a few *Ländler* in the style of his idol, Schubert. Then in his imagination the pieces began to connect, so that when reading the *Flegeljahre* of Jean Paul, they formed the shape of a masquerade. You can see the *Davidsbündler*—their names are not "Florestan" and "Eusebius" yet, but the characters in Jean Paul, "Vult" and "Walt."

It is unfortunate that here in Europe you never hear the *Humoreske,* the eight *Novellettes,* or the *Gesänge der Frühe.* And you never hear the wonderful fugues, Op. 72, and the four pieces of Op. 32. Did you know that Schumann composed *thirty Kinderszenen?* You wonder, where are they? My thesis is that they are all completely assembled in the *Albumblätter,* Op. 124. You could take from that and put together a second *Kinderszenen.* A few more things have come to light, so if I had occasion I could make, let's say, one more record side still of unrecorded pieces. But otherwise it's complete, and I'm very glad to have done it. I don't think I would have had the courage later on.

I would say Schumann is the only composer of all times who really was equally gifted as a poet and as a musician. He could have become a poet, probably above Heine, a poet of the quality of Eichendorff and Mörike. He was gifted for both. And that is a great lesson for pianists, because we must learn to "speak" with our fingers.

Peter Frankl

In the 1960s Vox Records had become famous for recording entire works of composers. But when they came up with the idea of doing Schumann, after the success of my Debussy, at first I was taken aback. He wrote so *much,* and what can one *do?* And then, as I played through the major cycles, I thought, I will give a second thought to this. I found an incredible treasure house of music. I did the first volume of the five sets of "Vox Boxes" in 1973. Most of them I did in the Decca-London studios in London. I think only once I went over to Paris to record some of the pieces. Later on, there was another box which was not released until later. It contained the duets and two-piano works and pedal-piano works. I did most of those with András Schiff. They were recorded also in a London church. The engineers were different, but the artistic director was the same. I wouldn't say that all of the work is equal in quality. There are pieces which I will never play again. But I was so fascinated that I started working on them and memorized most of them, with the exception, I think, of the fugues and maybe the *Album for the Young.* I would say I was on and off working on it for six years, one recording per year. It came to a total of fifteen records. I was able to do this since at the time I was at the beginning of my career, and I didn't have so many concerts. But soon I began concertizing more, so I had to take some time apart to learn those pieces and try them out at concerts. Twice a year I put aside a week or two, and I tried to arrange it so I could mix the familiar and the unfamiliar in each session. That way I wouldn't have at the end all the "leftovers." Unfortunately, I discovered the No. 9 of the *Fantasiestücke* too late to put it on the same disc us the rest of the cycle, which I would have loved to do.

On most occasions I used the Breitkopf & Härtel edition, which is the Clara Schumann edition, revised by Wilhelm Kempff. I believe that this is a very good edition; and of course the name of Clara Schumann has to be trusted. I don't know the differences in the Henle edition, but I very much trusted the Clara Schumann. Brahms helped her on that, although I admit he could have had different ideas from hers.

Charles Rosen

There's a great deal of Schumann's piano music that ought to be in the repertory but rarely gets in. I've read the *Intermezzi,* Op. 4, but I've never played them in public. Even the popular *Fantasy Pieces,* Op. 12, can be a problem, because I know in the original manuscript there were more than the twelve pieces we know. But they've been published separately. There's no edition in which you can get them all. And those Op. 5 *Impromptus* are also rarely performed. Above all, I wanted to do the first version of those *Impromptus,* because I had never heard them played in public, and it seems to me they are among the greatest pieces he wrote. However, they are very awkward pieces, and there are parts that don't quite come off. But it's quite obvious that with the *Papillons* it's *the* first work of genius, right at the beginning of his career.

I started being interested in the changes that were made in Clara Schumann's edition. The real trouble is a lot of modern editions only print the second version, the revised version of some of the early piano pieces. In almost all cases, I think, they are inferior. For example, the Dover edition reproduces the Clara Schumann edition, but whenever Clara prints the original version separately, they remove the original version and only print the revised one. So students who buy the Dover are not getting the best texts. The new edition of Schumann by Henle is a disgrace, based on the revised version, and the listing of the variants is inaccurate from beginning to end. I would like to get somebody just to reprint the first editions. All one would have to do is photograph them and put them out. It wouldn't be the perfect Schumann edition, because there are misprints, but it would be a lot better than anything we have. That may come about. . . .

It was so obvious in the Clara Schumann edition that the original versions were more interesting. She was very good, mind you, and it is still the best edition available (possibly excepting the Steingräber edition, edited by Hans Bischoff). That hasn't been superseded yet. The trouble is, Clara did not take Brahms's advice. He told her to reprint the original versions without any changes at all. But she made quite a number of changes, which are sometimes puzzling. The *Kreisleriana,* for example, is something of a mess in her edition. She prints the second version, but with the dynamics of the first version, which are more interesting. I don't object to anybody playing it that way, but I object to it being printed that way. In other words, I think pianists ought to have the right to choose what version they are going to play.

In the original version of the *Impromptus* he wrote an ending that is one of the most astonishing closures of anything he ever composed. You find that after the reprise of the gigue in the fugue, the theme disappears right in the middle of a phrase. The bass continues, but harmonies disappear, as well. Dissonances are left hanging, unresolved. The final tonic note is left unharmonized. It's quite extraordinary. But in the later edition, he revised and completely recomposed the ending to provide a more comfortable cadence. That's why I prefer playing the earlier versions of Schumann, because the first inspiration is generally the greatest. If you value that kind of spontaneity, the first inspiration is likely to be the best one. The funny thing is Schumann knew he revised badly, but he continued to revise—he couldn't help himself. George Sand said that Chopin, after writing the piece down, would then start revising. He would work and work—he was never satisfied—and when he got finished he would publish the original version! That was because of *all* the composers of that particular period, Chopin in a way had the most acute intelligence. I don't mean that he was a greater composer than Schumann, but in a way he was a much more critical composer, in spite of Schumann being famous as a critic! Put it this way: There are very few failures in Chopin; there are a lot of failures in Schumann—pieces that don't come off. Everything in Chopin, with three or four exceptions, comes off. A lot of pieces in Schumann don't quite work, including some of the greatest. Take the end of one of the greatest pieces of Schumann, the *Humoreske.* I've always wanted to play it in public, but I don't know what to do with the last two pages. It is far less interesting than anything which has gone on before. You've got twenty-five minutes of music which is absolutely great and two pages which are just good—not bad, but not at the level of what he'd done before.

There's a story behind how I came to perform the original text of the *Fantasie, Op.* 17, called originally *Dichtungen,* or "Poems." Alan Walker had discovered it in Budapest. It had been dedicated to Liszt, and the manuscript must have been given to him, which is how it came to be in the Budapest library. It turns out the last page is very different from the published last page. But in an article Walker published only sixteen out of the seventeen missing measures. I knew an excellent musicologist in Paris, Marta Gràbòsz, who has written on Liszt. She knew people at the Budapest library, and she offered to get me a photograph of the manuscript.

The original version of the last movement ended with a return from the first movement of a melody from Beethoven's *An die ferne Geliebte*. But with that return came an important change in the melody and harmony. When Schumann published it, however, he just crossed out the last page and substituted two measures of arpeggios. The original ending is quite beautiful, ending with a quotation from the last song of Beethoven's cycle *An die ferne Geliebte*. When I saw what it was like, I decided this was the version I wanted to play.

The *Davidsbündler Dances* is fairly accurately represented by Clara, because she prints the first version separately from the second version. And that's a fairly good printing. There are very, very few errors there. So you can always play the first version from Clara.

András Schiff

Somehow, Schumann still needs some championing, especially with the more obscure works. When you talk to a lot of pianists, they will say they love Schumann, but they have only a very scattered knowledge about a few of the big pieces, like the *Carnaval* and the *Kreisleriana*. Now, I'm playing things like the F-Minor Sonata in the original 1836 version. Why this work is the least played of all his sonatas blows my mind. Like all his works, it's a *desperate* piece with a lot of autobiographical elements in it. I am shocked by the unbelievable genius of it. And I have recorded the *Novelletten,* which is amazing. Maybe the length of all eight pieces has frightened away some performers. I don't know. But it needs to be heard more in public performance. If the public has difficulties with Schumann, it is more through the fear of being unable to follow the literary allusions and the constantly changing moods and incredible imagination. His very last piano work, the so-called *"Geister"* Variations, is one of the most moving documents in music, and it is very sad. You know, Schumann interrupted the third variation to make his suicide attempt. Later, after he was brought back to the house from the river, he composed two more variations. When I play the fifth variation, I feel a kind of hive of buzzing sounds going through my own head, like a beehive in the skull. At the time I was learning it, I couldn't get away from the piece. I'd like to make a documentary film for the BBC about that. I'm not very comfortable yet in front of a microphone and a camera, but I'm getting better!

Robert Winter

I think piano music from someone like Schumann didn't have a ready niche in the marketplace at the time. It was becoming much too difficult for the amateurs, for whom music had basically been aimed for a long, long time. Even most of the Beethoven sonatas had been written for intelligent amateurs to play. Schumann's music is music for the professional. It had very high standards, for the most part. You don't simply tell an amateur pianist who dabbles a couple of hours a week to play the first page of the Schumann *Fantasie,* for example. So I think it had trouble getting acceptance because of that. At the same time, his piano music is not concert-hall music. After he wiped out his hand, he stopped being a concert pianist. Much of it was not intended to be performed in a public arena like that. For that sort of situation you have to look at Clara Wieck-Schumann and Franz Liszt, who stood in the forefront of public performance, when their programs would include things like operatic potpourris. But think about something like the *Davidsbündler Dances,* and you realize it would not be the sort of thing intended for public performance. One always has the sense of this extreme intimacy between himself and the keyboard.

Hans-Joachim Köhler

My first edited volume of Schumann's piano music for Peters was published in 1975. It contained *The Album for the Young,* Op. 68. Children today can understand romanticism from it—not just as an epoch in music but as a basis in artistic and musical feeling, generally. Then came the early piano works, namely, the *"Abegg" Variations,* Op. 1, and the *Papillons,* Op. 2. While the former still shows Schumann under the spell of the concert virtuosity of the time, the latter reveals his interest in the literature of this time. In doing so, he hit upon his poetic principle, which purports to be something entirely different from, say, "program music." This was followed by the works written during his years in Leipzig. Schumann wrote them all at the college or in his apartment in *Inselstrasse.* The house is still standing where he moved with Clara after their marriage. As I studied these works, Schumann's life in Leipzig came to life for me, the residential building where he lived, the Thomas Church, and the old Gewandhaus building where Mendelssohn gave the first performance of Schumann's "Spring" Symphony. And I thought of the many visitors to whom he played his new works at the *Inselstrasse* residence, among them

Liszt and Berlioz and Mendelssohn. I sensed the problems which he must have faced when Clara Wieck's father, Friedrich, would not consent to her marrying Robert Schumann. I myself am living close to Schönefeld Church, where the wedding did take place, after all.

To me, the *Davidsbündlertänze,* Op. 6, the whimsical *Kreisleriana,* Op. 16, and the passionate *Fantasie* in C Major, Op. 17, seem like conversations with Clara. After all, for a long time he was not allowed to keep up correspondence with her, let alone to meet her. I came to realize that anyone who would play my editions ought to know all the things which are reflected in his music in subtle ways.

The Peters edition is different from others. Nearly all previous editions are derived from the first complete edition published by Clara Schumann after her husband's death. Of course, with the exception of the modern original-text editions by Henle in Munich and the Vienna Universal Edition, Clara's merits cannot be disputed. But she never gave an account of the alterations she made. Our edition sticks to the first edition that came into being during Schumann's lifetime. They are all kept at the Robert-Schumann-Haus at Zwickau, a newly built museum, erected on the site where he was born. Schumann had them bound in a uniform way and protected the collection like a gem. It was here that Schumann's last handwritten remarks after the printing can be found. I compared these first printings with the other available manuscripts. As compared with the more canonic editions, they show changes, especially in the bowings, and such dynamic specifications as *"forte piano"* and so on are given more precisely.

An important example is from the first of the *Paganini Etudes* from the Op. 10. In two places, two three-bar variants were inserted in our text. Schumann himself had announced them in the *Neue Zeitschrift für Musik* in 1836. However, there are some discoveries giving us a clue to the interpretation of other compositions which the editor finds more interesting and particularly delightful. Let me mention some of them: It is not known that the *"Abegg" Variations,* Op. 1, which Schumann presented to his teacher Heinrich Dorn as a sample of his skills, were patterned after something—namely, Chopin's *Variations on "Là ci darem la mano,"* Op. 2. It certainly does justice to Chopin's work. We must remember Schumann's article about Chopin contains his famous statement, "Hats off, gentlemen, a man of genius!"

As is well known, in the *Davidsbündlertänze,* Op. 6, a motif of Clara's serves as a motto for the cycle of eighteen pieces. I consider this small germ cell to be the starting point of all themes in the cycle. Robert Schumann succeeded in rendering Clara's thoughts in an infinite number of ways. That is the poetic idea underlying the work.

Op. 20 is entitled *Humoreske*. One passage of that lovely piece, which is performed very rarely (undeservedly so), is labeled "Innere Stimme" (Inner Voice). I have discovered that it almost coincides with a musical idea Clara had, namely with the theme of her Romance in G Minor, Op. 11, although the two melodies were created independently of each other. Schumann's excitement about his discovery manifests itself in the following words to her: "Each of your ideas comes from my own soul. I must thank you for the music I write."

I was particularly fortunate in finding the fair copy of the "Novellettes," Op. 21, although it was made by other hands. Only the last of the eight pieces, the most comprehensive one, was written down by Schumann himself. It contains a verbal comment, "Stimme aus der Ferne" (Voice from a distant place)—a reference to one of Clara's melodies in her "Nocturne" in F Major, Op. 6. He was in Vienna at the time, and it reminded him of her own true voice.

Perhaps I might add that in the *Waldszenen,* Op. 82 (Forest Scenes), he intended not only to publish the text by Hebbel for No. 4, "Verrufene Stelle" (Haunted Spot), but also a number of poems by various authors, including Joseph Eichendorff.

Garrick Ohlsson

I do have personal objections to a lot of Schumann's piano music. Schumann uses a lot of baroquish motor rhythms. A lot of his music has tremendous baroquish energy. Which does not endear it to me, but which endears it to a great many other people. That's one thing. I tend to dislike music that gets onto one rhythm and hangs on to it for dear life—especially dotted rhythms. And Schumann—well, it's one of his chief characteristics. As a matter of fact, often the most inspired and most joyous moments in his music are when he'll start the dotted rhythms going, and then . . . and then . . . I say, "Oh, God!" But this is just personal taste. Another thing I don't like is music which is constricted in range. A lot of musicians will tell you it's a problem in his scoring. Very often he'll score the instruments in the thickness of the middle range, and you don't know who's on top and who's on the bottom; and you can't really quite tell. And very often in the chamber music with piano, he'll start writing the stems to clarify things; so you'll have about five stems in one bar pointing in each direction. You're looking for the polyphony, and everybody's doubling every stem anyway, and everybody has *forte espressivo;* and it's like who yields what, because all you've got is this big pot of thick musical stew in which the ingredients are not very clear. Perhaps this has to do with the fact that I'm half Italian and I don't like food that is unidentifiable. Probably if I had observed this sort of thing to Schumann himself, he might have responded like Brahms did one time, when he told a critic, "Any jackass can see that!"

I suppose I belong to that long and not entirely dishonorable tradition of people who like to reorchestrate Schumann. And by "reorchestrate," I don't necessarily mean the orchestral music; no, I mean the voicing and registration. I've done a bit of that in the F-sharp-Minor Sonata when I've played it. There are times when I've decided, "For heaven's sakes, here comes the most important statement, but we've been in this sort of turgid middle area for such a long time," so I just lower it or raise it an octave. Most people don't even notice it.

VARIATIONS, CYCLES, SONATAS, THE PIANO CONCERTO, AND MUSIC FOR CHILDREN

The Beethoven Variations

The first utterance of a strong, youthful spirit has a certain individual, indestructible vitality. It may be rough, but it is the more effective the less one tries to bring it into conformity with what are accepted as the canons of art.

—Robert Schumann

Paul Badura-Skoda

I consider the so-called *Beethoven Variations* one of the first major works by Schumann, which only for external reasons became lost. I think Clara Schumann was too much afraid that works of Schumann's young age might spoil his reputation as a composer. I gave the very first public performance after this work was rediscovered— actually *discovered,* because no one had known of its existence. But the heirs of Schumann, believing that it was a minor work (which it is not), had kept it from publication. So I played it even before the first edition came out. It's a Henle edition titled *Variations on a Theme of Beethoven's Seventh Symphony.* I played it, very aptly, in the Schumann house in Bonn, in Endenich. That's where Schumann spent his last years. Immediately, it had a very enthusiastic reception. And since then I've recorded it and played it on a few concert tours—again to favorable response. But particularly in Germany, France, and even in Russia, people just love the work.

It's a work of Schumann's youth, in those early times of the 1830s when he was occupied with studying Beethoven. He worked at it for a relatively long period, I think, between the age of twenty and twenty-two; then he took it up again and left it in a half-finished form as the so-called "Skizzenbuch IV," not making it quite certain which order of the variations he intended. And I took this as a certain signal that I could rearrange them, and I arranged them differently from the printed version. I concluded it with the one with the most brilliant variations and a very short coda. Schumann kept rather strictly to the theme of the Seventh Symphony's second movement, at least in the majority of the variations. But a great deal of inventiveness goes into new and hitherto totally unknown piano figurations. In fact, he imitated his own work in his later *Symphonic Etudes,* where two or three studies with a different theme use exactly the same figuration.

The fantastic thing is that Schumann not only makes variations on the Seventh Symphony theme, but he ingeniously brings in quotations from the Sixth and the Ninth symphonies. And at one point he combines the opening measures of the Ninth with the harmonies and progressions of the Seventh Symphony. And there is one variation which I would call an "anti-variation," because it has actually nothing to do with the theme except the key. It's a sort of chorale prelude. It might belong to the variations the same way some of the nonthematic études belong to the *Symphonic Etudes.*

Papillons, Op. 2

> *In many a sleepless night I saw a distant picture like a goal. While writing down Papillons, I really feel how a certain independence tends to develop itself.... Now the butterfly flutters in the wide heavenly world of spring, and look at me—a child with heavenly blue eyes—and now I begin to understand my existence. The silence is broken.*
> —Robert Schumann, 1832

> *It is really in dreams that we grow butterfly wings, so that we can escape the narrowest, tightest prison and, shining brightly, fly up to the sky, to the highest sky. Every man really has an innate inclination to fly.*
> —E. T. A. Hoffmann, *Kater Murr*

Albert Boime

The key in the case of Schumann is the metaphor for metamorphosis.

The butterfly idea is one that's very appealing—the lightness of the butterfly, the metamorphosis of the butterfly, and then, of course, it also has its dark side in the form of the moth, which is the source of silk, as well. The butterfly is a constant image, not only in the nineteenth century, but even prior. The butterfly represented the soul, because it was related to the concept of metamorphosis. The butterfly emerged from another kind of being, it went through a stage of transition and transformed into another. So one talks about emancipation from one stage going to another in terms of the butterfly. It is a symbol for a freeing of the soul, a freeing of the mind, a freeing of creative expression. It's a constant in so many works. You quite rightly point out that Whistler used it for a monogram, for his work. The *papillon* is also a category that had been established by Jean Fourier, the great reformist of the nineteenth century. He said the *papillon* was the key to the new society, wherein everyone would do work that was consonant with everybody's personality type. And he wanted to have work that was meaningful, work that was appropriate for various people. He thought that was fundamental—including women's emancipation.

Eric Sams

The *Papillons*, of course, was one of Schumann's very first piano pieces. Here we have partners, friends, and lovers—allies in the great struggle—all dancing together and appreciating each other's life and art. It's a "papillon" because there's a motif that's the same backwards and for- wards. If you imagine to yourself what a butterfly looks like and draw that piece on a modern piece of manuscript paper, you can see that it resembles a butterfly's wings. And you can play that in any way you like. You can play it going down, then up. But also observe that in German, the word *larva* not only designates the larva of a butterfly, but it also means a "mask." Every time Schumann writes these pieces, he's project- ing a masked entity, the personality of a friend, onto music paper. That's exactly what Edward Elgar was to do later in the *Enigma Variations*. At the end of piece he does a very strange thing. He rolls the notes of the chord and, slowly, directs you to remove each note, from the lowest to the highest. It means the idea of disappearance. The imaginary figure disap- pears in front of your very eyes. The whole music is meant to symbolize a vanishing, which is a very strange thought, but then, Schumann in many ways had a very strange mind. Schumann is interested in pure sound, in pure sonority, and what he can do withdrawing veils of sound. This had a great influence on the later French school.

Hans-Joachim Köhler

The *Papillons*, Op. 2, are among the most popular of Schumann's compo- sitions, and they radiate natural freshness and vigor. As a matter of fact, they represent Schumann's first independent cycle. They abandon whatever

the *"Abegg" Variations* borrowed from the language that was in vogue at
the time. And they bring us face-to-face with the young Schumann, who
is looking for his own identity. The way they came about is also unusual.
In Heidelberg, where he had transferred from Leipzig in order to go on
studying law, Schumann began by composing a number of waltzes, some
of which were patterned after Schubert's dances. However, when he was
reading Jean Paul's *Flegeljahre,* it occurred to him all of a sudden that
he should choose the chapter on the "Masked Ball" for the setting which
might allow him to include his dances and contain autobiographical references. He decided to change and reassemble the pieces and to add two
new ones.

What are the *Papillons* all about? At that time, Schumann was grappling with many contradictions within himself, about his career, about
music, et cetera. It had occurred to him to try to think of himself as two
opposing personalities, "Florestan" and "Eusebius." The literature of his
own time offered him models for this. In the *Flegeljahre* he encountered
the two half-brothers, Walt and Vult. At a masked ball they both try to
win the affection of the girl, Wina, each in his own way. An exchange of
costumes leads to confusion. Walt, who has a vivacious nature, discovers
that Wina loves his sensitive and dreaming brother Vult. On the morning
after the ball, Vult goes away, playing the flute. Walt, who is still half
asleep, hears this but is unable to understand what is actually going on.
In a letter to Ludwig Rellstab, the editor of a Berlin journal, in which
Schumann asked for a review, he mentioned these words: "You will recall
the last scene of the *Flegeljahre,* the masquerade, Walt, Vult, Walt's dancing, the exchange of masks, confessions, anger, revelations, hasty departure, and the final scene and then the departing brother."

I was delighted to hold in my hands the thin novel that was once his
own. The pages of the aforementioned chapter bear notes that were written by him, where he assigns certain passages of the novel, numbered
one to ten, to the music sections, labeled "P-1" up to "P-10." There is no
doubt in my mind that the cycle came into being while he was cogitating
on this novel. The first dance, for example, reveals the sensitive and dis-
creet personality of Walt. No. 2 describes the dancing hall, which is "full
of zigzagging shapes moving towards each other." No. 3 describes "the
giant boot moving around, which was wearing and carrying itself." No.
7 contains Walt's urgent request that Vult change his clothing with him.
No. 9 and No. 10 refer to the English waltz which Walt, dressed in Vult's
costume, performs with plenty of enthusiasm. Schumann supplemented
this with the Polonaise, No. 11, which is not danced at the ball, but which
serves to characterize Walt. In the last piece, the twelfth, Schumann set

to music words noted down on the title page of the manuscript—"With delight Walt heard the fading sounds of the flute from the street below, though he did not realize that with them his brother was escaping." After we hear the chiming of the six bells in the clock tower, the notes die away. One senses that the notes of the flute are fading in the distance. I should add that rather than "depicting" specific scenes, the music is of a poetical, exalted type. Although we are free to associate the things mentioned, they are not intended to be exactly identical with the novel.

Erika Reiman

Papillons introduces us not just to Schumann's love of the novelist Jean Paul, but to his interest in the Schubertian *Walzerkette*, the "waltz chain." You see this in a lot of the literature of the popular music of the time. The most obvious examples are the waltzes of Strauss Jr., which last a good fifteen minutes each and give you a succession of idea, after idea, after idea. And Schubert's waltz chains—he does group them into bunches, sometimes—can be played on and on, in whatever order you wish. And Schumann employs this idea extensively all almost all the cycles, beginning with *Papillons* and extending through many of the cycles of the 1830s.

I don't think it can be denied that there are programmatic connotations in Schumann's *Papillons*. There are letters from that time where Schumann describes graphically the passages from Jean Paul's *Flegeljahre* that he correlates to the music. The basic storyline in the novel is that Wina, the daughter of a Polish general, is courted by the brothers Walt and Vult. Finally, at Fasching time [Carnival], everyone arrives at the masquerade ball, and we have descriptions of the costumes. For example, in No. 3, Schumann points to a passage in Jean Paul, where someone is costumed as a boot and is dancing around inside it. And No. 5 is a Polonaise, and Schumann points to a passage in the book about a Polish girl (Wina in disguise). And here's Vult (the Florestan figure) in the No. 11, who ultimately can't bear to lure her away from his brother. So Vult goes away, and the sounds of his flute disappear into the night air. *Papillons'* wonderful closing measures describe that. And at the very end, Schumann ties over six whole-notes in the same measure and directs you to release each, one by one. I wonder how that would sound on Schumann's piano, the one that he gave to Clara as a wedding present. I don't think it diminishes the *Papillons* to detect these programmatic considerations. I sit and listen to it, and yes, I can hear the program. But when I listen to his other piano cycles, also with their different keys and what meter you're in, or what motive you're hearing, I don't get precisely that same feeling.

Wolfgang Sawallisch

Personally, the *Papillons* was important for me as a boy, because it was the first connection between myself and the piano works of Schumann. I never did Schumann before I was seven or eight years old. I came to his mentality for the first time with the *Papillons*. After that, I played the *Faschingsschwank aus Wien* and the *"Abegg" Variations*. The *Papillons* are eight bars, sixteen bars, twelve bars—phrases that are very short but so expressive and so clear; and the musical diction and the *thema* is so significant, you understand, for the whole life of Schumann. I always feel that the best of Schumann is always in the short motif and how he works with it.

Intermezzi, Op. 4

> *The enemies of chromaticism should realize that there was once a time when the seventh interval was as conspicuous as, say, a diminished octave is now; and that through the development of the harmonic sense it has become possible to depict passion with finer shadings. And this has placed music in the ranks of the highest vehicles of art.*
>
> —Robert Schumann

Peter Frankl

I think the set of *Intermezzi,* Op. 4, is unjustly neglected. It came early in his career, around 1832, and it is very much like the *Papillons,* although more complicated, deeper. Again, every movement is full of contrasts, Florestan and Eusebius alternating all the time. There are many harmonic and rhythmic adventures. It was originally called "Fantastic Pieces," and that describes them very well! It has all the characteristics of some of the later masterpieces, particularly the *Kreisleriana*.

Take the first episode of the first piece. It's in A major, and it has the same character of portions of the *Kreisleriana*—the same atmosphere, the same *mysterioso* feeling.

The second piece is in E minor. It's very wild and stormy, but it's not as difficult as it may sound, since it's very well written for the performer. But, of course, you have always with Schumann all these so-called wrong accents. We are talking about the first episode of the second piece. You have it at the *last* beat of the bar, which the innocent listener would think is a *down*beat. You can find this sort of thing everywhere, particularly in the notoriously difficult coda of the second movement of the *Fantasie*.

And that makes it incredibly exciting, because you try to counterbalance it, to give the impression where the real beat is. It's always this irregularity and uncertainty which makes it incredibly exciting. In the middle section you see a quotation of lines from Goethe's "Meine Ruh' ist hin," a reference to *Faust*. He often uses song quotations, you know. In the *Fantasie* he uses Beethoven's *An die ferne Geliebte* (To the Distant Beloved). He wants to put his literary thoughts into the music. And there is this sotto voce character, a murmuring kind of sound. You have to use the soft pedal. Generally speaking, in piano playing—or whatever music we play—we have to give more justice to the speaking or the *singing* quality. Too many of my colleagues are ignoring this quality, the quality of the human voice. We have to do our phrasing in a way—even on a hammer instrument—to give it the quality of the human voice. And Schumann definitely requires that.

In the No. 3, in A minor, we have here the quality of the *Davidsbündler,* his Op. 6, which he composed very shortly afterward. The contrapuntal writing, this false rhythm, the contrast of sudden *fortes* and *pianos* is remarkable. And all the time you have to keep it light and humorous.

The No. 4, in C major, is a very beautiful movement. I believe it was originally supposed to be part of the *Papillons*. After a bold opening, it settles into an *allegretto simplice,* more of a *siciliano* character. The theme appears three times, but it's always increased in dynamics. Schumann starts with *mezzo forte,* then goes to *forte,* and then *fortissimo*. The coda is very, very beautiful.

The No. 5, in D minor, I think is in a way a very sad statement, because of these falling seconds. They contrast with the left hand's cello type of accompaniment. And then suddenly, out of the blue—even though it is *pianissimo*—it goes crescendo and becomes very energetic. Again, it's very much like *Kreisleriana*—constantly changing, full of surprises.

Finally, in the No. 6, in B minor, we have a fiery *allegro,* very much similar to the No. 2. I think this wildness has something to do with another craze that Schumann had at that time with the violinist Paganini. Technically, he was very much in debt to Paganini. His preceding opus had been a set of six *Paganini Etudes,* a piano version of six of the violin studies (but not like the Op. 10 set, which is a more freely adapted set of pieces). Later, he becomes more tender and more singing. There's a delicate episode he calls *alternative* that I like very much; and again it seems to owe much to the *Papillons.*

I think as you are now asking me about this, that I might perform the *Intermezzi* again in my repertoire. It's really fascinating to look through them. But obviously it's not as great a work as some of the later works. But you can find all the ingredients already here. I think it finishes very brilliantly, which is very rare in Schumann. Beside the sonatas, I think only the *Carnaval*, the *Faschingsschwank*, and the *Symphonic Etudes*—among the most popular works—finish so brilliantly. Most of the time, his most effective endings go very deeply inward—things like the *Fantasie*, the *Fantasiesstücke*, the *Kinderszenen*, the *Kreisleriana*, and the *Papillons*, where the sounds just dissolve away.

Erika Reiman

The *Intermezzi*, Op. 4, is a really crazy piece. As a result of this interview, I've been going back five years to my book [*Schumann's Piano Cycles and the Novels of Jean Paul*, 2004] and realizing that I had better program it in my own future performances. You never hear it, and it's fantastic! I have found only one recording of recent vintage, from the 1970s, by Christoph Eschenbach. The *Intermezzi* are a combination of harmonic and rhythmic inventiveness. The theorist Harald Krebs has brilliantly elucidated mathematically what is going on rhythmically in each movement. For example, he'll point out that in No. 2 we have a 6/8 meter, but the accents are on eighth-note number 3 and on eighth-note number 6 of each beat, so we are displaced by one eighth-note. So the first bars sound like a normal 6/8 with accents on one and four; but then, he's got the rhythm displaced, although the harmony is changing in the normal spot, on four—even though the accent is on six. In short, you suffer an aural confusion, but a delightful one. If the player keeps all this in the rhythmic tension, you feel like the music, not you, is in control. My favorite number is the No. 5. It has no established tonality, until measure 21. It's like the first page has been torn off and you're abruptly into something that's already been ongoing. And at this point, a contrasting idea appears. So we've had a twenty-measure sequence developing a chromatic descending motive, but with no clear key. The sequence of four dominant sevenths is never resolved. And then when it changes, there's this pseudo-baroque sawing away at the strings; and then darned if there isn't, in measure 29, a quotation of the "Grossvatertanz" from the *Papillons*. It's like a war between the sense that you're nowhere in particular, on the one hand, and a sudden crashing down to earth, on the other. It would take a pianist a while to get this down. And there's all kinds of hand crossings and two melodies that you have to voice out. And then you get to the "alternativo" and you have a Hegelian synthesis, a new melody in B-flat major and more sawing away in the bass. It's wild.

Carnaval, Op. 9

*I think these masks open a mine of the most delicious humor,
of the most striking irony, of the freest—I might also say the
most impudent—whimsy, although I think they lay better
claim to the external manifestations of human nature than to
human nature itself. Let me make a few observations regarding this composition, which owed its origin to pure chance.
The name of a city where a musical friend of mine lived
consisted of letters belonging to the scale, which are also contained in my name. And this suggested one of those musical
games which are no longer new, since Bach provided the model.*
                                        —Robert Schumann, 1935

*He reached the resounding, burning hall full of excited figures,
an aurora-borealis sky full of crossing, zigzag figures. . . .
Now he stood by the tranquil maiden, and the half-rose and
lily of her face looked out from the half-mask as from the
flower-sheath of a drooping bud. Like foreign spirits from
two far cosmic nights, they looked at each behind the
dark masks.*
                                        —Jean Paul, *Flegeljahre*

EDITOR'S NOTE
Carnaval was composed and published as Op. 9 by Breitkopf & Härtel in
1837. The spelling with an "A" is the French fashion. The work draws upon
characters in the commedia dell'arte, Schumann's friends and associates,
and several of his imaginary personae.

Albert Boime

Carnivals and masks are basic themes for painters. Masks belong to a
world of the unknown; they belong to a festival which is outside the
boundaries of normal civil discourse and which deliberately flaunt those
rules and regulations. If anything, authority is totally overthrown during
Carnival time. The mask has a double purpose: It conceals the individual
and conceals one's identity; and at the same time, it unleashes a new
identity, or emancipates the individual. So that one can do certain things
with the mask that one can't do in everyday life.

The painter Thomas Couture was obsessed with Italian comedy, which is related to Carnival and the various characters of Harlequin and Columbine and Scaramouche and the others. And they became a kind of allegory for working out various everyday themes that they wished to explore—but wished at the same time to give a symbolic, emblematic character. And carnival masks allowed him to explore these feelings without necessitating a kind of genre of everyday characterization. Couture almost felt the need to embed his subjects in some allegorical context. And Italian comedy seemed to lend itself. Since the seventeenth and eighteenth centuries, Italian comedy was prevalent. Molière made use of many of these themes. In the eighteenth century numerous painters take up the theme of the "unhappy clown." In Watteau we find "Pierrot." Of course, this is a theme that continues into the nineteenth century. The clown who makes everybody else happy but in reality is very sad. This is a theme that the artist, again—a kind of public/private dualism that's very appealing to the artist who has to work between the public and private, and between sketch and finish.

Couture kept an extensive archive of engravings. And it's certain Callot was one of his favorites, because I've seen numerous borrowings of Callot by Couture for his own work. So it's certain Couture would be familiar with these Callot engravings of the commedia. E. T. A. Hoffmann is drawn to them. As far as I'm concerned, Callot was a ready-made package of pictorial goodies that any artist of a later period could draw from and use and exploit.

Nancy B. Reich

Schumann spelled it C-A-R-N-A-V-A-L, which is the French spelling of what we call carnival. Most south Germans refer to the carnival season as "Fasching." Now it would probably be "K-A-R-N-I-V-A-L," because the Germans now have abandoned the letter C and use K for that hard sound. He wrote another work about this season, *Faschingsschwank aus Wien,* referring to the Carnival in Vienna while he was there in 1839.

We have been led to believe that Schumann was rather clumsy in his movements, but we have it on authority from a description by his sister-in-law, Marie Wieck, that in his youth he was a very graceful dancer. I don't know whether he danced in his later years. But certainly when he was younger he was a dashing young man who loved to dance and to carouse and drink. We know that.

Fasching was a time of celebration before the season of Lent. And it was a time when people let loose and, in Vienna, particularly, in Schumann's time, there was dancing all night into the morning hours. People wore masks and costumes. It was a time of intrigue and flirtation.

The aristocracy came to the dance halls and mixed in with the working classes and middle classes. I can never imagine that the mask ever really hid the identity of the people involved, but they pretended it did, and that pretense permitted them to carry on in a way which would have been prohibited, normally.

We have some wonderful firsthand accounts of life in Vienna by a north German named Johann Friedrich Reichardt, who was a composer, conductor, and critic. He wrote a series of letters about a trip he made to Vienna in 1808–9. Being a north German and a Protestant, he was quite astonished at the way in which the Viennese—Vienna was a Catholic country, of course—let loose during the Carnival time. I'm sure these same traditions extended right up to the dissolution of the Austrian Empire. Reichardt talks about the *Tanzlust,* the love for dancing, which during Carnival time is turned into a *Tanzwut,* a *passion* for dancing. He describes dances held in the Apollosaal, a very large dance hall. He also talks about the many places and the many balls held in private homes, where people could engage in secret trysts. He describes one ball at the palace of Count Razumovsky, in which one room was opened to the elements—this was probably early in February—and people danced away, dripping with perspiration, while the poor musicians were freezing and playing in their overcoats. We see this sort of thing in movies all the time. In fact, there was a great carnival scene in *Amadeus,* which I think was very typical and probably very authentic. You do get a feeling of the looseness and the flirtations which might have occurred. . . .

The music being played wasn't listened to so much as *danced* to. Mozart's only duty as imperial *Kammermusikus*—that was the one title he had until his death—was to write dances for the masked balls in the assembly rooms. The Ländler were country dances which had vigorous stamping and much turning and twirling. And of course, out of it and similar dances evolved the waltz. Even the minuets were lively dances and accorded much opportunity for flirtation. And those are dances which we listen to very calmly in the concert hall, but they were dances to which people in those days danced very lustily. The gulf which we have in our day between dance music, popular music, and so-called serious music, concert music, didn't exist at the time. The music which was written for the dances, for the balls and the Carnivals, was taken very seriously by the composers.

Peter F. Ostwald

In the *Carnaval* we see how Schumann's bipolar affective disorder was related to the seasons, as it not infrequently is. He would become more depressed during the winter months, and then in the spring his depression would subside and he would become more exuberant and happy, sometimes hypomanic. I think the change of seasons and the festivals associated them were be very important for him, especially Fasching. Other elements here include this dual personality, and he became aware of that quite early. Some of it was stimulated by reading Jean Paul, and some of it came to the surface when he was studying with Wieck and writing his *Papillons*. This duality of the butterfly and the metamorphosis of the larva played a great role in his thinking. Then there are the influences of the commedia dell'arte that appear in the *Carnaval*. He probably saw some of that when he visited Italy during that wild student trip of his.

Lawrence Kramer

Peter Ostwald says that because carnival time occurs in February, it is bound up with Schumann's bipolar affective nature; that carnival would represent a lot of things for him in a biological sense, an emotional sense—not just in the sense of masks and identities. That it is grounded inside him in a biological, a genetic way.

Do you believe that? I like Ostwald's book on Schumann very much. And draw on it for my work. I draw on it, as you can tell from the course of our conversation, to rely more on cultural frames of understanding than biological ones.

I looked at *Carnaval* in two different contexts. First, the literal question of European carnival practices—not so much as they were current in the Europe of Schumann's own day, but eighteenth-century carnival practices which had survived as customs in German university life. I'm talking about the kinds of things Schumann was experiencing during his short stay at the university in the late 1820s and early 1830s. That tradition is best described as entirely raucous, disorderly, insistent on overthrowing every hierarchy in sight.

The formal dancing and balls did happen, of course; and one of the interesting things about Schumann is that it's reported by reliable sources that in 1830 during carnival he went to a formal masked ball dressed as a woman. Which is important for the particular study I did. That kind of thing went on a great deal. But naturally, as the great Russian theorist Mikhail Bakhtin observed, carnival is "theater without footlights." And what basically happened during these carnival events is that theater spilled over into the streets. Everybody is a participant. Everybody is an observer. So even the ordinary hierarchical situation of spectator and the looked-at is overturned.

The influences on Schumann of the next-to-the-last chapter of Jean Paul's *Flegeljahre*—which is about a masked ball and involves these two brothers, Walt and Vult, and how they interact (they're both in love with the same girl)—can't be overestimated. I think that Schumann found in that chapter something so fundamental to himself, to the possibilities of human identity, that it reverberated both implicitly and explicitly throughout the music that he wrote in the early 1830s.

Most famously, what he found was the prototype for the two fictional characters by which he mapped out the alternate poles of his own identity, Florestan and Eusebius. The two brothers in the Jean Paul novel have that character structure. And that's the standard line on Schumann. And of course there's a good deal of truth to it. But my particular take on this topic, which I talk about briefly at the end of my book *Music as Cultural Practice* and more extensively in the essay on *Carnaval* in my *Musical Meaning,* a collection about gender in music: Schumann's Florestan/ Eusebius pair is not generally an expression of an instability within Schumann's sense of himself, but actually a stabilizing fiction. It actually manages to *contain* the mobility of identity which Schumann discovered in *Carnaval* and found in himself, and contain it within two relatively stable and relatively conventional figures. In fact, it was a much looser, more exciting, more disturbing, more threatening, more unknowable kind of phenomenon that Schumann was confronting. It came to the sense of who he was and what a person was as mediated through *Carnaval*.

The notion of social identity is something extraordinarily fragile, extraordinarily loose, artificial, and changeable. It was extremely important in eighteenth-century carnival, and the literary critic Terry Castle, who wrote a book about the subject, in fact said that as a social practice, these carnival festivities constituted a critique of the idea of the unified human personality—which is as strong on its own as the philosophy of David Hume, who dotted the I's and crossed the T's. And I believe it is that, that radical sense of the mobility of identity, both socially and sexually (the role of cross-dressing in these carnival practices is also very strong), and it shows up in Schumann's music, as well. . . .

You find examples of "cross-dressing," if you will, in Schumann's music. You can do that in two different ways, one of which is more profound than the other; but both make sense. The character of the piece, *Carnaval,* is a kind of musical metaphor for carnival masking, for masquerade, for *becoming* somebody else. The piece is set up in such a way that it breaks down a lot of different boundaries. People familiar with the piece will know that it is twenty-one little pieces, some of which are genuinely incomplete. And they form a kind of gigantic party that Schumann has put together. The pieces are of two different kinds: There are dance and marching pieces, and there are character sketches. I could pursue the implications of that, but suffice it to say that the dance pieces are devoted to a measure of *physical* energy, which is very fundamental to the carnival (people running through the streets, throwing things at each other, pelting each other with fruit, and doing other, more interesting things). And the character sketches speak to the notion that when carnival time comes, you can be who you want to be; you can be who you are afraid to be; you can be who you are told not to be.

And at the moment, I'll just focus on those character sketches. They also are of several different kinds, and the differences are very interesting. There are sketches of other musicians—Chopin, Paganini; there are commedia dell'arte sketches, figures drawn from the Italian pantomime, like Pierrot. I can't know for sure if Callot's commedia engravings are a source for Schumann's use of those characters. Or if there are other sources available. Schumann is a magpie. He picked up things from everywhere. And there is certainly enough, from the material he read, that he may have had more than one source. He may also have seen these things. If he was at the Munich carnival, he may have seen these things, as well.

But as for the third group of character sketches, they are of course people from life—his fiancée Ernestine von Fricken shows up under the name of Estrella, and then there's Chiarina, Clara Wieck. So what you get is a system of masquerades in which a bunch of barriers break down—the barrier between reality and fiction; between real persons and commedia dell'arte characters; there is the barrier of musical identity and competition (there's Chopin and there's Paganini). And then there's the gender boundary. If you wish, you can imitate your own fiancée; you can imitate the brilliant daughter of your tyrannical landlord. And so you can make all these crossings. And the spectrum of these crossings is the first level at which you can speak, if you wish, of music as cross-dressing—Schumann pretending to be Clara, writing like Clara, fingering like Clara. And the same thing with Coquette, the nameless flirt that also figures importantly in the cycle.

Now, the second level is really parallel with the first. Because what I've just said operates at the level of general impression and at the level of general expressive intention. It also operates structurally. And the piece is organized in such a way that many of the character sketches with distinctly masculine identities structurally interlink—sometimes are even finished by—the sketches with feminine identities. As if Schumann is gliding from one to the other. So you cannot disentangle them; you cannot disentangle one generation from another.

This is most noticeable in an important sequence of pieces early in the cycle, where you get "Florestan" and "Eusebius." "Eusebius" comes first but does not technically come to an end. It segues into "Florestan," which itself does not reach an appropriate closure—the standard tonic–dominant practice. And then that in turn goes into "Coquette," which actually finishes both the earlier pieces in its harmonic configuration at the very beginning. "Coquette" is followed by a very mysterious little piece called "Réplique," which is actually a very condensed variant repetition of "Coquette," which also repeats the progression by which "Florestan" and "Eusebius" have been finished. They're *not really* finished; there's a great deal of ambiguity surrounding the whole thing. And I hadn't even begun to talk about it, because there are other modes of cross-references involved in these four pieces, as well.

Then comes the kicker. After this sequence of pieces, there's a piece that is never played, the famous "Sphinxes," which is kind of a triple signature, which takes the musical letters of Schumann's name and arranges them anagrammatically. One of them spells "SCHA"—these are German designation for the notes; we don't have an H in English, but it's B. And then SC (which is A-flat), HA; and then "ASCH," which happens to be the name of the hometown of Ernestine von Fricken. So the anagrammatical play on Schumann's name provides a kind of clue to the structural play on the idea of identity. It also makes one aware that this can be seen as operating across the entire piece, because the "ASCH" motives are the main source of the thematic continuity of the cycle.

Rachmaninoff played the "Sphinxes." Which is lovely to know, because of course most people don't play it. As far as I can tell, Schumann never said that one shouldn't. Clara said, "No, no, you mustn't play those!" But Schumann is not on record for ever having said that. I've suggested that pianists should play them *if they feel like it*. I think he genuinely left it up to the pianist.

What conclusions do you derive from this? Does it matter, for example, whether he was intentionally doing what you say he was doing?

I don't think it ultimately matters. I have a rather skeptical view of people's intentions. I think we always act in webs of complicated relationships which overpower any intentions we can formulate. But I think that actually, as an off-the-cuff remark, he was quite conscious of it. The piece is so self-conscious in its design, so extraordinarily explicit in its allusions. An example of this—there's a little place in "Florestan" where there's a quotation of the melody from Schumann's *Papillons;* and he writes in the score,

"Papillons"—question mark. And the question mark is as interesting as yes, obviously a variation of a melody from the earlier cycle.

So I'm interested in the relationship between Schumann, Schumann's reception, and the world in which he is now received and to which he is now addressed. And I think that two things, briefly stated, matter about this. One is that in the nineteenth century there was a slow but very powerful upheaval going on in the question of what "masculine" identity was. And I think that to that degree a piece like *Carnaval* explores the limits of masculine identity and its relationship to other modes of identity, it is a significant document, both for its own time and for ours. So it shows Schumann experiencing something clearly at a terribly personal and psychologically real level, which is also representative of something that a lot of other people are going through that are either not articulate about it or articulate about it in less durable and appealing ways.

José Feghali

I've been playing the *Carnaval* since I was eighteen. And it was part of my program at the Seventh Van Cliburn Competition. You launch into those grand opening chords and, from the very first, the creative juices are flowing. Let's start with the four letters of his name, which correspond to the notes, S (which in German is E-flat), then we have C, then H (which is B in German), and A. Play them together and they sound strange, very modern. They appear in three different combinations, including A-S-C-H, the birthplace of his lady friend at the time, Ernestine von Fricken; and S-C-H-A, the letters in Schumann's own name. Schumann calls these note combinations "Sphinxes." He writes them out on the page, but few pianists play them. Rachmaninoff did, and he used tremolos to make them sound very mysterious. I often prefer to play them.

After the "Préambule," we meet the first of several characters from the commedia dell'arte, "Pierrot," and we hear the motif very clearly in the left hand. The most important thing about "Pierrot" is when the introverted kind of feeling of the motif is answered by a three-note thumbing of the nose.

Another commedia figure is "Arlequin," and you can imagine him jumping and falling, with the motif embedded in the notes.

Listen to the beginning of the "Valse noble," where we hear the motif in an almost Eusebius-like mood.

And indeed, "Eusebius," Schumann's dreamy persona, is next. What could be more poetic than this? It's absolutely a work of genius. Here you can trace the motif rearranged in its sequence.

"Florestan," the dashing, rambunctious side of Schumann, starts with the motif, but you have to play it very slowly to find it. Play it faster and it disappears into the notes. There is no ending here, just a crescendo to a *forte* and then—

—enter "Coquette." She comes almost out of nowhere, out of that tension of the "Florestan." She is teasing and, yes, coquettish; and the motif comes and goes in a flash. It's very well hidden.

You know, the "Réplique" has always been kind of a mystery to me, because it's skittish and Eusebius-like by turns. It's really more of a transition between "Coquette" and "Papillons." Play it slowly and you can pick out the letters.

Now, you can take "Dancing Letters" literally. The letters of the notes really are flying around—but then everything stops abruptly. "What happened?" you ask. You can imagine listeners in the audience sitting up in shock.

Of course, "Chiarina," or "Clara," comes in. It's usually played too fast. I know Clara had a fiery temperament, but I play it a little slower than that and reserve most of the passion for the second repetition (which he marks *fortissimo,* in any case).

"Chopin" has a few more harmonic progressions than you would expect. It's more "Schumann" than Chopin! The motif is very difficult to find here; but, you know, at the very end you hear a three-note version of it as a kind of "tail" to the piece. But normally, we would have heard them earlier.

"Estrella" comes in with a double *forte*. This is his girlfriend, Ernestine, and you can feel here how strongly Schumann must have felt about her at the time. A funny thing happens in the middle, where we have an almost *giocoso* moment, almost as if one of the commedia characters came in unexpectedly. But then Estrella comes back to end things in no uncertain terms.

Now listen to how the "Reconnaissance" starts. We pianists love to talk about this one; with those repeated notes for the thumb in the right hand, it's one of the hardest parts of the whole piece. Here the motif goes forwards and then backwards. And you can pick it out in the left-hand accompaniment, too. You almost want to dance to this—except in the middle, when you have a B-major quasi-contrapuntal dialogue working out between the hands. It's as if you have a violin line in the right hand and a cello in the left.

With "Pantalon and Columbine" I like to think "Pantalon" is one hand and "Columbine" is in the other. They seem to play against each other, one going up and the other coming down. And there's a wonderful canonic episode in the middle. It's almost pure chamber music, the viola line and the violin line clearly standing out.

The "Valse Allemande," or German waltz, has lots of moods in its brief span. The motif is especially clear at the very beginning.

"Paganini" would have sounded more square-toed if it had been written by anyone else. But Schumann staggers the hands, so one hand is going up and the other is going down. The juxtaposition of rhythms are not quite together, which creates an unsettled feeling. And it's marked *Presto,* which makes it extremely difficult to play.

The "Aveu" has a wonderful, *pianissimo* sound. After all, you're saying goodbye, right? Isn't it amazing how this piece of music can be based on the same motif as the other pieces, yet the mood is so absolutely different?

Both the characters of Eusebius and Florestan are in the "Promenade." You have Eusebius's statement, followed by Florestan; and then Eusebius again; then Eusebius pleading; and Florestan declaring himself again; et cetera. It is an incredible interplay between the two personalities, yet the piece holds together extremely well.

The so-called "Pause" is anything but. It begins with a rushing figure that repeats material in the "Préambule." You almost think it's going to end the piece—

—but you go right into the "March of the Davidsbündler." And there's our motif, right there in the first notes. And we get into this major battle with the conservative Philistines in the ¾-time "Grossvatertanz" (which we recall was heard in Schumann's earlier piece the *Papillons*). It is thrilling to listen to.

Carnaval is a piece of such inspirational depth and of such joy. I've lived with it for so long. Every time I look at this score, even now, I'm noticing things I've never noticed before—not only things in the printed page, but new ways of interpreting them.

Symphonic Etudes, Op. 13

Peter Frankl

It is interesting how many titles Schumann gave this piece. Like the *Clara Wieck Impromptus* and the *Davidsbündler Dances,* it went through different versions. First there was *Twelve Davidsbündler Dances,* then *Etudes in the Form of Variations,* and then finally it became known for its subtitle, *Symphonic Etudes.* That's how we know them today. Moreover, there are five more which were not published until Brahms published them much later. I picked out two of these so-called posthumous études—the fourth and the fifth—and mixed them in with the bulk of the work. These days I see that more and more people are playing all five and including them in the set. But I feel that Schumann must have had good reasons to leave them out, as beautiful as they are. Maybe he thought they distracted from the main line of the form. After all, he was very concerned with forms. Whatever, you might be justified to say there is no one authentic version. I think it is Schumann's most perfect work—a succession of small pieces enclosed within one major form. For my Vox recordings I decided to play all five of the posthumous variations by themselves, as a kind of "supplement" to the other side of the recording of the *Etudes*. I once tried that in a recital. I played all five of them in the second half of the program as one continuous, long encore! That last one, particularly, is a gem to finish a program—a "going away" type of encore, which I love.

I occasionally do the same with others of the "omitted" pieces of Schumann. For instance, occasionally I play the recently discovered ninth piece of the *Fantasy Pieces*, Op. 12, as an encore. Sometimes I play the original finale of the G-Minor Sonata. Even as an encore I play the extra Scherzo movement of the "Concert sans orchestre," the F-Minor Sonata.

Vladimir Feltsman

It was not so long ago—five or six years—that I learned the *Symphonic Etudes*. I chose to play them for my Carnegie Hall debut in 1987 for the second half of the program. [Note: The program was recorded "live" on the CBS Masterworks label.] For the first half I played Schubert's little A-Major Sonata, Op. 120, quite beautiful, but nothing much really going on. And there were also three pieces by Messiaen from *Vingt regards sur l'enfant-Jésus*. The Schumann is a beautiful work, a very important work. Besides, it was something "meaty," as you would say, for the public, and it reaches a very exciting climax. The audience loved it, and they gave me a standing applause. I think it's important, critical, to include all five of the so-called posthumous études. They weren't posthumous at all, of course; he had deleted them himself from the finished work. In my opinion, they bring the right balance to the whole shape. So it's not a matter of taste— whether you like the music or not—but of balance and form. As I wrote in my program notes, I think in this work Schumann has created a kind of "Carnaval" set of études. That's very basic for him, you know. He was always using masks, which is a very important concept in all romantic music—and in literature, painting, and poetry, for that matter. In these *Symphonic Etudes* we meet Mendelssohn, Paganini, Liszt, Chopin, Weber, and so on. And throughout it all we can see his face. And everywhere there are contrasts, contrasts, contrasts, only here they are heard in the sound and form derived from these other composers. Technically, there are sections that must be played very fast, like the Etude No. 9, *Presto possible,* which is very difficult to bring off. But you have to remember there was something wrong with Schumann's metronome. So when he speaks of, say, 120, the reality is more about 90 or a maximum of 100. The tempos should be a little slower.

Svyatoslav Levin

I first started playing the *Symphonic Etudes* during my second year in the Moscow State Tchaikovsky Conservatory. I had some freedom in choosing what to play after talking with my teacher, Yakov Milstein. I remember learning it during the summer break. I had very good guidance. I listened to recordings by Gieseking, Sofronitsky, et cetera. You had to wait long periods and stand in line and all that to hear these recordings. Now, with a mouse click on the Internet, you can hear everything very easily. But it doesn't mean as much, you know what I mean? Learning a piece was never just taking the score and playing it from beginning to end, but also knowing about its origins and traditions. That makes the music deeper and more interesting.

In 1833 Chopin published his Études, Op. 10. Only a little later, Schumann began working on what he first called *Variations pathétiques,* then retitled *Twelve Davidsbündler Etudes,* and then, by 1837, *Etudes in Orchestral Character for Pianoforte in the Form of Variations,* dedicated to his young English friend William Sterndale Bennett. Then later in 1858 Brahms discovered the other ones, now called the "posthumous" études. How you fit those five études into the perfect structure of the remaining twelve is a problem. They contain their own emotional climax, and you can't have too many emotional climaxes in the piece! The important thing for me was not to break them up, but keep them as a single group, but find the best place for them.

Despite the technical difficulties, what we now know as the *Symphonic Etudes* is very comfortable to play. Actually, you don't play it, but it *plays you*! It's a great feeling to play them. In other pieces you always worry, but here it's so overwhelming that you don't have time to worry about it, just give up to the torrent of music. I'm not saying it's easy by any means, but it's a *pleasure* to play.

The theme was by either by his first love, Ernestine von Fricken, or her father, depending on who you listen to. The word *Symphonic* in the title is important. Schumann wanted to go beyond the sound of the piano. Of course, he was not the first to do this. Schumann at that time was looking for all possibilities, and he felt he was competing with Chopin's Études. Here, Schumann is very sensitive to key relations, and all the variations/études are in relative keys, but it's implemented as mostly in C-sharp minor and E major and so on. The tonal plan is quite straightforward. In this regard, the composer Taneyev once said of his *Kreisleriana* that it was a great piece but had too much G minor!

The theme is simply stated in C-sharp minor. It's interesting that he ends the piece on the dominant. It's incomplete. He's preparing you for something to follow.

And that is the Variation No. 1, in the same key, a kind of march-scherzo with some polyphonic elements. The left hand introduces the march in the bass, and then the theme appears against that, interwoven into the marchlike material.

Variation No. 2 is very typical for Schumann. All the best of his talent is here. Plus, he loves to hide the theme. The theme goes into the bass as a foundation for a completely different melody on top. You only really notice it if you bring out the bass notes. But you don't do it all the time. With the repeats it would be stupid to always do that. And with the intensification of the music you have an orchestral texture.

The third piece (Etude III) is an etude and not a variation, at least "officially," or harmonically. The right hand has a pattern identical with Paganini's E-Major Caprice. The best way to work through material like this is to start with hands apart. That way you fully appreciate the simple but delicious line in the left-hand bass. It would be wonderful, by the way, if both hands played in exact synchronization, but Schumann displaces them a bit and it becomes very difficult. It's very showy and pleasant on the ear.

The next one, Variation No. 3, is a simple march-canon. What he does is to make strong *sforzando* accents at the beginning of each phrase, which turns your mind to the next voice—and which makes the whole so much more interesting. It is very strong and gives you the sense of a full orchestra.

And then comes the Variation No. 4, where you again get the sense of strings or woodwinds. Your right hand is very light, and the left hand follows it in a strongly accented imitation.

In Variation No. 5, syncopations displace the theme, which Schumann loves to do. When played fast, the leaps in the left hand are quite a task.

But now in Variation No. 6 for the first time there's a bright tonal shift. Strangely enough, all this time we've been in C-sharp minor, even though we've not felt any monotony about it. But we're now in E major. This piece is a kind of toccata. It chugs along like a locomotive. You must be careful to risk monotony. And the theme unexpectedly appears in C major, then repeats in B major, then back to E major.

Now, in Variation No. 7, you find most pianists playing it in all thirty-second-notes, but if you look carefully, you see Schumann also includes groups of sixty-fourths within the thirty-seconds. I am careful to observe that. The glissando effect of the sixty-fourths is like a trumpet. The theme is implied here; you can superimpose it against the note patterns. It's as if it's a ghost that is here, even if you don't hear it.

With the Etude No. 9, you have the marking *presto possible*. The theme is hidden in the flurry of notes in the right hand. I love the last few legato passages, very ghostly.

Variation No. 8 is very passionate, very symphonic. If you know what will follow—the ninth variation—you more appreciate the buildup of tension here. It is half toccata, half intermezzo, and it prepares you for the most beautiful part of the whole piece.

Everything points toward the Variation No. 9, which is in G-sharp minor. There is a murky quality in the left-hand pattern, in which one note, a D-natural, sounds repeatedly in it as a dissonance, or disturbance. It's actually a diminished fifth. Against that is a poignant melody. The key to understanding this is to separate the hands. You can easily sense the interplay of the contrapuntal textures. Now, everything would be fine if Schumann would allow you to play it that way, with two hands. But because this is played with the left hand, it becomes a challenge. You cannot physically play it that way. Also, since we tend to hear the top voice better than the lower voice, you have to compensate by playing the secondary voice a little bit louder than the main voice. That way, to the ear, they become equal. So if you want the listener to hear *both* voices, you have to play the lower one a little louder. Listen to this all together and you realize how unique this is. It's why Tchaikovsky considered Schumann the greatest. He loved him more than anyone else. Meanwhile, the piece builds and builds into a tragedy, then fades away into a kind of "farewell." This is very impressionistic. The dissonances seem very normal to the ear, which is ironic. This piece is probably, for me, the emotional climax of the *Symphonic Etudes,* a cry of the soul.

The Finale is in C-sharp major, but it's more comfortable to read and write in D-flat major, which is the same key. The theme is taken from an opera by Heinrich Marschner, *Der Templer und die Jüdin.* Today we wouldn't know this opera at all if it was not for Schumann! You hear it as a full orchestral triumph. Certain parts of it become obsessive with a dotted-rhythm pattern. He can't get out of it. The music can change, but the rhythmic pattern, this fanatical quality, keeps hitting your brain. Sometimes pianists struggle with the stretches in the left hand (those famous tenths). If you break them, the music loses something of its power. After this you have an absolutely beautiful melody against the dotted rhythm, which keeps going on and on. There's a section in which he modulates many times in quick succession. In four or five or six measures, he goes from D-flat major, to E-flat major, to A-flat, to E-flat, to G-flat, to F major, and finally to B-flat minor. And then the obsessive rhythm starts again. Now Schumann reveals his fullest fantasy. At the last repetition of the Marschner theme, you suddenly—and violently—shift to B-flat major. It's a shock, and it's exhilarating. He sets you up for this throughout the whole piece. And it brings you to a triumphal ending. Modulations like this in the nineteenth century were more shocking than they seem to us today.

Now we return to the issue of the five "posthumous" variations. Schumann probably felt they were either too sentimental, or not symphonic enough. I don't understand why he rejected them. But genius is genius. Anyway, Sofronitsky scattered the five throughout the *Symphonic Etudes*. I think Richter just put all of them somewhere in the middle. The first of these clearly sets out the theme in the left hand, while the right hand plays a kind of variation on the swirling pattern of the seventh variation. I don't like to play that pattern exactly as written, but vary it the way that Schumann instructs you to do in the seventh. We're still in C-sharp minor, by the way. The No. 2 is very beautiful. He sets up two pairs of phrases that follow each other in the treble and in the bass, then gives us a magical moment in tremolos, which gives us an impressionistic blurring of sound. And then, unexpectedly, we hear that same melody that was in the Variation No. 2 of the published version. It's a variation of a variation! This whole thing is ahead of its time. Now we come to the third variation. Ernestine's theme transforms subtly into a theme we know from *Carnaval*—a hint of "Chiarina," which was not Ernestine's theme, but *Clara's* theme! The Variation No. 4 is a bit of a mystery to me. It's a kind of waltz. I read somewhere that Schumann considered it a kind of mazurka. If you play it that way, it can sound very differently. You can do so many things here. But which? Finally, Variation No. 5 has a line in the upper register against a constant syncopation and accent displacement. You must keep that upper line smooth and legato.

So the question for me is, if you want to play all five of these together inside the main body of the published *Symphonic Etudes,* what do you do about this last posthumous one? What do you play *after* it? It is an agonizing choice. You cannot definitely play it before Finale, because you've already got the Variation No. 9 in that position, and that would put it too close to that variation, anyway. Besides, it's in D-flat major, which would lessen the impact of the Finale, which is also in D-flat. I personally cut all five in after the Etude No. 9 and then resume with the Variation No. 8 of the published set. It's always a compromise, but for me it's a logical solution. It's not that Schumann forgot about those extra five pieces, he just excluded them because they didn't fit his concept of the *symphonic* nature of the piece. But why did he exclude the second and third one? I don't know. He was ruthless in his cutting.

I have played this most of my life. As I look at it now, I know it is still in my fingers. Within a week or so I can get it back again. That's how absolutely *right* it is written.

Davidsbündler Dances, **Op. 6**

Please write and tell me how you liked the Davidsbündlertänze
*... not as though you were speaking to your fiancé, but as
though speaking to your husband, will you? ... Listen, and
you will hear the clock striking twelve at the very end.*
—Robert Schumann, letter to Clara, February 12, 1838

*Within him an abyss of figures and harmonies, of yearning
and voluptuousness had opened up, multitudes of winged
tones and nostalgic and joyful melodies passed through his
heart and mind, and he was moved to the depths of his being.
He saw a world of pain and hope unfold within him. . . . He
knew himself no longer.*
—Ludwig Tieck, *Der Runenberg*

Eric Sams

The *Davidsbündler Dances* is one of a series of works that conceive the world, the universe, the cosmos, as a kind of dance, especially one's own personal circle. The personal circle begins as a dance, and you imagine in it all one's friends, all one's acquaintances, all those who one has loved, living or dead. They are suddenly present as musical entities and are dancing and delighting us in their dancing, but also at the same time saying something significant about human life and circumstance. *Davidsbündler,* as the name implies, are his various friends and allies in the new German music that he was driving towards and did so much to establish in reality. Also notable, I think, is the Clara theme which unifies them. You find it in the D-Minor Symphony, but reversed here. One can't, after all, use the same theme over and over without some variation! *Davidsbündler* has it in retrograde form, that is to say, B, A-sharp, B, C-sharp. Well, the whole work begins with what's called a motto from Clara Wieck—her initials again. Schumann liked to be as mystifying as possible, even when the thing was entirely clear and simple.

It begins with the quotation from a mazurka that the young Clara had written. He transposes and reverses it. It's also reminiscent of a German folksong. For Schumann, it's about a new dawn in him, as so much of his music is. He's writing music which predicts himself into the future.

Charles Rosen

There are many special things about that work. You know, all of the dances in the *Davidsbündler* have something wrong with them rhythmically. For example, the first one is a waltz, where the melody is never on the first beat. And there are many touches in the writing that we might call "impressionistic." The work was originally published in two volumes of nine pieces each. You have to play them together, because the seventeenth piece is the same as the second piece. My feeling is that the work actually begins with the second piece and ends with the seventeenth piece. What is interesting is that the ninth piece and the tenth piece are both in C major. What you have is something unique even in Schumann, which is that you've got two harmonic centers: There's a concentration on B minor, which begins with No. 2 and ends with No. 17; and then you've got two books both of which end in C major. If the work is played with some feeling for that structure, it's quite clear to everybody in the audience that it really ends with the seventeenth piece. It's all over, it's gone back to the beginning. The last piece is an epilogue.

Jörg Demus

The *Davidsbündlertänze* is the most beautiful diary ever to be written in music. Schumann lays open for us everything that moved him during the years of crisis in his love to Clara, and he binds it all together into a musical wedding-eve party. The opus number is 6, which is a reference to Clara Wieck's *Soirées musicales,* her own Op. 6. He quotes her motif in the opening bars to unite the pieces on an emotional and mental level. In the first edition there are the initials F and E, which are Florestan and Eusebius, taking turns to tell us about their emotions, pains, and hopes. At the very end, we even hear his long-wished-for fulfillment of marriage to Clara. There is a deep bass note sounding midnight. In the epilogue, we see this inscription in the score: "Eusebius said this needlessly, and there were tears in his eyes." The great unity of these shorter pieces is remarkable. The second piece is repeated near the end, in the most beautiful section. The unity is so strong that it would be impossible to ignore any link in the chain.

Vladimir Feltsman

Schumann wrote the *Davidsbündler Dances* when he was knowing his love for Clara Wieck. And he was taking very seriously the literature on musical ideas by Jean Paul and E. T. A. Hoffmann; and he was reading, and playing with all his musical disguises and characters like "Florestan" and "Johannes Kreisler." For me, this is absolute nonsense. It's not interesting anymore. It is not needed to enjoy what is an excellent piece of music. In Russia we had our version of Hoffmann, you know. His name was Vladimir Odoevsky, and he was writing about the same time. He was educated in Germany and was a pupil of Schelling. In his strange novels and stories we can find a kind of Kreisler—a profile of the writer himself.

Although the *Davidsbündler Dances* have beautiful music and episodes, I don't intend to perform it. I can be definite about that. For me it is just shish kebab. It's pieces, pieces, pieces. There is no shape, no logic. Not like in the *Carnaval,* the *Humoreske,* or the *Symphonic Etudes,* which have balance and shape.

András Schiff

I'm sorry that Vladimir Feltsman feels that way about the *Davidsbündler Dances,* which is almost my favorite piano work of Schumann. It's wonderful. And so beautifully inspired. It's not an audience piece, certainly. But that doesn't decide its quality, or how effective it is. I particularly love the last section, a kind of gentle epilogue. After that very strong B-minor cadence, you go a semitone up to C major. Eusebius still has something to say. The tonal design of the whole thing is very important, because he closes the first half on C major, and then he returns to it at the very end. That can't be a coincidence.

Garrick Ohlsson

When you come to the piano cycles, like the *Davidsbündler Dances,* I confront a real personality thing. There is a lot of "in" stuff in Schumann—all the lettering and the names and the fact that the cycle goes toward the key of C in the middle and at the end—C means "Clara"—which is very beautiful and very touching. But sometimes I get impatient with "in" things and closed societies. Because somehow, I feel excluded. It doesn't make me feel warm and good. No, it makes me feel like I'm a voyeur peeking in on someone else's happy little thing. I don't mean to be nasty about this. I personally feel left out with all this "in" stuff, that I don't know the password to the secret door. Parts of the *Davidsbündler* are terribly beautiful, but I feel it starts to ramble—just as I am now! I just don't respond to this sort of thing. But maybe this is my own personal demon. I'm obsessed with why I don't like Schumann more than I do; because I really want to.

Fantasie in C Major, Op. 17

> *Through all the tones in this earthy, colorful dream, a quietly drawn-out tone sounds for one who listens secretly.*
> —Friedrich Schlegel, *Die Gebüsche*

Charles Rosen

A Beethoven melody from the song cycle *An die ferne Geliebte* [To the Distant Beloved] is everywhere in the C-Major *Fantasie*. Not just in the notes, but in the rhythm. I think one hears these things subconsciously. All those themes seem to go together so beautifully that when that theme from Beethoven recurs at the end, you don't think of it as a new theme, but one that sums up all that went before. And, in fact, that's what it's really doing. In any case, everybody would have recognized the Beethoven theme. (*An die ferne Geliebte* was very famous and had been arranged for piano by Liszt.) Moriz Rosenthal told me you don't get the root position of a C-major chord until the very last page of the first movement. Nobody before Schumann wrote a C-major piece that delays the C-major root position until the last page. That is a very radical thing to do. That's one of the reasons that I absolutely cannot accept Liszt's idea that the piece should be played "in a very dreamy fashion." No, Schumann asked that it be played "with passion throughout and with fantastic energy." If you write a piece in C major and never get a point of rest until the very end of the piece—then that kind of restlessness ought to be conveyed in performance.

That last movement sounds like an improvisation. In a letter to Clara he said, "I've been playing the melody from the last movement for hours." And he probably just sat there playing that tune for hours on end, extending it with sequences. I'm sure that's what he did. It's the sort of effect of improvisation in Schumann, and sometimes in Chopin, that you don't get in Haydn and Beethoven and Mozart. But the thing is, sometimes that effect of improvisation is an illusion. It took a lot of hard work to conceive it.

Richard Goode

Now that I've played a lot of Schumann, I know his sound world is very close to Debussy. You hear so much of that in the third movement of the C-Major *Fantasie*. I know Debussy loved Schumann, and that makes sense when you begin to think of the color characteristics of both. Schumann calls frequently for a certain kind of *blurred* quality in the sound. His piano playing has been described that he was a master of the ambiguous tone, of half tints, of voices that would come out and go back into the general texture. This is not the kind of transparency you would imagine in, say, Chopin's playing or Mendelssohn's. But, again, it's a world that's congenial to Debussy, a world of intimations and impressionist atmospheres. This is a challenge for the pianist. You find it not only here, but in the "Des Abends" [In the Evening] of the *Fantasy Pieces*, Op. 12, and in portions of the *Davidsbündler Dances*. You have to play in a manner in which each note sounds on its own; you have to create a sort of shimmering field of sound in which you're not conscious of each note but of the hovering harmonies. It's as if the melody arises out of this field of harmony, and you're not to be too conscious of the arpeggiated figures. Of course, the use of the pedal is very important, but you also have to play in such a way where your fingers are clinging to the bottom of the keys, so you produce the sound without letting the keys rise up. So, in effect, you're playing right *inside* the notes.

Kreisleriana, Op. 16, and E. T. A. Hoffmann

I like Kreisleriana *the best of all these things. The title can only be understood by Germans. Kreisler is an eccentric, wild and gifted Kapellmeister, a character created by E. T. A. Hoffmann.*

—Robert Schumann, 1839

Now they heard one melody after the other, joined together by the strangest transitions, by the most unfamiliar chord sequences. From time to time a sonorous masculine voice could be heard which sometimes drained all the sweetness of the Italian song, sometimes broke off suddenly, changed abruptly to serious, somber melodies, sometimes became a recitative, and sometimes interrupted with strong, violently accented words.

—E. T. A. Hoffman, *Kater Murr*

Charles Rosen

Schumann certainly had role models. E. T. A. Hoffmann was one. Hoffmann was one of the greatest writers of the period, and his influence is felt everywhere in Schumann, particularly in the great piano cycle *Kreisleriana,* which takes his name from one of Hoffmann's creations, the mad conductor-composer Johannes Kreisler. If you need a romantic role model, Hoffmann was about as good as they come. Here was a man who wanted to become a musician. I mean, the name "Amadeus" was *his* choice. He was certainly the greatest music critic that ever lived. His articles on Beethoven, written in 1811, are still among the finest ever written about that composer. He knew a lot about music, obviously, and was also the director of the Berlin opera. By profession he was a lawyer and a judge. At the end of his life he got into great trouble. He was on the "Un-German Activities Committee," which was investigating people suspected of having ties with the French. They were put in jail for political reasons. But Hoffmann kept releasing them as fast as the Berlin chief of police was arresting them! This was in the early 1820s. Hoffmann's last work, "Meister Floh," was never published in its entirety until almost one hundred years later, because of its virulent attack on German justice. He wrote a remarkable novel, *Kater Murr*, about Kreisler and a tomcat. The cat finds a manuscript of the life of Kreisler and writes his own autobiography on the back of the pages. And it's all sent to the printer that way. In other words, the cat sees everything that Kreisler sees, but of course he doesn't understand any of it. He only understands it his way, which is completely blinkered. It's quite funny, because the cat is a very pretentious student of German philosophy, who's been reading Fichte and idealistic philosophy. Hoffmann was a fairly good composer and a very great music critic.

Anyway, he does become a terrific model for Schumann—much more even than Jean Paul Richter, whom Schumann had claimed to be his model. The title of *Kreisleriana* is E. T. A. Hoffmann's. It is one of Schumann's greatest pieces. And what it does contain is that wonderful contrast you get between the extraordinarily wild romanticism, like the life of Johannes Kreisler, and that bitter satire, like Kater Murr. That sort of contrast runs through a lot of Schumann's music. It goes through the *Davidsbündlertänze* and the *Carnaval*. You have this sort of wild romanticism followed by music which is sarcastic. Chopin is different. Chopin, on the other hand, displays little sense of humor, except in some of the early rondos.

Edmund Battersby

I have recorded the *Kreisleriana* on my replica of an 1824 Graf fortepiano. Of course, *Kreisleriana* is about the crazy *Kapellmeister* Johannes Kreisler. And you have to remember that Hoffmann's original writings about Kreisler feature a crazy kind of narrative organization. There's this tomcat, Murr, who messes up the pages of a manuscript, so that everything is mixed up and the storyline is confusing. Well, that's what Schumann's music is all about. Several portions of this piece are really expressing exactly those grotesque qualities. Schumann gives you inversions, mirror aural images, and displacements of the right and left hands, as if the person is at odds with himself. There's certainly a madness here. One can hope Schumann himself is in control! All I can say is that the music is exceptionally well organized. And when you have someone as multidimensional as Schumann, you find music that is likewise unusual and going off in all directions, sometimes at once! Schumann composed it in 1838, most likely on that very model. Playing it on that instrument reveal how works like the *Kreisleriana* show him to be a forward-looking "acoustician," if I may put it that way—a composer with a special hearing that is still to be fully revealed to us. Even in his string quartets and symphonies he went for a different kind of sound than any composer of the period. The use of fifths in the A-Major String Quartet, that kind of reediness that he got out of the strings, was quite extraordinary and misunderstood for many years. Same thing with the symphonies. People used to take out the doublings because they didn't think it sounded good. But this was a Schumannesque sound that is now accepted. In the piano music in the early part of the century, some of the editions of the piano music rearranged notes and hands, because it was not thought to be orthodox, as if there was something wrong with his thinking and he didn't know how to work the textures and registers. Now we realize he did know what he was doing. He was the extension of Beethoven in his sensitivity to the piano. The most Schumannesque piece of Beethoven is his A-Major Sonata, Op. 101. That's pretty much uncontested. We have the rugged, marchlike dotted rhythms we associate with Schumann, along with the loveliness of tone and melody and use of imitation.

By the time Schumann is writing *Kreisleriana* in the 1830s, many pianos had a beautiful array of pedals. Some came equipped with bassoon stops, with a piece of parchment placed on the strings. That was more in line with Mozart and Beethoven than with Schumann. Broadwoods, English pianos, had split damper pedals that leave the bass clear and staccato while the treble was dampened. The Graf on which I recorded *Kreisleriana* had a moderato pedal, which gave the dreamy effect we associate with Schumann. Schumann was able to play music for several measures on the same pedal, mingling the harmonies, producing a sound that wouldn't be offensive to the ear at all. And because of the transparency of the textures, the voices of the music are in relief. Thus if you listen to his music on a piano of the time, you do not have the thickness that some people associate with him. You hear everything. (You can blow on the strings of my Graf with the pedal down and hear beautiful sounds.) When my recording first came out, a friend of mine played it and called me up and complained that it just didn't have that "Schumannesque richness." I said that that this so-called richness is something that has been imposed on this music by the kinds of instruments we have today. Even at the end of the nineteenth century, Bechsteins and Bösendorfers were much thinner instruments than the Steinways we're now used to. Of course, a lot of this has to do with the power needed for today's concert halls. You have to sacrifice something; you can't have the richness and the transparency both.

My piano in this performance is a replica made by Rodney J. Regier of Freeport, Maine. He copied it from an 1824 instrument by Conrad Graf. It's magnificent. It would be identical to what the Schumanns had when they were married. Graf was the foremost piano maker, and he never put iron in his pianos, even past 1830 when everybody else was doing it. It was made entirely of wood, no cast-iron frames. Without question Schumann, or Clara, or Liszt would have played his *Kreisleriana* on this kind of instrument.

Performance of the *Kreisleriana* on this instrument allows several parts of the music to come alive in a way that has perplexed pianists for years and years. For one thing, after you finish with the very wild, fast note-play of the opening of the first movement, marked "Äußerst bewegt," you have a beautiful middle section coming out of nowhere that has always seemed to me like roses falling from heaven. It demands an incredible change of color. And on the Graf, the effect is possible, partially through the use of the moderato pedal with the sustaining pedal to create a halo and a *pianissimo*. It's almost impossible on any other piano. And then in the recapitulation you have the quick change back to the first section, and it's stunning.

All through the *Kreisleriana,* Schumann presents a lot of compositional and pianistic challenges that are sometimes baffling. One of them is how he staggers left and right hands to create a harmonic displacement and a rhythmic displacement. On the Graf, these come through with a clarity and independence of the voices. Now, that first piece is confusing, but the pianist *shouldn't* be confused. He must be very clear about what the confusion is. In the opening you have two-note slurs, but you still have downbeats. And you have this very strong left hand in octaves which is on offbeats. And the question is, where is the beat, and where is the emphasis? This comes through so naturally, if you just do what he says on the Graf piano.

You see the same thing in the last movement, marked *Schnell und spielend,* where he marks that the bass must be "light" and "free" throughout. On the modern piano, because you need pedal sound, and because you need the articulation of the rests and slurs of the right hand, and because you have this bass falling offbeats in octaves in very low notes—well, the results can sound muddy and unclear. But on the Graf it's like oil and water, a peaceful coexistence, if you will.

The whole piece is about contrast. And one of the most extraordinary contrasts comes in the third piece, marked "Sehr aufgeregt," which has a very jerky opening of triplets against a detached bass. But the middle section is sort of "out of nowhere," as if heaven has descended upon Earth. It starts with a middle voice that has a beautiful rising scale, met by an upper voice and then a lower voice, and they are kind of like ships gliding by one another. Unfortunately, on the modern piano one boat has to stop to let the other by. But on the Graf they all just keep going. It's absolutely the most aural and visual effect. I just adore it.

Walter Klien

I first came to Schumann when I read the Johannes Kreisler stories by E. T. A. Hoffmann. I was crazy about them. Schumann without Hoffmann is unimaginable. Every note of the *Kreisleriana* comes from him, combined with his anxieties over Clara and her father. I first played it very early in my career. Only now, much later, am I coming back to it. It's always new to me, somehow. So many surprises. In the first and the eighth pieces you have almost a musical "photograph" of Kreisler. And not just in this piece, but in so many others by Schumann, like the *Fantasiestücke*. The seventh piece is very wild and always goes faster and faster. The last part goes back to a lyric mode, which is the way it finishes. The eighth poses difficulties in memorizing. Always the bass line changes, but it has to be played exactly as he wrote it, which is very, very hard. The right hand is completely crazy, it's walking around, but not normally, you know? Very often in Schumann, the left hand doesn't know where the right hand is going, and vice versa. It all leads to Freud, I'm sure, this kind of division. It has to seem improvised, although it is really very controlled. It has no end, really. Listeners aren't sure when it's over.

In the second section of the *Kreisleriana* you find a remarkable passage leading back to the theme after the second intermezzo. These are unbelievable bars. There's no tonality, a kind of "Tristan"-like quality. It's as if you can't see and you're in a fog, groping, lost. The music is completely *nowhere;* and then, slowly, comes this unbelievable return to the theme. Except now the theme sounds different, because of so much that has gone before. Schumann opens doors to landscapes that you've never seen before, but sometimes he gets lost, he gets completely lost. Alban Berg's favorite composer was Schumann. I can understand that. He wrote a long piece about the "Traümerei." You can study and study this music, but once you're on the platform, you are on your own.

Fantasiestücke, Op. 12

> *Unlike my* Carnaval, *where one piece interrupts the other,*
> *which some people find difficult to endure, in my*
> Fantasiestücke *the listener can spread out more comfortably.*
> —Robert Schumann, letter to Clara, January 24, 1839

Jörg Demus

What do we have in the *Fantasiestücke?* Thoughts of Schumann's love for Clara and his friend Anna Robena Laidlaw (to whom it is dedicated), of his schooldays, of his favorite writers, of his questions, of his prophecies of new music. He tells us this in the music. In the first piece, "Des Abends" [In the Evening], he is the precursor of Debussy. I mean, who wrote the next "Arabesque" after Schumann?—Debussy! Who wrote the next "Traümerei"?—Debussy and his "Reverie"! And if I play the "Prophet Bird" from the *Waldszenen,* my friends ask, Debussy? No, Schumann! I am always fighting with my pupils, because "Des Abends" is written in two and it's performed in three, with syncopated rhythm. This kind of rhythmic complication is called a "hemiola." It takes away from the banality of the song. Everything wavers, because it's what happens in the evening, with the bells and the wind blurring the sound. We find this effect again in Debussy's "Cloches à travers les feuilles."

The second piece, "Aufschwung" [Soaring], is a piece on horseback. Only that people don't own horses anymore, so this has been forgotten. But the rhythm says that. He had already written one for the *Jugendalbum* ["Wilder Reiter"], so he didn't want to call this the same name.

As a young composer, Schumann had marriage on his mind. In the next piece, the "Warum" [Why?], Schumann used the piano to declare his love for Clara. It's a duet, isn't it? In the soprano and bass, you hear the same words, or notes—eight times. Now, I ask you: Are you a halfwit to say the same thing eight times? Schumann is a young man; which question does he ask eight times? "Clara, liebst du mich?"—"Clara, do you love me?" It's there, engraved firmly. The question keeps hanging. And what is his rhythm? A syncopated rhythm. It's a heartbeat, of course. A heartbeat.

Later we have "In der Nacht" [In the Night]. Here is a piece where we find his favorite writers, together. We think of E. T. A. Hoffmann, we think of Jean Paul Richter, and we think of Austria's greatest poet, Grillparzer. There is the manly and weird, for Hoffmann; and there is the German sunny side of Jean Paul. But there is also Grillparzer's writing about the Greek myth of Hero and Leander. Schumann wrote to Clara,

"You will find the story of Hero and Leander in my piece, 'In der Nacht.'" Leander crosses the Bosphorus on a stormy night, and we have agitation in the music. At the convent he embraces his Hero. And she sings something beautiful. It's one of Schumann's most beautiful moments. But while she sings, you hear in the accompaniment the ocean outside going on and on. And at some time maybe a window flies open and you hear more of the ocean sound. It's an anticipation that joy will not be forever, that Leander must go back in that agitated ocean.

"Grillen" is, how do you say it in English?—"Jokes"? "Whims"? But I think it is meaning an insect, a cricket! Sometimes it sings, sometimes not. If you come near it, it stops. So you say in Germany to somebody who is very moody, that he has "crickets in his head."

The next is "Fabel." It is a story of animals. So, maybe Grandmother is with the grandchildren, and they say at the beginning, "Please tell us a story." First is a funny one and you are just twenty centimeters ahead of the wolf, who already has his teeth in your behind! So it's a very funny piece. Maybe it was too difficult to be a part of the *Kinderszenen,* which was composed at the same time. But if you think of the first measures, it's practically identical with "Der Dichter spricht" (The Poet Is Speaking).

"Traumeswirren" is all a tangle, like you have eaten too much and it sits on your stomach. And in the middle you hear this poor man snoring. Schumann writes a 144 metronomic mark, so you should play it that way, very fast.

Finally, "Ende vom Lied" [The Song Is Ended] is about Schumann's student days in Heidelberg. What does one do there but drink beer and say, "Now we go home and speak bad about our teachers!" So this piece is a "Studentenlied," a "student song." And he wrote in a letter, "In the end, it seems that 'Hochzeit and Sterbe Glocken'—wedding bells and death bells—are mixing. So he didn't want the *Fantasiestücke* to end frivolously. He wanted to give it a deeper meaning and make it into a cycle.

Novelletten, Op. 21

For the past four weeks I have done practically nothing but compose. I sang along with the stream of ideas that came flowing toward me. I'm playing with forms.
—Robert Schumann, letter to Clara, February 11, 1838

Ronald Brautigam

I have played the *Novelletten* publicly and recorded it; and despite its length I have found it most satisfying, both to the performer and the audience. It is true that the entire set is quite long, about forty minutes, but at the same time there's so much variety in the individual pieces that I have never had the feeling that it gets a bit much for the listeners. There's no question that they should be played as a complete set. The fact that Schumann had them published in two separate volumes says nothing: The *Fantasiestücke,* Op. 12, were also divided into two volumes, and yet we wouldn't dream of cutting them up into little helpings! Among many reasons why I consider them a unified work is the fact that the "Stimme aus der Ferne" appears twice, in Nos. 5 and 8. That clearly indicates that the No. 8 marks a "return," or at least a "reflection" back to the No. 5. Schumann was too good a composer to repeat himself like that without good reason.

As a whole, the *Novelletten* are extremely busy, very robust, masculine, generally good-humored. They give you a kind of catalogue of all the styles and moods Schumann has been up to when he wrote them in 1838. Other cycles, like the *Kreisleriana* and the *Fantasiestücke,* Op. 12, have their moments of rest, with long, beautiful adagios to charge your batteries for the next piece, like the "Traumeswirren." But the eight *Novelletten* are all fast movements with alternating slower intermezzi. At times the writing is almost orchestral. The harmonies and modulations are far more adventurous then in most of his other piano works. To me, the *Novelletten* sometimes feel like the "*Symphonic Etudes* meet the *Fantasiestücke*"; or "*Kreisleriana* meets the Piano Quintet." They are almost a catalogue of his pianistic and compositional art.

Considered separately, for the moment, the first one, in F major, reminds of the "March" movement of the *Fantasie* of 1836. It's the ideal curtain raiser for the set. The second, in D major, is fiendishly difficult to play. It's one of the highlights of the set, and we know that Liszt loved to play it. Its Intermezzo always reminds me of the second movement of the *Fantasiestücke,* Op. 73, for clarinet and piano. The third, in D major, is confident and boisterous, reminiscent of some of the *Davidsbündler.* The fourth, also in D major, is very elegant, a ball scene in 3/4 time, rather like a similar episode in the *Papillons.* No. 5, in D major, is a polonaise on a grand scale. Its proud character is interspersed with wonderfully contrasting intermezzi. The "sehr lebhaft" section may have been based on the Scottish folksong "Lang Hae We Pairted Been," possibly from Herder's *Stimmen der Völker.* I'm sure Schumann had a copy of this; Brahms did, too. It must have been a tune that stuck in his head. The sixth, in A major, has lots of different keys and mood changes and lots of abrupt dynamic contrasts. There's a lovely melody in measures 107–30, which is divided between both hands—very typical of Schumann. The No. 7, in E major, has a "Rhenish" quality. Was he thinking of this piece when he composed his "Rhenish" Symphony later in 1850? Best of all, it has an A-major section marked "etwas langsamer" that is one of Schumann's loveliest and most graceful melodies. Then at last we come to a grand finale, the No. 8, in F-sharp minor. What a wealth of musical ideas! I agree that perhaps the ending is a bit too long and repetitive, but what a piece!

The piano writing generally is sometimes quite thick, which is what I mean by its orchestral character. It's almost as if these pieces were studies for symphonies. You have to be careful to bring out the melodies without sacrificing the underlying harmonies. This can be a very tiring business! There are no real adagios, or rest points; the music goes on and on, slightly relaxing at times, but unfortunately nowhere easy. I sometimes feel like I am conducting a Bruckner symphony, trying to hold it all together without losing tension! You have to introduce all the new material that keeps popping up without losing the overall structure. But as long as you keep an eye on where you are and what you want with your material, the music will not fall apart.

Humoreske, Op. 20

> *I have been all week at the piano, composing, writing, laughing, and crying, all at once. You will find this state of things in my Op. 20, the* Grosse Humoreske, *composed in a week.*
> —Robert Schumann, letter to Clara, 1839

András Schiff

The *Humoreske* reminds me of a huge improvisation. It must sound like that. It's not really about "humor," as we think of it, but about moods. But there certainly are many wonderfully bright and lively moments, particularly in the second section. Some people think Germans don't have a sense of humor (and some of them don't!), but Beethoven and Schumann, they can make you laugh out loud. The real difficulty here is to make the individual sections hang together. They must. They must form a huge arch. I have to admit I'm still not sure how one achieves this, certainly.

Anton Kuerti

While some of Schumann's piano works can be considered as cycles, some do not. For example, the *Novelletten* consists of eight pieces which are not meant to be all played together. I once played them together in concert, and they are much too long as a set. It takes almost an hour. It would be a bit cruel, both to the audience and to the music, to put them all together without at least an intermission. I really adore them. But they clearly do not constitute a poetic cycle the way something like the *Kreisleriana* does. I wouldn't dream of playing them individually, the way you could with the *Novelletten*. You cannot find any thematic resemblances between them, or in terms of key relationships. They certainly don't end anywhere near the key they started in. But yet, they appear to me to have a continuity, a thread, some mystical, emotional cement that binds them together.

On the other hand, there's no question but that the *Humoreske* should be played as a unit. I've played the *Humoreske* quite often. It doesn't come to full stops, fermatas, and cadences at the end of the individual pieces. And the structure itself demands it be regarded as a single unit. For example, even though the introduction stands apart from the rest of the piece, it does come back at the end of the first big section. It's a wonderfully tentative, almost meek beginning with immensely subtle harmonies, with a rather Schubertian modulation at the end of the first phrase—a sinking down of a major third. It seems to be very improvisatory at first, just one basic melodic fragment which is repeated and extended, and which ends with a slowing down, a gradual dying out, preparing the way for one of the parts that really corresponds to the title's connotation of "humor."

There are so many wonderful and unexpected moments. Like the wild, running Intermezzo near the middle of the work. It's one of those things which I think is purposefully *dumb*. It's like "Pierrot" in the *Carnaval*. It's a blatant gesture, like sticking your tongue out. It's very difficult to play it with sufficient speed, but you have to do so to make those intentionally "dumb" repetitions make sense. What is so nice is the way it fades into the distance, ending up in a sort of beautiful echo, receding ever further into the distance. Elsewhere, Schumann does a very curious thing in the section marked "Innere Stimme." It's written on three staves, and in the middle is a melodic line that is not meant to be played! Every pianist has to come to grips with that. It might be possible to play all three staves, but it's clear to me you should not do so and instead just keep that hidden voice in your mind. And just before the concluding block, we have a section marked "Mit einigem Pomp"—a sendup of everything pompous and ceremonial. It really lives up to its title.

If the *Humoreske* has a weakness, I think it's the very last section. Although it's quite beautiful, it's a repetitive, large block of material which, coming so late into the work, flags a bit. I mean, until now, you've had so many wonderful contrasts of ideas and poetry and daring—but then comes this "Zum beschluss" (In Conclusion). It's a bit like the dinner speaker who says, "In conclusion" about fifteen minutes before he finally winds up the piece. It's one of the few places—perhaps the only place—in Schumann where the thought has crossed my mind to make a cut. Now, I would never make a cut in the last movement of the F-sharp-Minor Sonata, because it is magnificent as it stands, and with daring and intensity you can make it work. But the *Humoreske* as a whole takes twenty-five to twenty-six minutes to play, which makes it hard to maintain the interest of the audience and the concentration of the pianist. But at least Schumann leaves us with this wonderful final coda. He's really and irrevocably made the decision to bring things to an end! It's a wonderful, chromatic swirl of rapid notes, harmonically very daring. He redeems the stalling with a shouting exuberance.

There is no lack of new, fresh, imaginative ideas here, carried off with sudden dynamic contrasts and high spirits. Some ideas naturally grow out of what preceded them, while others just appear abruptly and then disappear just as suddenly. This is just what those of us who adore Schumann—perhaps above all other composers—admire so much: a daring and incandescent spontaneity. Let that *be,* the composer seems to say; let inspiration be the guiding light. We sense no preconceived notion of how the music has to fit together.

Steven Spooner

One reason we don't have as many recordings of the *Humoreske* as some of the other piano cycles is because years ago Svyatoslav Richter made such a fine recording of it on the Monitor label. It's like Michelangeli with the Rachmaninoff Fourth Piano Concerto. They're such a wonderful recordings that other pianists are afraid to touch them. The Richter was one of my first experiences with it. Now, I thought, I don't have to play the *Carnaval*! Here is another incredible piece to work on.

Humoreske is rather like *Kreisleriana* in that it oscillates between two keys, here between B-flat major and G minor. And the pieces themselves are much longer than the individual sections in the piano cycles. It points up the idea that is often forgotten that at this time, composers didn't find so much of a distinction between a key and its relative minor. They're still in the same mode. Chopin can begin a scherzo in B-flat minor and end it in D-flat major. It's no big deal. So to write a cycle of pieces in B-flat and G minor, all the way to the end, is not so unusual. You're struck by the length and daring of it all. The keys lend a kind of familiarity and coherence to the experience. That helps, because there are so many mood changes and so many interconnections among the pieces that you hardly know where the divisions among them are. But in the final analysis, what might seem to be big and sprawling, even incoherent, really does have many interior connections.

You know, Schumann referred to this piece in a letter to Clara as the "Great" *Humoreske.* Yet this is almost not music for a concert hall. Imagine sitting in an audience of two thousand people and trying to understand the intensely intimate sense of it, wondering all the while what key you're in.

The music begins almost as if it has been going on already. The gentle theme is in B-flat major and shifts to G minor in just a few measures. Already we have the parameters of the keys. There's such *longing* here, but near the end it shifts to a more hopeful, comfortable feeling, yet ends in a minor IV. After playing this first part, most pianists will just say, "That's it! I must go on!" And, of course, the theme returns in one form or another several times throughout the entire work—as in the later section marked "innig," right after the "schneller" direction. This time it seems to drift, to wander off into some unknown place. . . .

The *Humoreske* is very *odd* at times. There are great outbursts, in sections with markings like "Noch rascher," when Florestan jumps in suddenly out of nowhere and just sort of takes off in a wild series of jumps and figurations. One such moment that pianists really love is the section marked *Sehr lebhaft,* almost halfway through the piece, where you can just cut loose. It's so exciting. It's not grateful to the performer, that's for sure. And here you find a *stretto,* where you build up the motifs in a very tightly wrapped bunch, when they speed up and step on each other. It's a really manic idea. But look again, slow it down, and you find a link to the *Humoreske*'s opening melody.

And take the famous passage marked "hastig." This is always talked about. He writes it on three staves. The melody is in the bass, the lower stave, and the right hand plays an accompaniment pattern in the top stave. But if you look carefully, you see that the right hand is actually outlining the "inner voice," which appears in the middle stave. That middle staff is marked "*Innere Stimme,*" which means you are *not* to play it (even though he notates it with stresses)! In other words, that which is "not to be played" is already implied in the right hand. So many pianists will try to bring out those notes. And what you will hear, as a result, are several melodic lines intertwined. And that is followed by an indication, "*Wie ausser tempo,*" which is a very unusual marking. It gives you a kind of "off" feeling, a rhythmically *off* feeling, for an entire extended section. This whole sequence is very strange.

So you come to this kind of Teutonically sturdy march, which is very extended, a study in imitation in the chords in both hands. It doesn't seem to be going anywhere, until you get to this magnificent passage that ends it, with sharply accented discords, followed by a series of held chords, like a written-out improvisation that holds you breathless. He writes it out with those held notes so that you *can't* rush it. And there you hear echoes of the "hastig" section. It can cast a spell over an audience.

The whole B-flat/G-minor interaction is in the rather melancholy, rhapsodic section marked "Einfach und zart." But you can kill it if you play it too slowly. There's even a dancelike quality, though it's not a happy piece.

The *Intermezzo* section is full of a scurrying, baroque energy. He was so much about staying in a line of the great German masters, like Haydn and Beethoven. Not so much Schubert here. This strikes me as a Beethovenian string-quartet texture. Compare it to the musical static in the *Grosse Fuge*—it doesn't have to make sense; it's all about the workmanship. Playing it at speed and clarity is a real challenge, especially when the right hand has to switch to octaves without any lessening of the pace. Like Beethoven, it's purposely insensitive to the pianist. Once, when Beethoven was asked by a violinist to simplify some passages, he replied, "Does that man really think I give a damn about him and his violin?" I love that! The music speaks *first*, and the instrumental concerns are secondary. Liszt would never write a passage like that! He's never that uncomfortable for the pianist.

As we near the end, we have this section marked "Mit einigem Pomp." Most pianists will really run aground here in the phrasing. Again, I turn to Richter. Instead of playing the two-measure statement in separate phrases, which interrupts the flow and gets tedious, he'll keep them connected, not allowing the tempo to lag until you get to the big moment when it morphs from minor to major. It's a great example of doing what a composer *means* instead of what he *says*! You just let it grow on its own.

One of the hardest things about this last movement, which is marked "Zum beschloss," is keeping it aloft, if you know what I mean. Playing it too slow, or doing too much with it, will kill it. Richter ennobles it with his simplicity. Just play what's there. You have this buildup of sequences which, believe it or not, resembles the figures in the baroque section we've already talked about, only at a slower tempo. So you build and build and then, suddenly, magically, you must melt into this ritardando passage, where you shift from A-flat major to B-flat major. That leads to a murmuring kind of dream world that brings back that theme heard earlier in that rhapsodic section. It's there for just a second. And then—well, this drives my wife crazy—you have this wonderful series of ascending chords that to modern ears sounds very much like the chord progression and rhythm of the pop song "Only Fools Rush In." No kidding. You can sing the words, "Well I can't help falling in love . . ." right along with the chords! Sorry about that! As soon as I played this piece, that's exactly what I thought.

Did the person who wrote the pop song know about this piece? Anyway, there's this hymnlike sense of satisfaction.

The final Allegro comes in with a furious flourish of sound. Swirling thirty-second-notes underpin a chromatic ascent in right-hand octaves. It's glorious.

You know, I've never had a student of mine play this. You need to play a lot of Schumann to get to this. It takes lots of experience, lots of time, and lots of temperament.

The Piano Sonatas

> *[The sonata] has run its life's course. This is indeed in the order*
> *of things, since we cannot repeat ourselves for centuries, but*
> *rather should think about producing what is genuinely new.*
> —Robert Schumann, 1839

Ronald Brautigam

When I was asked to record the complete Schumann sonatas for the Globe label in the late 1980s, I had to learn the First and Third especially for the recordings. I did them, along with the *Sonatas for the Young,* on two CDs. It was a wonderful chance to do those. Tackling a piece like the F-sharp-Minor Sonata makes a lot of demands on you. I had never played it before making the recording, so I had to learn it from scratch. I count myself lucky enough to be a very good sight reader so, specific technical problems aside, at an early stage I am able to give a rough reading of a piece. My way of really getting to know the music is by playing an entire movement through without stopping to correct my mistakes or embarrassing myself too much. I save all those for the next "reading," where I pay extra attention to the problems in question. Of course, some passages have to be taken out of their context in order to tackle the technical difficulties. In this way, I can slowly absorb the musical atmosphere, the structure, and the direction of the piece. A couple of months of fierce practicing was enough. With a normal musicality and a good technique, you get away with a lot of things.

It's a good thing that when I recorded it in those days I had a lot of "Florestan" in me! And in the First Sonata I think there's more Florestan than Eusebius. You should say it is FLORESTAN in capital letters and Eusebius in smaller letters. There's an imbalance. The first four pages of the sonata form are all fandango before you get one page of slightly softer, more melodic material. He is actually obsessed with the fandango rhythm. It's slightly too much at times, I find. But I recorded it at an age when I didn't think about all those things. If I started learning it now, I might get lost!

In that third movement you have some very strange music. He's making fun of the old regime, the polonaises, the *à la burla*. It's like the "Old Major" shows up to strut around pompously. For a German, Schumann had a great sense of humor; but he was too serious a composer to go too far with the jokes. And the *ad libitum* nature of the oboelike recitative is really unusual.

I sometimes have the idea with this First Sonata that it's almost as if he's writing a study for a symphony, with its length and the bigger shapes and the bigger forms. The thick chords of the opening of the last movement are not really very pianistic, and the second subject has more of a cello character, and there's celli and double- basses and violas, to my mind, at least. I have never played this piece in public. No, no! I'm only human! I've played the Second Sonata a lot in concert, with the original Finale, but not the first one.

Charles Rosen

I particularly love the F-sharp-Minor Sonata. When I first looked at it, I thought there were going to be problems. But I wanted to play it anyway. I immediately thought of things that didn't seem ever to have been done with that piece that were just crying out to do. But it's also the one which is strangest in construction. It has an extraordinary introduction, and an Allegro derived from an early fandango he wrote when he was eighteen years old. The introduction is really a complete piece in its own right. The Scherzo has a very funny joke in the middle, which is followed with a recitative imitating an oboe, or bassoon. The last movement is full of extraordinary tone color, which no other work of Schumann in sonata form has. Not even the great Violin Sonata in A Minor, which is his most perfect sonata. The fact is, I've had less trouble playing it than other works. It's the last movement which is supposed to create all the trouble. It seems to fall to pieces and stops all the time. What most pianists try to do is hurry over the fermata, thinking they can hold it together. I believe the way to play it is to let it fall apart. And then it suddenly starts to come together all by itself. In a way, if you trust Schumann, it works out better.

Eugene Istomin

Schumann was young, and this First Sonata has more magical marvels of inspiration in it than four times that many sonatas could have—just one idea after the other in an excess of zeal. But he got himself into a problem of fitting them into a sonata form. He recognized this himself. For example, in the last movement he has this rather stolid theme which has a rhythmic pattern that becomes tiresome when repeated. The pianist can grow weary. And audiences, too (my audiences, at least!). That's the sad thing about this piece: After the marvelous promise of the first three movements, particularly the first two, the audience begins to tire. And yet I feel I must find a solution to this, that somehow I must play this work, because it's too marvelous not to play.

Uriel Tsachor

The Schumann Sonata in F Minor, Op. 14, the so-called "Concert sans orchestre," has been part of my musical experience for many years. I first heard it in 1974, at age sixteen, when I received a two-LP set on the International Piano Library label in NYC of a recital by Arthur Loesser entitled "Con Amore." I was immediately struck by the work's melancholy and stormy character, combined with its transcendental virtuosity and orchestral color. I knew I wanted to play the work but also realized at that time to do it justice was beyond my technical and musical abilities. . . . Since those early stages of my musical development, I have learned most of Schumann's large-scale works, but due to many circumstances I did not learn Op. 14 until 2004. Since then I performed it many times in Europe and the USA. All three of these sonatas are vastly different in character. The first sonata was conceived in 1832–34, when Schumann first met Clara. They were working together on a composition, and Schumann felt the urge to combine themes by them both. Op. 14 was composed at a turbulent time when Schumann was separated from Clara and unable to communicate with her, not even by letters. The one in G minor, Op. 22, was completed last in 1838–39, towards the resolution of Schumann and Clara's personal circumstance. While you could not exactly call it "happy," it is more relaxed and compact in its expression. For several reasons, the Op. 14 is my favorite. Like the other two, it's based on the descending five-note "Clara" motif and its derivatives. The piece is truly transcendental in its technical demands, complex cross-rhythms and cross-meters. The shifts between explosive outbursts and brooding moments are perfectly balanced. Schumann's tempi are fast, especially the *Prestissimo possibile* of the finale—which toward the end shifts to *Più presto* ("yet faster"). You have to create the feel that you are on the edge of your capacities yet keep things under control. The thick textures must be carefully voiced, as I believe they convey Schumann's own mercurial personality and conflicting states of mind.

Anton Kuerti

The "Variations" movement on an "andantino" theme by Schumann's beloved, Clara Wieck, is the centerpiece of the F-Minor Piano Sonata. It is quite a magical piece. But the theme is curious. You could look at it and say, here's something by a rather amateurish composer. There are three four-bar phrases; each is repeated, and they are tied together mainly by their rhythm. And each one, each section, consists of four measures which are repeated. But that opening is actually highly imaginative, very unconventional, and it sets a wonderful mood. It doesn't end in the tonic; rather, it ends without ending, leading immediately to the first variation. Schumann then does a masterful set of four variations. It seems almost too few, but those four variations certainly span a tremendous emotional ground. He really transcends the theme. He drops the repetition of the four measures very soon after the second variation. Finally, after a powerful climax in the fourth variation, the music dies out in a very unique and individual way. We have three groups of F-minor chords, sounding out a total of nine times in a long diminuendo. It's quite a striking gesture.

Forest Scenes, Op. 82

> *The flowers that grow so high here are pale as death. Only the middle one grows dark red—not from the sun's glow, but from the earth which drank human blood.*
> —Friedrich Hebbel

Charles Rosen

The *Waldszenen* is a masterpiece. It's as beautiful as anything else in Schumann. But it's beautiful in a very different way. Unlike the early piano cycles, it has a kind of nostalgia. It's much more temperate, it's far less youthful. And above all, it's sort of Biedermeier—that is, you know, good solid middle-class music. You can see that even in the titles of the pieces, like "Lonely Flowers," "Pleasant Landscape," and "House in the Wood."

Tim Mitchell

During the Biedermeier period, after 1830, there is the tendency by composers, painters, and poets to retreat from extreme emotional states of nature in the romantic era and to draw back to a different kind of nature, something more confined and more secure. The Biedermeier painting will take the same kind of location that might have appeared in an earlier painting, say, a mountainous landscape, and instead of showing a monk standing and staring at the moon, it will have a family having a picnic in that same site. So the emotional tone is totally different. Suddenly, nature becomes an inviting location for a tour or a vacation you can take the whole family on. It's not a place to go contemplate your soul. It's a place to have a good time.

Christoph Eschenbach

There are moments in the *Waldszenen* that are very deep, very poetic, even very sinister. "Verrufene Stelle" [Haunted Spot], for example, comes from this poem by Hebbel. The poem is very disturbing. It says there was a place in the wood where probably there has been a murder, because one sees a red flower there which was nourished by the blood of a murder victim!

Conductor/pianist Christoph Eschenbach has appeared as conductor and soloist at the Schumann Fests in Zwickau and Düsseldorf.

Schumann did that with a spooky atmosphere, very excellently put into the music. And "Vogel als Prophet" [Prophet Bird] is the most known piece from this cycle. It is a very advanced, avant-garde piece from that time. You might call it an early kind of impressionism. Sometimes I play it as an encore in recitals without announcing the title of the composer. People come up to me and say, "Oh, this Debussy you played was marvelous!" But it was not Debussy, it was Schumann!

Ronald Brautigam

The *Waldszenen* gives me a sort of spooky atmosphere that I really love. To me, Schumann, much more than Chopin, is the quintessential nineteenth-century romantic piano composer, with the Rhine legends of Heine, the Lorelei, the castles, knights, haunted forests, the fairy tales, the black armor, even Greek mythology. When I first heard it, I was very much into ghost stories at the time. There was something there that immediately captured me. There's this special atmosphere about the dark German forest, not the English rolling hills with trees. I was reading some of the romantic poets at the time, but I have to confess I couldn't get through Schumann's favorite writer, Jean Paul. I did like E. T. A. Hoffmann, especially that very strange book *Kater Murr,* where after every third page you find yourself in a different story! And with Schumann, you often find yourself in a completely different world that lasts for only a few bars, and then you're back again where you started.

I had this idea that it was more fun to play the *Waldszenen* in a small setting, like *Hausmusik,* than to sit in a large concert hall and play them. I know everybody talks about the "Haunted Spot" or the "Prophet Bird," but the "The Solitary Flower" has always been a favorite for me. Actually, I played it eleven years ago when I was trying to select a new Steinway in Hamburg. It convinced me that I had the right instrument. I could hear all the voicing, and I could hear the clear difference between the right and left hand and all these in-between voices. I think it's such a wonderful, simple piece; but at the same time, it's a difficult piece. I know it extremely well, but if I sit down now at the piano and try playing it up to the third or fourth bar, things begin to get more complicated, so that I don't know what to do anymore! Then I have to go back to the score. It's one of those things that doesn't stay in your memory. The way he writes his voices is so special and unexpected, in a way. It's the same with the first movement, the "Entrance to the Forest," where you don't know where this phrase is going to, and when does it end, or has it already? It's very difficult to divide it into logical periods. Maybe it doesn't really matter that much; it's continuous music, and whether it's a downbeat or an upbeat doesn't matter. It's typical Schumann. He does what he wants, and he doesn't really care that much whether it all fits in. I could say to just trust him—but then, you don't have any other choice, do you? It's typical of all his late music, which is so difficult to play well.

Jörg Demus

In the *Waldszenen* you can easily follow the different stations of our forest hike: We enter ("Eintritt") with a song on our lips, with the sounds of the surprises all around us that are hidden in the forest. We see the "Hunters in Ambush," with the long, lurking notes of the hunter and the staccato triplets of the fleeing game. "Solitary Flower" delights us with its harmonic dissonances. "Haunted Spot" is from a dark and creepy poem by Hebbel. "Friendly Landscape" is shaped like a Chopin impromptu . . . what could be more amicable? "Hospitable Inn" is a beautiful folksong. You can feel the semiquavers of a cool drink slowly dripping down your throat. And now we come to the darkest, most enchanted area, where the "Prophet Bird" alerts us with a touch of foreboding. But then the "Hunting Song" dispels the gloom. And finally we are taking leave ("Abschied"), filled with gratefulness for our walk. We might look back and linger a bit, but there is no heartache.

Piano Concerto in A Minor

We must await the genius who will show us a brilliant new way of combining orchestra and piano, so that the autocrat of the keyboard may reveal the richness of his instrument and of his art, while the orchestra, more than a mere onlooker, with its many expressive capabilities adds to the artistic whole.
—Robert Schumann, 1839

Malcolm Frager

In 1967, through an unusual sequence of circumstances, I discovered the original manuscript of the Schumann Piano Concerto in A Minor. It was at that time in a private collection in West Germany, in a very small village. I had wanted to authenticate some of the metronomic tempo indications which are printed in all published scores of piano concerto but which almost no one follows. And I thought that the only way to do this would be to find the original manuscript. At that time there was no published catalogue of Schumann's works giving the location of extant manuscripts. So I wrote a letter to the town where Schumann was born, which is now in the German Democratic Republic, which is East Germany, and I decided there must be a Schumann museum there of some kind. So I just addressed the letter to "Schumann Museum, Zwickau, Germany," and a few months later I had a reply telling me where the manuscript was. And I went to see it, and was astounded to find that I had in my hands the original manuscript, with the orchestration we all know superimposed upon an original orchestration, never published.

Schumann was a composer who was considered very modern in his day, and he made several revisions of some of his most famous works. For example, he made revisions of the D-Minor Symphony, the F-Minor "Concerto without Orchestra" Sonata, the *Davidsbündler Dances*, and other works. And if you compare the two versions, you find in every case that the second version is less daring, more conservative, less shocking, more in tune with the banalities of the time.

And I discovered that this first version of the Piano Concerto was very much worth hearing, and I've been playing it now for some years, although I haven't yet published it. The concerto was originally written as a one-movement *Phantasie* for piano and orchestra, and he tried to get it published in 1841, but nobody wanted to publish it. So he laid it aside, and four years later he added the other two movements, the Intermezzo and the Finale. And he used, in the Finale, some of these themes which are in the original version of the first movement—which proves to me that it was not until he had completed the entire concerto that he went back and reorchestrated the first movement, the original *Phantasie*. And at the same time, he deleted some of the ideas which he had already developed in the last movement. I did record the *Phantasie* with the original orchestration in Germany with Marc Andrae [1973]. It was the first time it had ever been recorded. And I've been playing it more and more of late, as I believe in it very, very much. All other recordings are of the normal revised version, which was published in 1845. I've written about all of this in an article [Malcolm Frager, "The Manuscript of the Schumann Piano Concerto," *Current Musicology* 15 (1973): 83–87].

"Point/Counterpoint": The Contrapuntal Studies

*Most of Bach's fugues are character pieces of the highest type;
some of them truly poetic creations, each of which demands
its individual expression, its individual lights and shades.*
                                        —Robert Schumann, 1848

EDITOR'S NOTE

In Dresden in 1845 the Schumanns turned to contrapuntal studies. Robert wrote two sets of canons, his Opp. 56 and 58, for the then-novel pedal piano (a piano equipped with a set of organ pedals) and *Six Fugues on the Name B-A-C-H*, Op. 60. In contrast to their lyric elements, the *Six Fugues* are more traditionally conceived as contrapuntal works. The pedal piano pieces can be performed on organ, solo piano, and four-hand piano. Renowned organists Gillian Weir and Simon Preston provide a brief commentary.

Gillian Weir

Schumann wrote six fugues for the organ on the name Bach. I have played them all. He was one of many composers who used the name Bach as a source for his fugues. We might think it unusual for him, who wrote so much piano music, and who was at home in the salons of the nineteenth century, to turn to the organ and back to the style of Bach. When we think of "romantic," we tend to think of something perhaps less disciplined. Indeed, even here, Schumann indulged in emotions and dynamics that were more extreme than would have been customary in the earlier times. So many people have been fascinated by this "Bach" theme, or motif. It has in it the characteristics of something complex and interwoven rather than something that is expansive. The letters all relate to the musical scale. You might wonder about "H," because we say "A, B, C, D, E, F, G." But the Germans had one more. They called one form of B, "H." So, you get B, which is what we call B-flat, and then the letter A, the letter C, and the letter—the note—that we call B, or B-natural. They called it "H." So there you have a theme. And it happened to be a theme that worked very well for playing with, musically speaking. So Bach himself played with this a great deal.

Simon Preston

Yes, I have also played Schumann's canons and fugues. They're actually quite wonderful. Of course, some of them were really written for the pedal piano, which shows their ambition toward working directly for the organ. And they bought this pedal piano so they could learn it. But they never really got around to the organ, I don't think. Anyway, the Schumann pedal piano/organ pieces are actually splendid pieces. That little Canon in B Minor—I often play it on the organ. I think it's a charming little piece. And the fugues—they make a wonderful suite of pieces. We forget that he did know quite a lot about counterpoint, from his early studies in Leipzig. By the way, these are *romantic* fugues; they're not fugues in the Bachian sense, I don't think. They're more *Beethovenian* in a way. They are more than just a footnote to his composing career. That would be a pity to think of these works that way. Certainly organists do not. I know several organists who play these pieces. They're quite popular in England, no doubt about it.

Piano Music for and about Children

I do not deny that while composing, some children's heads were hovering around me, but of course the titles originated afterwards and are, indeed, nothing but delicate directions for execution and interpretation.

—Robert Schumann, 1839

EDITOR'S NOTE

Robert Schumann was neither the first nor the last composer to write music for and about children. No one, however, penetrated deeper or was more insightful into that world. As a result, countless pianists and singers, professional and nonprofessional alike, have received their first musical training performing these pieces. The *Kinderszenen* (Scenes from Childhood) appeared in 1838, the *Album for the Young* and the *Song Album for the Young* ten years later, and the three *Sonatas for the Young* and several sets of four-hand piano music in his last year of compositional activity. Later in life most of us return to this music, only now we are prepared to perform and hear it with new ears, sensibilities, and experiences.

Overview

Roe-Min Kok

I'm so glad we're talking about this, since music for children is rarely taken seriously, unless it's for its pedagogical value. I've always been fascinated by German culture and attitudes toward children and childhood. Romanticism is the age in which the cult of the child exploded. Romantics saw the child as a gateway to the unknown. Friedrich Rückert said (I'm paraphrasing), "Through children one can touch the future." Children are on a threshold, poised between preexistence and the future of their maturity. You see that in the writings of Herder a lot. In literature, Wilhelm Hey's *Fifty Fables for Children* (1830s) represented something new. They are animal fables in the tradition of La Fontaine. For the first time in children's literature, you see children talking directly with animals. Everything mysterious in life was thought to reside in children. You don't know what they're thinking; there is a natural quality about them. Even clothes are now designed specifically for children. Before the late eighteenth century, clothing for children was just a smaller version of designs for older people, as if they were just miniature adults. In the nineteenth century, German factories begin manufacturing toys especially for children.

Music especially composed for children was coming to the fore. There was music for children before Schumann, of course. You think of Clementi, and we know Bach's notebooks for his son Wilhelm Friedemann. But there is a pedagogical purpose there, nothing like the poetry that Schumann put into his music. When I was in London two years ago, I found in a music shop music for children published in the late eighteenth century. Most of it was on the same lines as the Bach pieces, meant primarily to teach children how to navigate the keyboard, train little fingers, and so on. What does really anticipate Schumann are pieces by Daniel Gottlob Türk, who is of the generation just before Schumann. His pieces were very popular. For the first time, they all had child-oriented, characteristic titles, like "The Castle," "Romance for Children," and so forth. His titles open up imaginative realms for the child. I would think that Schumann knew these pieces. He was extremely well-read, and he probably would have played them.

Album for the Young

Jörg Demus

At the time we are talking, we are at the Schumannfest in Düsseldorf [1991], and I am presenting all forty-three pieces of the *Album for the Young*. I am playing them on two Hammerflügels of the epoch, which means that one was a Viennese Hammerflügel, about fifteen years older than the *Album for the Young*, and the other was an early Bechstein piano, a German piano, made about fifteen years after the composition. So they encompass really very well the language of the *Album for the Young*. I sketched for the audience a little bit about the genesis of this work, which was written by Schumann in 1848, in this year of upheaval and revolution, which really means a kind of peaceful counterpoint, because he was a man who had his conflicts and everything in the interior, not in the exterior. Wagner went to the barricades and was a big revolutionary and had to flee Germany. Schumann retired into his inner self and wrote this album for children.

On September 1 of that year, Schumann's eldest daughter, Marichen, had her seventh birthday and was supposed to get piano lessons. Clara writes in her diary that the materials which teachers had their students work on were so terrible, so bad, that Robert decided to write some of his own that Marichen could use. So the first thing which came was a little album for Marichen, which is already a *Reinschaft* [fair copy], and which was presented to her as a birthday gift. She was delighted with it, and we can imagine that if her papa really composes something for herself, with what zeal she would study this! This is a manuscript which is still in the possession of the Beethoven-Haus in Bonn. I was able to have a photostatic copy, which contains some of the easiest pieces, of course. They are about so many subjects! There is "Erster Verlust" [First Loss], "Nachklänge aus dem Theater" [Echoes from the Theater], and in "Erinnerung" [Remembrance], he's reminded of the death of Mendelssohn, who had died just a year before. He was such a good friend, whom his daughter Marichen might still remember. And so all the sides of a child, the funny sides, like "Bärentanz" [Bear's Dance]; and the soulful side, "Armes Waisenkind" [Poor Orphan]; and the interesting sides, like foreign lands and people, "Sheherazade." All are brought in, and the child is never felt to be played down to. There are other pieces from composers which he transcribed, like a two-hand reduction of "An die Freude" [To Joy] of the Ninth Symphony, the "Trinklied" [Drinking Song] from Carl Maria von Weber's *Der Freischütz*, Mozart's Zerlina aria from *Don Giovanni*. And there is another group where he himself wanted to introduce children to the great masters, like "Erinnerung," for Mendelssohn, a composition for Niels Gade, and two quotations from Beethoven's works.

At first they were called *Familienalbum*, and then he changed it to *Weihnachtsalbum*, because it was meant for Christmas. The whole thing took not even a month. By September 27 he was finished with everything—forty-three pieces, plus about fifteen of them which he did not afterwards publish, which he crossed out lightly by pencil, and which I was able to retrieve from those three manuscripts and publish separately. And of course, since his handwriting is very difficult to decipher, he and Clara together had to make a fair copy for the engraver. The original is in the Schumann house in Zwickau. So there are three manuscript sources, and from those emerged the *Jugendalbum*. He meant them to be interspersed with rules, how to practice, how to make music, even how to live. Those became the famous *Haus- und Lebensregeln* [Rules and Maxims for Young Musicians]. In the second version, the printed one from 1850, they were included as an appendix. I think that every modern version now in print should contain those *Haus- und Lebensregeln*.

I was six when I first played them. I have a delightful brother who's very musical, Klaus—Klausi, he's called in Austria (I'm not Jörg, but Jörgi in Austria)—and he already had lessons with my great-aunt, who was a musician, a professional teacher. And we were a musical family. My mother played the violin. And so Klausi had piano lessons for a year. Which meant Jörgi wanted piano lessons, too! And they said, "No, Jörgi, you have school this year and you already have too much work." I said, "No, for my sixth birthday, I want piano lessons!" And so I had to be given piano lessons. And we had a very nice helping girl, Frieda, who was seventeen, eighteen years, very pretty, very nice. We loved her. One day, after six months, Klausi and I played the same piece—"Rundgesang" [Roundelay], No. 22—and Frieda calls from the next room, "But Jörgi is playing this better than Klausi already." Which was the end of Klausi's piano! He later became an amateur cellist, an art historian like my father, a poet, but he had no chance upon the piano with such a brother!

So we went right through the *Album for the Young*. In about two and a half years' time, from when I was six to eight and a half, we had mastered—not mastered, perhaps, but learned by memory—the complete *Album*. Beautiful as it is, it has absolutely a pedagogical purpose. The pieces are even arranged in that way. They offer a "Gradus ad Parnassum," in that they offer new difficulties in every piece—the first time the child uses a pedal; the first time he uses chords; the first time he uses the stretch of an octave; the first time he uses sixteenth-notes . . . and so on. The *Album* is divided into a section for the smaller children, and the other for grown-ups. By "grown-ups" he means those who are already able to play.

When a child plays the piano, it's very nice to know that the piece that they play is not simplified by somebody. This is an original work by, let's say, Schumann, in this case. Don't you agree with that? These Schumann pieces are so accessible to children that they can feel a contact with the composer. It's not been watered-down or diluted.

Well, of course, everything you say is true, but what's more true is a child feels that he is not really played down to, because Schumann seems to have a real feeling for the soul of a child. He really shows quite clearly that music is not just the fingers, but it's head, heart, and fingers, and all those three you should occupy for the *Album for the Young*. He said sometimes that he feels like a very big child himself.

Roe-Min Kok

I think it's in the *Album for the Young* that Schumann makes his most complete statement about children and childhood. It's completely suffused with a "feminine" quality—but about girlhood, not womanhood. It began as an album for his oldest daughter, Marie. Just look at the original cover art by Adrian Ludwig Richter, a very famous illustrator of children's books at the time. He had sought him out, but the publisher rejected the idea because it was too expensive. So he went to Schuberth next. Schumann paid for the cover by giving composition lessons to the illustrator's son. Schumann was always up-to-date with the artwork of the day. There are little vignettes of each piece, including one of Mignon. You see her as a trapeze artist, a little girl with a balancing pole in her hand, and she's walking on a tightrope. There is a rocking motion and a syncopated beat in the music, like Mignon dancing on the rope. It's fairly awkward to play, you know. I heard Gerd Nauhaus play it on Schumann's piano in Zwickau. It's curious, but you also find two little pieces that have three stars for titles. You can't even articulate the titles. Just "three stars." I looked into the memoirs of the Schumann children and found out they had asked Clara, "What do those stars mean?" She said, "Well, they are meant to be *you,* children. Whatever my husband saw or felt, he immediately turned it into music." What a cryptic remark!

There are many other works for and about children. I love the set of *Twelve Duets for Small and Big Children,* Op. 85, for piano four hands. Some of them are too difficult for children, because of the speed and coordination you need to play them. There's a "Birthday March," a "Bear's Dance," "The Fountain," and "Hide and Seek." The No. 8 ["Reigan: Einfach"] is one of his loveliest ideas, with a kind of flowing serenity. They're such fun! Nobody knows about them! You know, it's fascinating to figure out the fluid boundaries between music for children and music for adults. I came to the conclusion that, like good children's literature, the music speaks to people of all ages. It's the same kind of beauty you find in the Grimm tales and folktales. There are nuggets of teaching and truth that children and adults can appreciate on different levels.

Charles Rosen

I've always liked to play Schumann. Even as a small child I used to play the "The Happy Farmer" and "Knecht Ruprecht" from *The Album for the Young.* My teachers never gave me adaptations. It was important to play the real thing, the original. After the age of six, I don't think I played anything except really original pieces. There's a lot of easy work one can give children. I was taken to play for Leopold Godowsky when I was about eight. I was told he put me on his lap and said, "What do you want to be when you grow up?" And I said, "I want to be a pianist like Josef Hoffmann!" I'd never heard of Godowsky, because he didn't play in public. He had a tremendous reputation for being the greatest pianist who only played in private. But Josef Hoffmann was the greatest pianist I'd ever heard. A few years later I remember going to play for Moriz Rosenthal. He was in his midseventies at the time.

Claude Frank

Ever since my childhood I loved to play Schumann's little pieces about childhood. At that time in my home town of Nuremberg, there was the family, aunts and uncles and all of that; and when a visitor came, I had to come into the living room and play one piece or another. These included the *Scenes from Childhood* and the *Album for the Young.* As I think back on it, I marvel at how wonderful they are, how sophisticated some of them are, and how well they lend themselves to children's playing. Yet some of them are almost too sophisticated for a child, because there's just so much behind the notes that the child can't possibly express.

The first ones I remember playing from the *Album* were the No. 6, in A minor, "The Poor Orphan," and "The Wild Horseman." There you have something of a virtuoso piece for the child, say, at age seven or eight. "May, Sweet May" is an unbelievably beautiful piece, to my mind. Near the end of the *Scenes from Childhood,* you come to the "Child Falling Asleep," which does not close with the cadence in E minor but instead ends on the minor subdominant—a wonderful effect that is totally unresolved, floating. Then you have the "Knecht Ruprecht," one of the most famous ones that all the children played. I don't know how to translate it into English. He is an apparition, a rough fellow who makes his appearance at Christmastime and takes the children to task for their behavior during the past year. I remember that very well! But what we didn't know was that he was usually a member of the family! And he would come carrying boughs from trees. Depending upon whether the child was good or not, the good child would be given candy from some of the boughs, and the bad child would get a spanking from the other boughs! Since I didn't want to stop between the pieces, my mother, who knew them all by heart, would whisper the titles between each one. When I came to the "Fast zu Ernst," my mother said, during the first few bars, "Almost Too Serious." But the visiting aunt misunderstood and said, "Oh, no, I don't think so! I think it's perfectly fine!"

Kinderszenen (Scenes of Childhood)

Roe-Min Kok

Schumann is writing what we now know as the *Kinderszenen* in the late 1830s while he was in Leipzig and Clara was in Vienna. He wrote many letters to her at this time. They tell a very private story of his feelings for Clara. He's deeply in love with this brilliant piano virtuoso, who's nine years younger than he. I think he's shyly putting forth to Clara his thoughts about setting up a home and having children with her. She had told him once that he seemed like a child to her. And he writes her about wearing a child's white dress with two ribbons at the back, like wings, while he was working on this music. This is very tender music, not for show, with lots of *Innigkeit.* It's mistranslated into English, you know: It's not *Scenes of Childhood,* but *Scenes of Children.* I'm pretty sure that the "children" referred to here are actually Robert and Clara. And Robert appears as himself at the end in the section called "The Poet Speaks."

It's a popular belief that he placed titles on them only *after* he had composed them. I think Clara said as much later on. John Daverio referred me to some documents at the Boston University Library that had lists of titles Schumann had drafted *before* he began composing this music. He tried out different orders of the titles. It's proof that he did think of titles in advance. It's important to emphasize that we have to take very seriously

Schumann's titles. He was so literary, unlike any other composer. The titles are an integral part of the music. They are not merely secondary important, not at all. It is true that he did not want to be associated with program music—at least not with what he called the "tacky" kind which he found in Berlioz.

Erika Reiman

Every cycle up to the *Kinderszenen* has been based on a chain of waltzes with digressions in other meters. But the *Kinderszenen* is the first of the cycles that is simply episodic; the digressions, as it were, *become* the work. In a sense, when you look at his choices of titles—"Hobby Horse," "By the Fire," "Tag," and "Fast zu Ernst" ("I can't figure out this algebra, Mom!")—you move effortlessly from fragment to fragment. There's a motivic unity here. If you look at the opening measures of the first piece, the rising minor sixth and then the little scale going down. Schumann takes this apart in each, and the character and the meter and the mood is completely different. You don't feel like you're being jolted around, like in the other cycles. And in the quasi recitative of the last one, "Der Dichter spricht," with its little turns and the simple, held accompaniment, you could imagine Schumann himself is coming forward to speak. You hear this sort of thing in so many other works, like the slow movement of the G-Minor Sonata, in the No. 4 of the *Kreisleriana,* in the *Arabeske,* the *Faschingsschwank aus Wien.* What is this telling us?

Three Sonatas for the Young

Ronald Brautigam

It's one of Schumann's great gifts that the more simply he writes, the more beautiful and deep his music is. The three sonatas he wrote for his three daughters clearly show how much he loved his children. I don't think children play them now, certainly not as much as the *Album for the Young.* And older pianists may not want to play them because they're "children's music," although in reality the Third Sonata, the one dedicated to his oldest daughter, Marie, is actually quite difficult. It's the same with Mendelssohn's music for children. You have some of his most wonderful music, but no one ever plays it. I must admit, although I have recorded them, I have never played these little *Sonatas for the Young* in concert. There is just so much Schumann to choose from that just one life isn't enough!

Roe-Min Kok

The three *Sonatas for the Young* are neglected today. They are not easy. They are snapshots of Schumann's three daughters. All you ever hear is the first movement of the No. 1, in G major, the one for Julie, who was physically the most fragile. The second movement is a gorgeous set of variations. You can actually hear the voices of the mother, the father, and the child, woven contrapuntally. The third one, for Marie, is very virtuosic but rather whimsical. It's close to the *Davidsbündler Dances,* but without so much of the dance element.

I am sorry that there has not been more work on children's music. There's so much out there—music by Tchaikovsky, Bizet, Fauré, Poulenc . . . so much. Children's music is such a huge field.

7

"The Poet's Love"

The Songs of Robert and Clara Schumann

Commentators: Elly Ameling, Dalton Baldwin, Katherine Ciesinski, Roger Cook, Jörg Demus, Christoph Eschenbach, David Ferris, Rufus Hallmark, Thomas Hampson, Roe-Min Kok, Jonathan Kregor, Tim Mitchell, Nancy B. Reich, Eric Sams, Samuel Sanders, and Robert Winter

> *I'd like to sing myself to death, like the nightingale.*
> —Robert Schumann, letter to Clara, May 15, 1840

EDITOR'S NOTE

After a few efforts at songwriting before 1830, Schumann did not turn again to the form until 1840. That remarkable "song year," which marked the months before and after his marriage to Clara Wieck, saw more than 125 lieder for voice and piano, including the collection *Myrthen*, Op. 25, the Heine *Liederkreis*, Op. 24, the Eichendorff *Liederkreis*, Op. 39, the *Dichterliebe*, Op. 48, the *Frauenliebe und -leben*, Op. 42, and many others. Clara, too, composed some songs during this period. A second period of intensive songwriting for Robert came after 1848, with such notable cycles as *Liederalbum für die Jugend*, Op. 79, the *Wilhelm Meister Songs*, Op. 98a, and the *Elizabeth Kuhlmann Songs*, Op. 104. The *Maria Stuart Songs*, Op. 135, are discussed in the "Last Days and Works" chapter.

OVERVIEW

Robert Winter

The romantic song is a very curious thing. It plays a very critical role for both Schumann and for Brahms. It seems to have been prompted first of all by a resurgence of poetry. A very unexpected one, in a way. Actually, there had been already a fair number of songs by Mozart, by Haydn, by

Beethoven. It was a genre that was known but was relatively lightweight. The radical transformation comes with Schubert, for whom the song becomes the locus, the way of defining his style, the essence of his style. And that was true of Schumann, of course, not just in 1840 but throughout much of his lifetime.

I think Schumann is the most romantic of all the song composers, certainly until Hugo Wolf. Brahms is a bit more classic, a bit more restrained. In Schumann, especially in the cycles like *Dichterliebe,* every song is interdependent on all the others. None of them can stand alone. He carefully and meticulously groups the poems by Heine into his own essential cycle, almost becoming a kind of coauthor, if you will. I don't think Brahms knew how to do that kind of radical surgery. He has songs in opuses and they certainly work sometimes better when performed together—the integrity of individual opuses is respected. But with Schumann, even with things like the *Liederkreis,* Op. 39, which doesn't particularly tell a story, you have a series of moods that are unlike the more narrative cycles of Schubert. They really have a kind of magical kind of seamlessness about them. I think that was one aspect that Brahms couldn't quite match. For Brahms a song was rooted in the country, in the German peasant. It was less of a romantic excursion, if you will. But Schumann, the son of a literary father, had more of an imagination when it came to texts. I think Schumann's response to texts was in some ways more consistently imaginative than that of Brahms.

Eric Sams

There are certain problems to solve if you're talking about any corpus or body or work like these songs. Some questions arise, like what are the dates of these particular works? Are they late or early? You see, some of the Schumann songs have late dates, but they look remarkably like the early style; so it's possible to say in some cases by applying what seem to be the right principles of research, to give reasons for saying this is an early work; and then later on, if a manuscript of an early draft turns up with a validating early date, well, that's very gratifying.

What I'm very sure of is this—if you're looking for a way into these works, it helps if you know some German. But that's not essential. You see, in many ways it's better to approach German as a foreign language, as a native English-speaking person would naturally do, because it has to sound like magic. It *must not* sound like an everyday language so you have to know a bit of that; but given that knowledge, the song approach is the direct and immediate way into the heart of each writer's creative output. Of this I'm very sure, and once you've attained that central position, you

The late Eric Sams, Schumann specialist, in his home in Sanderstead, Surrey, England.

can then look out and explore all their other multifarious and fascinating facets.

I would like to think that my most significant works are my books on the song literature. The first love of any critic, musician, or poet is bound to be Schubert, because that's where the romantic song tradition, as I understand it, really begins. The birth of Schubert to the death of Hugo Wolf spans the entire nineteenth century, plus or minus three years. This is not a coincidence. The song is a romantic and individualized art form that defines the nineteenth century. I have tried to establish the work list for Schubert, Wolf, and Schumann in *Grove's Dictionary*. But one has to begin with Wolf because he's much more manageable than Schubert. Schubert wrote well over six hundred songs, and one feels he will never know them all. It's taken me about as long to compile a card index of them as it did for him to write them! So Hugo Wolf is more manageable. And then Schumann. So those are the two things that I really set out to do, to try to write books which would serve the purpose of informing people, telling them something about what the German text means and what the song is all about, and hopefully, making a few converts. If I'm spared, I shall try to do the same with Brahms.

In a conversation I've had with pianist Jörg Demus, he talked about the importance of the piano writing in the Schumann songs. He finds lots of figurations and motivic patterns that you can trace back to the solo piano works, where you see parallels and consistencies.

I entirely agree with that. In the songwriting of great masters, especially Schumann, you can certainly find parallels in the piano music. Indeed, I would be prepared to argue this quite strenuously. What the German lied is, in its essence, is a keyboard art form. This fact is usually withheld from singers because it's bad for their morale! But pianists know and musicologists know that it is a *keyboard* art form. It develops from piano music.

Some of the more obvious motifs throughout German music are the various devices to depicting nature. And the German art song takes a great deal of its inspiration from poetry which is drawn directly from descriptions of nature, so you have to have a musical palette, so to speak, like an artist with colors. You can dip in your brush and, musically, you can depict such ideas as the lisp of leaves, the ripple of waves, and so on. And Schumann has all these very typical associations. A song for example, the famous "Der Nussbaum" [The Nut Tree], has to depict the idea of waving foliage. Simple arpeggios throughout the piece which, though entirely unobtrusive, are heard in conjunction with the melodic line. Both conjure up in your mind the picture, the *sense,* of waving foliage. And there are all sorts of movements like this in a song called "Die Lorelei." Now, these movements are enhanced by more pictures which are derived from the heart of the German woodland. The main thing here is the traditional horn call. Anything like that means "the hunt." And this can appear in any sort of guise. In a song, for example, called "Im Walde" [In the Forest], there's a description of a hunting party that suddenly passes by and the music has the same kind of sound that would be written for horns in couples or in quartets. This helps to create atmosphere in songs that mere words don't actually tell you. And the music begins in a prelude, so that when the words begin, "It is already late, it is already cold, why are you riding lonely through the woodland?," you know about that before those words are sung. The scene is set. Another example is the famous song called "Mondnacht" [Moonlight], where just the piano part has repeated chords about the stillness of the night. The harmony doesn't move, and you are to understand that a long-held note in music often means or stands for the moonlight. Think of the Overture to Mendelssohn's *Midsummer Night's Dream,* or Debussy's "Clair de Lune." At the same time as you hear that, you hear in the left hand the notes E–H–E ("H" being "B" in German). What a musical word *marriage* is! *Ehe* means "marriage." Schumann has written to his fiancée, Clara

Wieck, that an idea has just occurred to him. What is it? Well, this song
is about the sleeping landscape and the beauty of the moonlit night. But
the words happen to begin with a metaphor—"It was as if the sky had
silently kissed the earth"—and in Schumann's mind, this music moves into
a dream of married love. And he actually sets the scene and creates the
mood by writing in music the word *Ehe,* in the left hand. Really, it could
hardly be more clear or explicit. The ideal Schumann song prepares the
listener in various ways for the musical ideas that are going to be expressed
in the poem. And it enhances those ideas in quite unexpected ways.

It's quite often said, and I have a certain sympathy for this asservera-
tion, that, after all, music is music and cipher is cipher, and never the
twain shall meet (or at least they never meet in any significant measure).
I can see why that's said, but it seems to me to rest on a misapprehension. One might say, for example, there can't really be a "Clara" theme,
because the letter B isn't really L and thus can't really mean "L." On the
other hand, the letter C isn't really the note C either. All these things are
symbols, and music itself is a symbol. Schumann did that, and Brahms
did it, too, and Elgar certainly did it, beyond any question. It can't be
any coincidence that great composers happen to have minds that work
in that way. It's not a very common characteristic among the populace at
large. I should be surprised if more than a tiny fraction of one percent of
people were interested in such ideas, but a very high proportion of great
composers are.

Are there some questions yet to be answered about the Schumann songs?

I haven't studied them in depth for ten years. I'm about to resume my book
on Brahms. It will take the same form as the Schumann. I can't think
of any way of improving on these, i.e., the simple textbook form that I
have tried to adopt from the beginning—essentially text and commentary and notes. It's admittedly a didactic form, but it's the simplest way
of expounding on these masterpieces. And I want to do that for Brahms
and Schubert, if that's possible. And in doing so, I want to say what their
motivic language is, also. Thus I'm looking forward to establishing—if
this is possible, and if I have time—a complete breviary of motivic writing,
even to considering the possibility of translating, let's say, Schumann into
Wolf or Schubert into Brahms, as one might translate from one language
into the other. Each is a separate language, but they all have a great deal
in common. They all use the horn passage, for example, to connote the
open air, but they all have their individual musical expressions, as well.
So what I would then like to do, if there is time to round off the whole

study, is a complete conspectus of musical language in the lied, from Schubert to Wolf.

They are languages that are interrelated, and interrelated in the same way that other languages—nonmusical languages—all stem from the same root. They all directly derive from the earlier, the eighteenth-century German tradition, from Bach through Haydn. It's amazing how many of these ideas you hear in the *Creation*. In the beginning was Haydn's motivic writing, which everybody heard and incorporated into the lied. So what you hear in the German nineteenth century is a bit of musical history. You hear the initial sources of the eighteenth century broadening and deepening and then, mystically, dwindling and ceasing altogether. What I think happened to the German song after Wolf was that it became essentially popular music. It became Gershwin and musical comedy and has broadened still further into pop music nowadays.

THE SONG ACCOMPANIST

Jörg Demus

Being an accompanist is a perfectly honorable profession. Clara Schumann wrote into her diary, "Today is a very happy day for me, because Robert said that my playing has gained so much in maturity and refinement, that from now on I would be allowed and qualified to accompany his songs." So it's a step up, not a step down. And the step up for me was a very big step, like a pyramid step or so up, because, guess what my first song recital in my whole life was? *Die schöne Müllerin* with Fischer-Dieskau! So where could I go from there? That was in February in 1952 in the Mozartsaal in Vienna. He had debuted there a year earlier. He had written to the concert house that for his next recital he wanted an accompanist. Independently of this, I had become interested in the song literature. I let it be known that if ever a singer wants to try me out, give me a ring. They said, we have a young baritone, twenty-three, twenty-four years old, from Berlin, who wasn't happy last year, and would you do it? I said yes, very gladly. So he came the day before the concert to our house. My mother made a nice dinner, and so we sat down. Immediately, I felt that he was knowing absolutely what he wanted, and he also made suggestions for my phrasing and tempo and so on. But I was accustomed from the very first that one had to be very attentive, very quick, because he doesn't rehearse very much. He has his definite opinions, so you have to play very well, and you have to catch it very quickly. You think of him as the captain and me as the helmsman going on a journey! But, anyway, this was my very first song recital in my life. Two years later I played for him in his first

Paris concert. And we worked for his first Liszt songs in the early 1960s. And we have done also Carl Loewe and many settings of C. P. E. Bach (I played on my own 1793 *Tangentenflügel*), Schubert, Beethoven, Brahms, and Wolf. I have written about our times together in my book *Abenteuer der Interpretation* [1976]. I talk about how quick he is to learn, about his wonderful gift of breath phrasing, his pure love of the poetry, all of that.

He has such a gift for both the lyric and the dramatic. He can go one to the other so naturally. He was not a chain-smoker then, but he was a very sound and healthy smoker, who smokes with gusto. When he sings, and he's not happy, he repeats many times. And when he has sung something for the fifth time, like the "Mondnacht" by Schumann, and finally he is happy, then for a reward, he will smoke a cigarette. I have been very lucky, because I have since also worked with many fine singers, like Elly Ameling, Elisabeth Schwarzkopf—certainly the greatest female lieder singer I know—Hermann Prey, Peter Schreier, Theo Adam.

That kind of recital is disappearing. That music we are speaking about, let's say, Schubert, Schumann, Brahms, is like a happy island, and we're on a ship which is continuously going in another direction. And first we still see the hills and the mountain and the houses and the harbor and the people waving, and it's receding; and if we add a little distance, we even see more clearly the overall shape of the island; and since we are receding even more, there will come a generation when this island will not be seen very clearly, so we have no definite knowledge anymore of how those things should be played. I mean, we can guess how Schubert perhaps accompanied himself, his songs, with [Michael Vogl], but there is no way to know. He was not so famous that people would describe exactly his playing, like Chopin, let's say, who had pupils, and passed it on to other pupils.

Schumann himself was not a performer anymore after he had ruined his hand. So those piano styles are handed down to us, let's say, by Clara or Liszt. But how do we know that they really played it as Schumann wanted? And so, what we need is a key to open up those treasures. And one of the most valuable keys, to me, is the lied, because in the lied a certain music is associated with a certain word or expression or mood or whatever. For instance, *Kreisleriana* by Schumann starts with the same flourish as song No. 7 in *Dichterliebe* ends. So you have yourself "Zerrissen, zerrissen mir das Herz." So I know *Kreisleriana* means "Zerrissen mir das Herz"—"She has torn my heart apart." It's like a language. Whenever I play Schubert's Impromptu in G-flat, the accompaniment, I know it's a *Bächlein* [brook], which is also *Die schöne Müllerin* [The Beautiful Miller's Daughter]. So we have certain motifs for a brook, for blue sky, for going by boat, for going on horseback. "Aufschwung," for instance, is a piece on horseback.

I know it just by playing "Freisinn." "Lasst mich nur auf meinem Sattel gelten," in the song. You get a thousand keys to the world of Schumann solo music through his songs, and in Schubert, Schumann, and Brahms. Why would not a musicologist, instead of writing over a sixteenth-century master, write a dissertation for his doctorate about the coincidences of motifs in Schumann's songs and his piano music? So that's a new theme which I give here, at the disposition of young musicologists! He wouldn't need to spend much time. If he goes with open eyes through the texts and the musical correspondences of Brahms's *Vier ernste Gesänge,* or of *Dichterliebe* or *Winterreise,* he will receive a thousand inspirations, a thousand symbols, a thousand rhythms and melodies and harmonic progressions, which will be meaningful because they are associated with a word which clearly depicts what is going on.

Christoph Eschenbach

I had a wonderful time performing the Schumann songs with Maestro Fischer-Dieskau. He is an incredible artist. Of course, we didn't do them in one session—or I mean one set of sessions. We did it over two years. This was good, because there was time to think about the program for the next session and rework it and live before performing again. There were three volumes for Deutsche Gramophone. For the first we did extractions from the early *Myrthen* cycle, the *Liebesfrühling* [Love's Spring], and the complete *Liederkreis*, Op. 39 (an incredible work!). For the second, we did the Heine *Liederkreis* and the great *Dichterliebe*, and some late songs from the 1849 year, with the *Liederalbum für die Jugend* [Song Album for the Young]. The third book was lieder from the last years, from Lenau and Goethe. Was there was an influence from other recordings? Not at all. On purpose I did not listen to these earlier recordings. I wanted to have my own approach, which was probably also the aim of Fischer-Dieskau. It was his idea to record them with me. He knew them, but at the time I did not. I found them to be wonderful, even the very earliest ones, bold, and with a mastery of sounds. Obviously, the genre song was very near to Schumann all his life, from these early songs to the very late ones.

We also did the *Melodramas.* These were music for a speaker, pieces for a narrator with piano. The piano is not to be an accompaniment but as illustration to the texts by Hebbel and Shelley. The music is an illustration to the text, and the text is rather freely put into it. Schumann does not forcefully say where the words have to sit, but you can derive it from the music and from the sense of what the music illustrates. The music itself is very bold, very strange, and the texts are also very strange. The first is "Schön Hedwig," a ballad, and the second, "Vom Heideknaben" [The Moorland Boy], is a very spooky story. The third one, "Die Flüchtlinge"

[The Fugitives], is very dramatic. You have to have a very good actor with a big voice, because the piano part is very *fortissimo* and dramatic. There are only three *Melodramas*, so you cannot do a whole evening of that; also, you cannot do them in a lieder recital, because the singers don't usually want to speak during a recital. Physically, they are very difficult, as well, because they treat the voice totally different. So it's hard to put them in a context; therefore, they're rarely done.

Samuel Sanders

Schumann is the one who really started this business of so expanding the piano's role that at times it takes over completely. The great song cycles, *Dichterliebe* and *Frauenliebe und -leben*, have magnificent postludes that are really solo piano pieces. It's finally the piano that really has the last word on the subject. Or you could call it a summing up. But again, it reinforces the idea of the inseparability of the voice with the piano. People ask me what the singer is supposed to do during such moments. Generally, if they are thoughtful musicians, they realize that the piece is *not* over until the last note has been played. They should stay in that world of that song, of that poem, until the last note has been struck. I'm always telling my student singers, "Don't slouch like that; the song is not over yet!" In a sense you're an actor or an actress, and you keep playing out that role, even when you are silent. Just the body language, or the body position, is saying so much.

Meanwhile, the piano writing is just beautiful. Schumann certainly knew how to write for the piano, and Brahms certainly knew. As a matter of fact, I wish that Mahler and Wolf had written for piano, because they write for it so beautifully in their songs. Of course, there are moments when the piano writing is really a killer. You have to have machine-gun wrists for all those repeated octaves when playing Schubert's *Erlking*. They never let up.

EICHENDORFF, FRIEDRICH, AND *LIEDERKREIS*, OP. 39

> *Dusk begins to spread its wings, trees shudder, clouds*
> *Drift over like ill-omened dreams. What does all this mean?*
>   —Joseph von Eichendorff, "Zwielicht"

EDITOR'S NOTE

A product of the fabled "Year of Song," this song cycle to poetry by Joseph von Eichendorff also shares a kinship with the imagery of the painter Caspar

David Friedrich. It was composed in the first three weeks of May 1840, just a few months before Schumann's marriage to Clara Wieck. The *Liederkreis* is one of the great romantic evocations of the German forest.

Rufus Hallmark

You find in Schumann's Op. 39 *Liederkreis* cycle a remarkable confluence and affinity among three creative artists of the German romantic period, Schumann, Joseph von Eichendorff, and Caspar David Friedrich. Schumann we know, of course. The poetry of Eichendorff conveys strong romantic images of the landscape, with mystical overtones and strong feelings of nostalgia. Some of our most sacred ideas of romanticism are here in frequently repeated expressions and ideas, like the preciousness of the solitude and mystery of the dark forest, the duality of twilight and night. When Caspar David Friedrich paints a landscape, it is not a beautiful, pastoral representation of a landscape like you would find in contemporary English painters or the Dutch painters. One senses there's something *behind* the picture; there's some other meaning. He paints a winter landscape, but it's not just the snow

Musicologist Rufus Hallmark has conducted original research into Schumann's songs.

and children playing in the snow and snow-covered trees, but it is a stark, black leafless tree in the foreground and the mountains in the background. You just can't help but feel that there's some strong symbolism here, and when one reads about Friedrich, reads his letters and what his friends said about him and studies all of his pictures, you begin to sense a strong religious symbolism there.

When the *Liederkreis,* Op. 39, was first published, it consisted of thirteen songs, and it began with a song that was taken out for the second edition and relocated, I think in the Op. 77 lieder group. It was from another Eichendorff poem, "Der frohe Wandersmann"—"The Happy Wanderer"—a bright D-major march song. It's so difficult with hindsight for us to appreciate how this cycle could have begun with anything but the F-sharp minor "In der Fremde."

All of these poems appeared interspersed in Eichendorff's little novella *Ahnung und Gegenwart,* which might be translated as "The Future and the Present," or "The Unknown and the Known." I've read parts of the novel, and it's a loose narrative about some characters who live on the land of a grand estate, and they have their ups and downs, and they talk a lot about the landscape and nature. Occasionally, one of them will recite one of these poems to another, or sit down and take up a guitar and sing. Robert and Clara copied these poems into their poetry book. All the scholars who've worked on this have not been able to make any coherent sense out of the order in which they appear in the *Abschriften,* as compared with the order in which the songs appear in Schumann's song albums in Berlin, or as they appear in the order of the printed cycle.

Eric Sams

There are two ways of considering German landscape in the nineteenth century. One derives essentially from the poet Eichendorff, and he is of course a part of a continuing German tradition. He didn't invent these things, but it was him for whom twilight scenes became a living and vivid actuality. In this way he inspired, I'm sure, all the French poets of the later nineteenth century. Any poem about a formal garden illuminated by moonlight where peacocks walk, where there are great extensive vistas like the garden of the Tuileries. Poems of that kind come from Eichendorff sources, and they also derive in part from *Des Knaben Wunderhorn*— that sensibility connected with the idea of Germany as a national, living, almost religious force. The power of the past, the power of the great castle, the power of the twilight scene. These pictures Schumann set to music, especially in the *Liederkreis,* Op. 39, and in some of the Wolf songs. These, I think, are the definitive clear statements of the mystery and the magic of night in German romanticism—the starry night, late birdsong, and above all, immense vistas of bygone splendor—which we are to understand these days are to be renewed if Germany is to be great again. That's one powerful force, the nationalistic force.

The other part of it is the personal relationship with nature. If you look at the paintings of Caspar David Friedrich, who is, par excellence, the preeminent painter of the romantic movement, what you see is an isolated figure in some kind of splendid romantic exultation on the top of a handy mountain surveying the local scene. This person is, as it were, the German romantic soul on its upward path, the bourgeoisie ever improving its lot in the world, making its way upwards literally and metaphorically. He has reached that exalted pinnacle as the result of a journey, notionally life's journey. There's nowhere to go after that but down again; but that's why you're shown that scene in that magic moment of time when total dominance is achieved: The romantic figure alone in the landscape, a bit puzzled, a bit worried, a bit perplexed about life and things and maybe wondering where one's road leads and where one's goal is to be found—but on the whole content with the idea of dominating a total landscape. And in Wolf's songs particularly in the later romantic era, you hear exactly such songs turned into music and usually finishing with a kind of hymn of patriotism in the postlude.

David Ferris

The notion of the romantic song cycle relates to the idea of the fragment—a very important concept in the literary and artistic ideology of the early German romantics. It ties into the belief that romantic poetry and romantic literature and actually all of human life is "a work in progress" and is fragmentary in the sense that it's always still searching, always yearning for some kind of complete wholeness. If you follow that idea through, it becomes clear that the notion of a complete, organized work is just impossible.

Certainly in the poetry of Joseph von Eichendorff, nature becomes a very important symbol. Eichendorff uses nature as a symbol for man's progress toward what is, inevitably, an unattainable perfection. For example, the nighttime is a time when you get a glimpse, an *"Augenblick,"* of eternity, a moment of epiphany when just for a moment you are completely one with nature. And you see this in several songs in the *Liederkreis* song cycle, in "Mondnacht" (Moonlight), "Schöne Fremde" (A Beautiful Strange Land), and "Frühlingsnacht" (Spring Night). They all express this idea of being in the moment. The time of twilight, on the other hand, is a terrifying time, a time when you can't really perceive the landscape very clearly. And so for Eichendorff this symbolizes how man is cut off from other people, from nature, even from himself, and is trying to get back to a state of perfection.

The landscape about which Eichendorff paints his images is symbolic of this more spiritual experience. At the same time, we need to remember that the early nineteenth century is the beginning of industrialization, a time when for the first time people are becoming aware that Nature can be destroyed by people. They're starting to see air pollution; they're starting to understand that these forests and all this wonderful stuff all around isn't necessarily going to remain untouched. That's one of the reasons you find almost an obsession in early nineteenth-century poetry with nature, as an appreciation and as something we ought to revere, to hold on to. (Maybe I'm saying Eichendorff is a proto-environmentalist!)

The Op. 39 *Liederkreis* was the third cycle he wrote. The first one was *Myrthen,* and in the middle of writing *Myrthen* he wrote the Heine *Liederkreis,* Op. 24 (that was in February–March and ended in April). Then in May he wrote the Eichendorff *Liederkreis.* And within a few days of finishing that he started writing *Dichterliebe,* which he wrote in about a week and a half. In my view it was Clara who actually selected the poems for Robert's cycle. We have a document that is known as the *Abschriftenbuch,* which is a notebook in which both Clara and Robert wrote down poems they were interested in as potential settings for songs. It includes many poems that were eventually set as songs and many that weren't. The Eichendorff poems are written down in her hand. While she was performing in Berlin, she wrote out thirteen that she liked and sent them to him while he was back in Leipzig. They were apart when he composed the cycle.

He began writing the vocal lines away from the piano and later wrote the accompaniments. The first piano draft we have is dated May 1, 1840, and the last one is not dated, but we know he finished it on May 22. So it was about three weeks of intense composition. If you're looking for a story here, you'll have problems. German novels of the time didn't have a clear storyline, either. They were a mix of some prose and some poetry. And several of the poems in the Eichendorff cycle originally appeared in his novels. Second, writers were much more interested in the ways narratives can be fractured and the ways in which you can play around with time than in the ways you could present a straightforward story.

Something else you have to remember is that concert performances in Schumann's time were very different than they are today. Programs were like variety shows, with recitations, piano performances, and operatic excerpts. It was unthinkable in Schumann's lifetime to perform complete versions of longer works. Indeed, the first complete performance of any song cycle would have been in the 1860s, when Clara and Stockhausen did Schubert's *Die Winterreise* and Schumann's *Dichterliebe*. And even in this instance, there were interruptions in the performance.

It is important that we understand that the *Liederkreis* is a transformation of the Christian schema. What Eichendorff seems to be interested in is the whole notion of transcendence—which comes through love of another person, or through death, or in a union with nature. One asks, "Where do I leave off, and where does nature begin?" That is what Eichendorff seems to be asking, over and over again. Thus the poem texts are arranged in two groups, or arcs, of six apiece. I differ from some other interpretations in that I see each of these as depicting a process, or cyclical progress towards the nighttime and the moment of transcendence. And there are two epiphanies, the first with "Mondnacht" and then at the end with the "Frühlingsnacht."

If you try to understand this work simply as an expression of love for Clara, then you end up distorting the texts and you force Schumann into a pigeonhole. If you really look at the texts objectively, love is really more of a secondary theme than anything else. I see it as more about this kind of spiritual transcendence. Love is just an aspect of it.

Tim Mitchell

Schumann draws upon images Caspar David Friedrich uses over and over again in his paintings. The blasted, leafless tree, just a bare trunk, but with a few new growths coming out of the base—that was the power of everlasting life. Mountains become a classic symbol of God itself, sublime and unchanging. The moon becomes a symbol of Christ: It reflects the light of the sun, God himself, the transmitter of the message. Moonlight was the symbol of faith, the power of God to save you. Color for Friedrich was like the moon; if you see lighter tones, golden tones, it referred to Christ. It could be directly translated into the Trinity—one color represents God, another the Holy Spirit, another the Son.

Friedrich's landscapes were like Schumann's music about nature—generalizations, summations, derived from diverse inspirations. Throughout his life, Friedrich finished his landscape paintings in the studio. They were culled from different drawings he had done in the countryside in different locations and different time periods. He would use a drawing of a tree done in 1806, let us say, as the principal feature in a landscape painting in 1824. The tree is from one part of Germany, the landscape from another. He might use a rock formation done on a sketching trip in 1812 in the Harz Mountains. That rock will appear in a landscape, the background of which involving Alpine peaks near Salzburg, done from another source, another sketch. So he mixes and matches. They seem almost photographically real. But almost none of his landscapes are true "veduti," that is, they are not visions of sites, views of a single site. They are always compilations of parts brought together.

A Dialogue: Elly Ameling, Dalton Baldwin, Rufus Hallmark, David Ferris, Tim Mitchell

Hallmark: The *Liederkreis* happens to be, since you've asked, my personal favorite of Schumann's song cycles. I'm drawn to these songs and their moody quality, their ambiguity, the beauty of the melodies, and the richness of the accompaniments. I love to sing it. I love to hear it. I think it's Schumann's greatest cycle, although there is no clear narrative shape. It's very close and very tight, and there are musical motives that occur from song to song. I'm sure Elly Ameling and Dalton Baldwin have explored that thoroughly.

Ameling: You can absolutely not compare the *Liederkreis* to, say, *Frauenliebe und -leben,* and not even to *Dichterliebe,* which has such a different subject—the ongoing love story of this man. And this is almost an ongoing love story of nature itself. The typical nature of these poems is in the woods, and where the brooks are, and the moon. Every song is about nature—not so much a person and that person's love affair or love troubles set to a background of nature; but nature is in the whole song, the whole poem, nowhere else so much as in this cycle.

Baldwin: It's not a bombastic work; it doesn't present enormous difficulties pianistically or vocally. But the musical quality of this cycle is so fine it's like the finest cut diamond, you know? You can't cheat, you can't cheat musically . . . Most of the songs are only two pages long. But there isn't one note too much.

Does it make a difference if a man or a woman sings these songs?

Ameling: I must say, I love to sing it still; strange to say that when you sing it so often! I believe it is a little better for a man. But only if you're quite aware of the social position of a man and a woman in those days. A woman, with a long skirt and high heels, wouldn't walk so much and so freely in the woods as a man does. A woman was just not so near to nature. She was more in the house . . . If you are not aware of that, you have no problem at all, because the text goes very well for the woman.

Hallmark: There's not a persona who is the narrator of this that is either strongly male or female. As I said before, it's not a narrative cycle, so it's much more easily adaptable to either a female or a male singer . . .

Ferris: I don't see any objection for either a man or woman performing it, or using two soloists in the same program. I think one of the things that's quite interesting about this cycle—and in this way it really does differ from the Heine cycles—is that I don't really hear one single, strongly identifiable narrator. And again, this comes back to the whole idea of identity, and whether one really has an identity or not. You're really hearing from different perspectives and different narrators; and yet each of these narrators is articulating the same kinds of ideas and the same kinds of feelings. And so I would argue that to hear it with one voice throughout or a couple of different voices throughout, it would be just as effective either way.

The very first song, "In der Fremde," should probably be sung by a male. In the nineteenth century, the figure of the wanderer, for obvious reasons, was more male than female; it was socially acceptable for males to go wandering around, and it wasn't socially acceptable for females. Moreover, if you look at the origin of that poem within Eichendorff's prose works, you find it was spoken by a female character.

Hallmark: "In der Fremde" depicts the reddening evening sky at sunset. He remembers the land of his childhood and the parents who are now dead. And he says, "Wie bald kommt die stille Zeit"—"How soon comes the quiet time when I, too, shall rest." "Und über mir rauscht die schöne Waldeinsamkeit." This single line has so much of Eichendorff: "Over me rustles the beautiful solitude of the forest." A lot of Eichendorff's imagery has to do with sound. "Rauschen" is a word that we encounter over and over again. And there's the idea of this compound word he's created, "Waldeinsamkeit," which is awkwardly translated or rendered as "forest solitude," or loneliness in the forest. And then he says, "und keiner kennt mich mehr hier"—"And soon no one will know me here, either; I will dissolve into the great nature, 'Gefühl,' and be gone." And that sets the tone.

Baldwin: And here we have the wind rustling in the beloved German forest. The whole cycle is bound by the forest, the German forest . . . The forest encloses you and understands your sorrow—in this case, the "Sehnsucht," the home of your birth and for your parents who are no longer there.

Mitchell: Usually, the figure in these scenes is alone. The poet says he goes to nature by himself. He doesn't want a companion. It's a personal experience, something he can only do by himself. Like a religious experience, it is singular, alone. And he has this feeling of "Waldeinsamkeit," is the feeling of being *inside* the forest and looking up at the gnarled trees with their serpentine limbs. A sense of an organic energy surrounds you.

The second song is titled "Intermezzo."

Baldwin: Palpitating, palpitating heartbeats. You know, we have the heartbeats in *Dichterliebe*, "Ich grolle nicht," and of course, in *Frauenliebe und -leben*. The heartbeat, the heartbeat. We find it throughout Hugo Wolf songs and Schubert songs—"Gretchen am Spinnrade," in the left hand. That's the heartbeat. Here, it truly is the ecstatic heart . . . You don't touch ground anywhere in this song until the end. It's all suspended, just as love should be. In the second act of *Tristan* you get that suspension . . . And that's the feeling you get in this song, suspended in some kind of ecstasy, although on a very intimate level.

In the third song, "Waldesgespräch" (Forest Dialogue), we meet our old friend the enchantress, the Lorelei.

Ameling: In "Waldesgespräch" this man is going on his horse in the woods and meets nobody else but "Die Lorelei," yes? And she says, "Oh, you're beautiful!"—and you know the story of the Lorelei—and he looks into the water and falls into her arms. Anyway, here she says at the end, "You will never get out of this wood again, because I have you and I will hold you, or keep you here."

Baldwin: "Waldegespräch," of course, is fun for me to play because I know Germany very well, and I've taken a trip up the Rhine countless times to where the Lorelei stood; and if you use your imagination, she's still up there, luring us round these dangerous waters. Part of it can be very mean and spooky . . . I find it a very effective song, and it gives rhythmic variety to the cycle, which is very effective at this point.

Mitchell: In German cultural history, of course, the Lorelei is probably the single most famous rocky outcrop in Germany. It is a cliff along the Rhine. And today when you take a Rhine trip on boat or train you go right by the Lorelei, and there's a flag on top and you can walk up there and look out. The myth comes from the Middle Ages. *The Lorelei* was a term for a siren, a woman who would sit at the top of this cliff and bring the seafarers, the river boatmen, to their death, crashing against the rocks below. Today the mountain is not very frightening when you go by train. But it certainly is a popular spot.

The fourth song in the Liederkreis *cycle is titled "Die Stille" (The Stillness), the kind of wintry scene found in many of Friedrich's paintings.*

Baldwin: This is footsteps in the snow. And that's what I always think of when I play it. In fact, I think of velvet shoes. There's a lovely little song by Randall Thompson—"We will go in velvet shoes, walking through the snow . . ." That's the way I play it: very soft-footed. But not one chord can be overweighted, you see.

Ameling: "Wie mir so wohl ist, so wohl!" That is almost "lachen und weinen," yes? Nobody can guess how happy I am and how sad at the same time. The utmost example of romantic feeling. Happy and sad at the same time. Like in *Frauenliebe,* you have sometimes, "Ich weine"—I can't find the phrase so quickly—but then she would say, "Ich lache and weine," and both are meant to be for happiness. They can laugh or smile and cry for happiness. Both are intermingled.

Hallmark: The most famous song is No. 5, "Mondnacht," or "Moonlight"; and, by the way, that is also Eichendorff's most famous poem. It is the most anthologized in German books for schoolchildren and college students. It is also the most often excerpted and sung song of Schumann.

Ameling: It's like a ray of the moon and it should be falling, the whole song, as still as a ray of moonshine.

Hallmark: You know, if you put yourself into this poem, you imagine yourself standing in a meadow maybe with trees around you that are in the distance. But the sky is open, full of stars above your head.

Ferris: It is to me a very good example of a fragment, or a form, a musical form that reflects the romantic poetry in that it's not really closed; and it leaves things open. One of the things that's quite striking about "Mondnacht," when you listen to it, is that it really feels for the most of the song that you're just floating, that you're not really going anywhere. And it keeps not resolving. And this is a way in which he evokes this sense of nighttime transcendence that is at the heart of this poem—this idea of yearning, of having a glimpse of something, but you never quite get it.

Baldwin: It's a tightrope performance—for the singer as well as for the pianist. Not one note can be out of place. It's all imbued in that beautiful, silvery color . . . The danger, I think, might be to play it too softly. . . . It's a hard song, and I think you can frighten the singer if you play it too softly. Give them a nice bed of sound just the same. And they feel a little more enclosed.

The sixth song of this cycle is "Schöne Fremde" (A Beautiful Foreign Land). It hints at a splendid land lying beyond the trees, like the vistas seen by Friedrich's solitary wanderers as they pause atop a high hill.

Baldwin: "Schöne Fremde," I think, is a better man's song than a woman's song, because it demands quite a bit of strength in the middle of the voice, and there's so much going on in the piano . . . It is a relief; by the time you get to this song, you feel like doing something a little more overt, tonally and emotionally. And it comes as a relief—"Schöne Fremde."

In some respects, the strangest yet most amazing song in the Liederkreis cycle is the sixth number, "Auf einer Burg" (In a Castle), a portrait of an ancient knight in his castle keeping eternal vigil over the valley below. Many of Friedrich's paintings contain ruins of castles and monasteries.

Ameling: "Auf einer Burg" is almost a static picture—static, frozen, and dead. I try to sing this song without vibrato.

Baldwin: I must say, "Auf einer Burg" is one of the most static songs I've ever played. And to bring it off successfully, you must be completely immobile. It's a frozen picture. There again, I think of a Caspar Friedrich painting of an old ruined castle along the Rhine, with the ghosts of some past time echoing in your ear. "Auf einer Burg," as we said, is absolutely immobile. It's a great masterpiece with these sparse open fifths. Great masterpiece—how he ever did it, I don't know. I use a lot of pedal, of course, on romantic music. Not as much as I do in French music, but I do use a lot of it. In this song, I use both pedals. I use the left pedal for the whole song.

Ameling: I think that this is the hardest song to understand for an audience, "Auf einer Burg"—this frozen song with the old knight sitting in his stone chair. (He was not stoned, but *of stone* by age!)

Baldwin: It's a deathtrap for us. The last phrase, when the singer says, "Die weinet"—singing all of that on a vowel sound—and to absolutely be with it is a very great challenge. I'm telling you some of the secrets of performing this cycle!

Mitchell: The Germans have a word, *Gipfelerlebnis,* which means being on a peak. It conveys the sense that can only be experienced by being on the top of a mountain range looking out across the valley. You feel you are at the top of creation. Friedrich in fact has a number of paintings showing figures at the tops of mountains, standing either at the very pinnacle or on the way to the pinnacle, almost at the top. In most of these, it's clear that he's trying to capture this unique sensation of being at the pinnacle of the world. It's intended to convey the divine experience, where the sky is as important as the land. The sky might dominate the entire painting.

"In der Fremde" (In a Foreign Land), the eighth song of the Liederkreis cycle, is virtually a repeat of the melody of "In the Castle," only performed uptempo.

Baldwin: The grace note figure in No. 8 is interesting. There's several ways you can do it. Here I keep it very even. It would sound too baroque for me if that grace note were too short.

The last lines reveal a surprise that the woman is long dead.

Baldwin: Yes, there is this surprise ending, the surprise ending that comes quite often in these Eichendorff poems. All of a sudden—"und ist doch so lange tot" (she is dead). Again, you see it is *zart*—tender—and secretive. It's a secretive cycle, indeed. Doesn't take a great voice, but it takes a singer with great vision.

The ninth song, "Wehmut" (Melancholy), is about nightingales singing the poet's song. It recalls the verdant tree-scapes of Friedrich.

Ameling: And then you get to "Wehmut," which is maybe the most heartfelt song, I would say—"Ich kann wohl manchmal singen / Als ob ich fröhlich sei." Here again, "lachen und weinen" combined. What a beautiful melody to that song, "Wehmut."

Baldwin: "Wehmut" is, I think, one of the most romantic songs that's ever been written. One of the most difficult to bring across, because you cannot cheat—you have to feel it deeply. Otherwise, the audience will know. There is music you can cheat in, and you can create an effect, but not in "Wehmut"; it's one hundred percent interior.

The tenth song, "Zwielicht" (Twilight), is one of the most sinister mood pieces in the romantic song literature, reminding us of the misty, darkling twilights of so many Friedrich landscapes.

Hallmark: Zwielicht means "twilight," and the poem says that this is a mysterious, even frightening, foreboding time of night. There are four stanzas in this poem. We have a long prelude of almost a baroque counterpoint—one voice, the melody starts, another one comes in, and then a third and a fourth join in. Then the voice enters. The second stanza says, "If there's one deer in the forest that you favor, don't let it go grazing alone at this time of night, because there are hunters in the forest with their guns and they are wandering everywhere. The third stanza says, "If you have a friend here on earth, don't trust that friend at this hour. He will look friendly with his mouth and his eyes, but he's thinking war with his deceptive peace." And then we come to the fourth stanza. Everything that's been hinted at harmonically in the counterpoint, and what's been hinted at in the text, now becomes explicit. . . . The poet finally comes to the clincher—just beware! many things disappear in the night—*beware!*

Ameling: "Dämm'rung will die Flügel spreiten, / schaurig rühren sich die Bäume"—This is a misty scene. There I feel almost a place and an atmosphere. I see the woods, of course, where they wander around. And the misty scene of that, yes. "Stimmen hin und wieder wandern . . . Hüte dich, sei wach und munter!"—"Be on your guard!" For what?—it is not told to us. For anything, anything that can happen to you. It has not the necessity to be told to us. It's not romantic to give every particular. It's unreal.

Baldwin: This is a problematic song, No. 10, "Zwielicht." Because of the ambiguity of the music and of the poem. It's shifting all the time between trust and doubt, light and darkness, and the darkness in your soul, too . . . And of course, there's a menace, there's a threat at the end ("sei wach und munter") in these chords—even though you might consider they're still *piano,* because there are no other dynamic marks in the whole song—have to have a bite to them.

Hallmark: And the voice ends with a recitative. This is a wonderful instance of closing a poem, a song, with a musical understatement. By *not* letting the music express or be a vent for the emotion, Schumann throws it all on the listener. The voice drops down to very low ranges for a tenor singing the cycle.

And then the mood brightens with the penultimate song, "Im Walde" (In the Forest).

Baldwin: And then the sun shines again—"Im Walde," back to the German woods and the little image of the marriage in the distance, a much happier marriage than in *Dichterliebe* ("Das ist ein Flöten und Geigen, Trompeten")— which is a bitter experience for the singer. Here, it's a happy experience.

But, as happens so often in the Liederkreis cycle, the mood of this song abruptly darkens.

Ameling: Yes, "Im Walde"—nothing here is outspoken; it halts all the time. It doesn't run, like Schubert's "Der Musensohn," from beginning to end, where everything is clear. No, here this is much more hidden, yes? "Und mich schauert's im Herzensgrunde"—this kind of shiver of the heart, huh? Yes, this is about all things that may happen.

Baldwin: And then, of course, you finish with this beautiful explosion of spring and love intertwined.

The crowning glory of the Op. 39 Liederkreis is the last song, "Frühlingsnacht" (Spring Night). It realizes the ongoing theme of transcendence achieved through man's union with nature. It recalls many of Friedrich's paintings of copses of trees crowned by starry skies.

Ameling: Yes, a shimmer of light and rustling, yes. Happy. Happy. We transpose that song up. Honestly. Because in the original key for me as a soprano and for many tenors, too, it's a bit low, and you have to have a nice ending (hums). So you want to have it higher . . . It's quite *jauchzen*—jubilant, I think.

Baldwin: It's a lovely closer to this cycle, which, as I say, doesn't have a great deal of unity, apparent unity. But the unity comes, I find, through the woods, through nature, and through the sparseness of the writing. Almost all of them are two-page songs, like the Wolf *Italian Songbook,* but of the highest, highest quality. There isn't one note too much.

Ferris: One of the things that I find quite powerful about "Frühlingsnacht," for example, is that here is one who ultimately is singing about love, and yet throughout this poem this person, this narrator, is clearly alone. There's no other person there. The poem ends with the proclamation "Sie ist dein," "She is yours, she is yours." But he is just imagining that all of nature around him is speaking this, or maybe perhaps singing this. It's a moment of convergence with nature, in which nature is speaking of what he is feeling and hoping for within him. And if you look throughout the cycle, you find this is the case. Even when there is a reference to love, it's always solitary.

HEINE AND *DICHTERLIEBE,* OP. 48

Oh, land of rapture, I long to come to you, for I see you clearly. Alas, it is all a dream. It dissolves like foam with the morning sun."

—Heinrich Heine, "Aus alten Märchen"

EDITOR'S NOTE

Another product of Schumann's "Song Year," the *Dichterliebe*, Op. 48, from Heinrich Heine's "Lyrisches Intermezzo" in the *Buch der Lieder*, was composed during the last week of May 1840. The poet recalls the love that bloomed in the month of May, but that it resulted only in his frustration, defeat, and final resignation. Both poetry and song are demonstrative of the so-called romantic irony/agony.

Roger Cook

Around 1826 Heine published the *Buch der Lieder*. It was not until the 1830s, and in part because of the musical settings that romantic composers gave to his songs, that the *Buch der Lieder* eventually became a famous book. The *Buch der Lieder* is really a collection of poems that were written over a span of about ten years, from 1817 through the 1820s. They were in iambic verse, four lines to a stanza, with short, usually two, three, maybe four stanzas. Many of the ones Schumann set to music were mostly those shorter ones. There's a lot of play with words and rhyme schemes, and they display a very keen sense of sound. In the preface to the second edition years later, he seemed almost apologetic about having bared his romantic soul in verse. By that time, in the late 1830s, he was back writing very politically oriented prose. He said that those poems were poems of his youth and would almost would be better read in browned, crumbling paper with dried flowers pressed between the pages. But he never could be totally cynical, and he retained an obvious ambivalence toward them. Still later in his life, he began to appreciate more the kind of moments of fullness that he thought romantic poetry caught, as opposed to the larger, more politically historical view of seeing yourself always working toward a future. At the same time, there's this aloofness about it all. It's like he's laughing at his own vulnerability, even while he writes about it. And yet he can still relish the passion of being caught up in those romantic moments. For me, the essence of Heine's poems is the idea behind unrequited love. It's not simply unrequited love and the pain that it causes, but that love itself, or a kind of passionate romantic love, contains as much sorrow as bliss. Many of the poems in the *Dichterliebe* cycle bring out that point. Even when love seems successful and happy, the pain and sorrow always wins out in the end.

Schumann's selection of Heine's poems in *Dichterliebe*, for example, is particularly oriented toward those songs that express the pain of love, but without the overriding critique of love.

The poems Schumann selects for *Dichterliebe* are from Heine's *Buch der Lieder*. These early poems, for Heine, were just like so many coffins. The idea in part is that the poet is killing himself by indulging his romantic feelings, by being caught up in the passion of writing love poetry. It is the poet building a coffin for his own heart, his soul, himself. In Schumann's other Heine cycle, *Liederkreis,* Op. 24, we found this in "Lieb' Liebchen leg's Händchen," or "Sweetheart, lay your hand on my heart," where there's a connection between love and death. In that poem, the beating of the heart becomes the carpenter who is inside his breast, making a coffin to bury him, his love, and his pain. Now, in the *Dichterliebe,* we find "Die alten bösen Lieder" ("The wicked old songs"), another good example of that. It is the last poem in Schumann's cycle. It begins with "Build me a huge coffin, because I'm going to place all my songs and my dreams in it." And of course those songs, those dreams, are the romantic passions and feelings. And then the final stanza of the poem says, "And [the coffin] has to be so big, because I'm going to put into it my love and my sorrow." So, the idea is yes, on the one hand, we're playing in the aesthetic world of poetry, words and verse. Yet at the same time, it's real, the pain is real, the pain that we create by becoming involved in that world is as real as any aspect of life. Even in a song like "Ich grolle nicht" (I Will Not Complain), when love is most blissful, in the moments where everything seems to be perfect, the bitterness and the sorrow break through. This is very typical Heine, something that's not so explicit in other romantic writers. The poet says, "And yet, when you say, 'I love you,' then I have to cry most bitterly." It's the ultimate truth that love will always end in pain.

For Heine it's not only the romantic poet who's suffering, but the woman who is also caught up in love. We know her pain, her sorrow, her torment. There are two kinds of women that appear frequently in his love poetry—the malicious woman who is leading the poor poet on and makes him suffer; and the one that becomes as involved in love as the poet himself. "Ich grolle nicht" is an example of that.

"Ein Jungling liebt ein Mädchen" (A Youth Loves a Maiden) is a rather unusual variation on this theme, because of the light, jaunty, capricious tone in the first two stanzas. It moves from one broken relationship to another until, in the final stanza, the poet says, "It's an old story." Here, in the last two lines is the actual pain—"but the one that it's happened to, his heart will break in two." It's interesting the way Schumann works with it—he has the jaunty music in the first two stanzas, it becomes darker in the third stanza, as one might expect, and then the music ends after the song goes back to the jaunty nature. And that is very in keeping with the Heine—that even after the dark realization of the worst kind of pain, there's nothing else we can do but realize that, after all, it's an old story . . .

We touch ground zero with "Ich hab im Traum geweinet," or, "I wept in my dream." He's dreaming and crying in his dream. The pain, somehow, is not real. But then, even when he wakes up, he's still crying. That's the kind of hard, brutal reality of the poem. As long as we are in the dream world, Schumann keeps the accompanying voice and piano separate throughout the first two stanzas. But then, when he wakes up, Schumann brings the music and voice together.

Many of these poems personify nature. Here is the romantic idiom where birds sing and flowers speak. This is where Heine pushes the romantic discourse to its limits, at least for him. As you read the poem, there's an ironic tone to it—nothing explicit, but an ironic tone that you can *feel*, even before its final twist. Whereas his belief in the pain and sorrow and the real intensity of romantic feeling is certainly genuine, I don't think he ever really felt quite at home with it. Instead, he uses this device almost as if he were making fun of it. That's one of his real geniuses, that he could combine the ironic parody with feeling that was intense and genuine at the same time. For example, "Im wunderschönen Monat Mai," or "The Lovely Month of May," is considered by many to be a perfect romantic song or poem. Eight simple verses, two stanzas, one of the verses repeated. But it's so beautiful in its simple, idiomatic description of nature. Yet every word, every tone falls so perfectly in place. Schumann's setting perfectly exemplifies that. There's nothing else to do with this poem. It's been set by many different composers. The ending doesn't have any flourish of finality to it; it's just what the poem itself is—a perfect piece that stands on its own.

One of the great dream poems is one that was ultimately left out of the published version of *Dicthterliebe*. In the first stanza of "Mein Wagen rollet langsam," or "My Carriage Rolls Slowly," the poet is sitting in a horse-drawn carriage, or wagon, on a journey. He begins to dream of his beloved, but immediately—and here is one of those strange moments in Heine that leaves you questioning—three shadowy figures appear; they smile, nod, and hop and make faces (almost as if they're making fun). Then they suddenly twirl and whirl in the fog, make a little kind of noise, a giggling, and they're gone. Schumann plays with this very well. He gives a sense of them dancing playfully, but there's that little bit of ominous feeling we sense about it all—particularly in that they appear only when he is thinking about his beloved. "Ich sitze und sinne and träume," he says—"I'm sitting and thinking and dreaming"—and we share his state of almost suspended animation.

And so we come to the penultimate song, "Aus alten Märchen winkt es," or "From the Old Fairytales." Heine and Schumann paint in words and music a magical land, a fantasy world where everything is wonderful and beautiful and strange and full of intrigue. It's an illusion he sees often in his dream, but when the morning sun comes, it dissipates into nothing but idle foam. Curiously, his most famous poem, "Die Lorelei," plays with this idea, as well. Both are in some ways statements about Germany itself. At least, they've been seen this way. The magical world of Märchen, or fairy tales, is something that is leading Germany astray. You get lost in this world of the imagination and fantasy—but then you crash to the rocks. Heine certainly saw the Germans as a kind of sleepy, dreamy people lost in the highest forms of romantic poetry—but it is a dangerous tendency.

I think, overall, Schumann does indeed do justice to Heine. I think he captures musically the essence of what Heine is getting at, even if he fails to address Heine's overriding philosophical or cultural view.

Heine and Schumann share a very strange fate. They both fall victim to an illness that to this day has been difficult to diagnose. And they both die within a few months of each other in 1856. The question of Heine's illness is a difficult one. It was a physical illness, but there were no signs of mental problems that might have affected it or might have made it worse. Despite a long period of excruciating pain and illness, Heine remained mentally very alert, talked about his physical and mental state in very clear ways. He broke down in 1848, but he remained extremely productive in those last eight years. There had been early signs of it back in the 1830s that were somewhat sporadic. And then in the 1840s he began to seek out medical treatment, trying to discover what it was. The symptoms were momentary lapses and momentary partial paralysis, particularly in his face. When the condition worsened in 1848, it became a permanent paralysis of one side of his face. The doctors didn't seem to help. They prescribed morphine and opium, which he did in fact take to help alleviate the pain. He wrote about his horrible fantasies while on opium. He had had suspicions of syphilis. He had had a number of illicit affairs. And there is a late poem in which he speaks of having a sexual affair with a maid who worked in the house. But he never says that explicitly. Due to his partial paralysis, he was virtually confined to his bedroom. He called it his "Matratzengrab," or his "mattress tomb." Yet, as I said, he still continued to write some of his most brilliant poetry and some of the most brilliant writing of his life right up to the end. But some of his themes changed. There was a kind of religious return, although it was by no means a return to some kind of collective, normal religious dogm0a. But the intellectual character, the clarity of his writing, never faltered.

I think it is for me one of the most amazing literary feats that I am familiar with. His wife, Mathilde, attended him. She remained very loyal to him.

Thomas Hampson

I've been working for quite a while on Schumann's *Dichterliebe*. In all of music there are few more vexing questions than why four songs from the original manuscript were omitted in the published first edition in 1844. That publication was significantly different from his original manuscript, what he called his "great Heine cycle," which was composed in a short time, from May 24 to June 1 in 1840. He *never* spoke of it as a "sixteen-song cycle," even two years after its publication. He always talked about the "*twenty*-song cycle." The published version lacked four of those songs, and there were many changes in dynamic markings, tempo and phrase indications, and the vocal tessitura at times was altered. The piano writing was not "prettified" but full of jarring dissonances. Some of the postludes were longer. Thematic material is more connected, song to song.

Now, I'm not saying that the later, altered version was published behind his back. Quite the contrary. I'm not even saying what was published is not legitimate. But it marks a unique event in all his lieder output. No evidence exists of what happened between the original manuscript with engraver's notes on it and the publication four years later of the first edition. The two versions differ so significantly that we are left with a plethora of ambiguous questions. Why the changes? Why did Schumann delete the four songs—if indeed it was he who did it? Now, I'm not saying I've found the answer or reasons for the changes; I'm not even saying there is an answer. I don't know what caused those changes. It's all supposition. But I think that the performance of the original manuscript can be very enlightening with regard to Schumann's relationship with the fabled "irony" of Heinrich Heine.

As I said, the cycle consisted, in its original form in 1840, of "Twenty Songs from the 'Lyrical Intermezzo' from the *Buch der Lieder*," his Op. 29. That manuscript we found in the Berlin *Staatsbibliotek*. It was way ahead of its time. Way ahead of its time in terms of vocal writing. When some of them were published later, they were changed and evened out and included in his Op. 142 and Op. 127. All of those four songs consistently evoked a dreamlike world, which provides an internal consistency among them. But that kind of vocal writing just had not existed in 1840. And I'm sure somebody said, "You can't write for the voice like that—that's a violin rhythm, that's a piano rhythm, but it's not a voice rhythm." And a syncopated articulation of a German romantic text in undulating 6/8 time did not exist in the vocal repertoire. I find that very exciting.

Singer Thomas Hampson has researched and recorded the original version of Schumann's *Dichterliebe*.

We know from the sketches in Zwickau, and from the letters also, that only two songs in the whole cycle were composed first at the piano, *for* the piano. Those are "Das ist ein Flöten und Geigen" and the "Aus alten Märchen." In looking at the published version, I could not understand why some of the songs had specific indications of tempo and dynamic markings throughout the song, yet other songs seemed to leave it up to the performer—sort of a "Do what you can with it!" But when I went back to have a look at the manuscript, *all* the songs had interpretive markings.

But five or six songs in the published first edition did not. And, of course, four songs were missing. Were they removed to clarify the cyclic unity? It's been assumed that Schumann did that himself. But there is no musical, autobiographical, or historical evidence anywhere that supports that conclusion. As far as I can determine, the exclusion of those four songs in no way improved the cyclic unity. I recall that after his death it was Clara who said that the first edition of Robert's works were the final word, not the manuscripts. She was very adamant about that. She even threatened to sue Johannes Brahms if he persisted studying Schumann's works from their original manuscripts rather than from their first published editions.

The order of songs as I see it now is: the first four songs from the published version; then I insert two of the removed songs, "Dein Angesicht" and "Lehn deine Wang" (a passionate song of intense beauty); and right after that we go back to the published version with "Ich will meine Seele tauchen"; then, later in the cycle, after "Am leuchtenden Sommermorgen" comes the other two removed songs, "Es leuchtet meine Liebe," which is a fantastic song—so far ahead of its time it's frightening (you think you're listening to Hugo Wolf)—and "Mein Wagen rollet langsam"; and then you go to the end of the cycle.

We looked into Rufus Hallmark's research material, of course, and went right back to the first editions of any writings on the Schumann songs. I think that it's always been a foregone conclusion, right up to Hallmark, that the first published edition is the final word, that Schumann's deletion of the four songs clarified the "story," as he put it, of the cycle. The Norton book and the Hallmark book have always stemmed from that premise. I can't agree with that. It just doesn't make sense. For one thing, when you go back to some early writings about the *Dichterliebe,* you hit on a very important person at the turn of the century named Viktor E. Wolff. In 1914 he actually did an analysis between the manuscript version and the first published edition. He observed that there exists no information in between those two. But he also references a man who worked with the engraver, and from that we know quite clearly that *Dichterliebe* was a title that Schumann came up with late in the day. We know, moreover, that Schumann was paid for twenty songs. We know that even when it was at the publishers [Peters], he was still talking about his *twenty*-song cycle. We know that in 1846 when he was writing about his works and the significant works he had achieved in his life, he was *still* referring to his twenty-song cycle. The specific deletion of the songs is without extant evidence. Wolf categorically said all the changes in the publication were to the detriment of the text. It resulted in a rounding off of speech patterns and the homogenizing of vocal lines to the piano. You have these additions of higher notes to match the piano line. For example, in the vocal line of "Ich grolle nicht," you have a high "A," even though it is completely and utterly contrary to the essence of the poem.

There's a very important consideration here: When you go back to the original setting of these poems, this whole sort of lame argument that he didn't set the irony of Heine's texts falls away. We're talking about very subtle differences, but if you move the ritard a couple of bars, and you take a crescendo out that wasn't there (like "Ich grolle nicht"), and if you put some of those tempo markings in; but more importantly, if you take the actual phrasings of the setting of the German text, as in "Wenn ich in deine Augen," for example, then you see a big difference. When you restore the syncopations in "Am leuchtenden Sommermorgen," you see the same thing: You have a man who by that time in the cycle has split apart in his relationship with nature and reality. He's living in a self-paradoxical psychology. Call it that for want of a better term. What happens is that his conflicted notion of reality and nature, which we know is disturbed, is conveyed in the syncopations. And when he thinks the flowers are talking to him—which is his perceived reality—that's when the rhythm stays even.

Knowing how Schumann's use of dissonance was so abrogated in the first edition bothers me a lot. For instance, when I first did the original version of the first song, "Im wunderschönen Monat Mai," in Boston and New York the critics wrote, "Well, what he did wasn't so ingenious, he just doesn't do the appoggiaturas in the first song." But that first edition just follows the right hand of the piano, which means, of course, there's no dissonance. But if you sing it the way Schumann actually wrote it, and those lines *diverge*, what you have, all of a sudden, is a completely different thought process. The poet is speaking about when "love awoke at the same time as flowers, and I made it clear to my love"—he is already making it clear that fate has denied him this love. Fate is the bad guy in this cycle. It is not the woman. This is not unrequited love. But we in America always assume that there must be an active and passive ingredient to notions like unrequited love, and that's simply not true. It is unrequited because it was *never allowed to be realized;* not because one of them was incompetent or something like that. It was because both of them were caught in separate spheres of their own existence. And that is exactly what Heine was talking about—his leaving of the romantic world and his opening of the modern world through his own poetry. And I think that's very significant. I think Schumann understood that far better than we've given him credit for.

My first performances of the twenty-song cycle were in the fall of 1992, first in Geneva and then in Vienna. It may or not have been a public premiere, but I don't claim that. We performed it in Ann Arbor for public radio. I will not record it before fall of next year. One, I don't have time; two, I won't record it until I'm in a tandem relationship with the publishing of it, so I can coincide the two; and three, I won't record it until we have a copy that is legitimately publishable. I can't tell you yet who my accompanist will be, but he is a master of the repertoire [the recording with Wolfgang Sawallisch at the keyboard was released by EMI in 1997]. When I perform it, I'm not relaxed onstage; I think that would be a very bad thing to be. I'm extremely focused, alert, intent on what I'm trying to do. I'm not concerned about presenting you a Schumann song. I'm concerned about *re-giving* you that song. I'm not nervous about you watching me, because you're not; you're actually participating in the same world that I'm re-creating for you. I don't think it has much to do with Thomas Hampson; I think it has a lot to do with Schumann, or Beethoven, or Rossini, or whoever. That's what is very challenging about a recital, both in its programming, its content, and then bringing it to life, both for the public and for the performers. You transcend different thoughts and worlds. That's what fascinates me the most. It's like a picture gallery, like going to an exhibition. And I'm just hanging different pictures on the wall for you for a couple of hours.

Do you know that for me—not just Schumann, but composers in general and works in general—works that just keep grabbing me are the ones that ask questions but don't give answers. I don't mean they're playing tricks with you, or that that they're ignorant. It's more about the asking of questions; it's more about the enormous mirror that they hold up to the human condition and ask you to sort it out yourself. *Don Giovanni,* for me, is a flawed work, but it's the flaws that make it universally accessible. Every performance begs the opportunity to do another performance or re-creation of it, to ask the question in a different context. I feel the same way about a great deal of Schumann's work. You feel that he is a man struggling to articulate, "Why?" Why life, why this context, why not the other context, why not—why the incongruities all around us? I think Schumann's unraveling musically and psychologically is more significant than his syphilis.

He tries in so many ways to inscribe his feelings in his scores. He does that at the end of another *Dichterliebe* song, "Flöten und Geigen." He writes in parentheses, "Vivat hoch!" Now, who's supposed to say that? It's wonderful! Can you imagine anything more damning as a composer than having to express your thoughts in a notational system like we have in Western music? I mean, we're talking about any composer who is grappling with the universals of human expression through music. How close they get comes and goes. They are trying to articulate something that is terribly personal, terribly pertinent to everyone's thought processes. I mean, look at a Mahler. Can you imagine, "Okay, Gustav, we love your mind and we love your thoughts and what a great individual you are with your devils and angels at the same time. But we just have one piece of bad news: You've got to write it in a 4/4 bar!" Can you imagine anything more damning? And I think our responsibility as musicians—and I mean from both camps, the musicological side and the performing side—is to gather together, hand in hand, look at it, and figure out what kind of breath, at what velocity, was going through that 4/4 bar at that time. That's what interests me.

Even when you understand the language there still is a realm of emotional and intellectual association to the song you're hearing, regardless of your understanding. You may know Schumann better than anyone else on the face of the planet, and yet Schumann will take you someplace that is above and beyond Schumann. The whole of a great work of art is infinitely greater than the sum of its parts. And we as musicians have to attend to more than "the trees," as it were; what we're really in the business of is the "forest." Regardless of how much you research and how much you study and how well you know the piece, there has to be in the re-creation of the piece, as much as in the receiving and perceiving of the re-creation of the piece, that moment that transcends any knowledge of the piece. That is very important.

The realm of the unanswerable is infinitely more pertinent, especially today in the music world, than the answerable. I think we've gotten way, way too preoccupied with finding the answers. I think the great masterpieces of music, of which there are infinitely more than we're exposed to today, are the ones that invite people to ask questions about their own existence, their lives and relationships.

SONGS FOR AND ABOUT CHILDREN

EDITOR'S NOTE

As he did for the piano *Album for the Young*, Schumann in his *Liederalbum for the Young*, Op. 79, gave voice to the world of childhood, from innocence to impending maturity. Notable in these songs is the appearance of the mysterious child-woman Mignon, a character in Goethe's *Wilhelm Meister's Apprenticeship*. In his *Liederalbum*, Schumann set Mignon's song, "Kennst du das Land" (Do You Know the Place?), from Book 3, Chapter 4. And in his *Wilhelm Meister Songs*, Op. 98, he set three more of Mignon's songs. The titles convey a sense of the child's anguish and uncertainty—"Nur wer die Sehnsucht kennt" (Only Those Who Have Known Hopeless Love, from Book 4, Chapter 11), "Heiss' mich nicht redden, heiss' mich schweigen" (Bid Me Not Speak, from Book 5, Chapter 16), and "So lasst mich scheinen, bis ich werde" (Let Me Seem to Be an Angel, from Book 8, Chapter 2). Apart from Schubert and Hugo Wolf, who also set many of them, only Schumann forged the Meister songs into a unified cycle. (For more about this fascinating figure in romantic thought, see the chapters on choral music and on romanticism.)

Jörg Demus

I've recorded all the *Song Album for the Young* with Elly Ameling, and it was a delightful experience. Schumann wrote them a year after the *Album for the Young*. He said, "I want to bring the best poets and folksongs suitable for the young, that go from easy and simple to more difficult." Even an amateur singer can do some of the *Volksliedchen* (Little Folksongs), but the last Goethe song, the "Mignon," of course, needs an accomplished singer. It reveals a young adult looking with doubt into the future.

Elly Ameling

I have done lots of Schumann on recordings with Jörg Demus. He plays it so beautifully. You know, Jörg is a hundred percent, all around. If you think of a musicologist, you usually think of someone who is dry, all theory. But Jörg's theory behind the notes is never dry. And that comes because he is a practical man at the piano. He has it all. Absolutely. Like Fischer-Dieskau, you know he knows more about song-singing than anybody else, but not in a dry way. I speak German, and I understand everything of it; and a German person sees a certain word in its context, its touch of color. And Jörg could make that clear to me. And it helped enormously. I must say this was a splendid idea of Philips Records, who asked me for this Op. 79, the *Liederalbum für die Jugend*. The first songs are simple to play. But towards the end of the cycle—the last song, actually, "Mignon's Lied" (Mignon's Song), which is sometimes called "Kennst du das Land?" (Do you know the land?)—he wrote himself, "I finished my cycle of 'youth songs' with—how did he phrase it?—"this child, Mignon, which has so much of the emotions of an adult person. Therefore, I put it here at the end of my cycle." So, he starts with the young kids and ends with the depths of a character, like Mignon. I think I did it for the first time, yes.

Roe-Min Kok

This "Mignon" song, "Kennst du das Land?," is very interesting. After the great success of the *Album for the Young*, the publisher asked Schumann to consider writing a companion album of songs of childhood, a *Song Album for the Young*. And he did so, and you have to admit there's a commercial motivation here. Anyway, at the end of the *Song Album* Mignon appears with her famous song, "Kennst du das Land?" The test comes early in *Wilhelm Meister,* when Mignon is feeling for the first time the rush of mixed emotions of love and sexuality toward Wilhelm. She comes to him and sinks to her knees and tearfully implores him to be her father. It's at that point we hear her song. The harper, who is outside, accompanies it with his harp. Mignon describes a strange land of oranges and lemon blossoms where she and her protector/father must go ("Dahin!"). Mignon is turning her face to the future. It's not a narrative. It's fragmented and wistful. If you talk to singers about it, they'll tell you how difficult it is to sing! (And it's very hard for me to teach it.) We look at it in comparison with earlier settings by Schubert and Beethoven. They really think Mignon is a little girl, after all, and they put more frivolousness and cheerfulness into their versions. But in Schumann there's this hint of a wise yet sad maturity that's just beyond Mignon's reach. I think of the very end of Novalis's *Heinrich von Ofterdingen,* when the child Fabel appears and spins a golden thread out into the future. It's a glorious image.

SONGS BY CLARA SCHUMANN

EDITOR'S NOTE

Among the hundreds of songs transcribed for solo piano by Franz Liszt were a set of ten songs by Robert and Clara Schumann. Clara herself transcribed many songs by her husband.

The Songs

Katherine Ciesinski

Just a year or so after Robert and Clara married, in 1841, Robert Schumann's Op. 37 songs, the *Liebesfrühling,* were published. And in that group of twelve songs he included three of Clara's, which he was very intent on bringing into major publication form. They're based on Friedrich Rückert poems which were very beloved. These are some of her most well-known songs, actually—"Er ist gekommen," "Liebst du um Schönheit," and "Warum willst du an die Fragen." I recorded those three on the Leonardo label, along with four others. One can certainly sense there is a musical relationship going on there. She has certainly the preludes and postludes that reflect the same form of lieder composition that Robert was involved in through his whole life. And there was a very beautiful harmonic language that she developed—actually more in many ways. They were more daring songs than his, because she dared to put little extra incidentals, accidental notes that I think Robert would have refined out of his final product. So in a sense you're seeing a more rudimentary—but not rudimentary in the sense of its power—but formative kind of musical language that Clara used; and that makes her songs very interesting, because they're not so predictable. Robert Schumann's music is well known and well beloved, and so it's always wonderful to hear the other side of the coin, so to speak.

Nancy B. Reich

While I was in the East Berlin Music Library, I found a *Liederheft,* a collection of Clara Schumann's songs. These songs were written down in her own hand but were obviously written at Robert's request. He had written the title page and had urged her through some entries in their joint marriage diary to do this, to put everything down. She was very careless about keeping her own compositions. So Robert had written everything out—the table of contents, too, is in his hand. They were all her songs. There was Op. 12, Op. 13, and Op. 23. She didn't feel, I don't think, that her things were worth keeping. They probably would have been lost if he hadn't brought them all together. She had doubts about her composing but none about her performing.

Piano Transcriptions

Jonathan Kregor

I have tried to track down the manuscripts of as many of Liszt's transcriptions of songs as I could. In 1872 Liszt published a set of *Ten Lieder by Robert and Clara Schumann*—seven by Robert and three by Clara. This is long after Robert is dead and long after he had any contact with Clara. Most of Robert's were from the Op. 79 *Song Album for the Young,* and Clara's were from her early songs. Liszt published separately at other times several more of Robert's songs, including the famous concert versions of "Spring Night" and "Widmung." There are several versions of "Widmung," which seem to have been created for different levels of piano proficiency—some that embellish them and some that tamp down the filigree. The manuscripts I have seen reveal that Liszt did them in a short period of time and made few corrections in them. In my opinion, they don't exhibit the flair and insight we might expect from Liszt as an interpreter of songs, such as he did in the Schubert transcriptions. This is the same period when Clara is arranging some of Robert's songs and is even playing some of Liszt's transcriptions. Unfortunately, there has been little work done comparing the versions of Robert's songs by both Liszt and Clara. I only know of one study, which is by a German scholar named Stefan Bromen, and it's from a German dissertation.

Clara's own collection of her husband's transcriptions, called *Thirty Melodies,* was published in Paris. They were adapted for solo piano, but the vocal line is indicated by the use of notes larger than the other notes. This is very helpful when the melody is buried in the accompaniment, which is often the case with Schumann. The song titles don't quite correlate to the original German titles. This leads me to think there's some sort of disconnect in how the French view him as a songwriter and how the Germans viewed him. It's possible that the texts in the French translated versions are not exactly like the texts in the German versions. I think there were "stock" poets who instead provided the requisite lyrics. That might have been the motivation for Clara to arrange them, i.e., to preempt any further mismanagement of Schumann's music in France. This is unclear.

The copyright issue is interesting. There is copyright as late as the 1820s in some countries. But Liszt is not paying royalties to anyone. He would get an upfront fee from his publisher, and that would be it. But nothing would be paid to Clara or Robert. I know nothing of any objections by composers or demands for payment from Liszt. There's no ASCAP at the time! Things change completely by the early twentieth century, when even an aleatoric piece like John Cage's 4′33″ would be covered by copyright.

8

"A Call to Awaken"

The Schumann Symphonies

Commentators: Marin Alsop, Christoph von Dohnányi, Lukas Foss, Margaret Hillis, D. Kern Holoman, Katherine Kolb, Erich Leinsdorf, Susan McClary, Peter F. Ostwald, Leon Plantinga, Wolfgang Sawallisch, and David Zinman

> *I believe it would be best if he composed for orchestra; his imagination cannot expand sufficiently on the keyboard. . . . May I succeed in persuading him to enter it.*
> —Clara Wieck, 1839

> *Now, many sleepless nights are followed by exhaustion; what is happening to me is what might happen to a young woman who has just been delivered of a child—so light, so happy, and yet ill and weak.*
> —Robert Schumann, January 1841 (on the completion of his First Symphony)

EDITOR'S NOTE

Robert Schumann's first essay in symphonic form came as early as 1831–32, when he wrote two movements of a G-Minor Symphony (sometimes subtitled "Zwickauer"). Eight years later, shortly after his marriage to Clara, he turned again to symphonic writing, composing the "Spring" Symphony in January 1841 and the *Overture, Scherzo, and Finale* a few months later. The Second Symphony was written in December 1845; the Third Symphony ("Rhenish") in September 1850; and the Fourth Symphony in December 1851 (revised from a version written earlier in 1841). They constitute the most important body of symphonies between Beethoven and Tchaikovsky. At the same time, as discussed here, they reflect the status of the orchestral forces available to the composer at the time, particularly at the Leipzig Gewandhaus.

Since Schumann's death in 1856, many composers and conductors have considered "retouching" his orchestrations. A few thought about it and then rejected the idea (Anton Rubinstein and Edward Elgar), and others did indeed issue their own versions (Gustav Mahler, Max Reger, George Szell, and Felix Weingartner). Alexander Glazunov and Frederick Stock rescored the Third Symphony. Other conductors, notably Leonard Bernstein and Marin Alsop, have preferred to retain the original instrumentations.

EVOLUTION OF THE ROMANTIC SYMPHONY ORCHESTRA

Leon Plantinga

We wonder about how the orchestras in Schumann's day actually sounded. We have always assumed that we know how nineteenth-century music and performance goes. That's because we have assumed there is a kind of continuous tradition that goes from Schumann and Berlioz to us. But we're more and more finding out that that's not the case. The kinds of performance traditions that we have inherited have basically been *late* nineteenth-century traditions and late nineteenth-century instruments. Those presumptions we have had—the use of metal strings, violin technique with the elbow held high and lots of vibrato, the need to bring a sound powerful enough to fill large halls—well, we're more and more revising that. The remarkable recordings by Roger Norrington of the Beethoven symphonies are revelations. You hear what the tympani was like—the effect of hitting a tabletop with a hard stick, a *crack!*, an explosive sound—which is very different from our sort of mellow and velvety tympani sound. We get new insights into the sounds that Berlioz and Schumann had in their heads.

D. Kern Holoman

The Leipzig Gewandhaus concerts in Schumann's time share with the Paris concerts the fact that they weren't closely associated with princely court orchestras and patronage. One of the interesting things about the nineteenth century is suddenly you have performing groups that redefine the tradition of what an orchestra is about in a variety of ways. In Leipzig a lot of things were going on that were similar to ways of thought in Paris, in Russia, and certainly in London (and for all I know, in Berlin and Vienna, as well). One of them is certainly the interest in the modern repertoire. Very quickly the Gewandhaus Orchestra, as in Paris, becomes very republican, very progressive, very experimental, very willing to bring musicians up from Dresden, very willing, as I understand it, to play whatever the conductor, like Mendelssohn, has written next. I think the dawn of conservatories in that period has a good deal to say about advancing orchestral techniques, which in turn has a deal to say about the ability of players to play the kinds of music that was being written.

Katherine Kolb

What we consider to be the classical orchestra nowadays was essentially formed in Europe in the 1830s and 1840s. The Beethoven orchestra really came more out of Paris and the Paris Conservatory than anywhere else. The players performed Beethoven without rival for at least ten years and maybe more. When Wagner came to Paris in 1839, it was the first time he had ever heard such an orchestra. The German orchestras also were becoming virtuoso orchestras at that time. The Gewandhaus Orchestra, far from having the size and brilliance of the Paris Conservatory Orchestra, nevertheless was in fact much more our kind of orchestra, because it was a permanent orchestra chiefly for symphonic music. It was trained to perfection. Ferdinand David, Mendelssohn, and Schumann were there. Berlioz was vastly impressed that they could play his music after only a few rehearsals. His *Treatise on Instrumentation and Orchestration* was published as a series of articles in the *Gazette musicale* in Paris. Never before this had there been such a full-scale treatment of the different instrumental groups within the orchestra. With Berlioz you have a wide range of different possibilities for each instrument. No instrument has just one given character. For Berlioz, it's all open; it can be many, many different things for each one. It's like what de Tocqueville said of American democracy—everyone can come together.

THE SCHUMANN SYMPHONIES

Susan McClary

There are very interesting ambivalences that run very strongly through Schumann's symphonies. He combines in them aspects of the "masculine" and "feminine." He is trying to create a fusion between the genres that he's very comfortable with—those which are fantasy-oriented and those which are larger-scale formal works. Listen to the Fourth Symphony and you feel a very interesting tension between the very forceful music in the outer movements and the very tender, lyrical romance that appears in the second movement. And that seems to me the strength in Schumann's symphonic output: as a creator one hears the same kinds of tensions you find in his critical writing, namely, this "masculine" attraction to the rational, the formal, the structural, forceful—but yet the refusal to give up on the "feminine" imagination, fantasy, and romance.

Peter F. Ostwald

For Schumann, the problem of how to make a living really arose in Dresden. When he was in Leipzig, he had been able to make ends meet with his newspaper and a legacy from the family that he always relied on. It was not until the move to Dresden that his interest in composing the larger forms required of a great composer at that time led to an interest in conducting. That was partly through his friendship with Ferdinand Hiller, and together they organized concerts. I don't believe he ever made much money from conducting. Even the job he later accepted in Düsseldorf was not a well-paying job. In fact, if you compare the salary with what Liszt was making in Weimar or with what Wagner was making in Dresden, what Schumann made was not at all impressive.

At any rate, he was not only conducting and hearing his own works, but those of his friends. He had a chance there to try out his own works; and he rewrote his D-Minor Symphony while in Düsseldorf (the two versions were quite different). He was very supportive of Niels Gade and Mendelssohn, much to the dismay of people in Düsseldorf who wanted to hear more French music, more Wagner and Liszt.

Most of the orchestras at that time were smaller than what we're used to today. But that orchestra in Düsseldorf was one that had to be complemented by amateurs. Let me put it this way: There were people that played in that orchestra who were not regular orchestra members, who were borrowed from the military band and from the dance orchestras of the city. Who was available at any given time was often a matter of chance. One reason why Schumann did so much doubling of the instruments was that he wanted to be sure that someone was available to play a particular voice. If the flutist was absent that particular day, there might be a violinist who would play.

I don't like Mahler's reorchestrations. They don't sound like Schumann to me. He likes to give melodies to instruments that Schumann hadn't intended, and it gives a richer, more Mahlerian kind of sound to it. But I have to admit I happen to be not that great a fan of Mahler. It even bothers me when I hear Schumann sounding like Mahler! I think Schumann has a very distinctive quality, and when a fine conductor takes on a Schumann symphony, he should be able to bring that out even if there's doubling.

There's so much here that is of a very high quality. Take the opening of the "Rhenish" Symphony. This is an absolutely incredible work in all respects—rhythmically, melodically, the way it's orchestrated. No apologies needed anywhere. The most problematic of the symphonies is, I think, the Second in C Major. He was, in fact, very severely ill when he worked on that symphony. And he noticed that himself. I've discussed this with Kurt Masur, and he points out that he really didn't know how to deal with these very lugubrious kind of chromatic events in the opening of the Second Symphony, until he understood what Schumann was experiencing. Then suddenly it made sense to him, and that helped him in shaping an interpretation of it. A really magnificent and altogether perfect movement is the great Adagio, one of the most profound music compositions ever written. But if it's done too fast, it doesn't work. A lot depends on the conductor of the orchestra.

Erich Leinsdorf

Beethoven cast a shadow over the entire century of composers who followed him. And his shadow is still with us, although the form of the symphony has undoubtedly run out of gas. I'm sure that writing a symphony was almost "de rigueur" for the romantic composers. However, I don't think the symphony was Schumann's métier. But he wrote four masterpieces, all of which have this combination of melos and harmony, along with an inner warmth that ranges from elation to the tenderest feelings. One particular difficulty he had was scoring for the string instruments in the tutti orchestra. When he writes for chamber music, it is totally different. When you look at his string writing, you always see that he writes as if for the piano. It is a fact. It is not idiomatic.

By contrast, his friend Mendelssohn was a different type. He was absolutely perfect and was always on the surface of things. Schumann was never perfect and always delving deeper into things. His sense of form is unusual for the time. His symphonies, like the Third, were free in their formal structure, and its fourth movement was considered inappropriate, because polyphony was not a typical thing in symphonies, notwithstanding Mozart's finale to the "Jupiter" Symphony. The critique of Schumann's Third was entirely against that fourth movement.

I would say that Schumann's orchestra ranged from between forty-five to forty-nine players, depending upon if you have trombones or not. In all the thirty-seven movements of Beethoven's nine symphonies, he uses trombones in only five movements. So in thirty-two of the thirty-seven movements there are no trombones. By contrast, Schumann used trombones in all his symphonies.

He was writing for the Gewandhaus Orchestra. Now, it is my impression from later correspondence about the Meiningen Orchestra, between Hans von Bülow and the young Richard Strauss, that we can easily calculate that these orchestras averaged eight woodwinds, four horns, two trumpets. If you go to forty-five players, that would mean thirty strings, which today is less than the first and second violin section of a major symphony orchestra. These orchestras were mostly opera orchestras. There were not so many concert orchestras in those days. The symphony concert was only an occasional event, compared to the opera, which was a nightly event in the season. I have very little doubt that the orchestras Schumann knew were not very good. On the other hand, very soon thereafter, Wagner came along with his enormous demands, which seem to have been fulfilled. So we must conclude that the orchestras were capable of better things. It must have been a misfortune for Schumann to be working in the one locality where the orchestra members can barely live. He has to orchestrate according to those limitations.

Did you know that Gustav Mahler altered some of the orchestrations? He made a few changes which I think were unnecessary. For example, in the opening to the "Spring" Symphony, Mahler utilizes the chromatic horn, which has notes which Schumann did not have. Schumann's compositions don't need changes in voice leading or harmony. It's the same kind of error like that made by Rimsky with changing Mussorgsky's *Boris Godunov.* Mahler interchanged very often the oboes and clarinets, and he put the clarinets in the higher octave and the oboes in the lower octave, which of course produces a totally different sonority. I have no doubt Schumann did not want that. But the decision has to be made—do you want Schumann to sound, or not to sound? By all means, I think they should be edited in order to *sound* as well as they can sound. Don't forget, our orchestras are different, our halls are different, our ears are different. And I'm sure that if Schumann had had better instruments at his disposal, with more technical knowledge of the balances of the modern orchestra, he would have orchestrated differently.

By contrast, Leonard Bernstein insists that he plays Schumann in the original orchestrations. Personally, I don't think you can play Schumann in the originals without making some changes, certainly in the dynamics. Let me cite, for instance, when we speak of editing, the second movement of the First Symphony, that beautiful 3/8, which has that very gorgeous melody. It is carried the first time by the first violins in octaves. I don't like violins in octaves. The first violins in octaves weakens the carrying power, because half of them carry the lower octave and half play the higher octave. So what I do in my editing is let all the first violins play the upper octave and the solo cello play the lower octave. They are the same notes. Schumann has always had a great penchant for the solo cello. So I felt I was justified in using a cello part there. I have also written that Schumann uses in his writing baroque rhythmic notations. The dotted eighth plus sixteenths can equal a triplet configuration. And this is the case in the Fourth Symphony, where literal-minded conductors take this literally, and it is awkward to hear. Speaking of the Fourth, of the two versions I think, like Brahms, that the first version is the superior. It is much lighter in texture. It was actually an early work from 1841 and rewritten ten years later as his Fourth.

Schumann was criticized by contemporary critics for writing five movements for the "Rhenish" Symphony. The only five-movement symphony I can recall up to that time had been the Beethoven "Pastoral," with the extra movement, the "Thunderstorm." The traditional scherzo of the Beethovenian model is missing, replaced instead by the third movement, which is more or less an intermezzo. And then the fourth movement is an unusual chorale-like work with an almost baroque polyphony.

Christoph von Dohnányi

I have recorded the Schumann symphonies for London Records. We started with the First and Second symphonies in 1987. I am glad I was not forced to record them too early in my career. Sometimes I pity for some of my much younger colleagues who are being pressured by some recording companies to record them before they have had a chance to perform them at different times with different orchestras. For the Second Symphony, for example, I have already done it a lot, and lately we have played it on tour. I think there is not a single main orchestra that I haven't done this piece with, from the Vienna Philharmonic, to Berlin, to Warsaw, you know? And since it's such a great work, this adds to the possibilities for interpretation. There are some works, if you do them too much, too many times, you begin to realize the music is not so great. But the Schumann symphonies become greater and greater the more you do them.

Last summer in London as preparation I did a lot of reading by and about Schumann, and about how his symphonies have been interpreted. And I got hold of Peter Ostwald's biography, which I can tell you made me very jittery, because the pain of the composer was so real to me. I knew I would have to come to terms with the versions by my predecessor, Dr. George Szell, which have many retouchings and changes. And when I returned to Cleveland, I decided to use fresh parts, without the markings that Dr. Szell had made. And although the players already know this music well, we worked as if we had never heard it before. We questioned everything.

Our procedure is that after we have played the piece in concerts and on tour, then we are ready for the recording people. Then we record it in one three-hour session. I listen to the playback. Then I do some inserts as I think they are needed. And then I play it a second time. Because of the compact disc technology, we can do this more quickly than in earlier days. But we all have to be very brave and disciplined due to the lack of time available. This may be one of the first complete sets recorded entirely on compact disc [London Records, 1988–89]. That's something I'm not so informed about. I'm so much a "live" musician, I'm not really interested in that too much, you know? For me, recording is something I love mostly because it shows me where I am standing with the music, what I could do better. I learn a lot. I listen to a lot of recordings by others, but if I can get a hold of somebody directly, I'd rather listen to him "live" than in a recording.

About 35 percent of the players under me were here under Dr. Szell, including our concertmaster, Daniel Majeske. But that is not a problem for them working with me. No, this orchestra is much too good not to like "new adventures." They like a different approach. And they are very self-confident, and they know how good they are. They keep their personality yet are willing to work with me.

My predecessor at the Cleveland Orchestra, Dr. George Szell, did not trust Schumann's orchestrations very much. This had already been a traditional attitude. Even Brahms was suspected of not being able to orchestrate. People thought Bruckner couldn't orchestrate! But now, people like Stockhausen, Ligeti, all these people would be unthinkable without Bruckner. Schumann is another one. The Mahler versions are terrible. He like some others just thought they could do better than the composer with their retouchings and changes. He obviously thought that he knew better than others what Schumann wanted, like Richard Wagner did with Beethoven. I mean, these people tried to do the right thing. Dr. Szell did it because he believed in it. His manuscripts are here in the Severance Hall library. Oh, he changed a lot! He really did surgery, you know!

I happen not to believe in this. I think Schumann orchestrated tremendously well. I wouldn't say any of the Schumann symphonies are "muddy," as has been suggested. But I would say you have to shape the dynamics sometimes, as you have to do in Beethoven and so on. There was a time everybody thought that music had to sound "beautiful," know what I mean? You had to produce a "beautiful" and smooth sound, like a von Karajan. But beauty is something for a magazine. It's not for us. A so-called beautiful sound is nothing if it there is not *meaning* behind it. I have the feeling that Schumann insisted the music always serve the *meaning*. And that can mean that the music can sound *difficult*, as if he is trying to overcome difficulties of some kind, even with the instruments he composes for. So be it. I do not hide away from that. And we are there to help him make that clear. I trust Schumann's orchestration. I think he is a great, great composer with his own very special language. And I don't think he needs help in any sense of orchestration. He needs help in the dynamics, and that's all I do. And I change some of the dynamics in balancing so the main things would become a little clearer—the things which seem to me more important.

At the same time, of course, there are problems. He was writing in specific contexts and sometimes for specific orchestras. When Brahms writes about Schumann's orchestra in Düsseldorf, he says Schumann might have done things differently if he had had the Gewandhaus Orchestra. I was just now in Vienna, and because just now I am doing Beethoven's Fourth, I looked up the scores first used for the first performance. In Beethoven's hand everything is doubled, the winds, even the horns and trumpets are doubled. These composers had to be realistic, so they wrote for what they had available. But Schumann was trying to express too much into his music, from politics to religion, to feelings for Clara and later Brahms.

I am on record (so to speak!) as preferring the second version of what has come to be called the Fourth Symphony. I have studied them both very thoroughly. I never have performed the first version. Schumann himself thought the second version was the best. And if a composer improves something and okays it, I think I should follow him. It's true that Brahms preferred the first one. But I prefer to follow Schumann. There was something like a decade between the two versions. I think the first shows some awkward orchestration, and Schumann knew it himself. The second is much better orchestrated. The last movement generates so much excitement. He makes the string players do a lot of motion, you know, tremolo, thirty-seconds, and whatsoever they can do. Furtwängler reduced this when he performed it. But if you succeed in motivating an orchestra to try it as written, then something very exciting can come out of it. So Schumann wasn't all wrong. If you cannot motivate the orchestra to try to follow this excitement, then you might be stuck. At the same time, I have to admit there are certain things in the Fourth which can hardly be done. Those bass tremolos, those thirty-seconds, are really hard to do. Very hard to do. But you can do it, depending on the tempo. The tempo has to be very flexible.

Many people make a big deal about the fact that certain themes in Schumann reappear in later works by others, particularly Brahms. For example, there are themes in the First Symphony, particularly in the slow movement, that you can hear in the Brahms Third Symphony. I'm fascinated that in earlier days, when a composer used some material from another composer, this was regarded as a compliment. Now, in our day, people say, "For heaven's sake, we've heard this already!" We think everybody has to be outstandingly original. It has to be absolutely new. But if we are really honest, I can play some of the Christian Bach pieces and some of the early Mozart pieces for you, and you might not tell the difference. And how close is the early Beethoven to some of later Haydn? Nobody then would have said, "Oh, he stole this from this." What a ridiculous point of view! Music was in the air, everywhere, for everyone, and it was not a question of theft or anything like that. Perhaps an "homage" is a better way of looking at it.

If Schumann could hear his symphonies performed nowadays, he would be amazed. Because he couldn't even anticipate the kind of sound we have now. I'm absolutely sure of that. And let's face it, our ears are different and our times are different and our instruments are different. One's "ears" in those days, in a way, were much more sensitive, I'm pretty sure. And you would have been impressed by the *mezzo forte* of that time much more than by a *fortissimo* nowadays. But we use our own modern instruments. I absolutely reject the so-called original instruments movement.

Schumann was greatly criticized when he conducted his own symphonies. As a conductor, Schumann fell short where many conductors fall short. The older you get, the more the music is in your head, in your imagination. It was so strong for him that he did not realize what was happening with his players sometimes. That was his fault, and it accounts for what appeared to be a really amateurish way of conducting. He was actually sometimes not even hearing what was being played. Everything was in his mind. And people had to assist him.

David Zinman

I think in Schumann's day everyone was in the shadow of Beethoven and tried to write their version of what they thought Beethoven had done. They were stunned. I think Beethoven was the totally blinding light for them. Everyone was left to try and outdo Beethoven. Certainly you couldn't have a Berlioz or a Schumann or a Schubert or anyone else without Beethoven. So, for some, it was a wonderful opportunity for experimentation. And I think Schumann was a great experimenter not only in his piano music, but also in his orchestral music. At the same time, however, you can see a lot of Mendelssohn in his music.

You know, all of these composers wrote four-hand versions of their symphonies. They were usually performed first in such versions. Robert and Clara would play through a symphony that way. And when Brahms would send a symphony to Clara, she would play it first on the piano. Music was perceived that way. An actual symphonic performance was a real rarity and quite an occasion! People would already know the music through the piano version. That was their version of the gramophone, I guess.

Schumann left behind metronome markings for his symphonies. I went to the library in Utrecht, which has very fine photocopies of all his manuscripts. Some had metronome markings in his own hand and some in other hands. Schumann's balances of instruments work a little better if you don't play them in the Wagnerian style, but in more of a non-sostenuto. Throughout the history of music, composers tended to play others' music in their own style. So when Wagner conducted Beethoven, he did it in the style of his own music. And that's where the sostenuto—the sustained way, the Wagnerian way—of playing Beethoven came in. And it has stuck with us until this very day. The sostenuto idea is to make the phrasing as *long* as possible. In other words, prolong the line as much as possible. And what short phrasing does is make the pulse longer. In other words, if I can explain it to you, if you play the slow movement of the *Eroica* at the traditional Furtwängler tempo, the pulse is one . . . two . . . three . . . four. When Beethoven wrote 2/4 with a metronome mark of something like 82 to the eighth-note, the pulse then would be two. There would be one pulse to each bar. Which is a very slow pulse, actually. It's just that we transcribed the pulse to a larger area. So that the faster you make the music go, the slower the actual pulse is. The more you perceive that actual pulse, the more you see the line. From the time of the baroque period, if you saw a quarter-note, you always played it at half its value. It was just a tradition. Now, Beethoven wants it played at its *full* value. So he starts to write *sostenuto* over the note if he wants it long. Or, if he really wants it not stopped at all, he writes two eighth-notes tied to each other. That tradition wants to be broken, and the composers try to break the tradition in a way of notation and in a way of stylistic playing.

So we're going back to the origins. We're looking at the music from a different angle. We're taking away a lot of the fat and getting more to the essence. And in the tempi you see no really slow tempi, even in Schumann's adagios. They're all around 60 to 66, which are quite moving. His music takes on a different cast when thought about this way. Also, if you play it a little bit lighter, the balances come out better. As for his Fourth Symphony, I chose not to record the original orchestration, although I am fascinated by it. Eventually, I think, more and more conductors might go to that.

I do admit to a bit of retouching for my recordings. Sometimes in Schumann, as in the "Spring" Symphony, some of the instruments can get buried. I try to help that a little bit. Sometimes conductors don't like to step out on a limb and say, "I'm going to do something really weird." But the other day I saw Georg Solti on television talking about the Beethoven Fifth Symphony as though he had just discovered it. He suddenly decided to do the metronome marks—something I had done ten years ago. But now he's doing it. I think everyone will make the decision for themselves. But I feel, for myself, I want to look at music the way I want to look at it and try to answer the question for myself: What if I tried this? What if Beethoven was right in writing this metronome mark? What if Schumann was right in doing this particular dynamic? What would happen if you actually played it *the way it was written,* without any retouchings at all? What if we decided to do the Brahms phrasing the way he actually wrote it? Erich Leinsdorf wrote about this kind of thing. He called it "radical orthodoxy." In other words, in being orthodox, you're being radical. We played the Beethoven Sixth Symphony in Leipzig at the Gewandhaus in this, and they liked it.

Margaret Hillis

As for Schumann's symphonies, he made mistakes in the orchestral writing, like crescendos that come up which should be supported by tympani—but there's no tympani there! And there's what we call "doubling," which means that if the first violins are playing, the flutes and clarinets are playing along with them. You might have lots of instruments on the same line, playing octaves apart. The use of doubling is to stress something. And it is sometimes done for color, like a clarinet can be used to color the viola sound. Doubling is not exactly a "no-no," but its effectiveness depends entirely upon what is needed at any particular moment.

Mahler and George Szell both tinkered with Schumann's orchestrations. I think they both knew what they were doing. But you have to be very, very careful about what you do in order to crawl as much as possible into Schumann's mind. You have to know the score very well and not just do "pretty" things with it.

Marin Alsop

I am fortunate enough to have been with Leonard Bernstein when he was conducting Schumann. Toward the end of Lennie's life, around 1990, I went with him to a music festival in Sapporo, Japan. I conducted Beethoven's Second on the first half of a program, and he did Schumann's Second Symphony on the second half. It was a revelation watching him rehearse and perform the piece. I well remember him asking the violinists to stand up during the Scherzo, as a visual part of the virtuosic music! I don't think Bernstein subscribed to these notions that Schumann's symphonies have weaknesses that need correcting. He had great respect for Schumann, and that's how he approached all of the works that I saw him conduct. You know, he was not terribly shy at reorchestrating or reinforcing or cutting music, if he thought it was needed. But I never observed him taking anything to task in these Schumann symphonies. That has influenced my own views. I never looked at this music as having these weaknesses so many talk about.

I am naturally drawn to the Second Symphony for many reasons, not the least of which is that I had studied it with Bernstein. I remember programming it for my first season as music director at Eugene, Oregon, and later at Long Island and Colorado early in the 1990s. It's difficult to choose one of the symphonies over the other—it's like choosing one of your kids. It's not really fair. In all of them you can hear his special sense of *sound* and his respect for acoustics. He writes in such a way that you have "breathing room" in the music. It's hard to explain, but he hears things a little differently from anyone else. But over the years I have had the most experience with the Second. I love Schumann's ideas of metric modulation and segues and beautiful counterthemes that become anchors of the entire piece. And how he is able to foreshadow the tone poems that are coming; and how he can take the idea of a thematically linked, through-composed piece and at the same time maintain the symphonic form. He seems to have been a composer who both looked backward and forward at the same time in a very distinctive and personal way. True, you find almost obsessive rhythmic repetitions at times, but I don't approach those rigidly at all. The slow movement has a kind of inevitability in its rhythmic underpinnings and phrasings and arrival points. You have to manage the tempi so that it never falls away from that rhythmic purpose. And in the Scherzo there are these unexpected trios that are woven into the larger fabric. They're like clues to a puzzle that you can't quite grasp. I think this sort of thing was a huge influence on Brahms. And there's this sense of celebration in the last movement.

I think that the challenges for a young conductor are similar to those I have faced with Brahms and Mahler. Schumann's music requires maturity—not by age, but by musical experience. The symphonies for me personally gain in depth tremendously every time I do them. I'm always struck by their originality, even their occasional avant-garde qualities. I love all the orchestral music and am a huge advocate of the symphonies. The smallness of the repertoire allows us conductors to go so much more in depth; you can play them all in a weekend.

I do think there are some balance issues. Take the D-Minor Symphony, which he wrote in 1841 and revised later as his Fourth Symphony. You see how he looked back at his work and recognized that some problems needed to be rewritten. At the same time, you can manage those balances if you are doing your job. You can achieve a transparency that is very forward thinking, whereas the later version doesn't quite have that same transparency. Indeed, I personally prefer that earlier version. I may be influenced also by Brahms's advocacy of that version.

I also think the *Overture, Scherzo and Finale* is a wonderful piece. I hope to schedule it in future concerts. It would make a wonderful program opener. I find it charming and so Mendelssohnian and so whimsical. It's a delightful piece and has some fantastic counterpoint in the last movement. So far, I've only done it once, and it really was a hard sell then. I find many orchestras are resistant to Schumann in general. In fact, "resistant" doesn't even begin to describe the reaction to lesser-known works of Schumann! Orchestras are resistant even to the well-known works, as well! So it's very, very challenging. Try and get programmed some of the overtures, like the *Bride of Messina*. You hear from management that he "doesn't sell" and that sort of thing. But that's our goal, to engage our listeners to a one-on-one relationship with composers on a very basic, human level. If you only play a Schumann symphony here and there, and don't give people the wide palette of his compositions and his person, you're doing a disservice to your audience. You don't sneak him in; you have to put a spotlight on his work and on him. I think musicians are not nearly as reluctant as management can be. But often they don't know quite what to make of Schumann. It requires a real passion and commitment from whomever is on the podium. You hear about objections from string players that their arms are falling off from all those sustained tremolos. Well, that's nothing. Try and play the Schubert "Great" Symphony! That's a killer! Or you think of accompanying the Chopin Piano Concerti—you could die. You are on the G-string, holding whole-notes!

I have not yet done any of these symphonies with an orchestra of the original size of the Gewandhaus in Schumann's time. And I've always had reinforced strings. I even watched Bernstein doubling winds, but he had a proclivity to do that in many major pieces. That's not something I ascribe to, myself. I think most of the balance issues fall on the shoulders of the conductor. It's our fault if we can't bring off an effective performance.

You know, these days the pendulum has swung back a little bit to the "reinventing," as it were, or the repackaging of a lot of music. It doesn't sound sacrilegious at all to me to think about constructing suites of musical excerpts, maybe excerpts from unknown works like the *Faust Scenes* or the *Paradise and the Peri*—but to do it in a way that doesn't take away from the music and brings it to a new audience. I love the idea.

Wolfgang Sawallisch

I recorded all four of the Schumann symphonies in Dresden with the Dresden Staatskapelle in 1973. I feel it was a good recording, but I will not do it for a second time. I have to say that sometimes the musicians object to performing this music, generally. For them it is very difficult, because you never have big melodies, like a Tchaikovsky symphony. In the

Schumann there's always a break, and the melody is interrupted, and the second half of a phrase is performed by another group in the orchestra. Nobody knows exactly where are the main points of the orchestration. And this is difficult, because nobody is for sure. So you need a lot of time to explain to the players where the melody goes next and what is the *spirit* of his music.

Everybody says that the Great Dome in Cologne inspired the fourth movement of the "Rhenish" Symphony, and that is probably true. This is very descriptive, with the very long sound and echo effects, all those short entrances, one group after another—the first violins, the second violins, always with the big theme half a bar later, like an echo coming back. It is marvelous. Otherwise, the area of the Rhine certainly has no connection with that symphony except here. But it is not true that he was a bad orchestrator. I always go to the original scores. It's only during the first movement of the "Rhenish" Symphony that I have to correct the very fast tempo. I correct the sixteenth-notes for the contrabass players, because for them the eighth-notes are better. Otherwise, it's too fast and the sound is not good. That's the only correction I do.

I also prefer the original version of the Fourth Symphony. I am not happy with the later revision. Of course, I agree that in Schumann's time the orchestra and the musicians in the orchestra were probably not as good as they are now. The technical problems would have been more of a problem 150 years ago. I hate those Mahler orchestrations. I'm sorry, but it's true. I can't understand that big composers and great conductors have the opinion that the orchestration of Schumann is not a good one. Of course, it takes a lot of time to convince an orchestra, even a good orchestra, that the original orchestration can sound marvelous.

My own feeling with these works is that the form is generally classical, excerpt the five movements of the Third Symphony. But there is a passion and fire behind the notes. Even in the slow movements, when the theme is a very short one, there is inspiration of the heart and by sentiment—not *sentimental,* but sentiment.

Lukas Foss

Let's talk about Schumann in general, for a moment. There are composers you admire. You admire different things in composers. The composers you love are those where you admire not just the music, but the whole human being. And Schumann is definitely one of those. Verdi is definitely one of those. There are not so many. There are some where you say, "Well, I don't particularly wish to have known them, but I love the music." Wagner must have had *some* beautiful sides to him, because there is that in the music. There's a lot of love and resignation and beautiful things in the music. But there's also sides that you can tell in the music that must indicate that he was a much less beautiful person. But with Schumann, you can hear it in the music, you can hear the human being. It was absolutely wonderful, the heart, the mind, the generosity towards his colleagues. All of these things are so different. My God, so many composers are ungenerous.

Writing symphonies was the ultimate goal for the composers. But in a way, Beethoven stood in the way. Brahms waited a long time before writing his First Symphony, because he didn't think he was ready. Everybody expected that his First Symphony would have to be Beethoven's Tenth or Eleventh. They all felt they should be going on from where Beethoven left off, which of course is ridiculous. But obviously, you didn't really belong to that class of immortals unless you wrote symphonies.

So, next to the Beethoven symphonies, what do we have? We have two very great symphonies by Schubert, and we have some fine but lighter symphonies by Mendelssohn. And, of course, we have four great Brahms symphonies. The Schumann works are of the same importance, I would say. They are all important works.

We are supposed to think of Mozart as being light and elegant, whereas he's our Shakespeare. Or that Beethoven is always monumental and diabolic, completely forgetting all the serene music he wrote that is not at all *Sturm und Drang*. Schumann himself suffered from people saying that he was melancholic in his music. No, the music is full of fire, and there is no heaviness. Brahms is heavier than Schumann. That is absolutely a fact. The wonderful thing about Schumann is that he is an early romantic. Brahms is a late romantic. So Brahms has a "sunset" quality. But Schumann has—well, when Schumann says "romantic," he means the present and the future. It means the new, the new. He uses the cello in a romantic way, and you feel he is the first to use cellos in that way. You can sense that romanticism hadn't yet been exhausted. And that also is a very exciting yet lovable thing.

I agree with Schoenberg, who was aghast that people dismissed Schumann's symphonic writing as being badly orchestrated. Somebody put that in a textbook, and many textbooks now say that! This is, of course, complete nonsense. The symphonies are definitely orchestral in conception. It is true that here and there one wishes that something were a little bit different about the orchestration, and one can do something about it— but he is not merely a pianist who is suddenly writing for orchestra. No, there's nothing amateurish about Schumann. Later on, as he developed his orchestral style, he went in heavily for tremolos. That can be very hard on string players, and they get very tired. It's a little bit of "make-believe" excitement you get from a tremolo. So maybe reducing some of the tremolo writing here and there is wise. Mahler in his editing did just that.

I am particularly fond of the Second and Fourth symphonies. The Second has one of the great slow movements of all time. It's so inspired. If somebody asks you, "What is romanticism?," you say, "Go to the slow movement of the Schumann Second Symphony!" There is stunning string writing, with those rising violins and those sequences that go upwards, then settle down again. The one thing one might say is perhaps there is not enough of the *weird* in Schumann's symphonies, which you get plenty of in Beethoven and which makes Beethoven more true and fascinating. He gives you these really strange adventures into a no-man's land. You've got to make it as weird and crazy as it is—as surrealistic and unlovable, even, if you wish.

When I conduct the Fourth Symphony, I help myself to three sources—the original, which is simpler in the orchestration (more direct, if you wish); the late version from 1849, which has some additional music in certain bars (Schumann is always right when he decides something needs revision); and some of the Mahler revisions. It's completely nonsensical to use the word *original*. It's a misnomer. You cannot say that Beethoven's *Leonora Overture No. 1* is an "original" and that *Leonora No. 3* is not. It means the composer was dissatisfied and made another version. If Beethoven decided the first two overtures weren't good enough, you trust him. Therefore, it is totally wrong to play only the "original" version of Schumann's Fourth Symphony, for instance, and forget about all the wonderful and necessary retouching he did later.

I have a feeling that Mahler did his retouchings of Schumann when he was young. They are quite ruthless. Therefore, I don't like them on the whole. I share George Szell's view that, on the whole, they are not right. But now and then, especially in the little touches, the little retouches—like cutting out an instrument that's doubling or making something *piano* that's *forte*—are all right where they're sensitively applied. But where he acts like a teacher with a schoolboy and crosses things out and changes the harmony, then it's usually for the worse. I don't think the later Mahler would have done that. So finally what I did was help myself to some of Mahler's good ideas and some of Schumann's own good ideas, and wherever it's musical, always the later versions.

9

"A Little Haus Musik"

The Chamber Music

Commentators: Emanuel Ax, Hermann Baumann, Richard Goode, Bernard Greenhouse, members of the Guarneri String Quartet (John Dalley, David Soyer, and Arnold Steinhardt), Lynn Harrell, Heinz Holliger, Paul Katz, Nancy B. Reich, Michael Saffle, Richard Stoltzman, Charles Wadsworth, Peter Zazofsky, and Eugenia Zukerman

The objective and lyric elements intermingle and interpenetrate strangely but organically. . . .
　　　　　　　　　—Jean Paul, *School for Aesthetics*

My labor now is not just for my art, but for the daily, household life now all around me."
　　　　　　　　　—Robert Schumann, 1841

EDITOR'S NOTE

During the last fourteen years of his creative life, Schumann composed numerous works for a variety of instrumental combinations. Except for the Piano Quartet, Piano Quintet, three string quartets, three piano trios, and three violin sonatas, many of these works were intended to work interchangeably with other instrumental combinations. Biographer Nancy B. Reich and flutist Eugenia Zukerman provide an overview of these compositions and their performance. Musicians Emanuel Ax (piano), Paul Katz (cello), Heinz Holliger (oboe), Peter Zazofsky (violin), Hermann Baumann (horn), Lynn Harrell (cello), Bernard Greenhouse (cello), Richard Stoltzman (clarinet), and Eugenia Zukerman (flute) share experiences and insights. Also included are historian Michael Saffle and two members of the Chamber Music Society of Lincoln Center, director Charles Wadsworth and pianist Richard Goode.

OVERVIEW

Nancy B. Reich

The chamber works grew out of the study Robert and Clara pursued together of the works of Haydn, Mozart, and Beethoven. They both wrote of this in their Marriage Diary. They also owed a lot to the close musician friends with whom Clara played them. Of course, Clara was the pianist in everything he wrote, including the chamber works. She introduced them. They were always written with her in mind. And after his death she performed them constantly, especially the Piano Quintet. That became her signature work. It appears on many of her programs. Even during her performances with orchestras, she'd perform a chamber work, as well. It was the custom in the nineteenth century.

While in Leipzig she played with the leading violinist of the day, Ferdinand David. He was the concert master of the Gewandhaus Orchestra. She and David and Mendelssohn played these works publicly and in house concerts. In Dresden Clara was credited with setting up the first chamber music series, that is, public concerts at which chamber music was played. With the Schubert brothers—no relation to Franz, their name just happened to be Schubert—she premiered the piano trios. They would try them over in the home before publication, and after publication they played them publicly in Dresden.

Later in Düsseldorf, Clara performed them with Joseph Joachim and Brahms. These two men referred to Robert as "The Master." He was their idol. The works they all played together included Schumann's violin sonatas. Joachim was not only a violinist at the time, he was composing, too. Actually, the Schumanns had first gotten to know Joachim when he was only a child. He had come to Leipzig to study with David. Clara had even performed with him when he was a child prodigy. In fact, it was Joachim who told Brahms to go and meet the Schumanns.

Another friend at this time who played chamber works with Clara was Wilhelm von Wasielewski, the concertmaster in Düsseldorf. They were very fond of each other and found an immediate personal and musical affinity. He was a very cultured and literate man who wrote several books, including a biography of Robert [1858]. This caused something of a minor scandal, because despite Clara's help with Robert's documents, the resulting book upset her. She felt the book was unfair to Robert, because it hinted that some of his mental difficulties had surfaced very early in his life. This was something Clara didn't want to face. So she disowned the book and refused to read it.

Eugenia Zukerman

We flutists don't have any great romantic literature. We have no sonatas from Liszt or from Schumann, or even Schubert. The repertoire for flute is certainly smaller than piano or violin. But I think if we look at it historically, we can understand what has happened in terms of composers who have written for the flute. The flute had its golden age in the eighteenth century, when all the baroque composers used it as their melodic-line favorite, but as music changed, and grew more heroic and larger, and the symphony became larger, and sounds became larger and vibratos wider, the flute is an instrument that at that time was pretty much relegated to bird chirpings in the background. So we have to constantly pick away at the material to find more works that would work for flute. And in the twentieth century there has been a kind of renaissance of the flute. In fact, it is the instrument of the hour. It's the most popular instrument I think because, technically, things changed, and composers became aware of the potential of the instrument and are using it in very interesting ways.

But at least in Schumann's time you find a lot of music that transcribed well for flute. Publishers were saying to him, "Could you make this for cello, or horn, or clarinet, or even flute?" And so there are many pieces—I mean, Schumann's Op. 94 romances are written for oboe, but you can play in many other instruments. I have played them on the flute. But there are certain things I wouldn't touch. There's a transcription of the Mendelssohn E-Minor Violin Concerto. No, thank you. Even though the Franck Violin Sonata is played often on the flute; I would never do that. I was married for many years to the violinist [Pinchas Zukerman] who plays it better than anyone, and it just somehow would grate against me to do that.

THE STRING QUARTETS

> *The quartet has come to a standstill. . . . It is not a good sign*
> *that the later generation, after all this time, has been unable*
> *to produce anything comparable.*
> —Robert Schumann, 1842

EDITOR'S NOTE

Schumann's three string quartets, his Op. 41, were all written during the fertile, brief span of time from June 4 to July 22, 1842. The first is in A minor, the second in F major, and the third in A major. Discussing these works here are members of the famed Guarneri Quartet: Arnold Steinhardt and John

Dalley, violins, Michael Tree, viola, and David Soyer, cello. The quartet was founded in 1964. It is now in residence at the University of Maryland, and its members are on the faculty of the Curtis Institute of Music in Philadelphia. The quartet retired in 2009.

A Conversation with the Guarneri String Quartet

Arnold Steinhardt: The four of us have been together for twenty years. Interesting enough, there's only one Guarnerius instrument in our group, and that's the cello. Mr. Soyer has an Andreas Guarnerius from 1669. I used to have a Guarnerius del Gesù, but some years back I traded it in for a Storioni, which had been played by Emil Hauser, the first violinist in the Budapest String Quartet from its very beginning. When he left, he sold it to the succeeding first violinist, Josef Roismann, who played it until the end of the Budapest's career. All violins have pedigrees. There might be one or two quartets that have been together longer. The Amadeus has been together and intact for more than thirty years, I think. The group has remained intact. We are probably the oldest *American* quartet, at least. I would imagine during all that time we've been together I can count on my fingers the number of times I've been able to find time to hear other quartets perform. If I have a night off, I'd rather go to the movies!

David Soyer: Right now we're touring with Schumann's A-Minor Quartet this season. If I were forced to choose which of the three to take to a desert island, I might choose this one, the A Minor. No reasons, really—these things are always very subjective. Ask all four us the same question and you'd probably get different answers. These quartets are really wonderful works, better for the instruments than the Brahms. However, they are very difficult, thorny, with lots of problems, and that may have a dampening effect on the ardor of younger quartets.

Steinhardt: Working through problems in a string quartet is a metaphor for all kinds of life situations, of how delicately balanced is the social fabric is of our lives. We've certainly seen many disruptions in other groups, which might be a personality problem, or someone leaving the group, someone new entering the group, that sort of thing. There's a tremendous amount of wear and tear on all of us from the constant proximity we all have with each other and the constant chafing from rehearsing, criticizing, from arguing that goes on. It takes its toll, sometimes. I think in our early days, we each had our own cherished ideas about music and thought we had to defend them from everybody else. But as time went on, you find these positions will change, and you learn not to take a stand, or at least be more diplomatic about it. Three or four concerts down the road, things get worked out.

John Dalley: We go back a long time with the Schumanns. We've done them ever since we began. When we gave our debut in New York, the idea was to play two concerts of neglected works by famous composers. We played the F Major, which is very neglected and more difficult than the other two. Now we play them everywhere. Of all of them, I like the slow movements to them best.

Soyer: And we've recorded them for RCA. We were doing the Brahms quartets at the time, and it seemed natural to include the Schumann with them.

Steinhardt: Of course, we do that sort of thing only in recordings. We don't like to do "complete" things like that in our concerts. We present our concerts like a nice meal, with a first and second and third course and a nice dessert and coffee at the end. Not an "all this" or "all that." That's not doing a great service for audiences and for music at large. People go away needing antacids or something!

Dalley: It's true that the Schumanns pose their own problems, which means they're relatively neglected in concerts. There are basically two reasons for that. The string players face difficulties, a certain awkwardness in the writing. Moreover, I think people somehow dismiss his string music, I think unfairly. I'm guessing there. There's a kind of prejudice that I've found over the years. It's probably mostly that's it's hard to play.

Steinhardt: It saddens me that they are somewhat neglected. I feel very close to Schumann. I love his chamber music, as I love everything he's written. He's a very special composer. I find that his music is so wonderfully imaginative, daring, and inventive. Complicated music is complicated to interpret. But it's true some dismiss it as problematic. I don't think of them as problems, but idiosyncrasies that are part of his greatness, not problems. You have to figure out as a performer how to do phrases that go off in strange syncopations. You have to be a storyteller. Oftentimes these lopsided phrases and daring excursions to related keys have to be talked about. It's hard to resolve them sometimes.

Dalley: Schumann, of course, knew the piano, and there are places in the music where you see the pianist's intellect at work. For example, Ravel had more of an innate sense of each instrument he was writing for; and I think Schumann didn't have quite that kind of rapport for the string performers. His symphonies also have a kind of awkward quality, too, the way he wrote for the brasses and the use of doublings—more than one person playing the same note on the same octave, which results in a kind of squareness, a heaviness. Brahms had some problems, too, with his quartets. I think most string players will tell you that. He and Schumann are different, but there's still some awkwardness in both. Interestingly enough, Mendelssohn's quartets are neglected, too. I think there's a real stigma against his music, or certainly there used to be. Anytime you get into romantic music that wears its heart out front, it is something that people tend to back away from. And there's another Smetana quartet, which is wonderful, and a Grieg that is wonderful. It's almost an orchestral piece. And one by Sibelius. We get some flak from playing those. But we always get a fan of these, who comes to us and begs us to try them!

Steinhardt: You know, Schumann wrote them not just as isolated pieces but as works intended to be played together. He provided bridges between them. You can play one, and then transition right into the other, and then the other. It's an odd idea. I do know that once in Leipzig there was some *Hausmusik*—I think Mendelssohn was present—and all three were played that way. Later, he deleted the bridges. I would love to have been there to hear them that way. You know, it once was quite common that a performer, say, a pianist, would finish one piece on the program, and then he would run his hands over the keys and modulate gently and imaginatively to the next key, the key of the next piece. That would set you in the mood for the new key. I remember this specifically from a Josef Hofmann recital recorded at the Curtis Institute. I understand there was a tradition of that at the turn of the century.

We love the quartets and play them regularly. We enjoy them more, in a way, than the Brahms. In a certain sense, these are better written for quartet than Brahms. Of course, the Brahms is great music, but the textures can be hard to deal with. But Schumann is more lean and airy and grateful to the instrument. I consider his quartets as an amazing chamber-music gift. I don't think the string writing is a problem, but it's always a challenge to play. I don't think great music can be easy to perform. If it's great music, it's always going to be a problem. It's slightly quirky. There's odd edges and angles, but it's part and parcel of his genius.

On the whole, though, our talking like this fails to describe the music. You can't talk about music, because music is far too specific and language is far too inexact. I would rather leave such talk to the musicologists.

PIANO QUARTET AND THE PIANO QUINTET

EDITOR'S NOTE

Schumann's Piano Quartet, Op. 47 (1842), and the Piano Quintet, Op. 44 (1842), are among his most popular and enduring works. A Leipzig critic of the day greeted them with rapture: "These compositions are without reservation among the finest that recent times can show in this department. We have to admire anew the freedom and security with which he moves in a branch of composition new to him."

In late October 1986, the Cleveland String Quartet with soloist Emanuel Ax came to the University of Kansas to perform Schumann's Piano Quintet and Quartet. They were nearing the end of a road tour prior to recording the works in the Eastman Theatre on November 3–5, 1987. The compact disc was released that year on the RCA label. I caught up with cellist Paul Katz and pianist Emanuel Ax just moments after the evening's concert.

Paul Katz: Well, as we're talking, this is just within thirty or forty minutes from the end of our concert this evening, and I'm still feeling an exhilaration from having been just out there in what was a very exciting and thrilling experience playing the Schumann Quintet and Quartet with Manny Ax. So I'm on kind of a high right now—which is a bit like a runner's high. We love performing. For us, it's a renewal to be out there doing it. It's a tough life, traveling around, living out of suitcases, driving around for the three and a half hours that we drove today and will have to drive tomorrow. And it's the charge and the fulfillment and the whole creative process of being out there onstage that's just wonderful. I think both pieces are fantastically successful pieces, whether you're going by the applause meter or just whatever you feel in the air. The quintet is more popular and better known. It seems somehow to bring a bigger rise out of the audience. However, if I were to give you my personal preference, it's the quartet. I find it—and I hear lots of people say this—so buoyant and so full of life. It's really infectious music. I'm just crazy about that piece. Of course, both are marvelous examples of chamber music writing, and the quintet has more of a symphonic sense to it. But the quartet writing in general for the strings is a little more stylistic, and it's a little bit thinner kind of texture. Even the piano scoring, I think, is not quite as full in terms of numbers of notes in the chords and that kind of thing. I just find the tunes so inspiring. It's a great joy every time.

Emanuel Ax: I agree in that I think the quartet, in a funny way, is even more inspired than the quintet. It may be my favorite piece of Schumann. I don't think it's put together quite as simply and as effortlessly as the quintet, so I think you have to try very, very hard to use all your imagination to make things work. There are some pieces, like the Op. 109 Piano Sonata of Beethoven, the F-Major Ballade of Chopin, and the quartet, where one almost feels as if the music has been going on and on and on, and it only becomes audible at that moment we start to play. There's no real beginning. It's a very inspired kind of opening.

Katz: Oh, those cello solos in both! Undoubtedly the first movement of the quintet, that second theme, is my chance to shine. I have a duet with the viola, and I love playing it.

Ax: For me, certainly the slow movement of the quartet is one of the most inspired things ever written by anybody. And that's really—well, Schumann is one of those composers who is like the little girl who, when she was good, she was very, very good . . .

Katz: Yes, I find in that slow movement some of Schumann's most inspired writing. It's just a thrill every time. I can get gooseflesh during the concert. The viola plays it with the violin obbligato; and the violin plays it with the piano obbligato; and then the cello plays it even a fourth time at the end in a very reflective kind of setting.

Ax: Take the Scherzo of the quintet. The piano is such a huge instrument, so I can always play eight notes as opposed to one for everybody else. So obviously, I can be responsible for a lot more of texture and contrapuntal writing than any one of the other instruments. Second of all, most of the great composers of the nineteenth century played the piano. So they very much feel that the piano is an important instrument.

Katz: That Scherzo is nothing more than triplet scales, but it just wins the day. People tend to cheer at the end of that movement, and it's nothing more than descending B-flat scales. By contrast, the Scherzo from the quartet has a very smoky undercurrent. Even the lilting, fairy-tale aspects of Schumann can be delivered in very bizarre textures.

Ax: Right. It's a kind of *moto perpetuo,* a very scary one. I think it's a difficult movement to play well. You have to be very much together, first of all. Second of all, the sound has to be incredibly quiet and incredibly even. Anything that pops out disturbs the kind of eerie quality. In general, I think the connections among the movements are so important in this quartet. It's much more apparent in this piece than in a lot of other four-movement works. I think that's something Beethoven pioneered, in a way. The movements were not considered separate entities, but related elements drawn together.

Katz: Yes, that's so typically Schumann. And that's important. For example, one of the great stresses for—and probably nobody but cellists will care about this—is one of the strongest and most important links between movements. I refer to the final notes of the third movement of the quartet that lead into the opening notes of the Fourth. It's absolutely the work of a genius, the imagination of a genius. The character is so incredibly transformed, and yet it's the same notes. And we have to preserve that. Schumann comes up with this unique stroke here: He wants a low B-flat pedal at the end of the slow movement, and he instructs the cellist to tune the C-string down to a low B-flat. It's a famous instruction that's written right into the music. But I don't do it that way. I do it between the second and third movements, because I find it too disruptive to be plucking around down there while my colleagues are making beautiful music.

But what really brings down the house is the Finale to the quintet. Right in the middle of the excitement there a section that has a structural, formal backbone. It has a fugue that sounds almost baroque, with a certain quality of Bach in it. There's a lot going on. And then comes that last page. Well, that really cinches it. It's thrilling and exciting!

Ax: It's an exhilarating ending, and it's as full of ecstasy as almost any music I know. You can't help but lose yourself.

Katz: After tonight we'll go to New York for the recording sessions. The sense of continuity between "live" and recorded performance is terribly important. We like as much as possible to re-create the quality of the concert stage.

[Note: The following remarks by Mr. Katz came a year later, after the Schumann works were recorded.]

We recorded the quartet first, and then the quintet the first few days in November last year. I guess what was unusual about it was the hour in which these recording sessions took place. The Eastman Theatre was a busy place, and it isn't possible to get in during the day. So we started at 10:00 in the evening. And then we ran into some technical difficulties (I shouldn't be telling you this!) and finished the last movement of the quintet at something like 5:00 in the morning! We never really play longer than seven or eight minutes at a time. You do one movement and a complete play-through. Then you stop, listen, and discuss; then you go back and you rehearse the things you didn't like and you do it again. So you have to get yourself up for that seven or eight minutes over and over again. We all rely on each other, and we depend on each other and we feed on each other, and we inspire each other. So there's a positive side to it.

Afterward, I put Manny in the car and we went driving around Rochester, New York, looking around for an all-night diner so we could get some breakfast. We couldn't find a restaurant open at that hour. They didn't open until 6:00!

THE PIANO TRIOS

EDITOR'S NOTE

Unlike the string quartets, the three piano trios were written over the span of several years, the D Minor, Op. 63, and the F Major, Op. 80, in 1847; and the G Minor, Op. 110, in 1851.

Commentator Bernard Greenhouse talks about his experience as a cellist with the Beaux Arts Trio and the trio's recordings of these works.

Bernard Greenhouse

The original members of the Beaux Arts Trio were Menahem Pressler, Daniel Guilet, and I. Dan was French and had been brought up in the French tradition. I don't know if you realize it, but the French had more feeling for Schumann than the German public. They always chose Schumann on their programs. And Guilet knew this, and every time we went to France, we had to have a Schumann piano trio. And when it came to recording, he suggested that we do all three of the trios, along with Clara Schumann's trio. So we did them, and our first complete recordings were with him. That was in the early 1960s, I believe. We have talked amongst ourselves about the beauty of these trios. As a matter of fact, we've been a little bit disappointed that audiences sometimes don't react as much as we do. But they're an essential part of the trio repertoire.

The greatest of the three, for me, is the first one, in D minor. Oh, it's magnificent, and if he had only written this one trio, I would consider it a very important part of the trio repertoire. There's a wonderful moment in the first movement, marked *ponticello,* where the cello has this distant, far-off sound, perhaps an imitation of a horn. This is a technique where I have to play the instrument with the bow very close to the bridge. It produces an eerie sound. And then the violin joins in with the same kind of hornlike sound. It's spellbinding. It holds you breathless. You can see listeners perk up at this moment. At first they think something's gone wrong—with the instrument or the player! The slow movement has some of the most sensitive expressiveness of anything in literature. There's tears and sadness there, which carry over to the listener.

Some people like the Second Trio most. Certainly it's Schumann at his brightest. I think it proves that he was able to express all the emotional qualities expected of a great composer. It's quite different from the first. The real highlight, for me, is the second movement. It represents a quiet evening scene, with a beautiful sunset with all the colors of the sky and a feeling of great calm. I'm familiar with the ocean and sailing, and I hear in the music a series of waves which roll, one into the next, and create an undulating quality. Now, when you get to the Third Trio, I must admit that some of the cello writing is quite awkward. That's something where I wish he had been more of a cellist himself and a little bit more sympathetic to the performer! He does some peculiar things—he'll reach out for a high note out of thin air, where there's absolutely no chance to check the note you're playing. You find yourself suddenly going from the lower register into the top register without any chance to adjust.

MISCELLANEOUS CHAMBER WORKS

EDITOR'S NOTE
These works are arranged in order of opus number.

Charles Wadsworth
Members of the Chamber Music Society of Lincoln Center frequently perform and record many of these Schumann works. I feel comfortable with Schumann. His music feels good under my hands, and I feel a closeness with his message. That's not true with all composers; in fact, I'm normally very uncomfortable playing Beethoven and Mozart. What they ask of my fingers! Give me Ravel, Chopin, Schumann, Brahms, and I'm happy. The *Andante and Variations,* Op. 46, is a piece that enjoyed a number of performances back in the good old days in the 1930s and 1940s, when two-piano teams were popular. I remember when I was a youngster hearing Vronsky and Babin playing it. But in programming it for the Chamber Music Society of Lincoln Center, I wanted to restore it to its original instrumentation for two pianos, two cellos, and horn. It's an unusual combination, and I don't know why he did it, but the sonorities of the two cellos together with the French horn are so unbelievably original, the way Schumann used the richness of the lower register of the cellos in combination with the two pianos and the idiosyncratic writing for the horn. Sometimes you hear the pianos alone and as a duet, the

piano with the cellos, the cellos and horn as a trio, and all five instruments together. I had access to one of the great horn players, John Barrows, and two fine cellists, Leslie Parnas and Laurence Lesser. So we presented it in that form at Alice Tully Hall during our first season in 1969. For some reason, Schumann deleted some of the variations when he later wrote the two-piano version. We restored in our performance the wonderful alpine horn subject; the quotation from the postlude of the song cycle *Frauenliebe und -leben,* which has a beautifully mellow sound in the cellos; and an extraordinary, marchlike section which comes just before the finale. That is great fun, because it throws material back and forth, from one piano to the other, from Richard Goode to me, and back again. You have to be very careful about matching the exact length of those staccato notes. You shouldn't overpedal anything, so you can get this airspace between. And it builds up to a really rip-roaring climax at the end. I wouldn't hear this work any other way.

Hermann Baumann

I first came to Schumann through my mother, who was a pianist and who played for me many of his works. I was invited to play here at the Düsseldorf Schumannfest two of Schumann's works for horn, the *Adagio and Allegro* [Op. 70] and the *Variations for Two Pianos, Two Cellos, and Horn.* Schumann wrote them for two different kinds of horns. The *Variations* were written in 1844 for the hand horn, the *Adagio and Allegro* for the new valve horn. I think a festival like this gives to many people who love Schumann the opportunity to hear works from nearly all of his repertoire. My last teacher was with the hand horn. That's where you "stop" the notes by placing your hand inside the bell. That instrument taught me how to perform Haydn and Mozart. It is different from a modern valve horn, which allows you to play all the notes of the chromatic scale and which gives you a better low register. That's why it's so important for the Wagner orchestra and for Tchaikovsky, Brahms, and Mahler. Music like that would be impossible for the valveless horn. I am very interested in the history of both, along with the alphorn and any other kind of horn. Whatever I can find, I play! I even play hunting horns, but not to hunt, just to catch the right notes!

The valve horn was invented in 1813, but it took some years to find them in most orchestras. Schumann wrote the *Adagio and Allegro* in 1849, at the same time as his famous *Konzertstück* for four horns, to make the valve horn more popular and give it a new repertoire. He explored every possible effect, like arpeggiated sevenths and ninths and upward dramatic leaps. There had been little music for valve horn at that time, just a few pieces by Kalliwoda, who is not very well known now. There is a funny thing about the first performance of the *Konzertstück*: There were two hand horns still in the orchestra, but the soloists had to use valve horns. But the first horn soloist was not familiar with the valve horn, so he decided to perform it with the hand horn! Unbelievable for us! The situation was reversed later in 1864, when Brahms wrote his trio for violin, horn, and piano. This time the horn player didn't want to do it on the hand horn but preferred the valve horn! Already the valve horn was better known and more performed. Yet until 1896, the hand horn was still taught in Paris at the *conservatoire*. At our time now, many of us are going back to playing with the hand horn. I've recorded the four Mozart concertos with the valveless horn.

The *Adagio and Allegro* is fantastic music but very difficult to perform. It has no rests, no bars to rest. You play and play and play for ten minutes! I recorded it in 1981 with the Munich Philharmonic in an orchestration by Ernest Ansermet. I'm not able to perform it in that version very often. I prefer the original; but I must admit it does sound good with orchestra. We need more pieces like that for horn and large orchestra. And you can hear it in many other combinations of instruments, for clarinet, oboe, cello, et cetera. It wasn't just in the nineteenth century that you find so many different kinds of instrumentations like this; there was even more of this sort of thing in the nineteenth century.

When Schumann composed his *Variations for Two Pianos, Two Cellos, and Horn*, he scored it for hand horn. He gives the player more bars to rest, which he does not do when he wrote later the four-horn *Konzertstück*. It was a very good idea to combine the horn with the two cellos and two pianos. However, there's not a lot to do for me, except for things like the fanfares and some ornamental work. I'm looking forward for the first time to perform it in this original orchestration. You rarely find such opportunities these days, except in festivals like this. Otherwise, it's never performed, because it's difficult to get together artists of this caliber at the same time. I don't know why he did it later for just two pianos, but at least it meant it would be performed more often.

This is the center of my life, making music. Every day, twenty-four hours, I think about this, to make the horn more famous and not just a curiosity. When I read reviews about piano recitals, I read details about the music and performance. But we horn players also hope for better reviews that talk about the details and history of horn performance. More critics should be horn players and should know more about performance on wind instruments. We have such a great repertoire, and we deserve the same recognition that other performers get on their instruments.

Michael Saffle

In the early 1960s, when I was fifteen years old, I carried my clarinet and a copy of Schumann's Op. 73 *Fantasiestücke* to one of my piano lessons. My teacher, Edelgard Hainke, had already assigned me the *Papillons,* so she knew I knew something of Schumann's music. (Later we worked together on the A-Minor Concerto and the *Kinderszenen*.) She was a bit taken aback by the clarinet, however; I don't think she cared for it as a sound-producing mechanism. I explained that I'd come across the pieces in a music store and wanted to try them out. My idea was to master both parts, piano as well as clarinet, then record them together. (I had recently purchased a brand-new Wollensak reel-to-reel tape recorder so that I could play the solo part with myself.) I worked on the first piece at the piano, and we fooled around at a subsequent lesson with the tape recorder, which didn't produce quite the sound my teacher wanted. Finally she gave up and said, "Let *me* play the piano while you blow that . . . thing." It was my one and only attempt at playing chamber music on a wind instrument, although later I accompanied several wind players on recitals and played a lot of piano four-hands and two-piano music.

In fact, the *Fantasiestücke* were probably scored by Schumann for violin or cello as well as clarinet. I say "probably" because the "ad lib." string parts published in the original 1849 edition do not appear as such in Schumann's surviving manuscript. I've heard the pieces beautifully played on the violin, although I prefer the clarinet for several reasons. (Schumann evidently did, too; hence the "ad lib." designation.) One reason is historical: these pieces anticipate the rhythms and timbres of Brahms's late clarinet sonatas. Another is acoustic. Schumann's piano part is comparatively thick and lies mostly in the instrument's middle and lower registers. Played on the cello, the solo part would be difficult to hear and enjoy. No wonder that Schumann almost entirely avoided in these pieces the clarinet's low (or *chalumeau*) register, otherwise one of its most attractive features.

Unfortunately, the *Fantasiestücke* are often dismissed as examples of Schumann's so-called Biedermeier output. The term *Biedermeier* is frequently employed as a synonym for, or approximation of, early to mid-nineteenth-century "conventionality" or "domesticity." Biedermeier music, literature, and furniture are supposed to be "safe," if a bit stodgy, less than exciting. While the Op. 73 pieces work well in an intimate setting—none of the three numbers is altogether "virtuosic," although each of them (especially the third) calls for considerable skill from both performers—they are by no means mere *Hausmusik*. Instead, Schumann's churning accompaniment and soaring solo lines sounds "driven," even "passionate." The *Fantasiestücke* are powerful compositions that deserve to be heard more often, and to be appreciated for their conviction as well as their many charming details.

Heinz Holliger

I have been obsessed with Schumann since the age of fifteen. He is still the main composer in my life. I'm not only playing the oboe music, but I am also conducting as much Schumann as I can. I take him as seriously as a composer as I would take Bach or Mozart. And I would take his late output as very great music, and not just something from an ill brain. This is the tendency very much in the last ten years, to take also the last pieces and see them as great music. There have been so many stupid prejudices transported from one book to the other about Schumann. But we're learning more about him and his relationship with Clara, thanks to the publication of the original texts of the letters. And now we have new biographies of Clara by Dr. Nancy Reich and Eva Weissweiler. I think also the psychoanalytic study by Peter Ostwald, *Schumann: The Inner Voices,* sheds many new insights.

Schumann's Op. 94 pieces for oboe are a late work, dating from 1849. I think they are the most important works for oboe written in the nineteenth century. I recorded them in 1980 with Alfred Brendel on an album with other Schumann pieces [*Schumann: Works for Oboe and Piano,* 1980]. The oboe hasn't changed very much since 1870. Earlier in the century it was quite different. The authentic instrument of Schumann's time had a much lighter, transparent sound than we know today. More recently, bigger halls and our obsession for loud sounds has meant playing with a much bigger, "fatter" sound. You really have to make more noise to get to the ears of people in a four-thousand-seat hall. Humanity may go deaf in a hundred years!

Before Schumann's time, composers were writing for newly discovered, newly developed instruments. C. P. E. Bach could write for the new fort-epianos. Beethoven could write for the new Broadwood pianos. They were exploring new possibilities. But when new instruments like the clarinet and the valve horn were perfected, the oboe lost something of its inter-est for the romantic composers. They preferred the clarinet's soft lower register, you see. So they made friends with important clarinetists like Spohr with Helmstedt, Weber and Mendelssohn with Bermann. Brahms wrote his clarinet pieces because of his fascination with Mühlfeld. But this meant the oboe literature itself was reduced to a sort of virtuoso literature. When you look at Schumann's musical reviews you see notices of a lot of wind concertos, even a Trombone Concerto by Ferdinand David! But these were mostly by minor composers like Kalliwoda. From the start,

Schumann implied that all of his own wind pieces could be played on other instruments. The horn piece was even first performed on a violin and not on the horn. The clarinet piece has also an alternative violin part. The cello part was then added by somebody else. And the oboe romances are for hautbois or violin. It even says that on the title page. The pieces called "In Folkstyle" are actually written for cello or violin.

Schumann wrote those Op. 94 pieces for oboe, but he couldn't even find an oboist to play them, except for a local Dresden musician who played them once straight through at his home. They were never performed in public until probably around 1867 by an oboist called Lunden, with Carl Reinecke at the piano. And Joseph Joachim sometimes played them on the violin.

My album with Alfred Brendel came out of an idea Brendel had. First he wanted me to play some Schubert songs on the oboe and he wanted to record them with me. I told him I could do it with some later songs, maybe some Schumann songs, but with Schubert I was not really convinced. And then I told him, "I think it's much better to do some 'Songs without Words' by Schumann." I took over the idea of the multiple possibilities of instruments which Schumann already foresaw. All the other pieces on that album are also playable on the violin; so I thought I don't do any harm to when I played them on the oboe. For example, the beautiful "Abendlied" (Evening Song) had already been transcribed by Joachim for violin. It was originally from a group of twelve pieces for piano, four hands, Schumann's Op. 85. We played them in Henry Wood Hall in London. At the time I think it was the only project like it, but now there are many.

In pieces like this you see something of his compositional techniques. I think he was a real revolutionary of the nineteenth century. His development was nonlinear. He would take a little cell of three or four notes and then turn it into a spiral development, moving on and on, never straight, always with this circular motion. This is much closer to baroque music, like the Bach inventions. Many of his pieces develop this way. Take the No. 2 of the "Folk Style" set, which is in seven-bar phrases revolving back upon themselves. Look at the three notes, F–A–E, that he uses in the first of the oboe *Romances*. Music is a language itself, but you can't transcribe it into words. But I will try: At the beginning of that first piece I see a minstrel, who starts playing three chords on his lute. He then recites a ballad in a very free, *recitativo* style, something like, "Here, in olden times, et cetera." And then when it is finished there comes a regular, flowing motion in the piano, followed by a sort of aria, songlike music. But then at the end he writes a ghostly *scherzando,* and you have the feeling you don't know where you are. It's sort of a twilight thing, with those *forte* offbeats. Rather frightening. And then it goes back to this *recitativo* as in the beginning, but with a much more regular pulse in the piano. In the coda there is a heartbeat in the A, and then a chromatic "falling" in the music—you feel an urge to fall down, to sink. And then the piano takes the part of the oboe and the oboe the part of the piano, triggering a very dissonant chord, a diminished seventh with the A. Finally, it comes to a standstill, a sort of frozen standstill. And all of it is based on three notes, F–A–E—"Frei aber einsam" (free but lonely)—that soon will unite Schumann with Brahms and Joachim.

Richard Stoltzman

I've heard it said that Schumann's Op. 94 pieces are the finest pieces in the last century written for oboe. Well, I play them on the clarinet. It doesn't make any difference in my mind, and I don't think it makes in the minds of most listeners, who may have heard the piece played many times, what instrument it's played on. Schumann was a well-known composer in the nineteenth century, and he happens to have chosen the oboe for this. What's really important is that it's a piece by Schumann. But in the overall scheme of music of the nineteenth century, I wouldn't necessarily call it an important work. You know, the oboe's just an instrument, like the clarinet, the cello, or the piano. It matters who's blowing into or bowing those instruments to give you the true interpretation and color of the music. Of course, there are certain technical things, like range—I mean, you know, the oboe's range stops at a certain point and starts at a certain point, and you can't go beyond those possibilities. Okay, then, for sure, you would say, "Gee, I don't think I'd better play a piece that's written for oboe on some other instrument." I get that. But when I try to play the Schumann, I look for whatever I can find in it that's beautiful, and that seems to be friendly to the clarinet.

I think in vocal terms about those Schumann pieces. That means that I look for inflections of tone, color, and phrasing that are hopefully communicative and articulate—that is, in other words, not, say, metrically exact and always metronomically perfect. I try to think in an abstract way about either words or scenarios or gestures or something that I can equate with the pieces. For example, in the beautiful theme of the first piece, I don't have anything in my mind, but all I know is that the piano starts with a beautiful kind of questioning chord, and the clarinet answers with this held high note. It just seems to be a magical moment for the audience.

Peter Zazofsky

I played the Schumann violin sonatas for a Belgian label called Phonic that came out in 1981. I did a series of recordings for it. It was a small company, and it gave me much-needed experience in recording. My pianist was Jean-Claude Vanden Eynden.

Schumann being a pianist had difficulty writing for the violin. It's not music that plays easily on the violin. We have to use some unusual bowings and fingerings to make it sound. There are certain keys that work best on the violin. For instance, D major is a very popular key for violin concertos because you've got the open strings. If you're playing in D major, you've got the A-string and the E-string. Concertos that are based on keys that allow you to have open strings on the third or the fifth of a chord are the most brilliant-sounding. And after all, that's one of the things a violin concerto is supposed to do, sound brilliant.

There are passages that work more easily on the violin because they allow the violinist to draw over the four strings in a pendulum motion, which is natural for us. If a composer writes in a way that forces us to cross strings—two or three strings—and then jump back, for instance, that's not idiomatic writing, and it'll sound more awkward, no matter how gifted the violinist. Now, Brahms had the great experience of Joachim when he was writing his violin music. Schumann's acquaintance with Joachim maybe came too late to help him.

When I think of Schumann, one of the things that comes to mind is that in many places he doubles the same notes for both piano and violin. You have to try to avoid the dull tone that can result. And some passages that might work better on the piano he writes for the violin, and vice versa. He also tends to write a lot of passages with repeated sixteenth-notes, like in the Piano Quintet, which is "scrubbing" music. It's like you're scrubbing the floor with it. It goes on and on. Your arms fall off, and all of it is copying the texture of the piano. It sounds pianistic; it doesn't sound violinistic. But it does create a unique color. You can never mistake Schumann's music from other composers', because it has a certain muscular quality to it; which is fine. We wouldn't have it any other way. It's just that it's not very convenient for the violinist.

The First Violin Sonata, Op. 105, was composed in just four days, you know, in the fall of 1851. Three famous violinists were associated with it, and they all knew Schumann—J. W. von Wasielewski, Ferdinand David, and Joseph Joachim. It's great music as music. The first movement explores the dark, impassioned side of him.

The second movement is a lyrical intermezzo, a lovely little song with two interruptions. And there's a hint of the madness that became evident later in his life. There's a little bit of kookiness in the movement—or maybe quirkiness is a better word. The last movement is probably the least successful of the three movements. It's a kind of perpetuum mobile for the violin and the piano, both going at the same time. The whole movement is in sixteenth passages, and are there are a couple of snippets of melody that repeat. But mostly, it's a kind of "motor" music and very difficult to bring off successfully. Also, the metronome indication is so slow that the bow doesn't bounce properly at that speed. That's another thing when I talk about "unviolinistic"—there are certain speeds at which the bow will bounce comfortably and there are other speeds when it becomes very awkward. And this is an example where the speed is problematic.

He had a great gift for melody and a great rhythmic drive. The First Sonata is played a lot more than the other two. Violinists are not willing to buck the disfavor of the audience subjected to hearing it. I've played it live, with Jean-Bernard Pommier at the keyboard.

[Note: For a discussion by Steven Isserlis of the Third Violin Sonata, see the "Aftermath and Legacy" chapter.]

Lynn Harrell

Of Schumann's chamber works with piano, the only ones originally written for cello are the *Five Pieces in Folk Style*, a late opus [Op. 102]. They are wonderful. The first one, in particular, is fabulous! It's marked "with humor," and it took me a while to realize that didn't mean "ha-ha" humor. No, it means a kind of easygoing happiness. And it's followed by the lyrical "berceuse" of the second one—actually, it's marked "langsam," or "slowly"—and in the third you have those powerful major/minor changes.

As for the three "Fantasy Pieces," the Op. 73, they are originally for clarinet, but they work well for the cello, too.

The famous *Adagio and Allegro,* of course, was first of all written for the new valve horn. But I've got to say in some ways I think it works better for the cello, because you can play it with more delicacy and a slower tempo and not be concerned with breath. But if you have an extremely fabulous hornist, those powerful parts near the end work best on the horn.

I think that Schumann, along with a number of his colleagues, wanted their music to be played as often as possible, so sometimes they would write music that could be performed on a variety of instruments. By contrast, earlier, when Mozart would write for the violin, you couldn't really transcribe it for something else. By the time Schumann, Brahms, and Franck were writing sonatas for violin, viola, cello, flute, just about anybody would be able to play them.

Bernard Greenhouse

I think my first experience with Schumann's *Five Pieces in Folk Style* was with Pablo Casals. I must have been only about thirty years old at the time, just out of the Navy, and getting ready for a New York recital. It was with one of Schumann's pieces from the *Five Pieces* that I found a way of expressing myself which I hadn't found in any other work during my study period. There were things Casals could show me in Schumann, things that were so sensitive that they required new techniques of working on the instrument. For example, that second piece in the cycle is a very beautiful lullaby, and I spent at least three or four lessons in working on the expressive possibilities in just that one piece. And speaking of those pieces, Casals compared them to Grimm's folk tales. That was something he said before I even first put the bow onto the string. He felt that we should relate the music to some of the old German stories, and it was wonderful how just mentioning that brought a clearer conception to me or about how to perform them. And when he demonstrated for me, it became even clearer. You know, he reversed the order of the set and brought the last piece to the front. If Schumann had written only the *Five Pieces,* I would consider him a major composer for the cello. And the works that we cellists have stolen from other pieces, like the *Fantasy Pieces* [Op. 73] and the *Adagio and Allegro* [Op. 70], have added to our repertoire enormously. But with the *Five Pieces,* the Cello Concerto, and the chamber music, we can see the man had an incredible feeling for the cello.

Richard Goode

I have particularly enjoyed playing the *Fairy Tales* [*Märchenerzählungen,* Op. 132] for viola, clarinet, and piano. It's a very unusual combination, although you recall the "Kegelstadt" Trio of Mozart and some other things. Maybe Schumann was thinking of the Mozart when he conceived this. It's a nice idea, at any rate. It's a very late piece, and in some ways, it has many of the characteristics of late Schumann, including this obsession with the dotted figure. And it can be rather thorny for the pianist. But it's a very successful tapestry of textures and sounds. The third movement is really magical. It has one of the most beautiful outpourings in all of Schumann. It's very cozy, like a fireside you can warm up to. I think it represents in his style a new development, which very unfortunately he didn't live to continue. It's a heavenly sound that has the quality of *never closing.* Every cadence turns into a new opening. And the piece never comes to rest, somehow. There's this wonderful, free-floating, free-associational quality where one heavenly thing follows another. I guess you might say it has the *endless* quality of certain Wagnerian pieces. I find this whole aspect of Schumann fascinating—the way in which certain of these pieces develop a small vocabulary of motifs in such a totally natural way. You can have played them for years and still come across some completely new associations that you never had realized before. You're aware that they are less directed toward goals, but more as what I would call "texture" music. As a result, the overall shape and direction of them is not as clear as in his earlier music.

10

"Heaven Sent"

The Choral Works

Commentators: *Gerd Albrecht, Theodore Albrecht, Victoria Bond, Joan Chissell, John Daverio, John Eliot Gardiner, Margaret Hillis, D. Kern Holoman, Roe-Min Kok, Erich Leinsdorf, John Nelson, Elizabeth Paley, Leon Plantinga, Laura Tunbridge, Charles Wadsworth, and John Worthen*

> *The highest expression possible in music comes from chorus and orchestra.*
>
> —Robert Schumann

EDITOR'S NOTE

In the last seven years of his life, in Dresden and Düsseldorf, Schumann organized several choral societies (*Chorverein*) and wrote many part songs, ensemble lieder, and *Liederspiele* for male, female, and mixed groups. These ballades, romances, and folklike melodies expressed nationalistic sentiments and were designed primarily to be accessible to middle-class audiences. The larger choral works, *Paradise and the Peri*, *Manfred*, *Scenes from Faust*, *Requiem for Mignon*, and the choral ballads, have more ambitious priorities. We begin with an overview of the choral song tradition.

THE CHORAL SONG TRADITION

> *My Chorverein is a source of much joy, for I can try out, to my great delight, all the music I love.*
>
> —Robert Schumann, April 1849

Theodore Albrecht

We find at this time major composers writing choral settings that are heard in the German *Liedertafeln* and *Liederkränze*. Think of Carl Maria von Weber in the midteens after the Battle of Leipzig, after Napoleon has been beaten back from Moscow in 1812. He's setting things like "Lutzow's Wild Hunt," which is not just a hunt, but a patriotic expression. This leads in the early 1820s to *Der Freischütz,* which is a major patriotic opera. There's the "Hunter's Chorus" in that, with all those "Yo-ho, tra-la-la-las" that John Q. Public and friends would get together throughout Germany and sing. Even today, they sing it. Although somebody like Beethoven held himself very much aloof from this sort of thing, Mendelssohn got into it. We find a lot of Mendelssohn songs that have these sentiments (although recent research by Erich Werner has shown Mendelssohn privately thought this high-power patriotism rather distasteful). And, of course, there's Schumann.

Prince Metternich, hating as he did these tendencies inside Germany, forbade any *Liedertafel*-type organizations in the Habsburg Empire until something like 1835, when he had to bow and allow them in.

Generally, the men would assemble in the neighborhood *Lokal,* which was usually the local *Gasthaus, Gastette* of same sort. They'd have a back room. They'd go in through the front door, get a stein of beer or a glass of wine, go into the back, open up the singing books, and spend an evening—often two evenings a week—singing, practicing these choruses and songs, discussing politics, the world in general, and having a good time. Eventually the women joined in, as well. The *Damenchor* and the *Frauenchor,* the women's choruses, also grew up at this time. Sometimes they'd be in another room with their own piano, their own wine, their own beer. And at other times both women and men would join together for a *Gemischtenchor,* the mixed chorus.

It's only a matter of time before you have a ready-made repertory for these singing groups. They can not only sing something a capella like those wonderfully convivial Schumann *Romances and Ballades* [Opp. 53, 64, 145, 146], but they can also sing standard big works like Haydn's *Creation* or *Seasons.* And so you have the development in Germany of oratorio societies that nicely parallels the growth of them in England. And the minute that you put together an oratorio, you now need an orchestra. And many of the local theater orchestras became the local symphony orchestras. You also look to Wagner and Brahms, who wrote songs for these singing groups in the *Liedertafel* tradition. Anytime you see a full-blown male chorus in nineteenth-century German music, you'd better believe there is some *Liedertafel* influence there. Think of Wagner's *Meistersinger* and the "Entry of the Guilds." How do you think you got all of those guilds coming onstage singing those songs? You do it by inviting your local *Liedertafel,* or *Liedertafeln* (because most of the large cities that can put on something like a *Meistersinger* will have a half-dozen at least of these groups floating around town). That way you get a lot of people participating onstage and in the audience. This was the type of music making that Schumann came to when he took up his post in Düsseldorf.

Charles Wadsworth

We at the Lincoln Center Chamber Music Society like to perform Schumann's *Spanish Love Songs* [Op. 74] with all four singers and the two pianists grouped in a semicircle. And we angle the piano ever so slightly so that our backs are almost to the audience. Richard Goode and I can maintain direct eye contact with the singers that way, and we all can keep our eyes on each other. It makes for a tight sort of ensemble. Richard and I have performed it with Kathleen Battle, John Aler, D'Anna Fortunato, and Dominic Cossa. We were lucky to make a recording of it, too, around 1981, I think. I try always to get as intimate a feeling among the players and performers as much as possible, because that quality is in these eight songs. The warmth and loving tenderness is there, and you try to communicate to the audience. Even if you don't understand a word of the texts by Emanuel Geibel, you can still sense that warmth. There's so much variety here—everything you could ask for, from simple folk tunes, to love songs, to nature setting—in combinations of solos, two duets, a quartet, and a prelude and intermezzo for Richard and me.

THE DRAMATIC CHORAL WORKS

EDITOR'S NOTE

There are those who allege that Schumann's preoccupation in the last decade of his creative life with writing large choral works was a "fatal attraction," producing music that is little known and infrequently performed today. Now we see healthy signs of change. Here with overviews and specific commentaries on *Paradise and the Peri,* the opera *Genoveva* (an account of its North American premiere), *Manfred, Scenes from Faust, Requiem for Mignon,* and the choral ballads are Gerd Albrecht, Victoria Bond, Joan Chissell, John Daverio, John Eliot Gardiner, Margaret Hillis, D. Kern Holoman, Roe-Min Kok, Erich Leinsdorf, John Nelson, Elizabeth Paley, Leon Plantinga, Laura Tunbridge, and John Worthen.

John Daverio

I see a lot of Schumann's late choral and vocal music as a continuation of his love and passion for great poetry. This really goes back to his very first years, when he displayed an intense interest in fine literature, from Goethe to Byron. With his music for *Faust* he was dealing with something that had become almost a Bible to Germans. And with his *Manfred* music he drew upon his knowledge of Byron, which his father had translated into German. For the choral ballads he reworked texts taken from another master poet of the early nineteenth century, Ludwig Uhland. In his later years, the last ten years, Schumann becomes very interested in an overarching theme of redemption, which cuts across all his works, from the *Paradise and the Peri,* his biggest oratorio, to the *Pilgrimage of the Rose, Manfred,* and *Scenes from Faust.* And though it's certainly true that there are supernatural and otherworldly elements in these pieces, they are subordinate to this overarching theme of redemption, of being redeemed. We know very little about his theology. His biographer, Wilhelm Wasiliewsky, said that he had a private religion and was certainly not religious in a dogmatic sense. Like many Germans of the time, he had been raised with the Bible. Brahms says that he would oftentimes quote the Bible. He kept a book of reminiscences of his children, in which he would intersperse passages from Ecclesiastes with details from their lives. I think he knew the Bible as a literary document, but that doesn't mean he was religious.

Paradise and the Peri

> *I finished my* Paradise and the Peri *last Friday, my greatest work, and I hope also my best. . . . The story of Peri is from Thomas Moore's* Lalla Rookh, *and it is as though it was written for music. The whole idea is so poetic, so pure, that if filled me entirely with enthusiasm."*
> —Robert Schumann, letter to Verhulst, June 1843

Elizabeth Paley

One of the things that first grabbed me about Schumann's *Paradise and the Peri* was simply that, although it was one of his most popular pieces in his lifetime, it is relatively unknown today. It made his international reputation, and it was performed second only to the "Spring" Symphony. After he finished it, Schumann considered *Paradise and the Peri* his greatest work to date. He was very much aware that he was not writing a traditional oratorio in the Judeo-Christian sense. He was following a few recent precedents in works by Carl Loewe and Heinrich Marschner in writing something that is not overtly biblical. Certainly, in terms of its scope, roughly an hour and a half to perform; its mix of arias and choral sections; and its overall didactic effect, is like an oratorio.

Schumann took the story from Thomas Moore's *Lalla Rookh*. The text was published in 1817 and was an instant success, becoming one of the most widely translated texts of its time. It consists of several long poems with a framing story, kind of like an *Arabian Nights*. You have Princess Tulip Cheek (Lalla Rookh) traveling from her homeland in Delhi to Cashmere, where she is to marry the prince of Lesser Bucharia, which is part of Persia. Accompanying her is a poet, Feramorz, to entertain her. He tells her four different stories along the way. "Paradise and the Peri" is the second of the four stories. The others are "The Veiled Prophet of Khorassan," the "Fire Worshippers," and "The Light of the Harem." Of course, by the time the Princess has arrived, she has fallen in love with the poet and no longer wants to marry the king. But guess what?—It turns out in the end that the poet is the king in disguise! So they all live happily ever after. There are notes in Schumann's journals in 1840 indicating that at first he considered setting three out of Feramorz's four stories. The "Peri" section he initially considered making into an opera. Instead, it became a new kind of oratorio.

As for the "Peri" story, she is a "child of the air," a spirit with wings. She is the progeny of a fallen angel and a mortal, and is barred from Paradise. She asks the angel who guards Heaven how she can get in. Only by finding a gift "most dear to Heaven," she is told, can she earn her entry into Paradise. She goes on a kind of scavenger hunt, you could say, a quest. She first finds a drop of blood that is shed by an Indian youth who dies in his battle with the invading tyrant from Gazna. The second is a "sigh of self-sacrifice" by a maiden who dies with her lover, who has contracted the plague. It's the third gift that wins the day. It is the tear of repentance from a criminal that is shed when he sees a "lost child of Paradise," a young child, praying. That redeems not only the criminal but Peri herself, and she finally enters Paradise. So you have Eastern mythological creatures, the peris, sprites, water nymphs, and houris (a *houri* is a beautiful nymph). But even though there are references to Allah, the theme of repentance and redemption fits in well with Christian oratorio tradition.

There is this lure of the Orient at this time. I can't say that there is very much that is "exotic" in the music. There are a few places where we hear Western clichés of Eastern music—lots of open fifths and some janissary instrument combinations like the ophicleide, cymbals, piccolos, as in the big battle. What do we mean, anyway, if we say that music sounds "oriental"? I mean, the story goes all over the place, to Egypt, Syria, Palestine,

India, and you can't really accurately represent all of that in music. No, I think that most of the exoticism is in the text itself.

Schumann writes that he does not want to interrupt the flow of the music—he was invested in the integrity of the storyline—and he was criticized for that in the reviews. The music does indeed flow together with little distinction or breaks between the arias, recitatives, and choruses. There are very few stopping points. Schumann emphasized the drama in the story by mixing up the narrative with enactment and reflection. For example, in the original Moore text, Feramorz narrates everything. He tells us what Peri says. Schumann makes Peri into a speaking character. Her words are sung by a soprano and are heard in conjunction with a narrator's voice. Schumann's sketches show that at first he intended to include recitatives, but in the end he took them out as the passages became more songlike.

One of the challenges *Peri* faces today is that you can't just take one movement and perform it in concert. It's really an "all-or-nothing" piece; either you do the whole thing, or nothing at all. That's an unfortunate consequence of the piece's structure, because the emotional impact of the music—especially Peri's songs—is wonderful. Peri has some exuberant melodies, and there's a gorgeous, soothing lullaby [No. 17] shared by Peri and the chorus. Some of the choruses are wonderful—the sonorities just shimmer. One favorite spot of mine is the "Nile Genies'" song [No. 11]; it reminds me of a light and airy "Ride of the Valkyries," and it turns into the accompaniment for one of Peri's lovelier melodies. I admit, there are some slow parts, too. Sometimes the music drags, especially toward the end. But the leadup to that ecstatic finish [No. 26], where Peri is redeemed and joyfully sings that her task is done, holds us in suspense with a cadence that is waiting to happen. Schumann holds off and holds off. . . . And then Peri comes in with the words, "Joy, joy, my task is done!"—and at last the cadence arrives when Heaven's doors open. For musical closure, Schumann adds a choir of Blessed Spirits, who welcome Peri (something that is not in Moore's version).

Transfiguration and redemption are themes that reappear in most of Schumann's dramatic choral works. Often it's through a woman. You might think of Clara, I suppose. But it's not just any woman, but an ideal woman. In *Manfred* it's Astarte, who is idealized to the point of having no character of her own. In *Genoveva* you have the ideal wife, who's willing to sacrifice herself for her husband. The same thing in *Pilgrimage of the Rose,* where Rose sacrifices herself for her child. In the song cycle, *Frauenliebe und -leben,* you have the idealized picture of a woman and a wife. And of course, in *Scenes from Faust,* you have Gretchen as a redeemer. Gender roles like this can make me cringe, but they were part of an "eternal feminine" ideal, and the music itself is wonderful. The ideal was certainly not the nineteenth-century reality, and certainly not illustrative of Robert and Clara's own professional reality.

I haven't heard a live performance of *Peri*. My favorite recording is the one by John Eliot Gardiner. I'm not saying we need to hear the *Peri* every year—resources are limited, and we don't have the number of singing societies as in Schumann's day. I admit there are some things in *Peri* that seem outdated, but it would be nice if we could "redeem" the work, perform it more, and hear some of Peri's joy.

Margaret Hillis

I was involved several years ago in a production of *Paradise and the Peri* with Carlo Maria Giulini and the Chicago Symphony. I prepared the chorus. Giulini was usually the only conductor who always sent me very carefully marked piano and vocal parts, with crescendos and such worked out. But I didn't get it this time, so I had to work it out myself. I just know how he handles things and knew how he would feel his tempi and fugal passages. He always likes to do works that are unusual. And it's the only time I've ever been involved with this work.

It has some of the most beautiful music in it that I think was ever written, gorgeous melodies. The difficulty is that it doesn't hang together as one large structure. There's not enough contrast, which is where the weakness lies. But with Schumann it's just this outpouring of songs, like an evening of *lieder*. That often happens with people who are like, for example, Fauré, another master of songwriting. When he gets into larger forms, things don't really work. The problem with Schumann—and this is a problem you also run into with Mendelssohn—is he could get carried away with the beauty of the line and then start adding sugary elements to it. And I think he was considering the "middle" and "lower" classes of people who love folk music. They would even remember the fugue subjects, because they are highly melodic.

Schumann wants a big sound here. And the chorus amplifies the sound even more. There are so many things Schumann had to learn to know to build that kind of sound. Sometimes you use horns alone, and then, to change the color a little bit, you can double them with bassoons. Or you can use trombones and trumpets, but you can double that with horns to make a fuller and rounder sound. And maybe you've got a clarinet and an oboe playing in unison, but they might not be in tune—so you add a flute either an octave above or in unison with them and, suddenly, they seem in tune! You have to know that the double basses, for instance, if they don't have an instrument sounding an octave above them, running along their line, can sound like a bunch of bumblebees out in the back pasture.

They need something to tie them into the texture of the sound. When the cellos are doing something else, there has to be a horn or a clarinet or a bassoon that ties that sound into the texture.

John Eliot Gardiner

Several years ago I encountered a wonderful oratorio by Schumann called *Paradise and the Peri*. It was premiered in Leipzig in 1843 and was quite a success in its day. Now, however, it is woefully ignored. It is an exotic, poetic, and very expressive work with, curiously enough, some of the same qualities that I found so endearing about Handel: the very graphic orchestration, the wonderful mixture of a rhetoric gesture and great tenderness and poetry.

Yes, I plan to record it in Dresden with the Dresden Staatskapelle [it was ultimately recorded with the Monteverdi Choir and the Orchestre Révolutionnaire et Romantique and released in 1997]—the ultimate orchestra. The oratorio grew out of the kind of sanctimonious tradition around Handel's oratorios and which came to a further manifestation in the oratorios of Mendelssohn. These were works presumed to be edifying, morally edifying vehicles for a society trying to find their own moral values and rearticulate them in terms that they could accept in their own day. Schumann, who was a rebel in many senses, was showing his difference from his contemporaries—saying no, this is a secular oratorio. I'm not preaching, I'm celebrating something different: the spirit of man that runs through it, and the spirit of God, the spirit of divinity. He was very pantheistic.

Schumann, like so many of the romantics, was very interested in the East. I find this particularly appealing, personally. So much of the transmission of Greek philosophy, culture, astronomy, music into Western Europe came a result of the Arab invasions. We still have this unfortunate image of the Arabs as a very uncultured race. But, in fact, we owe them a huge debt in the West. They played a catalytic role in bringing to us during the Dark Ages of Europe the features of Greek philosophy and Greek thought and Greek culture.

Genoveva

> *In reading your poem,* Genoveva, *I was impressed by the wonderful material which it offers for music. . . . but I very much dislike the ordinary libretto style, and will not stoop to write tirades of that sort.*
> —Robert Schumann, letter to Hebbel, 1849

Victoria Bond

You know, ever since the first production in 1850 of Schumann's *Genoveva,* the criticism that has been leveled against this opera is that it's an evening of lieder and nothing much else happens. Well, that couldn't be farther from the truth. It is full of high drama and supercharged emotion. In my opinion, it's very stageworthy, too. It's not at all static.

There had not been any staged professional performances in America prior to the performance in June 1987 at Bel Canto Opera. That seems truly amazing, right? I mean, that kind of neglect is staggering. There've been concert performances, and the overture has been performed numerous times, but never the entire work staged. Incomprehensible.

Where did you get the idea of organizing a production of Genoveva?

That came as a result of research by several people in Bel Canto, particularly a board member, Jerrold Morgulas, who is quite a researcher and a very brilliant person and very committed. And he gave me a list of works to see which would interest me, and of course when I saw Robert Schumann's name, that sort of lit up all the red lights on my computer, and I said, "Yes." So I had a listen to the Kurt Masur recording [recorded in 1977 with the Leipzig Gewandhaus Orchestra with Dietrich Fischer-Dieskau as Siegfried, Edda Moser as Genoveva, and Peter Schreier as Golo] and absolutely fell in love with the music. From there it was a question of finding out where the materials were, and they were handled by G. Schirmer in New York, so there was no problem in getting the materials (although what we got were hopelessly marked up from a past performance, numerous cuts). I just shudder to think what that performance must have been like. I don't think it was a staged performance, certainly not in this country.

The scoring is actually quite light. My principal concern in reducing the orchestration was to maintain the richness of the music. The richness primarily comes in the string section, so I wanted to put together a decent string section in terms of numbers. We had far above a decent section in terms of players' quality. We had *I solisti di New York,* many young, wonderful freelancers. It was a joy; I mean, the harder the music got, the more they sort of took the bit and ran. They loved it. The wind parts are all in pairs, two flutes, two oboes, et cetera, and I reduced them to single winds, which is generally not terribly difficult because the winds act very much as soloists within the texture of the whole work, and there are very few moments when they actually have two solo parts that are not doubled in the strings. Then I reduced the four horn parts to two horns and three trumpet parts to one trumpet, and eliminated the trombone parts, rescored them in the bassoons and the cellos and the bass, reduced the percussion parts to one player who plays tympani and percussion. The string parts, of course, are all intact, and we had, as I say, wonderful quality in terms of string players, although if I had a less limited budget I certainly would have had a larger string section than we were able to afford; it was a chamber ensemble.

We knew that we were going to be doing this production a year before we actually did it, and we usually have a major casting in the spring for the following season. So when we do our auditions, it's a question of listening to what voices would be appropriate for which operas. And if we don't find all of the voices we need as a result of that major audition, then we will have separate auditions for specific voice types. And we assembled a really star-studded cast; we double cast it, one of the reasons being it gives the opportunity to twice as many young singers. Another reason, which is a very practical reason, is that if somebody gets sick, you don't get on the phone to an agent and say, "Get me a Genoveva," you know? This is not exactly a role that every soprano has at her fingertips or can fill in at the last moment.

The Genovevas were Bretta Lundell and Caroline Thomas; Golo was Neil Breeden; Siegfried, Bruce Haley and Jeffrey Ambrosini; Margaretha, Adele Nicholson and Debra Kitabjian; Caspar, Eric Coin; Balthasar, Charles Gafford; Drago, Jay Bonney; Hidulfus, Stephen White; and then, let me see, we had chorus master Greg Buchalter, assistant conductor Betty Prielozny, stage manager John Fisher. We had the tremendous challenge to make it stageworthy, or I should say to discover the stageworthiness within it, because it is very stageworthy.

Is it safe to assume that none of these singers knew about this work?

Oh, yes, very safe to assume. The director's name is Kathryn Weyand. And for our first session, we had, we assembled the entire cast, the double cast, and talked about the opera, basically—talked about Schumann, talked about the history of the opera, the plot of the opera; we just sort of had a lovely, informal party and spoke about *Genoveva* before we actually got started with any musical rehearsals.

They were very enthusiastic from the beginning. I'll tell you one thing that kept everybody's enthusiasm on a very high level was the nature of the music. The roles are challenging; the music is interesting at every moment. This is not a dull opera in any of its particulars. You know, sometimes you'll have an opera that has wonderful vocal lines and the orchestration or the instrumental parts are rather dull. I mean, I can think of many Bel Canto operas that fall into that category where singers love them, audiences love them because it's wonderful vocal writing, but the instrumental writing is from hunger. Well, this is not true of *Genoveva*. It has wonderful vocal parts, it has wonderful orchestral parts, everybody in the ensemble has something interesting to do, every last instrumentalist has a part that is fascinating, you know? You can take anybody's part out of context and it . . . there is so much to work on. So I think everyone was very challenged by the work and very excited about doing the premiere of it, and just doing it, period. We rehearsed for six weeks. We had very nice, simple but effective sets. And we all were on a high-tension wire for the opening night.

Let's go to opening night. When was it, and we're in the car and we're going to the theater and we tell the cab driver, "Take us to the Bel Canto Opera!"

Okay, let's see, the production was staged at the Fashion Institute of Technology Auditorium, which is at 227 West Twenty-seventh Street, and has a very, very lovely auditorium. There are always so many last-minute sort of worries—will the stand lights work, you know, is everybody there. Actually, what I do before a performance is completely close myself off, and I just try and not think about anything. I just blank my mind out, I meditate. So, I mean, it's a very useful technique in all kinds of situations, and I found it particularly useful in a situation such as this, because the very opening, the overture, starts out in high gear. You don't ease into this opera. You're there from the first moment, and you have to be "on." So there's no time to sort of rev up into it. And also my experience has been that one of the prime functions of a conductor is actually the scientific equivalent of a superconductor. The idea of transferring energy from one source to another with as little resistance as possible strikes me as a very apt analogy for what a conductor actually does. You know, when all things are working perfectly, you can self-destruct, you know, in a way because all the energy is just flowing. But the initial resistance to getting that energy started is enormous. I've made comparisons to lifting a 747 off the ground with your bare hands, you know. Everybody is nervous, they're worried, they're tired, they're, you know, cranky. Something is always wrong, you know, to get everyone out of the earth level of their daily mundane life and their worries about getting to the performance on time and missing the train and missing the subway and do I have all of my music and things like that. Focus, focus and concentration. Get that laser beam of intensity that happens when you have a hundred-odd people—sometimes very odd people—all working towards one goal. I mean that is such a heady experience, and in addition to the actual performers and all the crew, there's the audience, and that intensity and focus and concentration of the audience is a very potent element, as anyone who performs knows.

But then finally, when that curtain goes up, what is going on in this opera called Genoveva?

There's a segue from the Overture that takes us immediately into a very grand scene. Hidulfus, who is the Bishop of Trier, is kind of giving a pep talk to the armies to get them revved up to go off and fight the enemy and to fight for Carl Martell. (I was going to give everyone a bottle of cognac that said "Carl Martell" on it as an opening-night gift!) This is a very dignified, almost a popelike character, and the chorus is singing this Bach-like chorale at the beginning, which is very, very grand. And into this sort of tapestry backdrop we see the individual characters of Siegfried, who is the lord of the castle, and Genoveva, who is his bride. They've been married just a short time, and here he is already going off to war (what a life!). And she is distraught, to say the least. And he is trying to calm her and says, "Now, this is your obligation and your duty, and baby, if you're going to be married to me, this is the way it's always going to be!"

He assigns responsibility to various people in his castle, and the responsibility of his wife he assigns to his closest, trusted friend, Golo. Mistake number one. Now, Golo, first of all, does not like the idea of being left behind. He would much rather go out and fight for glory than he would sort of babysit Genoveva. But there's also another reason why he's very uncomfortable with this position, and that's because he's secretly in love with Genoveva. And all of these mixed emotions are going through his head after the wonderful choral exit, where everyone goes off to war and Siegfried leaves Genoveva. Genoveva, in a mood of utmost desolation, faints. And here she is, lying there helpless, and Golo, with all of these turbulent emotions going through him, goes to revive her, and as he holds her in his arms, the thought crosses his mind, the best way to revive her is with a kiss. I mean, you know, it does work in Wagner, why wouldn't it work in *Genoveva*? Actually, the story is very old; it's a medieval legend, so there is some precedent there. And so he does give her a kiss; she wakes up, and she thinks, of course, that he is her husband Siegfried at first. But then she realizes it's Golo, and she's a little bit taken aback, a little bit surprised. And watching this whole scene is the character who really catapults this whole plot, and that is Margaretha, a very interesting character. She is a sorceress. She had been an employee of the castle, and she was banished because she practiced sorcery, and she's got a chip on her shoulder ever since and would like to get back at Siegfried, who banished her. So when Genoveva leaves, Golo is left onstage alone to mull over what he's just done and the repercussions. And Margaretha says, "I saw what just happened, and by the way, I can help you." And so at first he tries to get rid of her; he's not interested in what she has to offer. But she does a very clever blackmail on him. Schumann's music for this is absolutely inspired, because we hear the way Golo regards Margaretha initially, and then we hear how her music gradually starts to infiltrate *his* music until he is, I believe, completely hypnotized by her. And at that moment, she knows that she has him exactly where she wants him, and they sing this wonderful sort of heroic duet at the end of the act.

But then after that, as is so characteristic of Schumann, the character of Golo does realize what he's doing; he's torn and tortured by that now. And he's very articulate about it.

Absolutely, he's torn in two directions, and he wants to right the wrong that he has done, but he's caught. And this of course happens in the second act. He's absolutely caught, and Margaretha now has him to such an extent, she really is almost like a devil that owns his soul. And he's thrashing about trying to wrest his soul back from her, but at that point it's too late and the only thing he can do is play out the drama.

In Act 2, Genoveva is pining away in her bedchamber. Siegfried's been gone—she's not really a liberated woman, let's face it!—and she misses him terribly. She feels the weight of the responsibility of the castle on her shoulders. And to make matters even worse, all of the servants are downstairs, getting drunk and being very rowdy. And Schumann sets this in such an extraordinary way, musically; he writes really some of his crudest music for them purposely, very . . . I can't even say folklike and peasantlike . . . and it's written for high clarinets in their most unpleasant register. I mean, this is not pretty, friendly music floating gracefully up from down below. There's definitely a touch of, you know, German expressionism here. It's a very uncomfortable scene. And she's getting more and more nervous as she hears them singing. And into this scene of consternation comes Golo, and she says, "Ah, Golo, I'm so glad to see you, what's going on outside?" And he says, "Well, they're celebrating, actually, because there's been a victory." And she says, "A victory? What's happened? How is Siegfried?" And he says, "Well, he's been victorious, he's won the battle." And she says, "How come I didn't hear about it?" And he says, "Well, good news travels quickly through people. I mean, he would not have been able to write to you and it wouldn't have gotten to you yet, but I'm telling you this is good news." And she says, "Oh, wonderful, let's celebrate. Why don't you and I sing a song?" And so Golo says, "Well, I haven't sung for a long time" (typical tenor response!). And she replies, "So much the better, your voice will be rested." So at that point he picks up a lute hanging on the wall, and they sing this lovely little duet. Schumann does the most remarkable thing in this duet, because it starts out in a very strophic, lyrical fashion, almost a medieval folk song ballad; but as each verse goes on, and Genoveva continues singing the melody, Golo steps out of the actual context, as though he were looking at himself from outside, and we hear his inner thoughts: "She's all alone. Her servant has gone off to tend to her sick mother. This is my opportunity. If I'm gonna make my move, it's now."

You're suggesting this becomes a kind of counterpoint to what she's singing?

Exactly so, it's a counterpoint. And the song is very calm, and his counterpoint is more and more agitated, and finally it's as though this monster that has been agitating underneath now gobbles him up. And he says, "I can't resist any longer, I have to tell you I'm in love with you." And she, who has been singing this lovely song very placidly, doesn't know what to think. I mean, she's completely taken aback. And she backs up from him, and he starts to pursue her, and she runs away from him. You have this whole kind of complete reversal of their relationship within just a matter of moments. So at the moment of greatest tension, she says to him, "You bastard!" And the way it's set is incredible. I mean everything stops when she says, "You bastard." And of course the word *bastard* must have carried a lot more implication at that time than it does now. I mean you call anybody on the street nowadays a bastard and it doesn't mean anything. But evidently this was such a deep insult to his character that he's completely turned off. And he just goes from white-hot to ice-cold, and he says, "You're gonna live to regret that remark" (I'm paraphrasing the words). So this begins his revenge on Genoveva.

The fascinating thing about Golo's character is that he has the elements of his own destruction within him, which is of course a wonderful analogy to Schumann's mental and physical condition, which has its manifestation in his music, as well. Golo has all of the elements for a great hero. You know, he is very brave, he's very gentle, he's a much more profound character than *Genoveva*'s Siegfried, who's kind of a cardboard character. He's just, you know, sort of a hero who's gone off to war. But Golo is the one who's been left behind; he's somebody who had been very brave in battle. But there is a fatal flaw to his character.

And he's a "watcher." We see him in so many of Schumann's songs: There's always a minstrel, an outsider, standing alongside, looking at the wedding of a beloved to someone else. He's bitterly gnashing his teeth on the sidelines.

Golo can't go off and fight because he's got to look after the shop. He's on the sidelines with Genoveva. His love for her is an impossible love.

In the scene where Genoveva is taken to the tower, we have really massive forces at work here. How successfully does Schumann work this out, in your opinion?

Extraordinarily successfully. I think he understands the mentality of a crowd gone wild. They've come into her bedchamber because she's been accused—falsely, as the audience knows—of having an affair, and she tries to plead her case. But they won't listen to her. And what happens is that the music gets more and more agitated, the tempos increase, and Schumann successfully builds transitions, like a stepladder, with the steps gradually increasing in intensity, increasing in tempo, increasing in drive, like a perfectly orchestrated hysteria of a crowd, until at the end they're singing, "Zum Turm mit ihr, zum Turm mit ihr," like a chant, you know? It's almost like a Nazi war cry that just is totally out of control. It's a remarkably exciting scene, and it grows and builds and builds and builds, and I tell you, onstage everybody's hair was standing straight up!

And Margaretha's voice comes in with some rather striking interpositions.

Yes, well, she always comes out of left field, you know; she's sort of the spark that's igniting this whole thing, and she keeps it going.

We've talked about elements of sorcery in this; let's move to the scene where Siegfried is confronted by Margaretha with a magic mirror. And he gazes at three pictures.

Golo has come to Siegfried and says, "Your wife is doing dirt behind your back." Siegfried is furious. He says, "Here, take my sword, take my ring. I'm gonna kill myself, but I want you to kill her first. So kill her with my sword and show her my ring and tell her this is what I think of her!" The mirror is showing Siegfried something he's not sure he wants to see. And the way Schumann sets this is with an offstage women's chorus. It's extraordinarily effective, with very, very ethereal writing in the orchestra. The voices are very high. It really completely captures the mood of something otherworldly. Whereas the human world is full of *Sturm and Drang,* the spirit world is very, very calm. It's on another plane completely.

As these images are delivered up to Siegfried, we have an effect that amounts to switching channels on a television. Scenically, how did you handle this onstage?

Well, as I said we have limited resources; we do what we can with mirrors, and the director had, I think, a very brilliant idea of how to set this, which I think is also very much in line with Schumann's writing. Rather than have a whole spectacle of what he sees in the mirror, we see his *reactions* to the changing images. Now, this, of course, would work even better in cinema. But it gives an actor a chance to really be the focus of the attention and how his mood goes from—"Oh, yes, it's my castle, how wonderful, I know that very pathway, and there's Genoveva"—to scenes that are less and less appealing. Finally, he sees her reaching out to who he thinks is his rival and kissing him. Siegfried is furious, and he smashes the mirror. Orchestrally and vocally, it's just so extraordinary a setting. I mean this mirror is like her soul—she will disappear in a puff of smoke, you know, when this mirror is smashed.

As a matter of fact, it's prophesied that she may disappear in a puff of flame if she doesn't right the wrong.

During all this there are some complicated twists and turns, and somebody is murdered. The ghost of the murdered man appears out of the shards of the broken mirror and says to Margaretha, "Unless you repent your evil ways . . ." It's really something right out of *Don Giovanni.*

The "mirror scene" in the opera is the one that has aroused the most savage criticism of people like George Bernard Shaw. He said it was trivial, completely lacking in any kind of drama. He criticized the orchestration—I think there's a high piccolo or something in there that he thought was "cheap." This one scene really does put Schumann on the firing line. How do you respond to that? Is it justified?

Oh, gosh, I think the mirror scene is absolutely the apex of the whole opera. I mean I love every scene, but this particular scene is where the whole drama turns around. I mean, without the scene you could not have *Genoveva.* This scene is absolutely integral and organic in the development of the opera. And as far as being dramatic, it is extraordinary, absolutely extraordinary. I don't agree with the critics at all in this regard, and I think it works instrumentally and vocally as well as stagewise. Siegfried smashes the mirror; the ghost of the man who was murdered appears to Margaretha and says, "If you don't repent your evil ways, you're going to be engulfed in flames like a salamander." And so that's the end of that scene, and Margaretha's just screaming . . . It's very histrionic. She has a wonderful, wonderful scene at the end of that act.

Meanwhile, back at the ranch, we find out that what has happened is that Genoveva is about to be executed. Golo gives her one last chance: Will you love me, or is this going to be the final farewell? And she says, "No, I wouldn't dream of it, I'm in love with Siegfried, I wouldn't dream of being unfaithful to him." Golo comes to her and says, "Do you know this sword? Do you know this ring? Your husband gave them to me and ordered me to execute you. What do you think of that?" It's quite a wonderful moment, you know. But she remains faithful to Siegfried to the very end. So then he tells his lackeys to go and kill her, and he leaves.

Meanwhile, while they're preparing to kill her, she sees a shrine and she rushes over to it and prays. A beautiful, beautiful prayer in the midst of all this chaos. They're too superstitious to hack her to bits while she's holding the cross. And then, of course, we have the deus ex machina. From offstage we hear the chorus of hunters. Enter Siegfried and Margaretha. Margaretha has explained to Siegfried that Genoveva is not unfaithful to him. Everybody ends up happily. The ending is a little bit disappointing, as far as all the drama that has been set up.

Big question: Where does Golo go? There is a problem with Golo, he just seems to kind of—doesn't he fall off a cliff or something?

Well, I must say the ending is dramatically disappointing. Musically it's not disappointing at all, but dramatically it's like Schumann was tired of writing it already and he wanted to just put an end to it. And so, I mean he sort of stuck an ending on it. But with the rest of the work being so powerful dramatically, I can forgive that.

I wish that he had written many more operas. If Wagner had only written one opera, then we really wouldn't be hearing very much of his music—his operatic output, that is. So I think that one learns best, particularly in terms of something as complex as stage work, by doing it. I can vouch for that from personal experience, being right now in the midst of writing my first opera. And with all of the ingredients that Schumann had to be a really great opera composer, I am truly sorry that he didn't have more encouragement to go on and do another opera after this.

Apparently Schumann's first night was something of a disaster. There were cues missed, and a letter wasn't delivered when it should have been, or something like that. These are things, I suppose, that any opera con-ductor certainly could identify with.

Absolutely. Absolutely. To get a work launched is an extremely touch-and-go kind of thing; you have to have a resiliency to bounce back after the most dismal failure and say, well, I'm going on to write the next one!

Do you think, then, that this thing will attach itself in some way to your own career; will people say, "Yes, Victoria Bond, she did the Genoveva*?*

Well, I would like to do it again, let's put it that way. I would like to do it many times again!

Leon Plantinga

Schumann's *Genoveva* suffered somewhat the same fate as Berlioz's *The Trojans*. They couldn't find audiences. Poor old Berlioz had to finally slice up his masterpiece into more palatable pieces to be fed to the audience. Schumann's opera was performed, of course, and did find a mediocre but short-lived success. But by the time it came along, it's already old hat because it's so much in the mold of the German romantic opera tradition. *Genoveva* is a wonderful opera. Wonderful things happen in that opera. But for German audiences clamoring for something new at every turn, it must have seemed something they had seen before, all the way back to Weber. *Genoveva*, like *Tannhaüser* and *Lohengrin*, is the last gasp of German romantic opera. There is no more after that. Wagner himself was aware of that, and he very consciously set out to provide something intended to be clearly new and fresh.

Manfred

> *Never before have I devoted myself with such love and outlay of force to any composition as to that of Manfred."*
> —Robert Schumann, 1849

Gerd Albrecht

I came to Schumann's *Manfred* through the famous Overture. When I decided to do the whole piece with the Berlin Philharmonic, I found out it had not been done since 1918 with Bruno Walter. But first I had to find out why it had not been done for so long, and I found out that the balance between Byron's text [1817] and Schumann's music [1849] was a misbal-ance. If you do the entire Byron poem, it would last two and a half hours. That's if you make no cuts in the text. Schumann gives you no sign what cuts to make. I believe he gave this to the conductors only. He let it be freely adapted. I have the feeling he wanted half music, half text. Another reason was the terrible translation available from English to German. So I made a new translation. Byron is hell to translate, though my English is rather good. And then I tried to balance out the text and the music. You see, melodrama is a very special kind of art. The difference between the spoken word, the sung word, and the music is so interesting and so exciting that I believe Schumann was right to do it this way. My performance in Berlin came in at sixty-eight minutes. I then did it in Vienna with the same cast, where we found it had not been performed since 1898. Eventually, I persuaded my recording manager to do it on record. And he said, "Yes, let's try it out; why not? And we did it in 1984 for Musica Mundi with the Berlin Radio Symphony Orchestra and four soloists, Gudrun Sieber (soprano), Gabriele Schreckenbach (alto), Alejandro Ramirez (tenor), and Harald Stamm (bass). For the recording we found a church in Berlin with marvelous acoustics. It came in at sixty-two minutes.

Manfred is a British *Faust*. The character is very divided, very conflicted: He is a hesitator, he is an actor, and he is disquieted. He is a neurotic, hypersensitive person, very romantic, but difficult to understand. I think Schumann was always drawn to this character. He was just nineteen years old when he writes about how disturbing he found the book. His musical version is more dramatic than *Genoveva*. The orchestration is the most sensitive that he ever did, in my opinion. The orchestration is not so thick. There's none of this "doubling" of instrumentation you hear so much about. For example, in the fourth number ["Hark! My soul would drink those echoes"], he calls for two English horns. Manfred hears the shepherd's pipe and feels a kind of self-cleaning, a rejuvenation, you would say. At the same time, we know it prepares him to die. When I did it, I stationed one horn in the orchestra and the other far away in the audience. And so it sounds like the sound is coming from two different directions. We did the same thing for the recording in the church. It's very dramatic in a rather sweet way. I know of nothing in Schumann more beautiful than the famous "Hymn to the Sun" and "Manfred's Death" ["O sun, most glorious orb . . . My life is in its last hour"]. Schumann allows for a wonderful balance here. Manfred compares the sun rising and sun setting with his own life. He says, "You are rising in the morning so strong and warming the Earth and me; and you then go down in the afternoon, and I feel cold." It's an image of nature which represents a man's own life and death. I have been discussing doing it onstage with a very interesting German painter and a stage director, Achim Freyer. When he heard my recording he said, "Please, let's do it onstage." We are still considering it.

Elizabeth Paley

For my PhD dissertation, I worked on Schumann's *Manfred*. Schumann set music to Lord Byron's poem about Count Manfred, who was suffering from guilt over the death of his beloved Astarte (who may have been his sister). Before I started, I had heard the famous Overture, but hadn't known that Schumann had written any incidental music. What we have here is an eclectic mix—one entr'acte, three songs, two "choral phrases," and nine "melodramas." Some of the music is quite eerie, and you hear a lot of torment and anger, but I think we have to be careful about taking that as evidence of Schumann's incipient madness. He can write music that *sounds* tortured, intentionally, not just because he might have personal issues. Byron didn't intend his poem to be performed theatrically, but there were subsequent traditions of acting out Schumann's setting with performers and musicians. There were even some "incidental texts," published in 1859—abbreviated parts of the poem, created to accompany the music—so you could hear all of the music without having to listen to all of Byron's poem.

Manfred employs a great deal of *melodrama*—meaning instrumental music coupled with declaimed rather than sung text. The disjunction between music and spoken text was often rather unsettling to audiences. Schumann took advantage of Byron's suggestions of the supernatural and accompanied the conjurations of demons and spirits with some of the most spine-tingling orchestral and choral music ever composed. Consider the summoning of Astarte in No. 10; the music is very quiet, sinuous, like a wisp of smoke, very disorienting. You don't get a strong sense of key or downbeat for a while. Another melodrama is the Requiem heard from afar as Manfred dies. Byron leaves the fate of the unrepentant count unclear, but by adding the Requiem, Schumann suggests Manfred is redeemed.

Scenes from Faust

I only wish I could have Faust's mantle for that day, in order to be everywhere and hear everything. How strange, the piece lay five years in the desk. Nobody knew anything about it, and I myself had almost forgotten its existence—and now in this unusual celebration it has come to light!

—Robert Schumann on the Goethe Centenary,
August 29, 1849

Erich Leinsdorf

I feel that Schumann was one of the few composers who truly understood Goethe's text. I can prove that more than subjectively by comparing various composers who took the *Faust* as their subject. Schumann understood the text much better in all its profundity than Liszt and far better than Mahler. Berlioz's *Damnation of Faust* is a different approach, and while it has elements of that book, I do not feel that it needs to be compared to Schumann. Goethe is, of course, for us who have been brought up in the German language, the non plus ultra. He occupies the same position that Shakespeare holds to the English literature student. He is as a poet the end of all things. Not as a dramatist. And *Faust* is a poem, not a drama. No question about it. Maybe Part One can be done as a stage play, and it has been done in Gounod's version. But the true greatness in *Faust* is the poetry.

I'm very, very fond of this work, and I have performed it a great deal. But it can be difficult for Americans to understand. It is not an opera, not an oratorio, but a collection of disjointed "scenes." When you take the two parts of the book, which have approximately eleven thousand lines in Goethe, you see that Schumann uses approximately only six hundred. Needless to say, unless you know the book from beginning to end, you cannot make much sense of the scenes Schumann strings together. The highpoint of his music is of course from Part Two, where we have "The Awakening of Faust," "The Approach of the Sun," "The Four Gray Women," Faust's death (which is a stupendous piece), and then the last scene. Schumann wrote two endings. I use the first one, which I think is far more appropriate for those last lines, *"Alles Vergängliche ist nur ein Gleichnis"* (All that Earth comprises is symbol alone).

I first encountered it simply by reading the score. All my life I have "read" music as voraciously as one reads words. During my first year in Boston, around 1966, I think, I was looking for a neglected and unperformed choral work that could be programmed with Brahms's *German Requiem.* Then I read an article about Schumann's *Scenes from Faust.* I did not know this work at that time. So I borrowed a score from the Boston Public Library. I was astounded. Here was a neglected masterpiece. I went to Hermann Prey, who was performing in the *Requiem,* and asked him if he would learn the scene of "Faust's death." He did, and it proved to be a great success. I then went in for four performances of the complete work, two in Boston and two in New York. I am sorry to report they were not successful. You can't have a text like this sung by people who do not know the language. Almost everyone, including the conductor, has to understand what they are playing. But since then, I've done it successfully many times in Europe, Frankfurt, Berlin. I've even done it in Milan (although I don't know what they got out of it!).

Hermann Prey has been my Faust from the beginning. I don't think I've done it with anybody else, except in Milan, when I had a nice Romanian baritone. Otherwise, Prey has been my man. He is certainly one of the two greatest male lieder singers and is thoroughly at home with the work of Schumann. Prey brought with him a conviction that went over to the other singers. This continues to be my main battle with choral works, that I never find sufficient attention to the texts.

Like much of Schumann's late orchestral writing, it's in need of editing. I have spent more than a year in editing the *Faust* score. If you perform these works precisely as they are printed in score, you would not be able to hear the singer. The instrumental accompaniments can emasculate the vocal sonority. You must take out some of the instrumental doublings, which was Schumann's major problem in orchestrating. And the Overture itself is problematic and needs extensive editing.

Schumann has given us many wonderful moments here. Faust's last scene with Mephisto is crucial to the meaning of the whole work. The ninety-year-old Faust has achieved what he set out to do, but to Mephisto (the incarnation of the negative principle), it is all a joke. Take as an example the irony of Faust's words, when he says about the land reclamation project, "*Wie das Geklirr der Späten mich ergötzt!*" (The click of spades—ah, how it heartens me!); but we know that in actuality Faust is digging *his own grave*. Such irony is never far away in Goethe's poetry. Never. So you have this flight of great romantic fantasy and, at the same time, this corrective of romantic irony, which is just as much a part of romanticism as the idealistic fantasy. Goethe is I think the greatest master of romantic irony.

And there's that wonderful moment in the fourth section of Part Three—which Schumann excerpted from the second book of *Faust*—when the angels sing, "*Gerettet ist das edle Glied / der Geisterwelt vom Bösen* (We have saved the noble one from evil). Now, what has happened here is that the remains of Faust have been taken away from Mephisto by the angels. Mephisto has been betrayed of his part of the pact. By the way, I must point out something that is not apparent to the reader of the Schumann score. I mean the moment when Faust dies. Goethe's words are "*Er fällt! Es ist vollbracht*" (It falls. 'Tis accomplished). These are the same words which you have in the Gospel of St. John as voiced by Jesus on the cross. And Schumann finishes the scene this way. But he left out Goethe's original, where we hear not only "*Es ist vollbracht,*" but Mephisto's mocking response to Faust's "*Es ist vorbei*" ("It is over"). He retorts—"stupid words." So there you have it—Schumann cut out the irony in his composition and left it only as "It is accomplished." In my own editing, I have added one *"vorbei,"* so that both versions—the "accomplishment" and "it is over"—are both represented in the performance.

These late works require complicated and costly preparation. I would like to test more of these choral works in performance.

Are American audiences doomed not to hear the other choral works?

There's always the same problem, and the problem in romantic composition is simply diagnosed—the four greatest composers of lieder, Schubert, Schumann, Brahms, and Wolf, have never been able to write along the lines of arias in operas. These four composers, who are the last word in lieder composition, together have not produced one viable opera. Wolf tried. Schumann's *Genoveva* is not really an opera. Schubert wrote a dozen "operas," but they are not operas that can live onstage. And Brahms never tried. I think personally that all the Schumann choral works suffer the moment you pit his orchestra against the voice. He was a lied composer.

Aside from the text problem, I am madly devoted to *Faust* and will always take the opportunity to perform it. But at the same time, I recognize its hybrid nature; and the greatest parts of it are songs; and songs with orchestra have rarely been successful. This includes the songs of Strauss, which have been orchestrated. If you compare Brahms's *Schicksalslied* (Song of Destiny) with Schumann, you see the difference between the two composers.

You don't need to defend Schumann by saying he was not a genius in everything. Nobody was. But with him it seems easier to spot the differences because of his unsurpassed greatness in writing for piano and in writing lieder. Those two categories show his inspiration at its best.

John Daverio

Schumann said once that the highest in musical expression is achieved through the forces of chorus and orchestra. There are many, many moods and characters and qualities that Schumann evokes in his *Faust* music. For example, I think that Schumann evokes a Gothic quality in the "Cathedral Scene" in Part One that is quite extraordinary. Gretchen is in the cathedral, and in the background a Requiem mass is being sung. Some commentators on the text think that it might be a Requiem mass for Gretchen's brother, who had been killed by Faust. In any event, Schumann sets its text to music—but in a kind of distorted form, as if this is how the disturbed and overwrought Gretchen is hearing it. That's really quite special. Later, in Part Two, in the "Midnight Scene" we find some of Schumann's most colorful orchestrations, filled with scurrying figures and contrasts between high and low textures. It's horrifying in the sense of nineteenth-century German opera, in particular Heinrich Marschner's *Der Vampyr*. (When Robert and Clara were living in Dresden, they had gone to the opera quite a bit, and Schumann wrote in his notebook critiques of this music.) In this particular scene, Faust, who has been involved in several noble projects, like trying to reclaim the land from the sea, is approaching the end of his life. He's visited by four gray hags, including Want and Care and Worry. "Care" is the principal figure here, and she winds up blinding Faust. His subsequent death is one of Schumann's most inspired and heartfelt passages. And here we find another quality in the music. While it might not be as gripping as the idiosyncratic nature of the earlier music, it is very important here. I refer to a kind of dignity and classic calm.

In Part Three, which he actually wrote first, and which is the longest of the three, we have "Faust's Transfiguration." It is divided into a number of sections, culminating in the ecstasy of the redemption. (Some readers of the Faust story might question the fact that Faust deserves to be redeemed at all!) This is extraordinary music. It builds up to a climax that displays the whole panoply of Schumann's vocal styles. There are lied-like passages, solos, and choruses in just about every style. The middle movement, which is built around the text "*Gerettet is das edle Glied*" (the noble member is now saved), starts with a choral statement of that text in a solemn, churchlike mode, followed by some solos, and concluding with the text in a driving, Handelian style.

Joan Chissell

When I first began research on Robert Schumann in the mid-1940s, there was no recording available of the *Scenes from Faust*, and I had to work entirely from the score. The earlier parts of Goethe he set later in Dresden, when he was very much under the influence of Wagner. The person who opened my eyes and ears to this music was Benjamin Britten. As you know, he ran a fantastic music festival at Aldeburgh, in Suffolk, where he lived. And he did the entire *Scenes from Faust* with Dietrich Fischer-Dieskau in the title role. It was absolutely a revelation. I was then working for the London *Times*, and it occurred to me to write about this performance. Because Britten was interested in what I had written, he suggested my name to Decca to write the sleeve notes for his recording of the complete *Faust*, which he did shortly after the festival performance. I was very happy to do that. Although I have always enormously admired Schumann's ending, especially the "Chorus Mysticus," I had never realized before how much original, striking, really dramatic music Schumann had provided for the earlier parts of Goethe's drama. In fact, I think it's almost more dramatic than parts of his earlier opera, *Genoveva*. When I had the chance to revise my book [1977], I did in fact rewrite large chunks of the *Faust* section. Later I got a very nice card from Britten, saying that he was pleased, and he thought I made the right musical points. It's one of my letters I keep in a very special place.

John Worthen

Schumann knows his Goethe very well. Goethe's in his head while growing up. Ask yourself, why does the young Schumann want to go to Italy? Because Goethe said, you go to Italy and your life is changed. So he goes. He even rereads Goethe while he's on the Russian trip in 1844. We know that. And what does a man read while traveling on sleighs through Russia? I guess he takes Goethe, at least!

What's interesting to me about the Faust legend in Schumann's time is the idea that the individual who is up against life and living has to find his own peculiar way to survive it. That is for me, a very nineteenth-century view as opposed to the eighteenth or seventeenth century. It's the individual finding his/her solution to life. Well, then, when Schumann picks up *Faust* and starts to work on it, he does the most extraordinary thing. Whereas someone else would've said, okay, we'll start with Faust and Margherite, right? Wrong. Schumann starts with the ending! He does an excerpt from *Faust, Part Two*, which was published in 1832, and which even then very few German people bothered about. The first part of *Faust* is great, but Part Two? Very, very dodgy. It's very undramatic, of all things. And it contains a great many characters you don't hear about very much, like Pater Seraphicus. Ordinarily, Part Two is omitted from *Faust* productions. I think Schumann actually may be the first person even to set *any* of Part Two.

So, Schumann starts off with the final scenes, the closing scenes of Part Two. He only chooses five hundred lines out of more than twelve thousand. It's just a tiny fragment. They deal with how Faust is finally reconciled to heaven, and heaven is reconciled to him. I think Schumann saw the drama within the drama. I just said Part Two is not dramatic. That's not really true, of course. Even if the external action is not very dramatic, the language is intensely so. Schumann's ear and eye for language and poetry is the saving grace here. And he sees what can be done with the internal drama of the poetry better, I think, than anyone else has ever done. Schumann is alone here, until Mahler, who of course transforms the same closing scene into his Eighth Symphony.

I guess people coming to this work who know only the more dramatic Berlioz Damnation of Faust *might be disappointed.*

There's very little overlap, really. For me, apart from the Overture—just to be personal here—the other scenes are not as compelling as the final scenes, which were written five years earlier and for different reasons. Schumann wrote the rest of the scenes incredibly fast, trying to get the whole thing up in time for the celebrations of the Goethe Centenary. Unfortunately, because he got ill, he missed the deadline. He had all the work done, though, so he went on to complete it a little while later. But it was written under pressure, and not, I think for the same reason as the earlier scenes.

He never heard it complete in his lifetime, I think. He did hear the closing scenes, because he plays them with his own choral society and orchestra in Dresden. That allows him to go away and revise it. He now knows how the orchestra actually works, or doesn't work. So he always does this. He loves hearing his work, then revising it, and then publishing it. That's the normal sequence. But the whole thing, no, he never heard it.

It's so different from the flashy supernatural claptrap you find in other versions, like the later film by F. W. Murnau [1926]. It shows you that Schumann is not that kind of person. All these attempts to say Robert Schumann was a romantic with a capital "R" are misleading. We are the ones who stick on a label like that and, in so doing, exercise an expectation. No, here he is not a romantic. He is interested in the Faust story because he knows that this story of redemption is a story of his time—and *our* time, to say the least. He does this in *Paradise and the Peri;* he does it in *Genoveva;* and he does it in Goethe's *Faust.*

Is he thinking about guilt? Some sense of his own guilt? Here is a postreligious age's attempt to say, how do we actually find our values? When it's not in obedience to an all-powerful God, how do we define our values and our functions in this world? And the answer is the human being can, in spite of everything, somehow come back and be redeemed, not by God or by heaven or by an angel, but through love and happiness.

Laura Tunbridge

The *Manfred* and *Faust Scenes* complement each other very well. They both respond to texts that are somewhat interrelated. Goethe read Byron's *Manfred* and thought it was a bit "hypochondriacal," or melancholy. He was saying that Byron was too young and romantic to understand this terribly tragic figure. He didn't really approve of the incest scene that runs through *Manfred.* But it was something that captured his attention, and when he came to write the second part of *Faust,* he wrote that into the character as a kind of Byronic figure who dies before his time. Schumann's two settings overlap each other in chronology, as well. The *Faust Scenes* took Schumann almost ten years to write, while he wrote *Manfred* quite quickly in 1848–49. They're both very dramatic but not necessarily meant to be put on a stage.

Interestingly, Schumann wrote his *Faust* backwards. He started in 1844 with what became Part Three. These final scenes had never been set to music before. Schumann, in fact, was the first person to try and write large portions of the Faust legend using Goethe's words, particularly the sections from Part Two. He found it difficult, not only because of the challenges of the literature, but also because 1844 was a period of intense depression for him. You have him writing to Mendelssohn that the first draft "is lying on my desk, but I really don't want to look at it." That implies he didn't think it up to scratch. So he puts it in a drawer until slightly later, when he hears some settings by Anton Radziwill at a soiree in Berlin. At that point he seems to have returned to the *Faust* music, at least in his mind. And then in 1849, the year of the Goethe Centenary celebrations, he performs his Part Three in Dresden, Leipzig, and Weimar. While that was happening, he was inspired to return to *Faust,* and he chose six scenes from Part One and Part Two from Goethe to make up the remainder of his work. Eventually, in 1853, he writes an overture to complete the whole work.

I think the *Faust Scenes* has some of Schumann's most wonderful music. As a whole it might not be entirely successful, but it shows him really trying to find a kind of middle ground between writing something operatic and writing something more along the lines of an oratorio. Some critics called the music of Part Three a kind of futuristic church music. The ending of Goethe's drama does indeed seem to synthesize Faust's redemption—Schumann called it a "transfiguration"—as a condition of the sacred and the secular. Faust is saved by Eros and Nature, the Eternal Feminine.

I frequently play for my students the scene set in the pleasant countryside. That is the first scene from Part Two of Goethe's *Faust.* We find Faust asleep in a lovely landscape, surrounded by spirits, including Ariel from Shakespeare's *Tempest.* When they wake him up, the sun is rising and he glories in the moment. It's one of the most significant moments in Goethe's poem: The sun is too bright for him, and it momentarily blinds him. At that point he turns and he sees a rainbow. The music shifts from a dramatic moment of the blindness and then shifts to a very carefully sketched idea of a rainbow. It's a lovely pictorial moment, a glorious moment of song.

John Nelson

I have many wonderful and memorable moments conducting Schumann, but I have to say the one that tops them all came in the middle of a political situation. I was conducting the Leipzig Gewandhaus Orchestra in 1989 in a performance of Schumann's *Scenes from Faust*. There I was, in Schumann's home, as it were, where he conducted that same orchestra and wrote so much music, including the *Faust*. As you know, every Monday there had been demonstrations in Leipzig at the *Platz* in front of the Gewandhaus. The first Monday that I was there, probably two hundred thousand people demonstrated and marched around the city. This went on for weeks and weeks until things started breaking down. And in the midst of this I'm conducting the Schumann. During the first vocal rehearsal I had all thirteen soloists in my room. They were all East Germans, except for a Czech lady who was singing the role of Marguerite/Gretchen. And the Faust was a man by the name of Egbert Junghans, a young and vibrant German singer. And when he came to the moment in *Faust* when you have the lines, "If you do not preserve your freedom on a daily basis, you will lose it"—the last soliloquy that Faustus gives when he's been blinded—this singer turned around to his colleagues and preached to them as he sang the part. He just looked at them, eyeball to eyeball. And he's saying, in effect, "If you don't preserve on a daily basis this freedom that you are demonstrating for, you are going to lose it." We were all moved to the quick.

A month before this, the people had come to Kurt Masur, the music director, and asked him if he could be put forward as the new president. His reputation was so high as a statesman/politician already that they felt he was somebody they could rally around. But he turned it down. I had met him already, years before, the first time I had been in Leipzig. He had asked me, "What do you want to do the next time you're in town?" And I immediately said, "I want to do Schumann's *Scenes from Faust*. "No," Masur said, "you can't do that. Because I'm going to do that. It's not been done by this orchestra in this century." Now, can you imagine that? In almost a hundred years this music by their own native son had not been performed! It's like an American orchestra never performing anything by Bernstein or Copland! So I let it go. But wouldn't you know it, a couple of years later, Masur gave me a call and gave me the go-ahead.

I'm the first to admit it's a problematic work. For me, it's like Berlioz—I'm a Berlioz freak—because I even love its defects. I feel I know them both. I love them, and I forgive them their faults. For every fault, I can tell you five glorious things in their music. One of the problems with the Schumann is that it was written at various times over almost a decade. And so it doesn't really hang together. If you have a sensitive ear, it doesn't hang together, musically. In Parts One and Two you have the mature, heady, weird and dark stuff, and all of a sudden you have Part Three, sunny, free-flowing, natural, light, and youthful music. It's just magic.

One of the faults most critics point to is Schumann's orchestration. I beg to disagree. The orchestral color is certainly not like Berlioz, but it is a specifically dark coloring which matches his personality and his music. Everywhere you look there are examples of marvelous tone colorings. When the blinded Faust dies, the horns literally cry out. By contrast, in the very first scene, where Faust is wooing Gretchen by picking petals ("She loves me, she loves me not"), the interplay of winds and strings is unbelievably tender. The tremendous choral scenes are beautifully orchestrated. I love it all. And I love him in all his various psychological states—even when he's in the insane asylum. My heart breaks with and for him.

D. Kern Holoman

I have a terrible time with "redemption" endings. I detest pieces that end in Heaven. Once Faust is swallowed up, I kind of lose interest in the story, quite frankly. It's Berlioz, not Schumann, who knows where Faust really belongs! But when things get pastel on you, like in Berlioz's *L'enfance du Christ* and the Fauré Requiem, all that heavenly stuff bothers me a little bit. So do paintings where you have a lot of pink. I don't think it's like that. I think it's more like the *himmlische Leben* in Mahler's Fourth Symphony, with people running around and eating and fishing.

Requiem for Mignon

> *His eyes and his heart were irresistibly attracted by the mysterious condition of this being. He reckoned her about twelve or thirteen years of age. Her countenance was not regular, but striking; her brow full of mystery. . . . This form stamped itself deeply in his soul.*
>
> —Goethe, *Wilhelm Meister's Apprenticeship*

EDITOR'S NOTE

Schumann composed the *Requiem for Mignon* in 1849, his "most fruitful year," as he put it. The message of hope at the end of the *Requiem* might have special significance, because it and the cycle of *Wilhelm Meister Songs* were both composed in Dresden at a time when revolution was sweeping Europe. The *Requiem* closely follows the description near the end in Goethe's *Wilhelm Meister's Apprenticeship* of the funeral ceremony for the mysterious child known as "Mignon." Roe-Min Kok investigates the strange attraction Mignon held out for Schumann. (See also Professor Kok's discussion of Schumann's "Mignon" music in the Piano Music and the Song chapters.)

Roe-Min Kok

Schumann, like so many artists of his time, was fascinated by this child, Mignon. You find her everywhere in his music. He knew about her from Goethe's *Wilhelm Meister's Apprenticeship*. As many scholars have shown, Goethe's novel is a *Bildungsroman,* a coming-of-age story about a young man who is involved with the theater and who has many experiences along the way toward maturity. Well, Mignon is one of the women in Wilhelm's life. She's a child of thirteen or so. She is very mysterious, nobody knows much about her. We sense she has had a checkered past, that she may have been abused. It's even hard to determine her gender at the beginning. There is a lot of androgyny here, which helps accentuate her strangeness. She's also portrayed as having darker skin, and we learn later she is Italian. She is very bright, but she has difficulty expressing herself, unless it's in song. This ambivalence is also enhanced by the metaphor of her rope dancing, which suspends her in the air above the ground. And there's the famous passage about her *Eiertanz,* or "egg dance," where she is so light and fragile that she doesn't even crack one egg when she dances quickly on them!

If you look at the writings of Schopenhauer, he describes adult women as big children. Consider this statement from the nineteenth-century stereotypical male point of view, and you see that the child and the woman share many common characteristics—they embody innocence, they belong in the home, they are tied to nature. Those categories belong together in nineteenth-century thinking about women. Thus Mignon belongs partly to the realm of womanhood.

We don't really know just what Mignon's relationship with Wilhelm is, either as beloved child or sister; but we do see that she gets jealous when he pays attention to other women. She probably has an adolescent crush on him. She's very excitable and agitated sometimes toward him. Then she goes away, and we don't hear much about her until we see her in a foster home. Towards the end she purportedly suffers a heart attack and dies. "My heart has beat too long," she says. It's only after her death that we learn that the Harper, another mysterious character in the book, is her father, and she is the product of his incestuous relationship with his sister.

Mignon's funeral is staged in the novel like a theater piece (after all, she had been a member of a theatrical troupe). Goethe's description is very ceremonial, and it takes place in a theatrical setting, a so-called Hall of the Past with tall pillars and tapestries and four young boys in feathered costumes. There are candles surrounding the bier. Two choirs are concealed in positions near the ceiling. "True music is intended for the ear alone," someone says.

Schumann, like so many artists of his time, was fascinated by this child. Little is known about how he came to compose his *Requiem for Mignon*, which is a faithful adaptation of the scene in the novel. When I was researching it, I found that even specialists closest to Schumann had not found very much material about the impulse behind it. Personally, I have ambivalent feelings about it. I have had friends express their dismay at my interest on music about the deaths of children. But my main intention is to know what fascinated him about Mignon and what he thought about her. Certainly, I love the music itself! You know, he was the very first composer to write Mignon's funeral scene to music. There's no precedent for this. That is amazing. The only other setting was by Ambroise Thomas in his later opera, *Mignon*.

It is apparent that a lot of people did not like Schumann's *Requiem for Mignon*, when it was first performed. It was more expected that in writing about children, you should show them at their peak, in all their innocence. But you do not show a child's funeral. That would be in bad taste, an offence to bourgeois sensibilities. Besides, they thought Mignon should have a better ending, by which they meant something more fitting to the tragedy of the young girl's death. That is what disturbed the critics. She was a street kid who had undergone many tragedies in life; so she should have had a more dignified funeral, something quieter and in better taste. Instead, unlike the solemnity of Goethe's text, Schumann at the end bursts into a celebration of joy. He was scolded for not treating the funeral more gently. I think he was very brave for doing it this way. Compare it with Schumann's other Requiem, which has the standard format with parts like Hostia, Sanctus, Dies Irae, and so forth. You don't have any of that here. It's more like an anti-Requiem, more like a small opera. I don't think he ever intended it to be staged.

I have researched the trope of children and death in nineteenth-century literature. There are many representations of this in Western culture, where you find illustrations of a grown woman with a baby—a "cradle to the grave" kind of thing. The child is a symbol of beginnings, but at the same time a portent of death. The child mortality rate was very high in the nineteenth century. But you don't find many overt references to this in music. Schubert's song "The Erlking" is an example. It's too traumatic a topic. But Schumann knew the subject only too well. He had lost a son, Emil, and Clara had miscarried twice. Besides the *Mignon Requiem,* you recall that he wrote a song, the "Cradle Song for a Sick Child" [Op. 78, No. 4]. Maybe works like this came not just from his own loss, but also were a kind of memento mori, a reminder of your own mortality.

Think of Mignon in connection with other choral works by Schumann, particularly *The Pilgrimage of the Rose,* where you have another doomed female figure, Rose, a fairy creature. Schumann changed the ending of Moritz Horn's original story, where Rose dies. Horn had sent it to Schumann, who said he would compose it only on the condition that the more grievous ending could be changed to a transfiguration of Rose to angel status. I love the version with piano accompaniment, and it's very delicate. The orchestration came later. I particularly love the part in the middle [No. 10] where Rose is drifting off to sleep, and then the little elfish chorus appears and pleads with her not to continue on her human journey! I am fascinated by how he treats the women's chorus—the range of richness and shadings of these combinations. Where did he get that from? Schubert, probably. This sort of transparency and strategic use of register also appear in Schubert's music for women's voices.

John Daverio

The *Requiem for Mignon* fits in with Schumann's preoccupation in his later years with the theme of redemption. Although as a teenager, his literary idol had been Jean Paul, he shifts to Goethe in the mid-1840s. There's a streak in Schumann which tends toward a certain kind of thoroughness. He wants to do all he can in a certain direction. In his last years he fastens on Goethe's two major works, *Faust* and *Wilhelm Meister*. He sets large chunks of both to important musical/dramatic works. *Wilhelm Meister* has lots of poems interspersed with it. He sets almost all of them for voice and piano. And around that same time in the late 1840s he composes the *Requiem for Mignon,* which appears near the end of the novel.

Mignon is an adolescent girl, whose origins are unknown and whose behavior is quite strange. It's not until the end of the novel that her back-story is revealed. She dies, and in the final book of the novel Goethe writes a kind of funeral ceremony for her. The text is well suited for musical treatment. It's very theatrical, virtually a little play enclosed within the novel. A large group of guests have been summoned to the lavish Hall of the Past in the castle of Lothario, for Mignon's funeral rites. Schumann crafts six interrelated movements that alternate between the singing of the boys (represented by soprano and alto solos) and the invisible spirits. It's really quite gorgeous. Although it is relatively brief, it is very moving, and it contains wonderful writing for the solos and chorus. It opens with a funeral march and a chorale that dominates the last three movements. There is a tone of noble simplicity from beginning to end. You can find many musical connections between this music and Schumann's *Faust Scenes.* I love this music. You come away from it with the message that the business of the living is to go on living fully instead of succumbing to foolish lamentation. I don't know of any earlier setting of this *Requiem.* There had been some settings of some of the *Faust* music, and there were

settings by Schubert of some of the poems by Schubert, but not of the
Requiem itself.

Choral Ballads

John Daverio

There are four late choral ballads that date from Schumann's Düsseldorf
years around 1852–53. Unfortunately, Brahms, Liszt, and Clara all
thought them indicative of a slackening in Schumann's powers. Thus they
are very little known today in the concert hall, although they have been
recorded [The *Sämtliche Balladen* were recorded and released on the EMI
label in 1988 with conductors Bernhard Klee and Heinz Wallberg]. I think
they are quite extraordinary, with very colorful writing for the orchestra,
solo, and choral forces. The four works have many evocative, colorful
moments. Three of them, *Das Glück von Edenhall* [The Fortunes of
Edenhall, Op. 143], *Des Sänger's Fluch* [The Bard's Curse, Op. 139], and
Der Königssohn [The King's Son, Op. 116], are drawn from old German
sagas by Ludwig Uhland, for whom this kind of world of chivalry, blind
minstrels, wild horses, and spectacular storms was very important. But
Vom Pagen und der Königstochter [The Page and the King's Daughter,
Op. 140], which I think is the greatest of his choral ballads, was not
from Uhland, but Emanuel Geibel. Schumann had set some of this music
before as song texts. I think that these ballads represent the culmination
of Schumann's interest in storytelling in music. We can hear this in his
early piano works, where there is no text, and then through the Year of
Song, where he sets a number of ballad texts, and in part songs, as well,
and finally in this culmination.

11

"Now It Grows Dark"

Last Years and Last Works

Commentators: Styra Avins, Ronald Brautigam, John Daverio, Peter Frankl, Lynn Harrell, Steven Isserlis, Roe-Min Kok, Susan McClary, John Nelson, Peter F. Ostwald, Leon Plantinga, Nancy B. Reich, Charles Rosen, Eric Sams, Wolfgang Sawallisch, András Schiff, Laura Tunbridge, Sarah Walker, Robert Winter, John Worthen, and Thomas Zehetmair

---

EDITOR'S NOTE

The first of these discussions begins with Schumann's arrival in Düsseldorf in 1850 to assume the post of municipal music director, succeeding Ferdinand Hiller. His responsibilities included organizing ten subscription concerts annually and managing the important "Lower Rhenish Music Festival." However, bouts of illness and emotional distraction increasingly hampered his ability to carry out his professional duties. Happier times seemed at hand with the arrival in late September 1853 of twenty-year-old Johannes Brahms. Schumann promptly proclaimed him the promise of new German music. But a few months later Schumann suffered a severe psychotic episode and attempted to drown himself in the Rhine on February 27. He was incarcerated on March 4 in an asylum in Endenich until his death on July 29, 1856. Ever loyal, Brahms sacrificed his own career during this time, supporting Clara and the family. The nature of his relationship with Clara has been debated ever since. In any event, they remained close acquaintances and colleagues until her death in 1886.

PRIVATE AND PUBLIC LIFE

[Schumann's] lips were pursed and he often brushed his thick, dark brown hair to one side. . . . He always wore black during his later years, and usually a top hat as well. This garb, taken

Robert Schumann, daguerreotype, Düsseldorf, Germany, 1850.

in conjunction with his quiet, unhurried manner, could have
led people to think he was a clergyman.
—J. W. von Wasielewski, *Life of Schumann*, 1858

Music Director in Düsseldorf

John Daverio

Schumann was especially prolific in the years 1848–49. Certainly he characterized this as his most productive period. He wrote in almost all genres; almost everything is covered. There are no symphonies from this period, but you have a lot of chamber music, choral music, songs, music for solo instruments—he did it all. Earlier, in 1840, he devoted a whole year to write songs. But later on his life, the creative drive, becomes more compressed. I think that artists go through various kinds of rhythms of productivity. And with Schumann, music just poured out of him. Sometimes this is taken to be a sign of manic behavior, which is understandable. We know that when he and Clara and some of their children took refuge in the countryside outside of Dresden during the revolutionary period, May 1849, he was terribly productive. So you might think this was a sign of some kind of mania. And yet when you read his household account books, it just seemed that he had gotten into a certain kind of creative rhythm. He liked to compose during the morning, and he did this also later in Düsseldorf, especially in the first year and a half. He had a regular schedule, or routine—get up early, compose for a few hours, lunch, take a walk, share lots of time with the kids. He fell into this rhythm. But periods of illness would interrupt it, when he simply couldn't work. This happened in Düsseldorf toward the middle of the second year, when he hit a kind of snag. Likewise, there was a lull toward the middle of 1853. Then in the summer and the fall, things picked up again.

Schumann and Clara had moved to Düsseldorf in the early 1850s. Apart from his composing, his job included conducting a largely amateur orchestra and chorus. And in order to get the most out of ensembles like that, it required a certain kind of personality type that was very different from Schumann's personality type. Mendelssohn had had essentially the same job seventeen to eighteen years before. But we know he was a much more outgoing personality type than Schumann was. So I think part of the problem in Düsseldorf stemmed from his personality—he tended to be more inward and withdrawn. From what we know, he was not a great communicator when he had to get up in front of the chorus and orchestra. He wasn't demonstrative enough and didn't know how to elicit a response from his players. When you add to that the fact that he suffered from various depressive phases and episodes in adolescence and adult life, this also adds to the problem. Finally, I think in those last years you begin to see manifestations of the illness that would take him over.

Well, there are reports of his mode of dress, and this comes from Wasiliewsky, his concertmaster. For example, was wearing all black unusual? As for his mumbling, there are reports to that effect that go back to the 1840s. I think we need to know more about the context of that. As for his not recognizing his children, that's more anecdotal. Clearly, there's strange behavior in these years. At one point, he reportedly is conducting a chorus and a mass by Moritz Hauptmann, and the chorus stops and he keeps on conducting. Obviously, there's something wrong here. He's having an aural delusion that the music is continuing. So this I think is clearly strange and unusual behavior. On the other hand, I'm not so sure I agree that other modes of behavior are so strange. He developed an interest in séances and table rapping. This has sometimes been adduced as a sign that he was losing it. Well, a number of the other people in his circle—upper-class, bourgeois types—were also interested in the same thing. It was a fad at the time. We have to be very careful to distinguish what might have been accepted at the time as normal and other kinds of behavior which are clearly and obviously strange.

Peter F. Ostwald

Schumann had a rather dreamy approach to conducting. He was listening mostly to music inside his head. He seemed rather unresponsive or insensitive to what was actually going on in the orchestra. He was notably rigid in his beating of music; he was not one who could be very flexible in giving cues and telling people where to come in. This I think was a reflection generally of his awkward social manner. He had this abstracted quality about him all his life. It was noted already when he was in his twenties. There's a wonderful description of the distracted, impractical Schumann written earlier by Ferdinand David, who was the concertmaster in Leipzig. He wrote a letter to Mendelssohn and mentions Schumann was very forgetful. They all noticed that when it came to administrative matters, he was not at his best at all. He wanted to leave that to other people. He excused himself from rehearsals and from board meetings, and he preferred to go home and compose.

He liked to isolate himself in the studio. And I think that's often the lifestyle of the composer. Even Beethoven, who was supposed to have wandered in the woods and parks and been inspired by nature, would seal himself up in his messy workroom and do his composing there. And that's the way one has to work, I think, very often, as a composer. Even today that's the life a composer leads, as opposed to the landscape painter, who works in the light, or the photographer who's out there looking at nature, taking in all the shapes and colors.

John Worthen

I think the allegations concerning his wretched conducting in Düsseldorf are overstated. For me, almost the biggest discovery in my book, which no one has mentioned to me, is Schumann's poor eyesight. He is shortsighted and therefore has an awful dilemma: If he wears any kind of glasses, or a lorgnette, to help him read, he will not be able to see the orchestra; if he doesn't put them on at all, he not only won't see the orchestra, but he won't be able to read, either. So he's really stuck. Relationships with an orchestra you can't see, as anyone knows, are bound to fail! Relationships with any group of people you're working with but who you can't actually see are going to be rough. And the fact that it was his eyesight rather than his hand which got him off military service in 1849, again, is a subject which has not previously been brought to the surface, I think. Yes, it is true that Schumann at that time still would have been eligible for military service.

Wolfgang Sawallisch

I think Schumann was not very lucky as a conductor in Düsseldorf. Nobody really knows what the problem was. Perhaps he was too weak for the platform, not a strong enough personality to lead an orchestra. Or you could say he was too gentle. He couldn't transfer his own wishes to the players. Certainly in his time, Schuman's music was not easy to perform. Even today, the orchestras always have some difficulties, the same trouble with the right interpretation. You know, it was the same with Brahms. He was not a good conductor, either, not even for his own works. It was the same for Bruckner. No one ever said that a great composer had to be a great conductor! Perhaps only Richard Strauss is an example.

Roe-Min Kok

I think I made a significant discovery concerning Schumann's last years in Düsseldorf. I spent a year there in 2000, attached to the *Schumann-Forschungsstelle*. That was the time when a cache of Schumann's letters, which had been found in the 1980s, was being organized. We're talking about more than two thousand letters from the later years of his life—many of them from Schumann to his publishers—that we had known nothing about before. I read them in their originals. I had had some training at Harvard in reading nineteenth-century German handwriting; but still, I needed some help from the Düsseldorf researchers. One amusing thing I must tell you is that it's a good thing Schumann grew shortsighted in his later years, because he enlarged his handwriting! I looked at his letters from the 1830s, in the smaller handwriting, and they're almost impossible to read. These particular letters were a real education for me. It was a lot of work to translate them. I am the first person to talk about them in English. What you get from them is a very different Schumann than you usually hear about, i.e., the romantic soul who is sick and composing while mentally unstable. Not only was he highly articulate in this correspondence, but the letters prove he had all his intellectual faculties about him in the late 1840s and early 1850s. He comes across as a more mature, practical, balanced person, not so much the idealistic fighter of his youth. I thought it was important to reveal this aspect of him. It's all a part of reevaluating the gradual course of his illness.

Crossing Paths: Schumann, Brahms, and Clara

> *It seemed to me there must appear a musician called to give expression to his times in ideal fashion. . . . and such a one* has *appeared , a young man over whose cradle Graces and Heroes have stood watch. His name is Johannes Brahms, and he comes from Hamburg.*
> —Robert Schumann, *New Paths*, 1853

John Daverio

When Brahms first arrived at the Schumann doorstep in the fall of 1853, the Schumanns weren't home. One of the daughters told him they were out for a walk. Brahms came back the next day. Every Schumann and Brahms scholar would like to have been on that doorstep! We know so little, but we have to make do with what we have. Although there are lots of unanswered questions about what went on, we have lots of tantalizing information in Schumann's household account books. Obviously, this was an extraordinary period. Brahms shows up, and Schumann recognizes him as the kind of messiah music was waiting for.

This is the youthful Brahms, of course, young, flaxen-haired, very handsome, part of a larger group of younger composers, younger musicians, who inspired Schumann in his last creative days. It was through Schumann's friend Joseph Joachim that Brahms first gained entry into the Schumann circle. He's a very impressionable young man, obviously extraordinarily gifted, but his knowledge and his encounters with the world were pretty limited. He had spent most of his life in Hamburg.

Exterior view today of the Schumanns' last residence, 15 Bilkerstrasse, Düsseldorf, Germany.

He went on tour with this crazy Hungarian violinist, Reményi. He had a brief encounter with Liszt. As a kid he, like Schumann, had been very much taken with the writings of E. T. A. Hoffmann. In this circle he now comes to realize he's not alone in the world, that there are other kindred spirits out there.

Schumann becomes a tremendously important influence on Brahms's music. We see that right from the beginning. There's a set of variations which Brahms began to work on not long after his first encounter with the Schumanns, his Op. 9 variations for piano. These variations are based on a theme by Schumann, a little piano piece from one of his later collections for piano. And he intertwines references to himself, Clara, and Robert in the work. In one of the later variations, Brahms quotes from the theme of Robert's Impromptus, Op. 5, which in turn are supposedly based on a romance by Clara. But that theme might actually have been derived from a theme Robert himself might have composed. It's complicated. Moreover,

Clara *herself* wrote some variations on this theme. It's very clear that in the Op. 9 variations Brahms has absorbed Schumann's own earlier keyboard style of writing, particularly in its toccata-like quality.

In the C-Minor Piano Quartet you also see the Schumann presence. We know that Brahms started on it in the mid-1850s, at the height of his contacts with the Schumanns. He destroyed it and rewrote it later on in the 1870s. We know about this earlier version because he writes about it in letters to Joachim, where he quotes some of the tunes and confesses that in writing this piece he had felt like Goethe's character of Werther, the young man who falls in love with a woman and commits suicide. Of the four movements, the first movement and the Scherzo are probably revisions of the earlier version. The second movement, which starts with that wonderful cello solo, was brand-new in the 1870s. You have a piece with a complicated genealogy, with two movements that date back twenty years, and two others that are almost brand-new.

Brahms once said there were three great events in his life—the work on the complete edition of Bach's compositions, the outcome of the Franco-Prussian War, and the relationship with Schumann. That really stayed with him to the end of his life.

Robert Winter

I think Schumann was one of the most generous great composers we've ever had. We know the story of how he heralded Chopin. But to have written an article about the twenty-year-old Brahms and to have called it "Neue Bahnen"—New Paths (something he wasn't claiming for himself)—was an extremely generous gesture on his part, and I think he was sincere about it. Strangely enough, I think Brahms was up to it, even though we might make a big deal about Brahms waiting until he was in his early forties to finish his First Symphony. I think Brahms was a pretty rugged type. I think he pursued the path he had set out for himself and was not dissuaded, like Bruckner, by criticism.

Brahms had a profound respect for Clara as a musician. And I think that's what helped salvage their relationship. Because, of course, if you look at all the other women in his life, they came in and out. Some of them stayed. But for the most part, Brahms kind of went through people—not in a manipulative, crass way, but he had a difficult time maintaining a relationship. He and Clara had so much to talk about and to deal with. And I think she, for her part, had a remarkable understanding of his compositional needs. She didn't try and turn him into Robert. She really let him be but was an extremely sympathetic ear for him—the kind of sympathetic ear that most composers dream of having but few have the chance to find.

Styra Avins

Eugenie Schumann wrote a good description of Brahms's arrival at the Bilkerstrasse home. Although she was just a baby at the time, she had heard about it later from her older sisters and mother. And we have Schumann's famous diary entry on the 1st of October, 1853: "Arrival of Brahms—a genius." Within just one day Schumann says this! It didn't take him long to figure it out! I can imagine something of Brahms's reaction to the Schumann household. Brahms must have been thrilled to find so many things dear to him—such as art (Brahms had a keen interest in graphic arts), fairy stories, a wonderful library, and the fact that the Schumanns' lives revolved around music. It must have made him feel that maybe he was not such an outsider, after all. He had certainly felt like he was the only one of his ilk among his acquaintances up to that point.

This is not the Brahms we think of in later years, with the pot belly and the beard. As a young person, the adjective that most often comes up about him is *liebenwürdig,* which means "sweet-tempered," "ingratiating," "nice." There's no English equivalent. He was an accomplished gymnast, you know. He loved to jump. He writes a letter to Clara, telling her how high he can jump! He's in his twenties at that point. He was smooth-shaven, anything but a bear.

Like Schumann, Brahms was an enthusiast of Jean Paul and E. T. A. Hoffmann. He identified somewhat with the character of Hoffmann's Johannes Kreisler. I do believe that knowing how Brahms identified with Johannes Kreisler tells you as much as you ever need to know about the internal life of this young man. Until he was thirty, he signed his music as "Johannes Kreisler Jr." Kreisler, you'll recall, was a young *Kapellmeister* whose poetic soul was utterly misunderstood by his peers. He has to spend too much of his time doing things that he detests. And of course, the teenage Brahms had to give piano lessons ad nauseam to indifferent young kids in Hamburg. One can assume his mental state mirrored in many ways that of Kreisler. I think I can make that connection.

He must have had a strange childhood. Biographers like Jan Swafford (Johannes Brahms, 1997) claim he played music in the Hamburg brothels as a youth.

Well, myths are wonderful things in biography, and this is a particularly entrancing one for a lot of people. Yes, there were brothels all over Hamburg, and there were tiny brothels in the neighborhood where Brahms lived. I have a list of them, and the number of women who worked in them, that was written by a doctor who attended the girls every week. But the brothels and dance halls were carefully kept apart in Hamburg. Now, in St. Pauli, a long walk from where Brahms lived, they were not. That's the sailors' quarter. Brahms's father, when he first came to Hamburg, had worked in St. Pauli. And probably this is the root of the misunderstanding. Brahms may have told somebody his father worked there, and they understood him to say he worked there. That's my guess as to how this all started.

Also remember that music was prohibited in brothels in Hamburg. They were rigorously controlled by the police. You were not allowed in a brothel until you were eighteen. Brahms looked like a baby. There's no way he could have passed for eighteen. And his parents were such God-fearing people, particularly his mother, to have allowed that. Brahms and his brother went to the best private school, one that was frequented by the sons of doctors and lawyers. What kind of parents would do that and, at the same time, haul their kids out of bed at night to play in brothels? It makes no sense.

Now, it is true that when Brahms graduates from school at the age of fourteen, he was playing in dance halls in Hamburg. There's no question but that he did that. And there's no question but that some of the dance halls were pretty rough. They had police on hand to make sure that nothing untoward happened. I have no idea whether Brahms played in ones like those. I do know that in his neighborhood there were two very high-class dance halls. He may very well have played there. Brahms himself told a journalist that at this time he made his living making arrangements, giving piano lessons, and playing from time to time in dance halls. Somehow, even that's been blown out of proportion.

What did Brahms know about Schumann's illness?

At the beginning, nobody knew that Schumann had syphilis, so there really was hope that he would recover. Very shortly before Schumann's death, Brahms had a letter from his mother saying, "I hear that Schumann is very ill and is not going to recover; poor boy." She's very concerned about Johannes and how this will affect him. Later, Brahms says that he hopes never again to live through something as awful as Schumann's mental breakdown. That is a very tough thing for a person to go through, let alone a young, romantic youth. The Schumanns had become like a family to him. He was more connected to them than with his own family. He revered Schumann, and he visited him frequently in Endenich; and, of course, we know he was already in love with Clara.

He wrote letters about visiting Schumann near the end. In one of them, written to their mutual friend, Joseph Joachim just a few months before Schumann's death, he tells of finding Schumann agitated and babbling incoherently, doing nothing but making alphabetical lists of cities. And there were those last terrible hours he witnessed between Robert and Clara. He went with her to Endenich. It was the first time she had seen Robert since he left Düsseldorf. Whatever fantasies or imagination Brahms might have had about his love for Clara at that point must have taken a terrible jolt. Schumann was in a horrible state and must have looked totally awful. Brahms says that in spite of his debilitation, Schumann flung an arm around Clara. It was the last time he saw the two together. It was all terrifying and horrifying, I'm sure.

We know for sure the next five years were really tough ones for him, emotionally as well as creatively. Schumann's "New Paths" article must have been a terrific burden on him. He wrote a very anguished letter to Clara, saying he had ceased to compose. Ideas weren't coming—at the age of twenty-one? There were six years of relative silence, with no new publications. But the amazing thing about him is that he didn't just sit and wallow in his terror. He simply—and heroically—decided he would somehow keep himself involved in music. He stayed in Düsseldorf because he was unwilling to give up his lifeline—the Schumann house. That household was Art to him. He didn't move into the house, by the way. That's a mistake of many biographies. That didn't happen until Clara moved again, about eighteen months after Schumann's death. Before then, he had a room near the house. He would come every day. He taught the children to read. He kept the household accounts. He catalogued the music library. When there were storms, he held the frightened children on his lap. He said in a letter, "The next time I'll know better how to do this." It's a wonderful letter. Eugenia left accounts of him playing with the children, doing handstands on the stairs. You don't think of Brahms that way. This was the first time he had responsibilities, but he rose to the occasion. Gradually his powers came back to him. There's a wonderful letter to Clara after he had gotten a job in Detmold: "My powers are coming back; it's a glorious feeling!" Those were very hard-fought years. He just didn't give up. It's a fascinating show of will. Except for that first distress after Schumann's suicide attempt, nothing would ever again get in the way of his composing.

There's no question that Brahms was deeply in love with Clara, almost obsessed. His surviving letters from this time are quite clear about that. However, by now you have to think the thought of a marriage to an older woman with seven children might be daunting. Also, Brahms knew

perfectly well what a marriage to an older woman entails, because he saw
the most awful example of that with his parents. He watched his father
and mother endure a horrible marriage, one that disintegrated and ended
in real tragedy. By contrast, he must have thought the Schumann marriage
was unique and could never be reproduced. And he also may have felt it
was too much of an expenditure of emotion on his part. You see him later
in life writing condolence notes to friends whose children had died. Every
once in while he would say, "Just don't have children." He was afraid of
loss, he really was. I don't think he wanted to face the possibility of a
wife who dies, or children who die. True, he and Clara did go together to
Switzerland after Schumann's death, as a kind of recovery. But before you
make too much of that, remember that he went with two of the children
and with Brahms's sister as nanny. He and Clara were never alone. When
he returned, he went back home to Hamburg.

Much later, in the late 1880s, Clara Schumann and Brahms agreed to
return their letters to each other. Allegedly, Brahms took his packet and
tossed it into the Rhine. Clara started burning her letters, but by the time
she got up to the year 1858, her daughter walked into the room and made
her stop. Lacking so many of her early letters to Brahms, we have little
insight about her feelings on getting these rapturous letters from him.
Actually, she did keep a few of his. That's a bit of a mystery. She kept the
ones that she thought were the most interesting. And of course in my view
that's all the more ammunition to support the idea they were *not* lovers.
She wouldn't have kept them if they were damaging to her. But they were
passionate love letters, all right, and I've included a number of them in
my book [*Johannes Brahms: Life and Letters*, 1997].

To me, Brahms is a classic case of a guy who's always involved in one
level or another with a woman, who always feels himself in love, and who
probably needs that kind of fantasy life. I think his relationships with
women were a stimulus to his music writing. Otherwise, in his later years
in Vienna, he went to prostitutes. You have to know what Vienna was like:
Everybody went to prostitutes. Prostitution existed on an industrial scale
in Vienna, according to Stefan Zweig. People have no idea what everyday,
middle-class, male life was like in Vienna. Brahms was totally normal.
The only different thing about it was that he didn't hide it.

Brahms was a very complex, deep man. To try and find one key to
his character simply doesn't work. This is a man of great humor, great
depth, and melancholy; but at the same time, externally he is a very positive, even cheerful person. Which is why I think many biographers get
something wrong about Brahms. I used to read program notes that Brahms
didn't have many friends. Well, of course, when you see the hundreds of

letters to him from his friends, you know it wasn't true. He also was the godfather to at least seventeen children. You don't ask a grumpy, morose misanthrope to be godfather to your child! So clearly there was another side to Brahms that many of his friends saw. In short, this is a person of tremendous variety, which is why I think some of his music has great popular appeal, like his "Lullaby" (which is the most famous lullaby in the world), and some is very abstruse, like the choral motets).

John Worthen

Brahms is, by Schumann's standards, uneducated. By Schumann's standards. Brahms grows up in Hamburg, and there were no books at home. His family is working-class. What is clear as a result of the last twenty years of Brahms scholarship is, as Styra Avins has pointed out so brilliantly, that most of the mythologies of Brahms's early life are absolutely not to be trusted, even though they come from Brahms himself. What he told Kalbeck [Max Kalbeck's biography of Brahms appeared within a decade of Brahms's death], and what Kalbeck wrote down, is simply not to be relied on. For Schumann, he is a kind of son, a raw individual who is actually going to make an extraordinary difference, who will be a different talent from anyone else the world has seen.

What actually happened in Düsseldorf between Schumann and Brahms, or between Brahms and Clara, over the years 1854–56 while Schumann is in Endenich is an absolutely mysterious area. Certainly upon Brahms's arrival Schumann is immensely impressed with him; and Brahms is immensely impressed by Schumann. That's been on the record for a very long time. He has access to the Schumann library, and it's a revelation to him. He becomes incredibly erudite and by his maturity knows as much about music and music history as any man alive. As Schumann taught himself about music everything he knew, Brahms teaches himself everything. While Schumann is in Endenich, Brahms becomes a substitute father to the kids. I love the story of Brahms sliding down the banisters and turning somersaults for them. Robert Schumann couldn't do that at this time in his life! Brahms is wonderful. He loves kids, and the kids love him, and he gets on with them very, very well. And I do have proof that the Schumann household notebooks in Düsseldorf are actually filled in by Brahms, who's living in the house at the time.

What I do not buy at any level is that the young Brahms had an affair with Clara Schumann. An infatuation, yes, and a frustration, yes again. And if she had said, "Come to my arms, Johannes Brahms," he might have said yes; or he might have said, "Oh, my God!" I don't know. But either way, he was infatuated, certainly. But while Robert was alive, I can't imagine that Clara would for a moment have considered a sexual advance by another man. If she had done so, I think she might have killed herself. He was immensely flirtatious, and loved women, and loved the attentions of women, and might even later on have considered marriage to the daughter, Julie. Clara anyway would have been down on that like a ton of bricks, because she also knew what happened to the professional artist who gets married. It's terrible for the wife. Of all the people in the world, she knew that.

Now, we know that, apparently, Clara did have some sexual relationships with Theodor Kirchner a little bit later; and if she did that, she might have had other relationships. But the trouble is, Brahms's best time for an affair with Clara is while he's in Düsseldorf, while Schumann is still alive; and that is the one time when he would not have had an affair.

I am convinced that all his life Brahms is under the sway of Schumann. What's not been talked about before is that Brahms does not get married because he knows what happens to the artist who gets married. He has seen Schumann busting a gut for years having to earn money by the yard to keep the growing family. It's appalling what Schumann has to do, and Brahms, I think, sees this, and decides, that way I do not go. And so a reason for Brahms not to marry is very clear to him; and Schumann is the great example of what happens to the great creative artist who gets married. This I think has not been said about Brahms before, and it's to me rather interesting. Brahms is clearly very attracted to women, he falls in love with them regularly, he goes to prostitutes very clearly for the rest of his life, as Schumann did early on; but what Schumann does *before* he gets married, Brahms does *instead* of getting married.

Brahms never gets away from Clara, though. And there's this wonderful story of his desperate attempts to attend Clara's funeral in 1896, which may have actually led to his own death. But he has to go. If there's one person whose funeral he has to go to, it's Clara. Not just because he loves her, but because he has been a part of her life for the last forty years.

Leon Plantinga

It is not generally appreciated that when Schumann wrote his "Neue Bahnen" (New Paths) article heralding the coming of Brahms, the *New Magazine of Music* was no longer what it had been at its inception. It was now edited by Franz Brendel, an ardent Wagnerian. Anyway, Schumann is, in a sense, asking who are the important composers now? And he answers himself, "There is this new fellow I want to tell you about, who is absolutely terrific. Nobody's heard of him. His name is Johannes Brahms." So he fills this article with extravagant praise for Brahms. And in long footnotes he adds, who are the *other* composers who are as good these days? He lists a whole bunch of names, none of whom we've ever heard of before. Completely missing from his categorization are both Liszt and Wagner. Both were the darlings of the journal. It's a kind of political twist to the event that's not appreciated. It's clear where Schumann stood. He did not approve of Wagnerism of any stripe. It must have been painful for him to see his beloved journal, to which he had dedicated ten of his best years, now being turned over to the so-called new music of Liszt and Wagner. Now, to be sure, Liszt was a wonderful character who was always very supportive of Schumann and Clara. Ironically, he was always supportive of Wagner, too, but usually was treated shabbily by him.

Susan McClary

You see in Brahms the same ambivalence Schumann felt about his "masculine" and "feminine" sensibilities. It's almost a direct legacy. You see, on the one hand, the small piano pieces, the ornamental devices and, on the other hand, the huge symphonies displaying the forcefulness of Beethoven. Even more than Schumann, he is determined that people understand that he is writing big works like this with, as it were, the same pen that Schumann claimed he found on Beethoven's grave. At the same time, as in Schumann, the inner movements are extraordinarily subjective, vulnerable, and coded as "feminine." And that tension remains prominent in Brahms.

Nancy B. Reich

After I wrote my book on Clara [*Clara Schumann: The Artist and the Woman*, 1985], I traveled to Sydney, Australia, where I was invited to speak at the Conservatorium of Music of New South Wales. During several other stops, I found a great deal of interest in Clara, even though my book had not yet appeared there. At the end of one of my lectures, a student asked me point-blank: "Was Clara's relationship with Brahms erotic or platonic?" The legends about her and Brahms had reached Australia and New Zealand, as well! My answer is that I think it was not a sexual relationship. I made that clear in my book. I think he was very much in love with her. It's the "Werther" story all over again: Here he is, in love with a woman who is married to his great idol and friend, and who is the mother of many children. As for Clara, certainly she had very warm feelings towards him. But what she felt was probably very often maternal feelings, sisterly feelings. As she got to know him, very soon she began to realize that here was a man she could turn to. He became her primary musical consultant.

In the asylum, during the clear times when Robert was able to write, he not only requested Brahms's music, but he wanted a picture of him to hang over his desk. During that time Brahms was close to the Schumann household in many ways. While Schumann was in the asylum, he took care of the children. He was often like a big kid himself. He really did help out Clara, not only with them, but with the bills. He tried to continue Robert's practice of recording everything that was spent. He recorded in the household books expenses for the school, for the girls, the servants' wages, et cetera. He really did step into the shoes of the father of the family.

He also wrote a series of variations, his Op. 9, *Variations on a Theme of Robert Schumann*. He wrote on the score, "Variations on a Theme, written by *Him* and dedicated to *Her*." Now, in that Op. 9, you see a very curious triangular relationship right there in the music. About a year before that, Clara had written her own variations, her Op. 20, on a theme from Robert's *Bunte Blätter* (Little Characteristic Pieces). On seeing her variations, Brahms took the same theme for his variations. And near the end of the Op. 20, Clara quoted a little melody she had written as a little girl. It was from her Op. 3 (a little melody Robert had used in his Op. 5). In the tenth variation of his Op. 9, Brahms quoted that little melody. It was really his first great variations piece. And there it is, a three-sided relationship among Brahms, Clara, and Robert, three great musicians who respected and admired each other's work.

Later, it has been suggested that Brahms became very attracted to the Schumann daughter named Julie. She was very beautiful, very sensitive, and rather a fragile and delicate girl. It might very well be that here was a young woman he could love. But it was out of the question for many reasons. Brahms never expressed any of this to Clara at the time. It was only after Julie's engagement and marriage to an Italian count that he indicated his feelings.

THE LAST WORKS

Whoever works in the same forms and conditions will become at last a mannerist or Philistine. There is nothing more harmful for an artist than continued repose in a convenient form; as one grows older the creative power itself diminishes and then it is too late. Many a first-rate talent only then recognizes that but half of his problem was solved."
—Robert Schumann, 1838

Overview

EDITOR'S NOTE

Before his incarceration in a mental institution in February 1854, Robert Schumann spent five incredibly productive years composing more than fifty works in a variety of genres and instrumentations. If the late concertos, songs, and piano and choral and chamber works have been generally dismissed as inferior and problematic, the fault may lie not with the composer but, as Cassius says, in ourselves. Scholars and performers disagree about how to assess and appreciate these works. While certainly his illness (an exact diagnosis remains elusive) hastened his breakdown and demise, it is debatable to what degree it influenced his music and how, subsequently, it may have prejudiced our perception and understanding of that music.

Charles Rosen

Are there differences in your own mind between Schumann's early works and the later works, either for piano or orchestra?

Yes, there are differences between early and late. But I'm not sure if it's a difference between youth and age. I'm less and less sure that it's a difference between sanity and a gradually increasing cloudiness of the mind, which is what happened to him. He may have feared near the end that he was becoming insane; and I think he went back to his early works and removed anything that could be interpreted as evidence of that. At the same time, I think that Schumann tended to burn himself out very fast in almost everything he took up. He starts with the piano music and for the first seven years of his composing life—between the age of twenty-one and twenty-eight—he publishes almost nothing but piano music. He did begin a few other things at this time, symphonies and such, but all the really great early works are for the piano. Then suddenly in 1839 he begins to compose songs, and he writes all the great songs within a year and a half. Then he took up chamber music. Towards the middle of the 1840s, when he was in his midthirties, he wrote two sets of pieces for the pedal piano, a piano with a pedal keyboard. The first set is absolutely glorious, and the second set is not very good. And I think what happened in all these cases is that he more or less burns out every single kind of music he writes.

He had started out with this extraordinary feeling for what we call "characteristic" music, that is, music that is actually *uncharacteristic*, that has an individual character of its own, that is like nothing else. And then he claimed that we have enough composers who can write characteristic pieces and nocturnes and songs, so now we need composers to write sonatas and symphonies. What he wants is to write much more formal, sublime music. As he got older, he wanted to become more classical. And he wasn't very apt at it. The composer who *did* that, and was successful, was Brahms. Brahms takes over this kind of neoclassical approach and mines it into very great music.

Is this a personal or professional burnout?

This may be disappointing, but I don't even think it's personal. I think that happened to almost every composer of his generation. It happened to Mendelssohn, who was at his greatest when he was sixteen or seventeen years old. He was always a fine composer, but he was never a composer of genius after the age of twenty (with a few exceptions like the Violin Concerto). Chopin dies young, so we can't tell what would have happened. For me, the really great pieces of Liszt are before 1850. Liszt remains a very interesting composer after that, but the kind of Liszt that we normally hear in concert programs is all finished by the time he's forty years old or less. And it's true, by the way, of poets. All the great romantic poets burn themselves out very young—Wordsworth, born in 1770, writes all his great poetry by the time he's thirty-five; Coleridge writes all his great poetry by the time he's thirty-four.

The style of music written by Schumann and Chopin and that whole generation born around 1810 valued spontaneity and improvisation more than anything else. And you know, that's a very hard style to sustain for many years. I think what happened was not so much that Schumann burned himself out, but that the style of Schumann and his contemporaries is the kind of music that you can sustain for only a brief period. Schumann sustains it, in fact, as long as anybody except Chopin.

Actually, one can see that Schumann kept his genius to a very, very late point. Even after he committed himself voluntarily to an insane asylum, there's that absolutely beautiful melody that Brahms used for his theme and variations for four hands. So he never really lost the genius. He kept it in fact more than Mendelssohn, in many ways. But it became harder and harder for him to exploit it.

Dr. Ostwald in his biography of Schumann speculates that late in his composing life Schumann found a "still point."

I think that's very sensible. When one looks at what other composers were doing, there's a comparable change. Chopin probably wrote less and less after he got to the age of forty because he was really sick. The amount he writes becomes very small in comparison to the early years. In the case of Liszt, too—Liszt continues, but the same kind of more classical, more sedate approach begins to be clear. He begins writing a lot of religious music, oratorios. The turning point in Liszt is the Piano Sonata in B Minor, which is in between the romantic and the classical modes.

András Schiff

I disagree with Charles Rosen that Schumann's genius ends after 1840. I have learned to respect the later works through my friendship with Heinz Holliger. He has showed me the way about late Schumann. I think Holliger is one of the most important living musicians and composers. Once I played with him his own interpretation of the *Gesänge der Frühe*. That was a great experience. I'm crazy about many of the late works, like the D-Minor Violin Sonata, which is phenomenal. When I visited Düsseldorf, I stood on the Bilkerstrasse at the gateway to the Schumann House. It was there that Brahms came. And it was from there that Schumann ran to the river and attempted suicide. He had been composing his last piece, what we now know as the *"Geister" Variations*. I just stood there, trying to picture that scene. That was very intense for me. It was then that I began studying the variations.

Eric Sams

In the later music, Florestan and Eusebius seem to disappear. At least they disappear in terms of his employment of the names. I think two things happened. First of all, one tired of it a bit as an idea; secondly, the personality became better integrated. I don't mean that the dual personality was in any way, in any serious way, neurotic. It's simply that with advancing age, the two halves or the two different aspects of one's personality do begin to foreclose. One gets a kind of foreshortening of the personality that does not mean the deterioration of age, but a better integrated personality. Second, we see the orderly progression from his youth, to maturity, to middle age, and to later life. One does begin as a young person with amazing notions, including various rebellions, revolutionary ideas, quite original ideas, which are to change the world. And later on, one discovers the world is on the whole very much the same place, though enriched by it. In Schumann's case he would have certainly seen there was no longer the need for him to have such amazingly original and unusual notions. Some have suggested that because his wife Clara was more Biedermeier, more bourgeois in her attitudes, it would have suggested to him that it was really time to settle down musically as well as domestically. But if taken too far, such remarks become calumnies against Clara, who was, it seems to me, in many ways the ideal musician, and who was really never,

never opposed to invention or originality on any kind of basic principle. And she was herself no mean composer. It's hard for me to believe that she would have chided Schumann for originality. I think it's just the ordinary progression of a composer's development. In many ways youth is the time for experimentation, and maturity is the time for retrenchment; and I think Schumann in that respect, as in so many, was typical of his age and indeed of great art generally.

John Daverio

It's sometimes said that Schumann's late music shows a lack of invention or inventiveness compared to his younger years, and that he will fasten on to a motive or tune and obsessively churn it out. That's a negative. But this same quality or characteristic is a positive when we talk about Beethoven's music. You can see this either as a sign of economy or lack of inventiveness. I feel that these negative approaches to the later music have been prejudiced by the fact that we know what happened to him. We know that he went mad. He had to be institutionalized. He suffered from mental illness. So it's easy to make a connection and say the music somehow suffers from this deteriorating mental state. I think that's a questionable step to take.

Laura Tunbridge

In my book [*Schumann's Late Style,* 2007] I am hoping to persuade people to bid farewell to our old images of Schumann and the late music, so we can consider them anew. I talk about the historical contexts of the music and its reception. I am one of several scholars, such as John Daverio, who have started to reevaluate the late works and revisit the biography. Some of this new interest has a lot to do with timing: We just recently had the 2006 celebration marking 150 years since Schumann's death. And coming up in 2010 we have the bicentenary of his birth. To be honest, we don't know the late music as well as the earlier piano music and the songs from the 1830s and the 1840s. There is a lot of music from the late 1840s and early 1850s that has just fallen out of the repertoire, and we're missing a lot of really interesting music. In some of it, around 1848–49, he was consciously interested in nationalist music and putting a populist message across. I think that hasn't translated so well into our time. He wasn't doing it as explicitly as someone like Wagner. But he was occupied with the importance of the German spirit and setting German texts to music.

In other ways his style and intention was changing. He was writing a lot for larger-scale forms, and writing in a more public way, if you will. There are quite a number of orchestral works, including the Third Symphony, which was written in 1850. Technically speaking, it marks the beginning of Schumann's late period. And there are several overtures, such as *Hermann and Dorothea* and *The Bride from Messina;* several concertos, notably the Violin Concerto and the Cello Concerto; some dramatic choral works, such as the four choral ballads; the *Manfred* and *Scenes from Goethe's Faust;* and chamber music, particularly the Third Piano Trio and two sets of *Fairy Tales;* and collections of songs, the *Lenau Lieder, Maria Stuart* lieder, and the "Elizabeth Kuhlmann" lieder. Add to that a few piano pieces, like the cycles, *Forest Scenes* and the *Gesänge der Frühe,* and you see that Schumann is writing in all the genres and for all the instruments that are available to him. His reputation was really doing very well. He was publishing a lot of music and starting to make some money from it, too. At a certain point it became so much that critics were saying, "If he wasn't producing quite so much, he would be producing better-quality music!" But I think that doesn't really happen until about 1853, which is the last year he was really productive.

I have devoted a lot of time to researching the books and paintings that Schumann was studying in this period. This is not the same man who had devoured the mysticisms and puzzles of Jean Paul, and the grotesques of E. T. A. Hoffmann. No, late in life he was reading Adalbert Stifter. I think I'm the first person to point out the significance of this. Stifter wrote quite a lot of stories—I particularly refer to the story collection *Bunte Steine* (Many-Colored Stones), from the mid-1840s. These are almost always in ternary form, framing narratives where some everyday occurrence would shift into fantasy and then return to the everyday. They return to "normalcy" after describing strange fancies. I conclude that they fantasize about "normality," rather than dwell on the fantastic. This is a reversal of someone like Jean Paul. Schumann uses this structure in spades in the songs and piano music of the time. We feel a kind of equilibrium, a sense of calmness, that you simply don't have in the earlier pieces.

We've been stuck with the traditional view that Schumann towards the end of his life withdraws from society. He's seen as increasingly melancholy and subject to various illnesses. That sort of view has really colored the way in which his music has been interpreted—how the whole of his career had been interpreted. My feeling is, we shouldn't make too close a connection between his physical and mental problems and the music, or we risk incarcerating him a *second* time—first at Endenich, and now in our attitudes toward him. Any obsessiveness we may think we see in the music might really be our own obsessions! By allowing his body into our own experience of the music, we increase our own potential to hear failure and sickness in it. Now, we can't just say, "We should take Schumann's illness out of the equation." But what I think we have to do is to put him and his music into a very different context. We need to take into account what was going on around him and what he was trying to do as a composer in the 1850s, not what he was doing earlier. It's a different context.

Because of the historical distance blocking our view, and the scant medical records available to us, we're never going to have a definitive answer for what was wrong with Schumann. In my mind it seems more likely that many different factors were in play. So he may well have had syphilis; he probably did, and certainly that is what John Worthen, his most recent biographer, has claimed. Worthen's book is a counterargument to Peter Ostwald's book. Ostwald had raised a lot of issues regarding Schumann's problems that people hadn't been prepared to entertain before. His openness of talking about Schumann's psychiatric condition in some ways paved the way for much of the scholarship that has followed. But Schumann could also have been suffering from other illnesses at the same time. So it's always very difficult to know just what was wrong. His wasn't a particularly "colorful" mental illness, if you know what I mean. When you think of the "mad artist," you have this notion about the romantic genius with extroverted, bizarre behavior. But Schumann was becoming much more introverted and melancholy. Eduard Hanslick, who knew Schumann, visited him in the asylum and wrote that he seemed just fatigued and sad.

Several works from these last years are frequently heard these days. I am a big fan of the Third Piano Trio. I also very much like the Second Violin Sonata, which in its day was much more successful than the First. But now the First, in A minor, has overtaken it. The four choral ballads really include some very illustrative music, particularly in the choral writing. The *Songs of the Dawn* is another late piece that I think is really quite astonishing. It's essentially his last piano cycle. At times it's as if he is writing for a keyboard physically bigger than the hand can accommodate. It's very difficult to know who these pieces were for, but there is something poetic about a man near the end of his career writing music signaling a kind of dawning. . . .

On the other hand, the Third Violin Sonata, the Cello Concerto, and the Violin Concerto are avoided by some performers; but others are convinced they can make a case for them. They're very difficult. Quite often what you find in Schumann's late music is a sense of containment, of a distillation of the musical language that is quite different from the earlier pieces. He always had a tendency to use sequences, but this becomes more pronounced later. It all has to do with him taking musical ideas to their furthest point.

The piano music is definitely not part of any modernist trajectory toward increasing complexity and harmonic freedom. Late in life, Schumann returns to writing music for children, to simple forms, music that moves away from eccentric and difficult forms. This is music that would help educate young musicians. So we see late in life Schumann returning to writing music for children, music that would help educate young musicians. This meant a return to simple forms, a moving away from eccentric and difficult music. I'm struck by the fact that when Schumann talks about Schubert's last piano sonatas, he seems to be describing his own music—music of greater simplicity of invention, avoidance of virtuosic novelty, and a kind of "endlessness" that is never obstructed for the sake of effect.

I think the attention John Daverio pays to the late work is very valuable, not least because it really encourages us to reengage with it. He writes about it in such an exciting way that it is a great contribution to the literature. It was about time that some of us Anglo-American scholars really did that! One of the things I find interesting about his approach is that in making a case for the late pieces he will say that they are examples of Schumann going back to what he did in his earlier music. So, for example, he talks about the early "Florestan/Eusebius" alternations of mood resurfacing in the First Violin Sonata. Now, there are indeed shifts of mood, but why insist they display the Florestan/Eusebius dichotomy, unless it might make us think better of the music? Rather, we just need to acknowledge that much of this later music, like the man, is *different*. There are cracks between the early and late works. Too many of us want to paper over the cracks to argue for some kind of redeeming ancestry. I am not here to "redeem" these works, just to point out that Schumann's biography and medical problems have unduly prejudiced our reception of them.

Charles Rosen claims that Schumann's late revisions of his early music render them less interesting. But that's almost as if you're expecting a composer to stay the same and to hold the same views throughout his career. As a mature composer, Schumann is looking back on what he wrote in his late twenties with different sensibilities and objectives. He was concerned with his public reputation at this point and wished to temper the music's eccentricities and difficulties. He was also concerned with musical education and how people would be able to play his music. He puts in more repeats in the piano music, for example, which is maybe to give people a "second chance" in their listening, to help them understand the music. He hadn't been concerned about that sort of thing in his youth.

I come away from studying this music with the sense that we are dealing with a cracked bell. The symbol of the bell recurs throughout his music. It tolls in the concluding piece of the *Fantasy Pieces*, Op. 12, and Schumann told Clara that it signified not just wedding bells, but the sound of a death knell. It's music that aims for greatness but is somehow flawed. It's difficult to reach a clear interpretation of these works, but it's worth trying.

Heinz Holliger

These days I'm conducting a lot of Schumann, and I've done many performances of the entire *Manfred* music. I suppose it's never been very popular because there's not enough music in it. There's a lot of text, and after the Overture the pieces are very short. Schumann called it only a "folio," that is, music wrapped around the text. He didn't want to overweigh the music. I have done my own adaptation with my brother, a theater producer. We retranslated a lot of it. Schumann, unfortunately, used a very poor translation of the Byron text. There is a very, very beautiful tape recording on Bayerischer Rundfunk of Rafael Kubelik with the whole *Manfred;* and he offered it to Deutsche Grammophon for free. But they refused it, and then he stepped out of the office and never did any more recordings for Deutsche Grammophon because he was so offended! In the future I want to do more Schumann, like a set of concert performances of his opera, *Genoveva,* and a lot of other choral pieces, like the *Nachtlied,* from a text by Hebbel. I have done it before in Helsinki, together with my own piece, a sort of Schumann portrait called *Gesänge der Frühe.* It's based on one of his last piano works, and I've transformed it for large orchestra, chorus, and tape. [Note: See the "Aftermath and Legacy" chapter.]

Peter F. Ostwald

Schumann changed in his approach to composition. He wanted to be a much more serious composer as he grew older. He and Clara were both dissatisfied with his earlier short pieces. From almost childhood on, he had wanted to write opera and symphonies. But he had some difficulties there, partly because of the lack of training. You know, Schumann was almost completely an autodidact. He did not do well with teachers. He trained himself, so that he lacked the technical ability of people like Beethoven. He did best with improvisatory ideas, fleeting moments. He had these great inspirations, and then when he had to work on them, he sometimes ran out of steam. So as his compositions become longer, there are stretches that strike one as being repetitive and somewhat dull. I suppose if he had spent more time in revising his music and had gone back very critically with the necessary musical ability and skills, he might have trimmed it and worked on it. But to say his music deteriorated, I think, is a great mistake because we find such wonderful compositions, such very successful works as the "Rhenish" Symphony, for example, which is a late work, or the Cello Concerto, which I think is one of his supreme masterpieces. He wrote that under very difficult circumstances in Düsseldorf.

The Mass and the Requiem are church pieces. They have some very great moments, especially the Mass. Again, I'm not a musicologist, and I don't think that what I have to say about them really counts very much, but I have the feeling that if Schumann had lived longer and had gone back to revise the works, they would be better today. He might have made certain changes. The Requiem was written under a kind of depressive fantasy. He thought that he was writing it for himself. That's not too unusual. Mozart had that feeling about his Requiem, which is also unfinished; and I think there have been a number of other composers who have written Requiems for themselves.

You know, I like *Paradise and the Peri* very much. It would be wonderful to do it as a kind of operatic piece or as a ballet. This is the problem with the opera *Genoveva*, too, which is so rarely performed. I think it's a difficult work, a very inward piece. Schumann has his characters talking mostly about what they feel and not about what they do, so it's a very private, sensitive work. It reminds me a lot of *Pelléas and Mélisande*. It's very dependent on the Thomas Moore story, which is rather old-fashioned, one of those highly romanticized things, like the *Arabian Nights*.

Nancy B. Reich

Schumann's doctor, Dr. Richarz, said he thought some of the alterations in Schumann's mental state began in 1852, about two years before he went to the institution. And this period included some of the works we hear today and some of the works we'll never hear because they were destroyed by Clara. She wrote to the publisher and said she felt it was important not to publish the things that "were unworthy of him." She didn't say it was because he was in another world—just that it was *unworthy* of him. Plus, she was trying to protect his reputation. We know there were some cello romances. Brahms and Joachim and she went over these, and they destroyed them. My friend Steven Isserlis, the famous cellist, has made a very imaginative film about this episode, *Schumann's Lost Romance*. [See his account in the "Aftermath and Legacy" chapter.] I was interviewed on camera for that. And yes, we know that Schumann did write some music in the asylum at Endenich. He had a piano at his disposal. He did play, and he did write down a few things during that time. He even wrote some letters to the publishers. But those letters were quite different from what he wrote earlier. First of all, in terms of the handwriting, they were easier to read, more clear. And they have a kind of simplistic expression. Clara treasured those letters, and they were later published. Now, it's clear from them he was in another state of mind. These works, too, were destroyed.

Selected Works

EDITOR'S NOTE
We begin with a commentary by pianists Peter Frankl and Ronald Brautigam about Schumann's last major piano work, the Gesänge der Frühe (Songs of the Dawn), Op. 133. Following that is a commentary by mezzo-soprano Sarah Walker on the *Maria Stuart* song cycle, Op. 135, and commentaries on three of Schumann's late, concerted works written at this time: Cellists Lynn Harrell, Steven Isserlis, musicologist Laura Tunbridge, and biographer Peter F. Ostwald offer contrasting views on the Cello Concerto, Op. 129; pianist Peter Frankl and conductor John Nelson on the *Konzertstück for Four Horns* (as transcribed for piano and orchestra), Op. 86; and Peter Zehetmair on the Violin Fantasie, Op. 131. Lastly, there is the strange story of three of Schumann's very last pieces, the Violin Concerto, WoO23; the Third Violin Sonata, WoO27; and the Five Romances for Cello (now lost). Steven Isserlis talks about the mysteries and controversies behind these works.

Songs of the Dawn

Peter Frankl

I haven't played the *Songs of the Dawn* for quite a while, but I think I ought to go into it again. Frankly speaking, I had the most trouble with this piece. It's an Op. 133, and it was sent by Schumann to his friend Joseph Joachim, while he was in the asylum. As very late Schumann, you can never be sure, *where does it go?* Sometimes it is accessible, but sometimes it really goes beyond our limits. It has moments of great serenity and great depth in it, but my God, you have to work hard for it! With this kind of Schumann I always have trouble. The *Gesänge der Frühe* are marvelous pieces, but you have to do some superhuman things to bring it out, like some of the other late pieces, such as the Third Piano Trio and the Third Violin Sonata. You know, I don't think at that time Schumann was interested in piano playing. He composed some of this music away from the piano. I think he lost interest a long time before that. He was, as the legend is saying, so dissatisfied with his own playing that he injured himself practicing. And he was never satisfied with the existing technique or existing instruments. Bach was not happy with his keyboards, and you can see evidence of Beethoven tearing up all the strings of his pianos.

If you look at the first page of the *Gesänge*, the one in D major, you think it's a relatively easy piece. But the polyphonic writing is sometimes awkward, and there are spans that are almost too wide for the hand. And there's something odd about the harmonies and the way it's worked out.

But for the ear it is a very beautiful and simple work. I compare it in a way to the slow movement of the Violin Concerto.

In the No. 2, in B minor, he is in his "Florestan" element. It's very busy and very passionate. It has an urgency in the triplets and some complicated composite rhythms. It's fiendishly difficult, and I don't think I have ever played it in public—one of the rare pieces that I didn't play.

Now, the third one in A Major is a "mad" piece, if I may say so. But it's the kind of mad piece which appeared in the last movement of the *Carnaval* and the Finale of the Third Piano Sonata, when he wants always to go ahead, faster, and then "as fast as possible." This is the fullest measure of romanticism. He's in a hurry all the time. You can do it with lots of accelerandos and you don't have always to be strictly in rhythm.

You see in the No. 4 what very often happens with Schumann: You have a beautiful melody, but which is very, very difficult to play. Some of the figuration of the accompaniment is in the same hand. But you have to think of nothing else but the melody. Try to forget the difficulties, and if you forget the difficulties you will be able to do justice more to the big melody climb. There is a magical modulation at the end when we go from F-sharp minor into F-sharp major. I think it's as simple as that. Very beautiful.

Finally, in the No. 5, in D major, you have this "end of lied" character. That's very typical of Schumann. If we think of it in retrospect, it seems to round off his piano music writing, as if he's saying farewell to it (although we know he did write another piece later). I love that lovely final section with its lovely legato broken chords and trill figures in both hands (and for all combinations of fingers!). And then, as is very often with him, he goes down to nothing, and it finishes very much in peace and tranquility.

Ronald Brautigam

The *Gesänge der Frühe* is what I would call "fragile" music. It's best, I think, to play it alone without an audience. That is probably how Schumann meant it. Some music works well in a concert hall, whereas other music needs the intimacy of your own study. It is one of the most moving of all his works, but it is also one of the most difficult. By the end of his life, his harmonic language creates a feeling of not belonging, of having moved on to a better world. I've always felt that the moment you play the first note of the first piece, it's already spoiled. It's really Schumann almost on his deathbed. It's the same as the theme from the *"Geister" Variations*, where everything you do is already too much. It's music that should play itself. He must have had large hands, because the chords in that first one can only be played if you break them. It's a shame, but it's the only possible way to play them. But as soon as you break those chords, it spoils the whole quiet and peaceful atmosphere. The third piece is technically very awkward, with those jumping chords and jumping octaves, but you have to try to keep it light and fresh. You're not sure where it's going, apart from going all over the place! There's not really a tune, just harmonies—a sort of "Ride of the Valkyries" gone wrong. It's a nightmare. But the fourth is absolutely fantastic, but also so difficult to keep the arpeggios light; and it doesn't stop, it just goes on and on. But you do keep going on and on, because it's such fantastic music; and in the end that's all that matters, even if you have to cut off one finger to make it fit the piano—or grow an extra one! The last one has a nice, chorale-like tune that you have to keep kind of *floating*, that doesn't touch the ground anymore. The same holds true for other music of this time, like the slow movement of his Violin Concerto. It's almost too beautiful to perform in public.

Maria Stuart Songs

> *I am going away, away; farewell to you, my happy France, where I found the dearest homeland of all, you the nurse of my childhood.*
>
> —*Maria Stuart* Songs

EDITOR'S NOTE

Schumann's last song cycle is based on texts that trace the tragedy of Mary Queen of Scots' departure from France and her plea for salvation in the moments before she was put to death. The songs are sometimes considered pendants to the *Frauenliebe und -leben* cycle in their voicing of a female sensibility. The poems have been mistakenly attributed to Maria Stuart.

Sarah Walker

I'm so glad you asked me to say a few words about the Schumann *Maria Stuart* lieder—so few people have heard them, possibly as they are considered by some (extremely prominent German) *artistes* to be lesser works, good only for singers who have retired! It is true that the cycle does not pose technical difficulties, but it requires great concentration and a very real sense of theater.

One of the reasons I love the Schumann *Maria Stuart* songs is because I particularly like performing characters and portraits. Roger Vignoles and I first put them into a program we did for the 1980 Edinburgh Festival, and we enjoyed them so much that we have put them into many concerts since. When we made our New York debut at the Frick Museum in 1984 we did a pair of "portrait" recitals called, after one of the cycles we were doing, "The Voice of Love." As I was at that time singing the title role of Elizabeth I in Britten's opera *Gloriana* at the Met, I was planning the first recital to be based on music that was, in one way or another relevant, to that period of English history. The *Maria Stuart* songs were perfect—they might have come out of the same box! Maria Stuart—or Mary, Queen of Scots, as she is known in England—was a great rival of Elizabeth I and was the heroine of Schiller's play on which Donizetti based his opera of the same name. The opera takes at least three hours and, charming though the music may be, I would far rather listen to the Schumann any day—they are infinitely more interesting and only take nine minutes, seventeen seconds! They are exquisite miniature portraits, encapsulating the whole story with more truth and insight than both Schiller and Donizetti. In each of the five songs Schumann gives you the essence of that particular period of her life, as if you're reading a book and turning the pages.

Mary spent her childhood in France and married the Dauphin, but when he died, she returned to Scotland as queen and, in the first song, "Farewell from France," we have her words, or they are meant to be hers—and may well be since both she and Elizabeth were very well educated. As the boat leaves the shores of France, she promises her childhood's nurse, "Part of my heart stays with you, and I'll never forget you." It is a beautiful, gentle song, but also bittersweet.

And then you turn the page to discover another picture: This is the birth of her son, and you are suddenly there with Mary, and she prays that the Lord will look down on them with favor and grant to her son his birthright. It's the most beautiful song, in which Mary's own ambition is masked by the hushed simplicity of the prayer. But she accepts that all will be "Not what I will, but what *Thou* willst."

And now you turn another page to find her imprisoned in England for many years and constantly writing letters to Elizabeth begging for a meeting. She is desperately trying not to offend Elizabeth but still wants to put her case strongly—"This letter is but a poor messenger; the storm of my enemies' advice obscures the truth of my love for you, and I fear their influence on your thoughts, dear sister."

After this passionate outpouring to Elizabeth, you realize in the next song, "Farewell to the World," that she hasn't been successful; and she knows that. "Now my enemies can be happy that I will never again be the cause of envy or hate; and my friends can be happy, too, because at last I'm going to a better place. Wish me joy."

And now we come to the final prayer. At this point I feel most clearly Mary's life passing before her eyes as she waits in her cell for the end. We review her departure from France, the birth of her son, the long imprisonment, and her fruitless requests to Elizabeth, her farewells to the world, to the present moment. She goes out of the door and there is the block—she sees it just before the opening, loud chord is played—but in her faith remains and sustains her in her final moment.

I really feel it is not necessary to speak German to understand these songs; the sometimes quite complex emotions that pervade them are so *clear* in the music that I don't like to have the distraction of a literal translation printed in the program, and so Roger or I will introduce the cycle from the stage, just giving the audience the gist. I really dislike people turning pages and rustling papers during the performance, and anyway, by the time they have read the text, I have finished the song! I want them *listening* to the music and understanding the song through what they see in my eyes. I must admit I feel a certain proprietary interest in the *Maria Stuart* lieder. If I were to listen to someone else sing them, perhaps not quite as I like it, I might get bored; if they do it better, I might get jealous! It is the most wonderful song cycle, and I hope you enjoy it!

The Cello Concerto

Lynn Harrell

The Cello Concerto is a late piece of Schumann. Although he wrote it around 1850, it was thought to be unplayable at the time. I don't think it was published until a few years later [August 1854], and he never heard it performed. [Note: It was premiered publicly with Ludwig Ebert as soloist in 9 June 1860.] His depression and his state of mind was of such fragility that any moment he would be wild and uncontrollable, and at another moment suddenly calm down and be very placid. Those are the undercurrents in this piece. For example, the cello line in the first movement is lyrical and beautiful. The syncopation in the orchestral accompaniment and the accentuations and the abrupt stopping and starting of phrases shows an alternating malaise and discomfort. But then you have the slow movement, and those conflicts seem to melt away. It is such a soft, dreamy, delicate "soft-as-a-Carebear-cloud" sort of thing. The cello, it just sings. It is a respite from the undercurrents of the first movement. So the second movement is like a sleep and a dream away from that. The last movement brings a return of a state of agitation, uncertainty, and some very uncomfortable cello writing. What happens here is that the difficult places are really very, very hard. Extremely difficult. They don't last long—only three of four seconds of that kind of real, extended difficulty. But unless you keep them absolutely in control, secure, and easy, then you've destroyed a much greater percentage of the musical utterance.

Laura Tunbridge

The Cello Concerto does indeed reveal some disjunctions between soloist and orchestra. The cello at times seems to wander into the distance,
toward some kind of extinction. Sometimes the orchestra breaks into the
dreams of the soloist. I wonder if that isn't like Schumann being haunted,
as he says, by melodies from elsewhere? I think beneath its surface we can
detect a body that beats. I am borrowing from Roland Barthes here. But
it's a body coming to an end.

Steven Isserlis

I first heard the Cello Concerto when I was twelve years old. It was a
recording with Pablo Casals. Later, when I was about eighteen, I played it
at Oberlin College, and I messed it up completely. I just didn't understand
how to approach it. But over the years I've been lucky to work on it with
a sympathetic conductor like Christoph Eschenbach, with whom I've
recorded it and played it in my film, *Schumann's Lost Romance* [1996; see
the "Aftermath and Legacy" chapter for Isserlis's account of the film]. It's
such a personal piece. I want to do it as a kind of chamber piece. I can't
think of a concerto *for any instrument* that is more personal and intimate.
The last movement is pretty classical, just sonata form: exposition with
two distinct subjects, development and recapitulation. I don't think he's
experimenting particularly there, except for the unique, beautiful accompanied cadenza. The first movement, however, is something else. It's very
difficult to pinpoint which phrases really constitute the first and second
subjects. The movement is like a continuous narrative. And there's such
an inner struggle there. I know that Gidon Kremer has played a violin
version of the Cello Concerto, which Schumann himself had authorized.
But I think it's a mistake. Nor would the Violin Concerto be successful
on the cello. The particular kind of lyricism of the Cello Concerto needs
the *depth* of the cello. And the violin just doesn't have that.

Konzertstück for Four Horns

Peter Frankl

The four-horn *Konzertstück* was originally written in 1849 and scored
for four horns and orchestra. I was really surprised when I found out
that there is a piano version, because I wouldn't think a piece for four
horns would transfer well to the piano. And, frankly, I still don't think
it sounds well on the piano. And there are some musicologists in London
who very much doubt the originality of this version. However, I was talking to the publisher, Litolff/Peters, in Frankfurt, and most of the German
Schumann experts are now saying that it definitely is an original work. It

was published in Schumann's lifetime. Obviously, if it was published then, Schumann must have been aware of it. And no other name is mentioned on the front page. Valve horns, which were just developed at the time, were a great fascination for Schumann. And in every Schumann biography that mentions the work, we see how fond he was of it. He really liked this piece extremely much.

It is claimed that if the horns were not available, he wanted to hear it on his favorite instrument, the piano. One would think the piano is a powerful instrument, but it's really very weak in comparison to four solo horns, plus the two which are already in the orchestra. But I thought that it was a challenge, so why not give a try? And I must tell you, I enjoyed it. I didn't give it the world premiere, but I certainly played the first performances in the United States and in England, Holland, Switzerland, and maybe other countries, as well. So I played it a few times before I recorded it with John Nelson with the Cincinnati Symphony in 1980. Walter Susskind was originally to be the conductor, but he just died about that time. I was very fortunate to get John Nelson to take over. It's a beautiful piece, altogether. The second movement is a real beauty.

The people at Vox Turnabout were very interested in such rarities. Since then another conductor, Marc Andrae, is actively specializing in discovering rarely played or early Schumann pieces (I know he has recorded Schumann's first attempt at a symphony, a work in G minor). He wanted me to record the piece again with a German orchestra in Cologne. But I discouraged him. I told him I just recorded it, and it would be silly that an unknown piece would be recorded twice within five years by the same pianist. Give an opportunity to someone else. So I didn't record it again.

John Nelson

Those performances with Peter Frankl came about because I was called in as a substitute conductor for Walter Susskind. He was the interim director at Cincinnati after Thomas Schippers died. He had brought this piece to the orchestras. Now, I'm not certain whether or not this piano version of the *Konzertstück* was Frankl's discovery or Walter's. But it was not mine. I simply walked into it with just a week's notice. We performed it four times before we recorded it. As far as I knew, nobody had known it even existed, and it had not been performed before. Peter was mad about the piece, and we were all happy to be a part of the project. We don't even know what prompted Schumann to arrange it for piano and orchestra. It's certainly an interesting piece, but to be quite frank about it, I don't really think it works in this version. It's a marvelous piece for four horns, and it was conceived for four horns. But hey, look at so many of us who swarm around the name Schumann. Everything is grist. I mean, if he wrote his tax return, we would be trying to come up with an unknown composition he might have made out of it! I think because we all too often play the same music, over and over again, we're hungry for new material. Even new material like this! Anyway, Peter and I look back on it with pride, because we both love Schumann. But really, after all, it's a relatively minor work in this version.

Fantasie for Violin and Orchestra, Op. 131

Thomas Zehetmair

I came here to Düsseldorf [1994] to the Schumann Festival because of Heinz Holliger and the Robert-Schumann-Gesellschaft. It is only here and few other places where we can do together a program like the Violin Fantasie, Op. 131. Heinz and I also did an all-Schumann program like this earlier in Ferrara. A festival like this is very necessary. We can address so many misunderstandings about Schumann's music, especially the late music, like this violin work. It's amazing how many prejudices there still are. But when the Fantasie was first performed, it got a wonderful reaction, from the audience and from the press. It was a piece with a lot of ideas. But a few years later, when it was known that Schumann's mental disease was growing, then suddenly the reaction was completely different. People were speaking about its weaknesses. It's now true of many of Schumann's violin works, especially this and the Violin Concerto. They say they're "ungrateful" for the violin. In my opinion, it's wonderfully played and it makes absolute sense. There's a special expression here which one has to find, and it has a very deep, emotional character. I first heard about the Fantasie about six years ago. I then studied the original manuscript at the library in Berlin. I found that the printed versions made many changes, which I have corrected in my recording with Christoph Eschenbach [Teldec Classics, 1989]. Both these late works were written in 1853 and dedicated to Joseph Joachim, who liked the Fantasie but refused to play the concerto. I have never heard it in concert, but I play it as often as I can. It's so strange to think it's unusual, because it is a wonderful piece.

Violin Concerto, the Third Violin Sonata, and the "Lost" Cello Romances

EDITOR'S NOTE

Near the end of her life, Clara considered either not publishing or destroying outright some of Robert's very last compositions. She argued that they were not up to the standard of her husband's legacy. The Five Cello Romances are lost irretrievably, presumably with Brahms's approval. Two works that barely escaped oblivion are the Violin Concerto and the Third Violin Sonata.

Peter F. Ostwald

The Violin Concerto has an interesting story. He wrote it at the request of Joseph Joachim. But Schumann was relatively inexperienced with the violin. He had studied it a little bit when he was in his thirties, but he was quite dependent on Joachim for corrections and asked him to help him edit the work. Joachim promised to come and play the concerto for Schumann in the hospital, but that never happened. I think it's an unfinished piece in some respects, but it's a very great piece. The slow movement especially is phenomenal. It has ideas that are very forward-looking. Yehudi Menuhin called that concerto the "missing link" between the Beethoven concerto and the Brahms concerto.

Steven Isserlis

Clara did not destroy the manuscript of the Violin Concerto. It was written in early 1853 for Joachim. It was rehearsed when Robert and Clara were visiting Joachim in Hanover in January 1854, but it was not performed. After that, it disappeared, and after Robert's death, Clara had it locked away, stipulating that it not be performed for a hundred years. That embargo was broken by a strange series of events. The violinist Jelly d'Arányi, who was a niece of Joachim, claimed that Schumann's spirit came to her requesting the concerto be found and performed. Eventually, in spite of the objections of Schumann's daughter Eugenie, the German violinist Georg Kulenkampff premiered and recorded it in heavily revised version in 1937, but in circumstances loaded with a dose of Nazi propaganda. Only a little later Yehudi Menuhin performed and recorded it. There's a story that a few days before Schumann's breakdown in January 1854, he claimed the angels of Schubert and Mendelssohn came to him with a beautiful melody. He immediately set it to music and composed variations on it for solo piano—a wonderful piece! The strange thing is that neither Schumann, Clara, nor Brahms noticed that the theme is almost exactly the same as the second main melody of the slow movement of the Violin Concerto! And you can even find it anticipated years before in a little song from his *Song Album for the Young*, his Op. 79, the "Frühlings Ankunft" [Spring's Arrival]. As a whole, the concerto is a magnificent work with both Handelian grandeur and some of the most gentle, inward-looking music to be found in any concerto. However, even a Schumanniac like myself has to admit that the last movement, a slow polonaise, is problematic. You have to play it with the right dose of swaggering good humor to preserve its charm. Part of the problem is Schumann's slow metronome markings. You have to remember that he wrote the piece at a time late in life when he found almost every tempo too fast.

The stories behind the Third Violin Sonata and the Five Cello Romances are intriguing. The sonata comes from late in 1853, when Schumann was surrounded by new young friends, Johannes Brahms, the violinist Joseph Joachim, and a young disciple, Albert Dietrich. Schumann came up with a plan that he and the others would jointly compose a violin sonata based on the initial letters of Joachim's rather gloomy motto, "Frei aber einsam" (Free but alone). So the so-called *F–A–E Sonata* was born, with a first movement by Dietrich, a scherzo by Brahms, and a slow movement and finale by Schumann. Joachim would be presented with it upon his arrival in Düsseldorf and, when he played it through, would have to identify the author of each movement. Guessing the composer wouldn't have been difficult, but sight reading the end of the finale probably gave him an apoplectic fit! A little later Schumann replaced the first two movements with two of his own, thus creating his Third Violin Sonata. Although his friends greeted this work with enthusiasm, it disappeared after Schumann's breakdown. It is likely that Clara demolished the fair copy of the sonata, but fortunately for us, a full sketch survived. But unlike the Violin Concerto, the Third Sonata had to wait a full hundred years to see the light of day. It was not published until 1956. Old prejudices die hard, though, and it is still shrouded in neglect. I have decided to kill the next violinist who says to me: "But Schumann only wrote *two* violin sonatas." I think that, having to endure that remark for so many years, I can produce quite a convincing case for the defense.

It's a wonderful work. It runs an impressive gamut of extreme emotions, from wild passion to the gentlest of musings. And there are also generous moments of deeply eccentric humor and crazy virtuosity. I have conceived a plan to avenge us poor cellists for those lost romances, by arranging this for cello. It is quite a task. It is one of the most difficult works I have ever played. But I'm so glad to have done it. Every performance constitutes a journey, both for players and for listeners. It stretches all of us to the limits. That is a feature of playing or singing Schumann: He demands our whole soul; anything less sounds tepid. And he is a composer who, even more than the other greats, depends on his performers. If you play it without commitment or understanding, the music can sound pedestrian. No, it must *fly*. To record it on the cello is even more of a mission. It is not a task that I approach lightly. But if pianist Dénes Várjon and I can bring this underappreciated masterpiece more firmly into the repertoire—and into the consciousness of music lovers—it will have been worth every demisemiquaver. [Note: The recording was issued in 2000 to rapturous reviews.]

Schumann definitely wanted his Five Cello Romances to be published. He wrote them in November 1853. He writes to the publishers, telling them about these pieces. Later, he asks that his Cello Romances be sent to the Endenich asylum, and he corresponded further with the publishers from the asylum. He even got a letter from Brahms, where Brahms tells Schumann that he and Joachim are fighting over which of the romances is their favorite. But they were never published. Ultimately it was not his decision. It was Clara, perhaps aided and abetted by Brahms, who decided to destroy them. No doubt she associated this music with a very unhappy time, which it certainly was. Now, she didn't destroy the Violin Concerto, but she did destroy the romances. Nothing survives of them. Not a note. It's frustrating, to put it mildly.

Styra Avins

Many people have attacked Clara for destroying some of Schumann's last compositions, including a series of romances for cello. I want to start out talking about this by mentioning that when Clara's last son, Felix, a very talented poet and musician, wanted to write something, she insisted that he do it under a pseudonym. She didn't want to risk anybody sullying the family name. We're not used to people being so tough on their own family members for posterity. You have to keep that in mind when you think about Clara's suppression of some of Schumann's late works. She asked Brahms's opinion. If Brahms had thought they were fine, first-rate works, he wouldn't have agreed with her. These last works are discursive, wandering pieces in some ways. Not everybody likes them. I am one of those people who don't think they're so great. They have beautiful moments, no doubt about it, but do I want to sit down and listen to the last violin sonata? Personally, the answer is no. This is a question of opinion. But to fault her in a moralistic way is not fair. I think one can understand what her position was without getting angry at her. Look at what Brahms did with his own music—how many pieces he suppressed and destroyed. He only wanted the very best shown to the public. And that's I'm sure the spirit in which these last works of Schumann's were suppressed.

12

"Let Us Drink Together of Lethe"

The Schumann Problem

Commentators: John Daverio, Erik Fokke, Peter F. Ostwald, Leon Plantinga, Nancy B. Reich, Eric Sams, and John Worthen

I haven't slept a wink with the most terrifying thoughts and eternally torturing music—God help me that I will not one day die like this.

—Robert Schumann, July 1838

There are men from whom nature, or some peculiar destiny, has removed the cover beneath which we hide our own madness. They are like thin-skinned insects whose visible play of muscles seems to make them deformed.

—E. T. A. Hoffmann, *Councillor Krespel*

EDITOR'S NOTE

The precise nature of Schumann's emotional, psychological, and physiological problems has long aroused diverging opinions and speculations. Recently, Schumann's medical papers have come to light, which have both clarified and confused the issues. In these pages we find sharp disagreements among a psychiatrist (Peter F. Ostwald); a medical doctor (Erik Fokke); biographers (Ostwald, Nancy B. Reich, John Daverio, and John Worthen); and commentators (Eric Sams and Leon Plantinga).

THE COMING STORM

Peter F. Ostwald

I think Schumann is a natural for a psychiatrist, because he's probably the best-documented psychiatric case that we have in the history of music.

He became interested in his mental processes quite early in life. It's characteristic of many creative people, that they're somewhat introverted and introspective. And the tendency to write a great deal about one's inner life was typical of the early romantics.

He was an exceedingly insightful person. This was, of course, a source of great fascination for me. He was almost like a patient in psychotherapy who has gone to all the trouble to reveal to you what he has observed about his suffering. And so Schumann proceeds, after the age of sixteen, to record almost every day his fluctuations in mood, his experiences, his observations, and that made him very, very interesting for psychiatric study. Romanticism had been very much still in favor among German intellectuals and artists. As a youth Schumann cultivated that kind of romanticism, and he indulged in thinking about himself as being "mad." He liked to read the works of other people who had mad experiences, such as E. T. A. Hoffmann, who described that in his stories about the character of Johannes Kreisler. And Schumann also read widely in the novels of Jean Paul Richter, which deal with the concept of the double personality as it was understood in the romantic era. He suffered from an inner disorder that we call nowadays an affective disorder. It would drive him into hypomanic episodes. He would actually enjoy them to a degree. He would use them creatively. He would write; he would become very productive. But he was also very, very fearful of losing control over himself, so that he had this double attitude towards his madness. On the one hand, he realized that it was something that pushed him into creative outbursts; on the other hand, it made him feel so sick and so unwell that he repeatedly sought help. As he grew older, however, his way of describing his symptoms changed. He began to refer to his problems as "illness," or "melancholia," rather than madness.

I can't help but be fascinated by a curious episode during Schumann's years in Dresden. Troubled by severe depression, he went to see a Dr. Carl Helbig, who practiced hypnosis, which in those days was called "magnetizing." Robert submitted to this. He had always believed in magic and a little later would attend séances. The hypnotherapy may have had a deleterious effect on his composing, for he seems to have turned away from it for a short period.

I don't happen to think that he had any mental deterioration. This is where I part company with so many people. I don't think that there is any real evidence of mental deterioration. First of all, I don't like the term *deterioration*. Surely, Schumann had serious problems in controlling his thoughts and his feelings. That came periodically. We know that happened to him in his adolescence, in his twenties, in his thirties, and in his forties. The only real evidence of quote "deterioration" I suppose would be in the very last phases of his hospitalization, and that's a problem, because we don't have enough information really to know what happened. My guess is that he became very depressed again in the hospital, that he stopped eating there, that he probably stopped cooperating with the nurses, and that he did undergo a kind of physical deterioration simply because he was not eating. You see that in prisoners who are starved or who starve themselves. You've seen that in concentration camp victims, and that's what happened to Schumann. He suffered enormously because he was not eating in the hospital. To that extent there was deterioration, and he finally died.

We can observe our mental states. We see this all the time in psychiatry. We can have terrible nightmares, for instance. We're fast asleep, but we have thoughts about being in another world, or we have the most peculiar ideas, sometimes the most frightening fantasies and hallucinations while we're asleep. That can also happen during waking states with people who are afflicted with certain types of mental disorder. There's no reason why someone cannot, at the same time, maintain a sort of awareness. Now, this fluctuates. There are also conditions we call "without insight," where patients lose the ability to recognize that they are mentally ill, but Schumann had a good deal of awareness, and I think that he realized that he was mentally ill.

Affective disorder refers to emotional disorder, to mood disorder. An affective disorder is one where there are intense feelings of sadness, much more than ordinary unhappiness. Schizophrenia is a different category of illness. Schizophrenia is manifested by a primary disorder in thinking, in the cognitive processes. I don't think Schumann was schizophrenic. So often in medicine you have disagreements over these things, and I don't think there's any point in hassling over the diagnosis, because there's so many tests we can't do on Schumann which we would like to do these days. If one wants to keep the idea of schizophrenia alive, one could accept the position that he had what's called a "schizoaffective" type of disorder, in which schizophrenic-like symptoms occur in the setting of a major depressive disorder.

John Worthen

I have a take on Schumann's mental condition which may be unique. I want it to be. I want to say it's also right. I think I'm the first person to have been lucky enough, just by timing, to have not only just read the Schumanns' diaries, which came out in 1987, but also to have had access to the Schumanns' medical records in Endenich. Parts of that were published in 1994, but I went to Berlin a couple of years ago and read through the complete notes by Dr. Richarz and the other doctors about what happened to Schumann in Endenich. That's now been published. It came out in the summer of 2006. It's in German. I'm the first person to be using that material for an English-reading audience. Jensen uses the 1994 materials only. There's the famous remark in which Schumann purportedly says, "I was syphilitic and cured with arsenic in 1831." Jensen does mention that. But I have been able to think more widely on the subject. Schumann mentioned arsenic, which was state-of-the-art in 1831. Mercury treatments had already been used for centuries, while arsenic was the coming drug. Schumann's doctor, Glock, in Leipzig, clearly had access to that, and used it. It would have done some damage to Schumann, certainly, because drugs of that kind used against the human organism are damaging. But it wouldn't have done anything apart from some local and incidental damage.

Of course, the trouble with treating syphilis in the primary stage—and no one knew this at the time, because the three stages of syphilis were not specifically known until the 1880s—was that you thought when it went away, you were cured. I was amazed to find in the 1830s a real expert on syphilis denying the existence of syphilis having three stages. So we're talking about doctors who don't know about how this disease is working in any way at all. We now know that only about 30–35 percent of people who are infected with syphilis go on to suffer the appalling and fatal tertiary stage. Otherwise, you get it, and it stays with you. It stays in the organs; it doesn't go away. The spirochete will go on reproducing, but if you're lucky, it won't reproduce very fast or in areas that particularly damage you. You might go to your grave carrying it. But Schumann was in that unlucky percentage. It did go full term into the tertiary stage.

Can we trace this in the various illnesses he suffered his lifetime? This has never actually been looked at. The information is all there in Schumann's notebooks and diaries, and occasionally in letters, wherein he talks about the illnesses he's having. One of the classic syphilitic symptoms, of course, is rheumatism, because the spirochete lodges in joints, which start to function badly. Another classic symptom is in blood vessels, and there's some evidence of Schumann having cardiovascular incidents later in life in the 1850s—including an incident in the summer of 1853, when Clara noticed he couldn't speak. His mouth didn't seem to work, which is the sort of small paralysis one associates with this. None of this says he was suffering from syphilis, but the likelihood of syphilis in his own accounts, as well as these other levels of what I call ordinary illness—the muscle twitching, the trouble with motor movements, the rheumatism, and so on—supports the conclusion that syphilis is probably the underlying cause behind them all.

I must admit I come to these conclusions with a degree of prejudicial thinking. My book is dedicated to my late brother, Peter, who died four and a half years ago of cancer of the brain. I watched him in his mercifully very quick last weeks, and it was very clear that he was crudely mad. But he wasn't, because he was suffering from an entirely physical illness. The brain is an organ of the body, after all, which damages and leads to extraordinary effects. This should be differentiated from mental illness, which on the whole is not physically based, and which is a function of other things altogether. Now, watching Peter die helped me—which is why I dedicated the book to him—and it helped me make this distinction between saying that madness is not the same as physical illness, although the results may be terrifyingly similar.

And all of this had been compounded by the fact that I still hear people referring to schizophrenia when I think what they're really talking about is the bipolar affective disorder; and the two are totally different.

Absolutely right. And that distinction, of course, in Schumann's case was made crucial in the fact that around the first decade of the twentieth century, the difference between the bipolar, then called manic-depressive, and the schizophrenic, was laid down, almost in stone, by the psychiatric movement as the two primary forms of mental affliction. And so if you decide that Robert Schumann is mentally afflicted, then he goes down one of those two paths, there and then.

In my discussions with Dr. Ostwald, he said that Schumann regarded "madness" as a very romantic thing as a youth. It was something to tease and play with. But in later life, he doesn't use the term anymore; he uses the term "melancholia," which might mean that perhaps he's now aware that madness is not something to play and tease about. It might now be altogether too real a possibility.

That's interesting, given the obscure nature of what happened to Schumann's sister, who died when Schumann was fifteen years old. Now, in what circumstances, and how she drowned, we're not going to know. It's possibly a suicide. It seems probable to me that it was suicide. Schumann might have been troubled by that. Melancholia is, I think, a little different in Schumann's case from madness. Madness would be something to be actually profoundly scared of, which makes of course his decision, his demand, to be put into a mental asylum in 1854 so extraordinary. If there was one thing he'd been trying to get away from all his life, it was the possibility that he might be mad. For him to say, I will go the asylum, as the only way out of a problem I feel is encroaching on me, is an extraordinarily courageous act. As someone once said, it may be a sane act to declare yourself mad. And I think Schumann was saying, "In order to be sane, I have to put myself in the place where people understand madness."

BREAKDOWN

John Worthen

Yes, I went to the site in Düsseldorf, actually, on the 27th of February, the very day that Schumann threw himself into the river. Schumann had been going downhill very fast. And he clearly was very angry with Clara, threatening her. By late September, he was denying her existence, referring to her as his dead wife. Anyway, I went to the site partly to find out how long it would take you to walk from the house to the river. And I knew where the pontoon bridge had been—it's not there anymore—from using an old map. And so I got to the river, the way that Schumann would've gone, finding out the streets he would've gone down, which are all still there. I must confess, I did consider putting on slippers and dressing gown, as Schumann had done, but my wife was with me, and she wouldn't have liked that!

But seriously, was there a thunderstorm at the time, and was there a carnival celebration going on?

Yes, all this was true. But it was just raining hard, not a real thunderstorm. You know, walking in slippers over cobblestones when it's wet is a hard business. I thought about that. It would've been cobbled all the way, and he would have been slipping and sliding. The only reason he wasn't stopped on the way to the bridge, I think, is because people everywhere were dressed in peculiar carnival costumes that day. When he gets there, he hasn't got any money for the toll, so he pays with a silk handkerchief. By now, this man is decidedly drawing attention to himself! I do discount the old stories of him diving headlong into the freezing flood and all that stuff. I think that's rubbish. I had looked into this in the police records to see how people commit suicide in rivers; and on the whole, they slip in feet first. They sit on the edge, they work their way forward, and they finally drop. I think that's what Schumann would have done. It must have taken him some time, because he was retrieved from the water almost immediately. I wanted to see how fast the Rhine might be flowing when it's flooded, because at that time of the year the water is coming down from the mountains, and it's very cold, about eight degrees centigrade.

How long would he be in the water? How long could he survive? Not very long. And the river's going fast. It was faster than I could walk. I tried that. These days it's a bit more hemmed in between the banks, but in those days it would've been a bit fuller, so I think about the same speed. So the fact that he came out of the water so quickly, so quickly as to sit the next day back at his desk, with no trouble, no colds, no nothing at all, shows he must've been gotten out of the water almost at once. That suggests that he had drawn attention to himself in one way or another. If someone is wearing only a thing like a dressing gown, a morning gown, it's actually rather hard to pull him out of the water, because the waistband will give and it will come off the shoulders. Much harder than if someone is fully dressed. For men, a trouser belt is the great salvation of suicides. They get hauled out by it. Schumann didn't have that. He actually slipped out of their hands, or struggled to get back in, and it took them a deal to get him out of the water. But they got him out, and wrapped him in blankets and took him home.

Was any kind of statement or document left by these fishermen?

Nothing like that. A medal was struck for the man who actually pulled him out. And there was a short account in the local newspaper about the man having been in the water—but not, of course, actually calling it a suicide attempt. You see, no one knew; he might have just fallen in. So no, there's not much about it, as there would not have been. In those days you didn't print lurid stories about a prominent director of music. Anyway, he was taken home. Something had to be done, clearly. A suicide attempt is not to be trifled with. Düsseldorf is a very Catholic city. Schumann is Protestant, of course, but that doesn't matter. As a Catholic town, he would be removed to a place which was good for him. And within five days after the event, he was on his way to Endenich—where he wanted to go.

Peter F. Ostwald

His breakdown was a horrifying psychotic episode. He had been bothered off and on by uncanny sounds in his ears. These turned into horrible hallucinations. He was very agitated, and he was, as he had been several times before, suicidal. He wanted to go to a hospital. He got all his things ready. He told his wife he wanted to be separated from her and to go into a hospital. He was afraid that he would attack her, but she apparently got down on her hands and knees and said, "How can you do this? Don't leave us. How can you leave me and the children?"—which again is an understandable reaction of a frantic, helpless woman under those circumstances, but the next thing that we know is that Schumann escaped from the house and tried to drown himself.

He was very severely suicidal. He not only jumped off the bridge and tried to drown himself in the Rhine, but even after he was rescued and put on a boat, he again jumped off the boat and had to be pulled back. But remember he did call attention to himself when he started to cross that bridge, so he alerted the toll keepers to the situation. In other words, he was not like one of these people who really set it up in such a way that he would definitely die. You know there are people like that who take poison and slash their wrists and blow their brains out. Schumann never went that far. I think to a certain extent he was ambivalent. And he did accept hospitalization after he was brought home. He was sedated undoubtedly by the doctors. They probably made every effort to distract him from his difficulties. He may not have been encouraged to write; he may not have wanted to write. I would assume he felt very humiliated and embarrassed about the whole situation. He wanted to forget about it.

DEATH IN ENDENICH—A DEBATE

Eric Sams

The syphilis theory is entirely consistent with the evidence that Schumann was a sane, ordinary, generally a rather happy human being, who was prone occasionally to melancholy as many people are, who happen to suffer from syphilis. He knew, you see, where that road led. He knew that it would lead to his madness and general paralysis of the insane, which is exactly what happened. A person who knows his fate that far ahead may be forgiven for occasionally having certain misgivings and indeed exhibiting psychic symptoms of one kind or another. Anyone would do that, any ordinary, normal person with that sword of Damocles hanging over his head would respond in exactly the same way. Now, I think that if Schumann had been a schizophrenic in the clinical sense, his creativity would certainly have been damaged. Creative schizophrenics, so far as I'm aware, who are at a very high level of artistic genius have not been observed. The fact is that schizophrenia damages creativity, and Schumann's creativity was not damaged. It's perfectly clear to me, therefore, that he was not a schizophrenic in any sensible sense of that term, certainly not in your accredited clinical sense of that term. No, this is the classic syphilitic syndrome of its time leading to madness and attempted suicide—exactly as in the case of Hugo Wolf, who was also syphilitic and attempted death by drowning. The clinical picture seems to me absolutely

The grave marker for Robert and Clara Schumann, Bonn-Endenich, Germany. It was commissioned by Clara and erected in 1880. She was buried there in 1896.

clear, and many distinguished philologists and venereologists have said exactly the same.

Accordingly, you object to Dr. Ostwald's theories that Schumann was not syphilitic, that he died of self-starvation?

I don't know of any reason for thinking that. I think it's quite common of cases of paresis, that during the ultimate stages of general paralysis the patient stops taking food. But that Schumann deliberately did so in order to starve himself to death seems to me merely theoretical, not to say hallucinatory. Dr. Ostwald's book was published in 1985. I reviewed it for the *Sunday Times* when it first appeared. My impression was that it doesn't rely as much as it should on actual hard evidence. What one has to do, I'm sure, in considering this or any other question, is to begin by soberly setting out the facts and, on that basis, offering some kind of general hypothesis And one begins by setting out on a piece of paper what those facts are and what their sources are. If one does that, I think one comes to the kind of conclusion that music historians have come to about Schumann throughout the ages, namely that he was, alas, a syphilitic. It seems sensible to explain all his physical ailments and symptoms, and indeed some of his psychic ailments and symptoms, as well, on those grounds and those grounds alone, unless one has clear evidence or proof of other intercollated conditions.

What about the Schumann children? Anything about their medical history that either supports or denies this?

The Schumann children had a very unfortunate medical history. Some of the girls were quite long-lived, and presumably they weren't touched by the illness at all. It is something, after all, that has its effects in rather unpredictable ways. But it is worth noting that Ludwig spent all his days in an asylum, and he suffered from some disease of the spinal marrow which is consistent with a syphilitic parentage. Clara suffered several miscarriages, and other of the Schumann children died young—Felix from tuberculosis at a very early age, and Julie, also early. The clinical picture is, again, consistent with the history of syphilis.

What about Clara, then?

I think Schumann as a proper citizen with special probity would have made absolutely sure that in accordance with the medical knowledge at the time, at least, that he was not infectious when he married.

Would Father Wieck have known anything about this or suspected?

I'm sure. And I'm sure that's why he objected so strenuously to the marriage, objected strenuously really beyond the bounds of all reason and conscience. He was determined to stop that marriage, and if your prospective son-in-law had syphilis, wouldn't you? But it was the kind of thing that wasn't said, and perhaps he wasn't in a position to say so. However, when Schumann first consulted a doctor, it was Wieck who went with him, because Schumann's father had died and Wieck was *in loco parentis*. He was the only father that Schumann had, and they went together to consult the doctor.

Does it bother you, however, that there's not a single reference to it in anything we know that Wieck wrote or said?

In the first place, I think these things were unmentionable. In the second place, Wieck was not in a position wholly to be sure. Everything he could conceivably accuse Schumann of, like drunkenness, he did. But drunkenness was comparatively respectable. Syphilis was, I suppose, the equivalent to AIDS now. One would be reluctant to make precise accusations if one wasn't actually medically sure oneself.

Peter F. Ostwald

I've never met Eric Sams. He's not a physician. But he seems to enjoy making the diagnosis of a syphilitic condition in everyone that he takes a look at. I just last night happened to read the article about Schubert in the *New Grove Dictionary of Musicians*. And Eric Sams had his hand in that one; and I was so amused to read the statement that the older view of Schubert having died of typhoid has now been debunked because it's been generally accepted that Schubert died of syphilis. Now, that's simply not true. If you look at the best medical writers on Schubert, they agree that he had syphilis, but they do not agree that he *died* of syphilis. Eric Sams seems to have that bee in his bonnet, and he's been very influential in Great Britain. On the other hand, some readers in Great Britain, including some very prominent neurologists, have written to me saying they're so happy that I was able to challenge that diagnosis with Schumann. Of course, I'm not at all convinced that one can reliably make the diagnosis of syphilis. In many of those people—even Hugo Wolf—I think there has to be a certain amount of skepticism about the diagnosis he had been given.

I don't think there's any speculation about Schumann's self-starvation. I think that's a fact. Knowing how often Schumann was suicidal—which has been well documented—having some sense of the tragic circumstances under which he lived in the hospital, and in looking at the writing that his doctors did about the problem of suicide in their hospital (how patients were tending in that particular hospital to starve themselves to death)—it doesn't strike me as too far-fetched an assumption that Schumann stopped eating because of a massive depression. I find it hard to believe the prevailing idea that he couldn't eat because his throat was paralyzed.

John Worthen

At this stage of his life, we know what was wrong, but whether it was the result of syphilis is more difficult to confirm. But he's clearly suffering from delusions and terrible problems with speech. He eventually becomes absolutely incomprehensible in Endenich. It's interesting that the doctors were checking his eye pupils. This is something which has not been mentioned much before. It wasn't there in the 1994 publication to which Daverio had access. The doctors were looking at the pupils. They did this because people had begun to realize that eye pupils are an indication of disease. Before Schumann even goes to Endenich, the artist Lorenz had noticed that one of Schumann's pupils was bigger than the other; and while he's in Endenich, on at least nine occasions the doctors check his eyes and they notice on a number of occasions that one pupil is considerably larger than the other. Now, this may have been an indication of syphilis, but it's not by any means conclusive proof. If the pupil does not react to light,

does it react to movement? We know that Schumann's pupil was not react-
ing to light, but we don't know whether or not it reacted to movement.
So what might have been good evidence to say, here's a syphilitic condition the doctors aren't aware of, is only reduced to saying here is a little
more evidence that probably it was syphilis from which he was suffering.

The autopsy tells us little, because what Richarz was looking for in the
autopsy was what he wanted to find. He was not a professional surgeon,
and people who commented on this said he did it very badly. What he
was looking for was the proof, which he wanted to give to Clara, that
Schumann's illness was of long standing and his death inevitable. And he
thought he found it in the condition of the blood supply to the brain and
in the existence of bony pieces of the skull pressing on the brain. Neither
of these two things would've had any effect on Schumann's condition at
all. The bony things he would've lived with, and the blood supply to the
brain was simply so mucked up by the autopsy happening twenty-four
hours after the death that you had no evidence either way. But Richarz did
the autopsy in order to tell Clara what she wanted to hear, that is, that her
husband was suffering from something absolutely inevitable and of long
standing and perhaps genetic. So it was bound to have happened. It was
not her fault or his fault, it was just one of those awful things. Richarz
could do that for Clara; and he sent her the autopsy. That's obviously why
the autopsy actually survives. Until Richarz's records turned up in Berlin
in 1994, the only copy was in the Schumann family possession. It wasn't
an autopsy done to be put in an official record anywhere.

Ultimately, the symptoms to me add up to a probable diagnosis of
syphilis. I wouldn't put it any stronger than that. You don't need to. The
suppositions that he was either bipolar or schizophrenic are not supported by evidence. Yes, syphilis fits the facts very well indeed. That's
all I can say.

John Daverio

I am part of a group of people who feel that the evidence is pretty clear
that Schumann had contracted syphilis early on in his life and that the
third and final stage was setting in during his Düsseldorf years, especially
in late 1853–54. One of the results was dementia, which manifested itself
in various ways.

A portion of Dr. Richarz's diary, or logbook, that gives an account
of Schumann's medical condition has been made available for scholarly
study. Richarz was not Schumann's actual attending physician. There was
another doctor who met with him almost every day. Richarz supervised
the place, but he wasn't in daily contact with Schumann, so probably
some of these notes represent paraphrases of the other doctors' accounts.

In one of the entries Richarz says that Schumann has been writing down all kinds of melancholy reflections. This may mean that he was keeping a diary while in the institution. And then Richarz goes on to quote one of the entries, where Schumann says, "In 1831, I was diagnosed and treated for syphilis." We know from the Richarz papers that Schumann burned a lot of papers, letters from Clara, for instance, including compositions, and perhaps this diary. I think that we can be 99 percent sure that what Richarz transmitted was indeed the truth, and that Schumann had been diagnosed with syphilis at an earlier time. Thus we can assume that Schumann was suffering from the tertiary phases of the disease. There's still always that one percent chance that we have some room for doubt. The surefire test for diagnosing syphilis did not come down the pike until later. So maybe he was *mis*diagnosed in 1831. I think that's highly unlikely. I just want to proceed with some scholarly caution and say we're not absolutely sure that was the case. But the available evidence points in that direction.

We also know from Richarz's papers that there were periods where Schumann refused to eat. Now, refusal to eat is not the same thing as suicide by self-starvation. He refused to eat in a number of cases because he thought he was being poisoned. He was suffering from delusions. We also know from Richarz's logbook that there were periods of time when Schumann ate perfectly normally. So I have a real problem with the suicide diagnosis. Suicide implies a certain kind of intent, that someone is saying I am consciously deciding to take my life. I don't think this was the case with Schumann. He was suffering from many kinds of delusional symptoms, and one of them was that he thought he was being poisoned, and he therefore he didn't eat. It's not a pretty picture. One of the problems I have with the suicide theory Ostwald and others have written about is that suicide isn't pretty, either. But it makes Schumann into a kind of hero, because it makes us think that in these last years he was trying to take control of his life and doing with it what he wanted. In fact, I really don't think that the intent was there. Schumann was not making himself into a modern-day Prometheus and committing a Promethean act.

Leon Plantinga

Schumann died because he was ill. It's simple, and as complex, as that. It's not entirely clear what the illness was. I'm fairly convinced by some of the more recent medical findings and opinions that the result of a syphilitic infection, probably much exacerbated by the treatments administered. It seems to me that Dr. Ostwald's opinion that he simply died of starvation has no basis in fact. There is not sufficient evidence for that conclusion. In general, it seems to me that we ought to be careful—even medical researchers ought to be careful—in this matter. It's hard enough for doctors to figure out what people are suffering from at the time, much less render a diagnosis long after the fact. There's so much we still don't know. We don't even know what the Black Death was. We say "bubonic plague," but how can we be sure?

Nancy B. Reich

It was long thought that the Endenich medical documents had been destroyed. Dr. Richarz—a man who didn't believe in restraints, force-feeding or straitjackets—was the director of this institution and evidently a very progressive psychiatrist. He kept these notes, and when he left the institution he did not leave them there, because he felt they had to be handled discreetly. Also I think he felt something of the confidential nature of these, because of the relationship between doctor and patient. It turns out his diagnosis was syphilis, and because of the stigma attached to that he was concerned they not be published. He took them with him and left them with a relative—I believe it was a nephew who was also a psychiatrist. This nephew was a great-uncle of Aribert Reimann, the contemporary German composer. Reimann inherited these when the uncle died, and he'd been asked not to publish them, either—to keep them confidential, even though the people involved had died. On the other hand, Reimann, who said he spent many sleepless nights over it, felt that it was important to have this information made public—if only to stop the many false legends that had sprung up about Schumann's last years. The excerpts I have seen of these notes make it clear that Schumann was a very, very sick man indeed. The stories that he was sent to the institution by his wife so she could carry on with Brahms—stories I hate even to repeat—have now been proven to be totally false. I always suspected they were, but now there's clear evidence.

    Schumann was really much sicker than we thought. There've always been stories that when Brahms or Bettina von Arnim visited him, he seemed fine and he was able to hold an articulate conversation. In fact, the story was spread recently that von Arnim said there was nothing wrong with Schumann; he had just had a nervous breakdown and should return to his family. She didn't know that he probably should have gone to the institution at least six months earlier because he was often depressed and, as we know, had even attempted suicide. He had asked several times—we know this—that he be sent to a hospital because he realized he was almost out of control; he had aggressive moments, as well as very depressed moments.

    Dr. Richarz says there's no doubt that it was syphilis. He wrote that Schumann told him he had contracted syphilis in 1831 and had been cured. Schumann thought he had been cured, but what happened was that it was in a latent period, which is common in syphilis. So, for some twenty years, he was not infectious, because neither Clara nor the children had it. Richarz saw him daily in the hospital and made notes on the visits. This was a progressive way of handling the patients. Schumann had a nurse or an orderly with him all the time, day and night. There were times when they had friendly conversations, and Schumann was able to talk. But one of the symptoms was increasing speechlessness, inarticulateness. He was unable to control his tongue. Richarz describes this deterioration over the two-and-a-half-year period. Schumann wrote notes because he knew they couldn't understand what he was saying. He couldn't control the muscles of his mouth.

The main question that is always asked is why didn't Clara visit him in the institution for two and a half years? Richarz's papers make it clear now: There were many periods when Schumann was very aggressive and would scream for hours. He would be hoarse the next day. It would have been impossible to have his wife visit him. She was told this. She was simply forbidden to visit him. People ask me, why didn't she go anyway, if she loved him? Well, she was a woman who was very conscientious and followed the doctor's orders. And I think she was also afraid to see him, afraid to see him in his condition, afraid that he might harm her or harm himself. He had no control over himself. It was a terrible situation. There were times when he was more articulate, and it was usually at those times that the doctor permitted visitors, like Brahms, Joachim, von Arnim. At a time when he could speak and was relatively calm. The other thing I learned was he didn't really die of self-starvation. His physical condition had deteriorated so much he couldn't eat; he could just swallow some wine and jelly and some other very light things. Even so, he had difficulty swallowing. The doctor speaks of paralysis in the muscles of the throat as well as of the legs.

Erik Fokke

Since his incarceration and death in the Endenich asylum, 1854–56, Schumann has been the subject of much speculation and controversy about the precise nature of Schumann's terminal physical and mental condition. His most recent biographer, John Worthen, demystifies and frees Schumann from 150 years of myth and unjustified psychological and psychiatric speculation. Based on Schumann's diaries, published for the first time in 1971 in the former DDR, and on a great many other, more recent sources, Worthen delivers an astute analysis of Schumann's mental problems after 1852—dementia paralytica, the last stage of syphilis.

This diagnosis can now be confirmed with the publication of the records that were kept by Schumann's doctor in Endenich, Franz Richarz, recording his meals, medications, pulse, respiratory rate, temperature, skin color, size of the pupils, stools, fantasies, rages, et cetera.

There exists a great taboo around the subject of dying by one's own hand, venereal disease, or mental illness. Richarz's records were therefore long kept secret, passing from the godson of Richarz's aunt to that godson's nephew, Aribert Reimann, who inherited them in 1973 and kept them for himself as his uncle had requested in the interest of doctor–patient confidentiality. After a long period of indecision, Reimann finally handed Richarz's records over to the Archive of the Academy of the Arts in Berlin in 1991. These medical records are unabridged and uncensored as published by Schott Music in 2006 in the book *Robert Schumann in Endenich (1854–1856): Krankenakten, Briefzeugnisse und zeitgenössische Berichte*. From the introduction by editor Bernhard Appel, we learn that not all records survived the violence of the Second World War and that of the original records, the periods March 4 to April 5 and April 26 to September 6, 1854, are missing.

Certainly one of the victims of all the speculations around the incarceration of Robert Schumann in Endenich was Clara Schumann. Her conduct during this period got a fairly negative description in many earlier biographies, i.e., that she had shoved her husband into the Endenich mental home to carry on a love affair with Johannes Brahms. Comments in Richarz's notes, such as ". . . physically attacked the doctor," ". . . spilled wine given to him at dinner into the stove because he thought it was urine," et cetera, justify in hindsight Clara's decision to turn her husband over to the care of doctor Richarz's clinic.

Syphilis is notorious for its uncommon patterns and can have an extraordinary range of symptoms. Generally accepted are the three stages of the disease, primary, secondary, and tertiary, described for the first time by the French venereologist Philippe Ricord in a monograph in 1838. The first stage of syphilis appears between one to eight weeks after exposure. The symptom is a small, hard, painless swelling, called a *primary chancre* at the site of the infection, which usually heals in one to five weeks. This is the "wound" that, according to Schumann's diary on the morning of May 11, 1831, Schumann's friend young doctor Christian Gottlob Glock saw on the fraenulum of Schumann's penis—and that Glock on June 4 bathed in "narcissus water." The ulcer disappeared, but that also would probably have happened even without the application of the water.

Around 1910 came Paul Ehrlich's chemotherapeutic breakthrough, the discovery of Salversan, the first real effective therapy against syphilis, before penicillin was introduced in 1943. The causative agent of syphilis, the spirochete *Treponema pallidum,* was identified in 1905 by the German zoologist Fritz Schaumann. It is this spirochete that in the second stage of syphilis enters the bloodstream and spreads through the body to cause symptoms, such as a general feeling of illness, fever, headache, a loss of appetite, and sometimes loss of hearing or vision. Many of these symptoms can be found in Schumann's diary in this period. This second stage lasts two to six weeks. After the second stage an untreated person will progress to the latent (hidden) third stage of syphilis. This latent period may be as brief as one year or range from five to twenty years. Although this third stage is the most destructive, a person may never experience illness in this stage and is no longer contagious. This is the period in which Clara and Robert had an intimate relationship. Being not contagious any longer, it explains why the children of Robert and Clara were free of symptoms of syphilis.

It is significant that, according to the records of Dr. Richarz, after his admission in Endenich Schumann wrote, "In 1831 I was syphilitic and treated with arsenic." Schumann also declared that he probably contracted his disease from a certain "Cristel," purportedly the housemaid of his piano teacher and subsequent father-in-law, Friedrich Wieck. This was at the time that Schumann rented a room in Wieck's house.

It is also significant that Richarz did not consider Schumann's own diagnostic suggestion in 1855—"syphilis"—seriously and regarded the remarks of Schumann as more a symptom of his mental state than a cause for "atrophy of the brain." It is also striking that only sporadically Schumann's own thinking is recorded, while we do learn that the composer had at least 150 clysters during his stay in Endenich and over 600 times the consistency of his stools is mentioned in Richarz's records. Seen from our generally accepted medical knowledge in 2010, Richarz's recordings are still very valuable, since many of his observations, together with what we now know from Schumann's diaries, lead us to the only possible diagnosis: syphilis. If Schumann was treated with the antibiotics we have today, the incarceration in Endenich would never have been necessary and Schumann's biography would have been quite different.

EDITOR'S NOTE

The following volume is recommended for further reading: Bernhard R. Appel, ed., *Robert Schumann in Endenich (1854–1856): Krankenakten, Briefzeugnisse und zeitgenössische Berichte.* Mit einem Vorwort von Aribert Reimann. Schumann Forschungen, vol. 11. Mainz: Schott Music 2006.

13

"Der Dichter Spricht"

Aftermath and Legacy

Commentators: Ute Bär, Erik Battaglia, Gordon Boelzner, Victoria Bond, Simon Callow, Joachim Draheim, Claude Frank, Heinz Holliger, Steven Isserlis, John M. MacGregor, Akio Mayeda, Margit McCorkle, Gerd Nauhaus, Peter F. Ostwald, Nancy B. Reich, Erika Reiman, Aribert Reimann, Helma Sanders-Brahms, Thomas Synofzik, John Taras, John C. Tibbetts, R. Larry Todd, Robert Winter, John Worthen, and Eugenia Zukerman

> *Follow us into our dwelling; in the temple there we shall dwell forever and guard the secret of the world.*
> —Novalis, *Heinrich von Ofterdingen*

> *Their works do follow them.*
> —Revelation 16:13

EDITOR'S NOTE

The first of these discussions centers around the nature of how Schumann's illness might be treated today. Moreover, our attitudes toward mental illness and its relationship with creativity have become a hot topic in academia and medicine. Commentators here are Dr. Peter F. Ostwald and psychiatric historian John M. MacGregor.

Second, after Schumann's death in 1856, Clara, with the advice and support of her good friend Johannes Brahms, continued to raise the children and enjoy a successful performing and teaching career. There is some controversy, however, regarding her decision to suppress from publication some of her husband's last works. Brahms biographer Styra Avins and cellist Steven Isserlis discuss the facts in the case. Meanwhile, Clara has become a role model for today's professional women. Commentators include Steven Isserlis, Nancy B. Reich, John Worthen, R. Larry Todd, Leon Plantinga, and Eugenia Zukerman.

Third, Schumann's music has inspired several ballets. John Taras and Gordon Boelzner talk about Mikhail Fokine's *Carnaval* and George Balanchine's *Davidsbündlertänze.*

Fourth, many contemporary composers have found inspiration in Schumann's works. The beginning of the twentieth century saw Arnold Schoenberg praising Schumann as a composer. His pupil Alban Berg wrote a few early works based on themes of Schumann. His Violin Concerto evokes the penultimate section of Schumann's *Davidsbündlertänze.* Berg's pupil, the theoretician and critic Theodor Adorno, composed *Kinderjahr* (1941) and orchestrated pieces from the *Album für die Jugend.* Other works from the first few decades of the twentieth century include Novák's *Variations on a Theme of Schumann,* Déodat de Séverac's "Invocation à Schumann" (from *En vacances*), and Ravel's orchestrations of portions of *Carnaval.* Among more recent examples are jazz pianist Giorgio Gaslini's recording of improvisations on the *Kinderszenen* and Tobias Picker's *Romances and Interludes* (1989) for oboe and orchestra, which derived from Schumann's *Romances,* Op. 94.

Included in the following pages are observations by three of today's most distinguished composers on their recent Schumann-derived works. Oboist/composer Heinz Holliger comments on his *Gesänge der Frühe* (Songs of the Dawn), for choral and instrumental forces (based on Schumann's last piano cycle); Aribert Reimann on his *Seven Fragments for Orchestra, in Memoriam Robert Schumann* (based on the *"Geister" Variations*); and Victoria Bond on her forthcoming opera about Clara Schumann.

Fifth, research on all things Schumannian is continuing apace in archives and Web sites all around the world. In Germany there is a resurgence of interest in Schumann's artistic/spiritual mentor, Jean Paul Friedrich Richter, in the Jean-Paul-Gesellschaft in Bayreuth. The Robert-Schumann-Haus in Zwickau and the Robert-Schumann-Forschungsstelle in Düsseldorf have become important centers of research and performance. A thematic catalogue was published in 2003, and a *Gesamtausgabe,* or edition of complete works, has been in progress since the early 1990s. Biographer John Worthen poses some unresolved questions; researchers Margit McCorkle, Ute Bär, Gerd Nauhaus, and Thomas Synofzik recount their ongoing researches; Erika Reiman visits the Jean Paul Museum in Bayreuth; and Erik Battaglia talks about his construction of a Web site devoted to the eminent Schumann scholar the late Eric Sams.

Sixth, for the Schumann enthusiasts, the cities where Schumann lived and worked—most of them in the former East Germany—are now open and available: Nancy B. Reich and R. Larry Todd conduct tours of modern-day Zwickau and Leipzig.

Seventh, the story of Robert and Clara fascinates novelists, playwrights, and filmmakers. Biographer Nancy B. Reich, pianist Claude Frank, educator Robert Winter, cellist Steven Isserlis, director Helma Sanders-Brahms, and actor Simon Callow take us backstage to look at the films *Song of Love* (1947),

Spring Symphony (1983), *Schumann's Lost Romance* (1996), and *Geliebte Clara* (2008). Performers Sting and Company have recently released on DVD a staged dramatic reading of the Clara–Robert letters, titled *Twin Spirits*.

And finally, plans are afoot for future Schumann festivals in honor of the Bicentenary Year 2010 of his birth. Conductor Marin Alsop of the Baltimore Symphony Orchestra, Thomas Synofzik of Schumann-Haus in Zwickau, and Steven Isserlis preview some upcoming events.

DIAGNOSING AND TREATING SCHUMANN TODAY

Peter F. Ostwald

Robert Schumann could be treated much more effectively today than he was in his own time. First of all, we would do a very thorough physical examination and try to correct whatever physical problems he had. You know, we don't even know what Schumann's blood pressure was.

The late Peter F. Ostwald, Schumann's biographer, San Francisco.

There were no blood pressure gauges in those days. And yet there are reports that he had a so-called apoplectic constitution, which suggests that he had high blood pressure. We just don't know. Nowadays, the first thing is to do a very careful physical evaluation, so that if someone has hypertension, that can be corrected with antihypertensive drugs. If someone has a heart condition, that can be managed. If somebody has a metabolic disturbance . . . we just don't know! Did the man have diabetes, did he have liver disease? We don't know. Did he have an infection? Did he have tuberculosis? We don't know.

These conditions could be remedied today. We could take X-rays of the chest, we could do a test for syphilis, we could treat those conditions with antibiotics. A bipolar affective disorder is eminently treatable today. We would probably use lithium salts. That's not a drug, it's a natural salt. It has a remarkable effect on controlling these drastic cycles in the mood. We know that there are abnormalities in brain metabolism associated with these affective disorders. These can be corrected with tricyclic antidepressant medication. And in the worst case, one can give electric convulsive treatment. That's not done very frequently anymore. But that definitely removes the depressive condition.

There's so much more that could be done. I would have loved to play chamber music with Schumann. I've treated a number of musicians this way, who didn't care to talk otherwise. Schumann didn't like talking all that much. I would have chatted with him as much as I could, but I wouldn't have pushed him to talk. I certainly would have encouraged him to compose. One of my most severe criticisms is of the doctor who was treating him in Dresden. There was a hypnotist who told him to stop working on his compositions. I think that was a terrible mistake. I would strongly encourage Schumann to try to compose. And I would try always to engage him in musical situations in which he felt comfortable and in which he would prove himself to be competent.

And as for Clara I would try to work with her very closely. I would try to persuade her to come to the hospital. I would try to get her to confront the situation. And I would see to it that she gets advice; I would listen to her and see what her conflicts are. I would not allow her to go off to London as she did without first dropping by and talking with me in the hospital to discuss her husband's case. We'd have a family conference; we'd talk about the children. I think nowadays we would face these issues quite differently than they did in those days. I am quite optimistic about it because Schumann had recovered from so many episodes.

I don't think I would have been made very welcome at Endenich! I think Dr. Richarz had his own ideas about how he wanted to handle patients, and I'm not so sure I would have sent Schumann there. I probably would have tried to treat Schumann closer to home. I know there was a mental hospital in Düsseldorf, and Schumann was afraid of it. I rather think there was a bit of a conspiracy going on there. You see there was Dr. Hasenclever, who arranged to get Schumann out of town. I think that was very convenient, because Hasenclever was one of the directors of the Symphony Society there, and Schumann had become a bit of an embarrassment. It might have been better if he could have been taken to England. There were some very fine hospitals there, as well as in France.

John M. MacGregor

I think the romantics have given us today a capacity to look with acceptance at all sorts of altered states of consciousness; to realize that the human mind has depths and kinds of irrationality which, while they may not be functional in day-to-day life, are profoundly important. That's the gift of the romantics to us—whether it's madness or hallucinatory states or whatever. They have made it acceptable for us to look at the stranger products of the human mind with acceptance and with curiosity and even with love. After all, the psychotic and the professional artists are both exploring the same world, which is the world of the unconscious. The only difference is that the professional artist descends into the unconscious, as it were, protected by a diving suit. And he's safe. Although it may be frightening, he's able to come back to the surface. The psychotic artist, however, never comes back; but he is occasionally able to send back messages from that world that we can share in.

There is still a tendency today to hide madness away. We're still looking at these people out of the corner of our eye with fear and some disgust. Ideally, I wish that could change. Most of us don't have the chance to get to know madness close-up. For the most part, it's not that frightening when you do. You need to encounter it in yourself first. If you don't have the chance to accept your own madness, you'll never be able to accept it in others. And that of course is why the romantics had a greater tolerance. They were confronting in themselves levels of psychological functioning we would have to call clinically mad.

Meanwhile, what we do with people who are mentally ill today is not all that better than in Schumann's time. Indeed, I think if were to choose to be insane in the nineteenth century rather than the twentieth, I would probably choose the nineteenth century! Because then there was more of an acceptance of psychosis itself, perhaps because they couldn't do much about it. Today we can't do much about it either, but we interfere with it massively. As anybody who has had experience with psychosis can tell you, today the mentally ill in hospital settings are not permitted to be psychotic for any length of time. They are administered massive doses of drugs and other things, which may or may not be good for them, but which does destroy their art-making potential.

It seems to me that today's psychiatrists need to be human, need to be profoundly human, if they're going to be any good at all at what they're doing. In our country it's rare to find a psychiatrist like the late Dr. Peter Ostwald, who has a humanist and arts background. Certainly some of the very finest psychiatrists have been drawn to the branches of art. Those people tend to be the best of our psychiatrists, with deep cultural roots as well as training in medicine.

Finally, we don't understand genius in the context of madness any more than we understand it anywhere else. Schizophrenia explains nothing about the great artist. There's nothing within schizophrenia itself that creates genius. We can't explain the ability to give form, to express, in profoundly beautiful and moving ways an internal world. We cannot explain the creative artist. We cannot explain the creative schizophrenic artist, either. So, that remains the mystery. Where does this incredible sense of creative form come from? Where does this incredible drive to give form to internal expression come from, and why are they successful? We don't know the answers to that.

CLARA SCHUMANN—LIFE AFTER ROBERT

To the moist, youthful luster of [Clara's] eyes, there has succeeded a fixed and anxious look. The flower crown, once so loosely woven in her hair, now scarcely hides the burning scars which the holy circlet has impressed so deeply on her brow.

—Franz Liszt, 1854

I always pray to God to give me the strength to successfully overcome the frightful agitations that I have lived through and that still await me. My true old friend, my piano, must help me with this!

—Clara Schumann, 1854

EDITOR'S NOTE

After Robert's death, Clara was left with the care of their eight children. They were, in order of age, Marie (1841), Elise (1843), Julie (1845), Emil (1846), Ludwig (1848), Ferdinand (1849), Eugenie (1851), and Felix (1854). Marie, the favorite of her parents, remained by her mother's side all her life and died in 1919. Emil died in 1847, just one year old. Ferdinand was wounded in the Franco-Prussian War and died a morphine addict in 1891. Elise married a businessman and spent several years in the United States, where three of her four children were born. She returned to Germany and died in 1928. Julie, "the pretty one," married an Italian count and, as the Contessa Radicati di Marmorito, settled in Torino, Italy, where she died of tuberculosis in 1872. Ludwig entered a mental hospital at the age of twenty-two and died there in 1899. Eugenie was the biographer of the family and, before her death in 1938, wrote two volumes of family memoirs. Felix suffered ill health most of his life and died in 1879. Somehow, despite a litany of familial tragedies, Clara continued to concertize and teach, establishing herself as one of the foremost pianists of the nineteenth century.

Steven Isserlis

On the surface, Clara had lost everything after her husband's death. Any possibility of marrying Brahms, now that she was officially "free," was not to be. Her children remained dutiful, but the relationships were hardly close and loving. In fact, the day after Schumann's death, she wrote to the two eldest girls, Marie and Elise, to tell them the news: "He was a wonderful person. May you, who loved him so dearly, become worthy of such a father. May you both try to make me as happy as possible." Later, her son Ludwig was taken to a mental asylum for reasons that remain unclear. She visited him twice and then abandoned him for the next twenty years. She buried her emotions in her career, which she followed zealously for the next forty years, always appearing onstage swathed in black.

Nancy B. Reich

In the years after Robert's death, Clara deplored any kind of showiness in her performances. Early on, she had expressed her disdain for Liszt's more flamboyant style (and she never played him later). Her style was always serious. She always wore dark dresses. And although she continued to play a lot of Schumann, she played more Chopin and Mendelssohn. She never played showstoppers, those big bravura pieces of her childhood and youth—her own, or anybody else's. She certainly could, but not then. I think she had emotional difficulty with some of Schumann's works. For one thing, she never had Robert's imagination. There was a capriciousness and a wildness which was not a part of her personality. Also, she may have been fearful in a way of them. They brought back painful memories. The F-sharp-Minor Sonata, which was dedicated to her, she didn't perform publicly until fifty years after its composition.

I might add that there were a number of other very talented women who made their living as Clara Schumann did. They were working women who supported their families as professional musicians. Of course, there were more singers than any other kind of musician. But many also were pianists, violinists, composers, editors, and certainly teachers. And most of these women, I would say ninety-five percent of them, were women who *had* to work. They were professional musicians just as the men were. And they had to go out and meet the competition and face the public. And this was their job. And they took it very seriously. And for most of them it was a family tradition. It wasn't merely a matter of being supported by a man. The myth was that musicians or creative figures in the arts always had to have a male mentor as supporter. That wasn't the case with most of these women musicians. Most of them were from families—not only were their mothers musicians, but their fathers were musicians. That was certainly true of Clara Schumann. Her mother was more skilled than her father, who was primarily a teacher. It was very true of Pauline Viardot Garcia, whose mother and father were musicians, whose sister was a musician, whose brother was a musician, whose children were musicians. These were families. It was true of Louise Reichardt, rather an unknown composer of lieder of the early nineteenth century, whose father was Johann Friedrich Reichardt and whose mother was Juliana Benda Reichardt, also a composer. Her aunts were performers of the court in Weimar. In fact, one of the beefs I have is that critics were often more interested in the *physical appearance* of the woman musician than in her talents as a musician. And I can cite many reviews where the women are described as presenting "a beautiful view of her figure from all sides," and so on. And yes, by the way, "her playing was quite admirable, too."

I think I said in the introduction of my book that Clara was not a feminist, because she didn't think of herself as battling for women's rights. She just sort of assumed that her place in the world was as an artist and couldn't conceive of the fact that some women might have a harder time. She felt very inadequate as a composer, but not as a performer. And I think this was due to that strong ego building she had as a child along with her father's great conviction that she was going to be a great artist. So she didn't think of it as a struggle. She wasn't an intellectual and was totally unaware of any movements which were already taking place in Germany during her lifetime concerning women's rights. I think Clara would not have thought of herself as a feminist, and I don't think of her that way. Compare her to Ethel Smyth, who came along a generation after Clara. They knew each other, because Ethel went to Leipzig to study with Heinrich von Herzogenberg, who was a good friend of Clara's. Smyth had to fight for her right to study music and to be a musician; Clara never did. And so Smyth was very aware of the problems that women faced, and her music was not performed because she was a woman. And people always said, "How could a girl compose?" But Clara took her own place in the world as if by right, and she did it very early.

John Worthen

Clara was tough beyond belief. After Robert's incarceration and death, she has to earn for the entire family, and pay the fees at Endenich, which amounted to six hundred thalers a month. Who else is going to earn for them? There's no other money coming in. Various people offer loans and so on. But Clara's a proud woman; she wants to earn, and she'll do it, and she does it. She is magnificent. And of course some of the children are ill. The boys die eventually. She has a most dreadful life, I think. I admire Nancy Reich enormously for having written that biography. I don't think I could. The truth is so difficult sometimes. You know, I found writing the last chapter of the Schumann book bad enough. I wouldn't want to have to write the tough story of Clara's survival, but I'm glad that Nancy's done it.

Eugenia Zukerman

I can understand today why professional women might regard Clara Schumann as a role model. I must confess I do. Against tremendous odds—particularly in the nineteenth century—she supported her husband and family while continuing to support them with her concertizing. Even today, it's difficult. I bear witness to that! And now I hear from a lot of people saying that they really enjoy my concerts and broadcast work on CBS, and they tell me that *I'm* a "role model" to them! Well, I've got to admit I'm tired of being a "roll," I want to be a bagel! But seriously, of course, I'm very, very flattered by that. But I don't so much see myself as much a role model as I do just a working mother who's trying to get things done. We're all looking for answers, and we all need role models, but I think it's a mistake to think that we can pattern our lives after anyone else's; we can say, "Oh, Clara did that, or Eugenia did that, so I can do that, too!" What we all face in common, I think, is to learn how to modify our professional lives with our personal lives.

I have been thinking about how Clara came through all this so spectacularly. She managed to be a wife, mother, and concert giver. And, of course, giving a concert in her time meant organizing the whole bloody thing yourself—renting the pianos, seeing that they were tuned, making sure the hall was there, making sure it was heated. Today I travel unchaperoned, but to do so in the nineteenth century I would have had to have been an actress or a dancer, and I would not have been held in the kind of high regard that we hold artists today. I think that women today are blessed and burdened—never more burdened and never more blessed. And everyone struggles to make their own balance, but opportunities have never been so vast for us, nor have we had such a burden of trying to do everything right.

I've done a bit of reading about Clara, and she had no compunctions whatever about taking the children out of the home and boarding them for weeks at a time with professional people and nurses. She would also leave them with Robert at home—although she was criticized a bit for that, especially when she would travel alone. I have very little patience with people who take exception to her mothering. She had an enormous task. She was a great artist, and she had that drive. She was a wife, and very much in love with her husband, whom she revered, whom she had to start taking care of at an early age. Those of us who are parents know how hard it is to be a parent with a career. And there's no way to do it right. The only thing you can do is to love your children and to listen well, and be there to guide them; but I can't fault Clara for doing what she had to do. If she were a man, would we have faulted her? Would anyone say anything about his sending them to his mother while he went on his concert tour? This is something women today have to deal with. I believe it's so important to deal with it without cynicism or bitterness. It just is true that a mother is a mother, and no one can take your place, and you have to try to juggle your work and your needs with your children foremost in mind.

BALLET MUSIC

Schumann's music conceives the world, the universe, and the cosmos as a kind of dance, especially one's own personal circle. The personal circle begins as a dance, and you imagine in it all one's friends, all one's acquaintances, all those who one has loved, living or dead, are suddenly present as musical entities and are dancing and delighting us in their dancing but also at the same time saying something significant about human life and circumstance.

—Eric Sams

EDITOR'S NOTE

Schumann's music has been the source for two ballets: *Carnaval* (Michel Fokine, 1910) and *Davidsbündlertänze* (George Balanchine, 1980). Fokine's *Carnaval* brought onstage all the characters from Schumann's *Carnaval*, Op. 9. The piano pieces were orchestrated by famous composers of the day, including Glazunov and Ravel.

Two men talk in these pages about these ballets. John Taras (1919–2004) performed in a 1942 revival of *Carnaval*. Balanchine's *Davidsbündlertänze* was his final principal ballet. The dances were performed to the piano's original instrumentation. Eight dancers, alternating in pairs and solos, enacted the passion, the doubts, and the ultimate tragedy of the romance between Robert and Clara. Gordon Boelzner (1937–2005) was involved in the 1982 revival of *Davidsbündlertänze*. Recorded on video by the New York City Ballet, Boelzner appears onstage at the piano, stage right. The dancers appear as four couples—Suzanne Farrell and Jacques d'Amboise; Karin von Aroldingen and Adam Luders; Sara Leland and Ib Andersen; and Heather Watts and Peter Martins. (Boelzner went on to become the music director of the New York City Ballet in 1990.)

John Taras

As I recall, Michel Fokine wanted to do a "carnival" ballet with Schumann's music for a benefit, a charity ball in St. Petersburg in 1910. I studied with Fokine years later, and he told me that he took the dancers from the Imperial Ballet, and he took an actor from the Dramatic Theater to play Pierrot (which was not a dancing part), and he put it together with Schumann's music for just that one performance. And then when Diaghilev organized the company for a Berlin trip, he took *Carnaval,* as well. Leon Bakst designed the costumes. For that production Harlequin was Leontiev, Vsevolod Meyerhold was Pierrot, Karsavina was Columbine. I'm not sure who the rest were, but Vera Fokine was in it, Ludmilla Shollar, and Bronislava Nijinska. A year later Nijinsky took on the role of Harlequin. He became famous, you know, for his checkered costume and his hopping and balancing on one foot. The Schumann piano pieces were orchestrated by Glazunov, Rimsky-Korsakov, Ravel, and others. It must have been quite extraordinary.

I was in a production of *Carnaval* years later, around 1942, I think, so I know it quite well. I played Pierrot. That's when Fokine was working with what came to be known as the American Ballet Theater. *Carnaval* was set in a sort of Biedermeier salon. All the pantomime characters come onstage, one by one, first Pierrot peeking through the curtain, then Harlequin, Eusebius, and Florestan, and so on. There were marvelous things—like the three ballerinas who dance to "Chopin"; a pas de deux between Columbine and Harlequin, which is interrupted by one of Columbine's suitors; and the entrance of the Philistines at the end, all dressed in black and carrying tightly rolled umbrellas. They are quickly chased offstage—I remember everybody rushing around! At the end, Pierrot is left abandoned, alone, in front of the curtain.

Gordon Boelzner

Here we are in the New York State Theater at Lincoln Center, in the offices of the New York City Ballet. In fact, we're in the office that Balanchine himself used when he was alive. I am the assistant music director of the New York City Ballet. I was solo pianist for many years, and it was in that capacity that I played the first performances of the *Davidsbündlertänze* that Balanchine choreographed.

My association with Balanchine began thirty years ago while I was still in music school. And it continued uninterrupted all the way to his death in 1982. And now I'm still working for the New York City Ballet.

Davidsbündlertänze actually began long ago with Igor Stravinsky. He had mentioned to Balanchine that he thought there was some very good Schumann music that would work for dance. Balanchine didn't know what to do, however. But much later he and I were talking and I suggested the *Dances*. Strangely enough, he didn't know so much music, and he didn't know this piece. I gave him a recording of it, and I gave him the music sheets. He looked at it, and he thought it was a very, very good idea to work with in dance terms. George was always very careful about taking really good music for his ballets. You know, he used Brahms's *Liebeslieder Waltzes* and the Schoenberg orchestration of the Brahms G-Minor Piano Quartet. And in the case of the Schumann, he thought it was so introspective that you had to be careful about not adding too much or overburdening it.

At the time he was faulted for his choreography, though, on the grounds that it wasn't "disturbing enough." I think he was attracted to the idea that he could depict the personality shifts of Schumann, that he could formulate them in terms of the characters of the dancers. But after a while he gave up on that and got much more general, creating a romantic atmosphere including some biographical elements of the composer and Clara. I was onstage, in period costume, playing the piano. I'm not sure just what or who I represented. That's undetermined. I guess my part is just as "the Piano Player"! George liked the way the piano looked onstage. And our settings were a vague kind of landscape, derived, more or less, from the paintings of Caspar David Friedrich.

The curtain rises and you see me seated at the piano. Surrounding the stage is a backdrop in violet and gray colors with lots of flying draperies and silks and things. In the distance is a vague image of a castle, and on the forestage there's an effect of a shining river, and you can't quite tell where it leaves off and the stage begins. I begin playing, and the first couple—there are four couples in all—rushes in. From there I play all the pieces in the exact order of the original work. At first you see only one couple per piece; then, later, they dance in different combinations. Their connections are never really fully explained. Although there are energetic moments in the ballet, there are also some strangely quiet moments, where the music is quiet and the dancers relatively still. George had the incredible confidence to just let the moment stay all by itself and not push things.

We didn't end up retouching the music at all. George thought, however, to slightly exaggerate the duality of the introverted and extroverted personalities in his choreography. It was a very emotional piece, partly because it was to be his last ballet. And at the end, when the "Schumann" figure disappears into . . . what—Death? Insanity? The suicide attempt in the river?—the "Clara" figure is left alone. But I can tell you that after George died, it was very disturbing to perform that piece. The first performance after his death was very emotional because, in a way, it seemed that by choreographing Schumann's disappearance he was anticipating his own death.

At one point in the ballet, several threatening figures hooded in black appear onstage. George always wanted to include them to represent the hostile critics of Schumann's music. Like the Philistines that appear in the *Carnaval* ballet. At that point, the lights go kind of crazy and curtains start billowing.

There was an obstacle to the ballet, in that people weren't quite sure how to pronounce the title! And they couldn't tell if it was a scene from another world, a dream, or what. But what Balanchine was especially good at was establishing a community of feeling amongst people that's not easily explained. And in my opinion, that makes it a very good ballet.

I recall that opening night as a lot of nerves and, then, relief. It was a very nice event because, first of all, it's not the kind of music you generally find in the ballet theater. But it was very rewarding to me as a musician, because it was music that wasn't too often done. Later we released it on video. I believe it was part of the *Dance in America* series on public television. It was done in Nashville, Tennessee, adjacent to Opryland.

I have never played that music anywhere else, or as a solo concert piece. When I hear somebody else play it now, I can't help but think of the ballet. I had a very good compliment one time when the great pianist Claudio Arrau came to the ballet and later told me I had played it very well. It's never been a very popular piece in the concert sense, and it has such a curious, odd ending. Very downbeat, even a little morbid.

NEW SONGS

Heinz Holliger

I am doing a lot of composing and conducting now. Something I intend to perform more and more is a work for large orchestra, chorus, and tape that I wrote in 1987 and based on Schumann's last piano cycle, the *Gesänge der Frühe* [Songs of the Dawn], He wrote it in 1853, when he was ill. He had dedicated it to Hölderlin's ideal figure of Diotima, which is interesting, when you know that both Schumann and Hölderlin ended their lives in madness. In my own version I quote texts by Hölderlin. In the first part, which is an a capella chorus, I quote "Die Sonne kehrt zu neuen Freuden wider";

in the second, "Elysium"; the third, "Schönes Leben!"; and in the fourth, "Geh unter, schöne Sonne." There are also quotations from other late Schumann pieces, such as the Violin Concerto, the *Requiem for Mignon*, the second *Concert Piece* for piano, and the *"Geister" Variations*, and so on. I haven't recorded it yet. [Note: In August 2009 a recording on the ArchivMusic label has been released of Holliger's *Gesänge der Frühe*.] It's important not to throw a new piece like this in the face of audiences. You have to give them some hints, or help, or play a few excerpts before doing the whole performance. They can then experience a "déjà-vu" feeling. You try to play a piece which can open a door to the other pieces. New works are the only reason for existence of the musician today. He has to be a part of the actual culture. Otherwise, he is a mummy and should be put in alcohol in the glass! Many times when you see players who do "authentic instruments," you find they are much more interested in modern music than average middle-of-the-road musicians.

But back to my *Gesänge der Frühe*. It's a sort of analysis of Schumann in the moment of his death. I haven't performed it in the United States, although I plan soon to do it. But we can't yet find a chorus able to sing it! It's a very, very difficult piece. It is only possible to be performed by a very professional chorus. I had incorporated Schumann into my music before. In a very early piece of mine, *Erde und Himmel*, a little cantata for tenor and five instruments. It was my first published piece in 1961–62. There I had a little quote from Schumann exactly in the center of the piece, from the song "Zwielicht," or "Twilight," from his Op. 39 song cycle. Nobody knew it was there, but it was.

Aribert Reimann

EDITOR'S NOTE

The performance in Düsseldorf in June 1991 of Aribert Reimann's *Seven Fragments for Orchestra, in Memoriam Robert Schumann* marked an important event. For the first time in many years, Düsseldorfers were able to hear the Robert-Schumann-Philharmonie of Chemnitz, a kind of sister city to Düsseldorf. "We are from the eastern part of Germany," explained the orchestra's conductor, Dieter-Gerhardt Worm, during a reception for the group after the concert. "We are from the area about twenty miles from Zwickau, where Schumann was born. Now, since the 'Change,' we are named 'Chemnitz' again. The orchestra is more than 150 years old, but only since 1983 has it been named the 'Robert-Schumann-Philharmonie.'"

I am here in Düsseldorf just for this concert of my *Seven Fragments for Orchestra, in Memoriam Robert Schumann*. I used the theme of his

"Geister" Variations. I heard my piece for the first time with this same orchestra a half year ago in Chemnitz. I wrote it over a period of four or five months in January 1988. It was commissioned by the Hamburg Opera. I had the idea several years ago when I was very occupied with Schumann. He's one of the most important composers in my life. I have the feeling of being very close to his music. I have played the song cycles with several performers over the years. At the same time I wrote this, I also instrumented the *Maria Stuart* songs for mezzo-soprano and small orchestra. I think other composers today, like Heinz Holliger, are also being inspired by Schumann's work. I wanted to evoke in this music the troubled state of Schumann's mind. The first fragment is for me like Schumann's mental condition, a kind of obsessive turning around of a theme in his mind. The second fragment gives us a sense of the high-pitched sounds in his head. They go higher and higher, in the strings, and then comes the theme again. At the end, the theme comes again as a high solo in the clarinet. It is bleak, yes? And it soon fades away into silence. It is performed quite often in the last two years. Although the acoustics here in Düsseldorf are very dry, I still have been able to hear things in the music I hadn't heard before! I'm very thankful the Schumannfest began this year with my piece. It is good to bring Schumann into our own time. He was a progressive composer and wrote many things that were different and so complicated to understand. He continues to be important for us in these days. This piece has not yet been recorded. Maybe one day. [Note: Herr Reimann explained during an exchange of e-mails in May 2009 that he has recently arranged Schumann's *Fantasiestücke*, Op. 73, for clarinet, flute, harp, and two violas. Currently he is completing a commission by the Vienna Staatsoper for an opera, *Medea*, based on the play by Grillparzer. It was premiered in February 2010.]

Victoria Bond

EDITOR'S NOTE

The following conversation between composer Victoria Bond and Clara Schumann's biographer Nancy B. Reich regarding Bond's opera about Clara was recorded in New York City on May 30, 2009.

Victoria Bond: I was with Opera Roanoke from 1986 to 1995. But now I consider myself a composer who conducts, rather than the other way around. I am now working on my fourth opera, about Clara Schumann. The title has yet to be determined. I am fascinated by the historical figures of strong women, and my second opera was called *Mrs. President,* about Victoria Woodhull, the first woman to run for president of the United

States. Clara Schumann is such a strong figure. Nancy Reich has been good enough to be my historical consultant.

Nancy B. Reich: I have been able to share with her the work I've been doing on the only diary from Clara's youth that survived. She was just seven years old when it was begun in 1827. Her father wrote some of the entries. It is an indispensable source of information about her girlhood. All of her personal diaries have disappeared except the first one, the one I'm working on translating with Dr. Gerd Nauhaus right now. What we do have, largely from Litzmann's biography, is an incomplete picture of her that says very little about her life as a composer and a mature member of a circle of like-minded women. I'm learning a lot more now from letters to and from her women friends, her students and companions.

Bond: Yes, Nancy and I talked about this project a couple of years ago. At first, the idea was to do something for young audiences, teenaged girls, particularly. It would be based on a book that Nancy's daughter Susanna wrote [*Clara Schumann: Piano Virtuoso*, 1999]. The book is a wonderful introduction for young readers of the story of Clara, Robert, and Brahms. But that version never got off the ground. Now I am more interested in a two-act opera that begins with her youth and marriage to Robert and continues in the second act with the aftermath of the marriage, the appearance of Brahms, and Robert's death. This story seems like the most obvious thing to bring to the stage, but I don't know of any other attempts to do so.

Reich: It is needed. Before my biography of Clara came out in 1985, I found while researching that there was little work being done about women in music. When Clara did appear in a book, she was identified primarily as the wife of Robert and a concert performer.

Bond: My opera will be a very intimate chamber drama with seven characters. In addition to the dual characters of a "young" and "mature" Clara, there's a six-member chorus, three men and women who "play" the different characters of Schumann, Mendelssohn, Brahms, Father Wieck, Clara's mother, and Clara's oldest daughter, Marie. They also double as members of an audience. A chamber ensemble of musicians will be visible onstage, but somewhat off-center to the action. It's all very compact. The opera will open with Clara onstage with her piano. She's at the height of her fame. And everybody involved in her life will be present with her.

Reich: I've never had a chance to ask you what drew you to this story in the first place.

Aerial view of Zwickau today.

Bond: Well, my mother was a child prodigy, a pianist, born in Chicago, who played with the Chicago Symphony when she was ten years old. Her father, a composer, Samuel Epstein, was her teacher. "Jane Courtland" was her professional name. Her father was overbearing, like Father Wieck, and very forceful.

Reich: Feelings that Clara had toward her own father, of course!

Bond: He played the double bass in the CSO. While just a teenager, my mother was already on the road performing. She studied with Carl Friedberg and, before the onset of World War II, with Bartók and Kodály in Budapest. She won a Liszt Competition and played all over Europe. She told me stories about traveling alone, and sitting alone in hotel dining rooms before concerts. It was only in the late 1930s, as things grew complicated in Europe, that her parents brought her home from concertizing. So when I read Nancy's book, Clara's story reminded me so much of my mother. There are gaps in accounts of her life. But here again, I go back to my mother and her own conflicts with her father—crying fits, confusions, et cetera.

Reich: It sounds just like Clara!

Bond: Right, I feel it gives me a real "feel" for what Clara went through as a child and later a young performer. My librettist for the new one is Barbara Zinn Krieger. She was the founder of the Vineyard Theatre in New York and "Making Books Sing," which is a company I worked for as a conductor. We have a treatment here, which Barbara has written. At this point it's very much in flux. Of course, there are certain dramatic moments that, as a composer, I want to focus on. In the first act we have the conflict between Clara and her father and her conflict between gratitude toward him and feelings of wanting to be free from his influence. His feelings for Robert change from kindness and interest as a student to anger as his daughter's suitor. I think I want to write a "mad scene" for him! All these characters are three-dimensional. He had his own reasons for what he did to her.

Reich: You don't want to smooth that over too much! I don't think he really wanted Clara to marry anyone. He really would have liked to keep both his daughters for himself. And Clara also had confusions about marrying Robert. Would her father reject her? Would she have to abandon her career? What kind of man was Robert? She knew already about his emotional complexities. But there's no question that she had really fallen in love with him while still only a child.

Bond: With all that in mind, there was nothing really inevitable about this relationship. It could have gone wrong at several key points.

Reich: Not so much on Clara's part, but perhaps with Robert, yes.

Thomas Synofzik, seen here with wife Katrina and son Ruven, is the current Director of the Robert-Schumann-Haus, Zwickau.

Bond: Then you have the "trial scene," which has great dramatic potential. Its resolution ends act 1. In act 2 we deal with the love story between Clara and Brahms, Robert's collapse and institutionalization, and death. It's not a question whether or not Clara and Brahms "did it," so to speak; but they obviously had so much love and respect for each other on such a profound level—

Reich: Yes, they were respectful of each other, but later on they did have arguments and there were strains in the relationship. But it was not a sexual issue.

Bond: I know that's the sort of thing people would want to see, but it's not a question that I want to answer.

Reich: In my research I have learned that Brahms did indeed profess his love for her in a letter to a friend.

Bond: So it is a love story in its own way. A story like this is what composers live for. Musically speaking, I want to include actual music by these characters. They are treated as "found objects," i.e., as layers of musical commentary to reinforce the structural foundation. I will be directly quoting them. And I will use the form of melodrama to combine music with the spoken text. I love the idea of music underlying the spoken words. It's interesting to think how I might use *silence,* too, as an element in the drama. I'm thinking about that now. For example, what about Schumann's death? How should that be handled? I don't know yet.

Reich: Yes, no one was there when he died, you know. Clara and Brahms had left to meet their friend Joachim at the train station. Right after Robert died, she was offered lots of money from friends, but she was determined to make her own way. And I felt in my research a sympathetic chord with her, because I had lost my husband three days after getting my contract for the book. Working on it helped me in my own difficult time.

Bond: So you see, Nancy, you and I both have a personal connection with this story! It's hard to describe the music I want to compose here. Music refers only to itself, and describing it in words is difficult. I'll tell you what fascinates me about this, though, is the harmonic, melodic, and phrasing of the music of these three people. It must be translated *through* me in my own voice. The material must tell me where to go. My music must *grow* out of that. For example, in those scenes of Schumann's breakdown, I would hope I can find a way to project the listener into his mind at that moment. It would be very easy to fall into a Hollywood cliché and indulge in all sorts of sound effects. No, the integrity of the music must be intrinsic. But finding that "voice," that personality of each of these characters,

Clara Schumann's biographer, Nancy B. Reich, with Gerd Nauhaus, former Director of the Robert-Schumann-Haus in Zwickau, Germany.

is a real challenge. I think of composing as two separate actions: There is the "finger painter," and there is the "critic." They must never be in the room at the same time. If the critic is in the room, the finger painter just goes to the corner and sulks. When there's no critic there, the finger painter thinks everything is just wonderful. When I am in the "finger painter" mode, everything is wonderful, everything is on the table. I take in all impulses. Everything is all good. And then the critic comes in later and says, "Out, out, out!" And at best maybe he finds one usable idea in that whole day's work. So it's important that they be kept separate.

Above all, I find it inspiring to spend so much time with such a strong woman. The number-one thing about this is that I love Clara, and I want the audience to love her also. That's what I felt coming from the pages of Nancy's book. I need to touch across the centuries a woman who is so strong and who has such a clear vision of her purpose in this world. Clara is such a person. In my opera, everything revolves around her. So far I have composed one piece. I can play it for you on the computer. It's an aria from act 1 built upon a theme from Clara's Piano Trio, where I split her into "young" and "old" characters who sing a duet with each other. I want to have the majority of the opera blocked out by next spring. I have a performance scheduled for April 2010. I impose my own deadlines. I learned to work with pressure like when I was working as a composer in the film studios orchestrating and arranging and ghost-writing for film composers. You learn to work against deadlines. You don't have the luxury of waiting for inspiration. You use every technical device at your disposal and do the best you can. Soon I'll be going to Brahmshaus in Baden-Baden for additional research.

Reich: Yes, Clara lived in Baden-Baden, too. And you can stay at the Brahms House. Their houses are within walking distance of each other. I have been there in the living quarters. You can sleep right in the bedroom that we think was Brahms's bedroom! Now they all speak English there, which is very convenient. The director, Ilka Hekker, is very helpful.

Bond: And the place itself is very full of Clara Schumann. Her spirit is very much present. [Note: Ms Bond plans to premiere excerpts from the opera in the fall of 2010.]

ONGOING RESEARCH, ARCHIVES, CONFERENCES, FESTIVALS

Erika Reiman

There is increasing interest in Jean Paul's influence on Robert Schumann. It was not always so. At the time I was researching my book on Jean Paul, around 2000, I may have been the only musicologist in the world who went to Bayreuth and went to the Jean Paul Museum instead of the Wagner Museum! Both are situated very close to each other, in fact. Bayreuth is not a very big place. The Jean-Paul-Gesellschaft is there, in a house, with many of his manuscripts, portraits, letters, et cetera. You can also visit it on the Web. It's a very active society and publishes an annual journal. The people there were very helpful to me. Schumann himself went to see his house. He was just fifteen when Jean Paul died. He also saw the palace, called "La Fantasie," which is just outside Bayreuth. It's a large eighteenth-century house for one of the local nobility. Jean Paul mentions it in several of the novels, a beautiful place where wonderful things happen. Schumann wrote in the sketches for *Papillons* a piece entitled "La Fantasie." I feel like the response to my book has been rather slow, up to now, but interest is growing. In a future project I would like to extend my ideas and methodology on Schumann's piano music to the works of his later years.

Courtyard entrance to the Robert Schumann Research Institute, Düsseldorf, Germany.

John Worthen

I come away from my biography [*Robert Schumann: Life and Death of a Musician*, 2007] with many unanswered questions. (A.) What kind of singing voice did Schumann have? I'd love to know. Graham Johnson says he thinks it was a light baritone. A woman in his choir in Dresden said it was a light tenor. But even more than that, when Robert Schumann gave Clara, say, *Myrthen* in September 1840, and they went to the piano and sat down, who did the playing and who did the singing? Or did they both sing and both play at the same time? I just don't know.

(B.) What really happened to his piano playing? He did go on playing piano all his life, very clearly. And not just as a composer. When he was young he had to play to compose. That wasn't true after about 1840–41. But he goes on playing. And some of the accounts of his playing reveal great facility and a tremendous use of the pedal. That may have been because he was covering up for a nonworking middle finger on his right hand. It may have been because that's how he played, or wanted his own music to be played. There was one occasion, quite late in his career, about 1848 or 1849, at a friend's party, where he was asked would he accompany Clara, and they did play together. I don't know any other documentation of them actually playing duets together. That was the only occasion they did so. It was at a private party, but at least he was heard playing with her. And apparently he could match her for playing, although of course if you're playing duets it's never quite as taxing as it is for solo work.

(C.) People will go on talking about Schumann's schizophrenia and manic depression as if I had never disputed that in my book. I know that will happen. I don't mind. In the end, I hope people will disagree with me enormously. That's what the book is written for. It's an attempt to sum up the situation of Schumann's biography. Let's clear the slate, let's start again. But people will go on talking about Schumann's hand injury being caused by mercury poisoning for the next fifty years, I am perfectly sure. What I'd like to do, though, is start by looking at the evidence; gradually, perhaps, the mythologies will start to vanish. Because they are mythologies. We all have mythologies about other people's lives. It's natural. It's part of our culture that we do that. In Schumann's case it's more than possible. You can give probable verdicts of what was really wrong with him, even a hundred and fifty years later.

Thomas Synofzik

The Robert-Schumann-Haus in Zwickau has three main functions as museum, research institute, and concert hall. As director I am responsible for all these things. I am responsible for the special exhibitions, which change every three months. For special occasions I am doing the guided tours, which we offer through our permanent exhibition, and I play on the original keyboard instruments. There will be a renewal in 2010 of the permanent exhibition with its eight rooms. I am responsible for our archives, which were founded in 1910 and today form the world's largest collection of original Schumann documents. Though our funds are extremely limited, we can do new acquisitions from time to time. My main research project is the Schumann-Briefedition, which started last year with two volumes of the correspondence with publishers and was continued this year with the publication of the correspondence between Robert and Clara Schumann and the Mendelssohn family. Concurrently, there are smaller research projects, i.e., Schumann's choir music and the interpretation history of his works.

Gerd Nauhaus

I am the retired director of the Schumann-Haus in Zwickau. I first came to Zwickau in 1967, when I worked at the Zwickau Theater as dramaturg for a production of Schumann's only opera, *Genoveva*. From time to time I visited the Schumann-Haus, which is a national memorial place, a museum and archive for Robert Schumann. It is located at 5 Hauptmarket. The bookshop of his father, August, no longer exists. He died in 1826, and two of Schumann's brothers kept the bookshop and publishing house until around 1840. August was a very interesting man. He made the first series of books of German translations of foreign classics, like Byron and Walter Scott. Some of Robert's books exist today and you can look into them. A lot of the books from the publishing house are here.

Three years later, in 1970, I got the position as vice-director of Schumann-Haus. It has many of Schumann's manuscripts, diaries, and letters. You can see the handwritten scores for *Genoveva*, the song cycle *Dichterliebe*, and the *Album für die Jugend*. We have on the ground floor a big hall where we do exhibitions and concerts, and on the first floor is a permanent exhibition of Schumann's life and work. There are also archive rooms and research places. We do many concerts here with famous artists, like Jörg Demus. We do Schumann Festivals every year, excerpt for every fourth year, when we have a Schumann Competition for pianists and singers. There are prizes for that. And the Town Council of Zwickau gives another prize every year to performers and musicologists and orchestras. Our greatest project in the past was the edition of the Schumann diaries, which was completed in 1987. We are now working on the edition of his complete works, in cooperation with Dr. Bernhard Appel and his colleagues in Düsseldorf. At the present I have been working with my friend the late Peter Ostwald, an American psychiatrist, who is very interested in translating the *Marriage Diaries* [the English translation of *The Marriage Diaries of Robert and Clara Schumann: From Their Wedding Day to the Russia Trip* was published by Northeastern University Press in 1993]. I do hope that in two or three years an edition will be available in America. It's very hard work, because Robert and Clara used forms of old words that are difficult for us now to translate.

In both Zwickau and Düsseldorf you will find many of the Schumann letters. The largest collection in the world is in Zwickau. His handwritten index, where he listed letters written by him and received by him, is placed here. One difficulty in Schumann research is that his handwriting is very hard to decipher. I have been able to learn to read them. Some of the manuscripts are very fragile and you have to ask for special privileges to examine them.

Nancy B. Reich

These days there is much interest in Clara. The centenary of Clara's death in 1996 occasioned many festivals and conferences and new publications. A film was made in Germany, *Spring Symphony* [1984], directed by Peter Schamoni, which starred Nastassja Kinski as Clara. A novel about Clara has appeared in recent years, J. D. Landis's *Longing* [2000], and my daughter, Susanna Reich, has written *Clara Schumann: Piano Virtuoso* [1999] for younger readers. And there are numerous performances, editions, recordings, films, radio and television programs, dissertations, articles in popular and specialty magazines, more biographies, even a Clara Schumann Piano Competition in Düsseldorf, Germany. Meanwhile, I have kept returning to Zwickau for several reasons. After the publication of my first book in 1985, I compiled a discography of her own compositions, numbering more than fifty works. The revised edition of my book came out in 2001 and contained not just a catalogue of the complete works, including published and unpublished arrangements, but new information I gleaned from Clara Wieck's girlhood diaries and from the *Briefwechsel* of Robert and Clara. In general, the new edition was an enlarged and more enlightened picture of Clara Schumann.

Recently I went back to Zwickau to go over the manuscripts of Clara Schumann's works. I did that not just because they have all the Clara Schumann autographs there—the original music she wrote with her own hand—but I was also interested in seeing Clara's letters in her own handwriting that had not been published, as well as her childhood diaries, from her birth to the day she married Schumann, which were the only diaries kept by Wieck and his daughter (also unpublished in entirety). I am currently working with Dr. Gerd Nauhaus, the retired director of Schumann-Haus, on the only manuscript still in existence. This is the girlhood diary from June 7, 1824, to September 13, 1840, the day of her twenty-first birthday. Litzmann, who had worked with Marie Schumann, her eldest daughter, had given many excerpts from all her diaries, and when his three-volume work was finished, all the diaries, excerpt for the very first, were destroyed.

Akio Mayeda

I have been chairing with Klaus Wolfgang Niemöller the *Robert Schumann: Neue Ausgabe sämtlicher Werke* [*New Edition of the Complete Works,* published by the Robert-Schumann-Gesellschaft Düsseldorf, edited by Akio Mayeda and Klaus Wolfgang Niemöller in conjunction with the Robert-Schumann-Haus Zwickau. Mainz, Germany: Schott, 1991–.] It is our intention to finally present editions of all of Schumann's works, writings, letters, and primary documents. This will take many years. The first volume was edited by Bernhard R. Appel of Schumann's Missa Sacra, Op. 147, which was a late work written here in Düsseldorf. It was being published in this year, 1991. It contains the full orchestral score, the autograph sketches, and information about primary sources. It's a coproduction between the Schumann Society in Düsseldorf and the German Academy of Sciences. I am assisted by others here at the Schumann-Forschungsstelle, the research institute in Düsseldorf. We oversee the entire series of volumes, while other scholars around the world will be contributing primarily to the individual volumes. It is very important to present an exact edition of this music. It builds upon the first attempt, which was supervised by Clara Schumann and published in thirty volumes and a supplement by Breitkopf & Härtel. The first volume of that was printed in 1879, and the supplement appeared in 1893. Johannes Brahms assisted her in this edition, especially with the orchestral works and, of course, on some of the piano works. In some cases Schumann had revised his piano works, so Clara and Brahms printed both, in order that pianists could make a choice.

Now in our time we see many gaps in that edition that need to be addressed. The volumes did not contain critical reports or other philological material. There are several works missing. The most famous example is the Violin Concerto [WoO 1]. Brahms and Joseph Joachim were of the opinion that it did not measure up to the standards of the composer, and Clara agreed. Nowadays, however, we hold that work in high esteem, and it will be an indispensable part of the new complete edition. Other missing works are the Third Violin Sonata [WoO 2], the five romances for cello and piano [Anhang E7, reportedly destroyed by Clara], the C-Minor Piano Quartet [Anhang E1], and the G-Minor Symphony [Anhang A3].

The Piano Quartet, which he worked on sometime during and just after his time in Heidelberg, around 1829–30, is full of symphonic ideas. Schumann wrote in his diary that he intended to write a symphony, but at the time he hadn't yet mastered full scoring, so he wrote this as a kind of exercise or learning experience. It was an ambitious work. The piano part is full of tremolos and octaves, and the string-quartet writing is a substitute for the full orchestra. Professor Wolfgang Boetticher edited the work from the autograph materials, which came to the University Library in Bonn in 1874. It was not published until 1979, but it was not satisfactory. It needs to be corrected. [Note: The Piano Quartet received the world premiere recording from the Boetticher edition in 1991 for RCA with André Previn, piano; Young Uck Kim, violin; Heiichiro Ohyama, viola; and Gary Hoffman, cello.]

A few years later, back in Zwickau and Leipzig, Schumann began work on the G-Minor Symphony. Schumann had had thoughts of a symphonic work before 1830. He was between his Op. 4 and Op. 5. But it was never completed. Instead, he worked on the first movement over and over. We know of three sketches for that one movement alone and two sketches for the second movement. All we have of the last movement are some incomplete sketches.

In working to restore these pieces to the public, we want to clear up the general sense that Schumann wrote only in cycles—first the piano, then the songs, the symphonies, the chamber works, and so on. We now know that he wrote songs before 1830, and that long before the quartet and the symphony his first work as a boy was actually a rather big-scale work, a setting of the Psalm 150, when he was just twelve or thirteen years old. It was for chorus and orchestra. I can't say that he had *learned* how to write such a work; instead, he was an autodidact at this point. He wanted to write music and gather with his friends in Zwickau and form an orchestra. It's very interesting that he began this way, with thoughts of a big-scale choral work.

Collaboration between the East and West is very important. Schumann was born in Zwickau, in what became known as East Germany, and he died near Düsseldorf, in the region of what became known as West Germany. But relations between Zwickau and Düsseldorf have for many years already been very good. For example, after the first Schumannfest and Research Symposium in Düsseldorf, several scholars were able to travel to Zwickau and Leipzig. And participants in the Leipzig Conference sent scholars to the second Düsseldorf Symposium. Those connections are improving as the years pass.

We can now make many corrections in the first edition, since over the years we have made remarkable progress in techniques of editing the music sources. Yes, it is a lot of work and a difficult task. We have to research in many archives, gather important examples from many journals. Schumann lived in many cities in Germany, and we find manuscripts and papers throughout the country. And we find his manuscripts in many places outside of Germany, in the British Museum in London, in the National Library and the Society of the Friends of Music in Vienna, and in many archives in the United States. Even the question of an "urtext" is complicated. You can go to a musical shop and ask for an "urtext ausgabe," but there may be two or three and they all vary slightly. The question of authenticity is very complicated. When people ask me how we can make a better edition than the one by Clara and Brahms, I simply answer, "Well, we are not Clara and Brahms. We can be objective." In that way we can go back to Robert Schumann himself.

[Note: Since 1991, more volumes have appeared from scholars Bernhard R. Appel, Ute Bär, Linda Correll Roesner, Margit L. McCorkle, Ernst Bürger, and Irmgard Knechtges-Obrecht, including separate volumes on the Requiem, Op. 148 (1993); the Symphony No. 3, Op. 97 (1995); the Studies and Skizzen (1998); the *Overture, Scherzo, and Finale* (2000); the three violin sonatas (2001); the Piano Concerto Op. 54 (2003); and the McCorkle *Thematic Catalogue* (2003). Dr. Ute Bär is representing the project at the Robert-Schumann-Haus in Zwickau.]

Ute Bär

There are various reasons for a new edition of Schumann's completed works. Formerly, in the years 1879–87, the Leipzig publishing house Breitkopf & Härtel released the complete edition of Schumann's compositions, compiled by Clara Schumann and Johannes Brahms. For one, the old edition did not have, due to missing proof of origin and false attribution of music pieces, all the compositions by Schumann. This is a common issue seen also with other great composers. In the case of Schumann, another problem was Clara Schumann's and Johannes Brahms's decision not to include some of Schumann's later material, as they believed it had been influenced by Schumann's declining mental health. Therefore, the time has come to publish the missing works in a new edition.

It thus became important to locate the still-missing sources of material and proofs of its composer, if there was no evidence of their destruction. Also, the old complete edition of Schumann's work was not a historically critical collection, and many sources were omitted, not explained in enough detail, and insufficiently informative on the history of origin, print, and reception of his works. One hundred years after the original release, it was time to create an edition of his completed works in their historical-critical contexts. Attempts to publish a pan-German edition in the 1960s failed due to the GDR's division politics, but the need for a new, more critical edition remained. Akio Mayeda voiced this need at the first Schumann-Symposium in 1981 in Düsseldorf.

This desideratum was followed up by the Düsseldorf Schumann Association. As a result there were intense negotiations with the Mainz Academy of Literature and Sciences and the publisher Schott Music.

An important prerequisite to realize the project was the acquisition of sources on Schumann's life and work. Therefore, the German
Research Community (DFG; *Deutsche Forschungsgemeinschaft*) assisted
in a project to locate Schumann autographs. A research department was
created at the University of Cologne's Institute for Music Studies. In
January 1986 this project finally led to the *New Schumann Complete
Edition*. The first volume was released in 1991 and contains the Missa
Sacra, Op. 147, a later work by Schumann composed in Düsseldorf. To
this day, sixteen more volumes have been published, among them the
Thematisch-Bibliographisches Werkverzeichnis (Thematic-Bibliographic
Work Catalogue), and a chronicle of Robert Schumann's life, illustrated
with countless images and documents. Now the *150th Psalm,* a work
created in the composer's youth in his birthplace of Zwickau, has a place
next to such well-known works such as the Piano Concerto, Op. 54. The
150th Psalm, thanks to the *New Edition,* saw its world premiere on June
8, 1997, in Düsseldorf. To this day, new sources and information about
other individual works is unearthed. For example, in the volume of the
edition published by myself, we find a CODA-version of a concert autograph for piano and orchestra, *Introduction und Allegro Appassionato,*
Op. 92, currently situated in the Music Division, Prussian Culture, of
the National Library of Berlin. The music scholars consult all possible
sources to follow the genesis of Schumann's work and the individual pieces
while compiling material for the *New Edition.* Thus the help of the State
Criminal Investigation Department (*Landeskriminalamt*) became necessary when it was attempted to make visible deleted texts and changes by
the composer with the aid of an optoelectronic method, while researching
the Third Symphony, Op. 97.

The source-faithful presentation of the works is imperative for the *New
Schumann Complete Edition.* The publishers have to become involved in
the process when misunderstandings arise in today's context. Every change
to the actual music text, however, will be clearly stated in the revisions
report. For example, the crescendo and decrescendo markers are noted
differently, depending on the source. Thus a precise positioning of the
markers, which one would expect in a critical volume, cannot be taken
at face value from any one source. The editor has to make a pragmatic
decision to solve the problem. Every single case of the sort is noted and
discussed in the revisions report.

The *New Schumann Complete Edition,* next to the critically revised
music script, contains a detailed English and German history of creation,
print, performance, and reception of the individual music pieces. A
separate facsimile contains reproductions of all drafts, work manuscripts,

example scores, et cetera. These document the scientifically claimed and developed sources, rather than stand as illustrative materials.

Margit McCorkle

I have been working on the *Robert Schumann: thematisch-bibliographisches Werkverzeichnis* since the early 1990s under the aegis of the Robert-Schumann-Gesellschaft Düsseldorf. It is being published as part of the evolving *Robert Schumann: Neue Ausgabe sämtlilcher Werke (New Schumann Complete Edition)*. I find that this kind of thematic catalogue is a tremendously exciting view of the way Schumann's career and music developed. I see it as nothing less than a tour of the composer's workroom. It documents his works, opus by opus, from inspiration to definite plan, from sketch to completed work, from rehearsal to premiere to first edition and reviews. In this way you can interpret the life principally through his works. Some of this kind of information has not been available before in this form. As a result of my researches, I have realized more and more that Schumann developed his career with a great deal of sagacity, in what he chose to do, when he chose to do it, and how he chose to do it. I would also say that much of his drive in his last years, in 1849–55, to compose was from an economical agenda as much as from inspiration. He was a first-rate publicist of his own works. Moreover, there is a decided political agenda, as well. He self-consciously attempted to write in all genres and to write works which no longer fit into any genres but crossed their boundaries. This was an aspect of his originality. Whether or not he always succeeded is another consideration. But you can see he developed this ambition very systematically. At the same time, he's publishing and writing letters to publishers, attempting to catalog his music and his writings, and reading inveterately. Before the Richarz papers about his illness came out, I had thought to myself that these activities must have caused a nervous breakdown. I see now how amazing it is that he did so much of what he did in the face of such problems.

Joachim Draheim

My recent Schumann projects for Breitkopf & Härtel include many, many editions of Robert's works, including choral works and the "study scores" of his four symphonies (with Jon Finson) and some lesser-known works like the "Variations on a Nocturne of Chopin" (a fragment sketch) and Clara's "Four Pieces," Op. 15. For the Wiener Urtext Edition, there are the "Arabeske," Op. 18, the *Kinderszenen*, Op. 15, the *Waldszenen*, Op. 82, and the *Complete Works for Four-Hand Piano*. There have always been close ties between Schumann and Breitkopf & Härtel, beginning with the first editions of the *Carnaval* and the *Kinderszenen,* and continuing on with many chamber works and two of the symphonies. This has continued long after his death.

Some of these publications date back to work where I was involved in finding and restoring to the public several of Schumann's unknown compositions. In the Berlin Staatsbibliothek I made a copy from manuscript of a fragment of a Schumann opera version of Byron's *Der Korsar* [The Corsair]. You know, he had tried to write operas several years before he produced *Genoveva*. In 1844 he asked a librettist, Oswald Marbach, to adapt the text. When he refused, Schumann probably wrote the text himself. He began to compose a chorus, the "Chorus of the Corsairs," with a beautiful postludium and some bars of an aria for

Exterior view today of the Robert-Schumann-Haus, Zwickau, Germany.

Conrad the Corsair. He orchestrated only a few bars of the aria before he abandoned the project. We gave the fragment its first performance in Karlsruhe in 1981. After that, we published it at Breitkopf & Härtel in Wiesbaden.

Another time, in 1987, I was in Hamburg at the Staat- und Universitätsbibliothek and I examined the papers of Joseph Joachim, the great violinist and friend of Schumann. I found there a copy of a violin transcription of the solo cello part of the famous Cello Concerto, Op.

129, from 1850. This copy was not in Schumann's hand. It was written here in Düsseldorf by a copyist named Peter Fuchs. It was not difficult to authenticate the manuscript. Schumann had written in his own hand the word "violin" on the first page and two remarks on the title page. The first remark was: "This Concerto has also been published in a transcription for violin"; and the second, "The closing has yet to be corrected." He also wrote in his own hand some cues and some notes. It means he thought he could publish his Cello Concerto also in a version for violin. Schumann was very practical and made several transcriptions for various instruments of his later works. But this version was forgotten. It is difficult to know when this was written. This version might have been the idea of Joseph Joachim in 1853. We don't know why he didn't perform it, but perhaps it had to do with his mixed feelings about Schumann's late works. The transcription was simple. The cello part was just transposed up an octave. But the ending is different in both versions. Schumann changed the last six measures of the violin solo, which means the orchestral part must also be altered. My edition was published in 1987 by Breitkopf & Härtel. It was not performed until November 29, 1987, by the Kölner Philharmonie with Saschko Gawriloff. Now it is being played by Gidon Kremer. I hope it will soon be performed by other violinists. Nobody could have thought that Schumann would have had this strange idea. There is no trace of it in his letters and diaries. Only in this copy which I found.

Schumann made his first serious attempt at a Piano Concerto in D Minor in 1839. The *Konzertsatz für Klavier und Orchester* was ultimately abandoned after one movement. It was written in Vienna and described in letters to Clara Wieck as something between a symphony, a concerto, and a grand sonata. The Belgian pianist Jozef De Beenhouwer found fragments of the manuscript in the University Library in Bonn. There was an orchestral score, a piano reduction, and a sketch, all in Schumann's hand, which is all but indecipherable! From these he reconstructed and completed the movement. One was for orchestra, and one was for solo piano and orchestral reduction. I assisted him and published my edition with Breitkopf & Härtel in 1988. It begins with a five-measure introduction that reminds you of the overture to *Don Giovanni,* and it goes on with some ideas that were more fully worked out a few years later in the famous Piano Concerto Op. 54. [Note: It has been recorded on the Koch label with Jennifer Eley, piano, and the English Chamber Orchestra conducted by Sayard Stone; and also on the Bella Musica label by Iva Maria Witoschynstkyi and the Collegium Musicum of the University of Karlsruhe, conducted by Herbert Heitz.]

Erik Battaglia

The "Centro Studi Eric Sams" is a Web-based project (www.ericsams. org) that I founded in 2006. It consists of the online publication of Eric Sams's complete essays and reviews on music, Schumann, Shakespeare, and other subjects, as well as letters and drafts. I'm also working on the Italian translation of Sams's *Complete Works* and on the first edition of his "Introduction to Schumann's *Papillons,*" which was found among his posthumous papers. It's my way to honor my dear friend and mentor, with whom I shared a friendship and correspondence of twenty years, since I was fourteen years of age. I shared with him my name, birthday, and a particular passion for Hugo Wolf. I first met him in London when I sought his opinion on an essay I had written on Wolf. Eric wrote to me two weeks later, with "collegial regards," as he put it. From that time on he was for me a sort of open (mind) university. Each of his letters was full of ideas and quotations in a sonata-like development (passing to new topics in a kind of "literary modulation," as he called it). He trained me in the "application of thought," a praxis he had inherited from his mentors A. E. Housman and Alan Turing.

Whereas Robert Schumann spent the first part of his creative life writing masterful piano music, and then turned to a second career as a lieder composer (his first song was derived from Shakespeare), Eric Sams spent the first part of his creative life writing masterful analyses of lieder and studying in depth the hidden details of the art of Wolf, Schumann, and Brahms (a work on Schubert was never finished); and then he began a second career as a Shakespearean scholar and revolutionized research on many aspects of the Bard's early life and works. However, just as Schumann the lieder composer simply went on writing poetic music (although now with words *en clair*), Sams the Shakespearean scholar simply went on as a cryptographer/detective investigating the Bard's creative soul and the poetic emotions, as he had done with the composers.

In Schumann, Sams had unveiled a world of Shakespearean images of experience, which he called *musico-verbal* images: motifs, inflections, themes—most famously the "Clara theme." This, however, formed only a small part of his Schumannian thesaurus. Nowadays that discovery is sometimes brought into question by scholars like the late John Daverio, thus forgetting that its wider inquiry was no less than cracking the genetic code of Schumann's music by means of quasi-scientific as well as linguistic procedures. Shakespeare's so-called image-clusters (a succession of associated images) are just like Schumann's song-motifs (for example, a flattened seventh, which means "heaven," or "skies"). A *pun* is, so Sams once wrote to me, something like an enharmonic modulation.

This approach doesn't alter or impede, as sometimes has been said, the force of Schumann's spontaneous expression. On the contrary, it contextualizes it in a frame of logical and therefore passionate beauty: Schumann as *Showman* and *Schaman,* as Sams put it once, playing with words on that composer's much-debated dualism. Even his critical analysis of Schumann's late songs—easily countered by the music's sheer beauty (not to be denied by anyone)—must be seen in the context of Sams's study of the composer's private musico-verbal vocabulary. From 1849 on Schumann, so Sams has claimed, rarely used these motifs anymore to express what he meant, or composed music that was "too beautiful" (vis-à-vis its words, e.g., Lenau's "Meine Rose").

In sum, this is something that only a musicologist, Germanist, composer, pianist, cryptanalyst, pun maker, chess player, Shakespeare scholar, crossword solver—in other words something that only Eric Sams—could have managed, decoding the music's hidden truth without spoiling the protective membrane of the *Schumann/"papillon"* wings. That method, the *Samsian analysis of song-motifs,* could and should become a musicological standard and replace (in the field of song research) the Schenkerian method and the mere literary commentary, both of which deal with poem and music as elements of a suspension, rather than of a solution. *"Lieder"-ature* was the apt word-concept "composed" ad hoc by Sams.

"What's in a name?" asked Shakespeare. "For Schumann, everything was in a name," answered Sams. May his own name be linked with Schumann's "for all times."

IN SCHUMANN'S FOOTSTEPS

Nancy B. Reich

You have to travel a lot to know the contexts of Clara Schumann's life. The first time I went to Schumann's birthplace, Zwickau, it was a medium-large city of 100,000 people in what was in the early 1980s referred to as East Germany (run by the Russian army). It was very smoky and dirty then, because there is an automobile factory there and a uranium mine just outside the city. The air was always full of soot, and it was hard to breathe. But in the center of the town you still had the old marketplace, which looked very much the way it did in Schumann's time. Although the amenities were lacking, the town had spent a great deal of money restoring this marketplace. No automobiles were allowed; it's a foot zone, or walking zone. Right in the corner of the marketplace is the house where Schumann was born. There were just a few people researching there, maybe four or five. Now Robert-Schumann-Haus in Zwickau has become a very popular place to visit. It always was a national monument, because it was the house where Schumann was born. But there are twenty-one staff workers now.

The musicologists in Zwickau were and still are particularly helpful and cooperative. During my early visits, I met Martin Schoppe and Gerd Nauhaus, who were directors of Schumann-Haus while Russia was governing East Germany. It was very difficult then even to visit East Germany. Schumann-Haus was managed by a man who had the Russian authority and had many Russian visitors who were always welcomed by him, but he always kept his eyes on visitors and scholars from the West.

Now the city is beautifully transformed, the air is cleaner, and the Schumann-Haus restored and renovated with its own concert hall added to it. There you can find all the Schumann materials and archives which at one time had been housed in the Zwickau museum. Downstairs is a reception hall and the concert hall, while up a marble staircase with a gleaming brass handrail, kept polished by an assiduous *Hausmeister,* is a small exhibition area with a room, for example, where you find the piano where Clara Wieck first played in a concert in 1830. There's one room devoted to her and portraits of all the children. And then in two or three very small, crowded offices are all the archives, hundreds, thousands of Schumann letters, the diaries, the household books, et cetera.

R. Larry Todd

Even though Leipzig has changed so much because of the bombing in World War II, you can still find today many traces of Mendelssohn and Schumann. There is still a sense of how the culture of the city was and still is intertwined. Even now, you can walk in the space of twenty minutes from the Thomaskirche to the Schumann House, which is a lovely museum, and then you can go to the Mendelssohn House, which is a fabulous museum, and then to the *Hochschule,* the conservatory that he founded—not the original building but the institution. In front of the Gewandhaus you can see the restoration of the statue of Mendelssohn that had been torn down in 1936 by the Nazi Reich. A replica has been unveiled, and it's now covered in flowers. Of course, the original Gewandhaus from the eighteenth century is long gone. On that site was built another concert hall, which burned down. During the time of East Germany a third structure was built on the site. It was one of Germany's great architectural accomplishments. If you had gone into that building in Schumann and Mendelssohn's time you would have found yourself in a smallish building enjoying a more intimate experience than you would have today. There were rules about where the women and the men could sit. The orchestra was only about forty-five instruments. We have to remember this when considering Schumann's symphonies, where the string writing works much better than when it is amplified to accommodate a one-hundred-piece orchestra. There's nothing quite like that here in the States.

And you can't forget the famous Coffe Baum, nearby, where Schumann and Mendelssohn and their friends frequently gathered in the 1830s. When I went there a few years ago, Christopher Hogwood and I walked in and sat down at the "Schumann-Ecke," or Schumann Corner. We heard the Vivaldi *Four Seasons* on the sound system, and we asked if they could change the music to something by Schumann, but they could not because it was an automated system. But we sat there and had a beer or two and a nice dinner. It was nice to sit there and try to imagine the Davidsbündler meeting there and planning out the *Neue Zeitschrift für Musik*. Certainly Mendelssohn would have enjoyed their company, and Schumann considered him a member of the group, but on the whole, he might not have agreed with everything that was said about criticism. He had a healthy distrust of musical journalism and criticism. He once said he had never gone to a musical symposium without leaving feeling he was somehow less musical than when he had entered. He said that music "is far more precise than the ambiguity of words."

These days in 2009 I've been traveling a lot, twice to Washington to the Library of Congress, and to New York, where we had the American premiere of my reconstruction of his Third Piano Concerto (the European premiere was earlier in January in Bavaria). I was in Leipzig for a documentary film about Mendelssohn. Yes, there's a lot going on. I can't really keep up with all of it!

THE HOLLYWOOD VERSION

History decomposes into images, not into narratives. . . . It would work on the principle of montage, juxtaposing textual fragments from past and present in the expectation that they would strike sparks from and illuminate each other. I needn't say anything. Merely show.
—Walter Benjamin

At the very outset, the writer of a sketch of this poet has to decide whether he will confine himself to what he knows to be true, or speculate at length on many things which he can see to be possible, or even probable, but which may, after all (especially in the light of later research), be entirely misleading.
—G. K. Chesterton, *Chaucer*

EDITOR'S NOTE

Extant motion-picture dramatizations of the life and music of the Schumanns display diverse interpretations and personal, public, and political agendas. In these pages are overviews by musicologist/educator Robert Winter and actor Simon Callow, and commentaries by pianist Claude Frank on *Song of Love* (1947), Nancy B. Reich on *Spring Symphony* (1983), Steven Isserlis on *Schumann's Lost Romance* (1996), and Helma Sanders-Brahms on *Geliebte Clara* (2008). These commentaries are supplemented by my own research into these films.

Author in front of Schumann's piano, Robert-Schumann-Haus, Zwickau, Germany.

Overview

Robert Winter

It seems to me that the subject of movies that dramatize the lives and works of composers is not only a serious subject, but it ought to be a mainstay of every music curriculum. To be honest with you, I've never seen a biopic about a composer in which I didn't find at least something interesting. I include these films in my own courses at UCLA. I live and work in Hollywood, so I've found that dishing out traditional biographical material—whether it was in a rudimentary textbook or standard biography—just didn't "live" for most kids. It just didn't come to life for them. I could jump up and down about Beethoven and the French Revolution and Napoleon, and realize the students barely remembered if the French Revolution came before or after Vietnam! So I began cautiously with films like *A Song to Remember* [1945], the one with Cornel Wilde as Chopin. Until recently the only way to get it was to tape it off of Channel 9 at two o'clock in the morning. So I would truck it into class and set up the VCR. It wasn't that I thought I would be substituting it for great, scholarly fidelity. No, I thought it would be a starting point for discussion. For a long time I had no discrimination about bringing in good ones and poor ones. Ken Russell's *The Music Lovers* and *Mahler* were radical enough that they were more likely to engage my students. I found, quite frankly, that the more I turned my classroom into a cinema, the better it worked for a class of hundreds of students. Within seconds of screening something like that, you could hear a pin drop, and suddenly the kids who were reading the UCLA student paper, *The Daily Bruin,* would hush completely, and afterward hands would shoot up and everybody was talking. Students all grow up watching television and are immersed in visual media. It's not that they are disrespectful of scholarly articles and books, they just find it hard to get a hook and climb the wall. Cinema gives them that hook. Scholars and filmmakers—and our students—are all reimagining the past.

Simon Callow

I have portrayed several composers on stage and on film, including Mozart in *Amadeus* [1979], Handel in *Honor, Profit, and Pleasure* in a television production, and Schumann. Schumann must have been a really, really interesting man. That split in his character went right down the middle of his brain. I played both aspects of him. The basic premise is that Roger Norrington is conducting the Salzburg Camerata playing Schumann's Second Symphony. In his hotel room, Norrington becomes aware of a violent argument between two men in the room next door. He confronts them, and it's Florestan and Eusebius! I play both roles.

Eusebius is played as a sort of chain-smoking, dark-spectacled, suicidal bohemian type. Florestan is impatient and heroic and so on. It becomes a battle to the death. Roger becomes Raro, the eminently sensible conductor who mediates between them. Somehow, it all involves Schumann's suicide attempt. This is all intercut with scenes of Norrington rehearsing the Salzburg Camerata, unearthing the thematic cross-references to the Bach quotation, the Beethoven quotations, and all the ciphers. The film was shot on a preposterously low budget, and it was rather ill-prepared. Everything was shot in a hotel room—*my* hotel room! Couldn't be nicer, except my room was filled with cameras and lights and I had only room to perch on the bed.

There's no reason why you should exempt composers from being fictionalized on film, when every other kind of artist has been. It simply boils down to how well you do it. There's an inherent temptation in overdramatizing the life of a composer, to make him seem more like his music. But their lives often bear little or no resemblance to their work. Most musicians sit down and work solidly at their music, whatever the internal drama might be that gives rise to the music. In reality, there are a few composers who did have tremendously interesting lives. You might seize on Paderewski, for example, or Berlioz or Wagner. But it wasn't an exciting life by the standards of adventurers, spies, and soldiers.

The big challenge is visually depicting the actual creative process. I think it would be true to say that 80 percent of the population is uninterested in art as such, and therefore not terribly interested in the creation of it. Very few filmmakers or playwrights seem to be interested in the actual question of creativity, the nature of creativity, the creative act. But that's an enormously difficult thing to portray. You can't really show somebody like Schumann writing music, sitting at a desk, scratching away. Onstage, it's just nonsensical. Better to show the artist as a man who struggles with something; or, in a more watered-down sense, a person who wants to become famous and much rewarded. It's probably done best in a novel. Instead, onscreen, you get these oversimplifications and whitewashings. That whole "blossom time" treatment of Schubert is very characteristic of the period. When I grew up, I read a "Children's Lives of the Composers"; and all such books were like that—Mozart and his pretty little chocolate-box clothes and his daddy and his lovely little wife, and things of that sort. You outgrow that. It's good for children but sad for adults. And it's very hard to tell the life story of a composer if you're relying heavily on the music, simplifying his life into a kind of balletic narrative. I have tried to write plays about Oscar Wilde, Wilhelm Reich, and Stanislavsky; and in every case you have to say, "What is it about this person that really interests me?" Just that, rather than, "What a nice piece of music!"

I think there's a surprisingly wide range of composer movies, from Cornel Wilde's *A Song to Remember;* to Dirk Bogarde's Liszt film, *Song without End* [1962]; the Schumann film *Song of Love* [1947]; Ken Russell's Delius film, *Song of Summer* [1968]; and the Chopin film *Impromptu* (1991); et cetera. Ken's *Elgar* [1962] and *Bartók* [1964] were also fantastic. In those days Ken was the closest thing to genius English television has ever had. He was trying to make films that would create the inner world of the composer.

Personally, I would love to do something about Reynaldo Hahn. Apart from being Proust's boyfriend, at the age of sixteen writing some of the most gorgeous songs ever written, he was a heroic figure during the war, running the Paris Opera. I'm very interested in the idea of the not-absolutely-first-rank composer who is nonetheless exquisite in his writing. Not so many myths there to stub our toes on, as you say. But it's extremely hard to raise money on a figure that's not so well known.

Sometimes the arbitrary use of music out of the biographical context can be damaging. I think more harm was done to Mahler by the use of the Fifth Symphony's "Adagietto" in *Death in Venice* than can be adequately computed. So now, every time you listen to Mahler's Fifth Symphony, you think of Venice. What the hell does that music have to do with Venice? And Rachmaninoff's Second Piano Concerto—who wants to think of Celia Johnson and Trevor Howard in *Brief Encounter* [1946] every time you listen to that? But you do. It's maddening. On the other hand, it has to be said that certain films have used classical music in a wonderfully interesting way.

The Films

Song of Love, MGM, 1947

John C. Tibbetts

Song of Love was Hollywood's first major feature film about Robert and Clara Schumann. An A-list MGM release in 1947, it starred Katharine Hepburn and Paul Henreid as Clara and Robert Schumann, Robert Walker as young Johannes Brahms, Henry Daniell as Franz Liszt, and Leo G. Carroll as Father Wieck. The screenplay was by Irmgard von Cube and Allen Vincent, and was based on an unproduced play by Bernard Schubert and Mario Silvia. It was directed by studio mogul Louis B. Mayer's favorite contract director, Clarence Brown, a veteran of earlier biopics, including *Conquest* (1937), about Napoleon and Marie Walewska, featuring Greta

Garbo and Charles Boyer; and *Edison the Man* (1940), starring Spencer Tracy. The classically trained Bronislaw Kaper supervised the music, William Steinberg and Dr. Alfred Scendre conducted the concert sequences, and Artur Rubinstein provided the soundtrack piano performances.

"In this story of Clara and Robert Schumann," cautions an opening title, "and of Johannes Brahms and Franz Liszt, certain necessary liberties have been taken with incident and chronology. The basic story of their lives remains a true and shining chapter in the history of music." The allusion to "certain necessary liberties" is an understatement. Consider the challenges the Schumann story as we have come to know it presented to the proprieties of the Hollywood Production Code of the 1940s: Schumann's psychological problems, the tensions in the marriage with Clara, his suicide attempt, the controversial relationship between Clara and Brahms all must be negotiated in accordance with the code's restrictions on the depiction of deviant behavior, adultery, and suicide.

These tensions weren't confined to just this film; indeed, they were being felt industrywide. Postwar Hollywood was in the throes of the so-called film noir period. Fed by wartime disillusionment and subsequent Cold War paranoia, and the influx of European émigré filmmakers who were master practitioners of expressionistic themes and techniques, numerous films were preoccupied with paranoia, psychotic states, and violent behavior. *Song of Love* added to the mix the spectacle of the "mad musician." Up to now, mad musicians had been stock cardboard villains, as exemplified by various incarnations of *The Phantom of the Opera* and the John Brahm thriller about a homicidal pianist/composer, *Hangover Square* (1943). *Song of Love* proposed to depict in Schumann a more psychologically complicated character.

My research into the MGM production files [MGM Production Files, Folder No. 1, Doheny Library, USC, Los Angeles] provides useful information about the strategies by which the film sought to circumvent and/or contain the controversies. To be sure, it is immediately apparent that the filmmakers were fully aware of Schumann's historical record. The studio research on Schumann's life and work and his relationships with Clara and Brahms is exhaustive and fills several thick bound volumes. Thus any distortions of the historical record onscreen were not the result of ignorance but were wholly *intentional*.

In memos, treatments, and scripts spanning July 26, 1945, to August 24 a year later, there is much indecision about how to handle the film's storyline, structure, and music. "Loyalty of Clara to Robert and his ideals is the most important feature of the film," noted script supervisor Ivan Tors, "and the strength she gains through love and suffering." However, from the outset, Tors was worried about what he called "a potential weakness," i.e., the downbeat tone of the Schumann story. "Sometimes it's too gloomy," he wrote. "The ending [Robert's incarceration and death] is unsatisfactory. The picture starts with a hope for happiness and ends with loneliness." Tors suggested a strategy that employed a flashback technique: "The story could open at a Schumann festival when Clara, a gracious old lady, plays 'Traümerei.' She's moved by the enthusiastic reaction of the audience and by memories of the past. She can see herself as a young girl in Leipzig when she listened secretly at Schumann's door when he was engaged in composing the melody." After a succession of memories, the story would return to the aged Clara at the piano. "This proves to the audience," explained Tors, "that in spite of her loneliness at the end, this gray-haired lady had had an exciting and sometimes very happy and full life."

Later memos contain second thoughts: Maybe the flashback technique should be abandoned for a linear chronology. Maybe Clara should be a little girl at the opening concert. Does she play Beethoven's "Moonlight Sonata" or a concerto by Chopin, Beethoven, or Liszt? [In the finished product, she plays an excerpt from Liszt's First Piano Concerto.] And what does Liszt play in the scene when he inadvertently insults Clara? [In the finished film, he plays his flashy paraphrase on "Widmung."] What to do about Clara's career obsessions? How can Brahms and Clara's love for each other be suggested but not made explicit? Should Brahms be present with Clara when Schumann dies? Should Clara reunite with Brahms in their old age? And how should Schumann's mental problems be suggested?

Studio records demonstrate that in the face of code pressure, the film-makers were determined to portray the Schumann relationship as one of unwavering love and devotion. This is suggested at the outset, not just by Clara's passionate declaration at the court proceeding, but by their duet performance on their wedding day of the "Dedication" theme, when in close-up Clara places her hands over his. The screen depiction of Clara's untrammeled love flies in the face of the facts of her vacillating loyalties towards both him and her father and her avowed doubts and chronic ambivalence regarding a future with Robert. References to issues that disrupted the relationship and outraged her father—Robert's alleged alcoholism, his womanizing, the possibilities of a syphilitic infection—are omitted entirely (as is the crisis engendered by his damaged hand, which curtailed a promising concert career). The potential scandal of a mature man falling in love with a mere child (Clara was only eleven years old when they first met) is sidestepped by the casting of an obviously mature Katharine Hepburn in the role. Moreover, the film would have us believe that after the marriage, Clara's desire to return to the concert stage was an unselfish gesture designed to allow Robert time to compose. The truth is that she was determined to pursue her career on her own terms, regardless of the demands of homemaking and childbearing, and regardless of the protestations of Robert, who either found himself confined to the duties of househusband during her tours or the unwilling companion on her tours, frustrated by the lack of opportunity to compose. In sum, the conflicts between his and her professional aims frequently disturbed the harmonious union that legend (and Hollywood) would have us believe.

The business with Brahms is likewise sanitized out of all recognition. The most passionate moment between him and Clara is simply a moment when Brahms is packing shirts as he determines to leave the Schumann house: Each time he places his shirts in his suitcase, she puts them back in the drawer. But at the moment when he overtly confesses his love, she slowly takes the shirts back *out* of the drawer and places them *into* his suitcase! Marital infidelity was a problematic, if not an outright forbidden, topic in the eyes of the code.

I was surprised to learn that the first story treatments indicated that *Song of Love* would conclude with an elaborate staging of Schumann's suicide attempt during the Düsseldorf Carnival of 1854. This is very interesting. Surely this factual event could be ideally suited for the Hollywood treatment. The script calls for a deranged and disheveled Schumann to rush through a crowd of costumed figures and clouds of confetti. He suffers auditory and visual hallucinations—distorted musical sounds and tolling bells—and follows a capering figure in Harlequin costume toward the river and his doom. As late as August 24, 1946, that sequence was still intact in the script. However, there is no record of such a scene actually being filmed. Certainly it does not appear in the released version. Instead, the film's penultimate scene shows his collapse while conducting his "Faust" music. Perhaps the Carnival sequence was axed due to budgetary constraints; or, more likely, the depiction of a suicide attempt proved to be too objectionable to the Production Code censors.

Likewise simplified, suggested, or expunged outright is the full extent of Schumann's mental instability. It was decided that his emotional and organic abnormalities could be suggested but not detailed. Thus the film elides any discussion of the history of insanity that ran in his family, of his chronic bipolar affective disorder, the syphilitic infection that compounded his mental and physical deterioration, his homicidal threats against Clara at the time of his breakdown, and the gruesome details of his incarceration and debilitated condition during the last twenty-eight months of his life. Instead, the film implies his attacks came on only late in his career and were probably the result of overwork and mental strain. There are no scenes set in the asylum, excepting Clara's last visit, when he displays a childlike, relatively peaceful demeanor.

In the light of these containments, it is amusing to glance at the publicity attending the film's release, which alluded to passions and horrors *not* present on the screen (but suggested for the sake of promotional titillation). "On his fingertips, the Love of Music," proclaimed one advertisement; "and on her lingering lips, the Music of Love!" Other headlines blared, "She FELL IN LOVE . . . and trouble . . . with a MAD GENIUS!"

At the same time, Bosley Crowther's review in the *New York Times* suggests the film bowed too readily to censorial demands: "It takes the lives of famed musicians—Robert and Clara Wieck Schumann and Johannes Brahms" and "laces them into the clichés of false and sentimental romance" and the "saccharine-sweet little glimpses of episodes in their domestic life—familiar troubles with the servant, laughing anxieties over the kids and touching necessities of rebuffing the romantic advances of 'Uncle Brahms.'"

On the other hand, the usual "liberties with regard to incident and chronology" were forgiven by the *Hollywood Reporter;* "since the purpose was entertainment above documentation, no fault can be found with the free adaptation." Hepburn's performance was "easily the best she has done in recent years" and Henreid's Schumann was "appealing though dolorous, with his best scenes the ones where he realizes he cannot escape the cloak of madness that is descending upon him."

In retrospect, *Song of Love* is a prime demonstration of classical Hollywood at work. "MGM really felt it was presenting something intellectual and of a high cultural order," says historian William K. Everson. "If a studio like that felt it was making money on 'Dr. Kildare' films and Red Skelton vehicles, it then felt it had to do something classy once in a while. I honestly feel that in films like these, in spite of the fact that history is distorted and diverted to a very contrived plot, they really felt they were adding to the cultural status of Hollywood" [author's interview with William K. Everson, New York City, 12 November 1980]. At the same time, I might add, *Song of Love*'s desperate attempts to reconcile the extremes of Schumann's world to the narrow confines of "respectable" Hollywood corresponds rather neatly to the Schumann's own lifelong struggles to construct "normalcy" out of the chaotic conditions of his life and personality.

Claude Frank

EDITOR'S NOTE

Pianist Claude Frank is celebrated for his mastery of the standard German piano repertoire of Bach, Beethoven, Schubert, and Schumann. He has also gained some notoriety, however, for his lightly satirical re-creation of *Song of Love*. Frank began his "performances" of it with his brother just after World

War II. He has since taken it "solo" as a one-man show to many social and
musical events. He describes it in this interview/"performance" dating from
1987 at the University of Kansas.

Well, I've been doing my version of *Song of Love* very often for people
ranging from as few as five to as many two hundred people at parties,
at benefits, in schools, after master classes, when we all felt that students
and people needed a diversion . . .

Two important musical themes that recur throughout the picture are
Schumann's "Traümerei" and the melody from the song "Widmung."
The first time we hear the "Traümerei" is when she plays it as an encore
after performing the Liszt First Piano Concerto. Her father, Professor
[*sic*] Wieck, is outraged. But Clara says, "No, Father, if you don't mind,
I'm going to play the 'Traümerei.' And young Schumann is there in the
audience, and she loves him and he loves her. We don't hear it again until
about two-thirds or three-quarters through, when Schumann is in the
insane asylum and Clara visits him for the first time. And the doctor says,
"Mrs. Schumann, there are good days and there are bad days. And today
is a good day." That's what's so tragic about it, because when she comes
into his room he's "composing" the "Traümerei" (which, of course, he had
already written years before!). And Robert says to her, "Of course I can
still compose. I composed it today. I wrote it for you." And he sits down
and plays but then crashes his hands down on the keyboard. It reminds
us that in later life Schumann became again like a child. But it also means
that now he's lost his reason. So I play it "straight." And of course, in the
movie Robert doesn't even finish it. He collapses on the keyboard. That's
followed by a later scene, when Clara Schumann gives her farewell recital.
She ends it with the "Traümerei."

We first hear the "Widmung" when they exchange wedding gifts.
Clara's gift to Robert is her diary, which is still "tabula rasa"—just blank
pages—intended to be written in when they are married. And then Robert
goes to the piano and says, "There is a little poem by Rückert, which I
have set it to music for you. It's your wedding present." And he starts
playing it. And he says, "Not much of a wedding present. But I hope you
like it." And he leaves out the middle part but goes right to the second
verse. This time Clara plays the upper register. Even after just this one
hearing, she's able to play along, one octave higher on the piano! You see
their hands, side by side on the keyboard. Of course, since she doesn't
know the postlude yet, she lets him play that alone.

The theme reappears a little later when the Schumanns attend a salon
concert in time to hear Franz Liszt performing "Widmung" in order to

help out Schumann at a soiree. Liszt sits down at the piano and says, "I'll play my own version of a song called 'Dedication,' by Schumann." But rather than playing it straight, he plays it with lots of flash and lots of notes. Clara murmurs, "Is this my wedding present? Is it dedication to love, or dedication to your *pyrotechnics*?" And Schumann, being a gentleman, says, "Well, it's very interesting." After Liszt has finished, Clara goes to the piano and, very tactlessly, plays it very simply and delivers a speech about what the values of Schumann's are as against Liszt's values. And she's quite unfair. She says her husband stands for simplicity and love, whereas Liszt stands for glitter and outward success. Anybody else but Liszt would have been offended. In fact, other people are offended and say to him, "How dare she do that to you?" But Liszt is inwardly very noble, and he just says, "She did more than insult me, she *described* me." That's a very important scene.

But before we hear it again, Johannes Brahms arrives on the Schumann doorstep. Actor Robert Walker really does resemble the young Brahms, who was actually very handsome. But here's Brahms, although we don't know who he is yet. He comes to the Schumann house and asks him if he may play something for him. And Schumann says yes; and he plays something anachronistic, the Rhapsody in G Minor (which, of course, he hasn't composed yet; but this is Hollywood!). When he chances to see Clara, he immediately stops. Clara says, "Who is it, Robert? His name?" He introduces himself and continues to play. That's a very, very interesting scene, because near the end of the movie when Brahms comes back to the Schumann house and finds the piano locked, he opens the piano to attract Clara's attention. She has buried herself in the house. There's a very nice kind of symmetry there.

Another theme, the "Arabeske," is heard in the background when Brahms tells Clara it is time for him to leave the house. Clara rushes upstairs and tries to talk Brahms out of it. It's a funny scene, because they're constantly exchanging shirts. She puts the shirts in the drawer and he puts them back in the suitcase. And so on. And then at a dramatic moment he tells her that he loves her. At that moment, guess what she does? She puts the shirts back into his suitcase! Clara cries and goes into another room and opens the door, and there is Schumann at the piano, composing the "Arabeske." Without looking at her, he says, "I had to take a little rest from my *Faust* oratorio. So I composed the piece and I called it 'Arabeske.' Do you like it?" And then he sees her cry.

By now we know there is something very wrong with Schumann. One of the symptoms of his disease is a repeated note he heard in his head (and which we hear on the soundtrack). Near the beginning of the picture there is a party at the Schumann house, and everybody is very happy and dances. But suddenly, as one watches, we hear that note. And when I perform this, I strike repeatedly a key on the piano. Just that one note. In another scene, the doctor of one of Schumann's children arrives. As he talks with Clara, they hear spooky music coming from inside the house. We recognize it because it's a piece called "Haunted Spot," from Schumann's *Forest Scenes*. The doctor finds Schumann inside a dark room, kind of stabbing at the piano, just pieces of the melody. He holds a candle close to Schumann's face, and he doesn't react at all.

He finally breaks down when he is conducting a portion of his *Faust Scenes*. He suddenly stops, waves his hands in the air, and collapses. We hear that insistent tone again. I still wonder why the filmmakers chose that. Maybe it's because they wanted a big piece that had orchestra and chorus.

That "Widmung" theme returns near the end. You see, all this time the romance between Clara and Brahms is unresolved. So it must have been in real life. But in Hollywood all knots must be tied. So we return to Clara and Brahms. It's been years now since Schumann's death. They are chatting in a picturesque beer garden. They lean their faces close together. When he asks her to marry him, we hear his "Lullaby" on the soundtrack. She reminds him of the responsibilities of taking care of the children. He says that he loves the children almost as much as he loves her. Then he suggests she is as lonely as he is. He knows all about being lonely. You know by this time that any moment she's going to say yes. Unfortunately, a fiddler comes to their table and plays the "Widmung" theme! Tears fall from her eyes. "No, Johannes!" she cries. "In reality the only one who needs me is Robert. Robert is still alive, and he'll be alive as long as this music is alive. And I'm going to see to it, Johannes, that his music stays alive as long as *I'm* alive." And there's a title on the screen: "And this was her decision to keep the music of Robert Schumann alive by playing it all over Europe until her dying days."

Spring Symphony (Frühlingsymphonie)

John C. Tibbetts

Presenting a stark contrast to *Song of Love* is *Spring Symphony* (1983), written and directed by the veteran German filmmaker Peter Schamoni, photographed by Gerard Vandenberg, and starring Herbert Grönemeyer as Schumann, Nastassja Kinski as Clara, Rolf Hoppe as Father Wieck, Anja-Christine Preussler as young Clara, André Heller as Mendelssohn, Gidon Kremer as Paganini, and Margit Geissler as Christel (Schumann's mistress). The music on the soundtrack was performed by Ivo Pogorelich, Gidon Kremer, and Dietrich Fischer-Dieskau.

The storyline is confined to the eleven years between Schumann's first meeting with young Clara Wieck during his music lessons with her father, and the premiere of his "Spring" Symphony shortly after their marriage. By this time, the film has made it clear that Schumann's selfishness and opportunism will imperil her own career and that the marriage is surely doomed. Earlier, Father Wieck had declared presciently to Robert, "Of course, Clara's fame is convenient for you. You wanted to get to where you never could alone by riding on her back." The corroborating final scenes need to be recounted in detail: We see Schumann and Mendelssohn at the piano working out a concluding passage from the first movement of the "Spring" Symphony. Clara hesitantly enters the room. She is obviously pregnant. "I don't want to disturb you," she says, "I only want to go out for some fresh air." Schumann ignores here and mumbles under his breath, "I just hope our place isn't too small for two grand pianos." Clara freezes in place. "What?" she asks, turning back to Robert.

Cut to the next scene, in the concert hall. Mendelssohn is conducting the "Spring" Symphony while Robert and Clara look on from the box. Robert's words again echo in Clara's mind: "I just hope our place isn't too small for two grand pianos."

This clearly revisionist chronicle doesn't stop there. Clara is seen as the product (and willing victim) of implicitly incestuous relations with her father. Moreover, some viewers might be surprised at the depiction of frank sexuality, between Schumann and "Christel" (the serving girl at the Leipzig tavern) and between Robert and Clara in bed together. Moreover, the film pulls no punches about Robert's excessive drinking in the café, his tortuous nightmares, his self-doubt, and, as has been seen, his ruthless opportunism toward Clara.

A particularly unpleasant scene has Father Wieck unexpectedly entering Schumann's rooms, interrupting a sexual interlude with the maid, Cristel. Hurriedly, the half-naked Cristel conceals herself in the next room, while Schumann (hiding his bare feet) brazenly declares to Wieck his undying love for Clara. Wieck, all unknowing of Cristel's presence, begs Schumann to give up Clara, so she "is not pulled down into the sewer of vulgar passion." How right he is, some viewers might mutter.

The trial scene is quite dramatic and brings out many troublesome issues skirted in the earlier MGM film. "The plaintiff has not only seduced my underaged daughter," declares Father Wieck to the court, "at the same time he has also made advances to another one of my piano pupils, whom I had expressly warned about him. My young, inexperienced daughter is totally blinded by the mystical visions and fantasies of Herr Schumann. In reality she's the poor victim of his hallucinations. The man can only plunge my daughter into misfortune, because he's insane." Cut to Robert and Clara, sitting stiffly, side by side, staring blankly into space. It's a troubling image. "There's no order in his life or his music," continues Wieck. "This man, who wishes to marry my daughter, was required to seek medical treatment for an emotional disturbance. It's also my sad duty to inform Your Lordship that the plaintiff's father died of a neurological disorder and that his sister has serious psychological problems as well and died very young of a mental illness. Would you, Your Lordship, turn your daughter over to a compulsive, degenerate debt-maker, an habitual drunkard?" The film then cuts to the Schumanns' marriage ceremony, with Fischer-Dieskau on the soundtrack singing "Widmung." The sledgehammer irony can hardly be missed.

Indeed, the critics were quick to respond: "[In the conclusion] Schamoni chooses not to emphasize the triumph both Schumanns must surely have felt," writes Michael Wilmington in the *Los Angeles Times,* "but intimations of some unspecified schism (here, it seems less from the impending tragedy than, perhaps, career quarrels). The scene crystallizes the way 'Spring Symphony' frustrates you—not because it's shallow or empty, but because it's so rich with potential that you're continually left wanting more: more passion, more music" ["'Spring' a Fragmented Look at Musical Lovers," April 26, 1986]. Television critic Gary Franklin noted that actor Herbert Grönemeyer portrayed Schumann as "the talented, creative, eccentric nut that he probably was," and cited his sexual and emotion frustrations and "lots of bed-hopping" as appealing to contemporary audiences [appearance on *Eyewitness News* (KABC-TV), May 4, 1986].

Nancy B. Reich

Peter Schamoni, the director of *Spring Symphony,* contacted me, because I think he was concerned about how some of its revisionist scenes would be received by popular audiences. On the one hand, he wanted it very much to be as factual and accurate as possible; on the other hand, he wanted to avoid it being too academic. And he was sort of treading a fine line between the theatrical, the dramatic and the scholarly world. Most of his questions to me were about factual issues. I went over the script and found a number of inaccuracies of names, of children of the Wieck family, Clara's mother, et cetera.

I think he really captured the atmosphere of Leipzig at that time, and the Coffe Baum, the coffeehouse where Schumann met with his friends. Those scenes were accurate and very well done. However, I think certain aspects of the relationship between Clara and her father, especially the incestuous overtones, were totally exaggerated. I had expressed a lot of dismay about that, but of course, I wasn't officially a consultant. I just expressed my feelings, and I guess he felt it was his prerogative as director and producer to make that decision. The end of the film foretells doom for Clara as well as Robert. You feel there are going to be conflicts in the marriage, conflicts between this great superstar of the piano and this struggling composer. That was quite clear.

I thought Nastassja Kinski did a fine job portraying Clara. But I didn't like so much the way Robert Schumann was handled. I think Herbert Grönemeyer was wonderful, and he really resembled the young Schumann. But I felt that Schamoni didn't acknowledge Schumann's true stature as one of Germany's great musicians, great composers and intellects. He made him out so often as a thoughtless, humorless, and womanizing young man. Of course, during his younger years there were many times when he was all of those things; he behaved as most young men do. But he was a great genius, and you don't feel that in the film.

Schumann's Lost Romance

John C. Tibbetts

Schumann's Lost Romance (1996), directed by Steve Ruggi, photographed by Tony Miller, and starring Anton Lesser as Schumann, Anna Farnsworth as Clara, and Vaughan Sivell as Brahms, also partakes of a certain revisionist agenda. Through an unusual combination of fictive narrative reenactments, on-camera interviews, and documentary footage, renowned cellist and Schumann specialist Steven Isserlis leads us in an inquiry into the fantasy glamour of the Schumann story. "Legend tells us that [the Schumanns] had this idyllic marriage until he cracked up and was taken to the asylum," explains Isserlis at the beginning of the film, "But I've always wondered how true that is, how idyllic their marriage was; and indeed how much of a saint she was." Moreover—and this is the heart of the film—why did Clara Schumann destroy the Five Romances for Cello and Piano, some of the last pieces her husband, Robert, ever wrote?

Isserlis invites us to follow him on his journey to seek some answers. His first stop is Bonn-Endenich and the cemetery where both Schumanns are buried. There he interviews historian Nancy B. Reich, Clara's biographer. Reich presents an overview of Robert's first meeting with little Clara, nine years his junior; and how Robert lived for a year with the Wieck family. Next we go to Düsseldorf, where Schumann lived since 1850 and where his career as a musician and composer crumbled. Here's the house on Bilkerstrasse where the young Brahms visited the Schumanns in 1853. Clara and Brahms were left in the house while Robert languished in the asylum. There is no doubt, confirms Dr. Reich, that Brahms was in love with Clara. Next stop: Endenich, near Bonn. Isserlis takes us into the former mental institution and tours the room upstairs where Schumann spent most of his time in the two and a half years he was there. "Legend has it that Schumann's music was traveling down a slippery slope by the time he arrived at Endenich," Isserlis says on camera. "I think that's absolute rubbish." Moreover, alleges Isserlin, Schumann did not die of syphilis, but of self-starvation.

Interspersed throughout this clever travelogue are brief *tableaux-vivants* of incidents in the lives of the historical characters. We see young Schumann rigging up a sling device to strengthen the fingers of his right hand ("God, why did you do this to me?"); Schumann and Brahms and Clara on a picnic (Schumann criticizes her sketch of Brahms: "Don't ever give up the piano"); Schumann and his guests sitting down to a session of table rapping in an attempt to contact Beethoven's spirit ("Music is the only thing that overlaps our world and his world"); Brahms visiting the Schumanns and catching Clara's eye; Schumann's leap into the Rhine and his subsequent rescue by two fishermen; and Brahms in Schumann's Endenich room, kneeling in bewilderment beside Schumann, who is scribbling and blotting writing paper, mumbling names, oblivious to his young friend.

Near the end, we have a key scene when Isserlis steps out of the narrative and conducts an imaginary dialogue with Clara—or with her ghost. In the ensuing conversation, he asks her (Anna Farnsworth) why she destroyed the late Schumann cello/piano romances.

"Remember, Herr Isserlis," Clara replies, "that these are deeply painful memories that you are stirring up so blithely. You have absolutely no conception of the pure flame of love that is my feeling for the noble memory of my husband. If I thought it best not to let ignorant eyes to fall on works conceived at a time of suffering and illness, then it was because I knew that he would have wanted it so."

"But he was actually very fond of the Romances," replies Isserlis, "and so were Brahms and you at the time. He even wrote to Brahms from Endenich about them."

"If you only knew how I suffered, what I went through before each and every discussion concerning my late husband's work, you would not talk with such callous stupidity."

"But that's quite a responsibility to take upon yourself," pursues Isserlis, "to rob the world of some of the last thoughts of one of the great composers."

"As a young man you have not lived long enough to understand this, but sometimes one must take drastic action in order to preserve the things one loves most in life. If I destroyed my husband's work, it is because I knew that the flaws in those pieces would tarnish the reputation which we had so carefully built up together. It's because of our hard work that you now recognize the mastery of those pieces; but in those days perhaps they would not have been received so generously, and my Robert's place in history would have been less secure."

"Lots of pieces were badly received in his time . . . It's the music itself that was going to survive, because it was so great. What was important was the quality of the work."

"Herr Isserlis, I begin to lose patience with you. Would you think I was so foolish that before I burned the original manuscript of the romances, I did not make sure there was a fair copy safely held somewhere? The cello romances are safe, Herr Isserlis, and one day when the time is right, the world will discover them."

"But how does one find them?"

But suddenly, Clara has vanished, leaving him—and us—uncertain and baffled.

Although the fate of the "lost" romances remains unknown, Isserlis's film reflects a growing attitude today that Schumann's late music has been badly misunderstood and undervalued—not just by Clara but by the world in general. Several on-camera testimonies by Isserlis, author John O'Shea (*Music and Medicine*), musicologist Joachim Draheim, violinist Joshua Bell, and conductor Christoph Eschenbach all dispute the claims that Schumann's late music is the product of a disordered mind. Such claims are branded "idiocy." Rather, the late music was the result of Schumann's ongoing exploration of a visionary direction in music.

"I think the craftsmanship of late Schumann is incredible," says Eschenbach, "because he has separated himself from the earlier work, and has become visionary. This is done consciously and produces the most daring harmonic things. Clara did not get it, maybe."

"I don't consider these works to be crazy," confirms Bell. "As you know, Schumann was incredibly emotional. These last works are very extreme and suddenly change from very dramatic to intimate moods. But that was Schumann. I think people are always trying to label him as being crazy instead of being very original."

Finally, Isserlis admits that as a result of his mission to investigate the fate of the cello romances, perhaps his "initial hostility" toward Clara has softened a bit. "It must have been hell for her to go through those difficult times with Schumann. And of course, it's a complicated story." And yet—"But I still find her cold and manipulative. I don't feel she really understood either Schumann or her children."

Steven Isserlis

I appeared in *Schumann's Lost Romance* in 1996. Jan Younghusband, who is now head of music at Channel 4, knew I was interested in working on a film about Schumann. She was then working with Initial TV.

She and the Rhombus Company and Channel 4 asked me if I would like to do a Schumann follow-up to a film I had already done for a television series called *Concerto*. She told me about Steve Ruggi as director, and he came onboard. From the start, Rhombus wanted us to pursue the format of interviews, fictive footage, and documentary location work that had been done in their other films. I can't remember who came up with idea that I appear on camera conducting the tour of Schumann locations. I had not been to some of those locations. We went outside Schumann's house on Bilkerstrasse, but we couldn't go in. There was a cellist living there at the time. At Endenich we went to the second floor, where we think Schumann had his room. It was horrible to see how small it was, and how he must have suffered. I was a bit traumatized, just standing there and thinking about him being stuck there for two and a half years. What an awful way for a great man to end. And that he died by himself. Clara and Brahms had gone to the train station to meet their mutual friend Joseph Joachim. They could have sent somebody else, don't you think? Maybe not. I suppose it didn't make much difference; Schumann may have been unconscious by then. When you read those notes by Dr. Richarz, you realize Schumann was more mad than the letters reveal. It is all endlessly tragic and endlessly touching, because he was such a wonderful man, a good man. What a dreadful way to end.

As I recall, it was my idea to bring in Clara's biographer, Nancy Reich, to talk about Clara. She was the "opposition," you know! Nancy and I don't quite see eye-to-eye on Clara. I can't stand Clara. She was horrible about Liszt, too, even when he was trying to help Robert. Horrible woman. And so cold to her children, it seems. But Nancy put out a good case for her. I know Clara had a bad time with everything, with her father, then with her husband going mad, et cetera. When I read her letters to her children, though, my heart breaks. Sinks! And then I remember what she did to those cello romances! Anyway, Nancy and I got on very well, and we became friends. I did like Anton Lesser as Schumann. And it was a wonderful opportunity to perform with Christoph Eschenbach on the Cello Concerto, which we did pretty close to the other filming. It was my idea to invite him and my friend Josh Bell on the project.

I wasn't all that keen on the final product of the film. If I were doing it now, I would have taken a lot more control over it. I was too "green" then. I don't think people liked the film all that much, except for the scene of my "conversation" with Clara Schumann! I quite enjoyed that! Although the actress had her lines, I couldn't possibly learn a part, so I insisted on improvising and decided to just talk out the scene the way I wanted. In a way, it gave me the opportunity to say to Clara what I would really have wanted to say to her, you know? Don't think I quite lost my grip on reality;

but yes, there was some element of that, I admit! I liked the little twist at the end, which was not my idea, when she gave the camera a little look that implied that she might have saved back a copy. But of course, that's rubbish. Wishful thinking.

I would love to get involved with another film. Certainly, if I had the budget and resources it might be a biopic on Schumann. But it would be *accurate*. You don't have to make anything up with him. I mean, it's *all there,* already. And that suicide scene, in the Rhine, with the rainstorm and the Carnival, it's all there. Pure Hollywood. It was so symbolic that the last symphony he conceived, the "Rhenish," was inspired by the Rhine River. A great director, who really understands music, could do it. As for the other films, I rather like the *Song of Love,* but I didn't care for the rather negative, humorless portrait of Schumann in *Spring Symphony.* Or do I might do a reprise on the radio of my "Words and Music" program with Simon Callow.

Geliebte Clara

John C. Tibbetts

Released in 2008, this film by veteran German director Helma Sanders-Brahms, allegedly a distant relation to Johannes, has created a considerable stir among Schumann enthusiasts. Featuring the noted German actress Martina Gedeck (*The Lives of Others*) as Clara, Pascal Greggory as Robert, and Malik Zidi as Brahms, it is not only the first film to depict a frankly sensuous relationship between Clara and the young Brahms (see Tony Palmer's 1996 biopic, *Brahms and the Little Singing Girls*), but its revisionist portrait of Schumann during the Düsseldorf years as an abusive alcoholic addicted to laudanum—Greggory's gaunt features and stiff, repellent manner create a decidedly unsympathetic characterization—has raised the ire of a few historians, including Nancy B. Reich. At least one critic has been positive, however. "Gedeck gives Clara a grounded quality that serves the role well," writes *Variety,* "and she's especially convincing in her piano-playing scenes. Co-star Greggory is stuck in the thankless role of Schumann, with no real chance to show his pre-madness personality, while Zidi expectedly steals the show as Brahms."

The story spans the Schumann family's arrival in Düsseldorf in 1850, when Robert takes up his new post as music director, and concludes with Robert's death and Clara's subsequent resolve to return to the concert platform. The story proper begins with Clara taking her bows after a performance of Robert's A-Minor Piano Concerto. Among the admirers is young Brahms. When the absentminded Robert drops his wedding ring from his balcony seat, the young man catches it—a not-so-subtle premonition of the role that Brahms will play a few years later. A few moments later, the Schumanns meet young Brahms when they drop in to a café, where he is lustily playing themes from his unpublished B-Minor Piano Trio. Heedless of the youth, Schumann leaves rather huffily, sneering at the "rabble" in attendance. Weeks later, during his first rehearsal with his new orchestra, his conducting of the first movement of the newly composed "Rhenish" Symphony is interrupted by auditory hallucinations that distract him so much that he loses track of the players altogether. Clara is forced to step in as a substitute conductor. The players' scorn quickly abates when she shows her mettle. Later, during the premiere of the work, she stands beside Robert on the podium as *both* conduct. Life at home, meanwhile, is plagued by Robert's drinking and increasing use of laudanum to forestall worsening bouts of headaches and tinnitus. One terrifying episode in their wine cellar finds him attacking Clara when she attempts to stop him from swilling down another bottle. He brutally slaps her, sending her flying against the wall.

The only bright spot in this domestic turmoil is the arrival of young Brahms. On the one hand, the boisterous youth captivates the children with his clownish handstands and somersaults; on the other, his open admiration for Clara irritates Robert, who immediately takes his measure and suspects him as a rival for her affections. Soon he is installed as a regular member of the household. Reluctantly, Robert is won over

Room interior, Robert-Schumann-Haus, Zwickau, Germany.

by Brahms's music. He announces to a postconcert party that the youth indeed holds out a bright promise for new German music.

While Robert struggles to complete the "Rhenish" Symphony—this seems to be the only work he is composing during the Düsseldorf years—Brahms is more and more openly flirtatious with the oddly ambivalent Clara. Schumann is too preoccupied with his own problems to take much notice. Finally, during Fasching celebrations, Robert, clad only in dressing gown and slippers, joins a crowd of costumed celebrants. "I should get dressed to leave the house," he shouts to them, "but since it's Carnival, I will wear my dressing gown as if it were a king's robe!" He leads the merry group to the bridge spanning the Rhine. He takes off his ring and presses it into the hand of a friend. "Please hand this to my wife with my kind regards," he mumbles. Then, laughing crazily, Robert plunges into the Rhine.

Back home, rescued from the river by fishermen, Robert can only groan, "I was in the Rhine, but not even he wanted me. . . . I jumped off the bridge . . . but it means nothing." At Robert's request, Dr. Richarz arrives from nearby Endenich. "If I cannot heal him, I'll have to close my institute," he mutters grimly. Against Clara's protests, Robert stiffly accompanies him to a waiting carriage. In the hospital, the doctor and his attendants shave Robert's head and in a gruesome scene apply a drill to relieve pressure on the brain. The sight that greets a nervous Clara on her last visit to the hospital is of a pathetic, wordless wreck slumped against the wall. Silently, she feeds him jelly from her fingers, while he attempts a few broken words.

In the immediate aftermath of Robert's death, Clara takes to her bed. Brahms comes to her and lies beside her. "I can't do this," she murmurs. "Who wouldn't want you to?" replies Brahms. She replies, "Robert, my children, the whole world. . . ." Brahms loosens her blouse and pursues, "Finally, I'm allowed to see my forbidden paradise. . . . I will sleep with other women but not ever with you; and with every one of them, it will be only *you* that I hold in my arms, to the end of my days. I will wait until you die and I will follow you. I will be with you in the Kingdom of Shadows, and I will lead you to him." The scene fades out as he caresses her breast.

In the epilogue, as in the beginning, Clara is once more at the piano. But this time she is playing the tortured strains of Brahms's First Piano Concerto, while Brahms stands by. End titles inform us that the two remained close friends for the rest of their days, dying only a few years apart.

Nancy B. Reich

Recently, I took the opportunity at the Museum of Modern Art in New York to see a new film, *Geliebte Clara* (Beloved Clara). I shall only mention it in passing, because the less said about it the better. The audience that night seemed very excited about the screening. But I was very upset, even angry, at the lies and errors in the film. In my opinion, the filmmakers seemed to know very little about Brahms and the Schumanns. Robert was portrayed as a weak and ill character, and Brahms was seen as just a kid who fell in love with Clara. It concluded with a graphic love scene between her and Brahms after Robert had died. It seemed like many in the audience enjoyed that, but it had nothing to do with the historical facts we know. I can only hope it will not have a release in America. Most people don't know about the Schumann–Brahms story and might assume what they're seeing is the truth.

Helma Sanders-Brahms

My film has been many years in gestation, going back to before the year 2000. My first choice in the casting was Daniel Day-Lewis as Schumann, Isabelle Huppert as Clara, and Jeremy Renner as Brahms. Claudio Abbado was going to conduct the Berlin Philharmonic. The maestro even thought at one point to portray Schumann himself, but I think he grew too impatient with the time-consuming delays in the shooting! Daniel intended to coproduce the film, but finances collapsed when the head of Babelsberg Studios, Rainer Schaper (who had also worked on Polanski's *The Pianist*), died. We were at a loss. The new studio chief wanted only to make a silly Hollywood kind of commercial film. We thought he had "Hollywood raisins in his head." So at that point everything collapsed. But I am happy now with the results after many years and with this cast. I know some critics have attacked the film for how I imagined some of the scenes between Clara and Brahms. But others have liked the film very much. I had already known about another German film, *Träumerei*, which had been made in 1944. It was very conventional, not political at all. It was the basis for the later Hollywood version, *Song of Love*. I feel that pain is the real basis for the story of these three people. I am fascinated with that darker side of Schumann, his moods and depressions; and how Clara suffered in those last years, all the while being loyal to him and his music; and the role Brahms played in protecting her and the family. All that is true.

Twin Spirits

John C. Tibbetts

Twin Spirits is a staged theatrical event devised and directed by John Caird for the Royal Opera House, Covent Garden and recorded on a subsequent 2009 DVD release on the Opus Arte label. The program begins with introductory remarks by Sir Derek Jacobi. Grouped around him, seated and standing, by turns, are the principals—Sting reading Robert's letters, Trudie Styler reading Clara's letters, and baritone Simon Keenlyside and soprano Rebecca Evans singing songs by Robert and Clara. Members of the accompanying chamber ensemble are pianists Iain Burnside and Natasha Paremski, violinist Sergej Krylov, and cellist Natalie Clein. Against a dark backdrop, the faces of Sting, Styler, and Jacobi are starkly captured in tight close-ups, the camera angles deftly grouping them in a variety of frontal and angle-reverse-angle positions. Save from a tearful outburst from Styler during Clara's recollection of Robert's death, the emotional register is moderate and restrained. Jacobi's brief interpolations include an affecting reading of Grillparzer's famous 1838 tribute letter to Clara. Apart from the expected excerpts from familiar music from *Kinderszenen* and *Dichterliebe,* there are choice gems of relatively unheard music: Rebecca Evans sings Clara's "Sie liebten sich beide," Op. 13, and Natasha Paremski plays the romance from her A-Minor Piano Concerto. Simon Keenlyside sings several of Robert's songs, including two Kerner songs (the valedictory, sweet melancholy of "Stille Liebe" from 1840 and the waking ecstasy of "Stille Tränen" and two Dichterliebe songs ("Wenn ich in deine Augen seh" and "Ich grolle nicht"). He and Evans also sing two duets, the "Là ci darem la mano" and Robert's charming "Er und Sie," Op. 78. Concluding the program is an exuberant performance by the piano trio of the finale to Robert's D-Minor Trio.

There are a few inaccuracies in the timeline and omissions in the story. The program begins with Robert and Clara's first meeting in 1830, although they had met more than a year prior to that. Conflicts in the marital relationship and hints of the controversies attending the Brahms/Clara relationship are discreetly omitted. I suspect some of the letters have been radically altered from their original sources. Robert's confession to Clara of his disturbed mental state, for example, smacks more of the scenarist's invention than any authentic source.

These are mere quibbles. *Twin Spirits* is a careful and loving musical and dramatic tribute featuring an ensemble of artists obviously committed to the story. "I was thrilled to be asked to narrate *Twin Spirits* about Robert and Clara Schumann," says Sir Derek. "It was so beautiful, and some of the music on it, which I hadn't really known before, I found very affecting." ("Music That Changed Me," *BBC Music Magazine* (November 2009): 122.)

[Note: Included in a second disc is an extensive on-camera commentary by Gerd Nauhaus, former director of the Schumann-Haus in Zwickau, about Schumann's life and work.]

THE 2010 BICENTENARY YEAR

Thomas Synofzik

The year 2010 will be dedicated to "Robert Schumann in Zwickau." We began our schedule of events in January 21–24 with a symposium and concert series, "Musik und Dichtung," which brought here to the Schumann-Haus scholars and musicians from all over the world. Next is our central event from June 4 to June 12, a "Schumann-fest," where there will be a stage performance of Schumann's opera *Genoveva,* a performance on period instruments of his Piano Quartet and Piano Quintet by the La Gaia Scienza ensemble of Milano, and appearances by artists such as Jun Märkl, Hélène Grimaud, and Daniel Barenboim. Several other smaller festivals will be held throughout the year, including competitions for pianists in April, choirs in October, and a public viewing of the most famous Schumann films in August. There will also be concerts with chamber and piano music in the Robert-Schumann-Haus every fortnight on Saturdays or Sundays.

Steven Isserlis

I was asked to perform Schumann's Cello Concerto in Zwickau for the Bicentenary Year on June 8, the very day of Schumann's 200th birthday. But I'm already scheduled to be in Hong Kong. That's too bad. But there is a big tour of Australia doing all-Schumann this summer [2009]. The next time I play the concerto is this fall in Leipzig. But I've got lots of performances of it next year, including the first two Piano Trios at the Salzburg Festival and my cello version of the Third Violin Sonata. And I can always hope that somehow a copy of those lost romances might surface, somewhere. Maybe even in Australia?! You know, the cellist for whom they were written lived in Adelaide for a time . . .

Epilogue

A Word with Dietrich Fischer-Dieskau

EDITOR'S NOTE
This interview dates from a master class given by Dr. Fischer-Dieskau in Düsseldorf on June 12, 1991. Maestro Fischer-Dieskau spoke in English.

Here at my master classes in Düsseldorf, the students have my book about Schumann [*Robert Schumann: Wort und Musik,* 1981]. When they come here it is important that they have some biographical background. They of course should know a lot. I try always to mix into the lessons some materials, some news about Schumann himself. And for the songs, they must know the piano music and of course the poetry of the texts. It's never enough, of course, because you have to also have *Fantasie,* the heart and the imagination, for Schumann. For Schumann that is the most important thing. Analyzing the music is not my task in this special field. I think that they can have from other people. My goal is the interpretation. So I have to tell them how to approach this music. And I show them, too. They must have the proper physical posture and have the proper way to hold the head. It's very difficult, of course. A combination of voice and interpretation is important. In former times, some of the lieder singers when they started had interpretation but didn't have a beautiful voice, which restricted them. And you must do both lieder and opera. I tell them they have better careers when they sing both.

I am very much involved in the Researching Center here in Düsseldorf. They are now publishing all the works, the *"Skizzen,"* all designs, everything that is there, so that the reader has a real chance to follow the way of the compositions. That has been done in the first Schubert *Gesamtausgabe.*

Schumann has always been a special composer for me. Always was. My voice teacher at the academy in Berlin in the beginning was Professor Weissenborn. No, this was not *Gunther* Weissenborn, who played piano for me in the early days. I'm talking about *Hermann* Weissenborn, who was a pupil of Muller, who was a pupil of Julius Stockhausen, who sang Schumann's songs with Clara Schumann. So I had a rather direct relation

Dietrich Fischer-Dieskau and Frau Dr. Gisela Schaefer of the Schumann Gesellschaft, Düsseldorf.

to these people! And I learned a lot about controlling the breath and interpretation at that time. I always sang Schumann. Always. Very important for me. My very first recital at age seventeen was *Dichterliebe*. And I sang him during my prisoner years in 1945, when I sang in the open air and in the hospitals, all over Italy. The prisoners of war were hungry for music. The different camps had different people. There sometimes were only twenty, sometimes over a hundred filling a big tent, or a hall. And at that time, even before coming back to Germany, I think I always was nervous. But that's always part of the interpretation . . .

If the world had not the German lied, we all would be much poorer. Now I think there is not so much interest. Maybe it depends or goes together with a loss in interest in reading, generally. Maybe. If you don't read lyrics and if you don't read the great poets, the German ones, then you have not so much interest in the lied. They go together.

But in the end we will not know what kind of man Schumann was. And it is good that we will not know. It's the same case with Mozart. We will have no idea how he managed to do what he did. And that's for a genius the best way. . . .

Appendix

In the Workshop

Commentators: *Marin Alsop, Edmund Battersby, Victoria Bond, Ronald Brautigam, Katherine Ciesinski, John Daverio, Jörg Demus, Christoph von Dohnányi, Christoph Eschenbach, Vladimir Feltsman, Malcolm Frager, Claude Frank, Peter Frankl, Richard Goode, Thomas Hampson, Steven Isserlis, Eugene Istomin, Hans-Joachim Köhler, Roe-Min Kok, Svyatoslav Levin, Susan McClary, John Nelson, Garrick Ohlsson, Peter F. Ostwald, Elizabeth Paley, Leon Plantinga, Nancy B. Reich, Erika Reiman, Charles Rosen, Eric Sams, Wolfgang Sawallisch, Samuel Sanders, András Schiff, Richard Stoltzman, R. Larry Todd, Sarah Walker, John Worthen, Peter Zazofsky, Thomas Zehetmair, David Zinman, and Eugenia Zukerman*

A SELECTION OF CONTRIBUTORS' TESTIMONIES, BIOGRAPHIES, AND RESEARCH INTERESTS

Marin Alsop

I grew up playing the violin, and the first piece I fell in love with was Schumann's Piano Quartet. I would play it with my father, Lamar Alsop, who was a violist, and my mother, Ruth, a cellist. My father was concertmaster of the New York City Ballet for thirty years, and my mother still plays in the orchestra at the age of eighty! Together with our friend Seymour Bernstein, a phenomenal pianist and pedagogue, we would play the Piano Quartet as our "party" piece. I think I was eleven or twelve the first time we played it together.

I wouldn't say this was my stepping stone to "stardom," but it was a wonderful introduction to chamber music in general and to Schumann in particular. At the same time, I realized there are symphonic implications in the Piano Quartet—the incredible lyricism, the poignancy of the melodic materials, and the abundance of counterpoint—that are all hallmarks of his writing which have helped prepare me for the experience of the symphonies.

In addition to my duties these days with the Baltimore Symphony Orchestra and the Colorado Symphony, I have found working with Scott Simon on NPR's *Weekend Edition* has been a wonderful experience.

Earlier, I used to work with Martin Goldsmith on *Performance Today,* and then I started doing little pieces about particular works; and then that graduated to the work with Scott. We have a great rapport. Typically, I'll e-mail him idea suggestions and we go from there. Another wonderful spokesperson for this kind of broadcast outreach is Bill McGlaughlin on the WFMT Network. I came to the Eugene Symphony two music directors after Bill. You know, I have absolutely no business doing this sort of thing, I have no background and no professional training in broadcasting; so as long as people cut me some slack, I'm happy to do it. You don't have to do any "dumbing-down" for these broadcasts. And I'm always impressed how curious people are, how intelligent they are, and how educated they want to become. I'm a good friend of Eugenia Zukerman and have worked many times with her at Vale. We met when she was doing *CBS Sunday Morning* and she did a piece on me. We hit it off immediately. We're both pretty irreverent types!

I have been lucky enough to receive several honors. From an artistic point of view, the BBC 3 Listeners' Award was very gratifying, because it is based on listeners' input. Having done so many broadcasts on the BBC during my tenure with the Bournemouth Symphony and the London Symphony, that was a real vote of confidence. It's very important to reach out to as wide an audience as possible. But then, on a more personal level, it was the MacArthur Award in 2005 [Note: The John D. and Catherine T. MacArthur Foundation Award]. It's such a prestigious honor, and it comes from out of the blue. You don't know you're even being considered. It was such a surprise. And the cash award, $500,000 over five years with no strings attached, was a real vote of confidence at the time when I wanted to get more involved in educational programs. It has enabled me to spearhead several initiatives. With the Baltimore Symphony I was able to launch the Orch-Kids project in West Baltimore, an extensive after-school program, in places where the schools have very strong needs. I've been working with first graders, and they're already playing instruments after half a year. It's very rewarding. After all the publicity of that phenomenal television series *The Wire,* you go to these places and you feel like you're in one of the sets for that series! One time at the Beautification Day we filled an entire trash bag with shards of glass. This is not the way children in America should be having to live. So I hope this program offers them a sense of possibility. In my position you try to be a citizen of the planet and get rid of this elitist label of classical music.

In my travels I've been able to visit some Schumann sites. In Düsseldorf I remember conducting the "Rhenish" Symphony at the Tonhalle. I mean, the Rhine is flowing there right nearby! I went for a run along the Rhine, and I couldn't help thinking that I was retracing some of the same path that Schumann took when he made that suicidal run for the pontoon bridge. I took advantage of the places where he lived. I visited the house on Bilkerstrasse where Brahms came in 1853 to meet Schumann. I stood there at the door and suddenly felt I was back there in that moment, when he and Clara listened to Brahms. There must have been such renewal and possibility then. And I thought about the special relationship Schumann and his wife had together. Absolutely fascinating, but it must have been filled with stresses. Unfortunately, I did not make it to the Endenich asylum.

Edmund Battersby

I suppose I am known primarily for my love of the fortepiano. I have recorded many pieces from the romantic repertoire on my replica of an 1824 Graf piano. My early training was with Barbara Holmquist, a pupil of Carl Friedberg, who had been a pupil of Clara Schumann. After I finished high school I studied at Juilliard with Sascha Gorodnitzki, an experience which was very different from the Holmquist years, I can tell you! Although I frequently play and record the fortepiano, it is just part of my education. I play new music also and have a special interest in Spanish keyboard music. I don't like to think of myself as a specialist in any particular area.

Victoria Bond

There had not been any staged professional performances of Schumann's *Genoveva* in America prior to my performance in June 1987 at Bel Canto Opera. That seems truly amazing, right? I mean, that kind of neglect is staggering. There've been concert performances, and the overture has been performed numerous times, but never the entire work staged. Incomprehensible.

Somewhere along the line in your own studies, did somebody hesitate to recommend you to conduct? Did they say that this is a rough world for a woman to conduct in, and why is that?

Well, yes, indeed, in answer to the first question, it is a rough world for anybody. It's rough because there are no guarantees. I mean, you don't get a degree at conservatory and have a job guaranteed at the other end. It's a risky business, but very exhilarating because you are gambling on something you believe in. I don't gamble on the lottery, but I do gamble on myself—and yes, there were people all along the line who said forget it, I mean—"You're just—there has never been anyone before, there has never been any woman before that is currently doing what you want to be doing." You see, I like very much destroying preconceived ideas about what an artist is, what a conductor is, what a composer is; I think it's lots of fun to break down those kinds of stereotyped images. I was once doing an interview and someone said, "What does it feel like to be a woman conductor?" and I hesitated for a moment, and I said, "Well, to tell you the truth, I don't know the alternative." So, you know, for me it's natural, it's normal.

You have your top 100, you know, favorite operas that everybody likes to hear—probably even smaller than 100, if we're really going to take a hard look at it—and most of the companies around this country, with the exception of one or two that are very adventurous, produce the same operas every year. Now, there's nothing wrong with those operas, they're wonderful operas, I love to hear them time and time again, they're like a beautiful jewel that you get more out of every time you look at it. But the thing is that the season of the American opera companies is rather limited, both in terms of the number of months out of the year that they perform, and the number of performances within each month. So if they're going to give five or six productions a year, they are going to give productions of, you know, surefire box office hits because, face it, government subsidy in this country is not what it really should be, and they have to put together their foundation with what they get from box office.

Ronald Brautigam

My first Schumann piece was the *Arabeske,* which I learned when I was eleven years old. I didn't really do more than one or two of the *Kinderszenen.* Luckily, not long after that, my teacher at the time had the good sense to also introduce me to the *Waldszenen.* It is still one of my very favorite Schumann sets, and it brought me to a lifelong understanding of his later piano works.

My father used to be a very good amateur pianist. He's ninety-one now. I was brought up with the sound of a piano in my ears. I was not pushed to be a prodigy. I had a very normal childhood. My parents insisted that I finish my high school, and then if I still wanted to be a musician, that was all right. Actually, I didn't practice all that much. My first teacher was a private teacher, and she was old enough that as a child I thought she was about 120 years old, or so! Her name was Annie Salomons. I was with her from six years old. And she helped prepare me for the conservatory when I was seventeen. She had a great influence on me. It wasn't so much that she taught my fingers—I seem to have been born with quite a good set of fingers—what she did was what she called the "consciousness of making music." I understand that now; it's finding what's behind the notes. At the conservatory I studied with Jan Wijn, and I was with him for seven years. Then I got a scholarship to spend time with

Rudolf Serkin, which was quite an eye-opener for me, I must say. We met many times informally, backstage, in hotel rooms, wherever we could get together. At the conservatory I was very much interested in composing, but luckily, that didn't happen.

It was with the *Arabeske* that I first realized something very typical of Schumann. I could never actually figure out where the melody was and where was the accompaniment. A note might seem to be in the melody, but then you see it's part of the accompaniment. Music like this can be very busy, in that the melody might be on top, somewhere in the middle, or on the bottom. I liked that about it. I just loved playing him, trying to find out where the melody goes!

I live now in Amsterdam, right in the center. This was where I was born and where I will stay. Between now [April 2009] and July I'll be traveling all the time. I have a wife and four cats, and that's about all I can handle! At the moment I'm preparing for three concerts in Finland next week. We're doing Haydn and Mendelssohn concertos. It's been a very rich Mendelssohn Year so far. I've done a lot of recitals and concerto performances. I will play the Schumann Piano Concerto quite a lot in the coming Schumann Bicentenary Year. But right now I'm still in the middle of the Beethoven project. I've finished recording all the sonatas, and the second installment of the piano concertos will come out on the modern piano. And I still have to record all the variations and piano pieces, which are still another eight CDs. I'm using my two fortepianos for those. I put them in the back of my car. You need one of these seven-seater family cars. The Graf is too big for me, but it is brought over to me from Prague.

Katherine Ciesinski

I recorded a group of Clara Schumann songs with bass baritone John Ostendorf for Leonardo Records in 1981. It was a new label at that time. The executive producer was Marnie Hall, the violist who I had met in New York and at various pickup orchestras and festivals. She started this record company, basically single-handedly, and as time has gone on, she's managed to get quite a nice library of recordings together. John Ostendorf was instrumental in bringing all the forces together to make our own recording happen. Through Marni's research and inspiration we rounded up a lot of material by four women composers of the nineteenth century—Fanny Mendelssohn, the sister of Felix; Josephine Lang; Clara Schumann; and Pauline Viardot Garcia. John and I split the recording between us and recorded isolated lieder of these wonderful, talented ladies. It was a great joy and a revelation to me, because I just had not taken the time before to pursue this particular repertoire. Some of Clara's songs remain unpublished to this day, as far as I'm aware, and I am pretty sure that Fanny Mendelssohn got some of hers published in her lifetime.

There's a real resurgence of this kind of research, going back into these ladies' lives and into their music. I think back in the nineteenth century, women were certainly still seen and not heard from, for the greater proportion of the time. But Clara and Robert had a special artistic relationship that really complemented their marriage and their love for each other. And I think Robert was very solicitous of Clara in getting her works published and some with his own Op. 37.

John Daverio

I came to know Schumann and his music in strange ways. By training I'm a violinist, and the first music I got to know was playing in an orchestra. And I have to say as a teenager playing in various orchestras that Schumann was not my favorite composer to play. But when I played the First Violin Sonata, which is a fairly late work, I grew very fond of it. That was without really knowing very much about his life, the biography, the controversies, et cetera. What I'm trying to say is the seeds to my scholarly reaction to the later Schumann were planted earlier when I didn't know how controversial this music is. Now, what I try to do as a Schumann scholar is to try to separate out from the music what we know about all the terrible things that befell him. Let's try not to prejudice ourselves with our knowledge of that when we try to evaluate the music itself. And I've found this very unusual and interesting thing—that the very same qualities in the late music can be taken in either a positive or negative way. I'm certainly not the first person who has attempted to reevaluate Schumann's late works. This effort was already under way in Germany twenty to twenty-five years ago by two German scholars, Reinhard Kapp and Michael Struck. In part, what I have tried to do was synthesize and take into account some of the leads in their work and add my own thoughts.

Jörg Demus

I have the most delightful anecdote about working with Elly Ameling. We were invited by the Italian Radio-Television for a very elegant concert in one of the most beautiful palaces of the whole world in Venice, a kind of elaborate salon with silk-covered walls and candlelight. And we were to do Schumann and Schubert. I would play some piano pieces, and she would sit in lovely silk dress in a rococo chair. Then she would get up and sing. Let's say, I would play a *Moment Musical,* and she would sing "An die Musik" [To Music], and so on and on. Well, she had this lovely décolleté, and the technicians from the radio planted one of those big, old-fashioned microphones in the front of her décolleté, just to catch every vibration of her vocal cords. She said, "This couldn't be." They said, "We are paying for this concert, and therefore you have to accept what we say!" So, fine, here came the clarinetist, and we made the proof recording in the afternoon before the concert, so that they should get the balance. So I play my preludes, the clarinetist plays his preludes, and Elly opens her mouth and sings. But she is singing very LOUDLY! I look at Elly, and I think, "Is she mad?" She just twinkles back at me. She knows what she is doing! So, the technicians race out, draw the microphone a little farther away. But she continues to shout and shout and shout, until the microphone is removed from the décolleté. The rehearsal is finished.

Christoph von Dohnányi

I first became acquainted with the Schumann symphonies while I was in Berlin before the war, attending concerts by Wilhelm Furtwängler. Later, of course, on the other side of the ocean, I heard George Szell conduct Schumann many times. I quickly realized that Schumann did not fit comfortably into our concept of the so-called "romantic school," which sometimes people think means highly emotional and anti-intellectual. This music is neither only one or the other. There's a famous statement by Beethoven, when he says, in effect, "My music will be listened to with a brain." Schumann, of course, was a highly intellectual man, which certainly doesn't mean that he didn't have emotions. But he, like so many other romantics in Germany and France were very, very highly intellectual people. Furtwängler, of course, knew this. He never would be carried away by the emotions. Instead, he was very attentive to the *form* in Schumann. And that is a different issue, which brings with it its own challenges.

Last summer in London [1986], as preparation for my recordings, I did a lot of reading by and about Schumann, and about how his symphonies have been interpreted. And I got a hold of Peter Ostwald's biography, which I can tell you made me very jittery, because the pain of the composer was so real to me. I knew I would have to come to terms with Dr. Szell's own versions, in which he had made many retouchings and changes. And when I returned to Cleveland, I decided to use fresh parts, without the markings that Dr. Szell had made. And although the players already know this music well, we worked as if we had never heard it before. We question everything.

Christoph Eschenbach

As we speak, we are just now in Düsseldorf [June 1991], where I will do a Schumann Marathon at the Tonhalle on Saturday. That means about eight or even nine hours of Schumann solo and chamber music. We just had a press conference where we reflected on why one should do marathons and why not—and how they are done, and so on. The day and evening will be arranged with a few breaks, so people can come and go as they please. I will moderate the marathon.

Schumann and Bach have always been my first favorites, since I was a little child. Mozart came much later. But Schumann was very dear to me from the beginning of my musical thinking. And of course I've played a lot of Schumann, made recordings of a lot of Schumann (including my first recording for Deutsche Grammophone), and accompanied Fischer-Dieskau in Schumann's songs. I am now performing a lot of the symphonic music—all the symphonies, along with lesser-known pieces like the *Faust Scenes* and the overtures to *Genoveva* and *Die Braut von Messina*, the *Overture, Scherzo, Finale*. For example, I often do the *Bride of Messina*, because I love the piece. It's a great piece. It comes off well for the audience. It's very exciting, with an incredible, mysterious introduction, followed by a great, dramatic storm. It's a strong piece. All the orchestras I come to do not know this piece. In fact, most of them have never played it, including the Berlin Philharmonic and the Boston Symphony! It's amazing that these pieces like this which are so good are still not known at all. So I fight for them a bit. I care very much for them, and I want other people to love them, too. You know, there is great prejudice against some of these works, and the marathon will address that.

Vladimir Feltsman

I have played a lot of Schumann's music since my childhood. In speaking about Schumann, we're speaking about the highest point in romantic music. We who play piano are very lucky to have a number of major works by him. It's mostly beautiful music, and it's very well written for piano. It's joyful to play it, even in the physical sense of the word. However, I don't think of him as the greatest composer in the world, of course not. He reaches a point where he fails to continue. If I may make the comparison, he's like a beautiful flower which begins to die before it reaches its full bloom. He is the most beautiful flower of the romantic school, but he's dying already. At the highest point of his life he is already dying. Maybe that sounds a little mystical, but it's very clear to me. It was not so long ago—five or six years—that I learned the *Symphonic Etudes*. I chose to play them for my Carnegie Hall debut for the second half of the program. For the first half I played Schubert's little A Major Sonata, quite beautiful, but nothing much really going on. And there were also three pieces by Messiaen. The Schumann is a beautiful work, a very important work. Besides, it was something "meaty," as you would say, for the public; and it reaches a very exciting climax. The audience loved it, and they gave me a standing applause.

Malcolm Frager

You can trace my interest in Schumann—and my subsequent discovery of the original version of the A-Minor Piano Concerto [see Frager's account in the "Piano Music" chapter in this book]—with my first studies with Carl Friedberg in New York from 1949 until he died in 1955. He himself had studied with Clara Schumann! He was a very great teacher, not just a good teacher. And what I mean by that is that he was very inspired and helped his pupils to really gain a deeper conviction of what music meant in human life, what each individual composition had to say, what the composers really wanted to put across; but he never was involved very much in the discussion of technical matters, in problems involving the development of the fingers.

I first met him in Kansas City. My parents sent me here to take a series of lessons which he was giving at that time at the University of Kansas City (as it was then called). I was only thirteen. I was very impressed with what he knew, and whom he had known, and I wanted very much to go and study with him in New York. And my parents said, "Well, are you sure you want to go away from home so young?" And I said, "Yes, I want to go to New York and study with him." So they had a consultation with my teacher in St. Louis, which was my hometown, and he said, "No, you should really send Malcolm instead to Philadelphia to study with Rudolf Serkin, who has since become a very close friend." But I said at that time, "No, I want to go to New York, and I won't go anywhere else!" It's quite amazing, because I was only fourteen, and yet I knew exactly what I wanted to do. And finally my parents agreed, and my father—I think in those days there weren't too many airplanes—took the train up to New York and arranged for me to live with a family and go to a tutoring school. And the next September I went up to New York and started studying, and I never have regretted that I made that decision.

I was just twenty-five or so when I won the Leventritt and the Queen Elisabeth. It was the first time anyone had won both. The Leventritt isn't held anymore. That's when I really began touring and playing more extensively in public. Performing in competitions can be quite horrendous. The atmosphere is a very intense one, and I think in large measure one's success is determined by the way one psychologically meets the challenge of performing under pressure. Now, I'll tell you what happened to me. I had participated in a number of competitions, and hadn't really been too happy with the results, either with the way I played, or with the way I thought I was recognized, and finally I saw that I was going into those competitions in order to get something, in order to get a prize. Now, this should not be the motive of any artist. An artist should go onstage to give something, to share something, to communicate something. So I spent quite some time pondering that, and I reached the conclusion that the fear of participating in a competition is largely the fear of what you think others are going to think of you. And I decided that instead of going into the competition, which at the particular time was the Leventritt competition in New York City, with a desire to get a prize, recognition, concerts, or whatever—I would just play those pieces that I truly believed in, to the best of my ability. And I kept fighting with myself, and reminding myself that my job was not to get but to give. Now, that's a very simple thought, but it helped me to feel free when I played at that competition. And I'm sure that the success which I enjoyed was the result of coming to grips with those underlying issues. And the same was true the following year when I went to Belgium. Not everyone who has a busy career has been involved in competitions. It is one way to be heard, yes. And for some people it is an important thing. It was very important to me at the time. But I'm sure it's not the only way to establish a career. There are many other ways, too, and there probably are ways that no one's even thought of yet.

Like I say, I want to perform those things that I really believe in. For example, I'm very fond of the father of the entire romantic era, Carl Maria von Weber. He was born in 1786 and died the year before Beethoven, in 1826. A few years ago I recorded his two piano concertos, and I've played two of the four piano sonatas and a number of other works that he wrote for piano. I am very fond of Weber because he was an original thinker and expressed what he had to say in a way that no one else had ever done up until that moment. Now, some people think of Weber as old-fashioned and slightly superficial. I think this is a mistake. He had a tremendous influence on the entire nineteenth century, and even someone like Debussy said that Weber was the greatest composer of the nineteenth century. Wagner all his life was trying to write a German opera that would equal those of *Der Freischütz*. And I've seen a great many of the other Weber operas, *Oberon* and even some unknown works, like *Abu Hassan* and *Peter Schmoll.*

I have a son who's now fifteen, and if you asked me if I would send him to New York to study, I would say no. But New York isn't the same today as it was in 1949. I wouldn't send a fifteen-year-old child alone to New York today. And to whom you would send someone, at any age, is a very difficult question, because it's hard to know just which teacher is the right teacher for an individual student. You have to judge in each case what it is that the student needs to learn, and what the best environment for him would be. It is very important to find a teacher that you really believe in, that you really trust. It's not the same as a marriage, of course, but you can see some parallels. There are some elements of a teacher–student relationship which are comparable—the sharing of confidence, and the ability to allow complete freedom. A teacher should never restrict a pupil, should never hold the pupil in his control. The entire mission of the teacher is to enable the student eventually to become his own teacher.

Claude Frank

Like so many pianists, I came to Schumann through Beethoven and Schubert. I suppose many people think of me first with the music of Beethoven and Schubert, but Schumann has always been a great personal favorite. I started on the piano at age six with a teacher in Nuremberg, Germany, my hometown. The piano was in the living room. From that time I took lessons very seriously. At age eleven, I played for Artur Schnabel, who was in Italy at the time. He said to my mother, "Yes, this is serious; there's no reason why the boy shouldn't pursue this as a life." I was not at all nervous. Nervousness came in much later, in leaps and bounds! I practiced my stuff and I knew instinctively that Schnabel would recognize something of value that was there, whether I made mistakes or not. For better or for worse, I still feel that way with audiences. That's why I do allow for clinkers, because I feel the message of the music comes through, no matter what. The perfect surface for me is not an end. You can call that sour grapes; or maybe it's because I'm not capable. It may be. Anyway, to get back to Schnabel for a moment, I wasn't worried about making mistakes. I probably did. I played a Schubert impromptu for him. Again, I was too young to be frightened. I was eleven. And I heard Schnabel played Beethoven. When it was over he said immediately, "Another piece," so I played a Beethoven rondo, which I had heard on a recording by Schnabel; and I tried to play it exactly as he did. He said to my mother, "Yes, there's no reason why he shouldn't make music his life, and I recommend that he'll be with me eventually, but he's still too young. For four or five years he should study with one of my most advanced pupils." I wasn't supposed to know this at the time—this was all very old-fashioned and very European, and children weren't supposed to listen in on plans for their future. He recommended one in Paris. And that's what we did! It was a good time to leave, anyway, for political reasons (Hitler and all). I studied with this French pupil of his, who died during the war. But Hitler also saw to it that we left France. So, three years later, in 1941, I am fifteen, and it was time to knock on Schnabel's door. And I said, "Here I am." I also studied for years with his son, Karl Ulrich, except for my time in the army during the war.

I have a photograph of Schnabel in my studio. I have to admit, I do feel Schnabel's spirit when I play. As Schumann says in his "Aphorisms," "Always play as if a master were listening."

Peter Frankl

As a young man I never thought that one day I would ever learn an entire repertoire of such a composer as Robert Schumann. But after recording six records of piano music of Debussy for Vox Records in the early 1960s, I began to consider the possibilities. I have felt a great affinity for Schumann since early childhood, and I began learning the major works, beginning with the *Carnaval,* as a teenager.

In Hungary, where I did all my training, I had a very healthy musical background, mainly in the Germanic tradition, especially Schumann and Brahms. I got "hooked" to play Schumann. Somehow, I always felt very near to his nature, this very improvisational nature of his works, the short character pieces, with their lack of traditional form. Later on, I fell in love more and more with the deeper works, like the C-major *Fantasie,* the *Davidsbündler Dances,* and the *Fantasiestücke,* Op. 12. A special favorite of mine, when I still participated at competitions, was the *Symphonic Etudes.* I made a special "hit" when I played it at the Rio de Janeiro Competition, where it was a compulsory piece.

In my so-called "entry" to the New York concert scene, I played at the Ninety-second Street Y what all my colleagues thought was a suicidal program—all three Schumann sonatas in one program. I started with the G minor, continued with the F minor, and finished with the F-sharp minor. I must tell you, it received very favorable, overwhelming critical acclaim, and the public enjoyed it enormously. Under normal circumstances, I don't think I would play them all that way, but I was inspired. It was a kind of "self-celebration" after finishing in 1980 all the recordings of the complete Schumann works. Then I played a cycle of five Schumann recitals in London. It was a special event.

Richard Goode

It was through Beethoven that I came to Schumann. I remember as an adolescent loving the late music of Beethoven. It is not only a summation of classical composition, but for me it turned out to be a gateway into a different era, the romantic century and the inspiration for Schumann. I was a kid growing up in Brooklyn when a young man came to the house and played the *Pathétique* on our upright piano. The impact of it was very strong. The lights flickered and the piano shook. I won't say that remains the paradigm of the way Beethoven or Schumann or anyone else should be played, but certainly it's one of the elements you can find in the romantic repertoire. I began studying with a very fine teacher, a woman who was the aunt of Joseph Szigeti. She had graduated from the Budapest Conservatory and had a wonderful grounding in a fine musical tradition. From then on, there was never a doubt that I wanted to be a musician. I then had a succession of excellent teachers, Claude Frank, Nadia Reisenberg, Rudolf Serkin. And I've been lucky enough to play and record some of the late Schumann pieces with Charles Wadsworth and the Chamber Music Society of Lincoln Center.

Thomas Hampson

My passion for Schumann and lieder singing was a late phenomenon in my life. I wasn't a particularly good student, but I've always had a predisposition to language and sound. In fact, when I did my SAT tests to get into college, the scores were pretty abominable. And you know how they sort of blipped out things that you might be able to get into? Mine had only one blip—very faintly on the form—"slightly inclined toward the humanities!" I think I'm a good student now because there is a passion for information and knowledge and understanding, particularly in music, that's been awakened in me. For example, I've come to realize that we talk too much about a *composer's* songs. The *Dichterliebe,* Op. 48, is not a cycle of songs by Schumann. It is by Schumann *and* Heine. Or the *Liederkreis,* Op. 39, is not by Schumann, but by Schumann and Eichendorff. Sometimes the partnership is in balance, sometimes it's more to the favor of the poet. Now, that's certainly a mode of thought that Fischer-Dieskau has brought us. I think we should stay true to that, exploit that, go a step farther and be exploiting much more the entire historical, sociological, and psychological context of both the poet and composer in the birthing of these songs. We need our performing artists to be more attentive—more attentive to the detailed analysis of contexts, social, historical, musical, of the origins of these pieces. All of my repertoire is born out of this kind of curiosity. And all the records I've made in the solo repertoire have been my own projects realized by different record companies.

Steven Isserlis

Schumann is very much a part of my life. I've been playing all his cello music for many years now. I'm never far from Schumann. He is the ultimate romantic artist and the most autobiographical of composers. You don't think of any rules with him. He invites us into his life. The more you read about his life, the more you know about the music; and the more you know the music, the more insights you get into his life. That's not always true of other composers. Think of Bach.

I don't actually remember when I heard Schumann for the first time. I do recall when I was eleven or twelve, picking up a volume of his letters. And I knew right away this was a wonderful man. Even in translation, one could feel his romantic idealism and strength of character. (It's very annoying how many of the letters and such have yet to be translated into English.) I also remember my mother saying her favorite music was Schumann's *Dichterliebe*. So I grew up already with a feeling that Schumann was a wonderful figure in music. I probably came on quite strongly about him when I organized a big eight-day Schumann festival in 1989, "Schumann and His Circle," at Wigmore Hall. There were many musicians, including András Schiff, Heinz Holliger, the Takács Quartet, and pianist Olli Mustonen, and many others. During the eight days, we played all Schumann's chamber music. And we also had pieces by his friends, Ludwig Schuncke, Mendelssohn, Chopin, and Brahms. The festival opened with a script I cowrote with actor Gabriel Woolf for a program called "Words and Music." In later years I wrote another "Words and Music" script, this one about the last years of Schumann's life, which has been performed several times with my friend Simon Callow doing the readings. I'm very proud of these programs. They have led to many more Schumann programs over the years.

Eugene Istomin

Alexander Siloti was my first teacher. He was Rachmaninoff's cousin and older than he. I was a boy of six when I was brought to him by his daughter, Kyriana. He was the one who first persuaded Rachmaninoff to have lessons and play professionally. Siloti was himself a pupil of Anton Rubinstein and Franz Liszt. He was very eccentric and could be very profane, but he was a great, noble Russian and the person through whom all the great musicians went to St. Petersburg before the Revolution.

I knew Rachmaninoff. I played for him when I was seven years old, and he did what anybody would do, kiss little babies on the forehead, and he did the same with me. I played for him a Beethoven sonata, Op. 49, one of those little kiddie sonatas that he wrote. He had an apartment in West End Avenue in New York City at the time, around 1931. I do remember how he looked. I wasn't frightened, I was impressed with his hairbrush head and parchment-like creased face. Subsequently, I heard him play a number of times, I would say a dozen times before his death, including his last concerts in Philadelphia and New York in 1942. He did have a dour, sad expression; but he was ill then. The last time he played, I was a student, and I sat on the stage of the sold-out Academy of Music in Philadelphia with another of my teachers, Rudolph Serkin. Rachmaninoff came out of the stage door at the end, looking just as you might imagine, with a big hat over his face and a very "don't-talk-to-me-anybody" look. That was the last I saw of him. He died the next year.

I received the Leventritt Prize in 1943, which was the number-one prize in wartime United States. The entire prize was the appearance on a Sunday-afternoon radio broadcast with the New York Philharmonic. I was seventeen years old. I didn't play very well. I was frightened to death of being on the stage of Carnegie Hall with all those microphones. I almost fainted and landed in the first row of that sold-out Carnegie Hall. But somehow I got through the performance and the next day started getting fan mail from everyplace. That was a different era, you see. My career began, and I started making mistakes ever since!

Hans-Joachim Köhler

When I was asked by Peters in 1972 to publish Schumann's solo piano works and vocal works on the basis of his manuscripts and early printings, the great master came through in a manner in which I had perceived no other composer before. I learned that he was not only concerned with romantic music, but that he drew his decisive inspiration from the subconscious. Schumann was unable to create music unless he was inspired by immediate experiences. At the moment that he went into music, he apparently perceived himself as a single organism that embodied music, poetry, and the human call at one and the same time. I came to see him as an opposite of Bach, the great thinker among musicians. And since we Germans are always concerned to look for principles, in Bach and Schumann I hit on two counterprinciples; and I realized at once that in my awareness and feeling, that one required the other. The time to tackle the editing task had come.

Between 1972 and 1975 I thoroughly acquainted myself with Schumann's life and thought. You know, it was a tragedy in the lives of millions of citizens of the GDR that from 1961, the year when the Berlin Wall was built, until November 1989, that they were not allowed to go to distant countries. I was compelled, for example, to work on thirty volumes of Schumann's piano music (that contained forty compositions) within unbearable confines. The project called for plenty of precision and artistic empathy. Among the many manuscripts that made an indelible impression on me was Clara's diary. Much of it had been kept or supervised by her father. During the years that saw her burgeoning love of Robert Schumann, it is a shocking symbol of regimentation. Whenever a threatening word was used, her father's quill pen was applied forcefully. On the other hand, Clara's childish handwriting struck me as tremulous and small. Schumann's housekeeping book, which has meanwhile been published, reveals a contradiction that is hard to explain. How was it possible for such a prolific person to reveal such exactness in handling money? The diaries, on the other hand—especially the one he kept together with Clara—are replete with wonderful observations. If you immerse yourself in Schumann's inmost personality, his thoughts seem to come to life and to have been generated just a minute ago.

Roe-Min Kok

The first Robert Schumann piece I learned was "The Happy Farmer." It came complete with a drawing of a smiling, striding figure, hoe swinging from his shoulder. For me he looked just like Malay rice farmers I had seen working in rural areas of my native Malaysia. It was terribly exciting to connect visual memory to the musical meanings in the swinging meter and cheerful melody—the music literally came alive! Thus my path to Schumann wound through complex and interesting byways of ex-empire. I was born in the 1970s into a Malaysian-Chinese family, within which Confucian teachings about the importance of a good education prevailed. My parents' ideas of what a good education constituted came not from Confucius, however, but from their educational experiences under British expatriate teachers in Malaysia. Many English practices remained after political independence was achieved in 1957. In this context, I learned English, read English children's literature, ate orange marmalade and Marmite, and took up the piano. These practices were part and parcel of the colorful multicultural landscape of Malaysian society, populated mainly by Muslim Malays, Buddhist and/or Christian Chinese, Hindus, and Christian Tamils. I'm not surprised that even as an adult, I've remained drawn to children's music by Schumann. Their titles, and how or why these reference German/ethnic customs, are tremendously special. Like themes in folk and fairy tales, they really put on the table the big questions in life: everyday work, love, death, family, marriage, rites of passage. The beauty of it all is that they are meaningful across cultures, as my example shows!

Svyatoslav Levin

My first Schumann as a boy in Soviet Russia was the "Wild Rider" from the *Album for the Young*. It's still in my fingers. Old instincts. By age thirteen or fourteen I was very interested in Schumann, because I liked program music with literary references and that sort of thing. I was also reading E. T. A. Hoffman in Russian translation. Those things by Hoffmann and the other romantic writers were all available. Schumann was wonderful for a young performer, things like the *"Abegg" Variations,* the *Carnaval,* the *Kreisleriana.* Later, I decided that music doesn't need those externals, which can sometimes be an unnecessary burden.

Schumann has always been very highly regarded in Russia. He and Clara visited Russia in 1844. I had a chance to read the original newspaper notice about their appearance in St. Petersburg. Schumann wasn't yet known in Russia as a composer by the majority public. The article announced that the "world famous" virtuoso Clara Wieck was arriving; and by the way, her husband was coming, too. Nowadays, only professionals remember Clara, and everybody knows Schumann.

At the Moscow State Tchaikovsky Conservatory there were several great pianists in the 1960s, 1970s, and 1980s. My greatest impression while I was there was hearing Svyatoslav Richter playing the *Symphonic Etudes,* the *Fantasie,* and accompanying some Schumann songs. I met him several times. He was a very close friend of my teacher Yakov Milstein. Milstein shaped me as a performer. He was one of the most prominent Russian/Soviet musicologists. He wrote a book dedicated to Liszt, and it's still considered an important source on him. He also edited works by Liszt, Chopin, and Scriabin. His knowledge was exhaustive. We worked on Schumann's *Kreisleriana* and *Symphonic Etudes.* I still use those scores.

There also was, and still is, a wonderful Georgian pianist, Elisso Virsaladze, and her Schumann was also great. Another great musician was Rudolf Kehrer. I also spent many hours in the class of Dimitri Bashkirov. And we cannot talk about Schumann in Russia without talking about Vladimir Sofronitsky. He was a legendary pianist but was unknown in the West. He died in 1961. You should hear his *Fantasie* and *Symphonic Etudes.* He was also unsurpassed in his playing of Scriabin. He was married to Scriabin's daughter. It is said that when he met Richter, he saluted him as "genius," and Richter saluted him as "God."

In Moscow there were several piano schools. One was by the legendary Alexander Goldenweiser, and his most famous student was Grigory Ginzburg. The biggest school was Heinrich Neuhaus, a person of enormous influence in Soviet Russia. He attracted the most talented young pianists. There still exists a recording of Heinrich giving a lesson in the *Symphonic Etudes* to a student, Alexei Nasedkin. He was considered Heinrich's *second* most famous student. The first was Richter. So can you imagine being *second*? Also in that group was Emil Gilels! Another famous piano school belonged to Konstantin Igumnov. My teacher, Milstein, was one of Igumnov's favorite students and his assistant for many years.

Was there a "Russian" approach to Schumann? Well, there are tendencies that could be applied to many musicians all around the world. At the mid-nineteenth century with Anton and Nicholas Rubinstein, you see a kind of performance style that emphasizes that intentions be absolutely clear and strongly projected. A good example was Rachmaninoff, who is the highest point of what the Russian piano school could offer. Josef Hoffmann could also be considered as belonging to the Russian school. Applied to Schumann, it brings out the maximum of his duality and artistic expression. Yes, those are common words that might not seem to mean much; but you take into account the intensity and clarity of approach and bring out the artistic expression from that.

Susan McClary

Robert Schumann is practically a case history of shifts in gender coding in the nineteenth century. He fascinates me, because he was trying to break down those barriers and those categories and create fusions which have tremendous implications for the proper construction of the bourgeois male subject. This is an agenda that runs all the way through the literature of the nineteenth century, as well—what some people call the "feminization" of the bourgeois male subject. This means, simply, permitting male access into areas that had previously been understood to be in the female domain, i.e., feeling, vulnerability, and sensuality. I am interested not only in the cultural context within which artists produce their art, but also in the ways in which the artwork is informed by certain kinds of attitudes, particularly understandings about gender; and, likewise, the way artwork then shapes people who come in contact with it. Gender and sexuality are always constructed socially. The arts are some of the most important media by means of which societies reproduce and transmit their ideals and ideas about borders of gender sexuality. I feel that one of the very important agendas of the romantic artist was a new construction of "masculinity" and a reorganization of what is meant by "feminine." And that's where I sometimes have problems. Sensuality, subjectivity, imagination need not be at odds with the intellectual, the rational, and those dimensions that already had been understood to be masculine. The Enlightenment had been concerned with creating categories and binaries and realms that are mutually exclusive.

John Nelson

A concert schedule like I have is very typical of the conductor who must be on the road all the time. For example, right now, I'm preparing Schumann's *Paradise and the Peri*. In five weeks I go to Lyon to do Berlioz's *Beatrice and Benedict,* which is a new production at the biannual French Music Festival there. Earlier, I did it in St. Louis, Indianapolis, and Paris. This is my fifth "go" at it. And after that, for the next three months, I'm a week here and a week there. I come back to the New World Symphony in Florida for guest concerts and recordings. And there are choral festivals in Estonia, where the most musical people in the world live. Here is a people who for the last three hundred years have had only nineteen of them spent in freedom! And many thousands of people from all over the world come to sing, all in their native dress, all under your own direction! How does one handle it all? Well, I was brought up in a very religious environment, and that is still a major part of my life. Which means that in my philosophy you take things one step at a time; and you are grateful for where you are; and you let the man upstairs take the next step for you. At the same time, we are in control of who we can develop into. The outer level is the result of what's inside. If you get those things mixed up, then you're in real trouble. A very wise man said to me when I left my post at Indianapolis that you can be less stationary but more centered. That has happened to me; I feel at home everywhere.

Garrick Ohlsson

I am one of the pianists who do have problems with Schumann. I don't know if the others pay him lip service or not, but it's true that among musicians he's a deeply, deeply beloved figure. But at the same time, among chamber players, they do admit to problems. But generally, the heart is so warmed by the music that most musicians feel, "Yes, it's problematic but deeply fulfilling." There's something about my temperament and Schumann's which don't mix. Which is my loss, I suppose, although I've played a good deal of Schumann and admire his great genius. And that's not lip service; I really mean it. That doesn't mean that I'm problem-free with the music. I've played a great deal of Schumann, including the Piano Concerto and the solo works, including the *"Abegg" Variations* (one of my favorites), the *Davidsbündler,* the *Carnaval,* the G-Minor Sonata, the *Humoreske,* the *Symphonic Etudes* (which I've just played once). You know, you can fall in love with somebody, but the more you get to know them, you realize that perhaps it's not such a good match, after all.

Peter F. Ostwald

As a psychiatrist and a musician, I was always very interested in the possible connections between madness and creativity. I've found a few cases of musicians who were mad. Now, Schumann happens to be one of those, and it was very exciting to find out, first of all, that no one had ever seriously investigated questions around Schumann's madness; and secondly, that there was a great deal of interesting material that could be reviewed and could be utilized to reconstruct the evolution of Schumann's problems and to begin to relate the problems to the way he worked and the way he wrote his music.

I have been a musician all my life. I began studying to play the violin when I was eight and have continued ever since. In addition, when I was in my adolescence, I became very much interested in psychoanalysis and read a lot of Freud's works, especially on dreams. My father was a doctor, and he had all those books available. He encouraged my interests in that direction, because he didn't think it would be very practical for me to be a musician. He thought I should do something practical like being an electrician or a plumber or a doctor. Nonetheless, he was very supportive and always allowed me to have lessons; and he gave me a nice violin, so I was able to keep up the two interests; and after completing medical school, I specialized in psychiatry.

I had my principal psychiatric training in New York, which was a wonderful place to be, because there are so many musicians there. When I moved back to California, I met my wife-to-be, a pianist from Canada. Together, we've maintained a very lively interest in all things musical, and there's always a lot of music at the house. In my work at the University of California–San Francisco, where I am a professor of psychiatry—I am the director of a clinic here which specializes in the disorders of performing artists—I have always chosen to do projects that bridge the gap, so to speak, between music and medicine. Some of my early research was in the field of acoustics, for instance, specifically questions like hearing disturbances and speech disorders. I became very interested in the diagnostic meanings of babies' cries. That was a fascinating field, and of course I've always been very interested in the problems of musicians. I treat a lot of patients who are musicians or performing artists.

Well, my book is finished [*Schumann: The Intimate Voices*, 1985]. It received a Deems Taylor Award in 1986. My publisher [Northeastern University Press] told me to go to New York for the ceremony at the Lincoln Center Library, where composer Morton Gould presided over the ceremony. Actually, it was very good timing, because the paperback edition was about to come out, and there was just enough time to place a sticker on the cover. There was a problem, though, in Great Britain, where the book was published under another title, *Schumann: Music and Madness*. It's a much more provocative title. It led reviewers there to expect much more musicological analysis. I'm not a musicologist, so they will find it disappointing.

But the questions about Schumann have not been entirely resolved in my mind. As a doctor and a psychiatrist, there's nothing I can do for Schumann except to write about him, to write as honestly and truthfully as I possibly can and learn as many facts as I can. I don't think the subject has been exhausted by any means.

Elizabeth Paley

I discovered Schumann in my early teens, when my piano teacher gave me a copy of *Papillons*. I think back to something Roland Barthes wrote: that there are two kinds of music, what you *listen* to and what you *play*. Schumann is one who may be "minor" if you just listen, but "tremendous" when you play him (even if you play him badly!). I confess I've never been particularly fond of simply listening to *Papillons*, but I certainly enjoy touching the piano keys and making those little butterflies come to life. In college, I did a lot of accompanying for voice students and became interested in the ways music and text supplement one another to convey meaning. Schumann keeps the pianist well occupied in the song cycles *Dichterliebe* and *Frauenliebe und -leben* (although the storyline of *Frauenliebe und -leben* is regrettably archaic) and other lieder. Schumann had become enough of a habit for me as a pianist that when it came time to choose a topic for my music theory dissertation, I swore I wouldn't include him. I wanted to examine how music and text interact in genres other than songs, and so I turned to incidental music—music composed to accompany plays. I planned to include Beethoven's/Goethe's *Egmont* and Mendelssohn's/Shakespeare's *A Midsummer Night's Dream* and was looking for another piece to round out the group. That's when I came across the Schumann/Byron *Manfred*. So there I was, back to Schumann! I had heard the famous Overture but hadn't known that Schumann had written any incidental music, let alone this musically eerie, highly experimental assemblage. *Manfred* employs a great deal of *melodrama*—instrumental music coupled with a declaimed, rather than sung, text. Thanks to the film industry, modern audiences are quite familiar with melodrama, often to the point that we don't notice the music behind a movie's dialogue. In the nineteenth century, however, melodrama was still a relatively new concept, and the disjunction between music and spoken text was unsettling enough that melodrama was often associated with the supernatural. Schumann took advantage of this in *Manfred*, accompanying the conjurations of demons and spirits with some of the most spine-tingling music ever composed. So despite my original plan, Schumann assumed a prominent place in my dissertation.

Leon Plantinga

I started out in music primarily as a performer. I was a pianist and played a lot in public and entertained foolish adolescent thoughts that I was going to be a professional pianist. At some point, though, I became interested in academic and literary things. I did continue to perform music very seriously, even when I knew it would not be my professional career. I was more and more interested in questions like, how does one *talk* about music; how does one really achieve musical understanding? Those two issues are essential to any study of the life and work of Robert Schumann. When I came to Yale as a graduate student in 1959, I remember coming in the door, sitting down, and taking a German exam. Wouldn't you know that the material I was required to translate was one of the "wilder" reviews of Robert Schumann! That really impressed me. And I thought, maybe this is really the direction I'm supposed to follow! Later, I had the opportunity to examine one of the original sets of all twenty volumes of the *Neue Zeitschrift für Musik*. There was every chance that Schumann had held these very volumes in his hands. You could check them out from the library in those days, which I did for years!

Like many of us, I grew up on the treatments—I should say, *mis*treatments—of Schumann by the German scholar Wolfgang Bötticher. During World War II he wrote two huge volumes that had been commissioned by the German government. They have subsequently received a lot of negative criticism, rightly so. The worst thing Bötticher did was to tamper with evidence. For example, he added crucial words in sentences to make Schumann appear "properly" anti-Semitic. He used evidence in ways that seem to me quite impermissible in trying to establish political motivations, rather than following an objective interest in science or knowledge. At this point in time [1990] they have not been translated. Bötticher had a particular ax to grind. He talked about what he called "Charakterlogie," or "characterology," in English. This was a synthetic product popular in Nazi Germany and officially sanctioned by the state. Subsequently, he did some pretty good work in editing the piano music. For a good stretch of time, he was the only person who had access to some documents that had been generally unavailable since the war. Now they are available, for the most part, in Düsseldorf, Zwickau, and the University of Bonn. These consist of sketchbooks and other precompositional materials. For the record, I would like to make a distinction between what Bötticher did during the war and after the war.

Nancy B. Reich

It seemed inevitable that I would not write about Clara Schumann until I myself reached my middle years. I spent my childhood in upstate New York in Ithaca, where we had a music class every day. I went to high school in New York, to the Music and Art High School, which was a marvelous school—was and still is (but now is called the LaGuardia High School of Arts). I took my bachelor's degree and my master's when I was young, in my twenties, and got married when my husband left to serve in the army in the Second World War. When he returned and was getting his doctorate in physics, I was teaching music appreciation and theory at Queens

College; and I continued teaching until I was forty, with children in high school and in college. I then decided to go back to graduate school. At that time the whole feminist movement in the United States was growing, and I understood a lot more then about being a woman, being a mother, being a musician, and trying to have a family and a career. And I don't think I could've written with this kind of perspective when I was a young woman just starting out. I didn't have that kind of understanding.

I received my doctorate when I was forty-seven. I must have seemed like an old lady, you know, compared to the others. Even when I was a graduate student years ago, my peers were young women, usually twenty years younger than I. They would say to me, "Oh, Nancy, you're a real role model!" And I would sort of resent it. I didn't want to be a role model; I just wanted to go ahead and do my work. And I keep hearing this all the time. But there were advantages to being older. For one thing, I was able to concentrate better, even though I had all these family responsibilities and I was teaching at the same time to earn additional money. I really wanted to do research. I wanted to do it more than I wanted to do anything before. It's all doubly important to me now. We know women live longer than men; that women are often widowed in their forties or fifties and sixties. And I always felt (and this was partly my mother's influence) that you really had to do something constructive, that you really had to contribute in some way to the world. My mother was a woman of great energy, probably like Clara Schumann. She was determined that her daughters would be well educated and have careers. I never knew, for example, that girls didn't have the same opportunities for education that boys did, because my mother, who was a widow very early, insisted on this. Anyway, that doctorate opened many doors to me, and I really hope to continue working into my seventies and possibly into my eighties.

I suppose my book on Clara [*Clara Schumann: The Artist and the Woman,* 1985] began when I was invited to give a lecture at the Music Library Association in 1976. As I prepared a lecture on "Women and Music," I realized there was a book to be written which would look at Clara Schumann in a way that had not been done, which would look at her personality, her career, and her composing. I really felt at this point, as I've already mentioned, that everything in my life had led up to it. I was a musician, a musicologist, I knew German (my dissertation was about a male German composer), I was very aware of the feminist movement and what was happening in current interests in women's history. And I was fortunate enough to have the collaboration of an old friend from Music and Art days, Dr. Anna Burton, M.D., a psychiatrist and psychoanalyst in New Jersey, who helped me gain a fuller psychological understanding of Clara Schumann.

While I was writing the book, my husband, who had chronic leukemia for many years, but who had actually been my greatest support, died three days after I received the contract from the publisher. And so I lived through a period that was not unlike what Clara had to live through. She, too, had been in the middle of her career, when Robert died. I plunged into the writing of the book, working night and day, actually; and it was a great help in getting over this crisis in my life. I could understand even more how much Clara's career meant to her after Robert's death. My work, like Clara's concert career, became a great solace to me.

Erika Reiman

In addition to researching the relationships between the novelist Jean Paul Friedrich Richter and Robert Schumann, I have been busy performing in concert and recital works by Schumann and Brahms. I have always been interested in German language and literature and was fortunate to have access to an excellent department during my undergraduate studies at Mount Allison University. In the summer following my third year, I received a fellowship which allowed me to stay at school and research the literary connections with Schumann's music. I quickly realized that very little had been written about his relationships with Jean Paul. The existing literature dealt either with Schumann's own early literary attempts, all of which were heavily influenced by Jean Paul's style, or with the evident programmatic relationship between *Papillons* and Jean Paul's novel *Flegeljahre*.

It seemed to me that much more of Schumann's music must surely bear the mark of Jean Paul's influence more deeply than the extant scholarship indicated. John Daverio's work, particularly his first book, *Nineteenth-Century Music and the German Romantic Ideology* [1993], helped show a way to investigate and describe this influence.

I was interested in Schumann for a long time, and if you are interested in his piano music then you inevitably come to Jean Paul. I have German ancestry, so I studied German and music in college, so that helped a lot. I knew I wanted to do a thesis on Schumann's relationship with German literature. And my thesis advisor told me about Jean Paul (at that time John Daverio was just publishing). But I'm not sure if she really knew how complicated Jean Paul was. Her name was Gaynor Jones. She was until recently a professor at the University of Toronto. I think she's retired now. Except for Daverio, there was not much out there in English on Jean Paul and Schumann. Daverio had read some of him, but I've gone further on to the major novels, his *Vorschule der Aesthetik* (a kind of "Pre-School of Aesthetics"), and smaller novellas. I had a professor at the tiny school I went to at New Brunswick, Canada, who lent me twelve volumes in

German of his collected works. I did what I would advise anybody else to do when taking on Jean Paul—get a good German dictionary and set aside at least a year. Jean Paul's German is wild; the long and convoluted sentences, the range of vocabulary, and the incredible command of idiosyncratic German are amazing. Schumann even counseled Clara about the difficulties in reading him. Reading Goethe is a snap compared with him. I spent an entire year and a half getting through these works. But it was absolutely well worth it. The problem is that your commitment has to be great. I really don't think an adequate edition has ever been produced in German, much less in English translation. A modern reader needs much more.

Charles Rosen

There came a time in the early 1980s when I thought my Schumann playing was getting better. That's why I made the recordings of his so-called "Revolutionary Masterpieces." You spend a lot of time with one composer, get under his skin, so to speak—or *in* his skin. I recorded them in the early 1980s for a Dutch company, GLOBE Records, in the Netherlands, in the concert hall of Haarlem [they were later released in 1984 on the Nonesuch label]. The hall had fine acoustics on a Steinway that had been rebuilt by the technician of the Concertgebouw Orchestra. The hall is next to the largest church in Haarlem, which also has the loudest bells. We had to stop at each hour (and occasionally for a lighter tinkle at the quarter hour). I would have liked to include the sounds of those bells! A lot of those early pieces are radical, but for those recordings I just picked the six which were closest to my heart. I found the original versions better than the revisions, so I wanted to record the first versions of the *Fantasie,* the *Kreisleriana,* the *Davidsbündlertänze,* and the *"Clara Wieck" Impromptus.* The F-Sharp-Minor Sonata and the *Carnaval* are already so radical that I wanted them to be part of the project.

Eric Sams

I heard my very first Schubert and Schumann songs fifty-two years ago, so I'm quite familiar with these masterpieces and have been for some time. To learn them and learn *from* them means you bring to them love and respect and knowledge. Then you must say something about them to people who might not have had the chance I have had to know them quite so well. So it's two things, really. First of all, having received from Schubert or Schumann, or whoever it may be, some impulse and then to just propagate it like a radio wave to others; and, if possible, to make converts to this great music, which I have no doubt at all enriches and enhances life beyond measure for those fortunate enough to participate in it.

We are here in Sanderstead, Surrey, which is near Croyden. It's really part of greater London, and I've lived here for some time. I was a civil servant, a career civil servant for my working life, but I took the opportunity of early retirement and have spent ten happy years doing the kind of things that I really like to do, including writing my *Songs of Robert Schumann* [1983]. The essential thing for the researcher is to belong both to the British Library, the Library of the British Museum, and the Students' Room, where they have all the great manuscripts, including some Schumann and Schubert and Mozart. Best of all is the London Library, which has a million books and is well stocked in music and the German nineteenth century. I haven't done much research outside of London.

When I volunteered for the Intelligence Corps during the war— this happened to be, I discovered later, at a time when Churchill had decreed that secondary schools and young persons generally be combed and groomed and, if possible, be recruited for this very purpose—the interviewer had certain questions to ask. One of them was, "Can you play chess?"; and as you might imagine, the second was, "Do you like crosswords, and are you good at them?" And so on. But to my surprise, the third was, "Do you like music, and can you read a musical score?" It seemed to me then, and it has seemed to me ever since, that there is a clear correlation between music and cryptology. One point being, for what it's worth, that generations of composers, whether they're interested in cipher or not, have thought of music as a kind of communication and, in particular, a secret language which is accessible only to the initiated.

Thinking like a detective is the right way to approach all problems, even musical ones. It's not coincidence that people like Sherlock Holmes, or Hercule Poirot, or other detectives in fiction are notorious for approaching the problem always in the same kind of way, which is to first set down the facts. You provide the reader certain lists of suspects, motives, and the actual facts of the case, especially times and dates and alibis. Of course, the process of inductive inference is dependent on getting, if possible, all the facts and getting the right facts. And you might by an unfortunate mischance get the wrong facts, or the facts might lead you to a mistaken conclusion. There's no cure for that. The process is ineluctable. You have to follow these steps in solving crossword puzzles. You have certain conditions you have to comply with. You can't just write in anything that comes into your head. It has to be the right number of letters, and so on. Chess problems are faced with the same strategy: You actually have a design or pattern on the board which is there, which is given. The only way from the data to conclusion is by means of these accredited processes of inductive inference.

Wolfgang Sawallisch

It is a very big honor for me this year [1988], when I was voted an *Ehrenmitglied* [honorary member] of the Schumann-Gesellschaft in Düsseldorf. This is one of the most important societies for a German composer. I am the third member, following Dietrich Fischer-Dieskau and Claudio Arrau. I come to Düsseldorf because Schumann was the music director here [1850–54] and composed much music during that time. He gave a lot of his personal energy to the musical life here. I liked Schumann always, from my very first remembrance. I began as a pianist, you see, and my first connection with him was with his piano music. I am very proud of my recordings of the Schumann symphonies, which I did fifteen years ago [1973] in Dresden with the Dresden Staatskapelle. I feel it was a good recording, but I do not plan to do it a second time.

Samuel Sanders

During my time at Juilliard I was taught by a very great accompanist, as well as a fine voice teacher, named Sergius Kagen. He was an editor for music by Debussy, Brahms, and Purcell. He was a very learned musician and a terrific pianist. One of his voice students was one of our leading performers today, Jan DeGaetani. Juilliard is now giving a degree in accompaniment. I prefer the term "collaboration." I take a little bit of credit for starting that master's program there, and it's now being taken over by a former student of mine, Margo Garrett. There are a number of other schools now in the country that have similar degrees.

When I started out, I was playing only for singers. I played not only for my teacher's lessons at Juilliard, but for our other vocal teachers. One of my classmates, for example, was Tatiana Troyanos. I remember that she and I used to go over to Staten Island together to play for concerts sponsored by the Lincoln Center. I also worked with Jan Peerce. My best friend is a singer, whom I met even before I went to Juilliard. He's the very prominent tenor Robert White. We've done a lot of work together, and done a lot of concerts, and in a way he was really the first person who got me to realize that there's more to piano playing than playing the piano at Hunter College, which was our undergraduate school. And to this day we perform together with a lot of fun, a lot of pleasure.

Gerald Moore was one of the greatest of all accompanists. I would say he's my idol, quite unashamedly. He died recently [1999] at the age of eighty-seven. I always say Moore was to the piano what Pablo Casals was to the cello and Andrés Segovia was to the guitar—they all legitimized the profession of accompanist and made people aware of what that function is all about.

I think it is fate that brought me together with Itzhak Perlman. It's fitting, in a way. We perform together quite a lot. And we both have disabilities. Because of his polio, his big cause is to help facilities which would assist others who are disabled. I, myself, was born with a very serious heart defect. The trouble is, you can't see a heart defect as readily as you can somebody who has crutches, but it's been a huge handicap for me, for my entire life, and it's included three surgical procedures—three heart operations, that is. Many of the problems he and I have to face are the same ones for so many other people. What Itzhak is accomplishing for so many people, he's also accomplishing for me. So I have my own personal debt of gratitude to him. I have my own charitable enterprise, which is a chamber music festival in Cape Cod every August. We do benefit concerts sometimes. We did one in conjunction with Cape Cod Hospital several years ago, which is an excellent facility and the biggest one on Cape Cod.

My physical difficulties got me into music in the first place. I began as a solo pianist. I played on a Young People's concert with the New York Philharmonic when I was sixteen. My mother had told me to play the piano, since I was so limited in many other activities. I wouldn't say that I particularly love the piano now, but I love music. And the reason that years ago I chose chamber music and accompanying was because I happen to like the piano in conjunction with other instruments. I happen to like the sound of it better with other instruments, rather than as a solo instrument. If I had had my druthers as a musician—had I been born healthy (let's put it that way)—I probably would have chosen the bassoon. That's my favorite instrument. Don't ask me why. I just like the sound of it better. It appeals to me, you know. It's just one of those things. I guess it's why people fall in love with somebody and other people don't.

Along with Bach, Beethoven, and Brahms, there's another "B" in my life: baseball! I'm passionate about it. That's something I share with the great Eugene Istomin, even if he *is* a Detroit Tigers fan! It's something else I'd be doing if I were stronger. For part of the time that I was brought up in the Bronx, I lived a block from Yankee Stadium. And I see so many analogies between baseball and the art of the accompanist. You know, the less experienced a pitcher is, the more the catcher has to take care of him. When I'm working with a young performer, I'm extra-cautious, because I know that I'm working with a less experienced person. I guess you could also say that, like a catcher—or any ballplayer—we pianists have to sit on the, well, the *bench*!

András Schiff

Schumann was always very close to my heart, still is, and always will be. He is a great challenge to interpret, because both the player and the listeners need to have an unusual amount of fantasy and imagination. I was lucky in my Schumann playing to have found inspiration with several remarkable pianists. Annie Fischer is a wonderful artist. We became very close friends. No one else has been able to get the dualism of Eusebius and Florestan and the essential capriciousness of the music the way she could. I met Charles Rosen years ago while I was still living in Hungary. He asked me to help him out on research he was doing into Schumann's original piano scores. I went to the Czerny Library in Budapest to investigate the "other" ending of the C-Major *Fantasie,* the one where the quotation from Beethoven's *An die ferne Geliebte* returns at the end. I did, and I completely agree with him that usually the first editions and versions of Schumann are much more revolutionary and exciting, at least for more than 90 percent of the time. I especially prefer the first version of the F-Minor Sonata, the 1836 version, which I now play.

My life with Schumann has taken me many places. I remember receiving the Robert Schumann Prize in Düsseldorf in 1994. I stood on the Bilkerstrasse at the gateway to the house where Schumann lived. It was there that Brahms came. And it was from there that Schumann ran to the river and attempted suicide. I just stood there for a while, trying to imagine that scene. It was then that I began studying his last piano piece, the *"Geister"* Variations. Recently, I read John Daverio's new biography of Schumann. It is really extraordinary. I'm almost finished with it now. I have it here with me as we talk! He really understands Schumann, especially the late works.

Richard Stoltzman

Yes, I play a lot of Schumann on the clarinet. People have the idea that the clarinet doesn't have, say, the same kind of mature voice as a piano or a violin in major classical repertoire. They're surprised to hear the clarinet playing Schubert, or Schumann, or Brahms, or Debussy, or Poulenc, or Hindemith, or Bach—you know, composers they recognize. They realize that something is going on besides a demonstration of clarinet technique. A clarinet recital can be just as pleasurable an experience as hearing a piano recital, a violin recital, a vocal recital, or going to any kind of concert. But the clarinet has never been, what would you say, a real hot item on the recital circuit. Instead, you associate it with the big bands of the 1940s and 1950s, with Benny Goodman and Woody Herman, and Artie Shaw. And think of the Dixieland sound, with people like Pete Fountain. As for me, I'm just trying to play the music, and it happens that I play it on the clarinet.

Growing up, I didn't have any role models to emulate, except my father, who was my first teacher and who taught me so much marching band music. But when I got to Yale University, I heard the Brahms Clarinet Quintet for the first time. Keith Wilson, who was my clarinet teacher, played it. I was overwhelmed that this great piece of music had a clarinet in it. I determined that someday I would play it. Little did I know I would make records of it and play it hundreds of times! So that music encouraged me, and I began playing and spending summers at the Marlboro Music Festival, which was an education in itself.

And what often happens to me is that people who by accident or design show up at one of my concerts are very surprised and come back often-times afterward and say, "Gee, you know, I never thought the clarinet could sound like that"; or "I didn't know the clarinet was supposed to sound like that"; or "I didn't know you could have fun like that at concerts." I take them as compliments.

I never really set off with any kind of aspirations to have a solo career, nor did I imagine that I would be a torchbearer for the clarinet as a "legitimate" voice. I just like to play, and luckily I've been able to reach people. I don't know whether it's the clarinet that's doing it so much as just the music itself. I'd like to think that it's the music.

R. Larry Todd

A lot has been happening in Mendelssohnian research since I edited with Jon Finson *Mendelssohn and Schumann* [1984] and my biography [*Mendelssohn: A Life in Music*, 2003]. The impetus of that first book came from a conference in 1982 at Duke University, where new findings from scholars were presented. Certain stereotypes about the man and his music that had been impeding research were addressed. For example, George Bernard Shaw had attacked his "kid-glove sentimentality" and accused him of "dreary fugue manufacturing." Something of that persevered well into the twentieth century. What we had to do was peel away the layers of Victorian sentimentality that had accrued to Mendelssohn and get back to the original figure—who he was, what he was like, and what was the significance of the music he was writing in the 1830s and 1840s. We knew at the time of a surprising number of compositions which he didn't finish, such as an unfinished symphony in C major, dating from the late 1840s, an unfinished piano concerto in E minor, also from the 1840s (which it appears he was working on around the time he was considering the Violin Concerto in E Minor), and an unfinished Piano Sonata in G Major. [Note: Professor Todd's notes accompany a world premiere recording of the E-Minor Piano Concerto on the Koch label, with Jennifer Eley, piano, and Sayard Stone conducting the English Chamber Orchestra.] We did not yet have a *Thematic Catalogue* of all his compositions, which was incredible for a composer of his rank. We did not have all his music in print yet. There were still early works as a student, early operas that had not been published, and many, many letters not yet published.

Now, here we are in 2009, many years since our first talk at Bard College, and we are on the verge of resolving many of the gaps and misunderstandings about Mendelssohn and his relationship with Schumann. For example, we are getting closer to a *Thematic Catalogue*. Finally, we have in sight a complete catalogue of his music. According to Schumann, Mendelssohn claimed he had published only about one-fifth of the music he wrote. So a lot has remained in manuscript. In the 1970s there was an attempt in Leipzig to organize a new catalogue, since most of his manuscripts were in East Berlin. That foundered. Then, in 1997 for the sesquicentenary of his death, Breitkopf & Härtel launched the collected *Leipziger Ausgabe*. A few of us were brought in to Leipzig to consult on it. It will amount to about twenty volumes. They are planning to finish it in 2047, on November 4, the Bicentenary of his death. As for the *Thematic Catalogue*, there will be one published this fall by Ralf Wehner in Leipzig. He's putting the finishing touches on it as we speak. We now have a much clearer idea of what he wrote and when he wrote it than when you and I last spoke in the 1990s. Bärenreiter has announced a project to publish a critical edition of all his letters in twelve volumes—the first one is out, taking us up to 1830. They number in the thousands. He was a superb letter writer. They are works of a high literary quality. Of course, that means correspondence to and from Schumann will be popping up in the later volumes. We also have the so-called *Gegenbriefe,* the letters written *to* Mendelssohn. It is hoped they will be published, as well. Would that that can happen! It would be a huge archival treasure trove for anyone investigating the Mendelssohn circle. With all of this happening, there'll have to be a revision of my own Mendelssohn biography, for sure! It's already been translated into German and many new plates added, some in color. There's also a *Catalogue raissonné*.

These things are happening in large part because of changes in attitude toward him. His rise was so meteoric, he was so lionized in his lifetime, and he was the darling of the Victorians, that later in the century some began to distrust him. Wagner's attack on his Jewish ancestry—he was actually baptized a Lutheran when he was seven in 1816, which we didn't know about a few years ago—was damaging. (The religious affiliations of the Mendelssohn family are actually quite a complicated story.) Moreover, Mendelssohn's "Victorian" reputation made him an easy target. But now in the twenty-first century we are in a period of rehabilitation and revival. His star is on the ascendancy, and he's regarded as a more complicated figure than before. And his life and his family were fascinating, whether you're interested in his music or not.

Sarah Walker

I'm singing Mahler and Schumann this evening. Tonight's recital comes after a week of very different theatre work. I've just come from a run of Handel's *Julius Caesar* at the Met in a marvelous edition by Charles Mackerras designed especially to suit these huge, modern opera houses. Handel is very good for the voice, you know—you can't get away with anything less than good singing. And one must not "sell" Handel on emotion: Schumann, yes. Handel, no. Handel is "instrumental" in character. Audiences more familiar with a diet of nineteenth-century operas will need to make some adjustment to their expectations.

However, I digress! You mentioned the recording Roger Vignoles and I made of the Schumann *Maria Stuart* songs. Recordings can be rather like ambassadors—they give us a chance to get to know one another a bit before we meet. My home is in London, which is where much UK concert work is centered, of course. My husband, Graham, and I are very lucky— we are able to spend a lot of time together. A large proportion of my career is on the concert platform for lieder and orchestral work, and that takes up far less time than opera. I also work at home with Roger Vignoles. Roger and I were at the Royal College of Music together but, as he is a few years younger than me, we only actually did one concert together then. We didn't really start working together until some fourteen years later when he approached me after hearing a lieder concert I took part in for the Aldeburgh Festival with Graham Johnson in 1978. He suggested that we should work on preparing some song repertoire and that I should make my debut at London's Wigmore Hall. That was really the start of our partnership. We have had a wonderful time since then traveling the world, visiting many international festivals and making lots of recordings.

John Worthen

I've been thinking and writing my *Schumann* [2007] for ten years. I've traveled extensively, looked at the music, gathered an extraordinary library for myself of Schumann's music. Even now, not all Schumann's music has been recorded. There were times when I was living in Budapest and that Radio Bartók would occasionally play a Schumann oddity, which I would tape off air there and then.

How did I make the move from my D. H. Lawrence studies to a biography of Robert Schumann? Well, I don't think I ever actually did move from Lawrence to Schumann. I was an academic once, you see, in the old days, and as an academic I did all the right things. I wrote biographies, big ones, six hundred pages long; and I did editions, scholarly editions, lots of those, with all the footnotes. But I began to ask, in the middle 1990s, when I was getting into my middle fifties, what shall I do with the rest of my time as an academic? I didn't want to stay. And so I took early retirement at age sixty, primarily to write books. At that time I published *The Gang,* my biography of William Wordsworth, Dorothy Wordsworth, Coleridge, and Sara Hutchinson. One of the things I had realized—and this does impact on Schumann, as well—is the impossibility of doing a book about a single person. A biography is constantly going into the circles around the central character. It's the stone thrown into the pond, where the ripples spread outwards. And once you start writing about Lawrence, you start writing about Frieda, you start writing about his mother, his brother, his sister, his background, his friends—there's no end to it! And I also thought, what about a biography of someone in a different field of the arts, but who had a decidedly literary bent?

And that's how Schumann came into my life. At first I didn't know much about Schumann, other than that he wrote some music and had a wife called Clara. But over the years I have been educating myself; and I found myself, say, in the middle 1990s, thinking that Schumann is the only person I would want to write a biography of, who was not only a composer but a most literary person. When it comes to his notebooks and diaries, there's a wealth of material, such as the incomparably great edition by Gerd Nauhaus. On the other hand, the difficult thing about any Schumann biography, for me, are the letters. I always say, never write a biography of anyone whose collected letters have not been published for you.

I'm interested in trying to understand people from the inside, as much as from the outside. Being an academic I must exercise restraint, but I don't think it makes you cautious, necessarily. I mean, academics can be wild. I think what I want to say about people's lives is, there's always more than one thing going on at a time. Like all human beings, they have times when they're depressed, and they have times when they're exhilarated. And certainly Schumann had black times, and certainly Coleridge had black times, and certainly Lawrence had black times. But there are the happy times, as well.

So here I am, someone writing a biography of Schumann who wasn't a musicologist. Actually, this clears out of the way a good deal of baggage. I can go to conferences, music conferences, and feel that I'm absolutely at ease with the people that are there, because I'm not competing. The only Schumann scholar I've actually met is Nancy Reich. It's not getting to know them so much as reading their books and commenting on their books. The biography I've been most concerned with is the Peter Ostwald biography, because it stands in a way as a monument to the way that Schumann is now thought about. And almost every time you listen to a radio program saying, "Robert Schumann was doing this," it goes back to what Ostwald has written. However, I think a lot of what Ostwald was doing was very, very dubious. He was an intelligent and serious man; he knew about music and he could write well. So in those ways, it is a good book. On the other hand, by my standards, it cannot actually be a *very* good book, because it's actually wrong. And that is, he's not done his research, or he's been the victim of his own prejudices. He knows the answers before he finds them. So I suppose I've contested with him either implicitly or explicitly quite a lot in my book. I come across as very combative, I suppose. I think all my biographies are in an odd way contentious.

We biographers should never think that the historical and biographical record of events was somehow preordained and inevitable. The estimable historian Niall Ferguson talks about this. We need to pause constantly and consider the *alternatives,* the possibilities, the *might-have-beens,* as another approach to historiography. That's why, as I was talking about earlier, the reason why the biography that concentrates solely on a single individual is in a way such a terrible deception. It implies we all traverse our lives exactly as we want to, exactly as our nature tells us to. And we don't. We bump up against things all the time. Other people impinge upon us as we impinge upon them. And oftentimes what we do is take a path of least resistance, rather than actually one that we choose. And therefore, biographers have to consider these possibilities. It seems to me absolutely crucial where writing biography. When you're writing a biography, that subject becomes a member of your family for a while. So you get engaged with your subject, and in the end you mourn his going. I have now finished the book. I always feel that the reviews a book gets are like epitaphs on a grave. Because however close I've been to Schumann over the last ten years, it's now become something that it's in the past for me, as well. And I'm sad about that.

Peter Zazofsky

When I was a teenager, I was first trained as a chamber player. One of the most important relationships I established in my musical life was with the pianist Malcolm Frager. He was older than me, and he had always been a role model to me. I was a very nervous twenty-year-old when I finally called him at Tanglewood about playing with him. I thought he would never be interested in playing with a kid he didn't know. But he immediately invited me over. Not only did we play through a couple of sonatas, but we played that night for four hours, and the next day, and the next day. I was amazed not only at his knowledge, but his openness to a youngster. I've never met anybody like that. I've certainly had occasions where when I played for a great master; it didn't work out that way. "He's too busy, don't bother him." That kind of thing.

To this day, as a violin soloist, I'm jealous of the vast repertory available to chamber players. And I enjoy the *society* of chamber music. As a soloist, it can be a lonely life, and a lot of time alone in the practice room. Too often, you know, if you're invited to a city to play chamber music one year, it's unlikely you'll be invited back the next year to play as a soloist. It's an unfortunate fact of life. But my parents from the beginning had encouraged me as a soloist, and I began in that way as early as 1974, when I was nineteen. But at least as a soloist you have the chance to work with orchestras, and I love to do that as much as the conductor will allow me. I very much enjoy playing the nooks and crannies of the repertoire, both older and newer music. That includes Szymanowski on the one hand, and maybe the Schumann violin works on the other. I played the Schumann pieces for a Belgian label called Phonic that came out in 1981. I did a series of recordings for it. It was a small company, and it gave me much-needed experience in recording. My pianist was Jean-Claude Vanden Eynden.

Thomas Zehetmair

I studied with my father in Salzburg at the Mozarteum and later in Paris. Now I'm teaching in Berlin. I have worked a lot with Heinz Holliger, with whom I share a passion for Robert Schumann. Heinz is going to write a violin concerto which I will premiere next year [recorded in 2004 for ECM Records with Holliger conducting]. I am here in Düsseldorf [1991] at the Schumann Festival because of Heinz and the Robert-Schumann-Gesellschaft. It is only here and few other places where I can do a program like the *Fantasie,* Op. 131. Heinz and I also did an all-Schumann program in Ferrara. A festival like this is very necessary. We can address so many misunderstandings about his music, especially the late music, like these violin works. It's amazing how many prejudices there still are.

David Zinman

By the time I came to the Baltimore Symphony Orchestra, I had already been conducting two Dutch orchestras and recording for Philips in Holland. But when I came to Baltimore, one of the first priorities was to get a recording label. We had heard that Telarc was one of the up-and-coming labels with great sound. We made our first record for them, the Berlioz "Marseillaise" and some overtures. For Telarc, you had to make the balance; the conductor does it. They don't do it with their mike system, *you* do it. So what we got with Telarc was a true performance. It was a fantastic learning process for me. We have now completed our Schumann cycle and we're starting a Tchaikovsky symphony series. And as you know, we've just signed a contract to do American music for Decca Records, which is London Records in England. This is a good thing for us, because music has always been all about trying to get out of established molds. Beethoven wanted to change the way music was. So did Schumann, and Mahler. Traditions want to be broken, and many composers try to break those traditions. But sometimes conductors don't like to step out on a limb and say, "I'm going to do something really weird."

Eugenia Zukerman

I identify so much with Clara Schumann, because, like her, I am a mother and a professional musician. And when Clara's husband went to the asylum and later died, she was left with the raising and support of the children, while still maintaining her concert career. I and so many women these days face many similar challenges. And not only have I continued my music, but for some time now I've been enjoying a career with the *CBS Sunday Morning* news show.

I play the classical flute. I'm not a great improviser or jazz player. Although, when I was a freshman at Barnard, I accompanied Tony Montanaro's mime troupe, so I sort of played accompanying sounds and things. That's about as far out as I've gotten. And now that you ask, I also remember being on tour with Peter Schickele and his PDQ Bach show; and I was the slide whistle soloist and balloon soloist, too! So I've done a few far-out musical things besides the classics.

My instrument, the flute, became the instrument we know today in the 1840s when Theobald Böhm revamped the mechanisms of the flute. And then the flute hadn't really been tampered with until the last fifteen years, when makers began to see that if you move the tone holes just fractions of inches, you could get a different intonation. There's been little experimentation with the physicality of flute performance since the eighteenth century, not like a piano, where you tinker with the interior and roll golf balls across the strings. That sort of thing. No, that's because flutes are generally made of precious metals, and you're not going to bash a gold flute like mine around! What you do experiment with is the natural resource of the flute, *and that is the player:* And that is how you create the sound, how you blow into the instrument, how you can sing and play at the same time.

I played a silver flute for a very long time. And silver flutes are silvery, bell-like, with a very direct, very piercing kind of a sound. Whereas, with a gold flute, you are able to create, or at least I as a player have the illusion of being able to create, a warmer, more golden, more mellow sound, more diffuse sound. Whether or not this is true is disputable. The density of the metal has to come into play here, because gold is heavier than silver, and it is reflected in the sound that is created, and therefore it must have a physical reason. The flute maker sure makes a difference. My flute was made in Japan by the Sanyo Corporation that has something called "new scale," and that is slightly altered so that I feel that I can play better in tune. Unlike a stringed instrument, the newer the flute, the better it is. And you have to take care to polish it. I mean, you don't spend hours and hours doing it, because generally they don't get very dirty, but you must take care of it, swab it out, et cetera. Nowadays people are playing baroque flutes, which are the wooden flutes, the five-keyed instruments, and there are many players who play them absolutely beautifully and brilliantly. I, myself, find it a limiting thing to do. I think that—and this might be iconoclastic—but I think composers would be delighted to have their compositions played as best as possible, and you play them best on modern instruments.

People are always asking me how I can hold my breath for so long? Which is interesting, because, of course, you're never holding it. You are taking a deep breath and you are gradually letting it out. You have to find a way to expend the air so that it lasts the longest possible time. Breath control is the unending struggle that a wind player has, because you have no resistance. In other words, there's no reed in your mouth against which the air is resisting. So you are like a singer; you have to really dole it out.

We musicians are always looking for ways to inform the public. The traditional format of concertgoing has been around for several hundred years, and people are exploring ways of changing it. I have experimented with talking about the music during my performances. I note a difference in an audience's response to me when I speak to them and when I don't. They like to know about the music you're playing, and they like to know it from the performer, so if you can say something interesting about the piece before you play it, it's much more interesting for an audience than reading those program notes. And it makes it come alive. But I have an ambivalence about all of this, because there's a part of me that would like the music to speak for itself. We do, however, live in the age of personality.

Which brings me to my other career. As I said, another very important part of my career has been broadcasting on *CBS Sunday Morning*. My very first CBS broadcast was a trial by fire. I interviewed Virgil Thomson, who is one of the great icons of twentieth-century music. He was very hard of hearing, and a little feisty—absolutely terrific, but a little feisty. I was very well prepared and very much in awe of this man and his life. Not just as a composer, but as a writer, he's superb. So I went into the interview, and I think the very first question was something like, "What was it like living in Paris in the twenties with all the great writers?" And he misheard me, and he said, "You made that all up!" He had heard something totally different. And we proceeded to have the strangest interview, because he didn't quite catch what I was saying. And I also got to interview Aaron

Copland, which was very interesting, because Copland's memory of the present is not very keen, but his memory of the past is absolutely sensational. I have done pieces on people for whom I have such a reverence that I can hardly speak when I walk into the room, like Segovia, or like Nathan Milstein or Isaac Stern. And I've also done pieces with my great friends, like Yo-Yo Ma, Jean-Pierre Rampal, Misha and Cipa Dichter.

Index of Commentators

CD Notes

This compact disc includes three "chapters." It opens with a twenty-six-minute analysis of Schumann's *Carnaval*, Op. 9 [CD track 1]. Pianist José Feghali, Gold Medalist at the seventh Van Cliburn International Piano Competition in 1985, plays and discusses the motivic transformations of Schumann's most popular piano cycle. Joining in the discussion are Professor Lawrence Kramer of Fordham University, author of *Musical Meaning* (2002), and Professor John C. Tibbetts, author of this book. Actor Mark Robbins provides the voice of Robert Schumann.

Second, celebrated Dutch pianist Ronald Brautigam presents a complete performance of Schumann's *Novelletten*, Op. 21 [CD tracks 2–9]. This is one of Schumann's greatest, albeit relatively neglected, piano works, an eight-part cycle written in 1838, at the peak of Schumann's pianistic powers. Brautigam has won acclaim for his recordings of Schumann and for his recent cycle on fortepiano for the BIS label of works by Mozart and Beethoven. "I love to play Schumann's *Novelletten*," says Brautigam. "They are extremely busy, very robust, masculine, and generally good-humored. They give you a catalogue of all the styles and moods Schumann was up to when he wrote them in 1838."

Third, the CD features a promotional spot for the acclaimed radio series *The World of Robert Schumann* [CD track 10]. This fifteen-part program—written, produced, and narrated by John C. Tibbetts—has been heard worldwide on the WFMT Radio Network. "It may be aptly described as a documentary of Wagnerian proportions," wrote *Gramophone* magazine. "This aural tapestry of interviews, dramatizations, critical comments, and biographical and historical analysis [is] a feat of radio craftsmanship [that] weaves the raw materials into a unified whole, refusing to let any significant time pass without some insight into Schumann's life and times." For information how to acquire an attractive boxed set of this series, contact the author at tibbetts@ku.edu.

CD TRACKS

1. *Carnaval* discussion (26:29)
   José Feghali, piano, with John C. Tibbetts and Lawrence Kramer

2. *Novellette* No. 1, in F major: Markiert und kräftig (5:23)
   Ronald Brautigam, piano

3. *Novellette* No. 2, in D major: Äusserst rasch und mit Bravour (5:53)
   Ronald Brautigam, piano

4. *Novellette* No. 3, in D major: Leicht und mit Humor (4:31)
   Ronald Brautigam, piano

5. *Novellette* No. 4, in D major: Ballmässig. Sehr munter (3:21)
   Ronald Brautigam, piano

6. *Novellette* No. 5, in D major: Rauschend und festlich (8:50)
   Ronald Brautigam, piano

7. *Novellette* No. 6, in A major: Sehr lebhaft, mit vielem Humor (4:11)
   Ronald Brautigam, piano

8. *Novellette* No. 7, in E major: Äusserst rasch (3:16)
   Ronald Brautigam, piano

9. *Novellette* No. 8, in F-sharp minor: Sehr lebhaft (11:06)
   Ronald Brautigam, piano

10. Radio promotion for *The World of Robert Schumann* (5:58)
    John C. Tibbetts with Peter F. Ostwald, Nancy B. Reich, John
    Browning, Elly Ameling, Lukas Foss, and Paul Hume

All recordings copyright © 2010 Pandemonium Productions, L.L.C.™